This book is due for return on or before the last date shown above: it may, subject to the book not being reserved by another reader, be renewed by personal application, post, or telephone, quoting this date and details of the book.

HAMPSHIRE COUNTY COUNCIL
County Library

 100% recycled paper

Jane Hawking

MUSIC TO MOVE THE STARS

A Life With Stephen

MACMILLAN

First published 1999 by Macmillan
an imprint of Macmillan Publishers Ltd
25 Eccleston Place, London SW1W 9NF
Basingstoke and Oxford
Associated companies throughout the world
www.macmillan.co.uk

ISBN 0 333 74686 4

1 3 5 7 9 8 6 4 2

A CIP catalogue record for this book is available from
the British Library.

Phototypeset by Intype London Ltd
Printed and bound in Great Britain by
Mackays of Chatham plc, Chatham, Kent

FOR MY PARENTS

La parole humaine est comme un chaudron fêlé où nous battons des
mélodies à faire danser les ours quand on voudrait attendrir les étoiles.

Gustave Flaubert

Human expression is like a cracked kettle on which we beat out music
for bears to dance to, when really we long to move the stars to pity.

Contents

Part Three

Part Four

Acknowledgements

IN MUCH THE same way that Elgar dedicated the *Enigma Variations* 'to my friends pictured within', this book is itself intended to be an acknowledgement – a gesture of profound thanks to all the people, friends, colleagues, students and family, whose help and encouragement over the years brought a positive influence to our lives. The mention they receive in the text can scarcely do justice to their contribution. There will doubtless be many other people who deserve to be mentioned and whose names I have omitted through oversight or lack of space. To them I apologize and trust that they will feel able to include themselves and their part in the story as it unfolds.

Specifically I should like to thank Professors Kip Thorne, Jim Hartle, Jim Bardeen and Bernard Carr for helping to clarify some of the more abstruse and intractable scientific issues which I, a non-scientist, have had to address in the course of the writing. I am grateful to Kip Thorne for allowing me to quote from his eminently lucid and readable *Black Holes and Time Warps* (W. W. Norton & Company, 1994). I am indebted to Dr Brandon Carter for invaluable discussions on many issues, scientific and otherwise, and to Professor Peter Dronke for his advice on some of the finer points of medieval scholarship.

Susan Hill of Macmillan, who encouraged me to write this account, has allowed me complete freedom to tell my story in my own time and in my own way. I am extremely grateful to her for her acute professional judgement, her editorial skills and her encouragement.

I am indebted to my mother for putting her phenomenal memory at my disposal and to the several friends who have recalled a detail here or there which might have eluded me. I have been encouraged by the support my children have given me in undertaking to tell the story of our lives and I hope that they will not find the finished product a source of embarrassment.

Finally I wish to thank the two people who have lived patiently with the writing process over the past three years: Tim and Jonathan. The latter also deserves a debt of gratitude, not simply for much reassurance and many constructive discussions but also for painstakingly proof-reading the manuscript.

Prelude
July 1995

WELL, HERE I am, back in Seattle twenty-eight years older, almost to the day. I hope I may be somewhat wiser but whether I would do things differently these days, I cannot tell. I have changed in appearance, of course, as one might expect after such a long interval, but then, all those years ago, I was very young. Inwardly, I can only say that I am at last beginning to feel the burgeoning of a new self-assurance and a resurgence of morale, both of which have suffered a steady erosion over the decades. I am discovering the luxury of time, previously a scarce commodity. I have time to contemplate and review all that has happened to me since I was last here and place it in some sort of perspective. I also have time to try to think constructively about the future. As I sit out on the balcony in the warm sun looking towards the shimmering lake and the white mountains, I realize that with this visit to Seattle, a whole era has come full circle. The threads drawing that circle together complete a vast tapestry of human experience, containing a rich kaleidoscopic pattern of people, family and friends, many of whom are still very much alive. That circle encompasses events, both momentous and tragic, which the memory depicts in vivid colours. From neither – people nor events – could I or would I willingly alienate myself.

The idea of the self-contained circle permits me to regard those events and some, but by no means all, of the people with a certain detachment. I hope it will become a philosophical mechanism through which I shall be able to extricate myself from the emotional tangles of the past and consequently view it with some objectivity. This is essential if I am ever to proceed independently with my life and weave for myself and those I love new circles of experience. Without that detachment, I shall be trapped, like a fly in a spider's web, in the strands of that one circle, never able to escape, forever doomed to be devoured by the past in a futile attempt to wrestle with it. Time and the unravelling of the yarn will tell.

If I decide to write the story, it will have to be written in a balanced rather than a sensational fashion. It will be a work that only I can write since only I have the full knowledge of the subject: to do justice to its subject, it will have to aspire to be a work of literature. Moreover it will have to be a work which will draw the sting of venom and leave me free to live the rest of my life without being haunted by shadows from the past. It will have to account for all those years of my young life and acknowledge the selfless contribution to our survival made by that close circle of other people, my family and our friends who have really cared about us.

On the other hand, it will also have to reveal the heart-breaking reality faced daily in an uncaring society at large by disabled people and their carers, the battles with officialdom, the lonely struggle to keep going and maintain a sense of dignity, the tiredness, the frustration, the anguished scream of despair. It will be directed at all politicians and government officers who regard the disabled as an embarrassing drain on resources, and I shall also want it to become prescribed reading for all neurologists, medical students and nurses – in short for anyone in the medical profession – who currently seem to have such a sketchy awareness of the ravages of motor neurone disease and its effects on the personality as well as on the physical body: that will be the justification for including the sort of intimate personal detail which otherwise might well be criticized. It is however by no means a foregone conclusion that such a book will ever see the light of day since the attendant publicity could mean the loss of the treasured privacy which I have only just acquired.

Seattle has certainly changed. It is more assertive, more self-confident, though it is still recognizably the same city, just as, deep within, I am still the same person. The city has grown, enveloping Lake Washington to the east, and downtown, in a frenzied cluster as if space were at a premium, the skyscrapers are taller. They stand on the waterfront like a huddle of Venetian merchants from another continent and another age, scanning the horizon for their cargo-laden vessels, their post-modernist tinted plate-glass squinting into the Pacific sunsets, reflecting a dazzling glory of coloured lights. I am not sure of some of the subtler changes that may have taken place, since my memory of that last time in Seattle is dominated by domestic features, the house, the car and the diaper service, not forgetting the drycleaner's, the pharmacy and the store down on the corner of the street. I frequented those stores often; expanded and modernized, they are still in business. There are aspects of America which are more durable than one might expect. Change here consists of expansion rather than destruction, unlike in England where, if you close your eyes for five minutes, you can be sure that the whole landscape will have been mercilessly transformed. Mature trees will have been rooted out, old houses destroyed and local shops demolished to make way for anonymous offices, supermarkets and motorways, all bearing the mark of insensitive planning and self-regarding architecture.

Nevertheless, I have had great difficulty in identifying the house where we lived for eight weeks all those years ago. Our present house happens, quite by chance, to be just across the highway from the street, 47th Avenue north-east. I have a clear picture of that spacious, single-storey, brown weather-boarded house with its long concrete path of steps down to the road and have tried to find it, driving slowly up and down the street, but in twenty-eight years it will have been redecorated many times, painted white perhaps, enlarged and even remodelled. Trees have grown in the gardens and in the street, and the new children's hospital has blocked the clear view over to the west, to the distant, snowcapped mountains of the Olympic Peninsula on the other side of Puget Sound. Once from the front verandah I saw a light aircraft fall out of the sky over there and, although I telephoned the emergency services to warn them that the pilot was parachuting down, I never found out whether he landed on the earth, in the mountains or in the sea.

This time our house overlooks the blue waters of Lake Washington. We can clearly see the floating bridge straddling the lake to the pine-covered hills where Robert, my eldest son, works at Redmond. We can just make out the gash in the lakeside where Bill Gates, his boss, is building a mansion, 75 per cent of which is underground. Why anyone should want to build underground in such a setting on the lakeshore is incomprehensible to me, but then I have often been surprised by the attitudes of scientists and mathematicians. Of course, the Gateses' house does not have the advantage of the majestic view of Mount Rainier which greets us from our balcony – or 'deck' as the Americans call it – like an upturned Christmas pudding with cream flowing down its sides, through a blue haze in the morning and a pink haze in the evening. I gaze at it now, looking south across the lake and over mile upon mile of pine forest. We have been lucky; the mountain has been 'out' as they say, almost every day, except when we travelled the 100 or so miles to see it close at hand. Then it veiled itself coyly in a thick mist but emerged as soon as we arrived back home as if capriciously playing a childish game with us.

Ironically, Mount Rainier was one of the few sights we did manage to see back in 1967, thanks to Gillian and Geoffrey Pinfold, who had come over from Vancouver Island and drove us all there and back in a day. Little did I suspect that my two-month-old babe-in-arms who, in the photos of that excursion, has almost disappeared inside his sleeping bag, would one day be setting out with ice-axe and crampons to scale that particular mountain. In Robert's language, those trips are merely 'walks'. As that was how he described his expedition to Meera peak in the Himalayas, I have my strong suspicions that he and I employ a totally different vocabulary for such activities.

I draw scant consolation from the fact that his younger brother, Tim, shows little enthusiasm for mountaineering since *his* every waking moment is absorbed in daydreams of motor racing. In Tim's opinion, the one redeeming feature of last weekend's tediously long drive to the Long Beach Peninsula was the unexpected discovery at the end of it of a go-kart track by the beach. Not for him the romantic views over the vast, luminous reaches of the Pacific Ocean, where the endless brightness of the western sky gleaming over the glassy water extends the horizon further than the eye can see. He was anxious to avail himself of every possible opportunity to perfect his karting technique, following the driving line, accelerating out of corners, making his kart wide to prevent competitors overtaking him. His ambition is to become a racing driver. On the one hand, it's difficult not to encourage him as he has well and truly infected us with his enthusiasm for the Grand Prix scene and Formula One racing. On the other, I, as his mother, am all too conscious of the heart-stopping risks and horrific dangers involved in that sport. Surely I never gave my parents so much cause for anxiety?

I was a serious, shy, studious child. Yet I realize, in retrospect, that I gave my parents much deeper cause for heart-felt anguish, not because of physically dangerous hobbies and ambitions, but because of the course on which I set myself when I was only a few years older than Tim and much younger than Robert is now.

I have learnt a great deal from my parents. Despite their forceful personalities and their inevitable anxiety at my decision, they never tried to dissuade me from my chosen path. Perhaps it was their experience of the war years which made them view the uncertainties of my future with a surprising degree of equanimity. When we were on holiday in Florence in the summer of 1964, my mother confided in me that she married my father at the beginning of the war because she wanted to nurse him herself if he were going to be injured or disabled. They have always, even now in their eighties, given me unfailing support while I, for my part, regret the succession of trials and tribulations with which I have repaid their devotion.

If my daughter Lucy were to bring home a rather arrogant, unkempt young man who was already suffering from the onset of an incurable disease, and subsequently declare that she wanted to marry him, how would I react? I cannot for one moment believe that I should greet the announcement with unalloyed pleasure, yet when one Saturday in the October of 1964 Stephen bowed to convention to the extent of asking my father for my hand in marriage, my father's only stipulation was that I should finish my degree and his only reservation, expressed in the mildest of terms, was that he was afraid that Stephen might become a millstone around my neck. Stephen gave him his sincere assurance on both counts whereupon the engagement suddenly became official: my mother thrust a set of silver family teaspoons into my hand with her love and best wishes, we went out and bought a discreetly pretty engagement ring consisting of a small sapphire surrounded by a floret of eight tiny diamonds for £26, and a few days later, an announcement appeared in *The Times* to the effect that Miss Jane Wilde, only daughter of Mr and Mrs George Wilde of 35 Townsend Drive, St Albans, was to be married to Mr Stephen Hawking, eldest son of Dr and Mrs Frank Hawking of 14 Hillside Road, St Albans. I was twenty and had just started my second year at Westfield College, London, studying French and Spanish. Stephen was twenty-two and was a research student in cosmology under the supervision of Dr Dennis Sciama in Cambridge. Just after his twenty-first birthday he had been diagnosed, in St Bartholomew's Hospital, as suffering from an atypical form of a rare condition called motor neurone disease.

Not only do I ask how I would react if Lucy were to present me with such a situation, but I also wonder how I myself would react the second time round if I were to find myself reliving the past endowed with the benefit of hindsight. Would I still have the optimism of youth, fired by the belief that all things are possible, or would my reactions be so coloured by my foreknowledge of what was going to happen that I would walk hastily away from such a prospect? This is a question that I have often puzzled over. Stephen would probably say that it is not a meaningful question since it is impossible to re-create that situation. I would point out to him that he himself has actively investigated the theories of the direction of the arrow of time, including the possibility of the reversal of that arrow. This was the sort of discussion that just occasionally we used to have, half teasing, half serious, always stimulating. He liked to think, and he was probably right, that in intellectual terms he had the upper hand; I was pleased if I could find the practical flaws in his arguments. Then his expression would dissolve into that wickedly mischievous grin which never amounted to an admission of defeat but which did just concede that I had made a valid point. Much of the strength of our relationship consisted in those moments of genuine, entertaining rapport. Alas, those conversations, usually conducted over the dinner table to the amusement of all the many people regularly present, became rarer and rarer and now they are no more. Does he miss them? I wonder. I do sometimes.

Part One

CHAPTER ONE

Wings to Fly

To say that it all began in Seattle in 1967 would be inaccurate; the Seattle circle is a device which helps me view those twenty-eight years it encompasses in a certain perspective and with a certain amount of objectivity. The story of my life with Stephen Hawking really began several chapters earlier, in the summer of 1962, five years before the first visit to Seattle. Possibly it even began some ten years earlier than that. When I entered St Albans High School for Girls as a seven-year-old first-former in the early fifties, there was for a short spell a boy with floppy, golden-brown hair who used to sit by the wall in the next-door classroom. The school took boys, including my brother Christopher, in Michael House, the junior department. I only saw the boy with the floppy hair on those occasions when, in the absence of our own teacher, we first-formers were squeezed into the same classroom as the older children. I never spoke to him and certainly he never registered my presence. Nevertheless I think my memory is fairly accurate because Stephen was a pupil at St Albans High School for a term at that time before going to a preparatory school in Radlett, a few miles away.

Stephen's sisters were more memorable because they were at the school for longer. Only seventeen months younger than Stephen, Mary, the elder of the two girls, was a distinctively eccentric figure, plump, always dishevelled, absent-minded, given to solitary pursuits and abrupt of speech. Her great asset, a translucent complexion, was masked by thick, unflattering spectacles. Philippa, five years younger than Stephen, was bright-eyed, nervous and excitable, with short, fair plaits and a round, pink face. The school demanded conformity: the staff of middle-aged spinsters was rigid in approach, both academically and in discipline, and the pupils, like schoolchildren everywhere, could be cruelly intolerant of individuality. It was fine to have a Rolls Royce and a house in the country but if, like me, your means of transport was a pre-war Standard 8, or even worse, like the Hawkings, an ancient London taxi, you were a figure of fun or the object of pitying contempt. The Hawking children used to lie on the floor of their taxi to avoid being seen by their peers. Unfortunately there was not room on the floor of the Standard 8 for such evasive action. Both the Hawking girls left the High School before reaching the upper school.

Their mother was a familiar figure long before I met Stephen. A small, wiry person dressed in a fur coat, she used to stand on the corner by the zebra crossing near my school, waiting for her youngest son, Edward, to arrive by bus from his prep school in the country. My brother also went to that school after his kindergarten year at St Albans High School: it was called Aylesford House and there the boys wore pink – pink blazers and pink caps. The loss of dignity was worthwhile because in all other respects it was a paradise for small boys, especially for those who, like Edward, were not of an academic inclination. Games, Cubs, camping and gang-shows appeared to be the major occupations of the school. Charming and very good-looking, Edward, at the age of seven, was having some difficulty relating to his adoptive family when I made their acquaintance – possibly because of their habit of bringing their reading matter to the dinner table and ignoring any other non-bookworms present.

A schoolfriend of mine, Diana King, had experienced this particular Hawking habit which may have been why, on hearing of my engagement to Stephen, she exclaimed, 'Oh, Jane! You are marrying into a mad, mad family!' She it was who first pointed Stephen out to me in that summer of 1962. Having just finished our A-levels, she, my best friend Gillian Phillips and I were enjoying the blissful period of semi-idleness before the end of term. Because of my father's position as a senior civil servant, I had already made a couple of sorties into the adult world beyond school, homework and exams – to a dinner in the House of Commons and, on a hot, sunny day, to a garden party at Buckingham Palace. Diana and Gillian were to leave school that summer while I was to stay on as Head Girl for the autumn term when I would apply for university entrance. That Friday afternoon we collected our bags, bulging with the books we – or rather they – would no longer need, and, adjusting our straw boaters, we decided to drift into town for tea. We had scarcely gone 100 yards when a strange sight met our eyes on the other side of the road: there, lolloping along in the opposite direction, was a young man with an awkward gait, his head down, his face shielded from the world under an unruly mass of straight brown hair. Immersed in his own thoughts, he looked neither to right nor left, unaware of the group of schoolgirls across the road. He was indeed an eccentric phenomenon for strait-laced, sleepy St Albans.

Gillian and I stared rather rudely in amazement but Diana remained impassive. 'That's Stephen Hawking. I've been out with him actually,' she announced to her speechless companions.

'No! You haven't!' we laughed incredulously.

'Yes I have; he's strange but very clever, a friend of Basil's [her brother]; he took me to the theatre once and I've been to dinner at his house. He goes on Ban the Bomb marches.'

We raised our eyebrows and continued into town. I did not enjoy the tea-party because, without being able to explain why, I had an uneasy sensation about the young man we had just seen. Perhaps our reactions had offended Diana, though she seemed perfectly equable and undisturbed. Perhaps there was something about his very eccentricity which fascinated me in my rather conventional existence. Perhaps I had some strange premonition that I would be seeing him again. Whatever it was, that scene etched itself deeply on my mind, easily to be recalled in all its detail of light, colour, form and background noise.

The holidays of that summer were a dream for a teenager on the verge of independence, though they may well have been a nightmare for her parents, since Spain in 1962 was quite as remote, mysterious and fraught with hazards as, say, Nepal is for teenagers today. Before I set off for a three-week language course in San Sebastian arranged by the University of Bristol, Lady Crathorne, the wife of my father's former boss, the ex-Minister of Agriculture, threw up her hands in horror and virtually told my parents that they would be lucky to see me alive ever again. This was a slightly surprising reaction since, in 1923 at the age of nineteen, she herself had travelled the world, albeit in a luxury yacht, and had encountered headhunters, seen convicts on their way to execution, and visited the opium dens of Hong Kong. I was amused by her alarm on my behalf but unconcerned. With all the confidence of my eighteen years, I was quite sure that I could look after myself and I was right. The course was extremely well organized and supervised by the Professor of Spanish at Bristol University, Professor Jack Metford. We were lodged in groups of four and were well cared for in private homes, which in cities in Spain are usually flats, *pisos*. I found myself in

Señora Vidaurre's *piso* with her family of grown-up children and three other English girls. At weekends we were taken on conducted tours to all the sights – to Pamplona where the bulls run the streets and to Loyola, the home of St Ignatius, the author of a prayer I and every other pupil at St Albans High School had had instilled into us from constant repetition:

> *Teach us, O Lord,*
> *to serve thee as thou deservest,*
> *to give and not to count the cost . . .*

I was almost as awed by this strange connection between an everyday aspect of my school life and a remote monastery in northern Spain as I was by the one and only bull-fight I have ever seen, gory and cruel in its brutality but spectacular and enthralling in its suspense, skill, excitement and colour. We spent our afternoons on the beach and the evenings out in the city or down by the port in restaurants and bars, savouring the local delicacies, stuffing ourselves with *tapas* washed down by *vino tinto*; we participated in the fiestas and the dancing, listened to the raucous bands and gasped at the fireworks. To my joy, I discovered that I could quickly make new friends outside the limited St Albans scene, primarily among the other teenagers on the course. I struck up a friendship with my room-mate, Belinda Todd, a vivacious girl with flaming-red hair from Bishop Auckland, and thereafter she and I went everywhere together.

The course catered for all ages. As we younger members found the moment we boarded the train in London, the group had its own dotty, very demanding elderly spinster; it also had a fair smattering of middle-aged students and a handful of people in their twenties as well. Spain was glorious – exotic, stimulating and exciting. The dark side of Spanish politics did not at that stage impinge on us at all. Those three weeks were carefree and invigorating, a time for experimenting with a taste of adult independence, away from home, family and the imposed, stulti-fying discipline of school.

On my return to England, I was whisked away almost immediately by my parents who, relieved at my safe return, had arranged a family holiday in the Low Countries and Luxembourg. This was yet another broadening experience, one of those holidays in which my father special-ized and had been arranging for us for many years, ever since my first trip to Brittany at the age of ten. Thanks to his enthusiasms we found ourselves in the vanguard of the tourist movement, travelling hundreds of miles along meandering country roads across a Europe in the process of emerging from its wartime trauma; we drove to cities, cathedrals and art museums which my parents were also discovering for the first time. That summer holiday of 1962 was a typically inspired combination of education, through art and history, and enjoyment of the good things of life – wine, food, and summer sun – although that particular year, because I had already spent three weeks in Spain, the element of seaside sun was less important. Holland was an education in art – Rubens in Antwerp, Frans Hals in Harlem, Rembrandt and the Rijksmuseum in Amsterdam, all intermingled with the war memorials and cemeteries of Flanders' fields. We drove as far as the German border but because their war memories were still too vivid, my parents flinched at penetrating Germany any further than Trier, with its massive Roman Porta Nigra.

Back in school that autumn, the summer's experiences lent me an unprecedented feeling of self-assurance. School provided only the palest and most inadequate reflection of the learning, awareness and self-reliance I had acquired through travelling. No longer the timid, gauche schoolgirl, I had emerged from my chrysalis into an independent-minded young woman who was determined to revel in her position as Head Girl. This elevated position afforded me the freedom to attempt comparatively outrageous things. Every year it was the duty of the sixth form to put on an entertainment for the rest of the school. Taking my cue from the new forms of satire appearing on television, I devised a fashion show, with the difference that all the fashions were constructed from bizarrely adapted items of school uniform. The show was so well advertised that on the day, the whole school clamoured for entry on the staircase outside the hall. Miss Meiklejohn, the stocky, weatherbeaten games mistress on whose terrifyingly masculine tones the discipline of the school depended, was for once not able to make herself heard in the din and, in desperation, had to resort to the megaphone which usually only came out for a blasting on Sports Day, at the Pet Show, and for the purpose of controlling those interminable crocodiles we had to form when marching down through every possible back street of St Albans to the Abbey to say our prayers at the once-termly services on All Saints' Day, Ash Wednesday and Ascension Day. Her fury knew no bounds as she stormed through the protective cordon. It was reminiscent of those memorable occasions when some poor ignoramus had the misfortune to stammer a request to go to the 'toilet' rather than the 'lavatory', or someone else, equally misguidedly, had said that she was just going to 'start' tidying her desk, rather than using the socially acceptable 'begin'. 'Start', we were told explosively, was only used for races. In a similar state of towering apoplexy, Miss Meiklejohn demanded to see me. It must have been as much of a surprise to her as it was to me to to find that she no longer had the power to intimidate me. I coolly pointed out that our performance was about to begin (I chose my words carefully) and we were ready to let the school into the hall. Her anger subsided and subsequently, with the rest of the normally po-faced spinster staff, she was seen to muster an attempt at a forgiving smirk.

I had another opportunity to assert my independence on Speech Day when my turn came to propose the vote of thanks to the visiting speaker. At the time C. P. Snow, with his warnings of the dire implications of the divide between the arts and the sciences, was a national figure whose opinions were much discussed and respected. I adopted his theme for my vote of thanks. I felt strongly about it then and although my opinions may be modified, they have not changed: I still continue to feel strongly about the issue today. However simplistic it is to say that scientists should make an effort to express themselves in terms that everyone can understand, or that students of the humanities should resist the urge to turn the television off as soon as science is mentioned – in short, that there should be mutual respect between the disciplines – today the message is even more cogent, so much so that I used it again for my theme when I returned to St Albans High School to present the prizes at Speech Day in 1995. On that earlier occasion as Head Girl I fell into a pitfall for which I was given a sharp rebuke by the Headmistress, Miss M. H. Gent: she told me quite curtly, as a parting shot when I left the school at the end of term, that I had detained the audience for too long. That was a lesson that I was only too happy to bear in mind when asked to speak at prize-giving a second time.

That term long ago in the autumn of 1962 was not supposed to be about putting on shows and making speeches. It was supposed to be about university entrance. Sadly it was not a success in academic terms and I began to wish that I had accepted the place that the genial Professor Metford had offered me at Bristol University in the wake of the course in San Sebastian. However great our admiration for President

Kennedy, the Cuban missile crisis that October had well and truly shaken the sense of security of many young people and dashed our hopes for the future. With the Superpowers playing such dangerous games with our lives, it was not at all certain that we had any future to look forward to. As we prayed for peace in school assembly under the direction of the Dean, I remembered a prediction made by Field Marshal Montgomery in the late 1950s: he was confident that there would be a nuclear war within a decade. Everyone, young and old alike, knew that we should have just four minutes' warning of a nuclear attack which would spell the abrupt end of all civilization. My mother's comment, calmly philosophical and sensible as ever, at the prospect of a third world war in her lifetime, was that she would much rather be obliterated with everything and everyone else than have to endure the agony of seeing her husband and son conscripted for warfare from which they would never return.

Quite apart from the almighty threat of the international scene, I felt that I had burnt myself out with A-levels. I lacked enthusiasm for school work after my taste of freedom in the summer and I was nursing a cracked, if not broken, heart for a dashing young Englishman, a banker, whom I had met in San Sebastian. Spurning the long train journey with the rest of us, he had driven across France in his Mini Minor to join the course with the aim of improving his Spanish in order to be able to sell the newly developed Hovercraft to Latin America. I do not know whether he succeeded in his ambitions because it was quite obvious on our return to England that he found the attentions of a schoolgirl an unwelcome embarrassment, although to be fair he did transport my newly purchased Spanish guitar back to England in his car for me and he did once take Belinda and me out to a very nice dinner in Kensington. This occasion only prolonged the agony, however, and distracted the mind from the serious business of university entrance, with the humiliating result that neither Oxford nor Cambridge was interested in me. The humiliation was all the more painful because my father had been cherishing the hope that I would gain a place at Cambridge since I was about six years old. Gloomily I remembered sitting in the back of our old Standard 8 as we drove through Cambridge on our way home from our holidays at my grandmother's house in Norwich, and my father saying, 'Now, Jane, if you work hard, you might come here to study.'

Aware of my sense of failure, Miss Gent was very sympathetic and went to some lengths to point out that there was no disgrace in not getting a place at Cambridge because many of the men at that university were far inferior intellectually to the women who had been turned away for want of places. In those days the ratio was roughly ten men to one woman at Oxbridge. She recommended me to take up the offer of an interview at Westfield College, London. Westfield was a ladies' arts college on the Girtonian model, situated in Hampstead at some distance from the rest of the University. Its main building was a beautiful porticoed early-nineteenth-century house to which late red-brick Victorian extensions, dormitories, lecture halls and a library had been added. Over the years the College had acquired houses on the Finchley Road, and in the 1960s it was the subject of one of the crash expansion programmes by the University Grants Committee. The gardens of the houses on the Finchley Road had provided the space for a new dining hall and a science block without sacrificing too many of their shaded green lawns. Westfield was soon to admit men for the first time in its history and to lose its status as a liberal arts institution by offering physics, chemistry and biology.

Thus it was that one cold, wet December day I set off from St Albans by Greenline bus for the 15-mile journey to Hampstead. The day was a such a disaster that at the end of it it was a relief to be on the bus home again, travelling through the same bleak, grey sleet and snow of the outward journey. There was some consolation in having a companion on the return journey in Sandra Wade, the sister of one of my brother's friends, who had also been to Westfield for interviews. I hardly liked to admit, even to myself let alone to her, how I had had to bluff my way through the Spanish interview which mysteriously seemed to hinge entirely on T. S. Eliot: all I had read of T. S. Eliot was Gus, the Theatre Cat; *The Wasteland* and the *Four Quartets* were still only titles on my reading list. After that uncomfortable exercise, I was sent to join the queue outside the Principal's study.

Mrs Matthews, a former civil servant and the widowed mother of two young children, had recently been appointed Principal. Although during the course of the next few years I was to get to know her and respect her greatly, at that stage she brought the style of the true civil servant to the interview, scarcely looking up from her papers over her horn-rimmed spectacles. I was feeling exceedingly ruffled and put out by the fiasco of the interview in the Spanish Department. I had nothing to lose and it was better to make her notice me, even if I ruined my chances in the process, so when in a bored, dry voice, she asked, 'And why have you put down Spanish rather than French as your main language?', I answered in an equally bored, dry voice, 'Because Spain is hotter than France.' Her papers fell from her hands and she did indeed look up.

To my astonishment, I was offered a place at Westfield, but by that Christmas, much of the optimism and enthusiasm I had discovered in Spain had worn thin. When Diana invited me to a New Year's party which she was giving with her brother on 1 January 1963, I went along, neatly dressed in a dark green silky outfit – synthetic, of course – with my hair back, brushed in the style of the period into an extravagant bouffant roll, inwardly shy and very unsure of myself. There, slight of frame, leaning against the wall in a corner with his back to the light, gesticulating with long thin fingers as he spoke, his hair falling across his face over his glasses and wearing a dusty black velvet jacket and red velvet bow-tie, stood Stephen Hawking, the young man my friends and I had seen lolloping along the street in the summer.

Standing apart from the other groups, he was talking to Ken Morris, a friend of his from Oxford, recounting that he had now begun research in cosmology in Cambridge under the auspices of a supervisor with an unusual name, Dennis Sciama – not, as he had hoped, Fred Hoyle, the popular television scientist. At first Stephen had thought his unknown supervisor's name was *Skeearma* but it was only when he arrived in Cambridge that he discovered that the correct pronunciation was *Sharma*. He admitted that it had been with some relief that he had learnt the previous summer – when I was doing A-levels – that he had gained a First Class degree at Oxford. This was the happy result of a viva, conducted by the perplexed examiners to decide whether the singularly inept candidate whose exam papers also revealed flashes of brilliance should be given a First, an Upper Second, or a Pass degree which was tantamount to failure. Stephen nonchalantly informed the examiners that if they gave him a First he would go to Cambridge to do a Ph.D, thus giving them the opportunity of introducing a Trojan horse into the rival camp, whereas if they gave him an Upper Second (which would also allow him to do research), he would stay in Oxford. The examiners played for safety and gave him a First.

Stephen had also taken steps to play for safety, realizing that he was extremely unlikely to get a First at Oxford on the little work he had done. He had never been to a lecture; it was not the done thing to be seen to be working when friends called, and the legendary tale of his tearing up a piece of work and flinging it into his tutor's wastepaper basket on leaving a tutorial is well documented. Fearing for his chances in academia, he had applied to join the Civil Service and had passed the preliminary stages of selection. He was all set to take the Civil Service exams just after finishing Finals. One morning he woke late as usual, with the niggling feeling that there was something he ought to be doing that day, apart from his normal pursuit of listening to his taped recording of the entire *Ring* cycle. As he did not keep a diary but entrusted everything to memory, he had no way of finding out what it was until some hours later when it dawned on him that that day was the day of the Civil Service exams.

I listened in amused fascination, drawn to this unusual character by his sense of humour and his independent personality. His tales made very appealing listening, particularly because of his way of hiccoughing with laughter, almost suffocating himself, at the jokes he told, many of them against himself. Clearly here was someone, like me, who tended to stumble through life and managed to see the funny side of situations. Someone who, like me, was fairly shy yet was not averse to expressing his opinions; someone who – unlike me – had a developed sense of his own worth and the effrontery to convey it. As the party drew to a close, we exchanged names and addresses but I did not expect to see him again, except perhaps casually in passing. The floppy hair, the long finger-nails and the bow-tie were a façade, a statement of independence of mind, and I felt that in future I could afford to overlook them, as Diana had, if I met him out in the street.

CHAPTER TWO

On Stage

ONLY A COUPLE of days later, an invitation arrived. It was from Stephen and was written in a beautiful copper-plate hand which I envied and which despite laborious efforts, I had never been able to master. I was invited to a party at his house on 8 January. I consulted Diana who had also received an invitation. She said that the party was for Stephen's twenty-first birthday – information not conveyed on the invitation – and she promised to come and pick me up. It was difficult to choose a present for someone I had only just met, so I took a record token.

The house in Hillside Road, St Albans, was a monument to thrift and economy. Not that that was untoward in those days because in the post-war era we were all brought up to treat money with respect, to search out bargains and to avoid waste. Built in the early years of the century, number 14 Hillside Road, a vast red-brick three-storey house, had a certain charm about it since it was preserved entirely in its original state, with no interference from modernizing trends such as central heating or wall-to-wall carpeting. Nature, the elements and a family of four children had all left their marks on the shabby façade which hid behind an unruly hedge. Wisteria overhung the decrepit glass porch and much of the coloured glass in the leaded diamond panes of the upper panels of the front door was missing. Although no immediate response came on pressing the bell, the door was eventually opened by the same person who used to wait, wrapped in a fur coat, by the zebra crossing; she was introduced to me as Isobel Hawking, Stephen's mother. She was accompanied by an enchanting small boy with dark curly hair and bright blue eyes. Behind them a single light bulb illuminated a long yellow-tiled hallway with heavy furniture, including a grandfather clock, and the original, now darkened, William Morris wallpaper.

As different members of the family began to appear one by one round the living-room door to greet the new arrivals, I discovered that I knew them all: Stephen's mother was well known from her vigils by the crossing; his young brother, Edward, was evidently the small boy in the pink cap: the sisters, Mary and Philippa, were recognizable from school, and the tall, white-haired, distinguished father of the family, Frank Hawking, had once come to collect a swarm of bees from our own back garden – my brother Chris and I had wanted to watch but to our disappointment, he had shooed us away with a gruff taciturnity. In addition to being the city's only beekeeper, Frank Hawking must also have been one of the few people in St Albans to own a pair of skis. In winter he would ski down the hill past our house on his way to the golf-course where we used to picnic and gather bluebells in spring and summer and toboggan on tin trays in winter.

It was like fitting a jigsaw together: all these people were individually quite familiar to me but I had never realized that they were related. Indeed, there was yet another member of that household whom I recognized: she lodged in her own self-contained room in the attic but came down to join in family occasions such as this. Agnes Walker, Stephen's Scottish grandmother, was a well-known figure in St Albans in her own right on account of her prowess at the piano, publicly displayed once a month when she joined forces in the Town Hall with Molly Du Cane, our splendidly jolly-hockey-stick folk-dance leader.

Dancing and tennis had been just about my only social activities throughout my teenage years. Through them, I had acquired a group of friends of both sexes – Ken, Steve, Chris, Ros, Bill, John, Susan, Mary and Graham – from various schools and differing backgrounds. Out of school we went everywhere in a crowd: coffee on Saturday mornings, tennis in the evenings and socials at the tennis club in summer, ballroom dancing classes and folk-dancing in the winter. The fact that our mothers also attended the folk-dance evenings, along with many of St Albans' elderly and infirm population, did not embarrass us at all. We sat apart and danced in our own sets, well out of the way of the older generation. Romances blossomed occasionally in our corner and in our sets, giving rise to plenty of gossip and a few squabbles. Usually they faded as quickly as they blossomed. We were an easy-going, friendly bunch of teenagers, leading simpler lives than our modern counterparts, and the atmosphere at the dances was carefree and whole-some, inspired by Molly Du Cane's infectious enthusiasm for her energetic art. Fiddle on shoulder, she called the dances with the authority of a benevolent games teacher (if, indeed, such a person exists), while Stephen's grandmother, her corpulent frame upright at the grand piano, applied her fingers with nimble artistry to the ivories, not once allowing the sausage bang of tight curls on her forehead to become ruffled. An august figure, she would turn to survey the dancers with a curiously impassive, inscrutable stare. It was she who came downstairs to greet the guests at Stephen's twenty-first birthday party.

The party consisted of a mixture of friends and relations. A few hailed from Stephen's Oxford days but most had been his contemporaries or near contemporaries at St Albans School and had contributed to that school's success in the Oxbridge entrance exams of 1959. At seventeen, Stephen had been younger than his peer group at school and consequently was rather young for university entrance that autumn, especially as many of his fellow undergraduates were not just one year older than him, but older by several years because they had all come up to Oxford after doing National Service (which had since been abolished). Later Stephen admitted that he failed to get the best out of Oxford because of the difference in age between him and his fellow undergraduates.

Certainly he maintained closer ties with his schoolfriends than with any acquaintances from Oxford, and the former were in the majority at the party. Apart from Basil King, Diana's brother, I knew them only by repute as the new élite of St Albans society. They were reputed to be the intellectual adventurers of our generation, passionately dedicated to a critical rejection of every truism, to the ridicule of every trite or clichéd remark, to the exploitation of their own independence of thought and to the exploration of the outer reaches of the mind. Our local paper, the *Herts Advertiser*, had trumpeted the success of the school four years earlier, splashing their names – Michael Church, Roger Fernyhough, John McClenahan, Michael Crampin, Basil and Stephen, among others – and their faces across its pages. Whereas I was just about to embark on my undergraduate career, their student years were already behind them. They were, of course, very different from my friends, and as a bright but ordinary eighteen-year-old, I felt intimidated. None of this crowd would ever spend their evenings folk-dancing. Painfully aware of my own lack of sophistication, I settled in a corner as close to the fire as possible with Edward on my knee and listened to the conversation, not attempting to participate. Some people were seated, others leaned against the wall of the large, chilly dining-room where the only source of heat was a glass-fronted stove. The conversation was halting and consisted mostly of jokes, none of which was even remotely as high-brow as I was expecting. The only one I can remember was a riddle about a man in New York who wanted to get to the fiftieth floor of a building but only took the lift to the forty-sixth. Why? Because he was not tall enough to reach the button for the fiftieth floor . . .

It was some time before I saw or heard of Stephen again. I was busily engaged in London following a secretarial course in a revolutionary type of shorthand, called Speedwriting, which used the alphabet instead of hieroglyphs and, like Hebrew and Arabic, omitted all vowels. Initially I accompanied my father to the station at a sprint to catch the eight o'clock train every morning, until I discovered that I was not required to be at the school, above Lilley and Skinner's in Oxford Street, quite so early. I could therefore travel at a more leisurely pace than my dedicated, hard-working father so I ambled to the station for the nine o'clock train and met a completely different commuting public from the jam-packed, harassed-looking, middle-aged breadwinners in dark suits. Rarely did a day go by when I did not meet someone I knew, unhurried and casually dressed, either going back to college after a weekend at home or going up to London for an interview. This was a welcome start to the day because for the rest of it, apart from a short break for lunch, I was confined to the classrooms of the Speedwriting School, surrounded by the clatter of massed old-fashioned typewriters and the chatter of ex-debs whose main claim to distinction seemed to be the number of times they had been invited to Buckingham Palace, Kensington Palace or Clarence House.

The revolutionary form of shorthand was easy enough to pick up but the touch-typing was a nightmare. I hated it. I could see the sense of the shorthand for that was going to be useful for note-taking at university, but the typing was tiresome in the extreme and I was hopeless at it, still struggling to reach forty words a minute when the rest of the class had finished the course and mastered all the additional skills of the secretarial art, like layout, spacing and tabulation, then folding the letter, placing it in its envelope – and even where to stick the stamp. Actually the shorthand would be of short-term value while the typing skills would prove themselves over and over again.

At weekends I could forget the horrors of typing and keep up with old friends. One Saturday morning in February I met Diana, who was now a student nurse at St Thomas' Hospital, and another schoolfriend,

Elizabeth Chant, who was training to become a primary school teacher, in our favourite haunt, the coffee-bar in Green's, St Albans' only department store. We compared notes on our courses and then started talking about our friends and acquaintances. Suddenly Diana asked, 'Have you heard about Stephen?'

'Oh, yes,' said Elizabeth, 'it's awful, isn't it?'

I realized that they were talking about Stephen Hawking.

'What do you mean?' I asked. 'I haven't heard anything.'

'Well, apparently he's been in hospital for two weeks – Bart's, I think, because that's where his father trained and that's where Mary is training,' Diana explained. 'He kept stumbling and couldn't tie his shoelaces.' She paused before continuing, 'They did lots of horrible tests and have found that he's suffering from some terrible, paralysing, incurable disease. It's a bit like multiple sclerosis but it's not multiple sclerosis and they reckon he's probably only got a couple of years to live.'

I was stunned. I had only just met Stephen and I liked him for all his eccentricity. We both seemed shy in the presence of others but were confident within ourselves. It was unthinkable that someone only a few years older than me should be facing the prospect of his own death. Mortality was not as yet a concept that played any part in our existence. We were still young enough to be immortal.

'How is he?' I enquired, shaken by the news.

'Basil's been to see him,' Diana continued, 'and says he's pretty depressed: the tests are really unpleasant and a boy from St Albans in the bed opposite died the other day.' She sighed, 'Stephen insisted on being on the ward because of his socialist principles and would not have a private room as his parents wanted.'

'Do they know the cause of this illness?' I asked blankly.

'Not really,' Diana replied. 'They think he may have been given a non-sterile smallpox vaccination when he went to Persia a couple of years ago, and that introduced a virus to his spine, but they don't really know, that's only speculation.'

I went home in silence, thinking about Stephen. My mother noticed my preoccupation. She had not met him but knew of him and also knew that I liked him. I had taken the precaution of warning her that he was very eccentric, in case she should come across him unannounced. With the sensible assurance of the deep-seated faith which had sustained her through the war, through the terminal illness of her beloved father and through my own father's bouts of black depression, she quietly said, 'Why don't you pray for him? It might help.'

Religious observance had been a large element in our upbringing. My brother Chris and I were marched off to church every Sunday and sat swinging our legs under the pew, our minds wandering far and wide, through hours of sermons which left us with only the vaguest impressions of religious truth. (The resultant confusion may partly explain why Chris, when he was small, prayed, 'Thine be the power and the lorry.') Then on Sunday afternoons we were sent back to Sunday school. The overdose of religious observance at the weekend was reinforced at school during the week by more observance and quantities of religious teaching, since the school was a religious foundation with a strong affiliation to the Church and provided bursaries to help the daughters of impoverished clergymen.

Despite the fact that many of the teachers were also parsons' daughters, Christian charity in the treatment of their pupils was not an obvious priority, although it is only fair to say that some, like the Deputy Head, Miss Partridge, were models of patience and good sense. Even she had her foibles: 'Don't ever let me hear you use the word "cross" for any purpose except to denote *the* Cross of Jesus,' she instructed a suitably awed but perplexed class of nine-year-olds, of whom I was one. Her favourite observation on the human condition has stayed with me all my life: in its stark simplicity, it is a universal truth. 'What,' she would ask, 'was the first thing you said when you came out of the cradle?' She never waited for an answer. 'I'll tell you; each and every one of you said, "It's not fair!" ' Although, at eighteen, I was beginning to shake off the automatic acceptance of all that I had been told and taught, and was harbouring some considerable doubts about the relevance of organized religion, certainly I had to concede that Miss Partridge was right when I considered what had befallen Stephen. Perhaps my mother was right too when she suggested that I should pray for him. There did not seem to be much else that I could do.

I was astonished therefore when a week or so later, as I was waiting for a 9 a.m train, Stephen came sauntering down the platform carrying a brown canvas suitcase. He looked perfectly cheerful and pleased to see me. His appearance was more conventional and actually rather more attractive than on past occasions: the appurtenances of the old *roué* image which he had doubtless cultivated at Oxford – the bow-tie, the black velvet jacket, even the long hair – had given way to a red necktie, a beige raincoat and a tidier, shorter hairstyle. Our two previous meetings had been in the evening in subdued lighting; daylight revealed his broad, winning smile and his limpid grey eyes to advantage. Behind the owlish spectacles there was something about the set of his features which attracted me, reminding me, perhaps even subconsciously, of my Norfolk hero, Lord Nelson. We sat together on the train to London talking quite happily though we scarcely touched on the question of his illness. I mentioned how sorry I had been to hear of his stay in hospital whereupon he wrinkled his nose and said nothing. He behaved so convincingly as if everything were fine, I felt it would have been cruel to have pursued the subject further. He was on his way back to Cambridge, he said, and as we neared St Pancras, he announced that he came home quite often at weekends. Would I like to go to the theatre with him some time? Of course I said I would.

We met one Friday evening at an Italian restaurant in Soho which in itself would have been a sufficiently lavish evening out. However, Stephen had tickets for the theatre as well and the meal had to be brought to a hasty and rather embarrassingly expensive conclusion to enable us to make our way south of the river to the Old Vic in time for a performance of *Volpone*. Arriving at the Old Vic in a rush, we barely had time to throw our belongings under our seats at the back of the stalls before the play began. My parents were fairly keen theatre-goers, so I had already seen *The Alchemist* and had enjoyed it thoroughly; *Volpone* was just as entertaining and soon enough I was totally absorbed in the intrigues of the old fox who wanted to test the sincerity of his heirs but whose plans went badly wrong.

Elated by the performance, we stood discussing it afterwards at the bus-stop. A tramp came past and politely asked Stephen if he had any loose change. Stephen felt in his pocket and exclaimed in embarrassment, 'I'm sorry, I don't think I have anything left!' The tramp grinned and looked at me. 'That's all right, guv,' he said, winking in my direction, 'I quite understand.' At that moment the bus drew up and we clambered on. As we sat down, Stephen turned to me apologetically. 'I'm terribly sorry,' he said, 'but I don't even have the money for the fare. Have you got any?' Guiltily aware of how much he must have spent on our evening, I was only too happy to oblige. The conductor approached. He hovered over us as I searched for my purse in the depths of my handbag. My embarrassment equalled Stephen's as I discovered that it was missing. We jumped off the bus at the next set of traffic lights and fairly ran all the way back to the Old Vic. The main entrance to the theatre was closed but Stephen pressed on to the stage door at the side; it was open and the passage inside was lit. Cautiously we ventured in but there was no one to be seen. Directly at the end of the passage we found ourselves on the deserted but still brightly lit stage. Awestruck, we tiptoed across it and down the steps into the darkened auditorium. In no time at all, to our joint relief, we found the green leather purse under the seat where I had been sitting. Just as we were heading back towards the stage, the lights went out and there we were in total darkness. 'Take my hand,' said Stephen authoritatively. I held his hand and my breath in silent admiration as he led me back to the steps, up across the stage and out into the passage. Fortunately the stage door was still open and as we tumbled out into the street we burst into laughter. We had been on stage at the Old Vic!

CHAPTER THREE

A Bumpy Ride

SOME WEEKS AFTER the Old Vic episode, as the Speedwriting course was officially coming to an end – though I still struggled hopelessly with the typing – my mother met me on my return home one evening excitedly waving a telephone message from Stephen. He wanted to invite me to a May Ball in Cambridge and would ring back for my reply. At about the same time she had also taken a call from a South African concert pianist, a protégé of my Aunt Marge, an elderly cousin of my father's who had gone to South Africa in 1910 to teach the violin and had stayed there ever since apart from occasional visits to England. Her most recent visit had been timed to coincide with her protégé's debut at the Wigmore Hall; he also wanted to take me out but, to my indignation, my mother had told him that I was not available. I silently resented this interference in my affairs: it was not as if I had so many offers of dates that I could afford to be choosy and, in any case, I rather liked the concert pianist.

The prospect of a May Ball, however, was tantalizing. When we were in the Lower Sixth at school, a girl had been invited to a May Ball. The rest of us were green with envy and lapped up every detail of a gala occasion which seemed to be the stuff of fairy-tales. We saw her off early one Tuesday afternoon and waited impatiently for her return two days later. The stories she told of dancing all night, of smoked salmon and champagne, of punting up the river for breakfast left us feeling like a whole classful of doleful Cinderellas. Unbelievably, my turn had come. When Stephen rang to confirm the invitation, I accepted with pleasure and began to think about what I should wear. That problem was soon solved when I found a dress in white and navy silk in a shop near the Speedwriting School in Oxford Street. It was just within my means.

With typical Cambridge contrariness, the May Balls take place in June, which was still some months away. In the meantime I had to start replenishing my funds, depleted by the purchase of the ballgown, for my travels around Spain later in the summer, so I signed on with an temporary employment agency in St Albans. My first assignment was a one-and-a-half-day stint – Thursday afternoon and the whole of Friday – in the Westminster Bank in Hatfield where the branch manager, Mr Abercrombie, a patient, well-meaning man, was a friend of my father's. I was first directed to the telephone switchboard but had no inkling of what to do as I had never worked on one before. Panicking at the flashing lights, I frantically pulled out some leads on the board and desperately tried to push others into the vacant holes, succeeding only in cutting off all outside callers and in connecting up the telephones of people who were sitting opposite each other. Finally I was summoned to Mr Abercrombie's inner sanctum where with polite restraint he asked if I would prefer to take down a letter. The Speedwriting did not let me down but the typing was as much of a disaster as the switchboard. By the time I had flung six sheets of the Bank's headed notepaper into the wastepaper basket, I was aware that all eyes in the office were upon me. Eventually, doubtless fearing for the stability of the Westminster Bank, someone suggested that I should go and make the tea.

Soon, after various other jobs and a stint in London, I was casting around for my next move when Mike Warwick, a neighbour with whose younger sister, Fiona, I used to climb trees, suggested looking for work in Welwyn Garden City where he had a job with Smith, Kline and French, a pharmaceutical firm. There were no openings there at present but he promised to keep a lookout and let me know when something came up. The great advantage of Welwyn was that Mike could give me a lift in his Mini every morning. Even with my employment record, it was relatively easy in those days to find a job and in no time I found myself working for a firm that manufactured pacemakers in Welwyn Garden City. The medical slant made the work much more interesting than anything I had done previously and I was gaining confidence in my secretarial skills. Mike and I had the friendly, fraternal relationship of long acquaintance, which meant that we could chat quite freely on our way to work in the morning, even if some of the topics under discussion – cars, motor racing and golf – were not exactly at the top of my agenda. As the date of the May Ball approached, I told him about Stephen. He whistled between his teeth. 'Poor devil!' he remarked.

Indeed, when Stephen arrived one hot afternoon in early June to take me to Cambridge, I too was tempted to whistle between my teeth. His condition had deteriorated visibly since I had last seen him that evening of the Old Vic escapade and I doubted that he was really strong enough to drive his father's car, a huge old Ford Zephyr. Built like a tank, it had apparently forded rivers in Kashmir when the family – minus Stephen who had stayed at school in England – had lived in India some years earlier. I was amused by the number plate; the letters read 'VOY', 'I go', the first person singular of the Spanish verb *ir*. I feared that the snorting vehicle might well go much too fast for the present driver, a slight, frail, limping figure who appeared to use the steering-wheel to hoist himself up to see over the dashboard. I introduced Stephen to my mother. She showed no signs of surprise or alarm, but waved us away as if she were the fairy godmother, sending me off to the ball with Prince Charming in a runaway glass coach.

The journey was terrifying. It transpired that Stephen's role model for driving was his father who drove fast and furiously, overtaking on hills and at corners, and who had even been known to drive down a dual carriageway in the wrong direction. Drowning out all attempts at conversation, the wind roared through the open windows as we sped at take-off speed past the fields and trees of Hertfordshire into the exposed landscape of Cambridgeshire. I scarcely dared look at the road in front while Stephen, on the other hand, seemed to be looking at everything except the road. He probably felt that he could afford to live dangerously since Fate had already dealt him such a cruel blow. This was of little reassurance to me, however, so I secretly vowed that I would travel home by train; I was definitely beginning to have my doubts about this supposedly fairy-tale experience of a May Ball.

Defying all road accident statistics, we actually arrived in one piece at Stephen's lodgings in a fine 1930s-style graduate house set in a shady garden on the corner of Adams Road, where the other revellers were busy with last-minute preparations. I was allotted an upstairs room by the motherly housekeeper and when I had changed, I was introduced to Stephen's fellow lodgers and research students, among them Nick Hughes and Tom Wesley, whose seemingly contradictory attitudes towards him baffled me. They talked to him in his own intellectual terms, sometimes caustically sarcastic, sometimes crushingly critical, always humorous; in personal terms, however, they treated him with a gentle consideration which was almost loving. I found it hard to reconcile these two extremes of behaviour. I was used to consistency of attitude and approach and was perplexed by these people who confidently played devil's advocate, arguing ferociously with someone – that is, Stephen – one minute, and the next not only treating him as if nothing were amiss, but attending caringly to his personal needs, as if his word was their command. I had not learnt to distinguish reason from emotion, the intellect from the heart. In my innocence I had some hard lessons to learn. Such innocence, by Cambridge standards, was boring and predictable.

We all went off to a late dinner at Millers', a first-floor restaurant on the corner of King's Parade. From where I sat, I gazed out at the pinnacles and spires of King's College, the Chapel and the gatehouse, darkly silhouetted against the vast, luminous panorama of an East Anglian sunset. That in itself was magical enough. We returned to the house for last-minute adjustments before setting out on the ten-minute walk across the watery green spaces of the Backs to the old courts of Trinity Hall, Stephen's college. Stephen adamantly insisted on taking his tape-recorder and collection of tapes across to the College to install in a friend's room, put at our disposal when we needed a break from the jollifications, but could not carry them himself. 'Oh, come on,' one of his friends grumbled benevolently, 'I suppose I shall have to carry them for you.' And he did.

Relatively small, unpretentious and tucked away from public view, Trinity Hall consists of a motley collection of buildings – very old, old and Victorian – enclosing lawns, flower-beds and a terrace which overlooks the river. We approached the College from the other side of the river, standing briefly on the high arch of a new bridge which, Stephen seriously impressed upon me, had recently been built in memory of a student, Timothy Morgan, who had died tragically in 1960 having just completed his design for the bridge. From the bridge, for all its sad connotations, we were regaled with a fairy-tale spectacle: it reminded me of the mysterious château in one of my favourite French novels, *Le Grand Meaulnes* by Alain-Fournier, where the hero, Augustin Meaulnes, chances across a brightly lit château in the dark depths of the countryside and, from being a bemused observer, finds himself drawn into the revelries, the music and the dancing, never quite knowing what is going to happen next. Here in Trinity Hall, bands were sending their strains out on the night air, the lawn leading down to the river was hung with twinkling lights, as was the magnificent copper beech in the centre, and couples were already dancing on a raised platform under the tree.

We entered the *mêlée* where I was introduced to more friends of Stephen's, an expansive Australian couple, Anne and Brian Young from Sydney, and then John Billingsley, effusive and authoritative, with his quiet, pensive wife, Ros. Together we made a beeline for our ration of champagne which was being served from a bath, then on to the buffet and the various entertainments: to the tightly packed Hall where on a distant stage an inaudible cabaret was taking place; to an elegantly panelled room where a string quartet was attempting to compete with the Jamaican steel band out on the lawn; and to a corner by the Old Library where hot chestnuts were being served from a glowing brazier. Our companions had drifted away, leaving us sitting up on the terrace by the river, watching the dancers writhe to the hypnotic rhythms of the steel band.

'I'm sorry I don't dance,' Stephen apologized.

'That's quite all right; it doesn't matter,' I lied.

Dancing was not totally out of the question, however, because later on, after yet another buffet and more champagne, we discovered a jazz band secreted away in a cellar. The room was dark apart from some weird bluish lights. The men were invisible except for their cuffs and shirt-fronts which shone with a bright purple luminosity, whilst the girls could hardly be seen at all. It was eerie. Stephen explained that the lights were picking up the fluorescent element contained in washing powder, which was why the men's shirts were so visible; as the girls' new dresses would not have been contaminated with Tide or Daz or any other detergent, they did not show up with the same ghostly light. In the darkness of the underground room, I persuaded Stephen to take to the floor. We swayed gently to and fro, laughing at the dancing patterns of purple light, until to our disappointment, the band packed up and went home.

In the early hours of the morning, the other colleges which had been hosting May Balls traditionally opened their doors to all-comers. As day dawned, we staggered down Trinity Street to Trinity College where, in a spacious set of rooms, somebody's extremely well-organized and mature Canadian girlfriend was preparing breakfast. Although she was issuing orders in a voice worthy of Miss Meiklejohn's, I was impervious to her commands. I just sank into an armchair and fell asleep.

Some kind person must have led me back sleep-walking to the house in Adams Road where I slept comfortably until mid-morning.

The day's programme for the May Ball partners had been planned with the efficiency of a modern tour operator, except that it was much more stimulating. As well as researching their Ph.Ds in Chemistry, Nick Hughes and Tom Wesley were much involved, as editors, in the production of a guide to the post-war buildings of Cambridge, *Cambridge New Architecture*, which was to be published in 1964. Stephen shared their interest and acted as a part-time consultant in the project. They were all anxious therefore to show the subjects of their deliberations to any interested parties. However sceptically these buildings are viewed today, in the 1960s they were the cause of great excitement, the assertive excitement of post-war development and expansion. Conservation was not yet a popular concern. Architects and planners were the darlings of a new society, the arbiters of taste, the dictators of fashion. Traffic problems were solved in one fell swoop by clearing meadows of trees and any old property which stood in the way for the construction of fast new roads. Likewise new universities and old were scrambling for grants to accommodate the post-war bulge and put up as many buildings as possible, never mind what gems of a previous century's architecture and landscape had to be jettisoned to achieve those grandiose schemes.

The tone of the age is echoed in *Cambridge New Architecture*. It was with a zealous, pioneering fervour that our guides pointed out to us, their impressionably ignorant female guests, the features of a selection of new sites, either recently finished or still under construction. We saw the Hugh Casson development of the Sidgwick Site and Churchill College – the memorial to Sir Winston, whose concern at the lack of provision for scientists and technologists in this country led to the foundation of the College in 1958. We were also taken to Harvey Court, the Gonville and Caius development, which pushed even the glowingly enthusiastic contributors of *Cambridge New Architecture* to resort to euphemism in their description. They were forced to describe it as 'an experiment which may eventually bully its occupants into enjoying the pattern of life it imposes'. In case this might seem too harsh a recantation of their beliefs, the writers added: 'And it *is* Cambridge's most courageous attempt at finding some new ideal solution to the problems of college residence'. As a sop to tradition, we visitors from less richly endowed corners of the country were finally allowed to take a quick peep inside King's College Chapel.

By this stage I had begun to make friends with some of the other girls and found that they were travelling back by train to London. When I told them about Stephen's driving, they insisted that I should travel with them. After lunch we all went out for a ride in a punt and then the question of the return journey loomed. 'I think it would be better if I went by train,' I hesitantly suggested to Stephen but he would not hear of it. Anxious not to offend him, I took my place once again in the passenger seat of the dreaded Zephyr. The return home was every bit as terrifying as the outward journey and by the time we reached St Albans, I decided that, much as I had appreciated the May Ball, I did not want to subject myself to that sort of dodgems ride ever again. My mother was in the front garden when we drew up at the gate. I tersely said 'Thank you and goodbye' to Stephen and with never a backward glance, marched into the house. My mother followed me in and reprimanded me severely: 'You're not going to send that poor young man away without even a cup of tea, are you?' she said, shocked at my indifference. Her words pricked my conscience. I ran out of the house to try to catch Stephen. He was still there, parked at the gate, trying to start the car. Slowly it began to roll back down the steep hill because he had let the brake off before getting the engine started. He jammed the brake on and came in for tea with alacrity, sitting with me in the sun by the garden door. As we excitedly recounted the events of the ball to my mother, he was attentive and charming. I decided that I really rather liked him and could forgive his road madness providing I did not have to experience it too often.

CHAPTER FOUR

Hidden Truths

A COUPLE OF WEEKS later we temporarily acquired an addition to our family: my parents had responded to a call for accommodation for visiting French teenagers from Autun in Burgundy and were hosts to a sixteen-year-old girl, Annette Martin. By an uncanny coincidence, her best friend Martine was lodging with the Hawkings, and one Saturday in June, not long after the May Ball, Mrs Hawking invited the two French girls and me to join her on a visit to Cambridge. To my relief, she drove sensibly, talked in a jovially concentrated intellectual fashion, and brought a splendid picnic – 'a cold collation', she called it – which we ate on the verandah of Stephen's ground-floor room in Adams Road. Thus my family and I were brought into closer and more regular contact with the Hawkings, and when Stephen came back to St Albans for a weekend, my parents invited him to dinner. They treated him with faultless hospitality, outwardly unperturbed by his appearance. He had reverted to his old Oxford ways. His lank, straight hair was longer than ever and the black velvet smoking jacket and the red bow-tie had become a uniform, adopted to defy the very conformity which my parents represented. They, for their part, may have taken comfort from the fact that this was to be our last meeting for some time as I was on the point of setting off yet again for Spain, this time on my own.

My parents had been given the address in Madrid of an elderly couple, the Lewises, friends of one of our local doctors, and they wrote to say that they had found me lodgings with a lady called Pilar near the centre of the city. Early one morning in July 1963, my father drove me to Gatwick. The student flight was due to leave at 9 a.m and arrive in Madrid at one o'clock, but take-off was delayed while repairs were carried out to an engine. I was not at all concerned, either by the delay, by the need for repairs, or by the fact that after take-off, water which eventually turned to icicles dripped through the roof of the aircraft. Nor was I worried by the discovery that the captain and his co-pilot were happily enjoying a glass of beer when we students were invited to look into the cockpit. Bill Lewis, who met me in Madrid, was much more anxious. 'I thought you must be coming via the North Pole!' he announced jokingly when finally I emerged from Customs at five in the afternoon. He took me home to meet his wife, who assured me of a warm welcome at their apartment every evening from six onwards, and then he delivered me to Pilar's address. Pilar was a small, vivacious, sharp-nosed, black-haired single lady who lived in a extraordinarily large, well-appointed flat just off the *Calle Serrano* round the corner from the Lewises.

It was not until the next morning at breakfast, over coffee and bread soaked in oil, that I met Pilar's other lodger, Sylvia Forde, an English girl who had recently come to work at the Embassy. Even with my hard-earned A-level Spanish, I found Pilar's vociferous gabbling difficult to understand; poor Sylvia was only just beginning to learn Spanish and was overwhelmed by it. 'I'm so glad to have someone to talk to,' she confided, 'I haven't been here long and I can't really make out what's going on.'

Together, after an evening or two spent in Pilar's company and a few introductions to some of her friends, we decided that we knew perfectly well what was going on. On a small scale, Pilar was running a disorderly house and was intent on procuring nice English girls for some of the flabby, ageing men of her acquaintance. Sylvia and I adopted the expedient of firmly locking our bedroom doors at night and I hastened to lay my plans for leaving Madrid at the earliest opportunity. In the meantime I rapidly took advantage of every precious moment in the capital city and its environs. In the course of the next week I surveyed a fair proportion of the 2,000 pictures on display in the Prado, and joined many a tourist bus: to the Escorial, Philip II's monasterial palace from where he directed the course of the Spanish Armada (which, annoyingly, the Spaniards insisted on regarding as a very minor disturbance in the course of their splendid history); to Aranjuez, the summer palace of later generations of Spanish monarchs, and, of course, to Toledo, the medieval city perched on a rock above the river Tajo, where in the thirteenth century Jews, Arabs and Christians worked in perfect harmony in the pursuit of learning, and where in the seventeenth, El Greco executed some of his finest painting, particularly the *Burial of the*

Count of Orgaz which was housed in a chapel near the towering Gothic cathedral.

With a group of students I went on the pilgrimage to the Valley of the Fallen, *el Valle de los Caídos*, supposedly the monument to the dead of both sides in the Civil War. A huge Christ figure, arms in the shape of the Cross, stands high above the valley in the Guadarrama mountains outside Madrid, over the grotesque basilica hewn in the rock which Franco, then Head of State, conceived as his own burial ground and memorial. In the valley beneath, according to the official tourist guide, combatants from the Civil War, both right- and left-wing, were buried. A conflicting version circulated amongst our group. It was gleaned from a wizened little old man sitting at the foot of the Cross who said that only the Fascist victims of the war were buried there and that the whole monstrous project was carried out using forced labour, that of the left-wing Republican prisoners. I began to understand why there were so many mutilated beggars on the streets of Madrid: they were the tragic, living remnants of the Civil War. An ugly, schizoid streak to Spain which I had not suspected before was revealing itself. In the mid-twentieth century, the country still bore out the disturbing contrasts depicted by Goya in the eighteenth- and early-nineteenth-century paintings and drawings I had seen in the Prado. Fortunately these depressing revelations were counterbalanced by the sheer kindness and hospitality of a Spanish colleague of my father's, Gabriel Baquero de la Cruz, who took me out of Madrid one weekend to join his family in their summer house in the mountains, not far from *el Valle de los Caídos*. That day in the cool of the pine trees, playing with Gabriel's adorable, tiny, dark-haired children and talking to his spinster sisters who, unbelievably, declared that they loved the rain and cool summer breezes of England, is sharply etched in my memory as one of the most blissful days of that summer.

Back in Pilar's establishment, Sylvia and I had the uncomfortable sensation that things were coming to crisis point. We had persistently refused to go out with her and her portly cronies in the evenings and, just as regularly, saucepans were now clattering through the air in the kitchen. The swift succession of cooks and maids meant that meals and mealtimes became a matter of chance. Feeling slightly guilty at leaving Sylvia in the lurch, I took evasive action and set off by air-conditioned train for the safety of Granada where I settled in for a protracted stay at a student hostel which housed an itinerant, mixed international community as well as Spanish students. They were a stimulating and unpredictable crowd, particularly the Spaniards among them. One minute they would be engaged in guarded but heated political discussions and the next, poetry would be flowing from their fingertips. Poetry seemed to be a release from the tensions of living in a police state where political discussion was a dangerous luxury. I was impressed by the Spaniards' grasp of politics, so unlike the British who did not seem to have any opinions at all. Here everyone held pronounced political ideas about the future direction of the country. Most people were quite certain that there would be another civil war on Franco's death, and given the strength of their opinions, I was not surprised. I would spend hours listening to them and then, to preserve my own sanity, would have to escape from the intensity of their arguments to wander the streets of Granada in the heat of the day, watching the gypsy children at play in front of their caves, or to stroll through the Moorish palace, the Alhambra and the gardens of the Generalife, astounded by the sheer extravagant beauty of the place.

Lulled into a dreamy slumber by the perfume of the roses and the playing of the fountains, I sat alone for hours under the arches surrounding the *Patio de los Arroyos*, the courtyard of streams, in the Generalife, and from there would gaze across to the forbidding walls which concealed the intricate, creamy lacework of the inner courtyards of the Alhambra. Dazzling in the sun, the city lay at my feet, its glare broken only by the tall, bottle-green spikes of the cypresses and the violent purple and pink patches of bougainvillea tumbling over reflecting white walls. A beautiful city but also a very cruel city. What other city could claim to have murdered its own most famous son? It was in Granada at the outbreak of the Spanish Civil War that the rebellious right-wing Francoist forces slaughtered the greatest Spanish poet of the twentieth century, Federico García Lorca, who, through the colour, rhythm and vision of his verse, had introduced me to Andalucía long before I had set foot on its soil.

During these long periods of solitary contemplation in a setting of such dramatically haunting beauty, I found myself overcome by waves of sadness and loneliness. In the past I had known moments of extreme dejection without being able to identify a precise cause. The reason for them was now becoming apparent and it was natural enough: I longed to have someone with whom to share my experiences. Moreover, I realized that the person I most wanted to share them with was Stephen. The early rapport between us, if not his handling of the motor car, had held much promise of harmony and compatibility. Because of his illness, any relationship with him was bound to be precarious, short-lived and probably heart-breaking. Could I help him fulfil himself and find even brief happiness? I doubted whether I was up to the task. Gradually I summoned the courage to broach these problems to some of my new friends and travelling companions, Spaniards, Americans, Danes and Belgians of both sexes. With the brusque certainty of youth, their advice was unanimous: 'If he needs you, you must do it,' they said.

Competing against this inner turmoil, the strong pull of adventure finally tore me away from the brooding magic of Granada and deposited me on a hot, smelly bus, crowded with market vendors and their wares – mostly still alive and flapping and squawking – on the slow crawl over the hills to Málaga. I was waiting in the bus station for the connection to La Línea, the last Spanish outpost before Gibraltar, when a man came up to me and asked if I would like to train as a Spanish dancer. To my surprise he explained that I had the right looks and figure. Although I was by now an old hand at fending off the predatory Spanish male, I was flattered. Despite my misgivings, the man appeared genuine. He was neither oily nor ingratiating but quite straightforward in his approach. He handed me a card bearing the address of his dance studio. With Lady Crathorne's dire warnings of the previous year still ringing in my ears, I was weighing up his offer when the bus for La Línea lumbered into view and hauled me out of temptation's way. Sometimes I have a faint twinge of regret that that bus broke all known records for time-keeping in Spain by arriving on schedule. Who knows what my story might have been, had it arrived just a few minutes later?

From La Línea I passed through the very physical border between Spain and Gibraltar, a barricade of green iron railings about 20 feet high with a gate at the customs post. Gibraltar with all its incongruous trappings of British colonialism was a convenient stepping-stone for my one and only trip to Africa, to Tangiers for my first encounter with the descendants of the people who had invaded Spain in 711 and stayed there for 700 years – the Arabs. I liked them. They treated me, a young English girl travelling alone, with great courtesy, and, unlike the Spaniards who automatically harassed any passing foreign female, showed no such disrespect. They were a dignified people, proud of their artistic skills which were everywhere on display in the booths of the Kazbah. They were also gentle and hospitable, curious to learn about life in Europe, as I discovered over many glasses of the hot, sweet mint tea with which they plied me whenever I bought the smallest item in their shops.

Quite a few more saucepans had been flung around in Madrid during my absence, according to Sylvia. Pilar was more and more dissatisfied with the return that she was getting from her paying guests, having doubtless anticipated sizeable bonuses of one sort or another, and had turned Sylvia out of her room so she was now sharing with me. This, we decided, was a good thing since there was safety in numbers but it was no good for Sylvia as a long-term prospect since I would shortly be leaving and she could not possibly stay in the house on her own. Because we had learned to cope with the situation, I had deliberately refrained from telling the Lewises the truth about the lodgings they had kindly found for me. I did not want to appear ungrateful for their help or their hospitality but the time had now come to apprise them of the goings-on at the *casa de Pilar*. I suggested that Sylvia should come with me to the Lewises' six o'clock cocktail hour and together we would tell them about the succession of decidedly repulsive male visitors. As delicately as possible, we would recount the story of their attempts to grab us when we returned home at night, usually sheltering behind the *serrano*, the nightwatchman, who kept the keys to the front doors of all the apartment houses in the street and who would appear at a clap of the hands to open the main door. We would lightly gloss over the shenanigans which went on all night in the other rooms in the flat, and of the ominous rattlings of our locked bedroom door handle.

As Sylvia and I recounted these tales to the captive audience of British ex-patriots on my final evening in Madrid, Mrs Lewis spluttered over her gin and tonic, while her other guests grinned in amusement at our story. Immediately the tendrils of the local grapevine started reaching out. There was no question about it: Sylvia would have to move as a matter of urgency, Mrs Lewis decided, deputing her husband to mobilize all their contacts in Madrid to find new accommodation for her straight away.

Most of the Lewis regulars, like Sylvia, worked at the British Embassy, although she had not met any of them before. They included a lively, spontaneous young couple, John and Maria Maud, who were on the point of leaving for a hardship posting to Cuba – Fidel Castro's communist fortress island – for which they were having to take with them every single item that they would need in the next eighteen months. I was as fascinated by the prospect that faced them as they were aghast at the conditions Sylvia and I had endured. I enjoyed their company and liked the other people I had met at the Lewises' gatherings. They were amusing but modest, a good advertisement for the Diplomatic Service which began to beckon as an exciting career prospect. I returned to England the next day, by student flight, sad to have left behind so many experiences, sights, sounds, acquaintances and intrigues but dazzled, if slightly bewildered, at the broad horizons and the array of contrasting possibilities that were opening up before me.

CHAPTER FIVE

Uncertain Principles

M Y ATTEMPTS TO get in touch with Stephen on my return home from Spain were unavailing. According to his mother, he had already gone back to Cambridge and was not at all well. I was busy preparing to leave home to embark on a new stage of my life in London and for the next few weeks that autumn my attention was totally absorbed as I was drawn into the academic and social whirl of the Westfield scene in particular, and London in general.

Academically the modern languages course was both demanding and stimulating. There were only nine of us in the first year in the Spanish Department and a motley crew we were: Carolyn Merrill, Susan Green, Janet Cousens and I were from conventional English backgrounds, Shireen Bilimoria came from Trinidad, Vicky Gibbs and Helen Riess had been brought up in Latin America, and Sister Mary Martin was a Catholic nun. For one year there was also the extrovert Liz Bloom from Golders Green.

We were blessed with a remarkably low student/teacher ratio. The teaching was not only very efficient but also very entertaining as many of the members of staff seemed to have become severely infected with the Spanish sense of humour, particularly the Spanish sense of irony, so that, even at nine o'clock on a Monday morning, Dr Alan Deyermond's erudite lectures on medieval Spanish literature could be relied upon to get the week off to a rousing start. His comical representations of the epic tradition, where adversaries had the preposterously theatrical habit of flinging cucumbers filled with blood in each others' faces, caused much hilarity, as did his expositions of the Book of Good Love, *el Libro de Buen Amor*, where Juan Ruiz, the Archpriest of Hita, constantly finds himself beset by the demands of the wild women of the mountains as he tries to go about his parochial business. Similarly in language classes,

Janet Chapman would point out the pitfalls of language. We may laugh at the Spanish for having their *lecherías* (dairies), she would say, but they will make fun of us for having our groceries (*grosería* in Spanish means rudeness). While I am bound to acknowledge the excellence of the formal teaching at Westfield, I am also eternally grateful for the subliminal influence of that ironic sense of humour, a humour which succeeds in highlighting the ridiculous and the absurd even when doom and gloom may prevail all around.

On the social front, Westfield was less successful. My room-mate, Margaret Smithson, a fair-haired girl from Yorkshire who was as witty as she was practical, quickly became a close friend, as did some of the other girls in my year, including Sandra Wade whom I had met at the interview. Otherwise, as a social scene, Westfield was not promising. Freshers' functions struck me as rather juvenile after all my extensive travels, often alone, throughout Spain, and despite Beatlemania which was sweeping the country, the Freshers' socials, or hops as they were known, were each and every one of them a dire disaster. Typically, the boys brought in from other colleges would stand on one side of the room and the girls on the other until the very last dance when the boys would peel themselves away from the wall to ask the by now sorely disenchanted girls to dance.

Fortunately, because we were in London and could come and go as we pleased, our movements were not bounded by the confines of Westfield College. Concerts, the theatre and the ballet were all within easy reach – which was how I came to be travelling on the Underground with a group of friends when we glimpsed the headlines announcing President Kennedy's assassination.

It was at about that time, November 1963, that I heard from Stephen again. He was coming to London for dental treatment and asked if I would like to go to the opera with him. This was a much more enticing prospect than any Freshers' hop. Though I had loved music since early childhood, I had had little formal training and had been to the opera only once, with the school to a performance of *The Marriage of Figaro* at Sadler's Wells. My single attempt to learn an instrument, the flute, was quickly aborted as a result of an accident at the age of thirteen on the frozen lake in the park at Verulamium, the site of the Roman city on which St Albans was founded.

One of our group of Saturday friends, Susan Driver, a serious, methodical girl, had long promised that she would teach me to ice-skate, so when the lake froze during a particularly harsh winter, she lent me a pair of skates and guided me on to the ice. She herself was so well coordinated it must have been a shock to find how clumsy her pupil was, for as soon as I set skate on ice I fell forwards, landing heavily and painfully on my face and hands. Over the next few weeks I was to become closely acquainted with the husband of the kind lady who picked me up from the ice; she was none other than the wife of the orthopaedic consultant under whose auspices my broken wrists were subsequently x-rayed, manipulated, set in plaster and eventually mended. I became the object of envy rather than sympathy in school because, for very obvious reasons, I could not take notes, do homework or play games. That episode spelt the end of the flute, although with due caution I did persevere with the ice-skating.

One Friday afternoon in November 1963, I met Stephen in Harley Street where Russell Cole, his Australian uncle by marriage, had his dental practice. Stephen walked haltingly, lurching from side to side as he advanced, making taxis rather than the Underground or buses an expensive necessity for journeys of any great distance. Curiously, as his gait became more unsteady so his opinions became more forceful and defiant. On our way to visit the Wallace Collection, only a short distance from Harley Street, he announced quite adamantly that he did not share the general hero-worship of the assassinated President. In his opinion, the manner of Kennedy's handling of the Cuba crisis could only be described as foolhardy: he had brought the world to the brink of nuclear war and it was he, not the Russians, who had threatened a military confrontation. What's more, Stephen declared, it was preposterous for the United States to claim a victory because Kennedy had agreed to remove missiles from Turkey to appease Kruschev. Despite the force with which he expressed his ideas and his difficulty in walking, Stephen was defiantly indefatigable, so, from the Wallace Collection, we made our way down Regent Street in search of a restaurant. We were just crossing Lower Regent Street when in the middle of the road, as the lights were turning green for the oncoming traffic, he stumbled and fell. With the help of a passerby, I dragged him to his feet and thereafter gave him my arm to lean on. Shaken, we hailed a taxi for Sadler's Wells.

The opera for which Stephen had tickets was *The Flying Dutchman*. It was magnificent, sweeping us away in the power of its music and the drama of its legendary tale. The Dutchman, cursed to roam the seas through storm and wind until he could find someone who would sacrifice herself for him in love, was a wild, hounded figure, loudly lamenting his fate from the rigging of his tossing ship. Senta, the girl who fell in love with him, was pure and innocent; like most Wagnerian sopranos, however, obesity kept her pretty firmly moored to her spinning-wheel. Sensing that Stephen identified closely with the hero, I began to understand his demonic driving tactics. His father's car was the vehicle for his *angst* and fury at the trick that Fate had dealt him. He too was flying hither and thither in search of rescue – in a manner that could only be described as foolhardy.

After that evening, I felt that I needed to find out more for myself about Stephen's condition. I made several sorties into central London, searching out old acquaintances who had become medical students and investigating the poky offices of various charities dealing in neurological illnesses. Everywhere I drew a blank. Either my contacts were out or had not yet learnt anything about neurology, or the charity officials were elderly clerks manning a dusty office for an organization about which they knew next to nothing. Perhaps it was better not to know. Was Stephen's fate any worse, I wondered, than the fate which threatened all of us? We all lived under the shadow of the nuclear cloud and none of us could count on our full threescore years and ten.

In the lull of the bleak winter days between Christmas and the New Year, I called on Stephen at home in St Albans. He was not expecting me and was on the point of leaving for London to go to the opera with his father and sisters. However, he was so obviously delighted to see me that I readily accepted his spontaneous invitation to accompany him and his father in a week's time to yet another opera, *Der Rosenkavalier*. Opera seemed to be an established family pastime in the Hawking household whereas I, a newcomer to the genre, was still assessing this hybrid art form. Though undoubtedly it could exert tremendous emotional power through the combination of music and drama, it could also appear ludicrous if for the merest second one's concentration lapsed; indeed, it demanded a lot of the audience in the suspension of their disbelief. The missing link in my appreciation so far, as I was to discover the next week, was the totally fanciful experience of grand opera performed in a grand opera house, where the performance on the stage was no more frivolous or improbable than the glamorous spectacle of the bow-tied, diamond-studded, fur-draped audience in the auditorium – not of course that the Hawking contingent subscribed in any way to this latter aspect of the proceedings, preferring rather to dress as if for a brisk hike on

the Yorkshire moors, complete with Thermos flask and sandwiches for
interval refreshment.

During the next term Stephen seemed to have access to an inexhaustible supply of opera tickets and was forever coming to London to take
me to Covent Garden or Sadler's Wells. I once ventured to suggest that
I would rather like to go to the ballet since secretly I still preferred
ballet to opera, but that suggestion was quashed with withering scorn.
The ballet was a waste of time and the music was trivial, not worth the
effort of listening, I was told. Chastened, I refrained from telling
Stephen of the occasion when I managed to get myself a ticket for
Romeo and Juliet with Fonteyn and Nureyev through the Student Union.
I went in a party of girls and we sat in the cheap seats, far back and
high up in the amphitheatre at Covent Garden, way above the Grand
Circle where the Hawkings usually sat. That performance was sublime
in its grace and innocence, its strength and colour, its elegance and
range of emotion. It left me deeply moved. It was not until many, many
years later that I learned that Fonteyn was then, at the age of forty-six,
working with manic frenzy to support her paraplegic husband, Roberto
Arias, who had been shot – not as was originally believed by a political
opponent, but by the disaffected husband of one of his many lovers. For
Arias, Fonteyn had sacrificed her passion for Nureyev.

Stephen was still coming to London frequently for seminars or
dental appointments and, increasingly, I found myself travelling to Cambridge to visit him on Saturdays or Sundays. Those visits, though
urgently awaited, often proved disappointing to both of us. The fare, at
10 shillings return, made quite a hole in my allowance of £10 a month,
and the course of true love did not run at all smoothly. It did not
need much imagination to realize that Stephen could not contemplate
embarking on a long-term, stable relationship because of the dismal
prognosis of his illness. A quick fling was probably all he could envisage
and that was not what I, in my innocence and in the still puritanical
climate of the early 1960s when the fear of an unwanted pregnancy was
a potent constraint, dared contemplate. These opposing perspectives led
to such tension between us that I often returned to London in tears and
Stephen probably felt that my presence was rubbing salt into the wound
of his trauma. He revealed little where emotional matters were concerned and he refused to talk about his illness. For fear of hurting him,
I tried to intuit his feelings without forcing him to voice them, thus

unwittingly establishing a pattern of non-communication which eventually would become intolerable.

I met Stephen yet again in Harley Street later that winter after an appointment with his consultant. 'How did you get on?' I asked.

He grimaced. 'He told me not to bother to come back because there's nothing he can do,' he said.

At Westfield, Margaret came with me to the meetings of the Christian Union. I hoped that in those meetings I might be able to gain some supportive insights for a situation in which I was rapidly becoming more and more involved and which was swiftly becoming more and more confusing. Like his parents, Stephen had no hesitation in declaring himself an atheist despite the strongly Methodist background of his Yorkshire grandparents. It was understandable that as a cosmologist examining the laws which governed the universe, he could not allow his calculations to be muddled by a confessed belief in the existence of a Creator God, quite apart from the confusion his illness might be causing in his mind. I was quite glad to get away from the tedium of regular Sunday church-going but was not inclined to abandon my beliefs completely. Even then, possibly under my mother's influence, I was convinced that there had to be more to heaven and earth than was contained in Stephen's cold, impersonal philosophy. Although by this stage I was completely under his spell, bewitched by his clear blue-grey eyes and the broad, dimpled smile which was all too rarely in evidence, I resisted his atheism. Instinctively I knew that I could not allow myself to succumb to such a bleakly negative influence which could offer no explanations, no consolation, no comfort and no hope for the human condition. I feared that atheism would destroy us both. Quite the contrary, I needed to cling to whatever rays of hope I could find and maintain sufficient faith for the two of us if any good were to come of our sad plight.

The meetings of the College Christian Union were not well attended and soon they were to be even less so. The topic for the term's discussions was the nature of divine grace. In a preliminary discussion it quickly transpired that the leaders of the meeting, including the young chaplain, whose name we irreverently traduced to the Rev P. Soopa, were firmly of the opinion that only baptized, confessed, practising Christians could receive divine grace, salvation or whatever else they liked to call it, and only they had the right qualifications to enter the kingdom of heaven. Margaret and I were so indignant that we walked out, furiously compiling lists of all those dearly loved, good people, friends and relations, who did not fully meet all the correct criteria.

Margaret and I held our own long discussions on these topics which we continued into the holidays when I went to stay with her and her family in Yorkshire. Mostly we found ourselves in agreement. We formulated our own philosophy, heretical no doubt to the scions of the Christian Union, that deeds were more important than beliefs and that loving one's neighbour was tantamount to loving God, if God was indeed all goodness. Margaret's father, a gentle country doctor, renowned for his dedication, was the shining example of our theory at work. For my part I was – and had been since my sixth-form studies – influenced by the Existential movement, or at least by my understanding of it. I was impressed, not so much by the harsh, impersonal atheism of Sartre for whom Stephen professed admiration, as by the more approachable writings of Camus and the humanity of the Spanish Existentialist writer, Miguel de Unamuno. The theory of life as a series of choices which demanded total commitment through definitive decision-making appealed to me with a far greater intensity than the narrow-minded orthodoxy of the student Christian Union. I felt the urge to commit myself but I knew that in doing so I would require the support of a greater force and I would need to feel myself part of a greater plan than mere agnostic or humanist doctrines could provide. This may sound more sophisticated than it really was. My basic motivation probably stemmed from a childhood fascination with the captivating pictures in my Bible. It was no more complicated than the commendation to 'Consider the lilies of the field . . .' meaning, I supposed, that one should not worry about the future because it would take care of itself if one tried to keep faith with fundamental principles.

I threw myself into the College debating society as an alternative to the Christian Union. Debating was one of my father's favourite pastimes, possibly because he felt his own considerable talents frustrated from constantly witnessing, but not participating in, daily debates in the House of Commons. In my later teens, he encouraged me to share his interest. For a pensive, rather nervous girl like me, public debating was ostensibly out of character. However, once I had overcome my initial bout of stage-fright, I revelled in the cut and thrust of the platform which helped me lay aside my timid, reserved image and find a self-confidence in public-speaking which I lacked in day-to-day relationships.

In that first year at Westfield, I undoubtedly made quite a fool of myself in my many unselfconscious and ill-considered utterances.

While I blush at the memory of some of those early performances in the debating hall, I am also aware that through them I gained a tenacity, a reluctance to accept defeat and a refusal to be fobbed off with feeble or facile argument, which even today can surprise people who do not know me well, and which over in the past thirty years have often been put to the test. One aspect of debating eluded me, however. I found it impossible to play devil's advocate: I could never argue for a cause that I did not believe in, and vice versa.

Language students nowadays regularly spend a whole year abroad. In the 1960s it was a luxury to be able to spend even a term in the country of one's target language. We Westfield students, including Sister Mary Martin, our plucky nun, set out by train and boat in late April to spend the summer on a pre-arranged course at Valencia University. We arrived in Valencia to find that no such course existed and all the University could offer us was a few classes in Spanish on Shakespeare. The only obligation on us was to collect our certificates of attendance at the end of the term, whether we attended the lectures or not. We went to just one class which made a travesty of *Macbeth*, and decided that enough was enough. I had had a lifetime's education in Shakespeare at St Albans High School and could not bear the thought of a supplementary dose in Spanish. My companions agreed, so thereafter, we went to the beach instead.

Hardly had we been in Spain two weeks when, though the others still went to the beach, I was forced to stay at home, confined to my room in the seventh-floor apartment with a blinding headache which at first I thought was sunstroke but which developed into a severe case of chickenpox. I was already feeling wretched. I missed Stephen badly: communication by telephone was out of the question and he did not write to me although I sent him many letters. The only comfort was afforded by my Westfield friends whose visits kept me in touch with the outside world, and by my landlady, Doña Pilar de Ubeda and her middle-aged daughter Maribel. Initially I had been awed by Doña Pilar's domineering character, but when I fell ill she was kindness personified. She promised that she would look after me as if I were her own daughter and she was as good as her promise. As I slowly started to regain strength under her tender care, I wandered into the kitchen where she gave me lessons in Spanish cookery, a far more useful accomplishment than learning Shakespeare in Spanish. She taught me how to peel an orange tidily in quarters, how to make *gazpacho* and *paella*, and she took me shopping with her. Luckily, with a spotty face and in the presence of such an august matron, I was spared the approaches of the men idly lounging around in the streets. By now I was feeling pretty disenchanted with Spain, with the generally constant sexual harassment, with the censorship which meant that whole pages of the imported copies of *The Times*, containing uncomplimentary reports about the Franco regime, were often missing, and at the frequent disappearance of student acquaintances when they were picked up off the streets and flung into jail without trial.

Back in Doña Pilar's flat, I sat in her living-room listening *ad nauseam* to the two records I had bought myself – Beethoven's Seventh Symphony and excerpts from *Tristan and Isolde*. The latter reduced me to an exquisitely painful state of woe. At last the longed-for moment came. Setting out by train for Barcelona on the first leg of the journey home, I was glad to leave Valencia behind, despite the succulence of its oranges and the all-pervasive perfume of its citrus groves.

My parents brought Stephen to meet me and the initial moment of reunion was happy but shortlived. I soon became aware that in my absence he had changed: his physical condition had not altered markedly, except that he now regularly walked with a stick, but his personality was overshadowed by a deep depression. This revealed itself in a harsh black cynicism, aided and abetted by long hours of Wagnerian opera played at full volume. He was even more terse and uncommunicative, apparently so absorbed in himself that when he offered to teach me to play croquet on the Trinity Hall lawn, for example, he seemed to forget that I was there. Throwing his walking-stick to one side, he issued curt instructions as I aimed my ball towards the first hoop, which it missed. He then took up his mallet and, croqueting my ball round the whole course, reached the finishing post before I had even had a second turn. I stood open-mouthed, amused and perturbed at one and the same time. This was indeed an impressive *tour de force* in which he scarcely bothered to veil his hostility and frustration, as if he were deliberately trying to deter me from further involvement with him. It was too late. I was already so deeply involved with him that there was no easy or obvious way out.

It was painful but perhaps beneficial that we were soon to be parted again: Stephen was about to set out for Germany with his sister Philippa, to worship at the Wagnerian shrine, the Festspielhaus in Bayreuth; they had tickets for the complete *Ring* cycle. Thence they were to travel by rail behind the Iron Curtain to Prague. Meanwhile I was to accompany my father to an international governmental conference in Dijon where I was to stay with a local family. The Célériers were a pleasant, elderly couple with a highly sophisticated twenty-five-year-old daughter, Régine, who had a job and a boyfriend. Although I spent only ten days or so in their house, for years afterwards Régine wrote long letters in a precise, flowing French hand and an elegance of style which I struggled to emulate. Although she was at work all day and often out in the evenings, I was not at a loss for entertainment because my father's conference, after a day or two of lectures and study sessions, generated its own entertainment in which I was privileged to share.

Since we were in Burgundy, the entertainment naturally revolved around the vineyards, the famous *clos* of the region. Consequently there began yet another stage, arguably one of the most enjoyable, of my education – the cultivation of a discerning palate. I was pleasurably introduced to the great names and the great bouquets of the region, Nuits Saint Georges, Côtes de Beaune, Clos de Vougeot ... The advertising slogan for Nuits Saint Georges aroused my curiosity: tantalizingly, the deep velvety wine was said to resemble '*la nuit des noces, douce et caressante*'. In my ignorance, my imagination tried to fathom what that might mean – unsuccessfully.

From Dijon we drove to Geneva airport to meet my mother and then spent a couple of days in our favourite retreat, high in the Bernese Oberland, at Hohfluh, a tiny village atop the Brenner Pass overlooking the valley of the Aare at Meiringen. The old Hotel Kurhaus no longer exists; it used to be a family hotel run by the Blatter-Wiegands whose hospitality was such that during one summer holiday some years earlier, they actually dismantled the doors of the verandah where we were sitting so that we could watch the display of folk-dancing which was taking place indoors in the dining-room. The hotel enjoyed the most magnificent scenery: every morning against a peerless blue sky, the crystalline white peak of the Wetterhorn rose serenely above the black rock, the dark trees and the green pastures to greet us as we gazed in wonderment across the valley. It was a convenient place to cross paths with my brother who was travelling round Europe with his friends in a Mini, painted all over with the Union Jack: in those days such a gesture had not acquired the distasteful jingoistic overtones of extreme nationalism.

From there we prepared for the next stage of our journey – to northern Italy.

Before we left Switzerland, my father took us to Lucerne, the medieval city on the edge of the lake of the same name, and showed us the sequence of paintings of the Dance of Death in the roof beams of one of the wooden bridges which spanned the river. He pointed out the white-clad figure of Death, selecting its victim and capturing him in a deadly embrace before whirling him faster and faster to his doom.

Where Spain had been depressing, Italy was ravishing; it was a feast for the mind and the senses. Art, history, music, light and colour met us and pursued us everywhere we went – Como, Florence, San Gimigniano, Pisa, Siena, Verona, Padua – in a vertiginous display of florid exuberance. One evening in Florence, after a day in the presence of Michelangelo, Botticelli, Bellini and Leonardo, my mother and I were leaning out of our hotel window, looking across the Arno to the Pitti Palace where we were to attend a concert. It was then, in an expansive moment, that she confided to me her reasons for marrying my father at the beginning of the war. That remark was prescient, for only a few days later, when we arrived at our hotel in Venice, the Hotel Dalla Salute, located on a secluded canal behind the church of the same name, the manager produced a postcard addressed to me. It was a view of the castle at Salzburg and it was from Stephen.

I was overjoyed to receive such an unexpected piece of correspondence. Could Stephen really have been thinking of me as I had been thinking of him? It gave me grounds for daring to hope that he was looking forward to seeing me at the end of the summer. The postcard was uncharacteristically full of news. He had arrived in Salzburg for the tail-end of the Festival which was quite a contrast to Bayreuth. Czechoslovakia had been wonderful and remarkably cheap, a good advertisement for communism. He did not mention that a bad fall on a train in Germany had deprived him of his front teeth and that many hours of painstaking dentistry by his uncle in Harley Street would be required to replace them. In the glow of romance, though conducted at a distance, Venice, with its canals, lagoon, palaces, churches, galleries and islands, became even more gloriously scintillating, yet, impatient for the possible opening of a new chapter in my life, I was not sorry to leave and return to Switzerland. From Basle we were to fly home with the car on board the aeroplane in a well-justified stroke of extravagance after the many thousands of miles Dad had driven single-handedly across the Continent over the years.

Stephen was pleased to see me on my return. Intuitively I understood that he had begun to view our relationship in a more positive, joyous light and had perhaps decided that all was not lost, that the future did not have to be as black as his worst fears had painted it. Back in Cambridge, one dark, wet Saturday evening in October, he hesitantly whispered a proposal of marriage to me. That moment transformed our lives and consigned all my thoughts of a career in the Diplomatic Service to oblivion.

CHAPTER SIX

Backgrounds

ONCE THE MOMENTOUS decision had been taken, everything else began to fall into place, if not entirely of its own accord, then with the help of some determination and effort. We sailed through the next year, carried high on a tide of euphoria. All that had been black and hopeless before was now bathed in a golden light of optimism and love. Whatever misgivings my friends and family may have had about Stephen's state of health, they kept them to themselves and the only comments I received concerned the eccentricity of the Hawking family.

Such comments did not worry me too much because I liked the Hawkings and regarded their eccentricities with a respectful fascination. They made me welcome, already treating me as one of the family. They may have economized on material goods, preferring the old and tried to the new-fangled, and they certainly did compromise on heating to the extent that people who were cold were brusquely told to follow Frank Hawking's example and wear more clothes, a dressing-gown for example, even during the day. Moreover, as I had already discovered, there were areas of the house which could be charitably described as distinctly shabby. However, none of this was particularly new to me. It simply indicated that this household had a set of priorities which were not so very different from those I was used to. My own parents had scraped and saved for years. We were not wealthy and we often had to make do and mend because so much of my father's income went on our education and on those wonderful summer holidays. We did not have central heating at home and I was quite accustomed to sitting by the fire with my face and toes burning while a freezing draught whistled down the back of my neck. At night in bed I would rest my numbed feet on my hot-water bottle, in the full knowledge that the agony of blistering chilblains would be the price to be paid the next day for such small comfort. By the morning, Jack Frost would have sculpted an exquisite ice garden of opaque fronds and ferns all over the window-panes. If our house was neater than the Hawkings', it was both because it was smaller and because my father had given up all pretensions to any prowess whatsoever as a handyman – and for good reason.

The sad story of his attempts to repair or decorate the ceilings in our house over the years bore out the galling truth that Dad was no expert in household repairs. Ceilings had a knack of frustrating his best efforts to protect or repair them. When, in the wake of my tenth birthday party, he tried to clear the snow which had been driving under the eaves all afternoon from the rafters in the attic where it was accumulating, he slipped on the wet surface and his foot made two dramatic and unexpected appearances through the upstairs ceilings. Then there was the hot June afternoon a year or so later, when he decided to rectify the bulge in the dining-room ceiling; he succeeded in removing the bulge by bringing the ceiling down on himself, creating a large hole and covering himself in bits of debris. His efforts to decorate ceilings were no more successful: the hand-roller and its metal paint tray, the revolutionary tools which were said to cut decorating time by half, proved quite unmanageable when manipulated, one in each hand, from the top of a ladder, with the result that the white paint descended in a pearly shower directly over his assistants – Grandma and me – who stood steadying the ladder beneath. Thereafter he decided that it was cheaper to pay professionals to do his odd jobs for him.

Rarely when I was present did members of the Hawking family bear out the stories in circulation about their habits and bring books to the table, although other guests were accustomed to this idiosyncrasy. They may have made an exception to their usual routine out of politeness to me, for mealtimes were generally sociable occasions, calmly presided over by Stephen's mother who kept remarkably cool in the face of the torrents of expletives which accompanied her volatile husband's not infrequent outbursts of temper. Frank Hawking's temper did not shock me unduly since my father, despite his wonderful sense of humour, could also flare up at seemingly slight provocation. I assumed therefore that such explosions were a condition of families and fatherhood. Apparently no longer subject to the savage black moods of the past, Stephen's placid, more philosophical nature promised a calmer lifestyle. Although he could be sharp and demanding, Frank Hawking was not hard-hearted. His outbursts were usually directed at the crass inadequacies of some inanimate object, like a blunt carving knife or a spilt glass or a dropped fork, never at people within the family circle. In fact, with young Edward who was given to tantrums particularly at bedtime, he was a model of patience and forbearance.

The talk at mealtimes was predictably intellectual, ranging over political and international issues. As Philippa had gone up to Oxford to study Chinese, the Cultural Revolution was a favourite topic of fashionable enthusiasm. I knew little about oriental history or politics and thought it expedient to keep quiet rather than betray my ignorance. Spain and France seemed very parochial and unglamorous by comparison with the Orient and nobody expressed any interest in them or their cultures at all. The Hawkings, in any case, knew all there was to know about France since Isobel had French relatives. They also knew all there was to know about Spain, since she and the children had spent three months living in close proximity to Robert Graves' household in Deya, Majorca, in the winter of 1950 when Frank was away in Africa, engaged on research in tropical medicine. Beryl Graves was a friend of Isobel's from her Oxford days and Robert Graves was regarded as an icon in the family.

When the supper table was cleared away, the younger generation would settle down to play a board-game. Stephen had been a fanatical games player since his early childhood and with his close friend John McClenahan had devised a long and complicated dynastic game, complete with family trees, landed gentry, vast acreages, bishoprics for younger sons and death duties. Unfortunately this game had not been preserved so we were reduced to playing ready-published games like Cluedo and Scrabble and occasionally the notorious Chinese game mahjong, played with delicately carved ivory tiles. I had already been exposed to Stephen's prowess at croquet and I received similar treatment when he offered to teach me to play chess. However, when it came to Scrabble, I did not need a mentor as I was confident of being reasonably competent at word-games, an art learnt as a very small child from numerous games of Lexicon with my loquacious and inventive Great-Aunt Effie when we lived in her house in north London. It soon became obvious from the reactions of my opponents, both Stephen and Philippa, that guests – certainly not those who only went to London University as opposed to Oxford or Cambridge – were not expected to win at games like Scrabble, where the intellectual stakes were high.

If there was not a quorum for board-games, Stephen and I would sit by the fire after supper while his mother regaled us with episodes of family history. I enjoyed listening to her and admired her as a role model. An Oxford graduate and, before her marriage, an income tax inspector, she was intelligent and witty yet totally devoted to her family, appearing to have no ambitions for herself at all. At the time she was teaching history in a private girls' boarding school in St Albans where her very considerable intellectual qualities were clearly under-rated.

With a bemused detachment, Isobel took upon herself the task of introducing me to her own past and that of the Hawking family. The second child of seven, she was born in Glasgow where her father, the son of a wealthy boiler-maker, was a doctor. Although her family moved by boat to Plymouth when she was still a young child, she had vivid memories of her grandfather's austere house in Glasgow where family prayers in the parlour, attended by every member of the household staff, constituted the only form of diversion. On her mother's side, she claimed descent from John Law of Lauriston, who after bankrupting France in the seventeenth century took himself off to Louisiana. In the telling, multifarious and far-reaching family feuds came to light: most of them concerned money for it appeared that cutting a miscreant out of one's will was considered an automatic and quite acceptable means of expressing profound and puritanical displeasure.

Stephen's father's family were of God-fearing Yorkshire farming stock. Their claim to distinction had come through an ancestor in the early nineteenth century who had been steward to the Duke of Devonshire. In recognition of this elevated position he had built himself a large house in Boroughbridge which he called Chatsworth, after the Devonshires' stately home. The family fortunes had fluctuated somewhat since those days with the consequence that, in the twentieth century, Stephen's grandfather's farming ventures had led to financial ruin and it was left to his grandmother to rescue her family of five children – four boys and a girl – from penury. This she did by opening a school in her house. Its success was said to be a measure of her strength of character. Money, wealth and its creation and loss were prominent elements in Isobel's story-telling, as was her marked tendency to judge others by their degree of intelligence rather than their integrity or likeability. Charm was regarded as a severe flaw in character and those unfortunate enough to possess it were to be deeply mistrusted.

As his mother was one of seven children and his father one of five, Stephen naturally had legions of first and a whole army of second cousins. My parents, on the other hand, were both only children, so I had no first cousins at all: I had just a few second cousins, one in Australia and the rest in rural Norfolk. It therefore came as quite a shock to meet so many people who not only were closely related, but also bore remarkable facial similarities to each other. On Stephen's mother's side, they characteristically had high cheek-bones, close-set blue eyes and wavy, chestnut hair, while the faces of his father's relations were all long and heavily jowled. Only my brother bore any slight resemblance to me, yet here were all of thirty-three cousins who looked like each other, depending which side of the family they belonged to, and who were all closely connected to Stephen.

Although quite a number lived abroad and divorce had been rather fashionable among them, I met many of them, their friends, husbands, wives and even their former spouses, during the course of that winter's succession of family parties. They treated me in a friendly and open manner, though they really seemed to be more interested in each other and in the animated exchange of family news and gossip. As an observer, I began to realize what an advantage a large family network could be: the loss of individuality was more than compensated by the sense of security which such a network could create. Despite ongoing feuds and several divorces, all these people could depend upon each other as a direct result of their close inter-relationship. Such bonds were a happy accident of birth whereas in my experience, friendships were much less easily made and had to be worked at. Because there were so many of them, they scarcely had any need of friends and could afford to disregard the outside world as they were sufficient unto themselves. This sufficiency lent them a confidence which enabled them to move with ease in any situation, assured of their own worth and untroubled by the self-doubt which had so often beset me. The novelty of this sense of extended family was exhilarating. By comparison my own immediate family circle of parents, brother and one grandmother and two great-aunts seemed a bit limited.

There was, however, one Hawking who notably lacked the self-assurance of the rest of the family. On hearing of our engagement, Stephen's Aunt Muriel announced that, as she put it, she 'just had to come down from Yorkshire to see what sort of girl Stephen was marrying'. Muriel was Frank Hawking's only sister. The youngest of the family, she had stayed at home to look after her ageing parents despite being a gifted musician. Now in her sixties, she wore the marks of frustration in her sad, drooping face and large, soft brown eyes. She was devoted to her brother, Frank, and to his eldest son, and dutifully admired the family's intellectual qualities although she herself did not share them. Her homely way of speech was often greeted with ill-concealed exasperation or ignored altogether by the other members of the family, although Stephen, who was her Methodist equivalent of a god-son, always treated her with a good-natured tolerance. Frequently I would sit and chat to Auntie Muriel, just as I would sometimes escape to Granny Walker's attic, to get away from the suffocatingly competitive intellectual atmosphere of the dining-room.

Stephen was no respecter of persons, other than his closest relations. His self-confidence restored, he delighted in bringing his Oxford ways into any conversation, deliberately setting out to shock with his provocative statements. My mild-mannered grandma was profoundly upset when I took him to stay with her for a weekend and he nonchalantly announced, in answer to her enquiries, that Norwich Cathedral was a very ordinary, uninspiring building. My friends he considered easy victims and he had no compunction in monopolizing the conversation at parties with his controversial opinions. To my mortification, he dominated the twenty-first birthday party of one of my oldest schoolfriends, Caroline Berman, by now an art student, with a vociferous and protracted argument about conceptualism in modern art. Stephen had not bargained with Caroline's equally pronounced views and encountered in her a determined and tenacious adversary, hence the length of the argument.

With me he would argue that artificial flowers were in every way to be preferred to the real thing and that Brahms, my favourite composer, was second-rate because he was such a poor orchestrator. Rachmaninov was good only for the musical dustbin and Tchaikovsky was primarily a composer of ballet music. So far, my knowledge of composers was embryonic; what little I knew was gleaned from the records – Schubert, Mozart, Beethoven and Grieg – that Dad had been buying on Saturday mornings for the past couple of years since we had acquired a record-player, from the concerts I had been attending at the Festival Hall and from those few bewildering visits to the opera. All I knew about Rachmaninov and Tchaikovsky was that their music had the power to move me profoundly; I knew nothing about Brahms's orchestration. It was only later that I found out, to my silent amusement, that although Wagner had despised Brahms, the feeling was mutual. As for the flowers, Blake's lines might have given Stephen pause for thought:

> To see a World in a Grain of Sand
> And a Heaven in a Wild Flower
> Hold Infinity in the palm of your hand
> And Eternity in an hour . . .

While I applauded Stephen's refusal to be drawn into small-talk, I was nervously aware that his youthful arrogance was in poor taste and I was worried that it was putting me in danger of losing me my friends, if not my relations. There came a stage when I even feared that he was jeopardizing my chances of any future academic activity. I was content to abandon all my budding hopes of a career in the Foreign Office for his sake, but I was unhappy about letting him destroy whatever opportunity I might have had for pursuing some sort of research. When I took him to meet my supervisor, Alan Deyermond, who was at that time encouraging me to think about doing a Ph.D in medieval literature, Stephen really excelled himself. Waving his sherry glass around as if the point he was making was so obvious that only a fool could disagree with it, he revelled in the opportunity to tell Alan Deyermond and all my contemporaries that the study of medieval literature was as useful an occupation as studying pebbles on the beach. Fortunately, as Alan Deyermond was also an Oxford graduate, he willingly picked up the gauntlet thus offered and gave Stephen a good run for his money. The argument was inconclusive and both sides parted on remarkably amiable terms. When I protested on the way home in the car, Stephen shrugged. 'You shouldn't take it personally,' he said.

The proof of Stephen's conviction that intellectual arguments were never to be considered a personal matter came in a surprising manner in the course of that same year. Professor Fred Hoyle, who had rejected Stephen's postgraduate research application, was at the time pioneering the use of television to popularize science. So successful was he that his name had become a household word and his popularity was enabling him to put pressure on the government to grant him his own Institute of Astronomy in Cambridge. It was a foregone conclusion that if his demands were not met, he, like so many other British scientists, would embarrass the government by joining the brain drain to the United States. He had power, popularity and the attention of the public and his recent theories were eagerly followed in the press, especially those which he was developing with his Indian research student, Jayant Narlikar, whose office was near Stephen's on the old Cavendish site in Cambridge.

In advance of publication, Hoyle's latest paper, expounding further aspects of the theory of the steady-state universe which he had developed with Hermann Bondi and Thomas Gold, was presented to a distinguished and respectful gathering of scientists at the Royal Society. Then the forum was opened to questions which, on such occasions, are usually fairly deferential. Stephen was present and bided his time until his raised hand was noticed by the chairman. Still a very junior research student who as yet had nothing of any note to his credit, Stephen struggled to his feet and proceeded to tell Hoyle and his students, as well as the rest of the audience, that the calculations in the presentation were wrong. The audience was stunned and Hoyle was ruffled by this piece of effrontery.

'How do you know?' he asked, quite sure that Stephen's grounds for disputing his new research could easily be dismissed. He was not expecting Stephen's response.

'I've worked it out,' he replied as the audience gasped, and then added, 'in my head.'

As a result of that incident, Stephen began to be noticed in scientific circles and through it he found the subject for his Ph.D thesis, none other than the properties of expanding universes. Relations between him and Fred Hoyle never advanced after that incident.

Arguments – scientific, impersonal or otherwise – notwithstanding, everything we did in the course of that academic year contributed to a common purpose, our forthcoming marriage, for which a date in July 1965 was set. As it was by no means certain that I should be allowed to stay in Westfield as a married undergraduate, my top priority was to win the consent of the College authorities. Without it, the wedding would probably have to be postponed for another year because we both knew that the promise we had made to my father – that I would complete my undergraduate course – was not to be taken trivially. Since a year was a long time in the course of an illness such as Stephen's, as his father persistently reminded me, his survival for that length of time could not be guaranteed. This unpalatable truth was a factor that I would have to bear in mind constantly whenever I looked to the future. In fact, however hard I tried to be optimistic and put it behind me, it would surreptitiously colour every step, every decision and every reaction like a darkly threatening spectre lurking in the background. In the first instance, it was now up to me to persuade Professor John Varey, the Head of the Spanish Department, and Mrs Matthews, the Principal, that the situation was urgent. Taking my courage in both hands, I first broached the matter to Professor Varey. His response was that the situation was most irregular but that if the Principal gave her blessing, he would not object.

As my previous – and only – encounter with Mrs Matthews had been at the interview in 1962, I was not hopeful of a propitious outcome. I made an appointment with her secretary to call on her at six o'clock one evening towards the end of the autumn term of 1964. At the appointed hour, I knocked with trembling hand at the green baize door which separated her flat in the Regency house from the administrative area of the College. Mrs Matthews evidently sensed my nervousness from the moment I walked unsteadily through the door. She bade me sit down and thrust a cigarette into one of my hands and a sherry into the other.

'What's the matter?' she began, frowning and looking me straight in the eye with an anxious concern. 'Don't worry, I'm not going to eat you.'

I took a deep breath and did my best to explain my relationship with Stephen, his illness, the prognosis and our plans to make the most of whatever time we had left to us. She never took her eyes off me and betrayed very little emotion. When she had heard my tale through without interruption, she came straight to the point. 'Well, of course, if you marry, you will have to live out of College, you understand that, don't you?'

My heart lifted slightly, aware that she had not vetoed our plans outright. I nodded. 'Yes, I know that. There is a room available in a private house in Platt's Lane.'

'Well then, that's fine,' Mrs Matthews replied, staring fixedly at the embers in the grate. 'Go ahead and make the most of the chance you have.' She paused and then, changing her tone to one of uncharacteristic absentmindedness, confided that she herself had been in a similar situation; her own husband had been severely disabled. She was only too well aware of how important it was to do whatever one knew to be right in the circumstances. Equally she agreed with my father that I must complete my education. She warned me that the future I faced would not be easy. She promised to help in whatever way she could, most significantly by conveying her agreement to Professor Varey.

I regretted that I never had the opportunity to talk to Mrs Matthews again. In my final year our paths did not cross and she left the College soon after I did. Perhaps there was no need to approach her again, even to thank her. At that moment she quietly and firmly gave me the courage and the help I desperately needed. I counted myself very lucky that she happened to be the Principal of that particular College at that particular time. Undoubtedly, had I been an undergraduate at either Oxford or Cambridge, my plight would not have received such a sympathetic hearing.

Having surmounted that major hurdle, all that remained was to arrange my accommodation at the Dunhams' in Platt's Lane, which was easily done. Mrs Dunham readily agreed to let the attic room on the third floor to me and both she and her husband proved to be hospitable and patient landlords: 'patient' because never once did they complain about my monopoly of their telephone in the study downstairs. Stephen had devised a way of ringing me for four pence, the cost of a local call, via all the intermediate exchanges between Cambridge and London; this meant that there was no time limit on our conversations every evening. Quite apart from the frenzied pleasure of daily communication and love-talk, we had plenty to discuss as we laid our plans for our future. The illness assumed the proportions of a minor background irritant as we talked about job prospects, housing, wedding arrangements and our first trip to the United States, to a summer school at Cornell University in upstate New York, due to start just ten days after the wedding.

CHAPTER SEVEN

In Good Faith

Now that my immediate problems had been solved at a stroke, I was quite confident that in my final year I could finish my degree in London by commuting from Cambridge on a weekly basis, especially since current social research suggested that married undergraduates consistently produced better results than unmarried students stressed by the frustrations of unfulfilled relationships. My father generously offered to continue paying my allowance to help cover the rail fares but the responsibility of finding a job and an income to support us both lay with Stephen. For his part, he was beginning to take his research seriously, realizing that he would have to have a substantial piece of work documented, if not published, to enable him to apply for a Research Fellowship. To this end, he started to expand the ideas which had caused such a stir at Hoyle's Royal Society lecture. He also found by way of compensation for his efforts that his work was actually enjoyable.

Consequently it was with more than just the joyful expectation of a young fiancé awaiting the arrival of his beloved that he greeted me in his rooms, now for convenience in the main body of Trinity Hall, one chilly morning in the February of 1965: he was actually expecting that I would put my secretarial skills to good use by typing out a job application for him. The look of horrified dismay that spread across his face as I walked into his room with my left arm bulging beneath my coat in a white plaster cast dashed all my hopes of even the merest display of sympathy. I was not expecting anything more than that because the circumstances in which the fracture had occurred had been too embarrassing to confess over the phone.

The truth was that Westfield hops had livened up considerably with the advent of men students in the College and the election of a more dynamic entertainments committee in the Students' Union. We now had proper bands playing sixties music, the Beatles and the Twist. I loved twisting and at a midweek hop had indulged in an innocent bout with someone else's boyfriend. The floor was highly polished, my high heels skidded on the slippery surface, and down I went, falling heavily onto my outstretched left hand. The searing pain was the wretchedly certain indication of a broken wrist – for the third time – so Margaret, my constant friend and room-mate, packed me off in a taxi to the Casualty Department of Hampstead Hospital. As it was already late at night, the emergency staff summarily despatched me, having bound my arm so tightly in plaster that overnight my fingers turned blue and I had to return the next day to have the plaster removed and the arm reset.

Still rather battered by this ordeal, I did not at first appreciate the reasons for the horror on Stephen's face – not, that is, until he indicated the typewriter he had borrowed and the pile of pristine white paper he had neatly arranged on the table. Dolefully he explained that he had been hoping that I would type out his application for a Research Fellowship at Gonville and Caius College: the application had to be submitted by the beginning of the following week. I was then overcome with guilt about the illicit Twisting and the broken arm and set to work with a will to write the application out in long hand, using my intact right hand. The exercise took the whole weekend.

To have stayed overnight in Stephen's rooms was unthinkable. On more than one occasion, according to Stephen, the eagle eye of Sam, the surly bedder and guardian of the College morals on Q staircase, must have noticed a scarf or a cardigan of mine carelessly left hanging over the back of a chair in Stephen's study. Scenting the whiff of scandal and a captive prey, for he was no friend to young lady visitors, Sam would put his head round the door of Stephen's bedroom in the early hours, expecting to catch me squeezed illegally into Stephen's narrow single bed. His expectations of a juicy scandal to report to the College authorities were disappointed because many of Stephen's better-established friends regularly offered me hospitality at weekends. The Australian couple, the Youngs, had a flat perched high over King's Parade, right opposite King's College Chapel; Rob and Marion Donovan, a recently married young couple from Cheshire, had bought a new house out in the country at Coton where Marion could keep her horse, and Ros and John Billingsley were the proud owners of a house in the Arbury area of Cambridge. Having acquired property and vehicles, many of these friends were also already in the process of producing offspring which, for our generation, was the expected progression of events. Ours was the last generation for whom the prime goals were quite straightforward: the ideals of romantic love, marriage, a home and a family. The difference for Stephen and me was that we knew that we had only a brief space of time in which to achieve those goals.

As, against all odds, the Fellowship application was actually delivered on time, Stephen assumed that the next step would be a summons to an interview. It was not to be quite as simple as that. On the strength of the notoriety resulting from his startling intervention in the Hoyle lecture, Stephen had approached Professor Hermann Bondi at the end of one of the regular fortnightly seminars at King's College, London, and had asked him if he would be willing to act as a referee for the Fellowship application. As Hermann Bondi was a neighbour in Hampshire of Stephen's Aunt Loraine and her husband, Rus the Harley Street dentist, it did not seem necessary to reinforce the request with a formal letter. Some weeks after the submission of the Fellowship application, however, Stephen received an embarrassed message from Gonville and Caius College. In reply to the College's request for a reference for Stephen Hawking, Professor Bondi had disclaimed all knowledge of any candidate of that name. Given the circumstances and the casual nature of Stephen's approach to him, it was perhaps understandable that he should have forgotten. The situation was rectified by means of hasty phone calls and Stephen was duly summoned for an interview where he had plenty of scope for impressing the members of the committee with his powers of intellectual argument, the more so since none of them were cosmologists, however eminent their reputations in other disciplines. In many situations thereafter, Professor Bondi and his wife were always warmly supportive of Stephen's cause.

The novel idea of admitting a cosmologist to their midst must have appealed to the Fellowship Committee, while for us, the appearance of Stephen's name in the list of Fellowhip awards was a cause for jubilant celebration and the opportunity to develop a growing taste for champagne. Everything was working out just as we had dared hope and the date for our wedding could be fixed, as planned, for mid-July. Oblivious to the gloom of medical prognosis and ecstatic in the happiness of love and the promise of success, we glided into that summer through a series of further celebrations with only a cluster of small bothersome clouds, such as my second-year exams, the question of accommodation and the hitherto unfamiliar evil of income tax, gathering on the horizon.

To our indignation, an unseasonably chill wind of hostile reality blew one of these small clouds all too quickly across our path, temporarily dampening our elation with an icily discouraging shower. Flush with the success of his Fellowship application, Stephen went – within what we in our youthful impatience considered to be a reasonable lapse of time, a fortnight or so – to call on the Bursar of Gonville and Caius (generally pronounced in Cambridge as 'Keys', the name of the second founder of the College, but written 'Caius' because of the Latinizing tendencies of the Renaissance). The Bursar coldly informed the newly appointed Research Fellow that, as he was not due to take up his post until the following October, it was highly presumptuous of him to seek a consultation six months in advance. As to Stephen's query, a matter which was uppermost in our minds, he certainly was not disposed to tell him how much salary he could expect to earn from the Fellowship. For good measure he decreed categorically that the College did not, furthermore, consider it a duty to provide accommodation for its Research Fellows. Smarting from such high-handed treatment, we were left to surmise roughly what Stephen's income would be and to find somewhere to live. Since there were plenty of married Research Fellows in Cambridge, we assumed that they managed somehow. As for accommodation, we rather liked the look of some new flats which were being built near the market square and put our name down for one of those with the agent.

So confident were we in ourselves and impatient for our future to begin that we did not allow such mundane problems to bother us for long. Indeed the attitude of the Bursar and those of his ilk simply confirmed Stephen's healthy disrespect for pompous middle-aged authority, a disrespect to which I was becoming a willing convert. We well knew that in our idealism we were deliberately flying in the face of common sense, defying all received wisdom, all that was cautious, conventional and ordinary. We were certainly not going to allow our grand schemes to be thwarted or our convictions undermined by petty-minded officialdom. Tilting at such bureaucratic windmills quickly became our personal version of sixties' rebellion. By contrast our main battle was with the forces of destiny. In this lofty undertaking, we could afford to ridicule the minor stumbling blocks put in our way by officious College Bursars.

Battling with destiny changes one's perspective on every aspect of existence so that only the major issues, life, survival and death, are of real significance. Everthing else is trivial by comparison. So far the forces of destiny seemed to be either dormant or on our side, for in spite of the obstacles, our foreseeable future in the Cold War atmosphere of the mid-sixties was beginning to look as secure as anybody else's. Stephen may have been inclined to ascribe the broadening of his horizons to the logical sequence of events dictated by circumstance. That is to say, the prospect of marriage meant that he had to get down to work and prove his worth in physics. In my simplicity I also believed that faith had a hand in determining our way forward. In a sense, we both shared a faith, an Existential faith, in our chosen course but I, encouraged by my mother and by my friends, particularly Margaret, was reaching out to a faith in a higher, benevolent influence, God perhaps, who appeared to be responding to my need for help and support by strengthening my courage and my determination.

On the other hand, while I was well aware that the Hawkings, for all their traditionally Methodist background, professed themselves to be agnostics if not atheists, I found their tendency to sneer at religious matters unpleasant. Stephen and I spent our first Christmas together just two months after our engagement. The fact that he came to morning service with my family produced raised eyebrows and snide comments on our return to number 14 Hillside Road. 'So do you feel holier now?' Philippa quietly enquired of Stephen in a tone laden with sarcasm. He laughed in reply while his mother remarked, 'He should certainly be holier, because he is now under the influence of a good woman.' It was difficult to know how to take these remarks; it was not easy to make light of them because they smacked of conspiracy and seemed targeted at an essential element, my faith, on which I would depend implicitly in the task before me. This cynicism was very different from the good-natured mirth in which I wholeheartedly shared when we analysed the various forms of the marriage service. I was appalled to find that according to the marriage service of the 1662 Book of Common Prayer, I was expected to become a 'follower of godly and sober matrons' and opted instead for the 1928 version which omitted that ugly phrase.

Success had a knack of breeding success and soon we were celebrating again. Another Saturday had been spent in Stephen's rooms writing out another application, this time for a prize, the Gravity Prize, endowed by an American gentleman who in his wisdom believed that the discovery of anti-gravity would cure his gout. It is unlikely that any of the essays submitted ever provided any relief for the poor man's suffering, but his generous prizes provided great financial relief to many a struggling young physicist. Over the years Stephen won the whole range of Gravity Prizes, culminating in the first prize in 1971. Although, to our vexation, Stephen's first entry missed the post that Saturday in 1965, his efforts were nevertheless to be crowned with a very timely degree of success.

Some weeks later when I had completely forgotten about the competition, Mrs Dunham urgently called me down from my attic to take a call from Stephen. He was ringing from Cambridge – for four pence – to tell me that he had been awarded a Commendation Prize, worth £100, in the Gravity competition. To Mrs Dunham's amusement, I danced round her kitchen in raptures. Stephen's £100 added to the £250 which my father had been accumulating for me in National Savings and which he had promised to give me on my twenty-first birthday would enable us to pay off Stephen's overdraft and buy a car. Later that summer, just before the wedding, Rob Donovan negotiated a very favourable deal for us with his father, a car dealer in Cheshire. We had the choice of two vehicles; one, a gleaming, red-painted, open-topped 1924 Rolls Royce, was tantalizing but quite impractical and rather beyond our means. At the other end of the scale, there was a red Mini on offer. Reluctantly we had to concede that the Mini was better suited to our purse and to our requirements, especially since one of those small clouds looming on my horizon was ominously marked 'driving test'.

As I had not enjoyed any success to date with my several attempts to overcome that particular hurdle, I did not suppose that turning up for the next test in a 1924 Rolls would endear me to the crusty, humourless examiner who, when last I encountered him, had failed me yet again. Dryly he commented, as he clutched his heart, that my driving was not that of a beginner but of a hardened driver; it was alarmingly carefree and much too close to the speed limit. He should have been grateful that, given my recent experiences, I did not exceed the speed limit or overtake on bends or hills or attack dual carriageways from the wrong direction. Ironically, considering his known driving techniques, Stephen still held a valid driving licence although he was no longer able to drive, so it was within the bounds of the law for me to drive on a provisional licence while he sat beside me. When finally in the autumn of 1965 I passed the dreaded test, it may have been because my *bête noire*, the chief examiner, was said to be in hospital suffering from a stomach ulcer.

All the successes and celebrations of the early months of 1965 seemed to be signposting our way forward, justifying our hope and excitement. Consequently my concerns became more intensely focused on Cambridge and matrimony rather than student life in London or social life in St Albans. One regrettable result of this changing perspective and relentless march into adulthood was that I was becoming distanced from my friends and contemporaries, both my student friends in Westfield and my old dancing and tennis friends in St Albans. The last time that I saw many of those early friends was either when we worked together in the sorting office at the Post Office before the Christmas of 1964, or at my twenty-first birthday party which Stephen's parents kindly agreed to host in their large, rambling house which was much more spacious than my parents' semi-detached.

Because the wedding was to be a discreet occasion for family and a few friends – or rather, as discreet as possible considering the size of Stephen's family, my twenty-first birthday was a good opportunity for inviting all the other people who would not be coming to the wedding. Our two mothers coordinated their efforts over the catering while I took charge of the decorations. In a final fling of student abandon, I lined the walls of the Hawking house with tourist posters of Spain, including a copy which I made myself of Picasso's pen and ink drawing of Don Quijote and Sancho Panza. I collected up records of flamenco music and set up fairy lights and candles round the garden as the weather was more like June than March. It was a glorious day, hot and sunny with bright, clear spring skies, and my happiness was complete. Stephen's present to me, recordings of the late Beethoven Quartets, could only be interpreted as the ultimate expression of our depth of feeling for each other.

That birthday was happily very different from the previous year when Stephen had given me a record of the complete works of Webern. Then we, the whole family including Grandma, had sat in a silent circle in our living-room listening to both sides of the record. Stephen sat solemnly in an armchair while Dad buried his head in a book, my mother immersed herself in her knitting and Grandma dozed off. I sat on the floor unable to control my fits of giggles at the incongruity of the spectacle. With great aplomb my family managed to appear totally unmoved by the assorted atonic clashes, lengthy inconsequential pauses and grating dissonances of the music while I, on the verge of hysterics, had to hide my face in a cushion.

When shrewdly questioned by my mother, Stephen explained that he had bought the record for me because he himself did not know Webern's music and wanted to find out about it. 'Very sensible, such a good idea,' she concurred. Mum had an unexpected way of keeping Stephen on his mettle. Once when he complained that a picture she liked was far too sentimental, she retorted that, at her age, it was her privilege to be sentimental. There were other such occasions on which her astuteness and wit won his respect.

In the event it was just as well that, *ingénue* that I was, I had already sufficiently indulged my fits of the giggles that afternoon of my twentieth birthday because the birthday treat which Stephen had devised for me that evening was a play in London in protest at the American use of the electric chair. It was not a jolly evening.

In 1965, however, my twenty-first birthday party went with a swing in the warm spring air under the coloured lights on the terrace. It was as magical as a fairy-tale but as in all fairy-tales, it masked a perceptibly hostile element. For the first time I sensed an ill-disguised frisson of displeasure in Philippa's attitude towards me. I wondered why she appeared to resent me. What had I done to antagonize her? Was it simply because, for one evening, I had been allowed to take over her home for my party, or did her reasons run deeper than that? Did she resent me because, as I came to suspect, she did not think me a good enough catch for her brother? After all, I was a mere London, not an Oxbridge, undergraduate and only my father, not both my parents, had been to the old-estabished universities. I did not have the natural brilliance of the Hawking family and had to work hard to achieve results, while Stephen could look forward to a meteoric career and she herself was already recognized as Robert Graves's protégée. We were not monied nor were we aristocratic but then neither were the Hawkings. Had it not been for the Gravity Prize, Stephen's spendthrift nature – a reaction to his father's parsimony – would have brought an overdraft to our marriage. Certainly my colourful posters of Spain and my flamenco records were rather crude and unsophisticated by comparison with Chinese wall hangings and oriental music. No doubt my loyal, undemanding friends were deemed rather naive and unintellectual by comparison with Oxford society. My liking for nice clothes – always bought in the sales – seemed to have condemned me as unforgivably frivolous and 'feminine', a term of abuse in the Hawking lexicon, while my natural reticence was taken for dullness. The conclusion that I was despised as an inferior being was inescapable. That Philippa could have found my faith and purpose confusing was improbable, especially as she evidently mocked both. 'Don't take it seriously,' was Stephen's answer when I told him of my anxieties on that score, but such a glib reaction was not sufficient reassurance. Perhaps I should have realized that for certain of the Hawkings I would forever just be Plain Jane.

From Mary, the elder of the two sisters, I received a more good-natured response. According to his mother, Stephen had found it hard to forgive his sibling for coming into the world barely seventeen months after his own birth. Mary, shy and gentle by nature, had found herself in an unenviable position in the family, poised between two exceptionally intelligent, determined personalities, Stephen and Philippa. In self-defence, she had forced herself into a fiercely competitive intellectual mould when really her talents, which lay in her hands and her creative ability, were of a much more practical bent. At school she had cultivated an aura of indifference to other people. At home this detachment still prevailed, partially masked by an ill-fitting cloak of awkward camaraderie. With an intense Yorkshire loyalty to her father, she, unlike Stephen, had taken up medicine and it was with her father that she communicated most freely.

Although through various friends in St Albans my parents had heard first-hand accounts of Frank Hawking's blunt, abrasive behaviour towards his staff in the Medical Research Laboratory at Mill Hill, towards me he was chivalrous and considerate. It was unfortunate that he did not present himself in a better light to the outside world since he was a sensitive man who possessed generous and honourable qualities. Repeatedly, with endearing Yorkshire directness, he impressed upon me how genuinely delighted he and his family were at our engagement, sincerely promising to help in any way possible. Understandably he was devastated by the diagnosis of his son's illness and, notwithstanding his pleasure at our marriage, his medical background forced him to take a strictly orthodox and pessimistic view. My father had come across information about a Swiss doctor who claimed to be able to treat neurological conditions such as Stephen's by means of a controlled diet, and he had offered to pay for Stephen to go to Switzerland for a course of treatment. With the doubtful advantage of superior medical knowledge, Frank Hawking dismissed the Swiss claims as unfounded. He, for his part, was only able to warn me that Stephen's life would be short, as would be his ability to fulfil a marital relationship. Moreover he advised me that if we wanted to have a family, we should not delay, assuring me that Stephen's illness was not genetically inherited.

Stephen's mother, who confided in me that she was convinced that the first symptoms of Stephen's condition had appeared in an unexplained illness when he was thirteen, also thought I should be fully informed of all the horrific developments which could be expected to occur as Stephen's condition degenerated. However, if the only treatments available were to be dismissed, rightly or wrongly, as crank quackery, I did not see much point in having whatever natural optimism I could muster destroyed by a litany of doom-laden prophecies without any palliative advice. I replied that I would prefer not to know the details of the prognosis because I loved Stephen so much that nothing could deter me from wanting to marry him: I would cook and wash and shop and make a home for him, dismissing all my own previous ambitions which now were insignificant by comparison with the challenge before me. In return I trusted that Stephen would cherish me and encourage me to fulfil my own interests. I trusted too in the promise that he had made my father that he would not demand more of me than I could reasonably accomplish. With all the innocence of my twenty-one years, I was confident that we could work together as an effective and harmonious team in our battle against the illness.

The plans for the wedding proceeded apace, attended by much to-ing and fro-ing between St Albans and Cambridge, and by the sort of disagreements typical of weddings everywhere: Stephen, supported by his father, refused to wear morning dress although my father and brother insisted on maintaining a proper sense of style. Similarly, Stephen refused to wear a carnation in his buttonhole since he thought them cheap and vulgar, although for me they were redolent in their colour and perfume of Spain. Roses provided a satisfactory compromise. My father thought that no wedding was complete without a few token speeches at which Stephen balked. The question of bridesmaids came and went unresolved, leaving a gap which on the day was ably filled by nine-year-old Edward as an impromptu page-boy. Happily it was agreed, without audibly dissenting voices, that we should be married in the Chapel of Trinity Hall by the Chaplain, Paul Lucas. The religious service on Thursday, 15 July would have to be preceded by a modest civil ceremony in the Shire Hall, Cambridge the day before as colleges are not licensed for marriages and the cost of a special licence from the Archbishop of Canterbury at £25 was deemed an unnecessary expense. Having deliberately chosen a small venue, we were then hard pressed to accommodate all the guests. Some friends and relations had to be axed from the list altogether while others were consigned to the organ loft.

In the midst of this confusion, I was tussling with Napoleon III, the Paris Commune of 1871 and my final French exams. Shortly before the wedding, Stephen attended his first General Relativity conference which that year was conveniently held in London. I joined him for the official government reception in Carlton House Terrace where I met many of the physicists who were subsequently to play significant roles in his career: Kip Thorne, John Wheeler, Charles Misner, George Ellis and one or two Russians. Many of them were to become lasting friends to both of us. It was at that conference that the world's relativists, including Stephen, were first seized by the fever of excitement at the black hole research (at that stage known much less graphically by the more pedestrian description of collapsing stars) that was to grip them for decades.

After the civil marriage ceremony on 14 July, intoned by the Registrar in among the filing cabinets and artificial flowers of the Shire Hall in Cambridge, my mother-in-law came up to me and with her wry smile said, 'Welcome, Mrs 'awkins, because that's how you'll be known from now on.' The next day, St Swithin's Day, Stephen's best man Rob Donovan skilfully manoeuvred us and our near and dear without mishap through the marriage service and the festivities in the precincts of Trinity Hall. This was quite a remarkable feat if only because of numbers of elderly relatives present and the immense width of Philippa's hat to which she had attached a superabundant display of foxgloves, delphiniums and poppies, rivalling the College gardens in their herbaceous exuberance. It was a happy day despite the grey skies and intermittent drizzle. At last, in the early evening at the end of the reception in the College hall where my father had publicly thanked Stephen for taking me off his hands, Rob Donovan dropped us off on the outskirts of Cambridge. There in a side street he had parked our lately acquired red Mini, complete with L-plates, well out of the way of my brother's mischievous designs. I settled myself into the driver's seat and, with Stephen beside me, cautiously pulled away from the kerb, heading in the direction of Long Melford in Suffolk and the Bull Inn. We were alone and that day was already a thing of the past.

CHAPTER EIGHT

An Introduction to Physics

ALL TOO SOON that first idyllic week of marriage was but a halcyon memory – a memory of winding Suffolk lanes and lush gardens, musty country churches and half-timbered villages. At the end of it, as we sat waiting for take-off to New York, having boarded the plane hours in advance of the other passengers, that week with daytime outings to sleepy hamlets, country houses and the coast, and long leisurely draughts of deep velvety Nuits Saint-Georges at night in the Bull Inn, famous for the medieval carving of a wild man in its blackened beams, was quickly superseded by the inexorable advance of science, the synthetic traditions and the pace of the New World.

At Kennedy airport, we were joining the queue of passengers at passport control when a tall, neatly dressed air hostess approached us, intently examining the file she was carrying. 'What are your names?' she asked, looking down a list.

'Jane and Stephen Hawking,' we answered, not expecting any special messages.

'Oh,' she said in some surprise, 'I don't have your names on my list. How old are you?'

Now it was our turn to register some surprise. 'I'm twenty-one and he's twenty-three,' I replied for both of us.

'Gee, I'm so sorry,' she gushed, 'I thought you were unaccompanied minors!'

Indignant at the insult to our maturity and our married status, we pulled ourselves up to our full height and passed through US customs to the helicopter which was to fly us over New York City to La Guardia airport for the connecting flight to Ithaca in upstate New York. Our first view of New York was depressing. As we flew just above the level of the skyscrapers through a dense smog, the buildings loomed out of the haze like giant pins poised to spear us on their tips. It was hard to believe that human beings lived and worked down there in that inferno. My suspicions that we had landed in a modern Brobdingnag were confirmed when we were ushered to the limousine which had been sent to collect us from Ithaca airport and take us to Cornell University. The cars, the roads, the buildings – everything – was ten times larger than anything I had ever seen; even the wide expanse of pleasant green countryside seemed to roll on for ever. Yet for me, a linguist used to the challenge of a foreign language only 23 miles away across the Channel, the most baffling aspect was that we had travelled thousands of miles only to find ourselves among people who spoke the same language as we did, even if like the rest of their country, the language had suffered a bout of inflation on the way.

Our lodgings consisted of student accommodation in a twin-bedded room on the third floor of a new hall of residence on the Cornell campus. As we were both well used to the student way of life, that was not a problem. What really unnerved us was that the third floor had been designated for family accommodation for the duration of the summer school and we were thrown in to survive as best we could among families of babies and small children who wailed all night or sat out in the corridor protesting while their parents held parties in the lounge area. This unforeseen circumstance spelt an abrupt end to the honeymoon which we had intended to resume on the American side of the Atlantic. Although some of the toddlers, like Robyn Kerr, the little daughter of the New Zealand physicist Roy Kerr, were undeniably appealing, a stay in a mammoth nursery was definitely not what we had expected.

The problems were compounded by the logistics of the campus. For the able-bodied these would not have presented any difficulty but since the hall of residence was the best part of a mile from the lecture theatre and we had no transport, it was a struggle for Stephen to get to the lectures on time. He could walk alone but progress was slow; he moved much more quickly if he had a helpful arm to lean on, so gladly fulfilling my new role, I went everywhere with him. Meals presented another problem. Living, as we still were, on student grants, we could not afford to eat all our meals in the canteen, but as there was not a single utensil in the kitchenette on our floor, we did not have the wherewithal even to make ourselves a cup of tea. Eventually one of the conference secretaries came to the rescue and offered to take me by car down into Ithaca to do some shopping at the nearest Woolworths. As we glided along in her enormous station wagon, I politely asked, by way of conversation, if she had ever been to Europe. She did not mince her words. 'No,' was her reply, 'you see, I don't like going places where they don't have bathrooms.' Thus silenced, it was pointless for me to attempt any further conversation.

Duly equipped with a saucepan, cutlery, mugs and plates, plus an electric fan to mitigate the heat, which, unlike Spanish heat, was sticky and humid, I set up an improvised home base for the first but by no means the only time in my married life, on the third floor of the hall of residence. Brandon Carter, who was a fellow research student with Stephen in Cambridge and had been a guest at our wedding, was an invaluable help: drawing on his childhood experiences in the Australian bush, he taught me how to make tea by the billycan method in a saucepan, the same one that was used for scrambled eggs, pasta, baked beans and all the other bedsit-type fare on which we depended in those weeks. Versatility was of the essence in this unforeseen introduction to the joys of domesticity.

Much of my day was spent in walking with Stephen to and from the lecture hall and shopping in the nearby campus store. To fill the intervening hours which were as short as the distances to any other place were long, I resorted to my studies in the library. Then, to vary the monothematic diet of Hispanic studies, I hit upon the idea of borrowing a typewriter and a desk in the secretarial office and began to type out the preliminary draft of the initial chapters of Stephen's doctoral thesis. The universes in question may have been expanding but they were littered with so many incomprehensible hieroglyphic shapes and forms – as well as conventional numerals and all the normal mathematical signs – dancing above and below the line, that it soon became obvious that this particular enterprise was going to become a typographical nightmare.

Although such a sudden encounter with the nitty-gritty of marriage to a physicist might not have been exactly what I had anticipated from the second week of the honeymoon, I was relieved to have some useful occupation. I was also glad to be able to witness Stephen's intense excitement at moving in international scientific circles where he was already becoming recognized. He was particularly gratified at the increasing collaboration between himself and Roger Penrose, a slightly older British physicist, on a mathematical project known as the theory of singularities or gravitational collapse. The theory proposed that any body undergoing gravitational collapse must form a singularity, a region in space time where the laws of relativity cease to hold because the curvature of space time becomes infinite. In the case of a star collapsing under its own gravity when its surface and its volume shrink to zero, Roger conjectured that the singularity would be hidden in what was later to be called a black hole. Stephen was confident that these equations could be reversed in time to prove that any expanding model of the universe must have begun with a singularity, thus providing the theoretical basis for the Big Bang. The equations would also provide him with a momentous conclusion to his thesis.

The arrival like a ship in full sail from her family home in Detroit of Roger Penrose's wife Joan, bearing one small child in a sling on her front and clutching another by the hand, while her elderly mother brought up the rear, afforded some relief from the tedium of life on the third floor. Joan had majored in public speaking, a useful attribute in controlling a family of boys – an even more essential accomplishment, as I was beginning to realize, for making one's presence felt in the world of physicists where wives, although there were plenty of them with hordes of small children in tow, were scarcely noticed. Some were loud and loquacious, others were inhibited and reserved, others were positively sullen and morose; the handful of wives who themselves had a background in maths or physics tended to adopt a more competitive, masculine style of behaviour, while those whose dormant, half-forgotten talents lay in other areas tended to be prickly and mistrustful. Physics seemed to have taken its toll of all of them in some way or other and, whether or not they liked each other or got on well with each other, they all had one thing in common: they were already, to all intents and purposes, widows – physics widows.

There were a few memorable diversions. Every day as we strolled across the campus, I grasped the golden opportunity to chat in Spanish to a Mexican couple who seemed as disoriented in Cornell as I was. One Saturday afternoon some acquaintances of friends of Stephen's parents hospitably invited us to join them at their summer house by a lake not far from Ithaca. Otherwise, our evenings were spent humming 'Waltzing Mathilda' over our single saucepan as it bubbled on the hotplate in the kitchenette on the third floor, while Brandon regaled us with lengthy accounts either of life in the Australian bush or of a dramatic sailing trip which was to have reached the Mediterranean through the Bay of Biscay but never got further than Cherbourg on account of the weather, or of his interest in the mathematician James Clerk Maxwell, in whose uncle's house in Pennycuik he had lived. When these topics were exhausted, the conversation normally lapsed into a sustained cosmological argument between him and Stephen while I washed up the saucepan and the plastic plates, wondering whether we were doomed to spend the whole period of the summer school confined to the campus of Cornell University and the third floor of the hall of residence.

Just as I was beginning to resign myself to an unchanging routine, Brian and Susie Burns, an Antipodean couple who had previously spent some time in Cambridge, offered us a lift in their car to Niagara. Our sudden first sighting of the Falls after the tedious drive through the endless, sulphurous suburbs of the city of Buffalo took our breath away. The might of the immense volume of dark water constantly on the move, relentlessly tumbling over the edge of the precipice, transformed into a mass of white foam and rainbow filaments of cooling spray, was as mesmerizing as the thundering roar was deafening. Our senses numbed, we stumbled across the bridge to the Canadian side to get a better view and stood hypnotized until it was time for us to take the short flight back to Ithaca as the Burnses had gone on to a different destination. Against a threatening sky, we boarded the small plane and took off amid thunder and lightning. For the first time in my life, I was afraid of flying.

The next weekend, Brandon and some friends arranged a sailing trip on Lake Ontario. We set out in a gentle breeze and, once out on the lake, the day slipped by. I swam in the green waters and Stephen sat back deep in thought, enjoying the clear blue skies and the sound of the water gently lapping against the hull. By late afternoon, our companions had long since ceased to share our pleasure at the calm, peaceful conditions and talked anxiously of sending up flares and putting out distress signals. Brandon helpfully remarked that this was not a situation he had had to deal with in the Bay of Biscay as there you could always rely on the wind. Somehow, much later that evening, we managed to limp back into harbour as, in a magnificent blaze, the setting sun, sinking from view on the blackened horizon, bathed our weary faces in its amber glow.

It was not until the last week of the summer school that someone – I think it was Ray Sachs, an extrovert Californian physicist, the father of four daughters – had the bright idea of organizing a social event, a picnic in a field, for families. There we were introduced to more wives and more children but the person who made the greatest impression on us was a quiet American from Texas, Robert Boyer, with whom Stephen had already established a professional rapport. Robert included me in conversation in a natural, friendly manner, and talked about matters other than physics. Indeed, it has to be said that individually many physicists could be quite charming, friendly and down-to-earth. In a group, however, their natural tendency was to slip inexorably into interminable discussions and arguments, almost always about physics. There was one rival topic of conversation, though, which increasingly exercised the minds not only of all academics but of all young people; that topic, Vietnam, was liberally aired at that picnic. The growing menace of the war was regarded with fear and loathing; it threatened to cut a swathe through the nation's youth for a cause with which only the bigoted and the military sympathized.

On the last evening of the summer school, as we sat on the steps of the hall of residence, gazing out at a full moon suspended in a translucent sky, I was introduced to Professor Abe Taub, the summer school's avuncular master-mind, who with his wife Cice was also taking the air and admiring the night sky. We listened in fascination as they talked of their life in California, of the views their house commanded of the Golden Gate bridge, of San Francisco and of the campus and science at Berkeley where Abe was the leader of the relativity group. I detected a tentative invitation from Abe to Stephen and a corresponding eagerness on Stephen's part to accept, though no formal propositions were made.

We wandered back indoors and were about to resume our conversation when without any warning Stephen, perhaps affected by a chill in the night air, was seized with a devastating choking fit, the first I had witnessed. The illness, seemingly long suppressed, suddenly revealed itself in its true terrifying fury. The lurking spectre stepped out of the shadows and grabbed him by the throat, tossed him about, shook him like a doll, trampled him underfoot, and hurled his rasping cough round the room till the windows rattled and the very air resonated with loud, panic-stricken wheezing. Wild-eyed and helpless in the grip of the enemy, Stephen was beyond my reach. Useless and frightened, I stood by, unprepared for this sudden encounter with the dreadful power of motor neurone disease, the hitherto unseen partner in our marriage.

Eventually Stephen managed to gesture to me to thump him on the back; I did so vigorously, determined to expel the invisible monster. At last it receded as quickly as it had come, leaving us drained and exhausted and the onlookers politely dumbfounded. This onslaught came as a great shock to us both, an ill-omen, warning of a hazardous future. Dreams of California receded into the mists of the fantasy from which they had begun to emerge.

By the time we returned to New York, the Cornell experience had rapidly turned me – at the age of twenty-one – into a rather confused follower of sober, if not godly, matrons. The demonic nature of the illness had announced its presence much more dramatically than in lameness, difficulty of movement and lack of coordination. As if that were not enough, I sensed that there was yet another partner lurking in our already overcrowded marriage. This fourth partner, as intangible as motor neurone disease, was no raging fury. Indeed, she first appeared in the form of a trusted and quiescent friend, signalling the way to success and fulfilment for those who followed her. In fact she proved to be a relentless rival, as exacting as any mistress and as alienating from families, an inexorable Siren, luring her devotees to deep, isolated pools of obsession. There she beguiled them with promises of untold treasures, making of them her darlings and her victims. She was none other than the power of physics, cited by Einstein's first wife as the correspondent in divorce proceedings.

New York City provided both a necessary respite from such sombre considerations and the opportunity to restore the balance of our relationship, away from the inveigling companionship of other physicists. Dr Hamilton Southworth, a medical colleague of Frank Hawking's, generously offered us a room in his Manhattan apartment for the weekend. It was ideally situated for our sightseeing excursions to the Metropolitan Museum, the Empire State Building, Times Square and Broadway. Unfortunately Broadway had little to offer in August, so, bizarrely, we spent the Saturday evening in a cinema watching *My Fair Lady*.

I had few regrets when we said goodbye to New York. As the bus drove into Kennedy airport, I looked back over my shoulder to the solid line of clearly etched skyscrapers standing to attention in a grey mass on the horizon and thought that I had never seen an apparition of such monstrous brutality. My thoughts turned sympathetically to the reactions of the Spanish poet Federico García Lorca, who was in New

York at the time of the Wall Street Crash in 1929 and expressed his repulsion in his collection of surrealist poems, *Poeta en Nueva York*. I shared his horror of the brash materialism the city enshrined, his indignation at the gap between rich and poor, his sympathy for the blacks and his anxiety for the welfare of the people who lived in those unnatural surroundings, so remote from the rich interplay of light, colour, countryside and folklore of his native Andalucía. Disturbed by many of my own impressions of America and its manufactured traditions, I was impatient to return to the manageable, if cramped, proportions and genuinely old-fashioned but less frenzied ways of the Lilliputian world where I belonged. My place was on a continent mellowed by history and a sense of poetic values, where I fondly thought there was greater stability and where people had more time for each other.

CHAPTER NINE

The Lane

ANY SENTIMENTAL ILLUSIONS I may have held about the stability of life on the European side of the Atlantic were quickly dispelled. My parents, who were waiting to meet us at London airport, were bubbling with the news that they were about to move, only thirty doors up the road, to a house which my mother had had her eye on for some time. While I appreciated their excitement, this for me was a slightly disconcerting development which I had not anticipated. In my absence, or perhaps even since the marriage, my home in St Albans where I had lived since the age of six had, without my realizing it, ceased to be my home, and the break with the past was now becoming irreparably set in bricks and mortar. Although when last heard of, the flat we had reserved over the market-place in Cambridge was not yet finished, we had as a matter of urgency to find a home of our own if only to house all our wedding presents. Loading our luggage and presents into the red Mini, Stephen and I set off for Cambridge and went straight to the estate agent's. The flats were indeed finished, we were told, but, as the agent had no record of our names or of our booking, they were all already let to other tenants. The Old World was beginning to look distinctly unreliable after all. Furthermore, as we were soon to discover, attitudes could be every bit as callous in Britain as in America.

We discussed our next move over a despondent lunch. Stephen decided to brave the Bursar of Gonville and Caius once again in the vain hope that he might be persuaded to help, even temporarily. Together we bearded the ogre in his den. To our surprise, the ogre had changed identity in the previous six months: the new Bursar was the lecturer in Tibetan. While enjoying a sinecure since there were never any students in his subject, he had time on his hands in which to oversee the financial affairs of the College. Unlike his predecessor, he did not snap Stephen's head off in affronted indignation but listened gravely, even sympathetically, to his request and then came up with a brilliant solution, so brilliant that it even coaxed a glimmer of a smile from his dour face. 'Yes,' he mused, 'I think we might be able to help – only in the very short term of course, because you know that the College has a policy of not providing housing for Research Fellows, don't you?'

We nodded with bated breath. He consulted a list. 'There's a room vacant in the Harvey Road hostel: it's twelve shillings and sixpence a night for one man so we will put another bed in and it will be twenty-five shillings a night for the two of you.' We had to suppress our outrage at such sharp practice because we had nowhere else to go, hotels being beyond our means. We vowed that we would minimize both the amount of time and money spent at Harvey Road.

Some years later it transpired that the same Bursar had run away with the wife of a well-known novelist and together they had set up a fish and chip stall in Chicago. They had to move on, however, because the local residents objected to the oily black smoke issuing from their business premises. When eventually he reappeared in Cambridge, I had the misfortune to sit next to him at a College feast. He never once opened his mouth, which made me wonder how it was that he ever made contact with the wife of the well-known novelist, let alone persuaded her to abscond with him.

Although the College authorities proved harsh and ungenerous, the staff, in the shape of Mrs Blackwood, the housekeeper of the hostel, could not have been kinder. This proved to be characteristic of the College servants, whether cleaning staff, workmen, gardeners, porters or waiters. Unfailingly they revealed qualities of warmth and friendliness often conspicuously absent in the rarefied atmosphere of the higher echelons. Mrs Blackwood warmed our room, aired our beds, brought us tea and biscuits that evening and breakfast in the morning. She even offered to do our washing for us but that was not necessary as our stay was to be mercifully brief.

In the intervening day, Stephen's supervisor, Dennis Sciama, had come speedily to the rescue by putting us in touch with a Fellow of Peterhouse, who wanted to sublet the house he had been renting from that College. The house was unfurnished but it was available immediately and moreover it was ideally placed for us, in one of the oldest, most picturesque streets of Cambridge, Little St Mary's Lane, within 100 yards of Stephen's Department. The Department of Applied

Mathematics, which previously had been housed on the Cavendish site, had recently moved to the building of the old Pitt Press printing works in Mill Lane, a narrow street which ran down to the river, parallel to Little St Mary's Lane.

Since number 11 Little St Mary's Lane contained not a stick of furniture, we had to grit our teeth, dip deep into our funds, savings and wedding present money, and go on a rapid spending spree to buy a bed and other basic furniture and an electric ring. While we were waiting for the bed to be delivered, I went out to buy provisions, leaving Stephen propped up against the bare wall of the living-room for want of a chair. To my astonishment when I returned, he was comfortably seated on a blue kitchen chair. He explained that a lady from down the road had come to introduce herself and finding him leaning against the wall, had kindly brought him the chair which we could borrow until we had more furniture. The lady in question was Thelma Thatcher, the wife of the former Censor, or Master, of Fitzwilliam House, who lived at number 9. Thelma Thatcher was to become one of the most benevolent and most entertaining influences in our lives over the next ten years. That evening we cooked our supper in the Cornell saucepan on the single electric ring; we drank sherry from crystal glasses and, using a box for a table, ate from our fine bone china, using our as yet untouched gleaming stainless-steel cutlery set. Stephen sat on the Thatchers' kitchen chair while I knelt on the bare white-tiled floor. No matter that it was somewhat improvised, we celebrated our good luck in having a roof over our heads for the next three months.

Guarded at its entrance by two churches standing sentinel – the Victorian United Reform Church on the right and the medieval Church of Little St Mary on the left – the Lane is hidden from the public gaze. Tourists discover it only by chance and now that, thanks to our efforts, the Lane is closed to through traffic, visitors to the two big complexes on the river front, the Garden House Hotel and the University Centre, have to gain access via Mill Lane which is not residential. Number 11 is the last of the main terrace of three-storey cottages on the right-hand side of the street, some of which probably date back to the sixteenth century. When we took up residence in 1965, the house had been recently renovated by Peterhouse, a college which, unlike Gonville and Caius, did provide its Research Fellows with accommodation.

Fine iron railings on the south side of the Lane enclose Little St Mary's churchyard, a wild, overgrown garden which, that September, was ablaze with reddening hips and haws and heavy with the scent of autumn roses. The few gravestones still standing were so weather-beaten that their inscriptions had become illegible, despite the spreading branches of the towering sycamore trees and the gnarling stems of the wisteria which sheltered them from the worst ravages of the elements. Here there were no forbidding, monumental lines of crude, white incised marble announcing the inexorable march of the Great Reaper. Nature had gently absorbed the dead of previous centuries back into her bosom, resurrecting them in a profusion of blossoms which trailed over the railings and reached out to caress the crooked old gas lamp which lit the street at night with its sulphurous glow.

Thelma Thatcher was the self-appointed warden of the Lane. She it was who had planted many of the rose bushes in the churchyard where she exercised Matty, her King Charles spaniel, wrapping each of the dog's paws in plastic bags in wet weather. As a matter of course, she took it upon herself to keep an eye on the well-being of all her neigh-bours, whatever their age or circumstances. Scarcely had a week gone by than she had lent us more chairs, tables, pots and pans, found us a gas cooker to borrow – from Sister Chalmers, the Peterhouse nurse, who was moving into a fully equipped College flat – set about finding us somewhere else to live on the expiry of the present tenancy, and served us innumerable glasses of sherry in the elegant, highly polished, antique-filled living-room of her fine, whitewashed old house.

In 1965 she must already have been in her seventies, though with her straight back, dark hair and stately figure she could easily have been ten years younger. She was a gifted raconteur: in one of her many stories she recounted her memories of a Quaker wedding for which she was helping to prepare the reception. During the religious ceremony, in Quaker style, all the guests were invited to contribute their own spon-taneous utterances to assist the bride and groom in their future life together. Thelma Thatcher's utterance was indeed a flash of divine inspiration: 'I think we've forgotten to light the gas under the tea urn!' she announced to the startled congregation.

Intensely practical, she detested the pomposity of many Cambridge academics and, in a manner which would have done justice to Joyce Grenfell, she delighted in playfully deflating their egos. Her style was aristocratic and assertive but with good justification, since it was always supported by deeply held and sincere Christian values. Woolly-minded liberals were a natural target since she regarded herself as a pillar of the establishment: as such, of course, she represented everything that Stephen professed to despise. In her, however, he met his match and had to respect her for her goodness and generosity even if, politically, she and he were poles apart. Initially her directness left us both speechless, out of politeness rather than acquiescence, but the unmistakable twinkle in her eye taught me to recognize a mischievous sense of humour in some of her caustic remarks. 'Socialists are so immature, don't you think?' she would goad Stephen, who out of deference for her age and gratitude for the excellent meal we were eating could only shift uneasily on his chair, hide behind his unruly mop of hair and slowly raise his fork to his mouth to avoid having to reply. Once back home we would belatedly rehearse the replies we might have made, including the retort: 'Socialists might be immature but Conservatives are just plain selfish!' It would of course have been the height of discourtesy to have drawn attention to the Profumo affair, the sex and spy scandal which had rocked the Tory government and the country in the early 1960s.

Over the next few months, Thelma Thatcher took us under her wing like a mother hen. She kept a careful eye on Stephen when I was away in London as well as attending to the needs of both her elderly husband who, according to her, had snatched her out of her cradle, and her lively, independent daughter Mary, the librarian of the South Asian Library, who was assembling a film archive on the domestic lives of the British in India.

All too soon, I had to return to my final year at Westfield. Parting from Stephen each Monday was desperately painful and the regime was hard for both of us. We knew we had to adhere to it because of the promise that we had made to my father. Stephen was just sufficiently capable of looking after himself to be able to live in the house, but every evening, unless invited out elsewhere, he had to make the long, hazardous trek down King's Parade on his own to eat in College. Anne and Brian Young, our Trinity Hall friends, unfailingly kept an eye out for him as he passed their window on the other side of the road, and generally one or other of the younger Fellows would see him home after the meal when he would ring me to report on the day.

For me, the routine was exhausting. I would leave for London on Monday mornings, spend the week in Westfield, living with the Dunhams, and then on Friday afternoons would join the commuters once again. In my anxiety to get home to Cambridge, to Stephen – and to Nicholas Pevsner's Friday evening course of lectures on Renaissance architecture – I would bite my nails as I watched the minutes tick by on the Underground, wondering how long the train would sit in the tunnel, fearing that I was going to miss the connection from Liverpool Street. For years afterwards, my worst nightmares were of being stuck in a tunnel on the Underground.

During the week, the pressure was on: translations, proses, essays, seminar papers, all had to be submitted on time, and the only time I had for doing them was in the evening. Weekends were taken up with shopping, housework, washing and typing Stephen's thesis, parts of which he would have written out in a scrawly, all but illegible long-hand during the week, and parts of which he dictated to me as I sat typing at our shiny new dining-table in the otherwise bare living-room. The trials of that pre-university Speedwriting course were now bearing fruit. The shorthand had been moderately useful for taking notes in lectures but it was the dreaded typing, the bane of my life, which was proving to be a godsend in tabling the laws of Creation since it saved us a mint of money in professional fees. The thesis, with the equations and signs, co-signs and coefficients, Greek letterings and numbers above and below the line, infinite and non-infinite universes, first glimpsed at Cornell, drove me to distraction. However, since it was a scientific thesis it was blessedly short. Moreover, I derived some small satisfaction from the knowledge that my fingers were consigning the beginnings of the universe to paper. The thought that all these mysteriously coded numbers, letters and signs were penetrating the secrets of that deep, black infinity was awe-inspiring. Dwelling on the poetic immensity of the topic for too long was counterproductive, however, as it distracted concentration from all the little dots and hieroglyphs above and below the line, any of which misplaced could have thrown the beginnings of the universe into dire disarray and upset the whole order of Creation.

I was not a little proud, too, to be able to make a contribution of my own, other than the purely mechanical one of typing. Stephen's use of English left much to be desired. His speech was scattered with expressions such as 'you know' and 'I mean' and his written style showed scant concern for the English language. If nothing else, as the daughter of a dedicated civil servant, I had been taught from an early age to use the language precisely with appreciation for its clarity and richness. Here was an area where I could join forces with Stephen and assist him on an intellectual rather than merely physical plane. Privately, I also viewed this as a modest opportunity to pursue my own personal crusade to bridge the gap between the arts and the sciences.

The weekends were also the time for buying more equipment and furnishings, for exploring Cambridgeshire and for seeing friends. We spent an entire Saturday afternoon in an electrical shop trying to decide whether we could afford the extra £5 for a larger fridge than the one we had budgeted for. Considering that Stephen's salary, as we had at last found out, was £1,100 a year and our weekly housekeeping, when we were both at home, was £6, apart from rent and other outgoings, an extra £5 on any item of purchase was a major expenditure. On Sunday afternoons, if the Mini could be extricated from the Caius communal garage, we would tour Cambridgeshire, looking at villages and churches, always with an eye for a suitable house or plot of land to buy. Sometimes our expeditions had to be abandoned before they had begun because the Mini was so impossibly hemmed into its corner by ageing Bentleys and Rovers that it would have taken a crane to get it out. Sometimes, too, its path was blocked by Neil McKendrick's Citroën which had to be pumped up with air before it would start. Neil, a charming, debonair Research Fellow, a couple of years senior to Stephen, was very patient with me in his attempts to demonstrate how to start his car, but I never mastered the technique and lived in dread of finding his monstrous vehicle parked behind the Mini, condemning it to imprisonment and us to immobility.

One Sunday afternoon, having manoeuvred the Mini out of the garage, we tried to visit the local National Trust property, Anglesey Abbey. As the car park was by the gate, a good half-mile from the house, I drove up along the leafy avenue to the main entrance, expecting a sympathetic welcome from the attendants for my partially disabled passenger. When I explained why we had driven as far as the house instead of parking by the gate, we were met with rudeness and intolerance. Either we could park at the gate like everyone else, we were sharply told, or we could go away. We chose the latter course and went straight home where I penned my first letter in furious protest, not only at the lack of facilities for the disabled in Britain but also for the scant respect with which they were treated. I sent it to the top, to the Director of the National Trust, and received a bland apology in reply. Through that incident, I discovered an unexpected role for myself as a campaigner for the disabled and their rights.

Often on our Sunday afternoon jaunts we would happen to be in the vicinity of the Donovans or the Billingsleys at tea-time and, clinging to the illusion of a spontaneous student lifestyle, would drop in on them. Only slightly older than ourselves, many of these friends had already embarked on the next stage and were about to produce their first offspring. Consequently we found ourselves drawn more and more into their pattern of domesticity, especially when I became the fascinated, slightly bemused godmother to two of the said babies, Jane Donovan and Berry Anne Billingsley.

Stephen was also being drawn into other circles, those of the Fellowship of Gonville and Caius. One Saturday evening in early October, I accompanied him as far as the College Chapel for the service of induction of new Fellows. The Chaplain, who greeted us at the door, suggested I should watch the service in secret from the organ loft and then, defying age-old tradition, he invited me, a mere wife dressed in my house-cleaning clothes, to dine at High Table. This was an unprecedented break with the past as it was a long-established rule in Cambridge colleges that wives – especially wives – were banned from High Table. This was the preserve of the Fellows who cultivated self-importance with the same exquisite care that lesser mortals might be expected to lavish on a prized stamp collection or a breed of racing pigeons. Their conversation revolved around the finer details of the most abstruse subjects – their own subjects, naturally, on which they could expatiate at length while avoiding the embarrassment of having to discuss subjects about which they knew little or nothing. To have expected them to lower themselves to the frivolous, superficial level of wifely conversation was clearly unthinkable. Mistresses were preferred to wives. Indeed, a Fellow might invite any woman to dine provided she was not his wife. It went without saying, of course, that undergraduates were also banned from High Table. Unbeknown to the College authorities, their renegade Chaplain had offended both hallowed rules. Not only had he invited a wife to dine when he invited me, he had also invited an undergraduate.

Stephen's induction was soon followed by attendance at his first meeting of the governing body of the College. Before he had time to understand the implications of what was happening that Friday afternoon, he found himself deeply embroiled in College politics. To his confusion, he seemed to have walked right into a maelstrom, a re-enactment of the C. P. Snow novel, *The Masters*. The only minor difference was that the wrangling over the Mastership in the novel was deemed to have taken place in Snow's own college, Christ's, whereas the scenes that Stephen was witnessing were taking place in Caius. Here was life imitating art in the most incredible manner. As Stephen discovered after the event, the charge against the incumbent Master, Sir Nevill Mott, was that he was using his position to favour his own protégés. At the time it was impossible to tell what was happening. The governing body was in an uproar, tempers were flaring and immoderate accusations were being flung about. As the result of a quick calculation, Stephen had the uncomfortable sensation that the votes of the new Fellows might be decisive – indeed his own might be the casting vote – but as they had little idea of what they were voting for, their voting pattern was fairly arbitrary. Stephen's introduction to College politics came to a dramatic end with the resignation of the Master that very afternoon.

As a cosmologist Stephen was something of a novelty in the College and he basked in the attention his subject aroused. He was however but one among intellectual equals. Chris Andrew, who like my father was a historian from Norwich School and Corpus Christi College, Jimmy Altham, a philosopher whose family came over with William the Conqueror, Edward Timms and Norman Stone were elected to Fellowships at the same time as Stephen. Like senior prefects, some of the established bachelor Research Fellows took a benevolent and curious passing interest in the unusual new boy. They had already cultivated a caustic wit to maintain their hold on the uncomfortable spikes of the intellectual ivory tower where they perched, but a few of them, John Casey, Jeremy Prynne and Konrad Martin, were also considerate to a degree uncommon among the Senior Fellowship. During the course of the next year, the ructions over the Mastership crisis subsided as the new Master, Joseph Needham, tearing himself reluctantly away from his gargantuan task of compiling the history of science in China, guided the College back to stability. Although I found him terse, apart from one memorable occasion when, over port in the Combination Room after dinner, he expansively warned me never to drink sweet French wine – Barsac and suchlike – because of its high diosulphide content, his distinguished wife Dorothy was to give me invaluable help in securing a foothold for myself in Cambridge academic circles. Dorothy Needham, all her scientific brilliance notwithstanding, was one of the most modest, likeable academics I ever had the good fortune to meet. Joseph Needham later proved to be one of Stephen's most valiant supporters.

CHAPTER TEN

Mistakes in Miami

ON THE STRENGTH of his thesis, Stephen was gaining a reputation for himself as a prodigy in his field. In response to his winning a share with Roger Penrose that winter in the coveted Adams Prize for an essay in mathematics, entitled 'Singularities and the Geometry of Space Time', his supervisor Dennis Sciama assured me that he was sure that Stephen had a career of Newtonian proportions ahead of him and that he would do all he could to encourage its progress. He was as good as his word. For all his ebullience, Dennis Sciama selflessly promoted his students' careers rather than his own. His desire to understand the workings of the universe was more passionate than any personal ambition. By sending his students off to conferences and meetings, whether in London or abroad, and by making them scrutinize and report back on every relevant publication, he dramatically increased his own fund of knowledge as well as theirs, and succeeded in nurturing a generation of exceptional cosmologists, relativists, astrophysicists, applied mathematicians and theoretical physicists. The distinction between these various terms was never quite clear to me, except that their identities seemed to change according to the titles of the conferences: they would all become astrophysicists if the next conference was a conference of the Astrophysical Union or relativists if it was a General Relativity conference and so on. That autumn the relativists of the July conference in London began, chameleon-like, to adopt the trappings of astrophysicists in preparation for the next conference in Miami Beach in December.

It was fairly late in the term when Stephen learned that funds were available for us both to go to Miami. I was doubtful about taking time off from Westfield even though I would only be missing a couple of days at the end of term, but, surprisingly, Professor Varey raised no objections, so on a dull December afternoon, after a long wait for the fog to lift at London airport, we took off. It was already dark in Florida when we arrived, so it was not until the next morning that we discovered that our hotel room was right on the beach, looking out over the turquoise waters of the Caribbean. Having just stepped out of cold, wet London after a hard term's work, I marvelled at the extraordinary unreality, the improbability of the situation, as though I had walked into a different dimension, through the looking-glass perhaps. This impression was to grow as the stay progressed. The warmth, blue skies and sunshine were certainly welcome, especially since Stephen's choking fits were becoming more frequent and his sister Mary had earnestly advised me to take him away somewhere warm for the winter. At least by a happy chance we had the prospect of a week in the sun.

On the opening day Stephen, together with his casually dressed colleagues, disappeared into the preliminary sessions of the conference while I explored the venue. The hotel, built in a curve around the swimming pool, looked remarkably familiar. Was this a sense of *déjà vu*, I asked myself, for I was sure that I had seen it somewhere before. Suddenly it dawned on me that this was the hotel where the opening shots of *Goldfinger*, the James Bond thriller, were filmed. It was in a room in that hotel that the girl had died of asphyxiation after being covered from head to toe with gold paint! The Hotel Fontainebleau was a modern concrete structure with marble floors, plate-glass and huge mirrors covering whole walls. In deference to its name it was furnished in every nook and cranny with Louis XV-style furniture.

The furnishings were not the least of the incongruities since the astrophysics conference was a major incongruity in itself. The smartly dressed hotel staff looked distinctly uncomfortable with the delegates who were by no means models of sartorial elegance in their open-necked shirts, shorts and sandals. One day I ventured into the conference hall, thinking to sit in for a while on one of the lectures. At first I was perplexed at not seeing any recognizable faces in the audience, then I noticed that the delegates' dress bore no relation to the clothing the physicists had been wearing at breakfast because these people were all dressed in dark suits with ties, their hair neatly brushed and brilliantined, all clean-shaven, with not a trace of a beard anywhere. I listened to the speaker for only a moment before realizing that I had made a terrible mistake: I had burst into the wrong lecture theatre. The lecturer was waxing lyrical on the advantages of biodegradable plastic coffins! This was a conference of Jewish funeral directors, a group with whom the hotel management was evidently much more at ease than with the untidy physicists.

Quite apart from their appearance, Jewish funeral directors and their lavishly turned-out wives also had the advantage – for the hotel – that they did what was expected of them, whereas physicists had a way of causing unpredictable complications. Funeral directors' wives had difficulty in moving their bulky forms any further than the gardens around the swimming pool where they lolled on sunbeds all day, never venturing to take to the water. English physicists' wives, however, preferred to swim in the sea, a preference in every way contrary to hotel policy which liked to keep its guests within its boundaries – for their own security, naturally. In addition, physicists and their wives were generally much too young, whereas the funeral directors and their families were all of a certain age, easily defined as within the law for the purposes of dispensing alcohol. The wife of one young English physicist, that is to say me, had to be turned out of a party where alcohol was being served, despite the intervention of a distinguished physicist, simply because she had no documentation on her person to prove that she had in fact reached the age of twenty-one. After dinner, the English physicists also displayed the inexplicable and disturbing tendency to want to stroll along the beach in the balmy night air and had to be restrained by armed guards, fearful that they might be conducting a raid on the hotel by the back door.

From the exotic colours and summer sun of Miami we flew into autumn – to Austin, Texas, a small university town which in the mid-sixties was trumpeted in the press as the home of the brightest and best in cosmology. George Ellis, who travelled with us from Miami, was spending a year in Austin with his wife Sue, whom I had met briefly at our wedding. As we were to stay with the Ellises for a week, this was my opportunity to get to know them both better and forge the beginning of a life-long friendship which would survive the vicissitudes of many turbulent episodes in all our lives. Pensive and reserved, George Ellis was the son of a much respected former editor of the *Rand Daily Mail*, a paper acclaimed for its resistence to apartheid in South Africa. It was at Cape Town University that Sue, the daughter of a traditional Rhodesian farming family, had met George. He overturned her previously unquestioned views on white supremacy, making of her a fierce opponent of the South African regime. Both George and Sue were now self-imposed political exiles from South Africa, adamantly insisting that they could never think of returning to live in South Africa while the injustices of apartheid were dominant there. Where George was thoughtful and introverted, Sue was outgoing without being overpowering, vivacious yet sensitive to the needs of others. A talented artist and sculptor, she bubbled with warmth and creativity, qualities which she was putting at the disposal of a school for deprived children near Austin. Her pupils were not merely the victims of broken homes and physical abuse, some were even tiny black child prostitutes who had been rescued from the Chicago slums and brought to Texas for rehabilitation. It was not hard to imagine what an asset Sue must have been to that particular school for she had a way of making an entertaining and fascinating artefact out of the smallest twist of paper, length of wire or handful of matchsticks. In addition, her caring friendliness made her instantly popular among children who from an early age had learned to mistrust adults.

In creating a structure to her life in Texas, Sue appeared to be the exception rather than the rule among science wives. For them there was little of any interest apart from the Max Beerbohm manuscripts and cartoons in the University Library, and the grid streets of opulent houses in a landscape dominated by black-billed, crane-like oil pumps, nodding up and down as they extracted the liquid gold from the yellow earth. The feeling of remoteness from the rest of civilization was overwhelming in an environment where even radio reception was a chancy thing. This sense of isolation was reinforced by the length of time, all of twenty hours, it took Stephen and me to get back to London via Houston and Chicago where we were stranded for hours by snow on the runway.

Though Stephen may secretly have harboured ambitions of joining the physics group in Austin, one salutary experience made me more than glad to put America, for all the advantages of its southern climate, behind us once more. We were visiting friends of the Ellises one Sunday afternoon when Stephen had a bad fall which resulted in his coughing up a spot of blood. As his worst fear was brain damage, he insisted on our hosts calling a doctor. Their consternation was remarkable. They were embarrassed that their guest had had a fall but it was truly unheard of for doctors to home-visit, let alone on a Sunday afternoon, and they doubted very much whether they would be able to persuade one to come. After a succession of telephone calls in which they grovelled embarrassingly, they were finally put in touch with a general practitioner who, as an exception, agreed to come and inspect Stephen. He received right royal treatment when he arrived. As he conducted his tests, which indicated nothing amiss, I tacitly observed the scene from the sidelines. America was a fine place for the healthy and successful but for the strugglers and the infirm, for people who, through no fault of their own but through accidents of birth, colour or illness, were less able to help themselves, it was a harsh society which cruelly bore out the Darwinian theory of the survival of the fittest.

CHAPTER ELEVEN

Learning Curves

OUR RETURN TO England from Texas on Christmas Eve heralded yet another change in our lives. After Christmas in St Albans we went back to Cambridge to resume residence not at number 11 Little St Mary's Lane but at number 6. Our tireless supporter Thelma Thatcher had worked hard on our behalf during the autumn term and had assumed responsiblity for finding us somewhere else to live on the expiry of the lease on number 11. She had rung the absentee landlady of the empty house at number 6, a Mrs Teulon-Porter ('such a strange lady, my dears') informing her that it was an absolute disgrace that there should be houses vacant in Cambridge when there were so many young people desperately looking for somewhere to live. Mrs Teulon-Porter had no choice but to respond to the urgent call and caught the first bus to Cambridge from her home in Shrewsbury. Despite the expressed misgivings about her strange personality, she was offered generous hospitality at the Thatchers' while she attended to her empty property.

Mrs Teulon-Porter was a small, wispy, grey woman, already advanced in years. As Fraülein Teulon, she had come to England in the 1920s, had bought number 6 Little St Mary's Lane and had then married her next-door neighbour, the late Mr Porter. Both she and he were passionate historians of folklore and were closely connected with the Cambridge Folk Museum, which might have accounted for Thelma Thatcher's conviction that they dabbled in the occult. Various items in the house testified to their shared interest: an Anglo-Saxon rune stone, probably from the churchyard, was incorporated into the fireplace; the doorscreen was a slice hewn from the trunk of an elm; the offcut wood from a cartwheel had been converted to form a heavy, curved stool, and an eighteenth-century postillion's box, made of oak, had been upended and attached to a wall to form a small cupboard.

Mrs Teulon-Porter seemed harmless enough to us – perhaps because she had been so well tutored by her hostess at number 9 – but her house, despite all its quaint additions and its ideal situation, struck us as very poky and gloomy, musty-smelling and sticky with Dickensian grime. The façade in red brick and stuccoed weather-boarding suggested Edwardian renovations, while the front rooms on all three floors dated from the eighteenth century, charmingly so if one could overlook the dirt. The two flights of stairs were narrow and steep but did not present any insuperable difficulties. The back of the house, consisting of kitchen and bathroom, looked out on to a dingy yard enclosed by other houses and a high back wall. The back of the house appeared to be on the point of collapse because the foundations had subsided so badly that the floor of the kitchen, and correspondingly its ceiling and the floor of the bathroom above, sloped at an alarming angle. Mrs Teulon-Porter did not appear to consider this eccentricity at all hazardous. According to a plaque in the outside wall, John Clarke had master-minded this exemplary piece of engineering in 1770.

It required imagination and Thelma Thatcher's no-nonsense approach to convince us that this really was our dream house. Certainly its situation was perfect, in the centre of town within easy walking distance of the Department. The front rooms, right opposite the old gas lamp, enjoyed a full view of the churchyard, wistfully poetic even in winter, and although the proportions of the ground floor were rather spoilt by the staircase of the house at number 5 which butted into the party wall, the two bedrooms were quite sufficient for our requirements. 'My dears, all it needs is a coat of paint, you'll be surprised what a coat of paint can do,' Thelma Thatcher declared authoritatively, determined not to let her masterly scheme be upset by trivialities.

Thus persuaded, we entered into negotiations with Mrs Teulon-Porter. Stephen boldly made her an offer of £2,000 for her property. Not surprisingly she turned it down, timidly averring with one eye on Thelma Thatcher that she would expect it to fetch at least £4,000 on the open market. She would however agree to let it to us for £4 a week until such time as we could raise the £4,000 needed to buy it. In the meantime we were virtually free to treat the house as our own and redecorate it at will. The arrangement was to everyone's satisfaction: £4 a week was within our means and the charms of the little house grew on us. Thelma Thatcher shepherded her guest back to number 9 and there plied her with such liberal quantities of sherry, or possibly gin, that the next we heard was that Mrs Teulon-Porter, before departing for Shrewsbury, had agreed to have the dusty old coal-shed and lean-to removed from the back yard and a second-hand gas fire installed in the living-room to relieve me of the effort of having to heave coal in.

Since the house was already vacant Mrs Teulon-Porter was content to allow us to start redecorating before moving in. As Stephen's thesis, finally completed with the help of an obliging secretary in the Department, was now at the bookbinder's, the time which I had previously spent typing it at weekends could now be devoted to my next occupation, that of house-painting. It was rewarding but bore worryingly little relation to the Spanish literature which I was supposed to be revising for Finals. However, as the house was in a truly depressing state and as we could not afford to have it professionally redecorated, I had to do it myself. Armed with a collection of brushes and a plentiful supply of white emulsion, I attacked the grimy walls of the living-room. My intention was to paint the two most important rooms, the living-room and the main bedroom, before moving in, and then tackle the rest – the third storey attic, the two flights of stairs, the kitchen and bathroom – more gradually over the ensuing months.

As I disliked the smell of paint, I usually worked with the front door wide open. The Thatchers were frequent and admiring visitors, plying me with cups of tea and encouraging comments. One day, Mr Thatcher paused as he was passing, bending his military frame slightly to peer in at the open door, 'I say,' he exclaimed, 'you look such a fragile little thing, but, by Jove, you must be tough!' From the top of the stepladder, I smiled, flattered by this commendation from a veteran of the First World War who still bore the disfiguring marks of that conflict on his gaunt face. A few days later we were told that the Thatchers had decided to pay their odd-job man to paint the living-room ceiling for us: 'Dear Billy's housewarming present to our new neighbours,' was Thelma Thatcher's way of describing her husband's extraordinary generosity.

The Thatchers' odd-job man, a somewhat portly version of John Gielgud, was a retired artist who filled in his time with larger-scale painting while his wife ran a print shop on King's Parade. He was an amiable man who, I suspected, derived much amusement from my initial attempts at wielding a paintbrush, though he was tactful enough not to show it. Under his benevolent tuition I soon acquired many of the tricks of his trade, like starting a wall from the top, or applying the brush in a circular motion over an uneven surface, or using a hard edge to paint a window-frame. Stephen's reputation in relativistic circles may have been rapidly ascending the ladder of fame on account of his pursuit of singularities, but my learning curve was exhibiting an equally dizzy but more erratic series of highs and lows, propelled upwards by intensive doses of medieval and modern languages, philology and literature during the week and brought to earth by a crash course in the skills of interior decorating on Saturdays. Finally, when I began to find the area of wall and ceiling still to be covered rather less minimal and rather more daunting than I had anticipated, we calculated that we could just afford to ask the decorator to paint the kitchen for us, a particularly unpleasant task since the grime and grease were probably as old as the house.

Although my parents had only just moved to their new house, they and my brother Chris came to Cambridge one weekend early in 1966, to redecorate the top-floor bedroom and, in token of his expressed willingness to help, Stephen's father spared a day from his globe-trotting to paint the bathroom while I applied a coat of enamel to the old chipped bath. Then, magically, fully justifying Thelma Thatcher's convictions, our tumble-down eighteenth-century cottage acquired the air of a des res. In the transformation, the angles of its floors and ceilings had become simply eccentric curiosities. In addition, our few pieces of furniture which various colleagues of Stephen's carried the five doors along the Lane fitted in perfectly, although, of course, when we bought them we had not given a moment's thought to the possible proportions of their eventual resting place.

Proud of our restoration of the little house, Stephen and I decided that the new Bursar of Gonville and Caius was due for another visit, especially as Stephen was by now beginning to feel more sure of his place in the College hierarchy. Early in the New Year, we had braved the annual Ladies' Night, Bishop Shaxton's Solace, when wives were officially welcomed to the College precincts and treated to a banquet, as if in compensation for the contempt in which they were held for the rest of the year. Bishop Shaxton had, in the sixteenth century, bequeathed the munificent sum of 12 shillings and 6 pence for the solace of every Fellow who suffered the deprivation of having to spend Christmas at home rather than in the College. The equivalent in modern terms of 12 shillings and 6 pence per head was sufficient to provide a lavish five- or six-course dinner with unlimited quantities of the best wines for the Fellowship and their spouses. Typically the meal would consist of soup, a whole lobster, an undefined small game bird each –

usually served complete with head and limbs – , a substantial creamy pudding, a cheesy savoury and then, of course, at dessert, the famous port – or claret – which tradition demanded should only be passed clockwise round the table. In theory it was a magnificent spread but in practice, College halls tend to be draughty places and usually the food was cold before it reached the table.

Our first experience of Bishop Shaxton's Solace was a chill one, and not only on account of the temperature of the food, the wine and the hall. We were seated on the same table as the former Bursar who had so scathingly dismissed Stephen's perfectly reasonable request for a job description before our marriage. That was bad enough, but our discomfort was compounded by finding ourselves placed out on a limb at the end of the table. After the meal, eaten in a frosty silence, an elderly band appeared from the shadows and struck up antediluvian foxtrots. I had never learnt the foxtrot as the advent of the Beatles had cut short my brief flirtation with ballroom dancing and now I could only watch in pensive, glum frustration as our tight-lipped dinner companions deserted us for the dance floor, where, like close-furled black umbrellas, they authoritatively steered their submissive, upholstery-clad wives round the hall, deftly exhibiting a precise, manicured display of ornamental footwork. I was twenty-one: all around me our dining companions were in their forties and fifties, if not their sixties. It was as if we had been propelled into a geriatric culture where our generation was deliberately snubbed as irrelevant. 'Look how much more elegant we are than you; don't you envy our finesse!' they seemed to be saying. The only consolation was that Caius, as one of the richest, most solidly based colleges, could probably afford to lend us a couple of thousand pounds – at a lucrative rate of interest of course – without the loan creating even the slightest blip in the College accounts.

We were well aware that no building society would even begin to consider the house for a mortgage, but Stephen, undeterred by his previous encounters in the Bursar's office, thought it perfectly reasonable to apply to the College for a loan so that we could improve our offer to Mrs Teulon-Porter. While he was ensconced with the Bursar, I sat waiting for him in the outer office and broached a matter of some delicacy to Mr Clarke, the white-haired bursarial assistant, who was much more amenable than the Bursar himself. My discussion began in the nature of a complaint. Why, I asked Mr Clarke, had he sent Stephen the application forms for a University pension a few weeks back when it was common knowledge that Stephen's life was going to be so drastically foreshortened that in all probability he would not qualify? Was it not a bit heartless of him to have sent the forms? Stephen had taken one look at them and with a weary gesture had pushed them aside, not wanting to contemplate arrangements for a future that others might look forward to but that was to be denied him.

Mr Clarke did not apologize for any insensitivity, quite the contrary. With the most convincing display of disingenuousness, he shook his head as if unable to comprehend my problem. 'Well, young lady, I just follow my instructions,' he said, turning his bright blue eyes on me from beneath busy white brows. 'My instructions are to send out the forms to all new Fellows, as all new Fellows are by rights entitled to a University pension. Your husband is a new Fellow so he is entitled to a University pension, just like the rest of them. All he has to do is sign the forms to establish his rights.' His words were still ringing in my ears when he added casually as an afterthought, 'No need for any medical tests or anything of that sort, if that's what you're thinking.'

I could hardly believe what he was saying. This was an area which, in our ignorance, we had tacitly dismissed as inapplicable to us. Now I was being told that it could be resolved with a mere signature and moreover would assure us of a commodity which neither of us had ever thought about before: security. For one afternoon's business we had both been remarkably successful and through our success had discovered this new goal in life, security, which suddenly assumed a comforting importance. Stephen had persuaded the Bursar to send the College land agent to inspect the house with a view to securing a loan and I had secured Stephen's rights to a pension. With a loan to buy the house and a pension, our status would gain the solidity of two firm anchors in an otherwise uncertain world.

The College land agent, Mr Reed, came to survey the house one sunny spring morning when the churchyard was bursting into a profusion of yellow blossom. Our optimism soon quailed before his dry, unsmiling exterior and when he issued his verbal summary of his projected report, our hopes were dashed beyond recall. Mr Reed gave us the strong impression that we were wasting his time by calling him out on such a nonsensical errand. Could we not see that the back of the house was falling down? And, as if that were not enough, the third-floor attic was a definite fire hazard. He would not risk sleeping up there, or even using it as a study himself, nor would he advise letting anyone else do so. A 200-year-old house was not, in his opinion, a sensible purchase. In any case, there were so many road building schemes in the offing that he would not be surprised if the whole Lane were demolished to make way for a new access road to the city centre from the west. He could not possibly recommend the property as an investment to the College.

Stephen was infuriated at such a short-sighted, unimaginative verdict, but despite his vociferous protests, the Bursar accepted the land agent's report. Some time later as we were driving past Mr Reed's office on the other side of the city, Stephen spluttered indignantly as he pointed to the premises. Like our house, the building rose to three floors but on a larger scale, a good 10 feet higher than ours. The third floor was quite obviously, from the discernible lighting, being used as office or study space. Furthermore, the whitewashed, gabled, timbered property bulged and leaned picturesquely in the manner of a decrepit *sixteenth*-century building. It made our little eighteenth-century house appear positively modern and well-kept.

There was no immediate solution to the problem, except perhaps to save as much money as we could to raise a deposit for an eventual mortgage on a newer house. A system began to evolve whereby Stephen earned the money through salary, teaching and essay competitions, and I attended to the family finances, paying the bills and saving as much as possible through careful housekeeping. Delicious scraps of streaky bacon came at 1s 6d a pound from the old Sainsbury's with its marble counters and endless queues; duck livers from Sennit's the poulterer's were nourishing and cheap; the market proved a veritable cornucopia of fresh fruit and vegetables, and the local butcher, Chris Badcock, introduced me to inexpensive cuts of meat – hand of pork and shoulder of lamb never costing more than 5 shillings – which proved no disgrace on the dinner table when we entertained our new acquaintances from among Stephen's contemporaries in the College and the Department and their wives.

Our frugal but productive domestic economic policy ran counter to the national trend which was one of feckless extravagance, encouraged by the recent Macmillan government's maxim of 'You've never had it so good'. Their aspirations aroused, workers expected high enough pay rises to enable them to afford the plethora of consumer goods, cars, fridges, washing-machines and televisions – many of them foreign – spilling on to the high streets. Discontent with earnings, overtime and pay structures led to strikes to force up pay which was then spent on another round of consumer goods. The Labour government elected in 1964 inherited from the Conservatives the dubious legacy of a nation engaged on a gigantic spending spree. In the spring of 1966, having exercised my right to vote for the first time, I joined the late-night crowds in Market Square to greet the success of the Labour candidate in the repeat election, called to increase the government majority and consolidate Socialist power. Sadly, our new MP, Robert Davies, died while in office and the Labour government was shackled by its mounting economic problems, more strikes and a constant preoccupation with the 'balance of payments crisis', the economic buzz phrase of the sixties. With a failing currency, Britain was having to relinquish its role as a world power. Home news broadcasts were dominated as never before by economics while the international background of the war in Vietnam and heightening tensions in the Middle East threatened to give rise to the anticipated superpower confrontation which would unleash the forces of the nuclear arsenals of both sides.

Stephen meanwhile had discovered a way of earning more money and improving himself in the process. He had wanted to study mathematics at Oxford but his father was convinced – wrongly as it happened – that there would be no jobs in maths in the future. Aware that he had already disappointed his father by not showing any interest in a career in medicine, Stephen compromised by agreeing to study physics. When he came to Cambridge as a postgraduate student, therefore, he had only a basic grounding in mathematics. As he was now working with Roger Penrose, an exemplary mathematician, Stephen felt himself at a disadvantage. He hit upon the happy solution of getting paid for teaching himself the maths course by giving undergraduate supervisions in it for Gonville and Caius College. Thus he steadily worked his way through the syllabus of the Maths Tripos, Part 1A, Part 1B, and Part 2. Needless to say, his progress far outstripped that of his students whose lack of application he found frustrating. One in particular, a tennis blue, spent far more time on the tennis court than was good for his mathematics, as Stephen pointed out in the end of term reports which I wrote down to his dictation. With Brandon Carter, he also attended some of the undergraduate lectures in mathematics, notably the course given by the genial Master of Pembroke College, Sir William Hodge. During the course of the term, the rest of the audience gradually drifted away, leaving Sir William lecturing to only three listeners, Stephen, Brandon and another colleague, Ray McLenaghan. They regretted that they had not taken the opportunity to slip away sooner but since their absence would have been extremely conspicuous, they felt obliged to stay the course.

It must have been during my final year in London that an uncle of Stephen's by marriage, Herman Hardenberg, spent a long period in hospital in St John's Wood, just down the road from Westfield, suffering from a heart condition. I used to call on him sometimes of an afternoon when the day's lectures and seminars were over. He was the husband of Stephen's Aunt Janet, a hard-working London GP, who once had touchingly introduced me to a cousin as her 'very special niece by marriage'. Herman was a Harley Street psychiatrist, a charming, gentle, cultivated man who liked to talk about the subjects that interested me, particularly the poetry of the Provençal troubadours, the subject of my special paper in Finals. He had been reading C. S. Lewis's *The Allegory of Love* and naturally approached the tensions of the poetry where the poet-lover languishes for his unattainable beloved from the psychological angle. He gave me references to some papers on the subject in a psychiatric journal but at that early stage, my interests were more linguistic. Then our conversation would turn to family topics: I entertained him with accounts of our life in Cambridge and our efforts to restore the house to a habitable condition. 'I hope the Hawkings are treating you well?' he once enquired cautiously, making little secret of his mistrust of that family. I calmed his fears on my account. That the Hawkings were eccentric to a degree which at times verged on oddity was well known; that they were aloof, with a deeply entrenched belief in their own intellectual superiority over the rest of the human race, was also widely recognized in St Albans where they were regarded with a mixture of suspicion, humour and awe. There were emotional upsets and outbursts and there had been some slight *frissons* in the air at the time of our engagement and the wedding, but these I took as part of the general tenor of family life. I had no very substantial reason to complain of the way they treated me. Indeed they always seemed delighted to see Stephen and me and welcomed us warmly to Hillside Road.

CHAPTER TWELVE

An Unimportant Ending

WITH THE APPROACH of summer, the trees and plants in the churchyard vied with each other to capture the attention of residents and passers-by in a riotous competition of ever more flamboyant colour and seductive perfume. As spring became summer, successive groups of tourists, particularly Americans, would come sauntering down the Lane. Many of them would press their noses to our windows in an attempt to peer through the net curtains into our quaint interiors, doubtless searching for medieval elves and gnomes. Not all were susceptible to the beauty of the Lane: there was the small boy who announced in a loud voice to his parents as they strolled along: 'Gee, Momma, I wouldn't like to live here: the Holy Ghost might come up and get yer!'

Susceptible though I certainly was to the newly revealed beauties of our surroundings, I could not allow myself to dwell on them. Apart from a brief celebration for Stephen's Ph.D in March, my every precious spare moment was spent revising, in London in the College library during the week, in Cambridge with my books spread out around me in the attic at weekends, or, that Easter, in St Albans where we spent the holiday quietly, staying with my parents.

The Hawking household, on the other hand, was in some distress. Stephen's younger sister Philippa had recently been taken into hospital in Oxford for undisclosed reasons which the family discussed among themselves in lowered voices without ever specifying the nature of the problem or making me a party to it. I shared Stephen's concern and was anxious to be able to visit her. I naively hoped that perhaps at last she and I would be able to talk and come to some resolution of those ill-defined, lurking differences, which like clouds flitting across the sun, cast fleeting dark shadows over our relationship as sisters-in-law. Because

I loved Stephen, I wanted to get on well with his family, to like them and to be liked by them. It worried me that this particular relationship seemed so fraught with difficulty.

As it had been arranged that Stephen's mother would drive us over to Oxford from St Albans in the old Ford Zephyr to visit Philippa, we arrived at the house in Hillside Road one April morning, expecting only to decant ourselves into the larger car before setting off. Isobel helped Stephen out of the Mini and walked up the garden path with him while I locked our car before catching them up. As they reached the steps at the porch, they turned, as one, to face me. Isobel was still holding Stephen by the arm. He looked at me intently but said nothing while his mother spoke. Unceremoniously, she came straight to the point: 'Philippa wants to see Stephen on his own, without you.' She paused for her words to take effect and then, seeing the blank expression on my face, reinforced what she had said: 'She does not want to see you so I will take Stephen over to Oxford and you can stay here.'

Blankly incomprehending, I said nothing but I looked from one to the other, expecting some sort of explanation, waiting for Stephen to offer some reason to excuse his mother's bluntness. As no such words came, I stammered a few awkward words of incomprehension. Isobel cut me short, adopting a haughty, sarcastic tone: 'Well, of course, no one, least of all Philippa, wants to upset this thing' – she stressed the word 'thing' disdainfully, as if that was the only adequate term to describe our marriage – 'between you and Stephen, so Stephen had better stay behind with you.' She sighed. 'We all know how possessive you are, so I'll go alone.' With that she turned on her heel and went into the house.

These cuttingly well-chosen words swiftly reduced me to small and contrite proportions. Obviously Isobel was shouldering a huge burden of worry, not only for her son but for her daughter as well. Her husband was frequently away in the South Pacific, Africa or India, leaving her to handle family crises alone. In this crucial situation I had no right to raise objections or complicate matters.

'No, no, I quite understand, that's all right, Stephen can come, I'll stay here, I have plenty of work to do,' I called after her, following her into the house. Stifling my tears, I momentarily contemplated going home to my parents. Pride and the fear of upsetting them held me back. I dreaded giving anyone cause to say or even think, 'I told you so!'

I sat down at the dining-room table, making a show of arranging my books while Isobel and Stephen went out to the Zephyr, parked under the old sheet of corrugated iron which served as an apology for a garage. I listened as the doors slammed and the engine turned over. Again and again it turned but it would not start. Eventually they came back into the house. Then they looked woebegone indeed; I could not but feel very sorry for them. 'Would you like to take the Mini?' I suggested. This idea was greeted with gratitude until Isobel found that she could not manage a floor gear change because she was used only to a steering-wheel gear lever. The only solution was for me to drive them both to Oxford.

While the rest of the party went hospital visiting, I spent the afternoon in the waiting-room, revising the great medieval epic poem based on the exploits in exile of the hero, *El Cantar de Mío Cid*. The time passed quickly as I became absorbed in the remarkably sophisticated psychology of the late-twelfth-century poem which deftly interweaves two main thematic strands into its texture, the public image of the invincible warrior and the private face of the devoted husband and father. When the Cid goes into exile, the poet describes his distress at parting from his family as 'tearing the nail from the flesh'. Later the poet documents how the eponymous hero's many attempts to be generous and encouraging to his cowardly, snobbish sons-in-law are misconstrued and turned against him. These sons-in-law abuse and leave their wives, Elvira and Sol, for dead in a dark, wild forest where eventually their bodies are found by their cousin, Felix Muñoz, 'the curtains of whose heart are torn apart by grief' at the discovery. The outrage is finally avenged and the Cid's family honour restored when his daughters are sought in marriage by none other than princes of royal blood. This epic tale, like a distant voice whispering down the centuries, told of the complexity, the variety and the unpredictability of human psychology. Even in the twelfth century, the poignant distinction between the hero's private life and his public image was seen as an authentic concept. As the Cid's public standing reached its apogee with his reconquest of territory from the Moors, his private life collapsed with the humiliation and disaster inflicted on his daughters.

On our return from Oxford, no further reference was made to the morning's episode. In the Hawking family tradition, it was brushed under the carpet with many other dusty remnants of psychological and emotional detritus, regarded as being too insignificant to merit any consideration. In that rarefied atmosphere, emotional issues were almost never discussed: they seemed to pose too great a threat to the intellect, to the dominant sway of reason on which the Hawking family seemed to depend for its sense of superiority.

It was therefore a surprise, just before the onset of Finals, to receive a letter from Philippa, addressed to me in a minuscule hand, at Westfield. She regretted the differences that there may have been between us but looked forward to a better relationship in the future, assuring me that she respected my desire 'to *try* to love Stephen'. I responded whole-heartedly to this olive branch. Nonetheless I was disturbed by the cryptic reference to my wanting 'to *try* to love Stephen'. I loved Stephen passionately and was as perplexed by that comment as my mother had been some months earlier when the rumour had reached her ears that the Hawkings were thinking of moving to Cambridge to set up a home there for Stephen. Did they not expect the marriage to last, she wondered indignantly. I was confused by these undercurrents. Why did Stephen's family, of all people, seem intent on undermining our relationship with such cynicism? What possible motive could they have for wanting to disturb our happiness? How could Stephen and I not appear to be possessive of each other when we were so recently married – especially when he was dependent on me for so much of his everyday existence? Why, above all, did they want to make me appear so inadequate?

As if to confound the doubters, we were closer than ever in the week of my Finals. Stephen came to London to give me moral support and stayed in my top-floor room in the Dunhams' house working on the singularity theorems and occasionally dipping into translations of the great works of Spanish literature, among them *La Celestina*, the down-market prototype of *Romeo and Juliet*, while I went out each morning to the examination hall. At the time of my stay in Madrid in 1963, I had not appreciated that Pilar, my landlady, was the perfect archetype of one of the most famous and entertaining characters in medieval Spanish literature, the old procuress Celestina, whose interweaving of diabolical forces into her spells brings about the deaths of her young clients, the star-crossed lovers Calisto and Melibea. Had I done so I might have studied her psychology with greater academic interest and less distaste. She certainly proved a fruitful source of inspiration in the exams, however.

After the afternoon session of Finals, Stephen and I would make off to Hampstead Heath or the gardens and house of Kenwood in search of respite from writer's cramp and mental constipation. We also visited my much-loved Great-aunt Effie, as irrepressible as ever in her late seventies, still living alone in her large house in Tufnell Park. By the end of the week I was just beginning to get into my stride, but the exams were already nearly over and I felt a huge sense not of relief but of anti-climax. The topics I had revised had proved elusive in the extreme and I knew that the First which was expected of anyone bearing the name of Hawking would prove just as elusive.

With the last flourish of the pen on the last page of the last Finals paper, I irrevocably signed away my student days. The Beatles record *Revolver*, which Stephen had given me for my birthday, seemed sadly incongruous. There were no parties, no celebrations, just a few hasty goodbyes before I stepped definitively into my other existence and we set off in the car to meet Roger Penrose who was to guide us out to his home at Stanmore for dinner with his family. We stopped in the car park of Stanmore station for Roger to collect his car, a battered old blue Volkswagen. Every tyre was flat. Undeterred, Roger drove to the garage round the corner where he pumped them all up. When we reached his single-storey house at the end of a cul-de-sac, tucked away from the stockbroker mansions, we were given an enthusiastic welcome by Joan and their two small sons, Christopher and Toby who had been the babe-in-arms at Cornell the previous summer. Now, at eighteen months, Toby was fully mobile and expressed his infectious *joie de vivre* by racing the length of the living room at full pelt, biscuit in hand, leaving a trail of crumbs across the navy-blue carpet, hurling his small person into an armchair, clambering on to the arm of the chair and then jumping off, the while declaring, 'Don't do that, don't do that!' I admired Joan's composure as she did battle with a vast array of pots and pans in the kitchen. Unperturbed by Toby's antics, she continued her preparations, regaling me with stories of her activities in various protest groups, while Stephen and Roger slid into a long discussion on their favourite theme, the singularities of space time.

The Finals results were more or less as expected, not brilliant but good enough to allow me to start working for a Ph.D. From my obser-vations of the dynamics of life in Cambridge, I could see that the role of a wife – and possibly a mother – was a one-way ticket to outer darkness. Even though there were moves afoot to admit women to certain of the more enlightened men's colleges, there were many well-qualified wives in Cambridge whose individual talents had been totally disregarded, spurned by a system which refused to acknowledge that wives and mothers might be capable of an intellectual identity of their own. It followed from this that there were many unhappy women in Cambridge and I had already met a sufficient number of them to persuade me that, dedicated though I was to Stephen's survival and his success, it was essential for me to preserve my own identity somehow.

My weekly commuting to London had come to an end at a propitious moment, for Stephen needed my help more and more. As my arm had to be available for him to lean on wherever he went, I walked round to the Department with him every morning, took him home for lunch, which – like every other meal – had to consist of meat and two vegetables to satisfy his enormous appetite, and collected him again in the evening. All thoughts of a career in the Foreign Office had long been consigned to the distant past, but even a simple job or a teacher training course was out of the question as my presence was so obviously constantly required in the small circle of the Department of Applied Mathematics, Little St Mary's Lane and the kitchen. A doctorate seemed to be the ideal solution. I could easily adapt my hours of study in the University library and my work at home to Stephen's schedule. Furthermore I was eligible for a student grant which was a welcome bonus.

The literature of the medieval period attracted me as a possible area of research but as our circumstances clearly would not permit me to travel to remote libraries in search of dusty manuscripts, I could not expect to edit a hitherto undiscovered text. My research would have to take the form of a critical study, using texts that were already published. This would not be difficult considering the facilities available in Cambridge. I continued to be registered, however, as a student of London University under the supervision of Alan Deyermond for various good reasons, the most cogent being that Cambridge Ph.Ds were subject to a fairly strict time limit of three years whereas there was no such restriction on the London degree and it seemed unlikely that I should be able to devote myself uninterruptedly to my thesis.

I did not embark upon my chosen field of research, the medieval lyric poetry of the Iberian Peninsula, straight away because, thanks largely to Stephen, another topic had presented itself as a subject for a preliminary research paper. As a result of reading *Le Celestina* while ensconced in my room during my exams, Stephen had come up with a bright idea which he put to me as we were driving back to Cambridge at the end of Finals week. Had I not realized, he asked, that the ultimate tragedy of death, destruction and despair in the drama was precipitated by the old bawd Celestina's rejection of a minor character, Pármeno, a youth who has a mother complex about her? The idea was a fascinating one which won Alan Deyermond's amazed approval: he was even more amazed when I confessed that the idea was Stephen's. I too was astounded at Stephen's powers of perception and invention which could focus on the essence of a problem in any field, my own included. My task was simply to flesh out the argument and justify the Freudian concept when applied to a text dating from 1499. The most gratifying aspect of the project was that it was a tribute to the success of our relationship: we were living and working in harmony, supporting each other, participating in each other's interests, despite the disparity of our chosen subjects, despite attempts to divide us and despite the inevitable difficulties of growing disability. We were very happy. We both gained confidence and courage from the strength of our mutual resolve and from our trust in each other. Then in the early autumn we found that I was expecting a baby.

CHAPTER THIRTEEN

Life Cycles

FOLLOWING CLOSE ON the confirmation of the pregnancy came the grim fulfilment of one of the unwritten laws of nature, whereby the advent of a new life heralds the passing of the old. Stephen's paternal grandmother, Mrs Hawking senior, whose acquaintance I had made just a month before, died at the age of ninety-six while Stephen's parents were away in China on an official tour of the country at the height of the Cultural Revolution. In August on a trip north with Isobel and Edward to visit ageing relatives, I had been introduced to Isobel's elderly maiden aunts in Edinburgh and, on our return journey, we had stayed overnight in the Hawking ancestral home in Boroughbridge in Yorkshire.

In the early nineteeth century, it was the ancestor who had been steward to the Duke of Devonshire and built himself the grand mansion which he, too, called Chatsworth who had also amended the surname from the vulgar 'Hawkins' to the more genteel 'Hawking'. With its sweeping staircase, high ceilings and bay windows, the Hawking Chatsworth had seen better days. Poor Aunt Muriel managed the vast house alone while at the same time attending to her disabled but still imperious mother. Like the house, Mrs Hawking was certainly a shadow of her former self but it was not hard to discern in her wrinkled features the domineering determination and fortitude of the woman who had raised five children and saved her family from bankruptcy. She lived in the drawing-room, the only room in the house which was still warm and habitable. The other rooms, including ours with its half-poster bed, were cold, dark, damp and not a little eerie despite Aunt Muriel's efforts to make them comfortable.

While his parents were away enthusing over the achievements of the Cultural Revolution, Stephen's younger brother Edward stayed with my parents. When he came to Cambridge to spend a weekend with us, he found himself, at the tender age of ten, obliged to cook his own Sunday lunch under his brother's instruction because I was suddenly laid low with an attack of morning sickness. It lasted all that day and into the next, and the next, and so on for week after week. An experienced friend suggested that the best cure was a cup of tea first thing in the morning before getting up. This was fine in theory but in practice I could not have a cup of tea without getting up to make it myself. My parents came to the rescue with the gift of a tea-making machine. Thereafter I was troubled by few effects of pregnancy and was able to resume my usual routine of study and writing with renewed vigour.

There was no shortage of helpful friends, all of them recent mothers, to advise on the pros and cons of hospitals, nursing homes, health treatment, prophylactic breathing, relaxation classes and breast-feeding. In despair at my ignorance in such matters, they even left their babies with me for practice sessions in changing nappies but it all seemed highly theoretical since, on the whole, the pregnancy was so straightforward and their babies were so well behaved. I was convinced that babies just ate and slept, whimpering a little from time to time.

My own health was unexceptional by comparison with Stephen's, which was beginning to require some management. Before leaving for China, Frank Hawking had read in a medical journal that a regular intake of vitamin B tablets might benefit the nervous system, which could also be reinforced by a weekly injection of a preparation called Hydroxocobalamin. The vitamin tablets could be obtained on prescription from the doctor – Dr Swan, also a Bart's man – with whom Stephen was registered in Cambridge, but the weekly injections were more of a problem since the surgery was on the other side of Cambridge and, in Stephen's opinion, a morning spent there waiting for an injection was a morning wasted. We tried it a few times to Stephen's growing frustration. One morning we arrived back home from the surgery at about midday to find Thelma Thatcher out in the Lane, broom in hand, engaged in her daily exercise of sweeping the road and the pavement. Noticing our despondent faces, she called to us, 'Dears, dears, what's the matter?'

I explained and she immediately came up with a solution. 'Oh, but that's easy! We'll ask Sister Chalmers to call in on her way from Peterhouse!' She hugged us both and then went off to get in touch with Sister Chalmers, the kindly Peterhouse nurse who had lent us her gas cooker when we moved into Little St Mary's Lane. At Thelma Thatcher's instigation, she was now commandeered into giving Stephen his injection at home once a week when she had finished her College surgery. In our household this coincided more or less with breakfast-time.

A similar problem arose when the medical authorities suggested regular physiotherapy to keep Stephen's joints extended and his muscles active. Already his fingers were beginning to curl and he could no longer write, except to sign his name. We attended just one physiotherapy session at Addenbrooke's, the new hospital on the outskirts of Cambridge, but by the end of it Stephen was so angry that he declared he would not squander any more of his precious time waiting around to be treated. It was Dennis Sciama who came to the rescue on this occasion. He persuaded the Institute of Physics to sponsor twice-weekly domiciliary visits by a private physiotherapist from its benevolent fund, whereupon Constance Willis entered our lives.

Constance was one of those stalwart English spinster ladies, cast in the same mould as the jolly-hockey-stick Molly Du Cane, the leader of the St Albans Folk Dance and Song Society. Constance had the same straightforward manner and eager openness as Molly, not embittered as some of the spinster schoolmistresses of her generation were. Before coming to stretch Stephen's muscles at ten o'clock on Tuesday and Thursday mornings, she would visit two octogenarian patients in Trinity College, Mr Gow, the eminent classicist, and the Reverend Simpson, formerly Dean of the College, principally to help them put their socks on.

Between them, Sister Chalmers and Miss Willis minimized the inconvenience to Stephen's routine, enabling him to work approximately the same hours as any of his colleagues. In reality, although he might arrive in his office later in the morning than they did, he usually worked later into the evening as well. He would spend long periods deep in thought and often at weekends would sit silently wrangling with the equations governing the beginning of the universe, training his brain to memorize long, complicated theorems without the aid of pen or paper. 'Celestial mechanics,' Mr Thatcher jokingly called it: 'I suppose your young man is busy with his celestial mechanics?' he would ask if Stephen had passed him in the street without acknowledging him, a common occurrence which, together with Stephen's reluctance to expend any effort on polite small-talk, tended to offend some of our more sensitive neighbours, acquaintances and relations, and for which I frequently had to apologize, explaining that my husband had to put all his concentration into remaining upright.

Bouts of morning sickness had prevented me from attending old Mrs Hawking's recent funeral in Yorkshire, with the result that at the age of twenty-two I had never yet been to a funeral. That omission was sadly soon to be rectified. That autumn Mary Thatcher, the only daughter of our neighbours, was planning an extended study tour of the Middle East where she would divide her stay of several months between Israel and Jordan. Just before her departure I saw her walking along the Lane hand-in-hand with her father whose pace had become slower and more halting. They disappeared from view into the churchyard. This poignant vision of father and daughter inscribed itself indelibly on my memory for it seemed that in those precious moments they were anticipating their final parting. Soon after Mary had left, her father fell ill and was taken into the nursing home where he died some weeks later.

As dry leaves danced through the streets before the biting December wind, Stephen and I stood hand-in-hand at the back of the cold, lofty church of the Holy Trinity, the Low Church which William Thatcher had attended in preference to the High Anglicanism of Little St Mary's. The stirring words of the funeral service, intoned as the coffin was carried into the church, sent a chill shiver down my spine:

> O death where is thy sting?
> O grave where is thy victory?

Man that is born of woman hath but a short time to live . . .

Watching and listening, I was haunted by the paradox that in one stroke, death had erased all the learning, experiences, heroism, goodness, achievements, memories of that life from which we were taking our leave. Yet within me, I was carrying the miraculous beginnings of a new life, a blank page on which the long process of learning, experience, achievements, memories had still to be written. Beside me stood the child's father, young and vibrant despite the onset of disability. His general health was good and his determination to enjoy life to the full and to succeed in physics was gaining strength by the day. Walking was difficult, buttons were a nuisance, mealtimes took longer and the brain had taken over from pen and paper, but his were mechanical problems which invention and perseverance could overcome. It was unthinkable that he could be a candidate for the sad ceremony we were attending that day. Death was the tragedy of old age, not of youth.

Youth is essential to the very existence of Cambridge, despite its medieval buildings and its fossilized Fellows who come home to roost in their dusty nooks and crannies. The magnetism of the place draws in wave upon wave of young people for three, or if they are lucky six, years and then thrusts them out into the real world, abruptly closing its doors behind them, leaving them rubbing their eyes in wonder as if they have suddenly been roused from a spell. Those brief years become imprinted on the memory as a carefree period which can never be recaptured. On the other hand, for those who manage to stay on there for longer, the floating nature of its population is – and was – an unsettling feature of life.

Although many of our schoolfriends had gone abroad – Diana King to Australia, John McClenahan to America, Gill and her husband Geoffrey to Canada – the society in which I was brought up had hardly changed during my childhood. Sometimes I had wished that it would. Now in Cambridge, recently acquired friends would be up and off with scarcely a by-your-leave, whether temporarily like the Donovans who went to Canada for a year, or permanently like the Australian couple, the Youngs, the envied occupiers of the Trinity Hall flat on King's Parade, who escaped to fresh fields on the other side of the globe. Before leaving with her husband, Brian, and her infant son, Derek, Anne Young showered me with all the useful ante-natal information she could think of – who was the best doctor, which was the best nursing home, where to go for pre-natal classes.

Each departure was a minor bereavement but the gap these friends left was soon filled by an influx of new arrivals. The Ellises, George and Sue, returned from Texas and we became close friends with our successors at number 11 Little St Mary's Lane, Peck and How Ghee Ang, who had come to view the house in November 1965, bringing with them their adorable baby daughter, Wan Ling, or Susan as she was known in English. The Angs were from Singapore but since they each spoke a different dialect of Chinese they had to communicate with each other as well as with us in English. Despite our disparate backgrounds, we and they had much in common. How Ghee was a Research Fellow in Chemistry at Peterhouse and Peck was expecting their second child. They were more advanced in their domestic comforts than we were, however, and actually possessed a television. It was in their house that we watched the English victory over Germany in the 1966 World Cup, the only football match which until then I had ever watched: it had me sitting on the edge of my chair in excitement.

There was also a flood of more transient visitors, particularly to the Department. Professor Charles Misner had brought his family of four beautiful blond children and his charming, aristocratic Danish wife, Susanne, to Cambridge for a year. Susanne heaped baby clothes and baby furniture in perfect condition onto me as their children progressively moved on to the next stages of development. I admired Susanne although I found the standards she set somewhat daunting. Despite the demands of a family of four, she managed to cook splendid meals, maintain her slender elegance, and present a generous and effervescent face to the outside world. Another visitor that autumn was our quiet American friend whom we had met at Cornell, Robert Boyer. He paid only a brief visit to Cambridge when, after a session in the Department, he came to dinner with us. He talked about his English wife and little daughter, and Vietnam, the main preoccupation of Americans in those days, as well as about singularities and physics.

One day not long after Robert's visit, the radio was blaring out the News headlines while I was preparing lunch and waiting for Stephen to come home. Since his return from Texas, George Ellis had regularly brought Stephen home at lunch-time on his way to eat at the newly opened University Centre on the riverfront at the end of the Lane. I listened in trepidation as the main item recounted a sniper attack in Austin, Texas. A madman had climbed to the top of the University tower from where he had shot at the lecturers and students crossing the square below. One of the victims had been shot dead. The report was all the more horrific on account of the familiarity of the scene. I could picture it in my mind's eye and realized at once that the sniper's targets could well include some of our acquaintances. Later that day we heard that Robert Boyer was the victim of the sniper's bullet. This was not death from old age, or from natural catastrophe like the recent Aberfan disaster, or prematurely from illness; it was death at the brutal hand of man. There was a sober truth in the stark words of the funeral service: 'by man came death . . .' Shocked and bewildered at such a cruel trick of fate, we searched for a lasting way of expressing our sorrow and our admiration for Robert Boyer.

CHAPTER FOURTEEN

An Imperfect World

ROBERT GEORGE WAS born, weighing 6 lb 5 oz, at ten o'clock at night on Sunday, 28 May 1967, just as Francis Chichester, the lone yachtsman, sailed into Plymouth harbour to be met by cheering crowds on his return from his round-the-world voyage. Robert's birth was received with private rejoicing of such intensity that when Stephen went to impart the good news to Peck and How Ghee the next morning, he was so overcome with emotion that Peck feared that I had died in childbirth.

Robert, in his eagerness to come into the world two weeks early, had taken me by surprise. In March, Stephen's sister Mary, his cousin Julian and I, together with thousands of other graduates, had all received our bachelor degrees at the mammoth London University degree ceremony in the Albert Hall, the occasion marred only by the absence of the Chancellor of the University, the Queen Mother, on account of her illness. Afterwards our parents treated us to a memorable party in a splendid venue, the Royal Society of Tropical Medicine, obtained for our use by my father-in-law.

Earlier in the academic year, Dr Dorothy Needham, the distinguished wife of the Master of Gonville and Caius, had taken me under her wing and introduced me to a fledgling academic society, Lucy Cavendish College, pioneered by two scientists, Dr Anna Bidder and Dr Kate Bertram, whose aim was to promote academic opportunities for mature women students in Cambridge. Association with Lucy Cavendish College allowed me to acquire MA status in the University and this in turn, most importantly, allowed me to borrow books from the University Library. By late spring, the *Celestina* paper, *Madre Celestina*, was at the printer's and I saw no reason to suppose that I would not be able to combine motherhood with research. On the last Friday in May, true to my usual routine, I spent most of the day blithely working in the University Library, assembling material for the thesis. I did not suspect that this was to be my last visit to the Library for quite a long time.

That evening, disregarding the strange tightening sensations in my thighs, I went with Sue Ellis, who was also pregnant, to a party for wives given by Wilma Batchelor, the wife of the Head of the Department of Applied Mathematics. On the Saturday morning, after an uncomfortable night, the tightening sensations were becoming stronger and more frequent, so I dashed into town to do a copious amount of shopping. Feeling rather ill as I heaved it all home, I called in at the butcher's for a few final purchases. Chris the butcher took one look at me and insisted on serving me ahead of the queue. 'Jane,' he said, 'I think you had better go straight home to bed!' I gladly followed his advice.

Later that day, at the height of a thunderstorm, How Ghee, who now had a second little daughter, Wang Ming, drove Stephen and me to the nursing home, the same one where William Thatcher had died. I soon wished that I had stayed at home or applied for a bed at the maternity hospital which, in those days, admitted only women from deprived backgrounds or those with complications. The ageing midwives in the nursing home in that era were every bit as crusty as, and actually more spiteful than, the spinster school ma'ams who had been the bane of my teenage years however much the two institutions they represented might have improved since then. As I walked down the corridor with Stephen leaning on my arm, I felt the onset of a strong contraction, like the tentacles of an octopus embracing and squeezing my abdomen. Assiduously following the techniques acquired in the newly introduced ante-natal classes, I leaned against a door-post and focused my attention on the much-practised breathing exercises.

'What on earth's the matter with you?' the steely-eyed Sister enquired harshly. She was much younger than the rest of her staff and should have known better. Appalled that anyone in her position could be so ignorant or so unsympathetic, I took no notice of her and continued my deep breathing. The baby must have been able to hear this exchange and decided there and then not to emerge into such a hostile world after all, because the procedure came to a complete standstill for the next twenty-four hours. He was probably as glad as I was that, in the event, he was not delivered by one of the midwives but by John Owens, a cheerful young doctor from the general practice surgery where I was registered. Meanwhile Stephen was my faithful companion, sitting at my bedside for long hours and even sneaking in on his mother's arm by the garden entrance at six o'clock the next morning.

I lay in bed, bored and frustrated, transported only by the magnificent, overpowering themes of the Brahms Double Concerto for Violin and Cello which I had memorized as my mantra, the music on which I had learnt to concentrate to distract my mind from the pain. I found that it also provided a diversion from the narrow-mindedness of the nursing fraternity. Those strains of music took me back to the week's holiday in Cornwall arranged for us by my parents that Easter, just two months before the birth. The cottage my parents had rented was down on the edge of the cove at Port St Isaac, a very long way from Cambridge. They probably thought, mistakenly as it happened, that this would be my last opportunity to travel for a long time. During that week Stephen, in concession to my tastes, had given me the recording of the Brahms concerto for a birthday present.

As Stephen's self-confidence had grown, so he had gained in fierce determination. During our stay in Port St Isaac, an afternoon's drive took us to Tintagel, one of the reputed homes of the Arthurian legend, perched remotely on the north coast of Cornwall. Disappointingly, the ruined castle was not visible from the village and according to the postmistress, the only approach was down a steep, rocky gulley, the Vale of Avalon. Stephen was determined to see the castle and, not wanting to deny him anything, so conscious were we of his shortened life expectancy, my mother and I, one on each side, guided, lifted, bore him down the wild, uneven descent, stumbling over the stones in our path with the wind blowing off the sea into our faces. The sapphire band of sea at the end of the path seemed to be receding and the castle proved elusive. After we had struggled on for about three-quarters of an hour, my mother was getting short of breath and was worrying about me in my advanced state of pregnancy, but Stephen refused to give up. By a happy chance, a Landrover appeared from nowhere, climbing the rough track back up to the village. We hailed the driver. He was loath to stop but paused to tell us that the castle was still a long way off, round a headland. We pleaded with him to take us back to the village. Finally, with brusque impatience and a hostile reluctance, he agreed to take just one passenger. There was no question but that that passenger had to be Stephen.

With similar single-mindedness, Stephen was pursuing plans to attend a summer school at the Battelle Memorial Institute in Seattle that July. With never a moment's hesitation, I approved the plans, seeing no reason why the three of us, Stephen, myself and the baby, should not enjoy seven weeks on the Pacific coast. My brief experiences with other babies, particularly my little god-daughters, made me confident that our baby would simply eat and sleep.

The joy the baby brought was intoxicating. Within minutes of his birth he was lodged in the crook of my arm, looking slightly purple but observing his surroundings with consummate unconcern as if he had seen it all before. 'A future professor' was my mother-in-law's predictable verdict on her first grandchild. When next he was brought to me, he had recovered from the birthing experience and had gained a healthy colour. His eyes were of the deepest, brightest blue, set in a neat, elfin face with rosy cheeks and pointed ears. He had no hair, only an incipient blond down in a whorl on the crown of his head and on the tips of his ears. The minute fingers, each equipped with its own tiny nail, clasped my own outstretched finger.

This beautiful little creature, the miraculous embodiment of perfection, had come into a painfully imperfect world. In the week after his birth, the Six Day War erupted in the Middle East with violent consequences which were to last throughout the decades of the child's upbringing and into his adulthood. In my simple, post-natal frame of mind, I was convinced that if the world were to be run by the mothers of new-born babies, rather than hardened old men inciting brash youths to violence, wars would cease overnight.

Gradually in the days following Robert's birth, we acclimatized to a new reality. Grandparents helped out for a couple of weeks and then we were on our own, evolving a dramatically changed lifestyle. Henceforth expeditions – to the Department or into town – involved three people plus a pram and a walking stick. Luckily George Ellis came to the rescue. Not only did he bring Stephen home at lunch-time, he also collected him after lunch and brought him home again in the evening. One afternoon, after a couple of weeks, when we had begun to achieve some faint semblance of normality, I considered that the time had come to return to my books and my growing card index of the language of the medieval love poetry of the Iberian Peninsula. The baby was fed and changed and placed in his pram out in the back yard under the blue sky. He looked comfortable and drowsy in the warm afternoon air. I expected him to sleep for at least an hour. Stifling my own tendency to yawn, I crept upstairs to my books and cards in the attic and spread them out on the table. No sooner had I found my place than a raucous cry came from below. I hurried down to Robert, picked him up, fed him and changed his nappy again. He did not really appear to be very hungry. I laid him down gently in his carrycot and went back upstairs, only to be followed by the same cry. This little scene was re-enacted many times that afternoon until finally I realized that this tiny baby was not hungry nor was he sleepy. He just wanted to be sociable so, at the age of one month, he started work on a Ph.D thesis, helping me by wriggling on my knee and gurgling while I tried to write. That single afternoon completely destroyed whatever illusions I might have held about combining motherhood with some sort of intellectual occupation.

It was then that I began to understand why another neighbour in the Lane, Elinor Shaffer, a Fellow of Lucy Cavendish College who had given birth to a son in March, had remarked that she found the prospect of motherhood challenging. Elinor was wiser than me. In my medical ignorance, I had no notion of the demands on the body of the birth process. I fully counted on being up and about my normal business within a week, little realizing that the nine-month gestation and the trauma of the long birth would take their toll of my strength. Nor had I realized that feeding the baby would be such an exhausting and time-consuming commitment which, combined with the topsy-turvy schedule of infant demands, day and night, would mean that I would often slip into a doze when eventually he went to sleep at whatever time of day.

As the summer advanced and July approached, I began to have severe qualms about the Seattle trip, especially as the arrangements were becoming more and more complicated. Charlie Misner, who had become Robert's godfather at his christening in Caius Chapel in June, wanted Stephen to visit him at the University of Maryland after the Seattle summer school, to talk about singularities. Both he and Susanne assured us that we should be welcome to stay in their large house in the suburbs of Washington, DC. I could not allow myself to appear half-hearted but I was not sure how we were going to get to Seattle in one piece, let alone further afield. The tiredness I felt as I tried to pack for the three of us, Stephen, myself and our seven-week-old baby, was devastating and unprecedented. I had not expected anything like this nor had I expected that my own body, previously so utterly reliable, would let me down so badly.

Somehow, assisted by a posse of anxious parents, none more so than my mother, we managed to check in at London airport on time on the morning of 17 July 1967. Our goodbyes were hasty because the airline promptly provided a wheelchair for Stephen who found himself obliged to sit in it and be wheeled directly through Customs and Passport Control to the Departure Lounge. Laden with Robert and assorted bags of provisions for the flight, I hurried along behind. The ventilation system at Terminal Three had broken down that day, the hottest day of the summer, with the result that hot air was being sucked into the building but none was being let out, making a veritable inferno of the Departure Lounge. We had just reached the Lounge when the loudspeaker announced that our flight was delayed.

While we sat waiting in the stifling heat, Robert eagerly gulped down the entire contents of the bottle of diluted rose-hip syrup which was supposed to last him all the way to Seattle. The first announcement was soon followed by another, inviting Pan American passengers to collect complimentary refreshments from the bar. I deposited Robert on Stephen's knee and went over to join the queue for our free sandwiches. When I returned, I froze in absolute horror at the sight that met my eyes. Robert was still safely sitting on his father's knee, smiling beatifically and leaning comfortably back against Stephen's chest with Stephen's arm around him. Stephen's face wore an agonized expression. Down his new trousers there flowed a vast yellow river, as abundant as the Yangtse in full flood. He sat helplessly trapped as the yellow tide streamed into his shoes. For the only time in my life, I screamed – I dropped the sandwiches and screamed.

Screaming may sound a pretty irrational reaction. Surprisingly it was the most sensible in the circumstances. In my dazed state, the one fact of which I was certain was that the situation was beyond my control and I needed help. My screams summoned that help with amazing alacrity. A portly, green-clad nurse appeared from nowhere and took charge. One severely critical glance at me was enough to convince her, quite rightly, that I was hopelessly unequal to the situation. In a flash, she commandeered the wheelchair and pushed it and its occupants, father and son, back through Passport Control and Customs, disregarding the officials in our path, to a nursery where she cleaned up the baby, leaving me the task of rubbing Stephen down. While we were in the nursery, the last call for our flight was announced over the tannoy. Unmoved, the nurse rang through to Central Control and told them that the flight would have to wait for us. Thus at the age of seven weeks,

Robert acquired the distinction of having delayed the departure of an international flight.

Stephen had to sit in those trousers for the whole nine-hour length of that spectacular flight. He sat in them over Iceland, etched in the sea like a jewel in a satin case, over the iceflows of the North Atlantic, over Greenland's snow-capped mountains where the valleys between the 10,000-foot peaks were filled in by glistening glaciers, over the frozen waters of Hudson Bay and the arid wastes of northern Canada. Then at last, signalling the end of Stephen's ordeal, Mount Rainier loomed on the horizon as we came in to land at Tacoma airport. A day or two later, I took the trousers to the dry cleaner's but Stephen refused to wear them ever again.

Part Two

CHAPTER FIFTEEN

Unsettled in Seattle

FOR MOST PEOPLE, even at the end of the twentieth century, a spacious, detached, single-storey house, lavishly equipped with all mod cons, including a dishwasher and a tumble-dryer, and an enormous car with powered and automatic controls, would be tantamount to a dream come true, especially when the house is on the top of a ridge, facing west out to distant snowy peaks. These provisions, made for us in Seattle in 1967 by the Battelle Memorial Institute, were certainly generous for they even included a twice-weekly deposit of clean nappies and the corresponding collection of the dirty ones by that singularly American institution, the diaper service. If such carefully made arrangements did not altogether fulfil my dreams, it was not because I was unappreciative of them, it was just that I was overwhelmed by the sensation of being washed up on an alien shore, of finding myself in utter isolation in the heart of luxury, of being deprived so soon after childbirth of the support, advice and help which the community and the family had provided at home. Here, in Seattle, I was solely responsible for both my ailing husband and my tiny, helpless baby. Like the London slum-dwellers who had been moved out of their soot-encrusted, back-to-back hovels into custom-built new towns, I longed for the security and familiarity of our crumbling little house, our network of neighbours and friends, and our versatile, manageable Mini. Here there was no George Ellis to give Stephen a helping hand round the corner to work.

The Battelle Institute, the secretary told me comfortingly, was very close at hand, only two miles or so away from the house. Two miles or twenty, it did not make much difference: Stephen had to be taken there by car and to take Stephen by car, I also had to take Robert. This meant helping Stephen dress and eat in the early morning, and then feeding and bathing Robert – in that order or in reverse – depending on whose needs were the most pressing. Then the car – a Ford Mercury Comet, a monster if ever there was one – had to be backed round to the front of the house and one by one, my two charges, Robert in his carrycot, and then Stephen on my arm, taken down the steps of the long path and settled, the one on the back seat and the other in the front. Methodically carried out in an unhurried fashion in the best of circumstances, this routine could have been tolerable. As it was, although we tried our hardest to minimize the number of morning sessions that Stephen missed, our good intentions were thwarted and the system reduced to breaking point because our darling baby, who had just learnt to sleep through the night in England, was now, in Seattle with an eight-hour time change, sleeping soundly all day and was wide awake and full of happy, sociable intentions all night. In addition Seattle was enjoying – or suffering – its most intense heatwave ever. Since Seattle is not renowned for hot summers, its buildings lacked the air-conditioning which is considered indispensable in more southerly American climes.

For some time, in a spirit of nervous self-preservation as much as anything else, I restricted my excursions to the Battelle Institute and the corner stores, notably of course, the dry cleaner's. I drove the massive car so slowly and with such trepidation that eventually, despite the heat, I decided to do what no American mother would have dreamt of doing: I walked down to the store pushing my carrycot-pram and loaded the shopping into it beside the baby.

It was with the jubilation of a shipwrecked sailor sighting a vessel at sea that I greeted the arrival of the Penrose family. There were now three small Penrose boys. Eric, the latest addition to the family, was eight months old, somewhat more mobile than Robert but frequently recumbent. When the two prams stood side by side, or the two babies were placed down together on a rug, Joan would remark that they were continuing the Hawking–Penrose dialogue.

Thanks to Joan, my social scene brightened considerably. She introduced me to some of the other delegates' wives, dispersed in their separate houses around Seattle. Among them was Mary Geroch whose husband, Bob, was working closely with Stephen and Roger. With a detached aplomb, Mary coped admirably with the company of four little boys and their mothers when Joan took us all out on various excursions to downtown Seattle, where I should never have dared venture alone. I browsed in the department stores and bought babyclothes, while Joan went off in resolute pursuit of a wig. Her daily research, the fruits of which she regularly reported to Mary and me, was most thorough. Wigs of Asian hair were cheaper because they were more plentiful and tougher. Softer, finer, Caucasian or European wigs were almost unobtainable and it was a Caucasian wig that Joan wanted. I never asked why she wanted one – although the question crossed my mind often – since Joan had a splendid head of long, fairish hair which itself could have provided sufficient volume for a perfect wig. Under Joan's influence, my confidence grew as I began to find my way up and down the freeway which runs on a north–south axis through the centre of Seattle. I even managed to locate an old acquaintance from Norwich, Susan Fish, the niece of Grandma's next-door neighbour, with whom I used to play during those simple but idyllic summer holidays of my childhood. Susan had married a Boeing engineer and lived near the Boeing Field on the south side of Seattle. I took Robert to visit her one afternoon. It was a mystery to me that she could bear to live so far removed from her home and family, but she seemed happy enough, if rather solitary.

Then one Sunday, even more adventurously, Stephen's map reading guided us to a ferry port and we crossed Puget Sound to the Olympic Peninsula where I took Robert down to the water's edge and dipped his toes in the shimmering but icy waters of the Pacific Ocean. He voiced his shocked displeasure in no uncertain terms. Another weekend we drove 150 miles north across the border to Vancouver to visit our itinerant Australian friends, the Youngs, who had come to rest for a spell in the University of British Columbia. For the whole journey, ten-week old Robert sat propped up between his father and me, asleep on the bench seat in the front of the car – only, of course, to remain awake all night. In two days, we took in the sights of Vancouver, Stanley Park and the totem poles, and went up into the hills to Simon Fraser University with its concrete piazzas and loggias which seemed badly misplaced, since Vancouver was as cold and misty as Seattle was hot and dry. Vancouver, however, did have the Canadian charm of being more relaxed and less brash than its American neighbour.

There were only a few excursions organized by the Battelle Institute. With the rest of the group we assembled one hot Saturday morning down on the waterfront for one of those rare treats. We were to be taken by ferry to Blake Island, an Indian reservation where we were to be treated to a meal in a big, old-fashioned barn, converted into a restaurant catering for tourists. While waiting for the ferry, Jeannette

Wheeler, the wife of one of the most respected American physicists, came up to introduce herself. That very year, as rumour had it, in a flash of inspiration worthy of Archimedes, while having a bath, John Wheeler had lighted upon the name 'black holes' for the phenomena that Stephen and many others were studying. Down on the Seattle waterfront, Jeannette, a tall, regal, grey-haired lady who, by all accounts, was a member of that select group, the Daughters of the American Revolution, took charge of Robert's pram while Stephen leaned on my arm. Two little old ladies peered lovingly into the pram. 'Oh, how cute!' they gushed at the sight of the sleeping infant. Unable to resist the temptation, one of them reached out to tickle Robert's toes, uncovered in the heat of the day. Scarcely had her fingers touched their curled, rosy tips than Mrs Wheeler barked at her to leave the baby alone. The poor little lady jumped out of her skin, cringing in fright at such a stentorian rebuke. She and her companion edged away nervously into the crowd as Jeannette muttered indignantly, 'What a stupid thing to do. You should never tickle the toes of a sleeping baby!' Personally, I thought a bit of tickling of Robert's toes might be a very good idea. If he could be woken up during the day, I might get some sleep at night. As it was, he slept for most of that day, waking only to gaze angelically into the weather-beaten face of the elderly Indian squaw who rocked him on her knee while I ate dinner at the long communal table.

At least on this particular excursion, my only responsibility, apart from attending to the baby's needs, was to push the pram with one hand and support Stephen with the other. The other excursions where I was also responsible for driving long distances to interesting places left me so tired and so strained that I was on my knees with exhaustion by the time my school friend Gillian Pinfold, née Phillips, came over to Seattle from Vancouver Island where her husband Geoffrey, an engineer, had a two-year appointment. Gillian – and Geoffrey who was able only to spend a weekend with us – were my salvation. Geoffrey drove us on long journeys, not least a day trip to Mount Rainier, collected shopping and helped Stephen in and out of the car, while Gill willingly gave a hand in the running of the kitchen. Moreover, for one week, not only could I relax, I also had someone to talk to.

While Gill was still with us, an incident occurred which we both remember with distaste. In 1962 Seattle had been the site of the World Fair. The token monument which the city retained was the Space Needle, a concrete pylon some 300 feet high, topped by a viewing platform in the shape of a flying saucer. On Gill's last Saturday with us, we went up the Space Needle in the express lift and admired the views over the sparkling green waters of Puget Sound and the white crests of the Olympic Peninsula to the west, and the rugged Cascade range of mountains to the east; to the south, the skyline was magically dominated by Mount Rainier, the massive, dormant volcano. The views did not disappoint us but with Gill carrying Robert and Stephen leaning on my arm, we soon wilted in the sweltering sun. When we really could not stand the heat any longer, we returned to the lift and joined the queue for the descent. Near us there stood a couple of girls, teenagers perhaps, but not so very much younger than Gill and me. They watched us, nudging each other; then, as we were all standing together in the lift, they started making spiteful, rude remarks about Stephen's appearance as he leaned languidly against the wall. True, he was no Hollywood idol and possibly in my attempts to keep the baby well cared for, I had been guilty of overlooking some of the details of his personal hygiene. In any case, the heat was enough to make anyone look bedraggled. As they laughed and giggled, my anguish grew. I wanted to slap their faces and make them apologize. I wanted to shout at them that this was my courageous, dearly loved husband, the father of the beautiful baby and one of the world's greatest scientists, but in my English reticence, I neither did nor said any of these things: I simply looked away, busying myself with Robert and trying to pretend that they were not there or that they were talking about somebody else. Never did an express lift, travelling at 4 feet per second, take so long to reach the ground. As we emerged from the lift, one of the girls glanced over Gill's shoulder at Robert. 'Is that your baby?' she asked me in perplexed admiration. 'He most certainly is!' I snorted scornfully. She and her companion hurried away, I hoped in shame. Gill remarked, 'What strange people!', understating what she and I both felt. It was a long time before I could come to terms with the anger and pain caused by such barbaric behaviour. The only consolation was that because Gill and I had stationed ourselves between Stephen and his adversaries, he seemed oblivious of what had happened.

After this episode I should have gladly returned to England forthwith. However, towards the end of the summer school, Stephen was offered opportunities which he could not – and which I would not have wanted him to – refuse. The possibility of a two-week stay at the University of California in Berkeley was mooted one evening at the

Battelle cocktail hour and immediately a Brazilian participant in the Battelle summer school offered us the empty flat of an absent friend. The offer was attractive in financial terms and since we had already come so far, another two weeks on the West Coast, in California of all places, did not seem a great hardship. I had not entirely lost the spirit of adventure which had taken me round southern Spain in my student days. This was to be our opportunity to discover for ourselves that Utopia with which Abe and Cice Taub had tempted us in Cornell in 1965.

Encumbered by quantities of paraphernalia – the wheelchair, the pram, the luggage – we flew down to San Francisco where I was required to master yet another enormous car, a Plymouth, and negotiate yet another maze of freeways. Fortunately Stephen was an excellent navigator, a better navigator than he had been a driver – except on those occasions when he would spot a turning at the last minute and yell at me to cross four lanes immediately to a freeway exit. We were also somewhat hampered by my unfortunate inability to distinguish right from left automatically. After swerving a few times and bumping over a few kerbs in good Keystone Cop style, we at last found the address of our absent landlords: a homely, two-roomed flat with bathroom and kitchen in an old wooden house with a distant view, through the haze and the mist, of the Golden Gate bridge.

The accommodation was much more in keeping with our style and age than the sumptuous Seattle middle-class, middle-aged house, but it posed a fearsome logistical problem. The flat was on the top floor of the house, the second storey. The Seattle routine, which we had hoped to leave behind in that city, had to come into play again, except that every outing now required not two but three trips up and down, not one but two flights of stairs. Robert, at fourteen weeks, was getting too heavy to be carried in the carrycot, so first the carrycot had to be taken down to the car; then I would take Stephen down, leaving Robert on a rug on the floor, then Robert himself. To compensate for this amount of inconvenience, we maximized the use of the car and often, of an evening or exceptionally of an afternoon, after meeting Stephen from work, would drive up into the parched hills behind Berkeley or sometimes, more adventurously, north along the San Andreas fault, a hauntingly deserted, marshy area where the cracks in the road testified to the tremendous natural forces lying dormant beneath the surface. Once we drove down to a desolate cove on a coastline not unlike

Cornwall's where, defying the American way of life, hippies lived free of the constraints of a materialistic society in shacks on the beach.

Abe Taub, the Head of the Relativity Group in Berkeley whom we had met at Cornell, secured a temporary appointment for Stephen in his Department and one evening he and his wife Cice invited us to dinner in their beautiful house high up in the hills overlooking the Bay. The house was further away than we expected and by the time we found it, the evening was already drawing in. Unable to see where to park as we arrived in the gloaming, I drove into a gulley by the side of the road. The wheels locked and the car was stuck. Dishevelled and shamefaced after trying unsuccessfully to heave the car out of the ditch on my own, I went to seek help from the Taubs and their distinguished guests, among them Professor Lichnerowicz, a highly sophisticated and influential Parisian mathematician. The men took off their smart jackets, rolled up their sleeves and set to the task with chivalrous gusto. When at last we were extricated from the ditch and shown into the house – embarrassingly late – Robert started to whimper. He had played this trick on us once before when we were invited to dinner with Bob and Mary Geroch in Seattle. He would appear to be sleeping soundly until the very moment when his carrycot was put gently down in a darkened side-room and then, as though sensing that there was a party elsewhere from which he was being excluded, he would start to protest. The remedy was simple: Robert had to be allowed to spend the evening on my knee at the table, alongside all the other guests. The Taubs remained unflustered in the face of so many disruptions to their genteel gathering. Cice, perhaps taking pity on my haggard appearance, invited me to accompany her and Madame Lichnerowicz to the Berkeley Rose Garden the next day.

The Rose Garden became my haven, a paradise of peace and solitude in the frenzied environment of the Bay area and a respite from the strenuous routine which our living arrangements had forced on us. It had a calming effect on Robert, who would lie in his pram under the pergolas watching the patterns of light on the roses and the leaves above his head. I would sit by him in the shade, breathing in the perfume of the roses, immersed in my book, Stendhal's *La Chartreuse de Parme*. At times I would pause and gaze out over the Bay. Although it was quite possible to imagine that these were the gardens of a *palazzo* in early-nineteenth-century Italy, the setting of the novel, my thoughts were irresistibly drawn to Spain, to the gardens of the Generalife above

Granada where only a few short years before I had painfully tried to envisage a future for myself with Stephen. That future had become a reality and had exceeded our wildest dreams. I was tired but resilient, and my happiness far outweighed my tiredness. Stephen was already recognized and sought after in scientific circles, for his breadth of vision, his intuitive grasp of complicated concepts, his ability to visualize mathematical structures in many dimensions and for his phenomenal powers of memory. The future stretched ahead of us in a very real physical sense: it was now embodied in the small, thriving person of our baby son.

If the future had acquired a reassuring aura of certainty, the key to that certainty lay in managing the present. Living each day as it came and living for that day, and not some fanciful mirage in the distant future, was becoming a way of life. From that perspective, the general outline of the future was fairly clear-cut: in the short term our star was in the ascendant. In the long term, the huge question mark that hung over the entire human race might well obliterate any need to make further provisions on the personal level.

The Vietnam war had escalated – to use the current coinage – into the ugliest of conflicts where the horrors of modern chemical science were being unleashed on a simple peasant population in the most cowardly manner. Tiny children were being sprayed with napalm and set alight; tindery villages were ignited from the air and great tracts of forest and cultivated land were being laid waste and rendered toxic for generations. A cynicism reigned on both sides, masked by the emotive cover of political ideology. In fact it was nothing more than blatant economic imperialism, propelled by the military industrial complexes of both East and West, and those military industrial complexes had run out of control. Only a spark somewhere else on our troubled planet would be needed to ignite a global conflagration. Indeed, perceiving the sort of nuclear threat from across the Pacific which we Europeans had lived with for years, the Californians were now busy installing shelters in the basements of their houses.

It was all the more important to take full advantage of the present. The trouble was that the present had an annoying way of being much more unpredictable than the future. It would not allow itself to be easily regulated and kept tripping us up by putting unforeseen obstacles in our path, plummeting us into untoward circumstances which we would certainly have avoided had we been able to anticipate them.

The Brazilian couple who had, with the best of intentions, found us the flat, also doubtless with the best of intentions, offered to take us on a tour of the sights of San Francisco. I was delighted. For once I should be able to sit back and enjoy a day out. The couple arrived early one Saturday morning, bringing with them a Brazilian friend who spoke no English. Like the chattering children in the school opposite our apartment on the day of an outing, Stephen and I clambered down the stairs brimming with excitement. We had decided that he would get in our friends' car first and then I should go back up for Robert who would travel on my knee. As we emerged into the street, we looked around for the Brazilians' car. Apart from our own Plymouth, there was only a battered grey Volkswagen parked in front of the house. 'Where's your car?' I asked our Brazilian host for the day. He looked at me in surprise. 'No, no, we are no going in our car, it ees too small for all of us. We must take your car.' Aghast, I turned to Stephen, hoping that he would take it upon himself to veto the expedition outright but he did not.

Why, oh why, did I not allow myself to repeat the screaming fit of that July morning at London airport? Politely I suppressed my dismay and with sinking heart unlocked the car. Stephen was to sit in the back with the Brazilian ladies and our 'host' would sit in the passenger seat in the front, directing me, the chauffeur, while holding Robert on his knee. One look at him was enough to make Robert bawl as he never had before. He bawled all day, across the Oakland Bridge, all through the hours of torrid, nose-to-tail traffic jams in which we sat roasting, all through Haight Ashbury, up and down all the steep streets of central San Francisco. I understood only too well how he felt for I would gladly have bawled my head off too. I wanted desperately to comfort my frantic, hot, uncomfortable baby yet there I was, unable to move from the driving seat, trapped in a senseless situation.

There was a lull when at last we reached Central Park. Distancing ourselves as far as possible from our passengers, we joined a large hippy peace gathering and sat on the grass with the flower people, swaying to the beat of the music. I looked around the lawns and saw people of my own age and generation, yet somehow I was already much older. They were savouring the luxury of freedoms which they were claiming from authority and from a complacently rigid society. They were idealistic and opposed to war. Stephen and I shared their idealism and hatred of violence. We too had claimed a comparable freedom in our fight against bureaucracy and narrow-mindedness yet, to maintain our difficult course, we were constrained to follow a routine as organized and as rigid as any imposed by the society against which they were rebelling. The Vietnam war, though we shared their antagonism to it, was not our main target. Our efforts were directed against illness and ignorance.

Robert calmed down briefly until we resumed our journey. When finally that evening we ended up in a restaurant on Fisherman's Wharf, I was too tired and too frustrated to keep up even a semblance of polite chatter in pidgin Portuguese, so we ate in silence until the Brazilians decided it was time to go home. The moral I learned from that experience was clear: never depend on other people.

Putting that moral into practice was easier said than done, for Stephen had already accepted a pressing invitation to spend time in Charlie Misner's Department at the University of Maryland. Washington, DC was on the way home, we reasoned, half-way home in fact, so another few weeks would not make much difference. Indeed, breaking the journey half-way would help us all, including Robert, to cope with the jet-lag. We also looked forward to seeing Stephen's sister Mary who, now a qualified doctor, was working on the East Coast, and to visiting Stephen's old friend John McClenahan who, with his lively, Spanish-speaking American wife and her three sons, lived and worked in Philadelphia.

On the flight east, we sat in the same row as a middle-aged lady who was convulsed with sobs and tears for the whole five hours of the journey. Since she occasionally cast longing glances at Robert, I gave him to her to cuddle for a while. A pale smile flickered across her face as he beguiled her with his tinkling laughter and his broad, toothless grins. As her companion leaned across the aisle to tell me her friend's story, she broke into sobs again: she was returning home from Vietnam where her only son had been killed. For her, words of comfort had lost their meaning. For the rest of her life she, like so many other mothers, both American and Vietnamese, would be scarred by the crass injustice which had taken that precious young life from her: a mother without a child, hers was a role too terrible to bear. The hippies were right: why should they consent to being used as cannon fodder when many of them had neither the right to vote nor even the right to buy themselves a drink, since the age of majority was still twenty-one? Many of them were lucky in that, as college students, their military call-up would be deferred temporarily and then their college professor would move heaven and earth to help the best students avoid the draft. Some would escape abroad, to Canada perhaps, uncertain when if ever they would be able to return home in safety. The son of the mother on the plane had not been so fortunate; those opportunities had not been open to him.

Life for mothers whose children were alive and well was not necessarily easy, as we discovered on arrival in Maryland. The Misners, so happy and relaxed in Cambridge, had come home to a crisis in their family life. Francis, their eldest son, aged five, was being rejected by the local primary school on account of his mild autism, which until now had not proved a significant handicap. His mother, Susanne, was engaged in a stressful daily battle with the unimaginative school authorities, trying to prevail upon them to accommodate Francis, a quiet, affectionate little boy, in their reception class. Naturally this dispute, with all its emotional overtones and its implications for the future, had a severely depressive effect on Susanne's normally sunny, positive nature.

Our visit was evidently not best timed, unless I could find ways of helping to compensate for the inconvenience of it by playing with the other delightful Misner children, by babysitting and by giving a hand in the kitchen. Shopping was out of the question because, here on the outskirts of Washington, I did not have the regular use of a car and, unlike Seattle, the house was not within walking distance of any shops. Although we saw Stephen's sister Mary, and hired a car for our weekend visit to the McClenahans, I was stranded. I was also at the end of my tether, exhausted and depressed.

As soon as we had arrived in Seattle all those weeks ago, Stephen insisted that Robert's intake be supplemented with canned babymilk, a move which, though it ensured that the ravenous baby was properly fed and probably saved time, undermined my delicately balanced maternal self-respect. Since then, the upheavals and the physical strain of so many travels with a small baby and a disabled husband had drained my reserves completely dry and I was no longer able to feed my child. I sat on the bed in the guest apartment in the basement of the Misners' luxury home in Silver Spring and wept at the breaking of the first priceless bond between my baby and me.

If the recourse to bottles had unhappy psychological repercussions for me, it had even worse physical consequences for the Misners. One evening Charlie and Susanne, who was at last beginning to relax a little from her daily struggle, put on a splendid dinner-party to introduce us to some of their friends. Robert was asleep and the Misner children had settled down. We sat round the table eating and drinking, talking and laughing, and then sank drowsily into comfortable armchairs while Charlie put on a slide show of charming family photos, taken in America and in Europe. In my semi-somnolent state of unaccustomed idle contentment, I suddenly became conscious of a bad smell – a very bad smell – coming from the direction of the kitchen. What's more, the bad smell seemed to be addressing itself personally to me. The ghastly, unbearable truth was soon revealed when other people began to frown and cough as they too detected the poisonous odour, while I squirmed uneasily in my armchair. Before dinner I had put Robert's plastic bottles and their rubber teats on the stove to boil. In the convivial atmosphere, I had forgotten all about them. The contents of the saucepan had evaporated completely, filling the kitchen with an evil black smoke which was quickly penetrating every corner of the spotlessly clean house. Utterly mortified, I would not have been surprised if we had been turned out into the street, baby and all, there and then. To Charlie and Susanne's lasting credit, they did no such thing and the next day, summoning a prodigious degree of charity, they even managed somehow to make light of the shameful episode. They must have been heartily glad to see the back of us some days later when they cheerily waved us and our four-month-old baby goodbye at the airport. Their relief at seeing us go could not have been greater than mine at the prospect of going home.

CHAPTER SIXTEEN

Terra Firma

THAT TRIP TO Seattle – and beyond – changed our lives, in some ways for better, in others for worse. The money Stephen had earned in lecture fees during those long months across the Atlantic had a healthy effect on our bank balance. On the strength of it we were able to go out and buy a badly needed automatic washing-machine and, in good American style, a tumble-dryer as well. This would have been an exemplary supply of consumer goods for any British household in the 1960s but Stephen decided, after one searing exposure to domestic reality, that our lifestyle demanded even more electrical aids. The domestic reality in question arose one Friday evening later that winter when we gave a large dinner-party for an eminent Russian scientist, Vitaly Ginzberg, who had come to Cambridge from Moscow on a three-month visit. Not only was the length of his visit exceptional in the repressive climate of the Cold War, but he had also been allowed to bring his glamorous blonde wife out of Russia with him. Judging by the amount of crockery and cutlery piled in the kitchen on the departure of the guests, the dinner-party in their honour could be counted a great success. Leaning himself against the kitchen wall, Stephen took pity on me and picked up a tea-towel. So disgusted was he by the waste of time occasioned by so much washing-up that the following day, Saturday, he enlisted George Ellis's help and went off into town to buy a dishwasher. His mother was later heard to remark that in her day people bought their houses before frittering their money away on such expensive luxuries. She omitted to mention that when her children were small, she had the benefit of a nanny as well as an able-bodied husband.

There were other less tangible effects of the American trip. It was well established that the phenomenon that Stephen was researching had an easily identifiable name: 'the black hole'. The name was inspired. It was much less cumbersome than 'the gravitational collapse of a massive star', the process predicted in the mathematics of the singularity theorems, and it lent unity to scientific research. It was, too, a name which caught the imagination of the media. As a result of the Seattle summer school, Stephen had firmly consolidated his position in international circles as a pioneer in this research and we had widely enlarged our circle of friends. Indeed, Bob and Mary Geroch followed us back to England where they installed themselves in a basement flat in London while Bob worked with Roger Penrose at Birkbeck College. From time to time they came to Cambridge bringing their dog Charlie with them. Charlie was highly suspicious of six-month-old Robert and cannily took refuge from him under the table, growling in peevish defiance at his advances. Bob was blessed with the endearingly singular quality of being able to laugh at his own mistakes. When Stephen took him to dine on High Table in Caius, he confessed to being so overawed by the surroundings, the company and the array of cutlery on the table before him, that he felt obliged to peel and eat a banana with a knife and fork . . .

Stephen calculated that by the time we returned to England in October, Robert had flown such a vast distance in relation to his age that even in his sleep he was, in theory, still moving. Fortunately Robert himself did not appear to be disturbed by this particular consequence of his first visit to America. I too had travelled far but unlike Robert, I suffered long-lasting and tormenting results from these travels. They had sown the seeds of a paralysing fear of flying which germinated and grew like a giant weed in my mind in the months and years after our return home. When I considered how much I used to enjoy flying as a student, only two years previously, this fear was both frustrating and incomprehensible.

It was some time later that a rationale for the phobia emerged as I struggled to come to terms with it. When I reviewed the events of those four months in America, I realized that the problem lay not with flying since we had flown in many different aeroplanes over vast distances without incident, but with the attendant circumstances, the stresses and strains of being wholly responsible, a mere seven weeks after giving birth, for two other fragile but very demanding lives. That onerous and exhausting responsibility slowly crystallized into a fear of flying for want of any other outlet. The simple fact of being able to rationalize the fear did not make dealing with it any easier. First and foremost, I was

ashamed to admit to such a weakness which implied a major flaw in my
character, especially when our lives were strictly governed by Stephen's
laudably brave maxim, that if there was physical illness in the home,
there was no room for psychological problems as well. Secondly, my
doctor, however sympathetic, could only prescriber tranquillizers or
sleeping tablets since there was no known cure. Thirdly, although
Stephen was aware of the problem, he could not understand it or take
it seriously. He was now so deeply involved in physics and so excited by
the marked success of his research that he wanted to avail himself of
every conference, seminar or lecturing opportunity across the globe.
Applied mathematics, relativity, astrophysics, astronomy, theoretical
physics, cosmology, the titles of the disciplines did not matter much,
they were all in a ferment, investigating their particular aspect of the
black hole.

Luckily the question of further travels did not arise that winter
which we spent in a comfortably stationary state, adapting to the routine
of academic life which for Stephen was much as it had been before we
went to America. His Research Fellowship had been renewed for a
further two years and now that Rob Donovan was also a Research
Fellow of Gonville and Caius College, Stephen could regularly count
on his help for going into College to dine once a week. My routine was
rather less predictable and consisted of a constant struggle to reconcile
the needs of the baby with the demands of the thesis. When I took time
off from the thesis to play with Robert, my conscience told me that I
ought to be working on the thesis. When I worked on the thesis, my
natural instincts encouraged me to want to play with the baby. It was
not a very satisfactory state of affairs; nevertheless it was the only way
I could maintain my intellectual self-esteem in an environment where
babies were disdained and regarded only as necessary facts of life.
Theses, on the other hand, were respected. In addition, Stephen's work
was beginning to bring him such acclaim that unless I too had some
academic identity, I was in danger of becoming a mere drudge. In the
late 1960s, the University offered no crèche facilities although, true to
its male chauvinist instincts, it had for many years boasted a rifle range,
reflecting the priorities to which it and the society it served adhered.

The fact that I was able to persevere with my research at all was
largely thanks to my mother and to the succession of nannies employed
to care for Inigo Shaffer, the baby son of our neighbours in the Lane.
My mother would often come over to Cambridge by train early on a

Friday, arriving just as I was taking Stephen to work, and would look after Robert so that I could spend the best part of the day in the University Library collecting books and other material to study at home during the following week. Sometimes Helen, Inigo's nanny, would keep an eye on Robert for an hour or so, or as the boys grew older, invite him to play with Inigo for an afternoon, leaving me free to return to the Library. In return, Inigo would come to us to await his parents in the early evening after his nanny had gone home. This system also allowed me occasionally to attend and give seminars in London, assured that my family were in good hands back in Cambridge: Robert was being well looked after and Stephen, helped by George Ellis, liked to have lunch occasionally with the rest of the Relativity Group in the newly opened University Centre.

Thus, by means of much coxing and boxing, I was able to embark upon my project, an investigation of the linguistic and thematic similarities and discrepancies of the three main periods and areas of popular love poetry in medieval Spain. While Stephen mentally roamed the universe, I travelled in time – back to the *kharjas*, the earliest flowering of popular poetry in the Romance languages, that is to say, the body of languages deriving from Latin. I began my research by documenting the vocabulary used in the *kharjas*, which consisted of little more than poetic fragments in an early dialect of Spanish from Muslim Spain, with the intention of extending the exercise to the Galician–Portuguese *Cantigas d'Amigo* of the thirteenth century and the fifteenth-century Castilian popular lyrics or *villancicos*. The *kharjas* had held my imagination captive ever since I was first introduced to them on the course in San Sebastian in 1962. Their history was as extraordinary as their content was appealing because they were, in medieval terms, a remarkably recent discovery.

The origins of Romance vernacular poetry had lain shrouded in mystery until the mid-twentieth century. Until then, the first extant poetry in the Romance languages was thought to have been the highly sophisticated love poetry written in Provençal, the language of southern France, by Guilhem, Count of Poitiers, who was born in 1071. The poetry implies a feudal and adulterous relationship in which the lover-poet languishes abjectly at the feet of his ladylove whose husband is absent, possibly away on a crusade. Prying eyes and slanderous tongues are a threat to this relationship which was neatly classified by latterday scholars as Courtly Love, the concept at the basis of modern, though moribund, notions of chivalrous behaviour.

In 1948, however, an Oxford scholar, Samuel Stern, was working on some lines of indecipherable Arabic and Hebrew hieroglyphs attached to strophic poems in those languages, known as *muwassahas* from Muslim Spain. He discovered that the hieroglyphs were in fact Arabic and Hebrew transcriptions of Mozarabic, the embryonic Romance dialect of Spain under Muslim rule. From Stern's discovery, it became clear that the *muwassahas* – lengthy classical odes, funeral laments and panegyrics to elder statesmen in Arabic or Hebrew and reputedly invented around the year 900 AD – culminated, not in indecipherable nonsense, but in a few lines of lyric poetry in Mozarabic, the domestic language of Muslim Spain, the language of the girls, wives and mothers living under Moorish rule, as opposed to Arabic, the official language of government and men.

Since the year 711, much of Spain had suffered domination by invading Islamic forces from north Africa, despite the efforts of the northern outposts of the Christian forces to recapture their lost territory. However puritanical the Muslim caliphs had intended the effect of their *Jihad* or Holy War to be, once inside Spain the invading forces had a tendency to succumb to the charms of the country and its native population, adapting to its indulgent lifestyle and marrying its womenfolk. The relative harmony between Arab and Christian also embraced the Jewish community, thus producing a flourishing, cultured, multi-lingual, multi-racial society at peace with itself – until, that is, it was attacked from the south by further waves of extremely fanatical forces, whereupon Christians and Jews migrated to seek refuge in the Christian territories of the north.

It transpired that the Mozarabic lines of verse, the *kharjas* (meaning endings), were snatches of popular lyric poetry which had been incorporated first by the Moorish and then by the Jewish poets into their longer poems as a type of refrain and written down in Arabic or Hebrew characters. The content of the classical ode, a funeral lament perhaps, would be adapted to the refrain by a transitional stanza in which the grief of the court at the death, say, of one of their elder statesmen would be likened to the grief of the Christian girl bewailing the departure of her lover in the popular refrain. A crude modern analogy might be a formal funeral ode composed by the Poet Laureate, in honour, say, of

Winston Churchill, incorporating snatches of songs by the Beatles, written down in an unintelligible shorthand. The use of the *kharjas* was more sophisticated than that simple analogy suggests, however, because they also provided the metrical basis for the learned *muwassahas*. The difficulties of their reconstruction into Latin script were compounded by the absence of vowel markings in both written Hebrew and written Arabic and by the nascent character of the Mozarabic dialect itself.

The discovery of the *kharjas* turned medieval European poetic theories on their heads. Here was evidence of a poetic tradition, the earliest extant example of which could be dated from 1042, some thirty years before the birth of Guilhem of Poitiers, and which, some scholars boldly suggested, could provide the archetypal verse structures for Provençal poetry. In yet another twist, it was suggested that the classical Arabic verse form, the *muwassaha*, was, in turn, originally based on earlier, undiscovered Romance verse forms. In addition, the quest for the origins of European vernacular poetry was a matter fraught with nationalistic overtones, since there was great kudos attached to being able to claim that one's own country was the source of such a significant cultural development. Not surprisingly, the discovery of the *kharjas* ruffled quite a few Gallic feathers.

This, then, was just the preliminary part of the maze of conflicting arguments through which I was expected to find my way as a novice research student and to which I devoted many hours in the University Library. My precious time was spent scanning the huge, green-jacketed catalogue volumes, pursuing arcane articles in unfamiliar journals, seeking out cryptic references in footnotes, and searching the stacks and the shelves up on the upper floors of the north wing for the numerous works of literary criticism on which I would write notes at home during the course of the following week. Just occasionally I actually came into contact with original medieval manuscripts, an unforgettable experience but not one which advanced my research very efficiently because the temptation to browse and marvel over the beauties of the illustrated initials and the precision of the script was far too distracting.

Though the prospect of having to plough my way through reams of critical material was daunting, I relished those hours in the Library. I loved the curiously deferential effect that that shrine of erudition produced on its worshippers as, like shadows, they flitted almost on tiptoe, scarcely daring to speak, through its vast, silent halls. The place itself imparted to each area of study a hallowed importance simply because, on some distant shelf or in some remote drawer, it contained the essential materials for the pursuit of that study. Each student, young or old, was wrapped in his or her own small capsule of scholarship, assured of the freedom of being able to read and write without interruption.

An even greater compensation for the tedium which some aspects of the research entailed was to be found in the poems themselves, which had first been edited and published by Stern, and subsequently and more fancifully by Spanish scholars. It was astounding to witness how the inclusion of a handful of vowels could breath a pulsating life into a dead sequence of enigmatic Arabic and Hebrew consonants. For example, Stern had transcribed one group of Hebrew script into Roman consonants thus:

> *gryd bs 'y yrmnl's km*
> *kntnyr 'mw m'ly*
> *sn 'lhbyb nn bbr' yw*
> *'dbl'ry dmnd'ry*

With the addition of vowels, the text reads as follows:

> *Garid vos ay yermanellas*
> *com contenir a meu male*
> *Sin al-habib non vivireyu*
> *advolarey demandare*

Apart from one archaic form, *garid*, and one Arabic expression, *al-habib*, the poem is now perfectly intelligible, even to a modern Spanish speaker:

> Tell me, little sisters,
> How to contain my grief.
> I shall not live without my lover
> I shall fly away to look for him.

This one fragment suffices to illustrate one of most distinctive features of *kharja* composition: the singer/poet is a girl. Her confidantes are her sisters, as above, or a mother figure. Overwhelmed with nervous excitement, the girl turns to her confidante in language reminiscent of the *Song of Solomon*, when her lover arrives at her door:

> *Que faray mamma*
> *meu 'lhabib estad yana*
>
> What shall I do, mother,
> my lover is at the door?

He comes with the glory of the dawn, for in these poems the lovers meet at dawn, unlike the Provençal tradition where sophisticated lovers part at dawn:

> *non dormiray mamma*
> *a rayo de mañana*
> *Bon Abu 'l-Qasim*
> *la faj de matrana*
>
> I shall not sleep, mother,
> in the morning light
> Good Abu 'l-Qasim
> the face of the morning

Anxiety is always a dominant emotions in these love lyrics. The fear of the spy is a potent force and the girl has to seek advice, sometimes from a soothsayer, in the face of uncertainty. She often laments the lover's absence: she complains that he has deserted her and sometimes we are led to believe that she suspects that she has a rival; in other poems the lover appears to have been sent away, possibly on a military campaign:

> *Gar que farayu*
> *Com vivirayu*
> *este 'l-habib espero*
> *por el morirayu*
>
> Tell me what shall I do?
> How shall I live?
> I am waiting for my lover
> I shall die for him

In a clear reference to her Christian background, she cries forlornly:

> *Venid la pasca ayun sin ellu . . .*
> *meu corajon por ellu*

> Easter comes still without him . . .
> my heart for him

For me, even more poignant than the poems of absence were those heart-rending lyrics in which the girl weeps in despair at her lover's illness:

> *Vaisse meu corajon de mib*
> *ya rabbi si se me tornerad*
> *Tan mal me doled li 'l-habib*
> *enfermo yed cuand sanarad*

> My heart leaves my body
> will it ever return?
> My grief for my lover is so great
> He is ill –
> when will he recover?

In one *kharja*, the only decipherable word is *enfermad* – ill – and in another the girl herself falls ill with the cares of loving:

> *Tan t'amaray tan t'amaray*
> *habib tan t'amaray*
> *Enfermaron welyos cuidas*
> *ya dolen tan male*

> I shall love you always,
> I shall love you always,
> my love,
> My eyes are ill with weeping,
> they hurt so much!

CHAPTER SEVENTEEN

Heavenly Spheres

ALTHOUGH IN TACTICAL terms it was sensible for me to be registered as a London Ph.D student, in reality it meant that I was very isolated in Cambridge as I did not belong to any particular group. London seminars and supervisions under the auspices of my supervisor, Alan Deyermond, were always stimulating and often amusing, but my opportunities for going down to London were infrequent. In Cambridge, where I read in the Library and wrote at home, I had no forum for discussion. Thanks to Dr Dorothy Needham, I had become an affiliated student of Lucy Cavendish College and, by dint of careful organization, which involved having Robert fed, bathed and tucked up in his cot, and Stephen's meal ready for him on the table, I managed to go out a couple of times a term to the Lucy Cavendish dining nights which took place in Churchill College.

As a recently founded society, Lucy Cavendish could afford to dispense with the outmoded trappings of collegiate life, some of which still pertain. Since some of its mature students were likely to be older than some members of staff, segregating students from Fellows was not appropriate, so, in this democratic setting, the most junior student could find herself sitting next to a very senior Fellow – Dorothy Emmett the theologian, perhaps, or Hilda Davidson, the Norse scholar, or Natasha Squires, the tutor in French and Russian, or Mrs Cheney, the medieval historian, or even the President and co-founder of the society, Dr Bidder. On meeting Stephen, Anna Bidder touchingly confided in me that she quite understood why I had married him when she looked into his beautiful grey eyes. Although there was a fair smattering of medieval historians among the diners, I was the sole Hispanist and it was sometimes difficult to find common ground, especially since these women, some of whom had four or five children, seemed to give the impression that they had combined families and careers effortlessly.

A solution to my problem of academic isolation came in a most unexpected form – through Robert's growing friendship with our neighbours' child, Inigo Shaffer. One of the guests at Inigo's first birthday party was a vivacious, auburn-haired, six-year-old girl, Cressida Dronke, who, peering out from behind a hideous pair of multi-coloured reflecting sunglasses, regaled the assembled company of very small boys and their astounded mothers and nannies with a long and fascinating account of a production of *Romeo and Juliet* to which her parents had just taken her. There was apparently nothing unusual in this early introduction to Shakespeare, for Cressida was a hardened theatre-goer; she had been attending operas at Covent Garden since babyhood when her parents had taken her there in her carrycot. This articulate, entertaining child was the daughter of Ursula and Peter Dronke, Oxford scholars who had moved to Cambridge, where Peter lectured in medieval Latin while Ursula taught and edited Norse poetry and Old Icelandic sagas.

I already knew of Peter Dronke from his awesome reputation as one of the most powerful and gifted intellects in medieval literary studies. His range of scholarship was not confined to medieval Latin. When I first met him he had just gained widespread and controversial renown for his comprehensive two-volume work, *Medieval Latin and the Rise of the European Love Lyric*, in which he disputed the popularly held notion of Courtly Love as a specific, identifiable literary genre, unique to Provence. His lectures on Dante's *Divina Commedia* were always packed out and he was regarded as an authority on every aspect of medieval literature, not least on my own area, the lyric poetry of the Iberian Peninsula. The happy chance meeting with the Dronkes led to my acquiring an unofficial, surrogate supervisor in Cambridge. Peter was always ready to share his vast fund of knowledge and to pass on helpful suggestions, constructive criticisms and useful references, while Ursula, aware of the unusual nature of my situation, was a constant source of warm encouragement.

Another important consequence of meeting Peter and Ursula Dronke was that they invited me to join the coveted informal evening seminars which they hosted in their own home during term-time. Those Thursday evenings began in a relaxed fashion with a brief social gathering, a glass of wine and light conversation with the other members of the group in the Dronke's softly lit sitting-room. Then we, the student

participants, would arrrange ourselves deferentially on cushions on the
mustard-coloured carpet at the feet of the distinguished dons and visiting
speakers who sat in the armchairs. After a few words of introduction,
the speaker would give his or her paper, followed by an hour or two
when brains would whirr audibly, vying with each other in their attempts
to grasp, analyse and then dissect the speaker's thesis. Only Peter could
truly be said to be the master of all the topics expounded in the seminars,
for their range was eclectic, covering most of late classical and medieval
European thought and literature, from the Neoplatonic *De Consolatione
Philosophiae* which Boethius, the fifth-century statesman and philosopher,
wrote while awaiting execution, to the *Rime* of Petrarch, languishing for
his idealized beloved, Laura, in fourteenth-century Italy. There might
be papers on the Arthurian romances of Chrétien de Troyes or on
Gawain and the Green Knight or *Beowulf* or the *Chanson de Roland* but
frequently the discussions, at a considerable remove from the lyric poetry
of the Iberian Peninsula, focused on the great medieval dilemma, the
debate between the theories of Aristotle, in whose logical, empirical
philosphy the universe and all living beings were governed by the inexorable scientific laws of Nature, and the Judeo-Christian tradition of
revelation according to which the universe was created by a disciplined,
loving, personal God to whom Man owed obedience. As I listened in
awed fascination, I was surprised and amused to find how close those
seminars brought me in philosophical terms to the study of cosmology,
albeit medieval cosmology.

Inevitably the discussions dwelt on the twelfth-century intellectual
expansion which emanated from Paris and particularly from the
Cathedral School of Chartres, where it was believed that God, the universe and mankind could be examined and comprehended by means of
numbers, weights and geometrical symbols, effectively turning theology
into mathematics. The intellectual stimulus of the period led to the
founding of new institutions on the model of the Italian *studium generale*,
the universities, of which Paris and Oxford were the most important
examples. Both Paris and Oxford were at the heart of a continued,
intense intellectual debate, in which primarily the nature of God,
Creation and the origins of the universe exercised the minds of scholars
and theologians. The vigorous renaissance which took place in the
twelfth century owed much to the innovative ideas coming from Spain,
where in the year 1085 the Christian forces had recaptured Toledo from
the Moors.

After its reconquest, Toledo became one of the richest cultural centres in Europe, renowned for its heritage of Arabic literature and its mixed multi-lingual population. Following the example of the Catalan monastery of Ripoll, Raimundo, Archbishop of Toledo in the twelfth century, organized this exemplary heritage into a thriving industry of scholars, translating into Latin not only Arabic and Hebrew works but also lost works of classical antiquity which had been preserved in Arabic. In Spain a number of Aristotle's works – many of which had already been translated from the Greek by independent freelance translators in Constantinople from about 1130 – were rendered in new versions from the Arabic with commentaries by the great Muslim philosopher, Averroës. The works of Aristotle's master and mentor, Plato, against whose spiritual and metaphysical philosophies he had reacted, had been preserved since antiquity in the continuous Neoplatonic tradition.

In the thirteenth century, Alfonso the Wise of Castile, an ambitious scholar-king with unfortunate, expensive aspirations to the emperorship of the Holy Roman Empire, expanded the role of Toledo as a major centre for translation and scholarship by participating in its activities himself. He pioneered the use of Spanish rather than Latin for all documents and attempted various historical projects in that language. His most important prose work in Spanish terms was undoubtedly his codification of all aspects of Spanish law but, for the outside world, the translations from Arabic produced at his court were of greater significance. These translations covered a wide range of interests. Thanks to Alfonso the Wise, a book on chess was translated from Arabic into Spanish. The scientific theories on the nature of light of Alhazen, the foremost Arab scientist of the eleventh century, were also translated, overturning the ancient Greek theory of light. The Greeks had supposed that the eye emitted beams of light which illuminated objects. Alhazen formulated the contrary – correct – theory according to which light is reflected into the eye from each point of an object. Thus in thirteenth-century Toledo were laid the foundations of perspective on which Leonardo da Vinci would build in northern Italy in the fifteenth century. Even more significantly, it was through the translation of Gerard of Cremona at Toledo that the *Almagest*, the great work of Ptolemy, an Alexandrian mathematician and astronomer of the second century AD, was brought into the mainstream of Western culture.

Originally written in Greek, the *Almagest* existed only in an Arabic version until Alfonso commissioned its translation in Toledo. Ptolemy's cosmological model of the universe was based on the Aristotelian concept of a stationary earth, orbited by the sun, the moon, the planets and the stars. In the Ptolemaic or geocentric model, the earth is fixed at the centre of the universe while the heavenly bodies, the sun, the moon and the planets, each move around the earth along the paths of their own fixed spheres. A system of smaller circular motions or epicycles is introduced to account for recognized inequalities in the motions of the bodies. Beyond the sphere of Saturn is the sphere on which the fixed stars are carried across the sky and beyond that is the *Primum Mobile*, the mysterious divine force behind the cyclical movement of the spheres. This perfect, circular movement which propelled the planets on their course created a celestial music, the harmony of the spheres. The Ptolemaic model of the universe did not actually coincide with the scriptural view of the universe as being made up of the heavens, a flat earth and hell beneath, but since it could be made to coincide sufficiently neatly with it, without drastically upsetting previously held views of God's place in the heavens and of hell in the depths of the earth, it became a tenet of religious dogma in Christendom until it was questioned by the Polish astronomer Copernicus in 1543. For the Christian Church the most important implication of this geocentric model was that Man, the inhabitant of the earth, was at the centre of the universe and that divine attention was focused solely on him and his behaviour.

Stephen came to one of these seminars about early cosmological models in the Dronkes' living-room with a colleague from the Department, Nigel Weiss, whose wife Judy was a member of the seminar. The two scientists were forced to concede that the thinking of the twelfth-century philosophers, Thierry of Chartres, Alan of Lille and, in the thirteenth century Robert Grosseteste and Roger Bacon among many others, was extraordinarily far-sighted, accurate and perceptive. Included in the ranks of these philosophers was a woman, the strong-minded German abbess, Hildegard of Bingen, who devised her own version of cosmology in which the universe took the shape of an egg. Hildegard of Bingen was far in advance of her times. Not only did she devise her own cosmological model, she also proposed that women must make good the social and religious failings caused by the weaknesses of men and, to that end, should follow her example by undertaking missionary journeys along the Rhine, preaching, condemning heretics and righting social wrongs.

Several ironies struck me in the course of these seminars, particularly during the one that Stephen and Nigel Weiss attended. The most glaring, of course, was that in the second half of the twentieth century the position of women in society, especially in science, had progressed at a snail's pace since the twelfth century, despite Hildegard's brisk and frequent affirmations of the strength and glory of women. As far as the cosmologies were concerned, I was amused by the reflection that though advances in science may be revolutionary in the twentieth century, certain conceptual links with older theories die hard. The Ptolemaic system, which had gained ready acceptance in the thirteenth century but had been supplanted by the Copernican solar system, still had a point of contact, however implausible, with an important cosmological principle of the twentieth century, the anthropic principle.

This was one of those subjects on which, during that period at the end of the 1960s and the early 1970s, Stephen spent long hours of concentrated argument with Brandon Carter, usually on Saturday afternoons when we drove out of Cambridge to the pastoral bliss of the country cottage which Brandon and his Belgian wife, Lucette, had been renovating since their recent marriage. Lucette and I would take Robert for long walks across the fields, converse in French about our favourite authors, painters and composers, prepare tea and supper, and still Brandon and Stephen would be engaged in an intellectual contest over the fine detail of the principle which neither was prepared to concede.

The anthropic principle, as far as I understood it from Stephen's explanations in those rare moments when we discussed his work together, left me wondering at its close philosophical affinity to the medieval cosmos. As in the medieval, Ptolemaic universe, Man is once again placed at the centre of creation by the anthropic principle or more precisely by what is known as its 'strong' version. The proponents of the 'strong' anthropic principle claim that the universe in which we exist is the only possible kind of universe in which we could exist, because from the time of the Big Bang some 15,000 million years ago, it has expanded according to the precise conditions, often involving chance chemical coincidences and very fine physical tuning, which are required for the development of intelligent life. Intelligent life is then able to ask why the universe is as it is observed to be, but this is almost a tautological question, the answer to which is: if our universe were any different, intelligent life would not exist to pose the question. In a real sense, therefore, mankind could still be said to occupy a special place at the centre of the universe, just as he had in the Ptolemaic system. Whereas

for the medieval populace, this special position was a strong statement
of the unique relationship between human beings and their Creator,
modern scientists appeared to be irritated or merely amused by any such
inferences being drawn from the anthropic principle.

Although the modern universe is most certainly not bounded by the
medieval concepts of heaven or hell, it is in many respects a more hostile
environment than its neatly organized medieval counterpart, if only on
account of its extremes of temperature and its vast expanses of space
and time in which the human race appears to live in solitary isolation.
In 1968 for a fleeting moment it seemed as if we might not be alone in
the dark immensity of space after all. One afternoon in February of that
year when I called in at the Department, the tea-room was buzzing with
excitement. A research student in radio astronomy, Jocelyn Bell, and
her supervisor, Antony Hewish, had picked up regular, pulsating radio
signals from outer space through the row of radio telescopes positioned
on the disused Cambridge to Oxford railway line at Lord's Bridge, some
3 miles out of Cambridge. Could these signals be our first contact with
extra-terrestrial life – little green men perhaps? Jokingly they named
the first sources of these radio waves LGMs. The excitement died down,
however, when the sources of the radio pulses were identified as neutron
stars, tiny remnants of stars, possibly only 20 miles across, with massive
densities of hundreds of millions of tons per cubic inch. There was no
chance that neutron stars could be supporting life.

While twentieth-century cosmologists might still retain some
tenuous conceptual common ground with the Ptolemaic system through
the anthropic principle, and might respect the intellects of the earlier
twelfth-century philosophers of Chartres, Oxford and even Bingen on
the Rhine, the Dronkes' medieval seminars served to bring into clear
perspective the vastly divergent modern approach to the subject of
Creation. The main intent of the twelfth-century philosophers was
directed towards reconciling the existence of God with the rigours of
the laws of science, towards unifying the image of the Creator with the
scientific complexity of His Creation. To this end, Alan of Lille
attempted to reconstruct theology as a mathematical science, and
another student of Chartres, Nicholas of Amiens, tried to make it
conform to Euclidean geometry, using geometrical symbols to explain
the Trinity. However eccentric these notions may appear nowadays, they
were undoubtedly genuine attempts to introduce a scientific objectivity

to the teachings of theology and to explore and explain divine mystery through numbers and mathematical structures.

Conversely, their intellectual heirs, some 800 years later, seemed intent on distancing science as far as possible from religion and on excluding God from any role in Creation. The suggestion of the presence of a Creator God was an awkward obstacle for an atheistic scientist whose aim was to reduce the origins of the universe to a unified package of scientific laws, expressed in equations and symbols. To the uninitiated, these equations and symbols were far more difficult to comprehend than the notion of God as the prime mover, the motivating force behind Creation. Strangely, to the happy band of the initiated, these equations were said to reveal a miraculous, breath-taking mathematical beauty. This revelation, reflecting the hidden wonders of the universe, was in turn a mystery approximating to Platonic proportions. In the fifth century BC Plato, Aristotle's teacher and a major influence on medieval thought, described a theory of Forms, or perfect heavenly Ideas, unrelated to the senses, discernible only to the mind. Each perfect Form or Idea had its counterpart in the tangible, corruptible, imperfect forms manifest on earth. The reverence with which modern scientists treated the mathematics of the universe suggested similar intimations of sublime perfection.

Unfortunately these intimations of perfection were not easily accessible to those who, like me, were not fluent in mathematical jargon and for whom equations were impenetrable. The number of people possessed of the talent required to appreciate these numerical expressions of transcendental reality was very small and I was not one of them. It would be a hopeless task for me even to try to learn mathematics. The best that I could hope for was that one day a scientist, maybe Stephen, would write a popular book explaining the theories, the equations and the wonder and excitement to me – and to the many other people who were mystified by this branch of scientific knowledge.

Another difficulty which apparently was a direct result of their obsession with mathematics was the irrelevance for these scientists of the concept of a personal God. If through their calculations they were diminishing any possible scope for a Creator, it was logical that they could not envisage any other place or role for God in the physical universe. Concepts which could not be quantified in mathematical terms as a theoretical reflection of physical realities, whether or not the actual existence of those physical realities was proven, were meaningless.

Human reactions in all their complexities, emotional and psychological, would one day, by means of a giant computer, be reduced to scientific formulae because, in effect, these reactions were no more than the microscopic chemical interactions of molecules.

In the face of such dogmatically rational arguments, there was no point in raising questions of spirituality and religious faith, of the soul and of a God who was prepared to suffer for the sake of humanity – questions which ran completely counter to the selfish reality of genetic theory. Questions of morality, conscience, appreciation of the arts, were best kept out of the arena lest they too were to become victims of the positivist approach. Since I did not have the mathematical language at my disposal, I was powerless to defend such concepts in the only terms that were acceptable to my debating adversaries and was therefore obliged to keep my own counsel, seeking to satisfy my own spiritual needs as best I could.

Still reacting against the organized religion of my childhood, I did not attend either of the two churches at the end of the Lane regularly but I sought sanctity in the garden of Little St Mary's, where Thelma Thatcher designated a small patch of ground by the railings opposite our house for me to tend. There, under the rambling roses, I could weed, rake, hoe and plant bulbs for the spring and roses for the summer while pondering deep mysteries, theories and realities. Robert and Inigo played, running along the winding paths and clambering over the mossy tombs, while I worked. The ancient, sacred garden sprang to life with the music of their bright young voices and our strip of ground blossomed with a pink and white striped rose, the famous *Rosa gallica*, named *Rosa Mundi* after Henry II's mistress, Fair Rosamund.

CHAPTER EIGHTEEN

Dangerous Dynamism

Since the churchyard garden was enclosed, Robert and Inigo could play there safely, letting off their inordinate amounts of excess energy. From his early infancy it was quite apparent that Robert was blessed with at least twice the normal fund of energy expected of a small boy. Quite apart from overturning all my notions regarding the sleep patterns of a new-born infant, he discovered, at about eight weeks, that his feet and legs were meant for standing on. Thereafter he would not sit down, insisting on being held upright on my knee or on the knee of anyone else with arms strong enough to hold him for any length of time in that position.

During our stay in Seattle, we were invited to take advantage of a free photographic session by courtesy of the diaper service. Like his grandfathers some fifty or sixty years earlier, Robert was expected to lie gurgling on a rug, peep out coyly from under a blanket draped over his head, and sit back smiling in a reclining seat. Naturally he resisted with all the means at his disposal. The photographer was beside himself with ill-suppressed rage at having the aesthetic standards of his profession thwarted by such obstreperous behaviour, but eventually when his nerves were reduced to a jittery mess, he wearily conceded defeat. Grudgingly he allowed my arms to appear in the shot, supporting from behind the twelve-week-old baby who, with his legs flexed, was firmly planted on his two small feet. In the other pictures, Robert can also be seen easing himself out of the reclining chair and frowning at the sheer ignominy of having to lie on or under a blanket.

By the age of seven months, this inventive child had found out how to dismantle his cot, so all the joins, catches and hinges had to be tied together tightly with string to stop him falling out. Nevertheless, no sooner had Stephen and I turned our backs each evening and crept away downstairs, yawning and fondly trusting that repeated readings of *Thomas the Tank Engine* had at last softly lulled our audience into the realms of sleep, than we would hear the tiny feet coming busily down the stairs to join us for our supper and whatever concert we might be listening to on the Third Programme. Since he could no longer dismantle his cot, Robert would vault over the bar and then drop on to the floor beneath. At about eleven o'clock we would all fall into bed together.

Even before he had perfected that degree of agility, Robert's dynamism had given us a quite a scare. In the spring of 1968, my parents took us to Cornwall once again, to a National Trust cottage at St Just in Roseland across the bay from Falmouth. This time we travelled in two cars and my brother Chris and I shared the driving of the Mini. Fortunately Robert was prepared to sit quite contentedly in the car, strapped into his child's seat, no matter how long the journey. When at last we arrived in the early evening, we adults sank drowsily into the comfortable armchairs in the sitting-room of the cottage. Meanwhile Robert, already able at ten months old to walk nimbly round the furniture, set off on a seemingly harmless tour of exploration of the ground floor. A sudden high-pitched scream from behind my back roused us precipitately. To steady himself, Robert had placed one small tender hand – his right – against an electric storage heater which, unknown to us, was turned to its maximum setting. The sight was pitiful. The heat had seared off the skin of the palm, and not surprisingly Robert was inconsolable. Luckily Chris's medical training came to the rescue. Thanks to him, Robert was pacified with a fraction of an aspirin – the only painkiller available – the hand gently treated and bandaged in a clean handkerchief, and we all, though shocked, managed to get a good night's sleep. Robert, Chris and I spent the best part of the next day searching out a doctor. Overnight the infant hand had swollen into one huge blister. The doctor, impressed at the quality of the first aid administered by a mere dental student, simply provided a pediatric painkilling prescription and more substantial dressings and thereafter commissioned Chris to continue to care for his small patient.

In the summer of that same year, the year of Robert's first birthday, the Angs left the house at number 11 Little St Mary's Lane to return home to Singapore. In true Lane style, the Thatchers gave an informal farewell party for them, to which we and the Shaffers were invited together with half-a-dozen or so other guests. By this stage Inigo and

Robert were completely at home in the Thatcher household. They adored Thelma and she reciprocated with a grandmotherly affection. They would call on her every morning, peering through her letter-box, calling 'Tatch, Tatch!' in the hope of being invited in to play with the collection of bright marbles on her solitaire table. They were frequent tea-time visitors, sitting at her elegant Regency table on her elegant Regency chairs, though as a precautionary measure she did apologetically cover the yellow-striped damask seats with plastic sheeting. At the Angs' party no one took much notice of the small boys who were happily amusing themselves until Thelma called for a toast to the Angs – How Ghee, Peck, Susan and demure little Ming – and their future happiness. We all turned to pick up our glasses of champagne from the occasional tables, only to find that they were all drained dry. From upstairs there came the sound of running water, of much flushing and splashing and peals of laughter. Two rather tipsy one-year-olds were having their own, much more entertaining party well out of sight of the adults in the Thatchers' bathroom.

Later that summer Stephen and I took Robert on his first bucket-and-spade holiday to the north Norfolk coast, where I encountered the unforeseen dilemma of needing to be in two places at once. As Stephen's speed of movement slowed down, so Robert's accelerated. Stephen found it difficult to walk across the soft, yielding sand and so did I, as I supported him on one arm and carried bags, bucket and spade, towels and a folding chair on the other. Robert, in the meantime, would be racing away, heading for the open sea. Luckily, on that coast, the tide goes out as far as the eye can see, and that week was a week of low tides by day so we managed to avoid undue mishap.

On the final morning I went upstairs to pack our bags, leaving Stephen and Robert downstairs in the main room at the front of the house. At the back, a sun room with an open mezzanine half-loft approached by a rickety ladder had been added to the cottage. We did not use this room, for obvious reasons, and kept the door to it firmly closed. After half an hour of packing I came downstairs to find Stephen sitting alone in the front room.

'Where's Robert?' I asked in bewilderment. Stephen gestured towards the back room. 'He opened that door,' he said, 'went through it and closed it behind him. There was nothing I could do and you did not hear when I tried to call you.'

Momentarily I glanced at the door in horror then burst into the room. There was no sign of Robert. My eyes travelled upwards and there, to my astonishment, was my little son in his blue tee-shirt and checked trousers, sitting up at the top of the ladder on the open mezzanine floor, cross-legged like an infant Buddha, blissfully unconcerned by the drop beneath him. I raced up the ladder and grabbed him before he had time to move.

If, on that first visit to the coast, Robert did not succeed in hurling himself into the sea, it was only because his legs were too short for him to get to the water's edge before I caught up with him; after depositing his father on the folding chair on the firmer sand midway between the dunes and the shore, I would sprint over the beach at speeds which could well have won me an Olympic medal. Over the course of the next two or three years, Robert regularly threw himself headlong into any available stretch of water, be it sea, pond or swimming pool, as soon as my eye was distracted for the merest second. On a later visit to Norfolk with the Ellises and their little daughter – dark-haired, blue-eyed Maggie – Sue plunged into the sea like lightning to rescue Robert who, without warning, had run straight into the water and disappeared. When we visited the Cleghorns, the parents of Stephen's schoolfriend Bill, out in the country, Robert made a beeline for their pond and fell in amongst the weed, the mud and the frogs. In the summer of 1969, when we spent the month of July at the University of Warwick at a summer school – appropriately enough on Catastrophe Theory – Robert excelled himself by jumping into the deep end of the nearby swimming pool at every opportunity. Happily on those occasions, as his father was safely ensconced in lectures and not dependent on my supporting arm, Robert had the full benefit of my attention.

The summer school coincided with that 'great leap for mankind', the Moonwalk, which we watched on television in the student commonroom. Giant leaps, small steps and all too real catastrophes narrowly averted, these sonorous terms seemed to sum up the essence of our day-to-day lives. Giant leaps were needed to keep up with Robert's mercurial movements, while Stephen's steps were becoming smaller, slower and more and more unsteady. Each morning I would drive Stephen from the student hostel where we were lodging to the lecture hall on the other side of the new campus. At Stephen's pace, the lecture hall was some five minutes' walk away from the car park, across courtyards and through a maze of passages. Robert would shoot out of the car as soon as it came to a standstill and hare away ahead of his father and me. The only consolation was that, at the age of two, he had an unerring sense of direction which led him through the tortuous route to the lecture hall where he would install himself in the front row. It became a standing joke among the other delegates that Robert's appearance in the early morning always heralded Stephen's arrival five minutes later. The lecturer would then adjust the order of his lecture notes, deferring any important results until Stephen arrived.

At home, we had to barricade the house to prevent Robert from escaping and throwing himself into the river. On our afternoon walks I was hard pressed to find a means of expending all his energy without exhausting myself, especially as he would never turn round to go back home until he was on the point of collapse, and then he had to be carried or pushed in the pushchair. Generally I left the pushchair at home because on our outward journeys when speed of reflex was all-important, it tended to interfere with the swiftness of my reactions.

'Put reins on him,' my parents urged sensibly, worried by my haggard appearance.

'You don't understand, he won't walk with reins on,' I insisted, to their disbelief.

'Nonsense,' they said, thinking that this was just another example of my crackpot theories about personal freedoms.

'All right, you try,' I replied defiantly, handing them back the set of pale blue leather reins they had just given me.

They picked up their cherubic blond, blue-eyed grandson, the apple of their eye, and carried him and the reins down to the broad path along the riverbank, away from the traffic. In no time at all, they were back at the house asking for the pushchair. 'You were right,' my mother sighed incredulously. 'When we put the reins on him, he sat down and refused to move. When Dad tried tugging on the reins, he kept his legs firmly crossed and when Dad lifted the reins, he just left the ground, and there he was, dangling in mid-air on the end of the strap!'

Never in all the long years of my education – especially, unsurprisingly, nowhere in all those reams of medieval literature – had I encountered one jot of advice on bringing up children. Apparently through the ages children had just happened and it had never been thought necessary to teach their parents how to look after them. I asked myself how such a fundamental responsibility – possibly the *most* fundamental responsibility – could be left so casually to chance and to instinct. If this was an example of the workings of the geneticists' selfish gene, this gene was intent on self-destruction. Undoubtedly some babies, like Maggie Ellis and my little god-daughters, were not as demanding as the exuberant, irrepressible little stick of dynamite that was Robert. Since they each had two able-bodied parents, perhaps the strain on any one parent was less than it was on me. From six o'clock in the morning till eleven at night Robert was full of golden smiles – cheerful, loving and utterly adorable – but his boundless energy brought me to my knees. I thumbed through the already well-worn pages of my only guide, Dr Spock's *Baby and Child Care*, searching for help and reassurance. Comfortingly, Dr Spock seemed to recognize the problem, which suggested that Robert was not unique, because he recommended the desperate measure of putting a net over the top of the cot to prevent the energetic baby from escaping at night. I could not bring myself to adopt this solution. It was too much like putting Robert in a cage and anyhow I feared he might strangle himself in the netting. Then I turned to my doctor who sympathetically recommended a glass of sherry – for me – in the evening 'at about six o'clock, when Robert has gone to bed', and also prescribed a tonic.

Early one morning in the September of 1969, I was aroused from my slumbers not by a sound or by a light but by a smell – a sweet, sickly smell which subconsciously I recognized as wrong. I opened my eyes to find Robert standing by my side of the bed with a broad grin all over his face and a viscous, pinkish liquid dribbling down the front of his blue sleeping suit. I jumped out of bed and stumbled down the stairs to the kitchen. A chair stood by the fridge and the floor was littered with empty bottles, all of them medicine bottles. One of the bottles had contained the sweet, syrupy antihistamine which the doctor had prescribed for Robert for a recent cold and earache, and which had a conveniently soporific effect; another had contained the stimulant which I had been taking to pep me up. At two years of age, Robert had pushed a chair into the kitchen, had climbed up on to the fridge and reached up to the shelf where, for want of a medicine cupboard, the bottles were stored. He had swigged the lot.

Leaving Stephen to fend for himself as best he could, I dressed in haste and ran with Robert in his pushchair to the doctor's surgery as fast as I could. The surgery, only a couple of hundred yards away, was just opening and we were given priority. As Robert was already beginning to show signs of drowsiness, Dr Wilson immediately sent us to hospital, half a mile away in the other direction, by taxi. There the nightmare really started as the seriousness of the situation became evident. Robert, his arms and legs jerking and flailing out in all directions, was taken from me and held down while his stomach was pumped out. At first the nurses were terse, only asking what medicines he had taken, then, when they had tried all the interventionary methods at their disposal to rid the child's system of the poisonous cocktail, one of them turned to me and said: 'He is extremely ill, you realize; there is nothing more we can do, we shall just have to wait and see what happens.'

Only once before had Robert's health given cause for anxiety. The previous winter, at the Ellises' suggestion, we had gone with them to Majorca for a week's holiday over the New Year. We had barely arrived when Robert fell seriously ill with a virulent strain of Spanish tummy which confined us to the hotel room for the whole duration of the stay. Unable to digest even plain water, he wasted away before our eyes like the innocent child victims of the Biafran war, while the local doctor debated whether to take him into hospital or send us back home in advance of the rest of the party. As soon as the plane touched down at Gatwick, however, Robert began to make a miraculous recovery. By the time we reached my parents' house in St Albans, he was ready to play his favourite game of emptying all the tins from my mother's store cupboard and rolling them across the kitchen floor.

That episode had been harrowing but this was far worse; it was the worst agony imaginable, the agony of watching one's child sink into lifelessness and approach the realms of death. They tied Robert down in a cot in a partitioned room on the children's ward and beckoned me to a chair in a corner. He tossed violently under the restraints placed across the cot to prevent him from hurting himself. Mechanically I sat down, too numb to speak or think or weep. Life drained away from my own body as our beautiful, darling child, our most precious possession, sank into a deep coma. This child had astounded everyone with his beauty, his happy nature and his liveliness. He was the living personification of all that was good and positive in our world and relationship. I, and Stephen too, loved him more than anything else. We had created him as a part of ourselves out of love, I had given birth to him and we had nurtured him with passionate love and care. Now we seemed to be losing him through a combination of circumstances – my tiredness, his energy and the inadequacy of the precautions that I had taken for his safety. It was my fault. If he died, I should die too. My brain was capable of formulating only a single thought expressed in half a dozen words. They revolved round and round in my head, stuck in a single groove, to the exclusion of all else: 'Please God, don't let him die. Please God, don't let him die. Please God . . .'

Every so often a nurse would come in to check Robert's breathing and his pulse. Pursing her lips, she would tiptoe away again while I stayed in my corner blankly staring into cold, empty space, clinging to my formula, repeating it over and over again. Some hours later, the Ward Sister came in. She went through the customary procedures and then, instead of tiptoeing away, pronounced that Robert was in a relatively stable though still critical condition. His state was not hopeful, all that could be said was that it was not deteriorating further. Coming to my senses at this slightest of changes, I was shocked to remember that I had left Stephen alone in the house, scarcely able to look after himself. Where was I most needed – here in the hospital with my comatose infant son or at home with my disabled husband who, without my help, might fall or hurt himself or choke? I must have mumbled a few intelligible words to the Sister because she sent me out to check up on Stephen. I ran down the road through the fine grey drizzle to look for him.

Thankfully George had come in to help Stephen get up and had taken him to work. By this stage he was having lunch in the University Centre, desperate for news but not knowing where to find us. I sat with him for a short while. There was nothing we could say to comfort each other because there was no comfort to be had in our situation, except that we both shared the same sense of utter, bleak devastation, enveloped in an unremitting pall of greyness. I watched as Stephen ate his lunch. I could not even bring myself to drink a glass of water. It seemed pointless to try. There was no reason to stay alive. How could I live with such grief? We were crossing the threshold into a dark chasm where all hope is abandoned.

Scarcely daring to return to the hospital, I left Stephen in George's care. I entered the ward fearful of what I might find. All was silent. A young nurse followed me as I tiptoed into Robert's room. He was there in the cot, still alive. He was asleep, lying quietly on his back, as beatific as a Bellini cherub. To my surprise the nurse's face lit up with a smile as she pointed to the sleeping child, 'Look, he's breathing normally now. He's sleeping it off and soon he'll come out of the coma, he's past the worst,' she said. Only tears, not words, could describe my feelings. Floods of tears flowed freely, tears of gratitude, relief and elation.

'You'll be able to take him home when he wakes up,' the nurse continued – indifferently now, as if this was just one more crisis in her daily round, forgotten as soon as it was resolved. I rang Stephen to tell him the good news, and at half past three, Robert began to wake up. 'You can take him home now,' they said. Within ten minutes he was discharged and we stepped out into the vivid reality of our everyday lives. Once back home, we sent word to our neighbours to come and join us for a celebration. They all came and we watched silently as if in a trance while Robert and Inigo pushed their toy cars round the floor, unconcerned and totally unaware of the day's drama.

That day Robert survived, but a little bit of me died. Some, though not all, of that extravagant youthful optimism which had fired me with so much enthusiasm now lay buried beneath a heavy burden of anxiety, that dull care in its ravelled sleeve, which once it infects the mind is never banished. I had come so dangerously close to the worst catastrophe that a mother can bear – the loss of her child – and was so ashamed at my own carelessness that I became neurotically protective, often irritating Robert and his siblings by my level of concern for their safety.

Luckily the experience seemed to have left Robert unscathed. Nor did it reduce in any way his fund of energy, as our visit to a conference in Switzerland the following spring aptly demonstrated. While Stephen spent his day plunged into the murky past of the universe in the conference centre at Gwat on the shores of Lake Thun, Robert and I went walking. This was where he discovered his passion for the mountains, the true outlet for his climbing instincts. When, later that week, we and the Ellises spent a few days in the family hotel at Hohfluh, high above the Aare valley where I used to stay with my parents, Robert was in his element. More than once, at less than three years old, he insisted on scrambling up as far as the snow-line while I, several months pregnant again, plodded along behind.

CHAPTER NINETEEN

Universal Expansion

A LESS DRAMATIC CRISIS than Robert's calamitous encounter with the medicines loomed over us as the 1960s drew to a close: Stephen's Research Fellowship at Gonville and Caius, which had already been renewed for a further term of two years in 1967, was in 1969 about to expire. There was no mechanism for renewing it yet again but because Stephen was unable to lecture, he could not follow the normal course of most other Research Fellows and apply for a University teaching post. Nor was there any point in expecting a full Fellowship since Fellowships, as opposed to Research Fellowships, are not salaried appointments. Fully fledged Fellows of colleges usually have University posts which pay their salaries while the collegiate affiliation is tantamount to membership of an exclusive dining-club, a highly intellectual one, of course, founded – it goes without saying – on the most estimable educational principles.

In 1968 Stephen had become a member of the newly opened Institute of Astronomy, a long, single-storeyed building, luxuriously fitted out and set among trees in green fields outside Cambridge in the grounds of the Observatory on the Madingley Road. Membership of the Institute accorded him an office, which he shared with Brandon, and a desk but not a salary. It was unlikely to provide him with a paid position as long as Fred Hoyle remained its director since Stephen had notoriously antagonized him at the Royal Society lecture several years before. In Britain, unlike America, other paid research posts were few and far between. Yet our experience of life across the Atlantic so far did not encourage me to want to move there, away from family and friends. The intimations of security on which we had come to rely began to look very precarious.

Such was the excitement generated by black hole research over the past four years, however, that Stephen did not lack powerful advocates: Dennis Sciama willingly took up the challenge, as did Hermann Bondi, whose help my father enlisted on our behalf. It was rumoured that King's College had a salaried Senior Research Fellowship which the governing body were prepared to offer Stephen. The authorities of Gonville and Caius bridled at these rumours and stepped in with a special category of Fellowship, a Fellowship for Distinction in Science, before King's had a chance to make their offer. Caius' offer of the Fellowship for six years, conveyed to Stephen in a letter dated 17 March 1969 from the Master, Joseph Needham, was accepted without a moment's hesitation.

With a secure job and a steady income, it was time for us to review our living arrangements. Again we drove out to the Cambridgeshire villages at weekends prospecting for suitable properties. We constantly came up against the intractable problem of transport: if we bought a new house in a village, even the closest village, I should have to drive Stephen to work every morning and collect him every evening. The pressure of such a routine could become irksome, especially as, early in 1970, I became pregnant for the second time. We were more and more convinced that it would be impossible to improve on our situation in Little St Mary's Lane. With help, Stephen could still walk to work in the Department in the mornings, though occasionally he would get a lift out with Brandon to the Institute in the afternoons for seminars and discussions. For Robert, there was a delightfully old-fashioned play-group, close at hand in the Quaker Meeting House just across the fen, and the University Library, awaiting me as and when I managed to find the time and the energy, was within five minutes' cycling distance. We were within a stone's throw of the centre of the city and the churchyard not only catered perfectly for Robert's outdoor needs but also fulfilled my gardening aspirations without imposing any responsibilities. The only drawback was that the house was so small and decrepit.

Our enterprising friends George and Sue Ellis had, by the sweat of their brow, bought and renovated a house at Cottenham, a fen village some 10 miles from Cambridge. When first they came across it, the cottage had a corrugated iron roof, dry rot and ugly Victorian paint and fittings. They stripped away the Victoriana to expose medieval bricks and woodwork, replaced the rotten beams, dug out floors down to bare tiles and replaced the corrugated iron with new thatch. Brandon and Lucette had effected similar changes to their dream cottage out at

Eversden in the heart of the country soon after their marriage in 1969. Even in Little St Mary's Lane, various neighbours had, with the aid of council grants, cleverly enlarged and renovated their previously ram-shackle dwellings, making of them sizeable, attractive townhouses.

We had already experienced the benefits of the modernization that Peterhouse had carried out on the house at number 11 during our three-month tenancy in the autumn of 1965. The Conways, an elderly couple, had transformed the house at number 4, and at number 5, the author and biographer of Rose Macaulay, Constance Babington-Smith, had imaginatively adapted the limited space in her narrow house to meet her bookish requirements. Having seen, with a tinge of envy, how versatile the houses could be, we realized that ours, which was certainly ripe for redevelopment, was no exception. However, we were caught in the proverbial catch-22 situation. We had saved enough money for a deposit on a mortgage for a new property, but because of its age, our house did not qualify for a mortgage; council grants were available for the renovation of old properties, but of course the College on the advice of its land agent had dismissed the property as a bad investment.

As we were debating how best to resolve this dilemma, a change of policy on the part of some building societies removed the problem altogether. Happily it was just then that building societies, including the one where we kept our savings, started giving mortgages – at a higher rate of interest – for the purchase of older properties. Moreover, an agreed mortgage from a building society had the added advantage that it would qualify us for an extra loan, at a low rate of interest, from the University. Quite suddenly, everything started to fall into place, although Stephen was sceptical.

The Conways at number 4 were justifiably very proud of their house. On the ground floor, two rooms had been made into one, creating an elegant through-room from front to back: a new kitchen had been built out at one side of the yard, and the first and second floors remodelled to provide a new bathroom, bedrooms and a roof garden. The size of the original property was not unlike ours and it seemed to me as I pored with pencil and ruler over scraps of paper that some of the Conways' ideas could well be incorporated into our house. They had employed a retired surveyor, the aptly named Mr Thrift, who came along to see us and discuss possibilities. His genial exterior concealed a true mastery of his profession for, from the moment we were introduced, I could tell that he would not dismiss all my projections as mere pipe dreams. Mr

Thrift and I set about drawing up detailed plans which enlarged the house seemingly beyond the bounds of probability, availing ourselves of every inch of space.

We investigated grants – both improvement grants and grants for the disabled – and as soon as we had our draft plans ready laid, we were able to apply to a building society for a mortgage. How unlike the odious College land agent the building society surveyor was! He inspected the house, glanced at the proposed plans and nodded. 'It'll be quite charming, won't it?' he said encouragingly, indicating that he would have no difficulty in recommending the property for a mortgage. We were now in a position to be able to approach Mrs Porter again with a more realistic offer for the house and this time she accepted. It really seemed that all things were possible. We had scant opportunity to enjoy being householders, however, because, shortly after we had signed the completion, all the furniture had to be stored away in the front bedrooms, and we ourselves had to move out to allow the builders to invade our property. Further loans, including a generous one from Stephen's parents, and improvement grants were enabling us to embark without delay on a major rebuilding programme.

George and Sue, with Maggie and one-year-old Andy, had gone to spend six months in Chicago, the home of the highly respected Indian theoretical physicist and Nobel prize-winner, Professor Subrahmanyan Chandrasekhar, and his wife Lola. Chandrasekhar, though a Fellow of Trinity College, had been forced to seek a post in America after being humiliated by Arthur Eddington – once a close friend – at the Royal Astronomical Society in 1933. Chandrasekhar had anticipated black hole research by predicting the ultimate collapse of massive stars under their own weight, only to have his theory scathingly ridiculed by Eddington and the astronomical establishment. Chandra, as he was affectionately known, became a full professor in Chicago in 1944 and a naturalized American in 1953. The Chandrasekhars lived in quiet seclusion, untroubled by the social unrest in the city around them, in the sort of style which only a childless couple can maintain. Everything in their flat was as white as snow, a thick-piled white carpet, a white sofa and chairs, white curtains, all in all, a white nightmare for a visiting mother, like Sue, with very small children whose fingers were permanently smeared with sticky chocolate.

Meanwhile, we took over the Ellises' eminently practical, child-oriented, converted country cottage in Cottenham for the duration of the renovations to number 6 Little St Mary's Lane. We were very grateful for the timely loan of their house but soon found that living in a village produced its own set of problems which had nothing to do with white furnishings. The house was delightful but the isolation was distressing, particularly because I felt sick all day throughout the pregnancy. In addition, I was increasingly beset by an intense, frustrated nesting instinct, not a side-effect I had experienced when expecting Robert, and one which undermined all attempts to work on the thesis. Stephen had to be driven into Cambridge to the Department each morning and collected in the evening, except on those occasions when he was ready in time to catch a lift with other Cottenham commuter neighbours. Robert was unsettled, missing both Inigo and his playground, and I sorely missed my friends in the Lane, especially the Thatchers.

It was only through living in the country that I fully understood the convenience of living in town; it was disconcerting to be an outsider in the centre of town, with no home-base there. I constantly gravitated towards my old home, disobeying Mr Thrift's advice to keep away because of the danger of falling masonry. The first time I went back to the house, the sight that met my eyes was one of sickening devastation, as if a bomb had blasted it. At the back, where we used to cook our meals and take our baths, was a bare empty space, open to the four winds. The old staircase hung askew as if by a thread, and the three-storey front section of the house was resting on a single rusty metal pole. Then I really began to have my doubts. My foolish optimism well and truly seemed to have carried me away this time. It was self-evident that, even if the old part of the house at the front, did not collapse altogether, the rebuilding – for that was what it amounted to – would never be ready in time for us to move back in before the Ellises' return from Chicago and the baby's arrival at the end of October. There was no chance of fulfilling my nesting instincts among that debris so I went back to Cottenham and made enough jam to feed an army instead.

My depression was not eased by the constant pounding of the news reports from the Middle East, which suggested that another confrontation between the Egyptians and the Israelis, and consequently between the Superpowers, was imminent. Not only were the Israelis and Egyptians regularly raiding each others' territory, but also a new aspect of war had reared its ugly head in the hijacking of civilian airliners. I became tense and irritable, and, I am ashamed to say, short-tempered with my nearest and dearest, with Stephen, with Robert and, to my lasting regret, with my dearly loved but very slow-moving grandmother who came from Norwich to stay with us for one very hot, enervating week.

At last, against all expectation, the house was in a sufficiently habitable state for us to return to it in mid-October. It was not yet finished and each day brought a succession of different craftsmen, plumbers, plasterers, painters, electricians, all uncomfortably aware of the protruding deadline – or rather lifeline – to which they had to conform. Once back at home, Stephen and Robert could resume their normal routines and I could get on with scrubbing floors, rearranging furniture, hanging brightly coloured curtains and preparing the new back bedroom for the baby.

This bedroom and a minuscule new bathroom alongside it occupied the space of the old sloping bathroom on the first floor. They overlooked a roof garden above the kitchen which, like the Conways', had been built out into the yard at the side of the house. The area of the old kitchen was now the dining area of the through-room. As in the Conways' house, it extended from front to back, supported in the middle – where previously I had seen the rusty metal pole – by a solid girder, mysteriously referred to as an RSJ. Resting on brick pillars on either side of the room, the RSJ formed a pleasing archway. In the rear wall, constructed of mottled pink, black and yellow old Cambridge bricks, Mr Thrift had carefully reinstated John Clarke's plaque, thus crediting the eighteenth-century builder with twentieth-century building techniques and probably presenting future archaeologists with a mystifying conundrum.

At the top of the house on the third floor behind Robert's attic, Mr Thrift had cleverly added a new room. On the plans it had to be described as a store-room because the ceiling was a few inches below the statutory height for a habitable room on account of a side window in the neighbouring property. However, when the building inspector made his final survey, he cast his eyes round the room and impassively commented, 'This could be quite a nice bedroom, couldn't it?' I hastened to point out to him in no uncertain terms that the room was full of boxes and suitcases in recognition of its expressed purpose. Soon afterwards, the so-called store-room found its true function as a magnificent play-room – safe, out of sight, out of earshot and out of mind.

A fortnight later, on 31 October, when the workmen had left, we gave a party and invited forty of our admiring friends to squeeze into our house – a felicitous combination of old at the front and brand-new at the back. The excitement and the effort of putting on the party produced positive results. The next day found me languishing in a state of some discomfort on the *chaise longue* which I had just finished upholstering, and that night I went into hospital. Long ago I had decided that I would never again put myself and a new baby at the mercy of the crabby old midwives in the nursing home, and insisted that this birth should take place, attended by Sister Lore Weiss, our serene, ever-smiling local midwife, in the maternity hospital.

In an unprecedented display of early morning activity, I gave birth to a daughter, Lucy, at 8 a.m on Monday, 2 November. Sister Weiss gave me all proper attention and then, naturally enough after being on duty all night, went home, leaving the baby and me in the care of the hospital nurses. As it turned out, 8 a.m. on a Monday morning was an unfortunate time to be born. As soon as the nurses in attendance at the birth had washed and dressed the baby, they went off duty, leaving me stranded on the delivery table while the poor little creature in the cot beside me but just out of my reach screamed until her face turned bright red. I longed to comfort her but I had been instructed not to move and in any case, in my post-natal daze, I feared I might drop her. I lay cold and helpless on the hard table, distressed that the tiny red-faced infant in the cot was receiving such a rude introduction to life and angry that none of these institutions which purported to offer a highly specialized service could get it right.

Birth and death, the two greatest events in the human life cycle, the framework within which all mortal experience is contained, are badly mismanaged in Western society. Death, old age and fatal diseases are an embarrassment which society would prefer either to disregard altogether or to watch dispassionately as entertainment on television. Birth, as described by Tolstoy, is 'the most solemn mystery in the world'. Yet the circumstances attending the births of both my babies had been singularly unsatisfactory and there was no reason to suppose that my experiences were – or regrettably still are – in any way unusual. Here in the maternity hospital the atmosphere was more wholesome than in the nursing home where Robert was born, but the place, as I was already discovering, was run according to the rigid demands of the clock and nursing shifts rather than the needs of mothers and their new-born babies.

After two days in hospital I was ready and longing to go home – so ready that I had put my coat on and had wrapped my pretty little pink-faced doll, now much calmer, in warm lacy shawls – when a doctor appeared and ordered me back into bed, explaining that he was going to attach me to a drip containing iron rations to replenish my own failing supplies before letting me go home. Regretfully I obeyed and, instead of returning home to Stephen and Robert, I sadly took refuge in my book, *Buddenbrooks*, Thomas Mann's saga of a Prussian family in the changing times at the end of the nineteenth century. That novel had held me almost as enthralled as Tolstoy's account in *War and Peace* of the fortunes of the Russian aristocracy during the Napoleonic Wars. Tolstoy had been my constant companion throughout that summer and early autumn, immersing me in a dual existence where I could escape the pressures of my own life by entering the lives of other people from another age. I was particularly glad of their company when I took Stephen to a physics conference in Liverpool; disappointingly for a former Beatles' fan, the local people were unfriendly and humourless. We stayed in the Stork Hotel, but no one, other than ourselves and Abe Taub, Stephen's benevolent Californian colleague, appeared to appreciate the irony of its name in relation to my prominent condition.

My reluctant patience in the maternity hospital was rewarded the following day when Lucy and I went home, probably in much better shape thanks to the iron supplements that had been pumped into me. It was good to be back in the Lane where in early November the last roses, sweeter and more intense than any roses in summer, were coming into bloom in the garden. Robert arrived home from nursery school with Inigo soon after midday. He flapped at the letter-box, peering through it in excitement, and then rushed into the house, demanding, 'Where's the baby, where's the baby?' As soon as he saw his tiny sister lying on a rug on the floor, he went straight over to her and gave her a kiss. Thereafter, although Lucy hardly allowed him to get a word in edgeways once she had acquired the power of speech, this fraternal relationship was one area where Dr Spock's good advice was never called for. Robert showed not the least sign of sibling rivalry. Nor did he show any disappointment that the new arrival was not the boy whose development he had monitored by putting his hand on my bulge, announcing as the baby kicked and stretched, 'Ah, he's digging a hole to get out . . .'

Although Stephen's father and brother Edward had gone to

Louisiana for the academic year in the cause of tropical medicine, his mother had stayed in England to be in Cambridge over the immediate period of Lucy's birth because Stephen was beginning to need much more help with his daily needs. He could still pull himself up the stairs but his walking was so slow and unsteady that he had recently, with the greatest distaste, taken to a wheelchair. While I understood that he considered extra help and aids such as the wheelchair an admission that the disease was advancing, his adamant resistance to them was disturbing: if only he could regard them in purely practical rather than emotional terms, they would make life easier for us all.

In the four days of my absence in hospital, my substitute on the home front needed to be someone with patience, understanding and stamina, whom Stephen could trust implicitly. George was his stalwart helper in the Department but he had his own young family to go home to in the evenings, so naturally Stephen preferred to have his mother to look after him when I was out of action. She stayed on for a few days after my return home and was kind, good-humoured and energetic though detached. The routine was exacting: the shopping and the washing had to be done, the house cleaned, meals prepared and Robert and Stephen looked after single-handedly. In the longer term, the carer was also responsible for all those chores which in a normal household would have fallen to the husband, like minor repairs, taking the car to be serviced, putting the dustbin out and so on and so forth. The days since that one occasion when Stephen had picked up a tea-towel to help with the washing-up were long gone. His illness made it impossible for him to help with the running of the house because there was nothing of a practical nature that he could do. He could not wire a plug, make a cup of tea or change a nappy. In fact I never expected him to try to perform any of those tasks as doubtless I would if he had been well. The advantage for him of his practical inability was that it allowed him unlimited time to indulge his driving passion for physics. I accepted that that was what he was bound to do and knew that he would have been most unhappy to have been distracted from it by considerations such as cookery, housework and changing nappies.

I was glad that Isobel and I seemed to have settled into a good relationship after the earlier tensions, although to my mounting dismay it seemed that if we needed help, Stephen's parents would take such requests seriously only if they came from him, not from me. After my return home my own mother took over from her to enable her to join her family in America where her restraining presence was urgently needed. In his detestation of reptiles, Stephen's father had disobeyed all local advice and had tackled a deadly cottonmouth snake which appeared in his back yard in a fight to the death with a broom handle. Stephen was to visit his family in Louisiana in December on his way to a conference in Texas, six weeks after Lucy's birth, but to my immense relief it was agreed that he should go with George and I should stay at home with the two children.

When all the grandparents had left, our routine changed again, revolving around the baby and Stephen, with a great deal of willing help from three-year-old Robert, Inigo's nanny and 'Tatch'. While cuddling Lucy one day, Thelma Thatcher told me quite casually that she had had three babies but only Mary had survived. By comparison with this sad glimpse into her earlier life, I counted myself very lucky to have two thriving children. Stephen, however, was worried about Lucy. She slept for long periods during the day and at night was positively angelic, so much so that he was convinced that there was something wrong with her. He expected all babies to be like Robert, active and energetic at all hours of day and night. Needless to say, I did not share this anxiety. I thoroughly revelled in the blissfully quiet period after her birth which was one of the most stable, contented periods in our lives, especially welcome after the activity of the rebuilding work.

The house was a delight in its brightly painted cleanliness and comparative spaciousness and the baby a source of great joy; she was so tiny that I could hold her in the palm of one hand, and so quiet that when the health visitor came to call, she did not even notice her as she lay beside me on the bed. Little Lucy observed conventional bedtimes, allowing me to run a fairly well-ordered household, care for Stephen and Robert, and sleep regular hours. At night I was also able to resume my reading of Thomas Mann and Tolstoy while Stephen was getting ready for bed. We agreed tacitly, since all reference to his illness was offensive to him, that it was important for him to continue to do as much for himself as he could, even if that took time. He could undress himself once I had loosened his shoe-laces and undone his buttons and then he would struggle out of his clothes and into his pyjamas while I lay reading, a precious luxury at the end of each long day.

Stephen's night-time routine was a slow one, not only because of the physical constraints but also because his concentration was always directed elsewhere, usually on to a relativistic problem. One evening he took even longer than usual to get into bed; it was not until the next morning that I found out why. That night, while putting on his pyjamas and visualizing the geometry of black holes in his head, he had solved one of the major problems in black hole research. The solution stated that if two black holes collide and form one, the surface area of the two combined cannot be smaller and must nearly always be larger than the sum of the two initial black holes, or more concisely, whatever happens to a black hole, its surface area can never decrease in size. This solution was to make Stephen, at the age of twenty-eight, the dominant figure in black hole theory. As black holes had become a fashionable topic of general conversation, it was also to make him a recognized figure of some fascination to the population at large. In Seattle we had been orbiting the newly named phenomenon, the black hole; now we had definitely crossed its event horizon, that boundary from which there is no escape. The theory predicted that, once sucked across the event horizon, the unlucky traveller would be stretched and elongated like a piece of spaghetti, never to have any hope of emerging or of leaving any indications as to his fate.

CHAPTER TWENTY

On Campaign

NINETEEN-SEVENTY, THE year of Lucy's birth, saw the passing of the Chronically Sick and Disabled Persons' Act, piloted through Parliament by the Labour MP, Alf Morris. Though the Act was promoted with the best of intentions by its advocates and hailed across the world as an historic breakthrough in asserting the rights of the disabled, the government refused to implement it fully for many years, leaving already hard-pressed individuals to conduct their own campaigns for its enforcement locally. However, the Act gave substance to our many complaints against the various public bodies whose buildings did not allow easy access to disabled people.

Carrying a small baby in a sling on my front while pushing Stephen in his wheelchair with three-year-old Robert trotting alongside, I was of necessity in the vanguard of protesters campaigning on behalf of the disabled and their carers. A high kerb or a badly placed step, let alone a flight of steps, presented the sort of obstacle which could turn an otherwise manageable family outing into a disaster. Not robust enough, at only seven and a half stones, to surmount the obstacle unaided, I would have to lie in wait, hopefully scanning the vicinity for a male passerby from whom I could humbly solicit help. Then I would have to hand my baby over to any nice lady who happened to be around. Together, the accosted male, Robert and I would heave the chair and its occupant up or over the hurdle, always wary lest the helper should lift the wrong part of the chair – the armrest or the footrest – which might come away in his hand. Finally I would shower the helper with gushing thanks before we continued on our way. Often, to my relief, helpers would volunteer before I had to importune them. Always, as they lifted the chair with Stephen in it, they would ask in amazement,

'What do you feed him on – granite? He weighs a ton for such a slight chap.' 'It's all in his brain,' I would reply nonchalantly.

Our letters of protest to the City Surveyor were met with a superior disdain, reminiscent of Stephen's early encounters with the Bursars of Gonville and Caius. The City Surveyor had never before heard of a disabled person wanting to cross the city as far as Marks and Spencer's, so he failed to see the need for such an expedition – as if disabled people and their families had no right to venture that far. Injustice, Miss Partridge's 'not fair' principle from St Albans High School spurred us into action. Our lances were again at the ready to tilt against the host of intransigent windmills which blocked our path wherever we went. Why should Stephen not be able to buy his own underwear in M&S like the rest of the nation if he chose? Why should he have to suffer restraints on his lifestyle other than those inflicted by an unkind Nature? Why should short-sighted bureaucrats be allowed to make life doubly difficult for him, when he, unlike those smug officials, the scourge of seventies' Britain, was using his restricted allowance of life to abundant advantage every day?

After many battles we succeeded in persuading the Arts Theatre and Cinema to make seating areas available for wheelchairs. The University began slowly to revise its provisions for access as did a few of the more liberal colleges. We took our campaign further afield – to the English National Opera at the Coliseum where our needs were immediately acknowledged, and to the Royal Opera House at Covent Garden where help was woefully inadequate, consisting of offloading the responsibility for wheelchair access to two elderly front-of-house attendants who, while valiantly struggling with Stephen up the flight of stairs to the orchestra stalls, actually dropped him. By a curious coincidence, the attitude of the City Council towards access for the disabled and the lowering of kerbs mellowed rapidly as Stephen's fame grew, but that was long after those strenuous years during which I pushed the wheelchair with two small children in tow.

Most of the colleges were slower to make adjustments, pleading impecunity or the impracticality of adapting historic buildings without contravening conservation laws. Often, college dining halls would be accessible only via the kitchens. Having wended our way through their treacherous obstacle course of steaming vats, sizzling grills and laden trolleys, we would await our turn at a creaking, smelly service lift among stacks of crockery, trays of hors d'oeuvre and cases of wine. Our late arrival at High Table would be greeted with pompous disdain, as if such disruptions were too frightfully embarrassing and boring and should be treated with contempt. Our battle with one college, so advanced in its eagerness to admit women but distinctly tardy in its attention to the requirements of the disabled, continued late into the 1980s.

Quite apart from steps and kerbs, there were many unforeseen hazards in the course of everyday life. Once, when I was taking Stephen with Lucy on his knee out for a walk across the fen, the front castor of the wheelchair stuck in a rut, jolting the frightened occupants out of the chair on to the muddy path. On another occasion, when Lucy was slightly older, we carefully avoided the ruts but came across another obstacle in the shape of an ice-cream van parked outside the back entrance to King's College. To reduce the amount of encumbering paraphernalia, I had left the house with only my door key, leaving my handbag at home. Stupidly I had not thought to put a handful of coins in my pocket. As we turned through the wrought-iron gates into King's, Lucy registered the presence of the ice-cream van. She had begun to acquire the power of language at ten months old when, lying on our bed, she had looked at the light-fitting and announced 'lat, lat', so demanding an ice-cream at the age of one was well within her capabilities. Refusing to take my apologetic 'No' for an answer, she slid off her father's knee to the ground at his feet, and staged a furious infant sit-down demonstration on the pathway. There was nothing I could do. I could not carry Lucy and push Stephen at the same time. Robert and I tried to cajole the agitated little ball of royal-blue garments and auburn curls, to no avail. The King's choristers paused on their way from the choir school in West Road to Evensong in the Chapel and stood wonderingly round her in a circle, perturbed at the spectacle of so much anguish in such a tiny person. After an eternity, a familiar figure, an acquaintance of Stephen's from another group in the Department, appeared on the scene and came to the rescue. While I pushed Stephen, he carried Lucy, still loudly proclaiming her indignation, home – without an ice-cream.

Because we had no time to read newspapers, we relied on my parents for useful snippets of relevant information culled from theirs. Often they would send us bundles of cuttings, sometimes about discoveries in astrophysics, sometimes about benefits for the disabled. Since in one of the latter it was suggested that disabled people could reclaim the cost of the motor vehicle licence, we approached Stephen's doctor for clarification. It transpired that the information in the article was ahead of its time: there was no mechanism yet in place for reclaiming the licence fee – that was to follow some years later – but Dr Swan suggested that Stephen might like to apply for a disabled vehicle.

This possibility – one which we had never considered before – began to open up exciting horizons. If he could manage the joystick controls of an electric car, Stephen would have a new, mechanical freedom of mobility in compensation for the loss of personal movement. An application was presented, the bureaucratic formalities completed, but just one hitch remained: the vehicle had to be parked under cover near an electric socket from which its batteries could be charged up overnight. We could provide no such facility. As so often happened, a solution came from an entirely unexpected source. Our problem was brought to the notice of Hugh Corbett, a genial retired naval commander now the Warden of the University Centre at the end of the Lane, and he unhesitatingly offered Stephen a parking space under cover by a plug.

Although disabled vehicles were severely criticized for their instability, the electric car which travelled at the speed of a fast bicycle enabled Stephen once again to be master of his own routine, dividing his working day between the Department in the morning and the Institute of Astronomy – to which he could drive himself – in the afternoon. On his return home in the early evening he would draw up, hooting, outside the house. Robert would rush out excitedly and clamber on to a ledge beside him in the car for the final hundred yards of the journey down to the University Centre. I would follow them down the Lane with the wheelchair to convey Stephen back to the house. By now we had learnt that no system could be completely trouble-free. The car was subject to frequent breakdowns and often we found it hemmed into its parking place by other vehicles. Once it overturned, giving Stephen a nasty fright, though fortunately no injuries.

In summer Robert, Lucy and I would sometimes take a picnic out to the grounds of the Observatory and visit Stephen in his office in the Institute of Astronomy. The children's high-pitched voices would race ahead of them along the plush carpeted corridors, like gusts of fresh spring air, announcing their presence to their delighted father. The expressions on Stephen's face were always a much more powerful measure of his emotions than his spoken words and on these occasions his smile conveyed his unmistakable joy in his children.

Fifty yards away, the Observatory had the appearance of an unusual but imposing country house. It was purpose-built in 1823 as an observatory with a dome in the centre and residential wings for the principal astronomers on either side. Like any other country house, it was set in carefully tended gardens and orchards. Donald Lynden-Bell, the director, himself a keen gardener, gave us a small patch in the walled vegetable garden on which to grow our own produce. (While the churchyard was ideal for growing roses and lilies, even I balked at the thought of growing vegetables in its soil.) Out at the Observatory the children set to with a will, chatting incessantly while they dug, planted seeds and watched them grow. Then at the end of the day we would proudly take our armfuls of beans and carrots and lettuces into the Institute to show Stephen before setting off for home ahead of him.

Those carefree afternoons spent on the verge of the country proved to be a respite from the increasing trials of life in Little St Mary's Lane. When we had chanced upon it in 1965, the Lane was a haven of tranquillity. By the early 1970s, it was in danger of becoming a thoroughfare of Piccadillyesque proportions. Peterhouse used it for access to their tradesmen's entrance, as did the University Centre, and it bore a constant procession of cars zooming down to the Garden House Hotel on the riverbank. Not infrequently a 10-ton lorry would misguidedly come down the Lane intending to deliver its load to the Centre or the hotel, only to find itself stuck half-way where the width of the road halved. The lorry would then have to back up to Trumpington Street, narrowly missing the façades of our houses and filling our front rooms with fumes.

If this was the main problem by day, by night our ears were assaulted by a barrage of thudding, thumping pop music from the Peterhouse so-called music room. The Fellows of Peterhouse had cleverly situated the music room – where regular pop sessions were held – as far away from the main body of the College as possible, in a room overlooking the churchyard. Perhaps they thought that it did not matter if the slumbers of the dead were disturbed. Unfortunately they gave little thought to the living of the neighbourhood for whom the nocturnal wailings, poundings and crashings were intolerable. Advance warning of an imminent session could be detected in the afternoon when the whistling testing of speakers, the occasional chord on a guitar, the crash of a lone cymbal would advise us of what was in store. On one such afternoon, Thelma Thatcher nodded in the direction of Peterhouse: 'Isn't it lovely, dear,' she said, 'I think they're having a *thé dansant*.'

More campaigning – this time not about disabled issues – was an urgent necessity to protect the Lane's tranquillity and its inhabitants' sanity. A succession of letters to the Governing Body of Peterhouse, anguished telephone calls in the middle of the night to the porters, all produced the same response: 'We must let our young people enjoy themselves.' The fact that we were not enjoying ourselves at all, even though we too were young and our children were even younger, cut no ice. Nor did the fact that many of the inhabitants of the Lane were septuagenarians if not octogenarians. Finally, in sheer desperation one night at about 2 a.m., when the children were whimpering at my feet and Stephen and I had given up all hope of being able to face the next day, I rang the Master of Peterhouse in his Lodge over on the other side of Trumpington Street, well removed from the din. After that a compromise was reached: the hours for full decibel power were curtailed and the volume was reduced after midnight so the inhabitants of the Lane could sleep undisturbed while the 'young' continued to enjoy themselves if in a somewhat muted fashion.

The traffic, a real danger for the three small children, Robert, Lucy and Inigo, who liked to ride their tricycles up and down the road and pay social calls on the neighbours, was a more intractable problem and one which demanded a more organized campaign. We held meetings at number 9 or in our house, and invoked the help of local councillors, among them Gwyneth Lipstein, one of those legendary Cambridge ladies renowned for their formidable energy and grasp of local affairs. Predictably, letters to the City Surveyor did not meet with an encouraging response. However, the complexion of the issue changed dramatically on account of a catastrophe which struck the Garden House Hotel in 1972.

The hotel was originally a large family house, built by the prosperous miller of the watermill at the end of Mill Lane in the early nineteenth century. At the end of the century it was occupied by Professor Arthur Cayley, the father of modern algebra, and in 1922, the mill and the neighbouring mill workers' cottages were converted to create the hotel where Stephen and I celebrated our first wedding ceremony – the civil one – and where subsequently we dined on our anniversaries. Stephen called it 'our local'. The staff, who were our neighbours in the Lane, were friendly, the atmosphere relaxed and the cuisine of good repute. Our association with the hotel became even closer when Stephen's slim, fair-haired French cousin Mimi and her Italian husband Sandro came to work there. Although Cambridge, with its reputation as an area of under-, rather than un-employment, was not particularly welcoming to them, Sandro, a hardworking chef, was generous with his talents in an expansive Italian way. He would cook us wonderful meals in his spare time and Mimi, independent but affectionate and much more spontaneous than Stephen's immediate family, was always willing to come and babysit for us in order, she said, to pursue her studies in child psychology. We saw Mimi and Sandro almost daily and grew very fond of them.

In February 1970, before Mimi and Sandro came to Cambridge, the hotel had found itself propelled into the international headlines as the target of a student riot, provoked by its participation in the Cambridge Greek Week with an evening of Greek food and entertainment. It was tempting Providence in that politically inflamed era to mount any promotion which might be construed as support for the type of right-wing military junta which had seized power in Greece in April 1967 and had sent King Constantine fleeing for his life in the December of that year. Nevertheless, the hotel's supposed association with his persecutors did not apparently trouble the deposed King as much as it did the students. One summer morning a year or so later, I was passing the time of day outside with Thelma Thatcher when she nudged me, pointing to a gleaming silver Rolls Royce which was turning into the Lane from Trumpington Street and was slowly attempting to squeeze its huge bulk along the narrow thoroughfare without scraping its shining bodywork on the railings. Most certainly it was heading for the Garden House Hotel and this was precisely the sort of vehicle we wanted to ban. I assumed that Thelma was going to stop the chauffeur and tell him to back out of the Lane and approach the hotel by Mill Lane instead. Not at all. She nudged me even harder as I stood there waiting for her to step out into the road and raise her hand with the authority of a policeman. 'Curtsey, dear!' she hissed. 'It's the King of Greece!' She curtsied low, smiling graciously as the car glided by. The car bore no insignia and it was scarcely possible to discern any passengers behind the darkened glass. How she knew that it carried the ex-King of Greece remains a mystery.

Catastrophe struck the hotel early one morning in 1972 in the form of a devastating fire. Inigo excitedly reported the news when he and his nanny came to collect Robert for school. The little boys had to walk past the burning building on their way and the shocking impression left on Robert, a sensitive five-year-old, gave him nightmares for some months afterwards. By the end of the day, the scene of so many happy family gatherings was nothing more than a charred, smoking shell. The hotel changed hands after the fire and the new management wanted to construct greatly enlarged premises with facilities for conferences on the site. Architectural considerations apart, an enlarged hotel would create an even more horrendous volume of traffic, so the residents of the Lane decided to oppose the plans with one voice. Just as both sides seemed to be heading for a confrontation, we realized that the two apparently conflicting aims were not as incompatible as they initially had appeared. The managers wanted a new hotel and we wanted the Lane closed. By joining forces instead of opposing each other, both objectives could be achieved. At a tense meeting of residents and managers expertly chaired by Thelma Thatcher at number 9, the great British spirit of compromise triumphed. On the one hand, the hotel's plans were passed unopposed and, on the other, the hotel supported the campaign to close the Lane to traffic, thereby restoring it to relative peace and safety.

If in Cambridge Stephen and I had begun to find ways of adapting and controlling our environment, elsewhere it was more difficult. On their return from Louisiana late in 1970, Stephen's parents decided to buy a country cottage. I hopefully suggested that a cottage on the east coast would be a marvellous asset for our family. We had taken several holidays in north Norfolk in rented cottages with the Ellises, and had also stayed comfortably at the Anchor Hotel in Walberswick, Suffolk where the accommodation consisted of chalets in the garden just a few yards from the beach. In both those areas, though the sand was soft, the terrain was level and manageable, allowing Stephen to be pushed to the very edge of the beach from where he could watch the four small children, Robert, Lucy and Maggie and Andy Ellis, at play.

Isobel's reaction to my idea was curtly dismissive. 'The east coast is much too cold for Father; he would hate having a cottage there,' she remarked. This puzzled me. Frank Hawking spent most of his time working in the garden in all seasons and all weathers – an exact replica of the hardy Mr McGregor in *Peter Rabbit*. Indoors he wrapped himself in a dressing-gown for warmth rather than install more heating appliances, leaving everyone else to freeze in the sub-arctic conditions.

Isobel went prospecting for a cottage with Philippa, who had come back from a two-year period of study in Japan, and returned rapturously enthusing over their find – a stone-built cottage overlooking a bend in the river Wye above a village called Llandogo in Monmouthshire, a place with lovely walks and views, streams where the children could play and woods to explore. It certainly sounded most attractive and, as I had never been to Wales, I was easily infected by their enthusiasm, the more so because in the spring of 1971 we had acquired a new car.

After giving valiant service, by the end of 1970 the Mini was showing signs of advanced senility. It would splutter to a halt at the slightest drop of rain and, because of its intricately compact engine structure, repairs were becoming prohibitively expensive. Finally, just before Christmas 1970, it broke down in the rain at night on the M1 motorway at Stevenage, mindless of its cargo of babies and their great-grandmother in the back. It was evident that it had reached the end of its useful life, but since we had spent all our savings on the house, our financial circumstances were somewhat straitened.

In the New Year, Stephen ran off an essay for the annual Gravity Competition, which had in the past helped us out of many a tight squeeze. Yet again it did not disappoint us. Indeed, this time it turned up trumps: for the first time in the many years of entering the competition, Stephen was awarded the first prize. The coveted prize enabled him to approach a relative of Professor Hoyle's who was reputed to have access to new Chrysler cars at reduced prices. Thus in April 1971, at a cost of £964, we took delivery of a sea-blue Hillman Hunter, glossy with new paint and about three times larger than the Mini.

Even so, the new car was barely adequate for all our luggage, as I found when I experimented with various ways of loading it for the exploratory trip to Wales in the autumn of 1971. Once the wheelchair, pushchair and travel cot were stowed away in the capacious rear section, there was little room for the suitcases. The next expedient was a roof-rack but that created its own set of problems: by the time I had packed for the four of us, closed the house, eased Stephen into the front seat of the car, folded the wheelchair and lifted it into the back, strapped the children into their seats, loaded their luggage, including the travel cot and the pushcair, and then heaved four heavy cases on to the roof-rack, I was so weary that the 220-mile journey – three times as far as the distance to the Suffolk or the Norfolk coasts – became an ordeal rather than an adventure. Even when the M4 opened shortly after our first trip, the distance still proved to be a major drawback.

Nevertheless, when we stopped across the Welsh border for a tea-break and saw the road signs in a foreign language and smelt the tingling damp air, our sense of excitement returned. At last we could truthfully tell Robert, who had been asking how much further there was to go ever since we left Cambridge, that we were nearly there. After some miles of open hill roads and then winding, leafy lanes, we reached our destination. The description we had been given of the cottage was most certainly accurate in every detail. Its position above the river Wye was truly magnificent. It commanded an uninterrupted view of the river, the valley and the tree-covered hills on the opposite bank where in a resplendent glow of radiant colour, autumn reigned in all its glory. A stream ran down the hillside beside the house. A path through the beech woods at the back climbed up over damp peaty undergrowth to the waterfalls at Cleddon. But not so very far away, on the Black Mountains and the Brecon Beacons, a chill wind raged incessantly and tested the stamina of even the toughest hill walker.

The house itself was certainly picturesque – whitewashed, slate-roofed, set into the green hillside, blue wood-smoke curling gently upwards from its chimney – and its attractions were undeniable. This faithful description had omitted several important details, however. The hillside was little short of vertical so that the only possible movement was up or down. A track 100 yards long to the blackberry thicket at the edge of the wood was the only stretch of horizontal surface suitable for a wheelchair. The house itself was reached by a flight of a dozen steep stone steps, slippery with moss and lichen. Inside, a long, steep staircase led up to the bedrooms and the only bathroom. It could not have been more inappropriate for Stephen. Although his father stood by, it took him ten minutes to get up or down the stairs to the bathroom and at least ten minutes to get up or down the treacherous steps to the road. All excursions had to be made by car because there was nowhere else for him to go.

The children loved the place and a part of me shared their enjoyment. The changing colours were breath-taking and the clear air refreshing. I relished my mother-in-law's meals. She was an excellent cook, except on those occasions when she chose to economize by serving us fresh ground elder or brackish nettles from the garden. Unlike Stephen, who would wrinkle his nose in disgust, I also enjoyed my father-in-law's home-made wine, especially the luscious, golden mead which he fermented from the honey produced by his own bees. After supper we would spend long, lazy evenings in front of the open fire, playing board-games until the children's heads started to loll sleepily. But on those occasions when I went out walking or climbing with Robert, I felt painfully guilty at leaving Stephen behind, sitting sadly indoors or out on the terrace. Nowhere could more effectively or more cruelly have emphasized the limitations of his disability. The house and its situation sent out the disturbingly clear signal that the Hawkings appeared to consider themselves exonerated of all basic responsibility towards us. If we chose to visit them, they would be prepared to help, but otherwise they seemed intent on leading their lives independently, with minimal consideration of us and our problems.

CHAPTER TWENTY-ONE

Upward Mobility

LLANDOGO WITH ALL its obstacles turned out to be a useful rehearsal for the following summer's excursion to the summer school in physics at Les Houches in the French Alps. The annual summer school on the lower slopes of Mont Blanc was the brainchild of Cécile de Witt and her American husband Bryce. Cécile was one of those capable women – not unlike some of the Fellows of Lucy Cavendish – of whom I stood in awe. The mother of four daughters, she was an outstanding physicist at a time when women physicists were rare. From her home in America she organized every detail of the conferences in her native France and invited her own hand-picked participants. At her summer school she supervised all the arrangements, led the sessions and climbed the mountains with the strength of a man. In her eagerness to invite Stephen to Les Houches, she commissioned a labour force, brought in bulldozers to construct a ramp up to the chalet where we were to stay for six weeks, and made every possible provision for our comfort. Cécile could hardly be blamed for the weather in the Alps that summer.

Stephen flew out to Geneva with his colleagues while my parents and I drove the rest of the family to Paris for the overnight motorail to St Gervais, some 20 miles from Les Houches. It was unfortunate that we happened to arrive in Paris on the chaotic weekend of *La Sortie*, the weekend in late July when the whole of France goes on holiday. Somehow Dad managed to find the motorail depot and somehow, with our small charges, we managed to fight our way through the massed hordes of travellers on to the train at the Gare de Lyon. The next morning, with the nightmarish journey behind us, the sun shone as we relaxed over a breakfast of coffee and croissants outside the station at St Gervais and it still shone, bathing the white peaks in glistening magnificence, as we excitedly embarked on the winding journey up the Chamonix valley to the very heart of the mountains.

Scarcely had we climbed the steep track to the summer school, a cluster of chalets and lecture halls set among meadows and pine trees, than the sun disappeared, a mist descended and it began to rain. It rained and it rained and it was cold. Water dripped from every roof, every gutter, every branch and every blade of grass and Cécile's carefully constructed ramp soon turned into a mud slide. In the middle of July, my father and I had to resort to feeding the wood-burning stove an endless supply of logs to keep the chalet warm and to dry the nappies with which every corner was festooned. Dear little Lucy did her best to help by spontaneously potty-training herself at the age of twenty months.

In these circumstances, despite the elevation and the vertical nature of all expeditions, Stephen was happy. From morning till night, he was surrounded by colleagues from all over the world whose driving passion was the study of black holes. Occasionally some of them went off in groups for the day, weather permitting, to climb Mont Blanc but that only added to the excitement and the tension and lent an additional aura of superiority to their corporate image. Nothing was too difficult for this breed of superhumans. They were capable of mastering the secrets of the universe and also of conquering any physical challenge on earth. Stephen of course was included in this category since it was generally accepted that he was fighting his own physical challenges with the gritty courage of a hardened mountaineer.

The rest of us – the hangers-on, the wives, mothers, grandparents and babies – were left to our own devices, to shop and cook and find our own entertainment. Raids on the local supermarket for its somewhat limited range of supplies provided eggs for a staple diet of omelettes cooked over a bottled-gas stove. Although there was a restaurant which catered for the delegates, it was too expensive for the whole family to eat there all the time and in any case the conversation at table inevitably veered, in the friendliest possible way, towards the rarefied subjects of black holes or alpine mountaineering in which we – that is, the family – were not able to participate constructively.

As and when the rain eased off, usually for an hour or so each afternoon, we would set off for a walk under the dripping branches, up the mountainside at the back of the chalet past the lecture hall into the wood to search for wild raspberries and bilberries. There we encountered another problem that I had not anticipated. While Robert, true to form, would charge ahead manfully, Lucy adamantly refused to walk more than a couple of yards at a time and would then put her arms up, wanting to be carried. Because I had come to regard Robert's limitless energy as normal, this reluctance puzzled me quite as much as her propensity to sleep when new-born had perplexed Stephen. Our progress up the mountain track was slow and rarely did we reach the clearing where the raspberries and bilberries grew before it started to rain again.

On one of these expeditions, an extraordinary thing happened, extraordinary for the children's reactions as much as for the phenomenon itself. For once Lucy was actually walking on her own two feet with Robert, 10 yards or so ahead of her grandparents and me. Bringing up the rear, I was enjoying an unaccustomed freedom of movement, unencumbered by any other person, small or large, when suddenly I saw the children stop in their tracks. They stood stock-still, whispering to each other very quietly. As we approached, they beckoned to us to lower our voices and pointed to the ground. There, wending its way across the path from one side to the other with apparently not a care in the world, was the smallest, most perfectly formed adder, the white diamond markings on its body standing out clearly against the grey. It took no notice of us as it slithered into the undergrowth. It was beautiful to watch, but even more striking were the children's reactions, as if some primitive instinct had warned them to stand respectfully quiet and still.

However high-powered their physics and impressive their mountaineering feats, the American participants at Les Houches brought a carefree atmosphere to the centre which helped to mitigate the effects of the rain. There was nothing superficial about their relaxed friendliness. After years of dutifully complying with the demands of their Mormon upbringing, Kip Thorne and his botanist wife, Linda, had made the break from its constraints to search for broader truths unshackled by religious dogma. Whatever their private thoughts, never once were they heard to voice any criticism of the rigours of their background. Indeed they brought the positive aspects of Mormonism, a deep caring and concern for their fellow beings, to a wider world.

The Bardeens, who had recently moved to Seattle from Princeton, were also there. Jim Bardeen, the quietest, most self-effacing physicist imaginable, was working closely with Stephen and Brandon Carter on the painstaking task of constructing the laws of black hole mechanics from the basis of Einstein's equations of general relativity. The new set of laws detailing the physics of black holes had caused a hubbub of excitement when their similarity to the second law of thermodynamics had become apparent, and it was this similarity which was driving cosmologists to attempt to narrow the gap between thermodynamics and black holes by putting the theory of black holes into the language of thermodynamics. The laws of thermodynamics are the laws which govern microcosmic operations; they dictate the behaviour of atoms and molecules, including their eventual decay into heat which they exchange with the objects around them. However, the conundrum that now faced physicists was that the laws of thermodynamics, although similar, could not work in the case of black holes because the predictions were that nothing, not even heat, could escape from a black hole. As a loose analogy in the terms of my own research, it seemed rather like the historic transliteration of the language of the *kharjas* from Arabic script where it made no sense, to Romance script where it acquired some significance, except that, as with the *kharjas*, there were still elements missing.

Stephen, Jim and Brandon were attempting to unravel this major enigma when, one afternoon, unable to endure another drop of rain, I bundled the children and their grandparents into the car and set off over the pass beyond Chamonix to Switzerland, convinced that the sun must be shining somewhere. Somewhere there must be a welcome transfer of heat from one celestial body to another, even if heat did signify decay, or 'entropy' in scientific terminology. Nancy Bardeen came with us. She enthralled the children, singing to them, telling them stories, sharing jokes and reciting poems, all the way to Martigny, where indeed the sun was shining, and back. Through the infectious gaiety which shone from her big brown eyes, Nancy bravely concealed a deep pain. Before her marriage, she had given up all chances of an academic career to nurse her parents, one after the other, both terminally ill with cancer. On their deaths she had became solely responsible for her mentally retarded younger brother.

It was also in Les Houches that Bernard Carr, Stephen's new research student, came bounding into our lives one wet afternoon. Bernard was certainly different from the expected run of research students. He was talkative, sociable, unselfconscious, the result perhaps of being sent to boarding school at the age of six. His conversation ranged wide with jovial bonhomie over many topics, often coming to rest on his other main interest, parapsychology, a subject which physicists, including Stephen, tended to regard with derision. For Bernard, however, coincidences and telepathic communication were significant. It was of profound significance to him that he should have chosen to pay an impromptu visit from Geneva – where he was staying – to Les Houches, unaware that Stephen, his new supervisor, had already summoned him in an undelivered word-of-mouth invitation through a third party. Bernard's early ambition had been to become a spaceman. As a child, to his mother's consternation, he had once spent a whole day practising for this end by standing on his head in the cupboard under the stairs, while his younger brother sat outside the door acting as mission control. His mother must have been grateful that his intellect destined him for the theory rather than the practice of space exploration.

When at last the sun consented to shine in France as well as Switzerland and the mountains appeared from behind the clouds, Kip and Linda offered to take Robert and me on a mountain walk up towards one of the glaciers, the *glacier de Bionnassay*, on the west face of Mont Blanc. Leaving Lucy and Stephen with my parents, we took the cable car from Les Houches up to a ridge from where we could look down on the toy chalets and villages dotted about the valley. The summer school down to our left was just out of sight behind the dark trees, while to our right a steep path ascended the mountainside, following the track of the funicular railway which crawled laboriously up from St Gervais to the top station at *le Nid de l'Aigle*, the Eagle's Nest. The dazzling whiteness of the mountain against the deep blue sky was intoxicating, leading us on, up and up, pausing now and then to share Linda's ecstatic delight at the wide range of alpine plants and flowers opening in the afternoon sun. We continued our climb, higher and higher, beyond the end of the railway line in the direction of the massive blue-grey expanse of the glacier, still searching for more specimens for Linda.

It was not until we reached the first of the climbers' refuges in the lee of the *Dôme du Goûter* that, as one, we realized that we were alone on the mountain. Far below, the trains had ceased to run and all the other walkers had melted away although the sun was still high. Eagles wheeled silently overhead, a distant stream trickled down the rocks, otherwise there was little movement: an eerie quietness prevailed. None of us had thought of checking the time of the last cable car down to the village. At a brisk pace, almost a run, we set off back down the track to the cable car station, more than an hour's walk away. Against all expectation, there in the station was a cable car with an attendant standing beside it. We ran to him smiling with relief but his expression was dour as he turned towards us, barring our way. He shrugged his shoulders with an implacable indifference and announced that the last cable car had gone at five-thirty and it was now nearly six o'clock; we would have to walk down to Les Houches. We pleaded with him breathlessly, pointing to our five-year-old who was – for once – beginning to tire. The man was impervious, hard as flint, of military rigidity. We turned away, anxious and angry. On the ridge above the station there was a hostel from where we tried to call the summer school but there was no reply; evidently the office was unattended. We dared not wait any longer as the sun was now lower in the sky, so we left money with the hostel keeper asking her to try to ring through and leave a message.

There was nothing for it but to head straight down the mountainside as fast as possible, taking the path when we could find it, scrambling through bracken and long grass when we could not. A patriarchal figure, like a St Christopher in a medieval painting, Kip carried Robert whose legs had borne him well for more than four hours but were now aching with weariness. Fighting our way through the undergrowth, we watched in disbelief as the cable car, carrying the same disobliging attendant, sailed over our heads on its homeward run down to Les Houches. The air grew chill as the sun sank behind the mountains and the sky darkened. We persevered, thankful at least that we were walking down the mountain not up it.

The village of Les Houches, glad though we were to reach it at long last, was by no means the end of the road. The summer school enclave was another three-quarters of an hour away out of the village, up the hillside further west. It must have been well after nine when we stumbled blindly into the brightly lit refectory where everyone was anxiously waiting for news of us. No message had come from the hostel and the worried group of family, my parents and Stephen, colleagues and students were fearing the worst. Tired but happy, we fell into each other's arms.

At the end of August, as we dodged the showers at the last social function of the summer school – a barbecue where a whole lamb was roasted over a pit – Kip made the suggestion that Stephen might like to visit Moscow for talks with the many Russian scientists whose freedom to travel was severely restricted. He promised to make all the arrangements for a private visit which could be timed to follow on from the Copernicus conference in Poland in the summer of 1973. Kip's well-meaning suggestions made my blood run cold. While Lucy was a baby, Stephen had travelled abroad to conferences either with George Ellis or Gary Gibbons, his first research student, or with his mother. Now that Robert was five and Lucy one-and-a-half, my period of respite from international travel seemed to be drawing to a close. Frequently Stephen would ask if I would go with him to conferences in far-flung places; just as frequently I would reply that I could not bear to leave the children.

Divided loyalties were beginning to tear me apart. Stephen was pursuing his career with an iron will, attended by astounding success, and conferences probably enabled him to feel that he was expanding his life as well as asserting his presence on the international scene. I would be the first to admit that it had been my genuine aim to help him achieve all possible success but since making that commitment, I had become the mother of his children and to them I owed an equal responsibility. On the one hand, it was obvious that Stephen required my help for many of his personal needs, but on the other, the children needed my help for all of theirs. Stephen wanted my love and companionship but he was assured of the former wherever he might be, and as for the latter, conferences did not allow much time for doing things together. I had enough experience of conference routines to know that spouses were tolerated as second-class citizens, while for the duration, personal relationships were of secondary importance. The children were small enough still to need a constant presence. Their sense of security was fragile and had to be fostered gently. If the future was insecure on account of the health of one of their parents, it was up to the other parent to compensate for that insecurity by not abandoning them more than was absolutely essential. From my own point of view, although I was confident that with their grandparents they would be in excellent hands, the prospect of being thousands of miles apart from them for any length of time was excruciating.

The scenario was set for a grim competition. Stephen would ask if I would like to go with him to a conference in, say, New York or Princeton or Dallas. Apologetically I would refuse because I could not leave the children. Such a lily-livered response would have been frustrating for any scientist who found himself on the threshold of that Aladdin's cave wherein were contained the most coveted, prized secrets of the universe, but for one who had overcome so many physical as well as intellectual hurdles on the journey towards that goal, it must have been maddeningly incomprehensible. With commendable restraint, Stephen never showed any anger. Instead, quietly declining to accept my reluctance, he would patiently repeat the same question week after week until I was reduced to a frenzy, overwhelmed with guilt at letting him down yet saddened by his lack of understanding. This pressure exacerbated the fear of flying which had pursued me ever since the extended tour of America in 1967, hovering like a great black bird of prey over my head whenever air travel was mentioned. I had flown only twice since then, once on the ill-fated winter holiday to Majorca when Robert fell sick, and the second time to Switzerland in May 1970. There had been a trip planned to a conference in Tblisi in Georgia in September 1968 but to my silent relief, many British scientists, including Stephen, refused to attend in protest against the Russian invasion of Czechoslovakia that August. My fear of air travel was not completely unjustified: in the late 1960s and 1970s not only did aeroplanes fall out of the sky with chilling regularity, they were also the favourite targets for hijackings by the growing bands of international terrorists.

The sum total of all the conflicting pressures – the anxieties, the fears and the responsibilities – doomed me to years of misery under the shadow of that black spectre. So terrified was I by the mere mention of travels abroad that I would gladly take the most circuitous route by any other means than air travel – which was exactly what Robert and I did in 1971 when Stephen was invited to attend a conference in Trieste. Stephen went by air; Lucy, only seven months old, stayed with my parents while Robert and I took the train. After a long hot journey across Europe, we stopped in Venice where Robert was so bewitched by the view from the top of the Campanile that he would have stayed there for ever. Only when the sudden clang of the heavy bells at midday assaulted our ears did he race for the lift. He also insisted on sitting down at a table in St Mark's Square outside Florian's. That was an expensive object lesson – the equivalent of £6 for a tiny cup of coffee – so the next time we passed by Florian's, we sat down on the steps around the porticoed square, only to be earmarked for target practice by the local pigeons.

The scientific meeting which took place on the shores of the Adriatic at Miramar outside Trieste took place in sun-soaked calm which was broken one evening by a hurricane which raged furiously through the small community, scattering the underwear which I had put out to dry on the balcony around the streets of the port beneath. When the turquoise sea grew calm again and I had surreptitiously collected up various personal items from the gutters, awnings and coffee tables, we decided to take a day trip by boat from Miramar to Yugoslavia, the most accessible of the Iron Curtain countries. For entry the procedures were quite simple. Visas were given out and money changed on board the boat for the couple of hours we were to spend in Capodistria, a sleepy village down the coast from Trieste.

Two years later, the proposed trip to Moscow via Warsaw was a very different undertaking. It was out of the question even to think of going to Moscow by train. Travel by air was indispensable. Applications for visas had to be sent months in advance. Both children had to stay at home and we were going to be away from home for nearly a month. My presence was compulsory as it was unlikely, in those repressive days after the fall of Khruschev, that anyone other than Stephen's wife would be granted a Russian visa to accompany him. The prospect haunted me with foreboding but this time there was no escaping: the plans were laid, the tickets were booked – paid for, as always, by some scientific organization or other – and, with some difficulty, the visas authenticated and extracted from the Russian embassy.

When I considered myself in the context of this situation, what I saw was intensely dispiriting. Why had my courage failed me so badly? How, in the space of a a few short years, could I have become such a pale shadow of the student who had travelled alone round Spain, blithely disregarding all parental concerns, revelling in the spirit of adventure, delighting in the unexpected and relishing air travel, even in a clapped-out propeller aircraft? It was as a very pale walking shadow that in August 1973, bound for Warsaw and Moscow, I slipped away from the children as they played happily in their grandparents' house in St Albans.

CHAPTER TWENTY-TWO

Intellect and Ignorance

ASTRONOMERS WERE FLOCKING to Poland in 1973 to celebrate the 500th anniversary of the birth of Nicholas Copernicus, the Polish astronomer whose dissatisfaction with the complicated mathematics needed to account for the movement of the planets in the earth-centred universe of Ptolemy's theory compelled him to develop a new theory of the universe. The Copernican theory supposed that the earth and other planets revolved around the sun, thus superseding the Ptolemaic theory which had become tantamount to an article of faith, both scientific and religious, though in fact it bore little relation to the biblical concept of a flat earth, above which was heaven and below which was hell. For me, on my first visit behind the Iron Curtain, apart from the day trip to Yugoslavia in 1971, Poland was a lesson in the nature of tragedy, the tragedy of history in a country which bore the scars of oppression and division, the philosophical tragedy for mankind of the schism between science and religion which resulted from Copernicus' theory, and the tragedy of genius.

Although Copernicus did not live to see how his theory was developed by Galileo in the next century, he must have been well aware of its iconoclastic nature. It might be true to say that he was the first scientist to open the Pandora's Box of science with its dual potential of advancing human knowledge yet of posing an uncomfortable dilemma which would test man's moral integrity. The theory well deserved the term by which it came to be known: the 'Copernican Revolution'. Since, according to Copernicus, the earth was no longer at the centre of the universe, man was not at the centre of Creation. Man, therefore, could no longer be said to have a special relationship with the Creator. This fundamental change in perspective was to liberate man from the oppressive medieval obsession with the divine image, enabling him to expand his intellectual capabilities and value his own physical attributes. It was one of the powerful influences behind the philosophy of the European Renaissance when architects built palaces rather than cathedrals, and artists and sculptors replaced the religious image with the human form, depicted for its own sake, for its beauty and strength. In scientific terms, the Copernican theory paved the way for the discoveries of Newton in seventeenth-century England where Puritanism, the consequence of Henry VIII's Reformation, had cleared rational thought of superstition, with the incidental and quite unintentional benefit of allowing the advances of the Age of Enlightenment to proceed unfettered by religious scruple. Within Catholicism, however, the Copernican theory produced an ugly reaction, the repercussions of which are felt throughout society to this day.

Perhaps afraid of its implications, Copernicus did not permit his work, *Concerning the Revolution of the Heavenly Spheres*, to be published until just before he died: a copy of the printed work was brought to him on his deathbed on 24 May 1543. Nonetheless he had not sought to hide its contents, for the theory had been widely disseminated over a long period and he himself had lectured to Pope Clement VII on the subject in Rome in 1533. It is quite conceivable that the Pope did not fully understand the implications of the lecture if it was presented to him merely as a simplification of the cumbersome Ptolemaic mathematics or perhaps he did not take it seriously, because it was not until some time later – in the seventeenth century – that it fell to Galileo Galilei to bear the full brunt of the Church's ire for his support and publicizing of the new system.

A charming popular account of the spy-glass ascribes its invention to children who were playing around with bits of glass and lenses in the workshop of a Flemish spectacle-maker and found that by putting two lenses together they could see distant objects plainly. The spectacle-maker saw the potential of the gadget for the toy market but when in 1609 Galileo heard of it, he worked out the underlying theory in one night and developed his own improved version, the telescope, which he demonstrated from the Campanile in Venice to that city's incredulous merchants. To their astonishment, they saw that the markings on a sailing ship on the horizon, two hours from port, could be identified in fine detail. Galileo then realized that his revolutionary navigational aid could be turned on the heavens. He built a telescope in Padua, discovered four new planets – in fact the satellites of Jupiter – and published his own water-colour maps of the moon. His observations convinced him of the incontrovertibility of the Copernican theory and when, somewhat naively, he publicized his proof of the theory, obtained from his observations in 1613, he found himself in bitter conflict with the Church for which the earth was irrefutably and theologically fixed at the centre of the universe.

In 1592, Giordano Bruno had been burnt at the stake for daring to speculate about astronomical matters yet Galileo was undeterred by Bruno's fate. Innocently supposing that no one would want to contradict visible evidence, he went on to become the main and most successful propagandist for the Copernican theory, especially because he published his findings in the vernacular language, Italian, instead of Latin. The attack on the traditional Judeo-Christian view of a conveniently earth-centred universe posed an unacceptable threat from within to a Church already struggling to contain the forces of Protestantism from without, and, under pressure in 1616, Galileo was forced to acknowledge the error of his ways.

The election of Maffeo Barberini to the Papacy as Urban VII temporarily alleviated Galileo's uncomfortable situation. Barberini was a highly cultured man and lover of the arts but he was also proud, extravagant and autocratic. He it was who had all the birds in the Vatican garden killed becaused they disturbed him. He was, however, a friend of Galileo's and helped to bring about a limited relaxation of the 1616 injunction by commissioning him to write a discourse explaining the two chief world systems – the old, Ptolemaic, and the new, Copernican (*Dialogo sopra i due massimi sistemi del mondo, tolemalco e copernicano*), on condition that the discourse should be completely neutral. Inevitably, when it appeared the book was seen as a categorical statement of the force of the Copernican argument and led to Galileo's arrest and trial by the Inquisition. He was sentenced to house arrest in his villa at Arcetri where, old, blind and captive, the king of infinite space bounded in a nutshell, he eloquently lamented the disparity between the vastness of his area of research and the limitations of his physical condition: 'This universe is now shrivelled up for me into such a narrow compass as is filled by my own bodily sensations.'

Despite the life sentence of house arrest, his creative powers were not dulled. A new manuscript, *Concerning Two New Sciences*, was smuggled out of Italy to Holland where it was published in 1638. Here, Galileo is said to have laid the foundations of modern experimental and theoretical physics and with it the scientific tradition moved north, away from the repressions of southern Europe.

Although Galileo was a devout Catholic, it was his conflict with the Vatican, sadly mismanaged on both sides, that lay at the basis of the running battle between science and religion, a tragic and confusing schism on the face of civilization which persists unresolved. More than ever at the end of the twentieth century, religion finds its revelationary truths threatened by scientific theory and discovery, and retreats into a defensive corner, while scientists go into the attack insisting that rational argument is the only valid criterion for an understanding of the workings of the universe. Both sides may have misunderstood the nature of their respective roles. Scientists are equipped to answer the mechanical question of how the universe and everything in it, including life, came about. The complexity of their calculations and the admiration their discoveries have attracted have led some of them to fall into the trap of believing that science has become a substitute for religion and that, as its great high priests, they can claim to have all the answers to all the questions. However, because of their reluctance to admit spiritual and philosophical values, some of them do not appear to be aware of the nature of some of the questions.

Since their modes of thought are dictated by purely rational, materialistic criteria, physicists cannot claim to answer the questions of why the universe exists and why we, human beings, are here to observe it, any more than molecular biologists can satisfactorily explain why, if our actions are determined by the workings of a selfish genetic coding, we sometimes listen to the voice of conscience and behave with altruism, compassion and generosity. Extrapolating from animal patterns of behaviour, evolutionary psychology in the latter part of the twentieth century has ascribed altruism to a crude theory by which familial and social cooperation would appear to favour the survival and spread of the species, but scientists still cannot satisfactorily explain why some human beings are prepared to give their lives for others. The complexity of such an anomaly lies far outside the scope of their purely mechanical grasp. Nor can they explain why so much human activity operates at a subliminal level. The spiritual sophistication of musical, artistic, poetic and even scientific creativity far exceeds that of any primitive function programmed into the brain as a basic survival mechanism. The gene is after all only a tiny component in the development of each individual human personality; to propose it as the determining force in the development of the human race when the debate over nature versus nurture still rages is premature.

Scientists can offer explanations but not truths, although it has to be said there are those among them who confidently aspire to answer the question 'Why?' as well as the question 'How?' but acknowledge that they are still very far from reaching that goal. Others more arrogantly even aspire to become gods themselves by denying the rest of us our freedom of choice and disputing our right to ask the question 'Why?' in relation to the origins of the universe and the origins of life. They claim that the question is 'inappropriate', as inappropriate as it would be to ask why Mount Everest is there. They dismiss the suggestion that the question 'Why?' is the prerogative of theologians and philosophers rather than scientists because, they say, theologians are engaged in the 'study of fantasy': belief in God can be attributed to 'a shortage in the oxygen supply to the brain'. Their theories reduce the whole of Creation to a handful of material components. They complain with a weary disdain at the stupidity of the human race, that human beings are always asking 'Why?' Perhaps they should ask themselves *why* this is so. Might it not be that our minds have been programmed to ask 'Why?' And if this is the case they might then ask who programmed the human computer. The 'Why' question is the one which, above all, theologians should be addressing.

Frequently over the decades of our marriage, stimulated by a scientific article or television programme, I found my mind exercised by questions of this nature and would try to discuss them with Stephen. In the early days our arguments on the topics rehearsed above were playful and fairly light-hearted. Increasingly in later years, they became more personal, divisive and hurtful. It was then apparent that the damaging schism between religion and science had insidiously extended its reach into our very lives: Stephen would adamantly assert the blunt positivist stance which I found too depressing and too limiting to my view of the world because I fervently needed to believe that there was more to life than the bald facts of the laws of physics and the day-to-day struggle for survival. Compromise was anathema to Stephen, however, because it admitted an unacceptable degree of uncertainty when he dealt only in the certainties of mathematics.

Galileo died on 8 January 1642, the year in which Newton was born and 300 years to the day before Stephen was born. Stephen adopted Galileo as his hero. When in 1975 he received a medal from the Pope, he took the opportunity to launch a personal campaign for Galileo's reinstatement. The campaign was eventually successful but was nevertheless seen as a victory for the rational advance of science over the hidebound antiquated forces of religion rather than as a reconciliation of science with religion.

In the sixteenth century, Nicholas Copernicus had led the life of a true Renaissance man, untroubled by the crises and restrictions that Galileo was to suffer on his behalf in the next century. He enjoyed all the advantages, the breadth of education and experience of that period of intellectual expansion and travelled widely, as far as Bologna, Padua and Rome. He studied medicine as well as mathematics and astronomy. He translated the Greek verses of Theophylactus, a seventh-century Byzantine poet, into Latin, fulfilled a number of diplomatic functions and presented proposals for the reform of various Polish currencies. Ironically, 500 years later, such broad possibilities were denied to Copernicus' modern compatriots as they celebrated his quincentenary.

From the scientific point of view, the great advantage of the Polish setting for the commemorative conference was that it provided a meeting place for all the great minds from both West and East since Russian physicists were able to travel to Poland, if not further afield, with relative freedom. For Westerners, Poland was certainly more accessible than the Soviet Union: our Polish visas came through automatically, whereas with Stephen's schoolfriend, Basil King, acting as my bodyguard, I had been forced more or less to stage a sit-in at the Soviet Embassy in London in order to prise the Russian visas out of the austere consular grasp. The only inconvenience of entry into Poland, as a number of male delegates found, was that the bearer of a passport was expected to resemble his photograph down to the last detail. Since the year was 1973, many of the younger delegates and students were sporting long hair and a fine bushy growth of beard, bearing little resemblance to their passport photos which could have been taken nearly ten years earlier when they were but whining schoolboys with satchels, and shining faces. The only means of persuading the Polish authorities that they really were who they purported to be and not decadent hippies intent on undermining the purity of communist culture, was to shave off their beards and cut their hair at the border post. They arrived in Warsaw looking like sheep from the shearer. Stephen was probably the only one among them whose hair was actually shorter than on his photo.

The Poland we witnessed in 1973 was a sad country, ravaged by

Germany and dominated by Russia. It was hardly surprising that the Poles regarded all foreigners, including ourselves, with suspicion. We were all tarred with the same brush: if we were not German, we must be Russian. Protesting our Britishness was of no avail because we and the Americans came from the envied affluent societies to which the Poles would like to belong but from which, to their resentment, they were barred. Plate-glass shopfronts bore ample evidence of Western, aspirations: inside the shops, the shelves were either bare or the goods they displayed were shoddy and prohibitively expensive.

Everywhere Poland showed signs of a country ill at ease with itself, caught on the horns of a dilemma between old and new, East and West. Torn apart throughout its history by both its neighbours, Russia and Germany, it had painstakingly reconstructed much that it had lost in the Second World War – especially, in fine detail, the old town of Warsaw. In contrast, Stalin's unwelcome post-war gift to the Polish people was a monumental municipal building which reflected his own megalomania rather than the needs of the Polish people. It was said of this megalith that the best views of Warsaw could be seen from it – meaning that only by viewing Warsaw from the Stalin monument could one avoid seeing it in the picture. In that building the Copernicus conference took place. It was approached from without by means of a long flight of steps. Another long flight of steps led down inside the building from the foyer to the conference area. Each morning Stephen's student, Bernard Carr, and I would carry Stephen to the top of the steps, sit him down on a chair and then bring up the wheelchair. Inside the building, for want of a lift, we would then take the wheelchair down the corresponding inner flight of stairs before carrying Stephen down to it. This process was repeated in reverse sequence at the end of the day, possibly also several times during the course of the day, subject to variations in the programme and the venue. Those steps did not impress us with Stalin's generosity to the Polish people: they impressed us only with his pompous conceit.

A repressive communism, imposed by Russia, which condemned peasant farmers to appear as lean as the emaciated cows we saw them herding along the country roads or the teams of scrawny oxen they drove across the fields, had produced a defiant reaction in the people. Poland was the most devoutly Catholic country in Europe: the Polish Church had become a symbol of national independence and nobly fulfilled its role as the defender of liberty, producing martyrs from among its priesthood. Nonetheless, I was perplexed to find strong reminiscences in Polish churches of the Church in Spain, so unlike the refreshing simplicity of English Catholicism which had resulted from the reforms of John XXIII's inspired papacy. As in Spain, churches in Poland were ornate, darkly lit, incense-filled, full of extravagant plaster saints and virgins, imbued with that distasteful air of superstition. Clusters of little old crones, draped in black, crowded round the porches and genuflected at the altars, just as they did in Francoist Spain. Polish independence as manifested through the Catholic Church was a conservative force, competing against a hostile political system with its own traditional opiate, whereas in Spain the attitude of the Catholic Church was equally conservative but was generally one of political compliance with the repressive regime.

Cracow, to which the conference adjourned for the second session, was more assured of its identity than Warsaw, since its monuments – Wawel Castle and the church of St Mary – had survived the war intact, but the vicinity of Cracow was tainted with the chilling notoriety of Auschwitz. There was no official excursion to the concentration camp. Some Jewish participants organized their own outing and came back communicating to the rest of us their devastation at what they had witnessed.

The only place in that unhappy country where I detected any sense of peace and integrity was at Chopin's birthplace, a single-storey thatched house set in a tangle of greenery at Zelazowa Wola in the country outside Warsaw. Although Chopin's family moved to Warsaw when he was a baby, he spent summer holidays at Zelazowa Wola, the country seat of his mother's aristocratic relations, the Skarbeks, and it was there that he put the finishing touches to his Piano Concerto in E minor. He also spent holidays with schoolfriends in the country. On one such holiday, he and his friends went on an excursion to Torum and found the house where Copernicus was born. Shocked by the condition of the house, Chopin complained that the room where the birth took place was born was occupied by 'some German who stuffs himself with potatoes and then probably passes foul winds'.

The old house at Zelazowa Wola, with its sparse furnishings, polished floors, family portraits and collection of instruments, modestly conjured up the atmosphere of life in a cultured Polish family in the early nineteenth century. It was not just the aura of unworldliness that held me spellbound but also the evocative silence. Mazurkas and waltzes hung on the air as though the main living-room were still echoing with the strains of a family party. Nocturnes wafted in on a scented breeze from the shady garden. The setting lent a visual, tangible dimension to that powerfully emotive music. Above all, the house spoke of peace, the peace of a devoted family which had nurtured that most seductive of Romantic geniuses, the genius for whom, according to his good friend Delacroix, 'heaven was jealous of the earth'. Like Copernicus, Chopin lived abroad for much of his life. He left Poland in 1830 never to return to his beloved homeland. His love for the young Polish girl, Maria Wodzinska, whom he met in Dresden, was thwarted by her parents who disapproved of the match on the grounds of Chopin's ill-health. Marriage to Maria might have taken him back to Poland. Instead he settled in his father's native country, France, where he formed a tempestuous liaison with the volatile woman novelist of licentious repute, George Sand, and died of consumption in 1849 at the age of thirty-nine.

The tragic experience seemed to be the hallmark of that stay in Poland, its resonances pursuing us to the very end, for it was in the scientific company of Claudio Teitelbaum, a young Chilean delegate to the conference, and his wife that strange fleeting poetic memories from my own past resurfaced. Although they were living in Princeton, the Teitelbaums had close connections with the government of President Allende – the newly elected socialist government of Chile – through Claudio's father who was one of Allende's ambassadors. They were part of the circle of dedicated left-wing reformers which included Pablo Neruda, the inspired poet at whose feet I had worshipped as an undergraduate. In 1964 Neruda had come to read his poetry at a gathering in King's College, London, and I still carried in my mind the sensual sonority – as rich and evocative as Chopin's music – that he brought to his love poems, caressing and emphasizing their lush strain of natural imagery. Neruda, a communist, was so deeply involved in Chilean politics that the presidency was within his grasp but he relinquished his ambitions in favour of his friend, Salvador Allende.

It was in Cracow, in the bare lounge of the hotel on the last day of the Copernicus meeting, that news reached us of the right-wing military coup against the legitimate Chilean government, allegedly with CIA support. Allende had died in the defence of the Presidential palace. The Teitelbaums were stunned not only by the death of their much-admired President but also by the death of their dreams for reforming the impoverished lives of the oppressed peasants of Chile. They with thousands of others were destined to spend many years in exile. Their destiny was fortunate by comparison with those who did not manage to flee the vicious reprisals exacted by the right-wing Pinochet regime. Two weeks later Pablo Neruda, a Spanish-speaking poet of genius like Lorca before him, died in the aftermath of right-wing revolution.

CHAPTER TWENTY-THREE

Chekhovian Footfalls

IF THE IMPRESSIONS I carried from Poland were confusing, Moscow was perversely reassuring in that there was no room for doubt among its citizens about their own political identity or ours. We knew – and everyone else knew – that the Soviet Union was a totalitarian police state and that there was little to be gained by hankering after a liberal democracy. The Muscovites politely recognized that we came from a privileged society without holding that against us. On the flight between Warsaw and Moscow, Kip warned us to behave as though our room in the hotel were bugged. He was not absolutely sure but it would be safer, he said, not just for ourselves but for all the colleagues we would be meeting, to behave with caution as if there were eavesdroppers listening to all our conversations. Stephen had visited Moscow once before, as a student, with a group of Baptists – strange company for one of such forceful atheistic opinions. Even stranger was the fact that he had helped them to smuggle bibles into Russia in his shoes.

Such reminiscences were hardly appropriate on the present occasion, which had acquired the importance of a high-level official exchange with all the concomitant VIP treatment. On arrival at the Hotel Rossiya, a massive square block between Red Square and the river Neva, we glanced around our suite, equipped with samovar and fridge, half expecting to uncover a microphone strategically placed to record our private thoughts. We did not however resort to the lengths of the diplomat in a joke currently circulating: he was said to have pulled up the carpet and snipped at the wires he found beneath it. A loud crash and a horrified shout came from the room below where the chandelier had fallen to the ground.

We had already noticed that the lift bypassed the first floor of the hotel; this was out of bounds and was said to be reserved on all four sides of the building, each a quarter of a mile long, for 'administration'. Moreover, many of the Russians who had come to meet us at the airport bearing welcoming bouquets of roses and carnations were reluctant to enter the hotel beyond the lobby. Significantly, in the light of their reticence, Dr Ivanenko, an elderly scientist of modest reputation, was only too pleased to sit in Kip's room for hours at a time, precisely enunciating, as if to hidden ears, all that he had achieved for Soviet science. It was Ivanenko who always accompanied groups of younger Russian astrophysicists to conferences in the West. We generally supposed that he was their minder, especially because they were forever inventing schemes for evading him. His own behaviour could be mysteriously unpredictable. In 1970, while we were at the conference centre at Gwat in Switzerland, he had disappeared during the course of a boat trip along the shores of Lake Thun, not to be seen again until he turned up some time later in Moscow.

The purpose of Stephen's visit to Moscow was two-fold. Primarily a theoretician, he had begun to dabble in the practical question of black hole detection. In this he was following the example of an American physicist, Joseph Weber, who had been conducting a solitary struggle to build a machine for catching the minuscule vibrations of the gravitational waves which were predicted to come from stars as they collapsed into black holes. We had spent several afternoons scouring rubbish tips in Cambridge for disused vacuum chambers which might be fitted up, in somewhat Heath Robinsonian fashion, with detector bars immersed in liquid nitrogen, to complement Weber's work in Europe. This aspect of black hole research had also been taken up in Moscow, at the University, by Vladimir Braginsky, an experimental physicist who showed us his laboratory and cheerfully gave me the remnants of a stick of synthetic ruby which he had used in his experiment. He was blessed with an extrovert nature which concealed the extent of his scientific foresight and revealed itself in his penchant for risqué political jokes even in a semi-public setting.

It was Braginsky who at dinner one night kept the company captivated with a torrent of jokes, interspersed with a succession of toasts in vodka and Georgian champagne. Not all his jokes were hysterically funny. Most had a political edge, as for example the one about transport: an American, an Englishman and a Russian were comparing methods of transport. The American said, 'Well, of course we need three cars, one for me, one for my wife and a motor-home for holidays.' The

Englishman said modestly, 'Well, we have a runabout for town driving and a family car for holidays.' The Russian said, 'Well, the public transport is very good in Moscow so we don't need a car in town and, when we go on holiday, we go in tanks . . .'

Stephen had also come to Moscow for conversations with those Russians, many of them Jewish, whose freedom to travel had been severely curtailed. Yakov Borisovich Zeldovich, a fiery, impetuous character, had been in the forefront of the development of the Soviet atom bomb in the 1940s and 1950s. In the late 1950s and early 1960s, like his American counterpart, John Wheeler, he turned his attention to astrophysics where the conditions inside an imploding star mirrored those of the hydrogen bomb. In consequence Zeldovich became a foremost authority in black hole research. However, because of the secrecy surrounding his earlier work, he never expected to be able to emerge from behind the Iron Curtain and come to the West to share fully the international excitement aroused by black holes. The seminal research in imploding stars which his group generated was broadcast to the outside world on his behalf by a rather shy and tense younger colleague, Igor Novikov, with whom Stephen developed a strong working relationship.

Like Zeldovich, Evgeny Lifshitz, also Jewish, suffered travel restrictions, as did the many gifted students who knew that they would have to wait years before receiving the coveted first travel permit, itself a passport to the rubber-stamping of further permits. Some were vociferous and intense, others reserved and pensive. However extrovert some of their personalities might appear to be, the impression that they lived under extreme tension was inescapable. It was not difficult to sense the undercurrent of fear. All were seriously concerned at the restrictions placed on their creativity by incompetent officialdom and all were afraid of the power of the KGB if they tried to improve their situation.

Kip had many conversations on this theme with his Russian friends while Stephen and I provided a useful front of social activity. One evening this previously successful ploy backfired. Throughout our stay, our hosts showered us with tickets for the Bolshoi – for the opera, *Boris Godunov* and *Prince Igor*, and for the ballet, *Sleeping Beauty* and the *Nutcracker*. Though Stephen was eager to attend the opera, he was much more reluctant about the ballet. Indeed on the only previous occasion when we had been to the ballet together, to a production of *Giselle* at the Arts Theatre in Cambridge, he complained of a headache in the first act and I had to take him home in the interval. In Moscow we were consistently in our seats in good time for the opera but when we arrived at the Bolshoi for the *Nutcracker*, the doors were already closing. We were hurriedly ushered into a side aisle and the doors closed smartly behind us. Kip, who had been intending to use the cover of the ballet to escape with a colleague, Vladimir Belinsky, into the streets of Moscow for surreptitious discussions on matters political as well as scientific, found himself trapped. He had come into the theatre to help us settle in, and when the doors closed, he had no option but to sit patiently through the first act of *Nutcracker* till the interval while Belinsky waited for him outside in the foyer. At least Stephen had a companion in adversity.

Although we were well aware of these cloak and dagger operations lurking in the background, we began to realize that Stephen's scientific colleagues enjoyed in a limited fashion a freedom denied to the rest of the people, the freedom of thought. In its ignorance, communist officialdom was unable to measure the significance of abstruse scientific research. Consequently it tended to leave scientists in peace as long as they behaved with caution and toed the party line – unless, that is, like Sakharov, they spoke out openly against the regime on overtly political grounds. Indeed, in his book *Black Holes and Time Warps*, Kip Thorne refers to the unnecessary fear he felt for the Russians Lifshitz and Khalatnikov when they courageously wanted to acknowledge the error of their claim that when a star implodes to form a black hole, it cannot create a singularity:

> For a theoretical physicist it is more than embarrassing to admit a major error in a published result. It is ego shattering . . . Though errors can be shattering for an American or European physicist, in the Soviet Union they were far worse. One's position in the pecking order of scientists was particularly important in the Soviet Union; it determined such things as possibilities for travel abroad and election to the Academy of Sciences, which in turn brought privileges such as near doubling of one's salary and a chauffeured limousine at one's beck and call . . .

Lifshitz's freedom to travel had already been curtailed when to his immense credit and with the greatest urgency, he had persuaded Kip on an earlier visit to Moscow in 1969 to smuggle a paper retracting the

The Sixth Form at St Albans High School. I am standing 2nd
from the right in the back row next to Gillian Phillips on my left
and Diana King on my right.

Wedding in Trinity Hall Cambridge, 15th July 1965. From left to right:
my grandma, Stephen's father, my mother, my brother Chris, Stephen, me,
Rob Donovan, Stephen's mother, Stephen's grandmother, my father.

Little St Mary's Lane.

Newly installed at 6, Little
St Mary's Lane, January 1966.

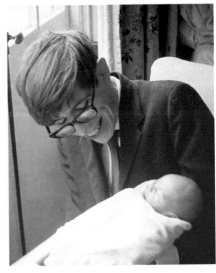

Stephen with Robert,
29th May 1967.

Above: 1967,
Washington State,
Stephen, Robert and
me with Gillian.

Right: Robert with
Stephen and my
father, St Albans,
March 1968.

Excursion *en famille*, Little
St Mary's Lane, 1971.

Stephen turning back
the waves, Brancaster,
summer 1971.

Right: Pirate look-out in the churchyard – Robert, Lucy and Inigo, spring 1972.

Below: Picnic on the Cam with my parents, Kip Thorne, Brandon, Lucette and Catherine Carter, John and Suzanne McClenahan and unidentified scientist with back to camera.

FRS, May 1974.

535 South Wilson Avenue, Pasadena, California, 1974.

With David Ireland and his son John (on my knee with Lucy),
California summer 1975.

Above: Christmas 1975 at West Road with Mary and Thelma Thatcher, my parents, Aunt Effie and Uncle Jack.

Left: David Hockney drawing Stephen and Lucy drawing Hockney, Cambridge, March 1978.

claim and admitting the mistake out of the Soviet Union. The paper was published in the West. As Kip thankfully remarked, 'The Soviet authorities never noticed.'

Stephen got on well with his Russian colleagues because they shared his intuitive approach to physics. Like him they were concerned only with the crux of any problem: the fine detail did not interest them and for Stephen, who carried all his theories in his head, fine detail was a hindrance to clarity of thought. Effectively, like him, they discarded all dead wood for a clearer view of the trees. They adapted this approach to whatever subject was under discussion, whether physics or literature. For me, their fascination lay in the impression they gave of having stepped out of the past, from the pages of Turgenev, Tolstoy or Chekhov. They talked about art and literature – their own and Shakespeare, Molière, Cervantes and Lorca as well. Like my student acquaintances in Franco's Spain, they recited poetry and composed verses for any occasion, including poems in Stephen's honour. To them, it seemed, one more repressive regime meant little because their country had always been governed by totalitarian regimes and had no experience of democracy, so, like generations of Russians before them, they found their solace in art, music and literature. In a society dominated by materialism, culture was their spiritual resource. Through them, I felt I could touch the soul of the country, the mournful soul of Mother Russia who always draws her exiled children back to her lonely rolling landscapes of rivers and birch forests. Their personalities shone out of the background of their bleak lives like the golden domes of the well-preserved though no longer functioning churches which would suddenly appear from behind the gaunt concrete blocks of modern Moscow, illuminating the grey dreariness with their gleaming brilliance.

These colleagues seemed just as happy to take us on cultural expeditions as to talk about science. Often our days were a combination of the two: scientific discussions would accompany our sightseeing. We wandered through the golden-domed cathedrals of the Kremlin, purged of their religious function by an officious communism which had not managed to eradicate their air of sanctity. We stood enraptured before the altar walls of icons and examined floors of semi-precious stone. We ambled through the art galleries, the Tretyakov and the Pushkin, and made the pilgimage to Tolstoy's homely wooden house with its stuffed bear standing on the creaky landing ready to receive visiting cards, and its little room at the back where the great man applied himself to his other passion, shoe-making. From Tolstoy's garden I picked up a handful of fallen maple leaves, rich brown, orange and yellow.

I asked to see a functioning church and was taken to both the extravagantly decorative, red, green and white church of St Nicholas in Moscow and the Novodievichy Monastery on the outskirts. With their wailing chants and mumbling, icon-kissing elderly devotees, neither could convey the essence of holiness with the power of the two decommissioned, empty little churches which stood abandoned outside our window at the Rossiya, dwarfed by the bulk of the hotel. One was brick-built, topped by a gold cross; the other was little more than a golden dome. One might have thought that in banning organized religion, the communist regime had actually encouraged the growth of an inner spirituality which was ever present for those who were receptive to it and alien to those who were not.

In the age of space travel, we were drawn back into the past through the lives of the dignified, poetic individuals with whom we were associating. There were few cars on their roads, their material possessions were scarce and their clothing drab. Health care was available to them free of charge but what we saw of it suggested that Soviet hospitals and doctors were to be avoided at all costs. During the second week Stephen needed a dose of hydrocobalamin, the fortifying vitamin injection which, in Cambridge, Sister Chalmers came to give him every fortnight. With some difficulty, his colleagues persuaded a doctor to come to the hotel. At first glance, I thought that it was Miss Meiklejohn, the terrifying, doughty games mistress from St Albans High School, who had walked into our room. She produced her equipment from a black bag, a steel kidney-shaped bowl, a metal syringe and a selection of re-usable needles. We both winced. Stoical as ever, Stephen sat quietly while she jabbed the bluntest of her needles into his thin flesh. Squeamish as ever, I turned away.

The endless, grey-raincoated queues in the shops where our friends bought their food brought back childhood memories of post-war London. Whether in GUM, the state department store on Red Square, or in neighbourhood shops, the system seemed expressly designed to discourage its customers from making any purchases whatsoever. First they had to queue to find out whether the desired items were available on the shelves, then they had to queue to pay for them in advance at the cash desk, and finally, clutching their receipts, they had to return to the original queue to claim their purchases. As privileged foreigners we could shop at the tourist Berioshka shops, which were greedy for our pounds and dollars. There, wooden toys, brightly coloured shawls, amber beads and painted trays abounded. I assumed that all the goods were produced in the Soviet Union until I chanced upon a pair of black leather gloves which bore the label 'made by the Coop, Blackburn, Lancs.'

In other Berioshka shops, foreign visitors could buy fresh and imported foodstuffs such as grapes, oranges and tomatoes, which for the average Russian were luxuries. If the food produced in the hotel, supposedly a first-class hotel, was any yardstick, the average Russian lived on an erratic subsistence diet of yogurt, ice-cream, hard-boiled eggs, black bread and cucumber. Such meat as the hotel managed to provide was usually either concealed in minute quantities in floury rissoles or was so tough and tasteless as to be good only for shoe leather. My smattering of Russian, learned in an evening class some years previously, was not much help in choosing from the numerous pages of the menu because, once we had made our selection, we would be told that it was 'off'.

For the first few days, we despaired of getting an edible square meal until one evening we discovered a restaurant secreted away on the top floor of the hotel, looking out over the red stars on the towers of the Kremlin. We found ourselves sitting near a Frenchman and watched in amazement as his meal was served. With the suave confidence of a Parisian dining in one of the best restaurants in his native city, he embarked on his first course. It consisted of a dish of caviar, smoked fish and cold meats, with a small glass of vodka. Then, while we pushed a flattened piece of chicken swimming in grease around our plates, his main course came to the table. Crisp brown slices of roast potato enveloped the *pièce de résistance*, a steaming, succulent baked sturgeon. Incredulously and enviously we watched him eat, savouring the aromas which wafted in our direction. It was not until he leaned back in his chair with a Gallic sigh and a gesture of deep satisfaction that it occurred to me that here was somebody with whom I could actually communicate. All I had to do was ask him in French where to find sturgeon and caviar on the menu. Obligingly, he indicated items 32 and 54, thus holding out the delectable promise of an acceptable diet for the rest of our stay. It was our bad luck that the very next day, the top-floor restaurant closed down and items 32 and 54 never featured on the menus of the other restaurants.

Mistrust of the next meal became a constant preoccupation during that visit. With some anticipation we looked forward optimistically to one of its highlights, dinner in the revolving restaurant of the Tower of the Seven Heaven, a radio tower, on the outskirts of the city. The tower, a space-age status symbol, was closely guarded – supposedly because of its strategic importance – and only special guests were allowed to dine there. Even they were not permitted to approach the tower directly but were frisked at the perimeter fence some 50 yards away, then led along an underground tunnel to the lift. Cameras were forbidden, we were told, since during the course of its heavenly revolutions, the restaurant passed by a milk factory. For 'milk', read 'armaments', Kip said. The milk factory came round with disconcerting frequency as we tucked into our first good meal in weeks. Nor was the ride a smooth one – the tower lurched drunkenly half-way through each cycle – which may explain why Stephen and I spent the next twenty-four hours competing for occupation of the bathroom.

It was no surprise to us that our Russian hosts were not at liberty to invite us into their own homes but there was one notable exception. On our last evening in Moscow we were invited to dinner at the home of Professor Isaac Khalatnikov, a beaming, expansive character whom we had first met at the General Relativity conference in London just before our marriage in 1965. The taxi delivered us unexpectedly to an imposing block of flats close to the river in the centre of Moscow. We had heard from contemporaries of the difficulties of family life in Moscow. Apartments were scarce. Entitlement to housing depended on one's standing in the Party. Newly-weds frequently had to live with their parents in two-bedroomed flats. Later, families would often take in surviving members of the older generation, particularly the *babushka*, whose presence was well-nigh essential, even in such cramped conditions, because it was she who ran the household and cared for the children while her daughter or daughter-in-law was out at work. We were astonished therefore to find that the Khalatnikovs' apartment was exceptionally large, consisting of several spacious, well-furnished rooms complete with television and hi-fi. Furthermore the food on the table was a veritable banquet which would not have been out of place at a Western dinner-party. The servings of caviar, meat, vegetables, salads and fruit were lavish and tastefully presented. Stephen and I were appreciative but mystified. Why, in a society which trumpeted its equality, did this family enjoy such an ostentatiously indulgent lifestyle?

Kip provided the answer: it had nothing whatsoever to do with Isaac Khalatnikov's distinguished scientific status, it was the consequence of his wife's connections. Valentina Nikolaievna, a rather sturdy blonde lady for whom my gift of delicate costume jewellery was singularly inappropriate, was none other than the Daughter of a Hero of the Revolution. In a nation where all were said to be equal, some were more equal than others. By virtue of her birth, Valentina Nikolaievna was entitled to all the prerogatives of the new aristocracy, including preferential housing and the right to buy her food in the Berioshka shops.

The maple leaves that I had collected from Tolstoy's garden proved to be an eloquent metaphor of the Moscow we saw in those weeks of our visit. It was with genuine relief that we joined in the cheers of the passengers when the London-bound plane took off in a swirling snowstorm in mid-September. Like the snow, the autumn leaves were harbingers of winter in a country where all those freedoms of speech, expression, thought, movement, which we took for granted were permanently frozen. Yet their vivid colours sang of our irrepressible friends, those courageous people stranded in that political wasteland. As winter approached in Cambridge, we realized that together with the leaves and the souvenirs, the wooden dancing bears and hand-painted china, we had brought back with us an unwelcome legacy of Soviet oppression. For several weeks after our return, we were unable to communicate freely in our own home for fear that the walls might be listening to us. If this was a measure of the psychological pressure that our friends lived under all the time, our admiration for them could only increase. Thrilled as we were to be back with our children, such a realization was sobering. How, we asked, would we cope in those circumstances?

At Christmas-time that year, my mother and I took the children to see the London version of the *Nutcracker* ballet at the Festival Hall. Lucy was entranced by the spectacle and thereafter insisted on being called Clara, after the child heroine of the ballet. She spent every spare minute dancing to a well-worn record and devised her own version of the Cossack dance by running the length of the living-room and kicking one small leg in the air before turning and racing back to the other end. Like father, like son, Robert was less enchanted by the performance and would have preferred his father's favourite Christmas-time treat, the pantomime. He fidgeted his way through the first half of the ballet and no sooner had the second half begun than he dragged his grandma out of the auditorium on the irrefutable pretext of having drunk too much orange squash in the interval. They were not allowed to return to their seats so my mother had to make do with a closed-circuit screening of the ballet in the foyer while Robert contentedly watched the barges plying up and down the Thames.

CHAPTER TWENTY-FOUR

A Chill Wind

THAT WINTER IN Cambridge we faced our own set of pressures, though ours were pressures of a psychological and physical rather than a political nature. The conference in Poland and the visit to Moscow, combined with the previous year's discoveries at Les Houches, had opened up new possibilities and new problems for black hole research. The secret aim of all physicists was to uncover the philosopher's stone, the as yet unformulated unified field theory which would unite all the branches of physics. It would reconcile the large-scale structure of the universe, about which Stephen and George Ellis had written a book, with the small-scale structures of quantum mechanics or elementary particle physics, and the theory of electromagnetism. Black holes held out the tantalizing prospect that they might hold the key to the first stage of this particular quest – through a solution to the enigmatic resemblance which their laws appeared to suggest between general relativity and thermodynamics.

Such was the lure of this goal that not only was Stephen intent on following up his Moscow discussions with consultations worldwide at every available conference, he increasingly spent his every waking hour immersed in such deliberations. The question of travels abroad came up with disturbing regularity. I repeated the canon of my excuses which began to ring more and more hollow by comparison with the importance and the strength of Stephen's ambition. It sounded feeble of me to claim that I could not contemplate a repetition of the strain of leaving the children when the future of physics was at stake.

At the same time, I was confused by Stephen's tendency to spend quite so many hours in the evenings and at weekends like Rodin's *Thinker* with his head bent low, resting on his right hand, transported to another dimension, lost to me and to the children playing around him.

However compelling the intellectual challenge of black hole physics, I could not fathom such depths of self-absorption, despite his phenomenal powers of concentration. Logically I would at first suppose that he was engrossed in a mathematical problem. In a tentative appeal for a reassuring word which would allow me to carry on calmly with my chores, I would cheerfully ask him what was on his mind. Since this question would often elicit no reply, I would quickly become anxious, afraid that something was amiss. Perhaps he was uncomfortable in his wheelchair? Was he not feeling well? Had I upset him in some way – perhaps by refusing to go with him to the next conference? As he would not reply or merely gave an unconvincing shake of the head, my imagination would start to run riot as I began to suspect that all these factors and many more, not least dejection at his deteriorating condition, were oppressing him unbearably. The position he adopted was, after all, that traditionally used by artists to depict depression.

Undeniably his speech was becoming indistinct, necessitating boring sessions with a speech therapist to try to redress the slur. Some people, whom we preferred to think of as deaf or stupid, could not understand him at all. He required my help with the minutiae of every personal need, dressing and bathing, as well as with larger movements. He had to be lifted bodily in and out of the wheelchair, the car, the bath, the bed. Food had to be cut into small morsels so that he could eat with a spoon, and mealtimes were protracted. The stairs in our house were now a major obstacle. He could still pull himself up – that in itself was recommended exercise – but he depended on the reassurance of having someone standing behind him for support. It was natural that when away from home, he wanted to have me with him all the time. Pent-up guilt at my own reluctance to take advantage of all those wonderful opportunities to travel the globe and frustration at the lack of communication would tie me in knots of anxiety and despair. Like the traveller who had the misfortune to fall into a black hole, I was stretched, tugged and pulled like a piece of spaghetti by emotional forces beyond my control.

A couple of days later, Stephen would emerge from his isolation. With a winning, triumphant smile, he would announce that he had solved yet another major problem in physics. It was only after the event that these episodes became a joke. As each new situation was marginally different from the previous one, I never learned to recognize the symptoms. At the time I could only worry that if I took no notice of them,

Stephen might really be feeling unwell and would think that I did not sympathize with him. On the other hand, if I allowed them to make me depressed and anxious, he might accuse me of being morose and irritable. Each time I would congratulate Stephen on his success, but secretly I realized that the children and I had joined battle with that irresistible goddess whose power I had first encountered in America in 1965, the goddess of physics who deprived children of their fathers and wives of their husbands.

For Stephen those periods of intense concentration may have been useful exercises in cultivating that silent, inner strength which would enable him to think in eleven dimensions. I could not tell whether it was oblivion or indifference to my need for communication that sealed him off with such impenetrably hermetic effect, and for me those periods were sheer torture, especially when, as sometimes happened, they were accompanied by long sessions of Wagnerian opera, particularly the *Ring* cycle, played at full volume on the radio or the record player. It was then, as I felt my own voice stifled and my own spontaneity suppressed inside me, that I grew to hate Wagner. The music was powerful, so powerful that I was irresistibly drawn into the sensual luxury of those hypnotic chords and thrilling modulations, but my daily round and common task did not allow me a single moment's respite from the unending demands of shopping, cooking, housework, childcare and Stephencare. From the kitchen or the bathroom or the play-room, I would be all too conscious of the power of the music, insinuating itself, asserting itself ever more insistently. I would try to ignore its beckoning strains, recoiling from it, knowing it to be far too manipulative for my confused state of mind. Where did the truth of those enthralling but ambiguous harmonies and discords lie? I was not strong enough for their mesmerizing influence and doubted the sincerity both of their charm and their inveigling nuances which presented my emotional range with too severe a test. The open clarity of Mediterranean culture was my touchstone, not the dark menace of northern myth where all heroes were doomed to premature death, and chaos and evil triumphed. Stephen might be as dominated by this demonic force as he was by physics, since both for him had become a religion, but I had to keep my feet on the ground. If I allowed myself to yield to the sombre tyranny of that music, the structure I had built around me would collapse and crumble to dust. Wagner came to represent an evil genius, the philosopher of the master race, the spirit behind Auschwitz, a threat to my optimism and potentially an alienating force in our marriage. The philosophy implicit in his music ran contrary to my simple belief that faith and perseverance could produce good out of misfortune.

Although in the early 1970s we attended the whole *Ring* cycle at the Coliseum and *Tristan and Isolde* at Covent Garden, our diet of entertainment thankfully was not limited to Wagner but was vastly eclectic. It ranged from Wagner, Verdi and Mozart in the opera houses, through performances of the Elgar oratorios, the *Dream of Gerontius* and the *Kingdom*, in King's Chapel or Monteverdi's *Vespers* in St Albans Abbey, to *Princess Ida* at the Arts Theatre, since, truly broad in his tastes, Stephen was a Gilbert and Sullivan fan as well as a Wagnerian. There was also a performance of *Hansel and Gretel* in January 1973 which terrified Robert so much that he took refuge under his seat for the whole evening. Apart from Wagner, Stephen's favourite entertainment was the *Footlights*, the university review in summer, and the pantomime in winter. For both of these he suspended his usually acerbic critical judgement. I often found the *Footlights* tedious since the standard of humour never quite matched up to the unrealistic expectations aroused by the *Beyond the Fringe* generation, and as for the pantomime, the smutty jokes wore thin through constant sniggering repetition.

To occupy those other solitary evenings at home when Stephen was immersed in thought but Wagner was mercifully suppressed, when the trappings of the day were cleared away and the children finally in bed, I bought a very compact piano on the pretext that Robert should start having lessons. In an environment where everyone was so naturally accomplished, it was embarrassing to admit that I really wanted to have lessons myself: I passionately longed to be able to play Chopin and Schumann, those nineteenth-century miniaturists whose music touched my heart. I took some lessons with Mr Hubert Greenwood, a retired school-teacher who, sympathizing with my ambitions, sensitively refrained from telling me that in my late twenties I was too old to learn to play. Rising to the challenge, he trained me in the basics of theory and harmony and, to my satisfaction, allowed me to choose my own repertoire. Robert also had lessons, with a young teacher who drew pictures for him of fairies dancing in the treble clef and giants stomping about in the bass.

Since he had started school, Robert, previously so happy and lively, was becoming much quieter and more reserved. He was only four-and-a-quarter when, according to local education policy, he was obliged to start school. I was convinced that this was too early and some time later when I read that the psychological difference between a four-year-old and a five-year-old is the same as the difference between a seven-year-old and an eleven-year-old, I knew that my reservations were well justified. In the more liberal climate of the late 1990s it is being acknowledged that starting formal school at the age of four is actually damaging to a child's development. Robert was a shy little boy and, when asked what he did in the lunch-hour, his reply, casually delivered, made me very sad. 'Oh,' he said with a shrug, 'I just sit on the steps.'

His primary school had an excellent reputation for bringing out the best in fast-learning children from academic backgrounds and was essentially a literary school where those children who could read quickly made rapid progress. Some years later Lucy, bubbling with creative and literary talent, flourished there. Robert, however, had great difficulty in reading. I feared that this might be a delayed effect of the medicine-swallowing episode, but my mother-in-law's comments were comforting. It was obvious that Robert was clearly just a chip off the old block, she said, because Stephen had not learnt to read until he was seven or eight years old. I then fully understood why the winter spent with the Graves family in Majorca had left such a profound impression on Stephen. If at the age of nine he had only just learnt to read, the daily sessions spent analysing the *Book of Genesis* under the eagle eye of Robert Graves must have been sheer torture. They certainly would have been so for Robert. Stephen wisely maintained that it did not matter what Robert read so long as he learned to read, whereupon every imaginable joke book and *Dennis the Menace* made their entry to the house and each mealtime was accompanied with interminable jokes of the 'Knock, knock', 'Who's there?' variety. Robert's reading improved dramatically.

Dyslexia was not a condition that was recognized in educational circles in the early 1970s. It was only thanks to the publicity given to it by the actress Susan Hampshire, herself a sufferer, that it came to the public notice. It was claimed that both Leonardo da Vinci and Einstein were probably dyslexic. We suspected that Stephen was dyslexic and were fairly sure that Robert was too, but, apart from a remedial reading class, there was no specific help for dyslexics in the state system. They were classed at best as lazy, at worst as backward, slow learners, already at the age of five consigned to a second-rate future. I knew that Robert was not backward: this was the child who at the age of four, when we were gardening one afternoon, had asked quite seriously,

'Mummy, who was God born inside?' This was the child who, at five, had sat down at the piano to explain the concept of minus numbers to me. 'Look, Mummy,' he said, 'all these notes going up from middle C are plus numbers and all the ones going down from middle C are minus numbers.'

I was sure that the emphasis placed by the school on literary rather than numerical skills was wrong for Robert. A new teacher who came to the school when he was just six announced that she was going to start an advanced maths group. I pleaded with her to let him join the group. She clearly found it hard not to laugh. 'But he can't read!' she remonstrated. 'How can he possibly do maths?' I persevered. 'Please just let him try.' With the greatest scepticism, she agreed to let him join the class for just three weeks. During that time Robert did not appear to be having any trouble with the advanced maths and he seemed much less tense. At the end of the three weeks, he brought a message home from Mrs Mehorney, the new teacher, saying that she would like to talk to me after school. She came out to meet me at the school gate. 'Mrs Hawking, I owe you an apology,' she began fulsomely, 'I really didn't think that Robert would be able to cope with the advanced maths when you asked me to let him come into the class, but I really must apologize because I was so wrong. He is extraordinarily good at maths and is way ahead of all the others.' But the maths class came to an untimely end after only two terms when Mrs Mehorney left to have a baby, and then Robert was back at square one.

As Stephen and I had blithely assumed that, in accordance with our socialist principles, our children would be educated in state schools, we were now presented with a resounding clash of loyalties. The needs of our child were not compatible with our political principles. The state system so far had not served Robert well. He needed to be praised for the subjects he could do well, notably maths, and he needed encouragement, not castigation, in those he found difficult, notably reading and writing. Only in the private sector could we be sure that the classes would be small enough for him to receive proper attention. The sonorously entitled Fellowship for Distinction in Science did not pay a large enough salary for us to be able to afford private education, nor did the Research Assistantships to which Stephen was subsequently appointed – at the Institute of Astronomy in 1972 after Fred Hoyle's departure, and also at the Department of Applied Mathematics in 1973.

But by another of those ironic twists of fate, the finance became available, in a way that we rather regretted.

In 1970, shortly after Lucy's birth, Stephen's lonely Aunt Muriel had died. Instead of enjoying her new-found freedom after her mother's death, she had simply wasted away. The money she might have spent on herself, by going off on a round-the-world trip for instance, she saved cautiously to provide for the uncertainties of the future. The future never came and the money was left to some of her great-nephews and nieces, among them Robert on whom she particularly doted. Of itself, the inheritance was not sufficient to finance long years of education but when set to work with an equal share from Stephen's father, it amounted to enough to buy a modest house which could be let quite profitably. Half the rent went to Stephen's parents while the other half contributed substantially to Robert's school fees. Cambridge was a good place for such a venture because properties were still fairly cheap and the floating population of visiting scholars meant that there was a constant demand for rented properties. With my experience of renovating our own house, I was put in charge of the project.

The house we bought, a two-bedroomed Victorian terraced house on the other side of Cambridge, had none of the charm of number 6 Little St Mary's Lane. It was conveniently placed, however, and promised to be attractive to visiting scholars. On a less ambitious scale, I repeated the renovation exercise with the help of an inexpensive but rather elusive builder, another of Thelma Thatcher's finds. His delightful manner suggested Irish origins though his accent was strictly East Anglian. I did much of the redecorating myself to economize, equipped the house with the necessary furnishings and advertised it for let. Although I had put a great deal of time and effort into the preparations, it was only when the house was let and supposedly off my hands that I realized what a burden this particular project was to become. The first tenants, a young couple, celebrated their domesticity by taking their oily motor-bike to pieces on the new carpet in the living-room. The next tenants deliberately flouted the clause in the tenancy agreement banning pets. When I called on them soon after they had moved in, a huge labrador came bounding out of the house to greet me. Its owner hauled it back inside and with a flood of expletives at my hesitant protests, slammed the door in my face. The whole house had to be redecorated at the end of each tenancy. This insight into the squalor of other people's lives was disheartening but since I was all too conscious of the need to save money for the ever-mounting school fees, I had no option but to take up the paintbrush for an intensive week of solo decorating once or twice a year. Sometimes this exercise had to be carried out even more frequently, as for instance one summer, when the wife of a visiting professor wanted the perfectly clean house redecorated in honour of her mother-in-law's pending visit.

Such taxing activity and wearing preoccupations left less and less time and energy for the thesis. I had succeeded in assembling material for the first chapter and was pleased to have alighted on a few original ideas of my own. I applied the idea of the mother figure of *La Celestina* to the *madre* of the *kharjas*, suggesting that the *madre* was more likely to be a go-between than the girl's real mother. I traced some close verbal reminiscences between the *kharjas* and the *Song of Solomon* and detected striking similarities between the *kharjas* and the Mozarabic hymns, the hymns of the native Christian populace under Moorish domination.

With luck, all other things being equal, I might be able to snatch an hour for the thesis in the morning while Lucy was at nursery school after I had taken Stephen to the Department. Keeping up with my own research stretched me to the limit of my capabilities. There was no longer any chance of broadening my grasp of other areas of medieval research, let alone the other fields and topics which came up for discussion at the Lucy Cavendish dinners. I was out of touch with the political and international scene and had scant time for reading. I had little to offer and little to gain other than a depressing awareness of my own inadequacy from either Lucy Cavendish or the Dronkes' medieval seminars. When I did attend one or the other, I had to bluff my way through discussions and conversations or else maintain a dull silence. It was an uncomfortable situation in which I felt a fraud. As I felt myself sinking further and further into the mire of my own intellectual incompetence, my attendance at both lapsed.

In Lucy Cavendish, I had just two friends, Pat Coppola and Hannah Scolnicov, with whom I felt at ease. Pat, an American mother of two children, was struggling to take up medicine in her early thirties, yet she never lost that totally un-British quality, the smiling unselfconscious spontaneity which enables Americans to reach out to other people with genuine interest. Hannah, an Elizabethan scholar from Jerusalem, was revelling in the respite which she found in Cambridge from the tensions of her war-torn homeland. She and I discovered that we had much in common. Although our circumstances were inevitably disparate, we were both trying to live normal lives and bring up our three-year-olds, Robert and Anat, against a background of tension and uncertainty. When we met, I had just given birth to Lucy and Hannah was expecting her second child. By the time Ariel was born the following summer, we had become friends for life. Moreover, in Hannah's husband Shmuel, a classical philosopher, Stephen had found an intellectual sparring partner. Both Hannah and Shmuel were so much more intuitive and perceptive than many people who had known us longer and supposedly better. When Shmuel's sabbatical year came to an end and they nervously returned to Israel with their young family, there was even less incentive for me to attend Lucy Cavendish and I became even more isolated and out of touch.

It did not matter much. Stephen's career was so obviously more important than mine. He was bound to make a big splash in the pond of physics whereas I would be lucky to make the smallest ripple on the surface of language studies. And, as I reminded myself often, I did have the consolation of the children, both of them lively and funny, loving and adorable. Many people who might well have stared cruelly at Stephen, absorbed by the freakishishness of disability – the same people who would have called him a cripple – were visibly nonplussed by the sight of a seriously handicapped father with such strikingly beautiful children, each one a miracle of lucid perfection. Stephen gained confidence through his pride in them. He could confound those doubting onlookers by announcing, 'These are my children.' The acute joy that we shared in their purity and innocence, their quaint sayings and their sense of wonder, gave us in turn moments of profound tenderness. In those moments, the bond between us strengthened till it embraced not just ourselves but our home and our family, reaching out to include all those people we valued most. The family, our family, had become my *raison d'être*.

Doubtless the Fellows of Gonville and Caius were right to exclude wives from High Table. What, after all, could a wife like me contribute to the high-falutin conversation of the Fellows except the trivia of motherhood? How could one expect eminent scholars who had never so much as paid an electricity bill in their lives and who spent all day and every day in the University Library poring over the literary criticism of the literary criticism of the literary criticism of some obscure text, to appreciate the poetry of blossoming new life or the anguish of watching a life in its prime being whittled away to the fragility of a straw in the wind?

I comforted myself that no amount of academic research or recognition could have equalled the creative fulfilment I derived from my family. If sometimes the long hours of child care and babytalk seemed unremitting, I was well compensated by the privilege of rediscovering the world, its wonders and inconsistencies through the eyes of small children. Happily my parents also revelled in this pleasure. Never were grandparents so keen to enjoy their grandchildren and never were grandchildren so indulged by their grandparents. The children brought my parents some light relief from their own anxieties, since they were very concerned for my grandmother whose health and memory were failing fast. When eventually she moved to St Albans from her home in Norwich, it was too late for her to settle with confidence anywhere else and all too soon, in her disorientation, she fell and broke an arm. I already knew when I waved goodbye to her one Sunday afternoon in early December 1973 that I should never see her again. I wept all week for that brave, gentle spirit whom I loved so much. It came as a great sorrow but no surprise when my mother rang the following Friday, 7 December, to tell me that she had died in her sleep.

CHAPTER TWENTY-FIVE

Balancing Act

THE GRADUAL DISAPPEARANCE of cherished friends from our social scene did nothing to alleviate my flagging spirits. My schoolfriends and college friends I saw rarely; either they had gone abroad or were raising families in other cities. The friends of the past few years were branching out, leaving Cambridge to climb the career ladder wherever the jobs happened to be. The Donovans had left Cambridge for Edinburgh where Rob was to become Professor of Physical Chemistry. Thereafter our contact with them and my little god-daughter Jane was sporadic, although, when we were able to meet, the strength of our friendship resumed in as lively and stimulating a manner as ever. We stayed with them outside Edinburgh in the summer of '73, just before the trip to Moscow. As always in the company of old friends, our conversations ranged far and wide, recalling those Sunday afternoon visits soon after our marriage. We would gossip about the Cambridge scene, the latest convulsions in Gonville and Caius, developments in science, the complexity of grant applications and friends dispersed across the globe.

When we spoke of the forthcoming Moscow trip, Rob insisted that we should not be lulled by lack of media coverage into supposing that in the post-Cuba era the arms race had disappeared into the attic of history. Surreptitiously, both Superpowers were developing a huge array of ever more sophisticated weaponry. Although the threat of nuclear warfare still hung over us all each time the Superpowers, like snarling dragons, caught a whiff of each other's presence in some contested corner of the world, it had not occurred to me, in my political naivety, that they were actually enlarging and refining their already enormous nuclear arsenals.

Rob's remarks worried and angered me. Now that we had children it was not enough to say that there would be consolation in all being blown up together. I was not prepared to stand back and let that monstrous apocalypse destroy the lives of my precious offspring. But what could I – or we – do? There was little use in appealing to the scientists who had developed these weapons in the 1940s and 1950s, many of whom were known to us on both sides of the Iron Curtain, because the decisions were now in the hands of politicians, the Wagnerian Hagens and the Alberichs, who were alarmingly untrustworthy: the devious Nixon in the United States and the inscrutable Brezhnev in the Soviet Union. It was almost harder to digest these unpalatable truths against the pristine background of Scotland's purple-headed mountains where the honey-laden air sang of biblical simplicity than in any man-made urban setting. Who could live at peace with the realization that the works of man, an ant on the face of Creation, were capable of destroying the timeless beauty of those hills?

The Carters, with whom we also used to spend so many weekend afternoons, had moved to France with their baby daughter, Catherine. There Brandon had taken up a research post at the Observatoire de Paris at Meudon. Rather like the Cambridge Observatory, the Observatoire was set in the grounds of a château but unlike its Cambridge counterpart, it commanded magnificent views over Paris. I missed Lucette greatly for many reasons, quite apart from the fact that she was the only person I knew in Cambridge with whom I could speak French. A respected mathematician, she was clever and articulate without ever being pretentious. Her sincere interest in people and her enthusiastic sense of family were not typical of the Cambridge academics with whom she had mixed. She was musical, imaginative and blessed with a delicate sense of poetry. It was Lucette who through her rhapsodic delight in the trees and flowers, colours and perfumes of the churchyard, introduced me to Proust.

The greatest shock came with the loss of the Ellises. Their departure was much more distressing because they were not simply leaving Cambridge to go to another job. They were leaving because their marriage had broken down. We identified so closely with them that when George and Sue separated, our own family seemed to be under threat. Our two families, each with two small children, had shared so much that we had become part of each other's support system. We had bought and renovated our houses, had our babies, gone on holiday and attended conferences, almost in tandem. On the one hand, George and Stephen had written a book, *The Large Scale Structure of Space Time*, together

and on the other, Sue, who was Lucy's godmother, and I had conferred and confided in each other over many of the crises of young
motherhood. George resembled Stephen in that he too could cut himself
off from the basic realities of the outside world, plunging out of the
reach of his family deep into the realms of physics. The many shared
and parallel experiences had built an interdependence into our marriages and when theirs failed, the solidity of ours was shaken.

Less obvious than Stephen's disability, the major challenge that faced
the Ellises was their self-imposed exile from their tragic homeland,
South Africa. There came the stage when George could no longer
ignore the call to return to South Africa, believing himself to be the
man of the moment. Sue, in contrast, could not reconcile herself to
bringing up her children in the midst of such injustice. They found
themselves in an impasse from which separation offered the only way
out. The involvement of the goddess physics was an implicit element in
their separation. Sue went to live in Germany and, after completion of
The Large Scale Structure of Space Time, George went back to South
Africa to make his contribution to the war against apartheid. The blow
was bitter. I tried rather clumsily to act as intermediary in the hope of
bringing about a reconciliation but it was too late. Quite apart from
genuinely wanting to help them in their all-too-painful circumstances,
my actions were not motivated entirely by disinterest because I myself
was not sure of our own way ahead if we were to be deprived not only
of George's physical help with Stephen, but also of the strong moral
reinforcement of their friendship.

All those friendships with couples who had now left Cambridge had
been formed in special circumstances. They were the product of
Stephen's contacts in the Department or in one or other of the colleges.
He had shared interests, usually scientific, with the husbands while I
discovered common interests with their wives. On the departure of the
Ellises, our very close, foursome friendships petered out. Although we
were on good terms with many of the younger Fellows of Caius and their
wives and had made new friends among the more recent postgraduates in
the Department, a subtle change occurred. I made many women friends
through the children but the husbands and fathers of those families did
not necessarily have much in common with Stephen. Often, because
they had not been in close professional contact with him, they were
understandably deterred by the difficulties of communication. Moreover I tended to make friends among people with whom there was a

perceptible bond of sympathy. They either had cause for sorrow in their own lives or they had some special knowledge of the needs of the disabled. Of all those several valuable friendships, two in particular, the most loyal and the most lasting, had very relevant points of contact with Stephen.

Among Constance Willis's team of assistants – 'Daddy's exercisers', as Robert called them – there was a slim, fairhaired girl of about my own age, Caroline Chamberlain. In the summer of 1970 Caroline ceased to practice as a physiotherapist because she was expecting a baby at the same time as I was expecting Lucy. As she lived nearby in the Leys School – the local boys' public school where her husband taught geography – we kept in touch and were brought into closer friendship after our little daughters were born. My mind was focused ever more exclusively on the problems of disability, for it sometimes seemed that a trap was closing over all of us, over the children and me as well as over Stephen. Information was pretty well non-existent and I began to depend on Caroline's fund of professional knowledge for guidance. At once practical and cheerful yet very sensitive, she was well aware of the array of difficulties we faced at every turn and would do her best to come up with an answer, be it a more comfortable posture, an item of equipment – such as a wheelchair cushion or a caliper – or the address of some useful pioneering organization. Even when Peter – known as Chippie, the most popular master in the school – became the house-master of West House, one of the boarding houses, and Caroline, now the mother of two small daughters, was obliged to entertain the boarders to breakfast on Sunday mornings, she continued to find the time to search out solutions and suggestions for our problems.

At the school gate, that traditional meeting place for mothers, I found another stalwart friend in Joy Cadbury whose children, Thomas and Lucy, were the same age as Robert and our Lucy. Joy's retiring gentleness confounded my perceived image of an Oxford graduate. Far from arrogantly vaunting her intellectual prowess at the expense of others, she played it down as if she were embarrassed by it, as if it were of absolutely no relevance to her present lifestyle. The daughter of a Devon doctor, she had fulfilled her real ambition – to become a pediatric nurse – after graduating from Oxford. Joy took our situation deeply to heart, always ready to take the children off my hands in times of crisis, always ready to give an unobtrusive hand when the strain was over-whelming. She was not unfamiliar with motor neurone disease, the incurable degenerative illness about which so little was known, for 250 miles away, her own elderly father was suffering its terminal stages.

In Devon, not far from Joy's family home in Barnstaple, I had other allies in my brother and his wife Penelope whom he had married in 1971. After Chris's first temporary job in Brighton, they had moved to Devon when Chris joined a dental practice in Tiverton. Penelope had trained as a drama teacher and prior to her marriage had taught in a secondary school in London's East End. She did not cultivate the expansive, overblown personality common to many drama teachers, rather her artistic nature showed itself in her interest in character and relationships. When we met, which was not very often, she and I would talk for hours about personalities, influences and emotions and the ways people communicated with each other, subjects which in the Hawking family were virtually proscribed. In Chris and his wife, I found a deep well of understanding and support; the drawback was that they lived so far away.

Not all new acquaintances could afford to bring me the unstinting encouragement which I found in Caroline, Joy and my relations. Some of my new friends were as marginalized as I was, though in different ways. Often they themselves needed support and turned to me for help. From the vantage-point of the physical illness which dominated our lives and which was so immediately obvious and clearly defined, I had only occasionally in the past glimpsed other tragedies which caused people to despair. With greater maturity I began to awaken to the many causes and complications of suffering. Some people were struggling with their emotions and with poverty after a traumatic divorce, others were alienated from their families, others were simply a long way from home. Many felt resentful and hurt, as though life had cheated them of their expectations. These situations and many others, at a remove from my own, I could regard with a certain objectivity and tried to give the sort of sensible encouragement which people like Joy and Caroline gave me. Ironically, situations which were closer to my own were much harder to deal with.

Some well-intentioned friends promised to introduce me to a woman whose husband had been paralysed in a car crash. I looked forward to this meeting, hoping that we might be able to bring each other the consolation of shared experience. It was hard even to mention the problems – the unending responsibility, the emotional strain, the aching fatigue of bringing up two small children unaided at the same time as caring for a seriously disabled person – without pangs of disloyalty. Stephen never talked about the illness, nor did he ever complain. His heroic stoicism increased my sense of guilt at even giving voice to the slightest misgivings. But it was the very lack of communication that was hardest to bear, sometimes harder than all the physical stresses and strains combined. Whereas I had hoped that there would be fulfilment in unity of purpose, in fighting together against the odds stacked so heavily against us, now it seemed that I had become little more than a drudge, effectively reduced to that role which in Cambridge academic circles epitomized a woman's place. When I could no longer contain my frustration and gave vent to it in tearful, angry outbursts, Stephen would attribute these periods of tension to the vagaries of the menstrual cycle or to the effects of the various pollen allergies to which I was susceptible. It was true that in the spring, tree pollens had a strangely depressive effect, unknown to medical science, on my system, but that was not the whole story. Fundamentally I knew that I needed help – physical help and emotional support – in keeping my beloved little family going.

On one occasion I summoned the courage to broach my woes – with the utmost caution – to Thelma Thatcher. Her response, if not a rebuff, was decisive in its severity. 'Jane,' she said, 'I say to you what I said to Mary when she came home from that conference feeling sorry for herself.' (Mary had been to a conference of people who, like her, were of restricted growth.) She continued, 'I said to Mary, count your blessings.' Like Mary, I knew that her answer was honest. She was right. We both had much to be thankful for – not least in my case, my family and Stephen's dedicated hard work and courage. Neither Mary nor I was destitute and neither of us had any alternative but to accept our lot, keep faith, work hard and make the best of it, as Thelma herself had had to do on losing her two infant sons. After all I was not unhappy: I derived intense happiness from the two most beautiful and enchanting children anybody could wish for – Robert with his silvery-blond hair, neat round face and wide enquiring eyes, and Lucy, auburn-haired with a pink and white skin as soft as swansdown. I was just tired – oh, so tired, exhausted from broken nights, back-breaking physical strain and the constant nagging sense of worry and responsibility. I was ashamed at having even attempted to unburden myself and slunk away to count my blessings as instructed.

Practical as ever, Thelma Thatcher called by the next day. 'I've been thinking, dear, you must have more help. I'm just going to call on Constance Babington-Smith, shall I ask her to send her cleaning woman along to you?' Constance Babington-Smith's cleaning lady, bustling Mrs Teversham, was a treasure of the first order, as was her successor, tall, angular Winnie Brown, a year or so later. Once a week, cleanliness and order were restored to our household. However, the housework was but a part of the problem. I still needed a sympathetic listener, someone who would patiently listen to my intimate anxieties with understanding and without reprimand. I was not expecting the flourish of a magic wand which would suddenly put everything to rights, but I did cherish the hope that perhaps the new contact, the woman with the disabled husband, would be the person who would listen and respond with more understanding than anyone else.

As I had never before encountered anyone in a similar situation, I was anxious to know how she dealt with the difficulties, the practical dimension of caring more or less single-handedly with severe disability and the emotional dimensions of insecurity and the onerous feeling of total responsibility for the well-being of very vulnerable people. Perhaps she could suggest ways of getting extra help on our very limited budget. I did not, of course, expect her to have an answer for the additional problem of life with an exemplary physicist for whom every topic for discussion, even on mundane family matters, was a potential battle-ground for an intellectual contest of wits which he was bound to win. I was confident, nonetheless, that we could pool our resources and give each other moral support.

We met and we talked on several occasions. It soon became obvious, however, that she felt the trauma of her own situation so keenly that there could be little worthwhile communication between us. My bright, positive vision was itself getting rather tarnished. Far from polishing it, that association threatened to cloud the vision with despondency. My attempts to appear optimistic and confident sounded trite and clichéd, more and more like a sham in fact, though I had to cling to them as they were fundamental to my way of life. She stayed in Cambridge for a couple of months and then went to Australia with a new partner, leaving her husband in a home for the disabled.

She had come to her own decisions, made her own choice in har-rowing circumstances. I identified easily with her in her circumstances but I could not allow myself to identify with her in her decisions. She was entitled to respect for the conclusions she had reached but her solutions brought me no comfort nor did they illuminate my way forward. In the last resort, I had to admit that Thelma Thatcher's stark philosophy of counting one's blessings was the only valid course. I had pledged myself to Stephen. In so doing I had committed myself to trying to provide him with a normal life. It was beginning to appear that that pledge meant keeping up a façade of normality, however abnormal life might become for the rest of us in the process. I had no intention of reneging on my pledge but, far from being reinforcing, isolated glimpses into the lives of others – such as the one I had just experienced – served to emphasize rather than alleviate my consuming isolation. Long ago we had discovered that there was no organization, no medical authority to whom we could turn for enlightened advice and assistance. Now, since there was no one to whom I could turn for personal support in finding a path through the maze of problems, I resolved to trust my own counsel, steering well clear of unsettling people and situations, pretending more than ever that ours was just a normal family, beset with a difficulty which was best kept confined to the background.

Even so, unavoidable incidents, casual phrases, chance circumstances would keep occurring. Sometimes they came from the most unexpected quarters. For example, when Stephen's father and I were signing the papers to set up an inheritance trust for Robert from Aunt Muriel's will, the solicitor asked for the names of the signatories to the trust. Without hesitation, Stephen's father announced, 'Oh, I think it had better be Jane and me.' Then, quite unnecessarily, with northern bluntness, he added, 'You see, it's very likely that I shall outlive my son – he is rather ill.'

I turned in incredulity to look at him. In my eyes, he was already an old man, white-haired and in his sixties. How could he sound Stephen's death knell so casually when I had never thought to question which of them might die first? His comment was the more ironic since the illness had long been a taboo subject, never discussed between Stephen and me and scarcely touched upon in the Hawking household. My every waking moment was devoted to convincing myself that we were leading normal lives and that we could enjoy a normal life expectancy. How could he so carelessly destroy the rock on which my castle was built? Or was it really nothing more than a castle in the air? In his remark I did not for one moment suspect any malice, only thoughtlessness or the Yorkshire tendency to call a spade a spade. Despite the lack of demonstrative emotion in family dealings, I believed that his love for his eldest son ran deep and that the illness, which was the ultimate irony for a medical man who had devoted his life to finding cures for other illnesses, had been a severe test of his emotional resilience. Hardening himself was part of his own defence. Nevertheless, his candid appraisal of our future, administered with the delicacy of a sledge-hammer blow, shook my own emotional resilience to the core. My brittle defences required sensitive handling; often they were overlooked either in the general concern of others for their own self-protection or in the morbid fascination which infirmity generates.

This aspect of human nature, whether displayed within the family or outside, was to become an increasing source of tension. Onlookers who had no connection with us had less reason to be sensitive than members of the immediate family. However, their reactions could be just as hurtful and the circumstances in which they emerged so unexpected that I myself would be stunned by a sudden brutal awareness of the contrasting extremes of our situation, the brilliant intellectual success and the hopeless physical incapacity. Each time one of those blows struck, it chipped away another little fragment of my fragile sense of security and opened up another crevice in the rock on which my youthful optimism was founded.

CHAPTER TWENTY-SIX

Event Horizons

ONE DARK, WINDY evening – 14 February 1974 – I drove Stephen over to Oxford to a conference at the Rutherford Laboratory on the site of the Atomic Energy Research Establishment at Harwell. We stayed in the Cozener's House at Abingdon, an old country house on the banks of the Thames which was in flood that winter. The rain pouring from heavy skies did not dampen our spirits, for both Stephen and I and a handful of his students were tense with excitement, anticipating a momentous occasion: Stephen was about to produce a new theory. At last he had reached a resolution of the black hole mechanics versus thermodynamics paradox which had been troubling him since the summer school at Les Houches. He had been spurred into obsessive calculation by the vexatious doubts cast on his earlier conclusions in the speculations of Jacob Beckenstein, a Princeton student of John Wheeler's. Beckenstein had been so struck by the similarity between the laws of thermodynamics and Stephen's 1970 black hole result that he claimed that the laws of thermodynamics and the laws governing black holes were actually the same laws. In Stephen's opinion, this claim was absurd, since to obey the laws of thermodynamics, black holes would have to have a finite temperature and would have to radiate, that is to say, the two sets of laws would have to coincide in all aspects, not just one. In his resolution of the question, Stephen's elaboration was innovative beyond all expectation.

Those intense periods of total concentration that the children and I had witnessed had led him to the conclusion that, contrary to all previously held theories on black holes, a black hole could radiate energy. As the hole radiates, it evaporates, losing mass and energy. Proportionately its temperature and surface gravity increase as it shrinks to the size of a nucleus, still weighing between 1,000 and 100 million tons. Finally, at an unimaginable temperature, it disappears in a massive explosion. Thus black holes were no longer to be considered impenetrably black and their activity could be seen to obey, rather than conflict with, the laws of thermodynamics. The long gestation of this particular infant had been cloaked in secrecy. For my part, I felt a certain vested interest in attending its birth since its rivalry for Stephen's attentions had already caused me such heartache. Bernard Carr was to act as assistant midwife, projecting a transcript of Stephen's lecture on slides to the audience.

On the morning of the lecture, I sat outside the lecture hall in the tea-room, idly flicking through a newspaper while waiting for Stephen's session to begin at 11 a.m. My concentration was interrupted by the raucous chatter of a gaggle of charladies in the far corner. Their spoons clinked noisily against the side of their cups as they stirred their coffee and their cigarettes filled the room with smoke. Irritatingly, I could not close my ears to their gossip, as pervasive as the smoke from their cigarettes, and found myself compelled to listen to their mulling over the conference and the delegates. To my bewilderment, one of them observed to her two companions, 'And there's one of them there, that young chap, he's living on borrowed time, isn't he?' Momentarily I could not think whom they meant. 'Oh, yes,' one of her companions agreed, 'a right state he's in, looks as if he's falling apart at the seams, can hardly hold his head up.' She laughed a light, callous laugh, amused at her own comic invention. Then, like darts striking my back, their barbed words pierced my consciousness and I realized that it was Stephen who was the subject of their ignorant chatter. Smarting in silence, I listened as they predicted his end in their crude, offhand manner. Stephen was being condemned behind his back, and all our past achievements, our bright vision of the future and our hopes were being summarily dismissed with a cackle and careless flick of a cigarette end into an ashtray.

When Stephen came rolling out of the lecture hall in his wheelchair, ready for a quick coffee before embarking on his lecture, I scrutinized him carefully from head to foot. He was alive certainly – alive with excitement and anticipation – but I had to ask myself if he really looked as if he were living on borrowed time, as if he were really falling apart at the seams. I had to concede that to a casual observer he probably did, and that concession to outside perceptions made me very sad. Fortunately such concerns could not have been farther from his mind. Firmly rooted in the physical world and as unaware as Don Quixote of unkind scepticism at his appearance and purpose, he was ready to charge into battle accompanied by his faithful Sancho Panza, Bernard Carr. I followed them into the lecture hall, still shaken by the grotesque truth which had so relentlessly forced itself upon me and which I was so loath to admit. I comforted myself with the reflection that those cleaning women had only seen the pitiable state of the frail body and were ignorant of the power of the mind and the strength of the spirit, conveyed so eloquently in that imperious cranium and those fine, intelligent eyes. My conviction that Stephen was immortal was nonetheless reeling from yet another severe blow.

With exquisite irony, Stephen reaffirmed his immortality in that very lecture, although at the time the chairman and some of the audience gave the impression that they thought he had taken leave of his senses. I sat on the edge of my seat holding my breath in suspense as I listened to Stephen, hunched in his chair under the lights on the stage, and read the slides which Bernard brought up on the overhead projector, clarifying the substance of Stephen's faint, whispering speech. In effect the lecture was given twice, once by Stephen himself and again by the slides, so there was not the slightest doubt about the message: black holes were not as black as they seemed.

Despite the clarity of the presentation, silence reigned as the lecture came to an end. It appeared that the audience was having difficulty digesting that simple message. The chairman, Professor John G. Taylor, of King's College, London, did not remain silent for long, however. Aghast at this heretical attack on the gospel of the black hole, he sprang to his feet, blustering, 'Well, this is quite preposterous! I have never heard anything like it. I have no alternative but to bring this session to an immediate close!' His behaviour seemed to me to be quite preposterous, reminiscent in fact of Eddington's attack on Chandrasekhar in 1933 except that Eddington used 'absurd' rather than 'preposterous' to describe Chandra's theory. Not only is it usual for a chairman to allow time for questions after a lecture, it is also a commonly accepted courtesy that he should thank the speaker for his 'extremely stimulating talk'. J. G. Taylor (not to be confused with Professor J. C. Taylor, the particle physicist who, with his wife Mary, was to become a close friend some years later) extended neither of these courtesies to Stephen; rather, he gave the impression that he would willingly have had him burnt at the stake for heresy. This conscious insult to Stephen was as intolerable as the cleaning ladies' mindless remarks. It implied a deliberate attempt to belittle him, suggesting that he had now proven himself to be incapacitated mentally as well as physically.

Whereas in the lecture hall one could have heard a pin drop, in the refectory after the lecture there was uproar. It was as if particles from radiating black holes were spinning in all directions, knocking the delegates sideways like skittles. Bernard settled Stephen quietly at a corner table while I went to queue at the counter for food. Still blustering and indignantly muttering to his students, J. G. Taylor stood behind me in the queue, unaware of my identity. I was rehearsing a few cutting remarks in Stephen's defence when I heard him splutter, 'We must get that paper out straight away!' I thought better of drawing attention to myself and went to report what I had heard to Stephen. Although he shrugged in a good-humoured way, he sent his own paper off to *Nature* immediately on our return to Cambridge. Since it was reviewed for the magazine by none other than J. G. Taylor, it was no surprise that it was rejected. Stephen then requested that it should be sent to an independent referee and, on the second time of asking, it was accepted. J. G. Taylor's paper was also accepted but died a natural death, while Stephen's marked the first step along the road towards the unification of physics, the reconciliation of the large-scale structure of the universe with the small scale-structure of the atom through the medium of the black hole. Undoubtedly the Rutherford experience served also to reinforce Stephen's determination to fight against all odds whether physical or in physics. The same experience left me proud but confused by the many hidden undercurrents it had revealed.

The theory of the evaporation of black holes paved the way for Stephen's election to the Royal Society the following spring at the unprecedentedly early age of thirty-two. In the seventeenth century Fellows had been elected as young as twelve years old, but that was in the days when privilege rather than merit ensured election. In the more recent past a Fellowship was an honour to which scientists aspired towards the end rather than the beginning of their careers, usually after acquiring a handful of honorary doctorates and serving on a few advisory scientific committees along the way. It is the crowning glory of a scientific career, second only in prestige to a Nobel prize.

We were informed of the election in mid-March, a couple of weeks in advance of the official announcement, giving me time to arrange a surprise celebration. I planned a champagne reception in the dignified setting of the Senior Parlour in Caius, to which Stephen's family, his friends and colleagues were invited, and I prepared a buffet dinner for a smaller, more intimate group of family and friends at home afterwards. There was no more fitting occasion on which to open the two bottles of Château Lafite 1945 which had appeared a couple of years back on the Caius Fellows' wine list at the remarkable – though erroneous – price of 45 shillings a bottle. The number of guests for the dinner-party was limited, therefore, not by the capacity of the house nor by the amount of crockery we possessed, but by the quantity of extremely rare old claret in the two bottles, just enough for everyone to have a taste.

On the evening of 22 March 1974, just before my thirtieth birthday, Stephen's students diplomatically steered him in the direction of the College where he was cheered as a conquering hero by friends and family, students and colleagues. The children did their best to pass round plates of canapés, caviar toasts, vol-au-vents and the miniature smoked salmon and asparagus rolls in which the Caius catering department excelled. Dennis Sciama agreed to propose the toast to Stephen and this he did very generously, listing all Stephen's many scientific achievements which, he said, would have more than justified his faith in him without this culminating honour of the Fellowship of the Royal Society. The children and I stood together in a glow of pride.

It was Stephen's turn to reply. He was well accustomed to making speeches in public these days but of course the party had come as a surprise and he had had no chance to prepare what he was going to say. He actually made quite a long speech, speaking slowly and clearly, though faintly. He talked about the course of his research and the unexpected way in which it had developed over the past ten years or so since coming to Cambridge. He thanked Dennis Sciama for his support and inspiration and he thanked his friends for coming to the party, talking as was his habit always in terms of 'I' not 'we'. With my arms round each of the children, I waited at the side of the room for him to turn towards us with a smile, a nod, just a brief word of recognition of the domestic achievements of the nine years of our marriage. It may have been a mere oversight in the heat and excitement of the moment that he did not mention us at all. He finished speaking to general applause while I blinked back prickly tears of dismay. Had Stephen forgotten us, forgotten all that I had tried to do for him, forgotten that while his mind roamed the outer reaches of the universe, my horizons had shrunk to the four walls of our narrow house, forgotten his pride in his two beautiful children – or did he consider all that irrelevant to the scientific importance of the occasion?

I was no saint, I was human; I needed reinforcement, encouragement and understanding as much as anyone else, more so perhaps given the exceptional demands made of me by the situation. I had loved Stephen for his sense of humour, his smile, the light in his eyes, his courage and his genius; I had supported him in all his scientific endeavours, I had fought all his battles with him, I had looked after his every need and I had urged the children to love and respect him, looking beyond the disability which made him so unlike other fathers. Now that his cup was overflowing with the sort of success that even able-bodied scientists scarcely dared dream of, could he not spare one little drop of appreciation for me, or was that something which like so many other aspects of our relationship I was supposed to intuit? How could I continue to maintain the bright illusion of normality if my own contribution to it was to be disregarded? As the mother of two young children and the wife of a severely disabled husband, I felt the emotional insecurity of my position keenly. Yet there was no shoulder for me to lean on and I had no other option; my future lay with Stephen and the children and I had to continue to give all I could for them, even if my own expectations produced only mirages.

Stephen was not naturally expansive or fulsome in praise. The Hawkings gave the impression of belonging to that class of English intellectuals who seem to regard any expressions of emotion or appreciation as a sign of weakness, a loss of control or a denial of their own importance. They were all, parents and children alike, capable of surprising generosity whether in giving presents on birthdays and at Christmas, or money when needed – Philippa for example, had given us many expensive and imaginative presents – yet strangely they seemed ashamed of demonstrating any warmth with that generosity. It seemed that generosity was acceptable in intellectual terms, a show of warmth and gratitude were not. Yet how could I doubt Stephen's love for us? Never counting the cost, he was magnanimous with presents and, at the end of a day apart, his face would light up with that wonderful smile when we were reunited. Tears had come into his eyes when Robert and I had finally returned from the ill-fated Mont Blanc expedition. Still, like the child at the end of a party, hoping for the token bag of sweets which never comes, I waited at the side of the room. The child knows that it has been a lovely party and that the oversight is trivial. She puts on a brave face because she knows that she has no right to cry and good manners forbid any emotional outburst.

A change was urgently needed, a change that would bring us a renewal of commitment, a new perspective and a fresh impetus. A change would be good for the children, too, and this was an appropriate time to make it. Lucy had not yet started school and Robert would be moving out of the state system the following year. By a happy coincidence, in the very week of the publication of the Royal Society Fellowship list Stephen received an approach – no doubt instigated by Kip Thorne – from Caltech, the California Institute of Technology in Pasadena, inviting him to take up the offer of a visiting Fellowship for the following academic year. The offer was lavish in the extreme. Quite apart from a salary on an American scale, it included a large, fully furnished house rent-free, the use of a car and all possible aids and appurtenances, including an electrically powered wheelchair to allow Stephen maximum independence. Physiotherapy and medical care would be arranged for him and schooling for the children. Stephen's students, Bernard Carr and Peter De'Ath, were also invited to accompany him.

The offer from the Americans who espoused our cause with generosity and imagination was even more opportune as our situation in Cambridge was much more precarious than we realized. Years later a close friend reported to me a scene witnessed at a somewhat frosty dinner-party in Cambridge in that period in the early 1970s. To the surprise of that dinner guest, Stephen's fate was sealed in a remark delivered with consummate indifference by a senior don. 'As long as Stephen Hawking pulls his weight, he can stay in this university,' the speaker announced, 'but as soon as he ceases to do that, he will have to go . . .' Luckily for us we were able to go of our own volition, not quite sure of what the future would hold, but in the event we were actually to be invited back a year later.

If an opportunity to exchange the icy chill of the fen winds for the warm deserts of southern California was to be welcomed, the obstacles associated with such an enterprise could not be lightly dismissed. Weighing up the advantages against the disadvantages preoccupied me most. Even though the theatricality of High Anglicanism was not greatly to my liking, I spent many a contemplative moment in Little St Mary's Church that Easter wrestling with this dilemma and all the associated problems while reflecting on the challenge of the immediate future. Whereas Stephen might well have mastered the 15,000-million-year history of the universe, my vision of the future had become restricted only to the foreseeable perspective of the next few days. I had learnt not to speculate on a more distant future, or plan for two, five, ten or twenty years hence. However, the next eighteen months demanded careful consideration, especially in the light of my past chaotic experiences on the west coast of America. I steeled myself to confront my personal problem, the fear of flying. At least this time I should not have to abandon my children because they, of course, would be coming with us, but that, in a changed perspective, was the least of my anxieties. Far more worrying was the question of how I was going to manage to travel a third of the way across the world, solely responsible for Stephen in his very debilitated state as well as for the children. Secondly, how should I cope for a whole year entirely alone, with neither parents nor neighbours on hand to help in time of crisis? Frequently in the past couple of years when I had been laid low with 'flu, headaches, backache and even pleurisy, I had been able to rely on my mother or Thelma Thatcher or my most loyal friends to come and help. No such help would be forthcoming in California.

In addition, one of the most perplexing stumbling blocks for some time had been Stephen's absolute rejection of any outside help with his care. He had always staunchly refused to accept any assistance, apart from snippets of advice from his father, which might suggest either an acknowledgement of his condition *per se* or of the fact that it was deteriorating. This attitude, together with his refusal to mention the illness, was one of the props which underpinned his courage and was part of his defence mechanism. I well understood that if once he admitted the gravity of his condition his courage might fail him. Equally I understood that the mere struggle to get out of bed in the morning might defeat him if he gave any thought to his plight. How I wished that he too could understand that just a little help to relieve me of some of the severest physical strain would contribute to an improvement in our relationship. If only he would spare me from that long blind tunnel where grinding exhaustion and constant pressure were squeezing and stifling my true self, still so full of hope and good intentions, but now becoming distorted and misshapen. Increasingly I was brought face to face with my own shortcomings, especially when my self-control gave way and my temper exploded at Stephen's insensitivity to my physical limitations. Contrition and guilt were the inevitable consequences of those explosions for me, the more so because his imperturbable façade was never ruffled. Could he not see how tired and physically spent I was – or did he not care?

In my mind's eye I formed a rosy picture of how I wanted to be, of how I saw myself, of how we could live if things were different. With more time and more resources of energy I would be less fraught, more patient and more relaxed. I could be a more stimulating companion, I could take a closer interest in current affairs and cosmology as well as my own research. I could take us out more often to the theatre and concerts. If only I had the chance to find myself and cultivate my waning self-respect, instead of feeling like a jigsaw scattered about a room, I would be able to encourage Stephen more wholeheartedly in those ambitions from which at present I shrank in dismay since they posed the threat of many a potential obstacle. We could still function fully as a couple, as companions and partners.

Dr Wilson had listened to my troubles and sympathetically shaken his head at the impossibility of helping someone who would not be helped. However, he conferred with Stephen's doctor and together they had tried to initiate a rota of domiciliary male nurses to lift Stephen in and out of the bath at least a couple of times a week. This embryonic plan was aborted as soon as it was conceived because the pleasant but elderly male nurse was able to come only at five o'clock in the afternoon and such an abrupt conclusion to his working day was, understandably, anathema to Stephen. Only a miracle could resolve the problems we faced and I certainly was not expecting to inhale a miracle from the incense-laden air of High Mass.

Nevertheless, as I spilled out of the church into the Lane with the other members of the congregation that Easter Sunday, there was an unaccustomed lightness in my step, occasioned by a sudden sense of relief as much as passing pleasure in the pale sunshine and the spring flowers. I was no longer haunted by the impossibility of our situation and the impracticability of well-meaning attempts from the other side of the world to offer us a welcome change of scene. Incredibly, thanks to the seeds of an astounding idea which had just floated into my mind with the graceful ease of thistledown gliding to earth, all things seemed to be possible again. Those seeds carried a simple message which took shape and blossomed with the beauty of the Easter lilies in the garden, bright and fresh, putting dark winter to flight.

That ethereal message contained the answer to my problems. As the idea took shape in words, it suggested with startling simplicity that we should invite Stephen's students to live with us in our large Californian house. We could offer them free accommodation in return for help with the mechanics of lifting, dressing and bathing. This was all the more essential since Stephen was no longer able to feed himself at all and needed a constantly watchful eye. With assistance from Bernard, he would not be humiliated by the unmentionable indignity of having to receive help from nurses – which he considered a detrimental step, an acceptance of the deterioration in his condition – but would be assisted by people from his own circle, if not family then at least friends, part of the household. Without a moment's hesitation, I hurried the few paces down the Lane to suggest the idea to Stephen. His first reaction was automatic rejection but when he had had time to think about it and realized that the fate of the Californian venture might hang on his decision, he changed his mind. I broached the idea to Bernard Carr and then to Peter De'ath who, after due consideration, agreed that it would suit all parties very nicely.

There remained one major function to be fulfilled that summer: Stephen's admission to the Fellowship of the Royal Society on Thursday, 2 May. We set off from Cambridge in good time for lunch at Carlton House Terrace, the fine eighteenth-century headquarters of the Royal Society overlooking the Mall. As we approached north London, the car began to lurch uncontrollably and the steering became heavier and heavier. We had no alternative but to press on with the journey, hoping against hope that we would be able to reach our destination. At last, tugging the resistant steering-wheel round, I turned with relief into the forecourt of Carlton House Terrace, there to embark on the well-rehearsed sequence of searching out the usual bevy of elderly porters, heaving the various parts of the wheelchair out of the car, assembling them, stationing the chair by the passenger seat of the car and then lifting Stephen under his arms and swinging him round from his seat in the car into the chair. Then the porters had to be instructed in the careful lifting of the chair up the inevitable flight of steps to the main entrance. This time the sequence was more complicated because the car as well as Stephen needed attention: the front nearside tyre was flat.

As on many occasions, help came from the least expected quarter. It was the Secretary of the Royal Society himself – a man of few words, flustered with the demands of the important guests and the significance of the occasion, for all of which he was responsible – who got down on his hands and knees, dressed in his smart dark grey suit, and changed the wheel for us while, unawares, we were being regally entertained to a formal luncheon by another Cambridge scientist, the President of the Royal Society, Sir Alan Hodgkin.

The admission took place in the early afternoon amidst much ceremonial in the lecture theatre. Speeches were made introducing each new Fellow who then stepped onto the platform to sign the admissions' book. When Stephen's turn came, a hush descended on the audience and the book was brought down from the podium for his signature. He inscribed his name slowly and carefully to a tense silence. His final flourish was greeted by a burst of rapturous applause which brought a jubilant smile to his face and tears of pride and joy to my eyes.

Stephen was not the only Cambridge scientist to be honoured that year, nor the only physicist from the Department. John Polkinghorne, the Professor of Particle Physics, was also being admitted to the Fellowship of the Royal Society on the same occasion. Having reached the apogee of his career in science, he was on the point of giving up physics to take up theology, that is to say, from being Professor Polkinghorne FRS, he was about to become an undergraduate again, embarking on the long haul of study for ordination, curacy and parish, with the particular motivation of healing the schism between science and religion which had originated with Galileo. In his opinion, science and religion were not in opposition but were two complementary aspects of one reality. This thesis would become the theme of his writings as priest-scientist. Although we did not know him well, I admired his conviction and was myself greatly encouraged to find that atheism was not an essential prerequisite of science and not all scientists were as atheistic as they seemed.

Part Three

CHAPTER TWENTY-SEVEN

Dear Friends

'O H, HI! MY name is Mary Lou and I live in Sierra Madre. And who are you? Where are you from?'

The speaker, a slight, tanned, bespectacled figure, exuding health and self-confidence, awaited our reply with a broad, friendly smile. We had only just arrived at the party, hosted by some English expatriates, a week or so after landing in Los Angeles, and were not yet accustomed to such uninhibited overtures. There was an embarrassingly long pause while we regained our composure and realized that the speaker was addressing us in the expectation of a reciprocally spontaneous reply. After all, it had taken the best part of ten years for us to be accepted and recognized at parties in Cambridge and even then, if people did come up to us, the style of approach was tinged with a certain diffidence. Of late some of the Senior Fellows – and more especially their wives – had regularly shown a benevolent and affectionate interest in us, but over the years we had become used to sitting trapped at the ends of tables or in corners on our own, never really expecting anyone to speak to us, always pleasantly surprised if during the course of the evening we happened to encounter a friendly face and a sociable disposition. Indeed, one of the kitchen managers had once confided in me that it was difficult to place us at table at College feasts because no one really wanted to sit with us. In College one always sensed a barrier of formality which permitted little external socializing. Small wonder then that we were unprepared for Mary Lou's initiative. Her exuberance was infectious and I attempted to convey our elation in my letters home to our families and friends.

535 South Wilson Avenue,
Pasadena, Ca. 91106, USA
30 August 1974

Dear Mum and Dad,

You cannot imagine how exciting this is!

The flight was very long – eleven hours – and two hours late in departure, but very straightforward by comparison with the last time we flew over the Pole when Robert was a tiny baby. As then, the scenery was dramatically beautiful, black peaks growing out of snowfields, mountains rising out of a frozen sea where occasional water holes glowed deep emerald in the ice, white specks of icebergs in Hudson Bay, then the deserts of America, the Salt Lake and finally the coastal mountains. Robert was fascinated, like a born traveller retracing his steps. In contrast, when we were high over the Atlantic, Lucy, quite unimpressed by the adventure, asked if we were on the ground yet . . .

It was of course about 2 a.m. (your time) on Tuesday when we touched down but we all revived on landing and were wide-eyed at the sight of so much that was new and unfamiliar – palm trees, huge cars, our own gleaming station wagon in which Kip came to meet us, freeways weaving in and out of the city in all directions, skyscrapers and, ultimately, the house with its white weatherboarding, looking much prettier than in the photos. It was dusk when we arrived and there was a light in every window – a Disney fantasy come true.

The house is as elegant inside as it is pretty out. And so comfortable! Huge sofas that you just sink into and bathrooms everywhere, all colour-coordinated, of course! Everything is brand-new, all the imitation-antique furniture, the towels, the china, even the saucepans! These people must think that we are used to an astronomical standard of living. If only they knew! I reckon that number six LSML would fit into this house at least four times.

The house is right opposite the campus so Stephen is actually closer to his office than in Cambridge. Like a small boy with a new toy, he is excitedly learning to manoeuvre his electric wheelchair. It is the same as the one he has at the Institute only much faster and will take him independently wherever he wants to go. It's years since he has had such freedom of movement, though the chair does balk at kerbs and steps and has to be lifted over them. This is a bit of a problem since kerbs are very high here as no one ever walks out in the street and the frame of the chair is very heavy. The two solid gel batteries each weigh a ton, not to mention the occupant. We have had engineers and administrators here all day attending to the wheelchair and making adjustments to all the other appliances. Nothing it seems is too much trouble.

The garden is rather bare and dusty. The grass needs a great deal of water which comes up from an underground irrigation system – no need for hosepipes or watering cans. It is however wonderfully exotic. We awoke the first morning and stepped out on to the patio to find a humming-bird hovering by a weird-looking plant, with spiky orange and blue flowers. All around the house are camellia bushes the size of trees and by the patio there is a huge Californian dry oak, just waiting to be climbed. Round the edge of the garden we have an orange tree in bloom and in fruit at one and the same time, two avocados, a fir tree and a small palm. So far, as it is so hot, we have eaten all our meals on the patio – just as well since the dining-room is so beautiful with its plush red carpet and its mahogany table, we hardly dare step inside the door, let alone eat our meals there.

The children and I went for a bathe in the Caltech pool this afternoon. Lucy fell in and did not like it at all but Robert will be swimming within the week. We are all so dazed with healthy, happy tiredness that Lucy has gone to sleep in front of the television and even Robert shows signs of dozing off. I think I may be asleep before him even so.

much love,
Jane

My father was due to retire from the Ministry of Agriculture on his sixtieth birthday in December 1974 after a long and dedicated career. My parents planned to celebrate his retirement by coming out to stay with us in California.

Pasadena, 22 September 1974

Dear Mum and Dad,

It will be wonderful to have you here for Christmas! There's such a lot to see. We have had several visitors already and, with them, we have begun investigating some of the local sights. Stephen's Trinity Hall friend Nick Hughes came with his wife, Janet, last week and this week, Sandra Wade, my Westfield friend (the sister of Chris's

contemporary Paul), came down from Berkeley. We had a great deal
to say to each other as it is four years since we last met. Peter De'Ath,
Stephen's other student, arrived the day before yesterday and is living
with us until he finds his own accommodation.

I am getting more confident at driving and today have done vast
quantities of shopping, all neatly packed into brown paper (not
plastic) sacks and carried out to the car for me by a smiling young
assistant who then told me to 'have a nice day!' What a change from
Sainbury's!

I am mentally compiling a list of places to take you to. Robert is
a brilliant navigator – he seems to carry the freeway map in his head
and, unlike his father, tells me where to turn off well in advance. To
the south and the west, there is ugly urban sprawl for miles, the
worst of America, placards, drive-ins for everything – food, cinemas,
banks, even animal cemeteries – and telegraph poles. Only four miles
east, at the end of our road, are vast expanses of mountain scenery,
parched to a cinder with flowers dried in full bloom, unscathed by
the mass of mechanized humanity beneath their heights.

The children have just returned, covered in mud, from playing
with Shu, the eight-year-old son of our Japanese neighbours, Ken and
Hiroko Naka, who unbeknown to us, lived for some time in Cambridge
before moving to the United States. Ken is a biologist and spends
his time analysing catfish eyes which I gather are some sort of scientific
oddity since they have a structure which is remarkably like that of
the human eye. Shu's conversation, which impresses Robert greatly, is
peppered with computer jargon. I should know because I collect the
children from school in the afternoon and while Lucy babbles on
irrepressibly, Shu conducts his own monologue which may just be
intelligible to Robert who nods knowingly, but not to me. The Nakas
are extremely kind: not only do they take Robert and Lucy to school
every morning, they also seem to be planning all sorts of expeditions
to fun-parks and beaches for the three children.

The children started school last Monday. On Sunday, Orientation
Day, we were summoned to meet their teachers at the Pasadena
Town and Country School and the next morning I delivered them
somewhat apprehensively to the school gate. At noon I went to pick
up Lucy from the nursery department and joined the car-queue of
waiting mothers, sidling round the block in their automobiles ('car'
is too short a word for these machines). As I edged to the school gate,

I gave her name to the teacher standing guard on the pavement and he hailed her over the loud-speaker: 'Loossee Hokking, Loossee Hokking!' he bellowed. No one came forward and there was no sign of Loossee Hokking among the crowd of small children waiting patiently in line inside the gate. A great commotion ensued. Could Loossee Hokking have been kidnapped – the worst fear of the school – on her first day? The place was in chaos. I parked the car and went in. The Principal came running out of her office and a bevy of middle-aged ladies scattered in all directions in frantic search of the lost infant. Loossee Hokking was not hard to find. She had liked school so much that she had taken herself off to lunch and was intending to stay until 2.30. Since then she has come out of school with Robert and Shu, sometimes temperamentally a bit the worse for wear as it's a long day for a three-year-old.

Both children are in their element. They are a healthy nut-brown colour and their hair is bleached by the sun, but unlike American children, they have kept their pink cheeks which are much admired. In less than a week Robert taught himself to swim – underwater, not yet on the surface – and Lucy allows me to drag her out into the deep water where she kicks hard. By Californian standards she is really backward since two-year-olds regularly jump off the boards at the deep end and swim lengths, thrashing up and down the pool like Olympic competitors.

Fortunately television here is a great disappointment to the children. They watch the educational network in the early hours of the morning before school but all the other programmes are made unbearable by the constant interruptions for the most banal advertisements, so the novelty of having a television has worn off very quickly and there is no cry of protest if I turn it off or even refuse to allow it to be turned on. They just go out for a ride on their bikes instead. As for the news programmes, well, by the time advertising, Watergate, national news, local news, smog reports and forecasts have all been accounted for in that order, there is precious little time – about five minutes out of an hour's broadcast – for the rest of the world. Stephen and I watch BBC imports in the evenings, all the programmes you have been watching but we have missed over the past few years through not having a television, like Jacob Bronowski's *Ascent of Man* which I find compelling and moving, and *Upstairs Downstairs*. Otherwise there's not much to do in the evenings.

The Thorne children, Brett and Keres, have generously donated cast-off toys, all in immaculate condition, and the bikes and other toys came from the Caltech visitors' pound which is managed by Ruth Hughes, an unassuming but outspoken lady in her sixties who takes visitors to Caltech under her wing. She was a refugee from Germany or Austria and her husband is a retired Caltech professor.

Stephen is certainly enjoying the independence which his electric wheelchair affords him and secretly I think he rejoices in being the star of the campus – where he sits in an air-conditioned office all day. As he says, he does not really care where he is so long as he can get on with his work. Ramps have appeared all over the campus as well as in the driveway to the house and no expense has been spared to make him comfortable. He has his own secretary, Polly Grandmontagne, a model of efficiency, and a physiotherapist, Sylvie Teschke, whose husband, a Swiss watchmaker, is anxiously anticipating the end of his livelihood because of the advent of quartz watches.

Bernard, Stephen's student, has begun to settle into the routine of life in our household. He is unfailingly cheerful and always smiling and it's nice to have someone to talk to, even though his timetable and ours diverge dramatically. He helps me put Stephen to bed at night and *then* goes out to parties! When he comes home in the early morning, he often sits up watching horror movies till dawn because he says he suffers from insomnia – and then he sleeps till lunch-time. Yesterday I went upstairs to rouse him in the middle of the morning and found him sleeping soundly with his body in the bed and his head on the floor!

The children are clamouring for a swim!

much love,

Jane

That autumn Mary Thatcher came on a tour of the United States, to lecture on her newly released film archive of the lives of the British in India. Los Angeles was to be one stop on her extensive itinerary.

Pasadena, 25 October 1974

Dear Thatchers,

How nice to hear from you both – and even nicer to hear that Mary will be coming to visit us! I am so glad that her film is arousing such well-deserved interest. Perhaps she should compile another archive – on the lives of the British abroad, substituting America for India. There's no shortage of material here: Caltech fairly bristles with British scientists and their families, many of whom are putting down roots.

We are sorry that Mary's stay is to be so short. The Huntington Gardens, only a few minutes from here, are *de rigueur* for a visit. They are vast and beautiful, divided into fascinating specialized geographical and botanical areas – a viciously prickly desert cactus garden, an Australian area with eucalyptus trees but no kangaroos, a jungle area, row upon row of camellias which should soon be coming into flower, a Shakespearean knot garden, a classical Japanese garden complete with bridge, house, gongs and a mysteriously philosophical Zen garden, mostly raked gravel dotted about with a few significant rocks.

In the Art Gallery I could stand for hours gazing at Constable's *View of the Stour* if it didn't make me feel sentimental. In the Museum, the Gutenberg Bible and the Chaucerian manuscripts must be the envy of every European museum, but then you see, you have to come to California to see the best of European art. If it's not here in the Huntington, it will be in the Pasadena Museum (at present being enlarged with a new collection), in the fabulously overendowed Paul Getty Museum at Malibu, or Hearst Castle on the way up to San Francisco. Mr Huntington made his money on the railways and married his aunt to keep it in the family. When you see her portrait, you may wonder if he didn't pay a rather heavy price for the privilege!

Talking of being sentimental, we shall look forward to hearing news of the Lane and our neighbours, of yourselves and of Inigo. Robert and Lucy send him lots of love. Here everything is so bright and brash that there is no room for those subtleties of life that we know so well, the grey skies, the respectable shabbiness, the crumbling piles, the diffidence, the snobbery. Here the skies, the colours, the landscape, the people, their behaviour and their use of language are all starkly well-defined, honest and devoid of nuance.

And the food! It's gargantuan. Mary should bring a supply of doggie bags – we can send enough food parcels home to last for months. It's so stuffed with additives, it would probably keep too. Perhaps you would also like a few of the fifty-two avocado pears which fell off the tree last weekend when we were away in Santa Barbara? We hurriedly picked them all up on our return on Sunday

evening and stored them in the bottom of the fridge to save them
from the weekly cleansing operation by the gardeners who come with
shears, brooms and a vacuum-cleaner. They cut back, tidy up and
hoover the lawn but never plant anything. I don't think they would
recognize a weed if it stared them in the face! What would they do
with the churchyard?

all love to you both!
Jane

30 November 1974

Dear Mum and Dad,

In a few days there'll be no more commuting from St Albans to
London at 8 a.m., just the long flight from London to Los Angeles!

I hope you will be able to stand the pace here. Don't imagine that
you are coming to California for a rest. We live in a constant social
whirl. As our house is closest to the campus and is so large, it has
become the venue for the Relativity Group's entertaining this year.
Kip and Linda have a lovely old Spanish-style villa up in Altadena but
that is some way out of town and the area around them is so thick
with thieves that as soon as they buy anything new, it disappears. The
same goes for any cars parked in the street. So we have some of the
parties here instead, cocktail parties, dinner parties, evening drinks
parties – not to mention Lucy's birthday party to which she insisted
on inviting the whole class plus teachers . . . Soon we shall be cooking
a turkey for Thanksgiving. I don't know how many people will be
coming but I'm leaving the traditional trimmings like pumpkin pie
to the Americans who know how to do those things. There's no
accounting for some of their tastes anyhow. Some people came to
dinner last week and I served them a beef casserole. To my amazement
they added autumn strawberries from a bowl on the table to their
plates of stew!

We look forward to introducing you to our new friends, especially
the other Fairchild Fellows in Stephen's field, the Dickes and the
Israels. Bob and Annie Dicke from Princeton are very much like
you. He is intellectual and an excellent pianist, and she is warm and
grandmotherly. The children and I often go to tea with her and
swim in the pool at their block of flats, grandly known here as
'condominiums'. I don't remember whether you have met the Israels
before. We first met them when they came to Cambridge with their

ten-year-old son Mark in 1971. They live in Edmonton, where
Werner has established a Relativity Group, but hail from much farther
afield. Werner was born in Berlin but was brought up in South Africa,
while Inge was born of Russian parents but was brought up in Paris
and later Dublin. They are very cosmopolitan in outlook but gentle,
humorous and immensely knowledgeable without a trace of affectation.
Mark, now thirteen, is at school in England, at Dartington, which I
think is a source of great anxiety for Inge. I would also like you to
meet Lea Sterrett. She is the administrator of the Fairchild
programme and has become a real friend to us. She told me that her
husband is disabled.

A special message for Chris – do tell him about our experiences
with the dentist. He will be horrified! Robert developed toothache
last week – although I had taken him to the school dentist just
before we came out here – so on Thursday we went to see a dentist.
California style. Potted plants, plush carpets, soft sofas and piped
music greeted us as we entered the surgery. The dentist came out to
talk to me after he had inspected Robert's teeth. 'Well, Mrs Hokking,'
he began, then paused for his words to take effect, 'this will be quite
an investment . . . those young molars need remedial dentistry, stainless
steel crowns . . . around one hundred and eighty dollars, I would
estimate . . .' I can imagine Chris's reaction but what choice do I have
except to pay up?!

The children and I have joined the local library. I have been avidly
reading the biographies you recommended, *Richard III* and *Mary,
Queen of Scots*. Robert took out a book on the British Empire which
struck me as rather excessively patriotic, but not bad for a child who
only a year ago was accused of being backward. I also have an addictive
new interest thanks to another Caltech wife, Tricia Holmes. Tricia, who
is Irish, has introduced me to the evening choral class at Pasadena
City College. Once a week we sight-sing our way through a major
choral work. I'm not a good sight-singer but it is very exciting. Last
week it was Brahms' German Requiem, this week the Mozart
Requiem and so on. Later in the year we shall be doing the St Matthew
Passion over *two weeks*. The approach reminds me of the way Americans
travel in Europe, a day in Paris, a day in London, two days in Venice,
perhaps.

Since I last wrote we have taken in another migrant to fill up some
of the space in this house. Anna Zytkov, a young Polish astrophysicist,

has moved in until she can find somewhere to rent. No sooner had
she arrived than I suggested a game of tennis, apologizing in advance
for being so badly out of practice, not having played in years. We were
just starting to play when Anna fell over, breaking her ankle. Since
then, in her immobilized state, she has built the most beautiful, fully-
furnished dolls' house out of a large cardboard box for Lucy for her
birthday. It is a real work of art, so delicately and imaginatively crafted
that it makes the garish plastic artefacts that one sees in the shops
look monstrously vulgar and clumsy.

Tricia Holmes' little girl, Lizzie, is more or less Lucy's age. Lizzie
and Lucy go to ballet together so the ballet shoes are in use again
and this time it's the real thing, no messing around with nursery
rhymes and free expression but no tears either. The teacher is young
and rather seriously American. Her reservation is that she might be
teaching Lucy by the wrong method . . .

We shall have a full house at Christmas. I think Anna will have
left by then but in addition to the six of us plus Bernard, George
Ellis will be coming to stay for a couple of days when he and Stephen
return from a conference in Dallas on the 21st, and on the 23rd, Philippa
will be coming over from New York where she is working at present.

We will be at the airport at 5 a.m. on the 16th to meet you! Be
prepared for all the usual end of term activities at the school, just as
in Cambridge, and for a huge party here on the 21st . . .

much love till 16th December, J

14 January 1975

Dearest Thatchers,

Now that the dust has finally settled after a riotous Christmas and
all the visitors are safely back home, I shall interrupt my mammoth
spring-cleaning to thank you for your letters and cards and to wish
you a Happy New Year.

It was such a treat to have Mary here in November but I am glad
for her sake that she missed one particular Californian experience
that I could well have done without. In early December, Stephen went
off with his entourage to a conference in Dallas. While the children
and I were alone in the house, we had an earthquake one night, not
the sort of little tremor that rattles the house like a passing lorry (I

should say 'truck') regularly every afternoon, but a real earthquake, so real that it was mentioned in the news bulletins the next day.

I awoke in the middle of the night to find the bed and the floor shaking beneath me. Our instructions are that we should run to the porch in the event of a quake but I am ashamed to say I was too terrified to move, literally petrified. When finally I recovered my senses, I ran upstairs to see if the children were all right. They were both sound asleep! I went back to bed, turned out the light and then it happened again! An aftershock so they say, but it was just as frightening as the first one.

We never had a dull moment at Christmas. If there had been earthquakes, we probably should not have noticed them (just as Stephen failed to notice a major earthquake in Persia in 1962 because he was travelling cross country on a bus at the time and was suffering from dysentery). In quick succession during the course of the previous week, all our visitors, Mum and Dad, George Ellis and Stephen on their return from Dallas, and Stephen's sister Philippa, arrived in the middle of the night and then we gave a party for forty or so friends and colleagues who enjoyed themselves so much that they stayed till after 2 a.m. To prove it, we have a photo of a very distinguished elderly physicist, Willy Fowler, practising yoga on the living-room floor at 2 a.m.!

Sixteen people came to Christmas dinner which meant that the children had a ready-made audience for their conjuring show. Robert was given a conjuring set and he, with his ebullient assistant, regaled us with a winningly innocent first attempt at sleight of hand – a change from the constant diet of riddles and jokes which bemuse us and keep the children in ecstasies of laughter. The contrast between his quasi-professional opening gambit – 'If you want to ask questions, please ask them after the show and not before it' – and the disarray in his box of tricks, his pleasure when a trick actually worked and his suppressed irritation at his show-stealing assistant, not to mention his gaping toothless smile, were most endearing. You would have loved it!

After Christmas my parents went to Santa Barbara and thence to San Francisco while a friend of Philippa's came to stay here. At last we summoned the energy to take the children to Disneyland for a day. The queues were long and the children managed to ride on only two attractions each, which was very disappointing. We did have a good vantage-point for the lavishly produced Disneyland parade, though, but even that was a bit of a disaster because it was Lucy's misfortune to be offered an apple by the wicked witch in the Snow White section ... Here in Pasadena on 1st January we had the City's own parade, celebrating the American heritage with a hundred or so floats decorated entirely with millions of orchids and roses. Americans do bring a seriously professional approach to all their activities.

Early in the New Year we drove over to Death Valley, a national desert park, 300 miles north-east of here. It is a weird primeval landscape, a giants' playground where the Valley floor is littered with sand dunes here, volcanic craters there, and slag and sand-coloured rock protuberances everywhere. Vast salt flats below sea level are all that remain of a deep ice-age lake. On all sides the Valley is enclosed by rugged snow-capped mountains which in their many-hued stratifications bear witness to enormous geological upheavals in the dawn of time. In summer Death Valley is said to be the hottest desert in the world. Consequently it is almost barren of vegetation, only cacti, desert holly and the creosote plant survive among its hostile rocks and stones, and only the tiny, prehistoric pupfish can withstand the extreme saltiness of its few shallow creeks. Constantly changing colour with the movement of the sun, the landscape is magnificent and awe-inspiring but not beautiful. The sorry tales of the pioneers who tried to cross the Valley in 1849 and the ghost town remnants of the gold prospectors' dreams together with the sterility and silence of the place, invest it with a menacing and forbidding atmosphere. My mother remarked how dynamic, tough and persevering those pioneers must have been and added that we shouldn't be surprised to find those same qualities in modern Californians, especially the women, the descendants of those pioneers. She's right.

We came home to a nice surprise. We had already organized a small farewell party for my parents so it was a happy coincidence that we could on the same occasion congratulate Stephen yet again and celebrate the award, jointly to him and Roger Penrose, by the Royal Astronomical Society of the Eddington Medal. I am so thrilled for him. We are told that this is all very prestigious but are not really sure what it signifies as the announcement came as a complete surprise. Nevertheless, it did have the effect of reminding Stephen to pay his overdue subscription!

The children send hugs and kisses. Lucy was determined to come back to England with her grandparents so that she could come and see you! She packed her suitcase specially and was so indignant when the plane took off without her that we had to make a quick dash to the nearest Kentucky Fried Chicken outlet to calm her down. The children are now back at school but as they come out at 2.30, there is plenty of time for swimming – even in January! Robert is getting quite proficient and would be able to swim a length if only he would allow his head to come out of the water to draw breath. Everyday Lucy proclaims that she is going to swim alone but when it comes to it she has second thoughts. Her swimming coach insists that she should jump off the board at the deep end . . .

all love, J

I often had to resort to general letters to allow me to keep in touch with my friends:

April 1975

Dear Friends,

You may find it hard to believe, considering the bad write-up that this area gets in the world's press, but we have become really fascinated by the whole Los Angeles area. Its cities and skyscrapers may be sitting astride some of the most critical geological faults in the Earth's crust but the expansive lifestyle expresses a confidence and an enthusiasm for progress which by all accounts seems to be sadly lacking in Britain at the moment. At any event, this year has been a useful exercise in perspective. From this distance Britain appears as a small offshore European island which would do well to settle down to its rightful place within the Common Market instead of dwelling on past glories and lost greatness. I just hope that when Martin Rees casts our proxy votes in the referendum, he won't find that Stephen's vote has cancelled mine – as he did, to my dismay, in the General Election!

Stephen is thoroughly enjoying Caltech and is getting up to all sorts of mischief. He and Kip Thorne have concocted a bet. Stephen bet Kip that the constellation Cygnus X-1 does not contain a black hole, as he felt he would need some consolation in the form of four years' subscription to Private Eye if that actually proved to be the case. Kip for his part was content with just one year's subscription to

Penthouse magazine if, as seems likely, Cygnus X-1 does contain a black hole . . .

Otherwise, I don't really know what Stephen is up to these days. He seems to be making contacts with particle physicists which I suspect means that his interests are moving way beyond the event horizon into the heart of the black hole. He has been attending lectures by two eminent particle physicists, Richard Feynman and Murray Gell-Man, whose gentlemanly behaviour towards each other conceals an arch rivalry. Stephen was present when Feynman turned up at the first of a course of lectures by Gell-Man. Noticing him in the audience, Gell-Man announced that he would be using his lecture series to conduct a survey of current research in particle physics and proceeded to read from his notes in a monotone. After ten minutes, Feynman got up and left. To Stephen's great amusement, Gell-Man then heaved a sigh and declared, 'Ah, good, now we can get on with the real stuff!' and proceeded to talk about his own recent research on the cutting edge of particle physics.

Winter here was scarcely noticeable as such, though it has rained in the past few weeks. When it rains, it really rains hard for two or three days. Then the sun shines again in a brilliant azure sky and the clouds clear from the mountains revealing the full splendour of the peaks sparkling with fresh snow. The rain has suddenly brought spring to the canyons which were so brown when we first arrived. Now they are green and lush while the roadsides and cliffs by the beach ripple with wild flowers, orange poppies, blue lupins, sunflowers and daisies.

We did not let the rain interfere with our activities. On George Washington's birthday in February, I took the family out for a drive and came back several hours later having driven 350 miles! We climbed up through the swirling icy mists of Mount Palomar to the world's largest telescope, and then crossed the scorching dryness of the Anza Borrego desert where the flowers were coming into bloom.

Stephen's mother and his Aunt Janet came to stay for the month of March. While Isobel was away in New York visiting Stephen's sister, we and Aunt Janet piled into the car and went off to the Joshua Tree National Monument, a high desert area above 3,000 feet, where the Joshua Tree produces its lily-like flowers at this time of year. At a lower elevation, there is a forest of cacti appropriately called 'jumping chollas'. One of them jumped at me, inextricably implanting its barbs in my leg, a rather mean thing to do to me on my birthday I thought, especially as the children had already sat on my birthday cake in the back of the car! Aunt Janet's medical expertise came to the rescue – of my leg, not the cake.

The children, Annie Dicke and I have just returned from Catalina Island where we spent the weekend. The island is a gem, unspoilt and free of traffic, but what impressed us most was the trip we took in a glass-bottomed boat. The sight of the tranquil, gleaming world of the seabed where seaweed grows to a height of twenty feet and fish, unaware of our presence, dart with a quicksilver grace between its branches, held us entranced. I wondered how we could be so ignorant of the silent beauty and mystery of that other world which is literally at our feet and on our shores. It also made me realize how easy it is to live in murky ignorance of other phenomena which touch our own existence.

Stephen is now in England, probably at this moment paying a flying visit to Cambridge, en route to Rome with his parents and Bernard. There he is to receive the Pope Pius XI Gold Medal for Science from the Pope, at the full session of the Pontifical Academy on Saturday. I think the notion of the Big Bang as the point of Creation appeals to the Vatican. At last Galileo has found a champion. Stephen has to give an address to the assembly and is going to use the occasion to make a special plea for the rehabilitation of Galileo's memory – three hundred and thirty-three years after Galileo's death. I trust that the days of the Inquisitor General really are over!

Jane

CHAPTER TWENTY-EIGHT

Undercurrents

OTHER ASPECTS OF the Californian experience provoked a more reflective response which would have introduced a jarring note to the generally buoyant nature of the letters home. This might have worried my family so mostly I kept these reflections to myself.

October 1974

At three years old, Lucy may be a backward swimmer but apparently I am a really retarded mother. In this country, if you don't have a job by the time your child is two, you are regarded as a miserable failure and are missing out on 'personal fulfilment'.

Ruth Hughes is a remarkably perceptive person. She has been very concerned for me as well as for the children and astounded me by the observation she made when I was introduced to her. She said that she had first seen Stephen in the Athenaeum, the Caltech Faculty Club, and while everyone else was praising his courage and brilliance, she had said to herself that there must be someone equally courageous behind him or he simply would not be there. Nobody has ever said anything like that to me before and it quite threw me off my stride. I was most touched and did not know how to reply, except with an embarrassed laugh.

People are spontaneously friendly and welcoming but I have a faint, lurking suspicion that this is an example of success breeding success. Now that Stephen has attained a position of some eminence, reactions towards him are noticeably different from those we encountered on our earlier trips to America. This is still the land where the majority of the population subscribes to the Protestant work ethic, loving success and deploring failure, with little sympathy for those who have not grabbed the opportunities it offers them. This may sound ungrateful when you consider how generously we are being treated. It's only an outsider's observation.

They ooze self-confidence, these nice people, and are quite certain that they have the best of everything here so why bother even to think about going anywhere else? Their eyes glaze over politely if you try to talk about Europe! They do have a point. They already have a good proportion of European art treasures in their museums. Not only do they have the best of everything, they have most of everything as well. The wastage is sickening. Gargantuan meals are served on beds of salad which no one is expected to eat and, in a land which cultivates an image of youth and fitness, I have never seen so many grossly obese people. This is strange when you realize that we are only half an hour from that shrine of shapeliness and glamour, Hollywood. Perhaps the competition is too discouraging for most people so they give up.

December 1974

I await the onset of 1975 in the certain conviction that my brain is turning to putty. I have had to abandon all hope of working on the thesis for lack, not of time for once, but of facilities since there's not much awareness here of medieval lyric poetry. I never dreamed that I would ever find myself *missing* the University Library! What a strangely ambivalent relationship I have with that institution! I have taken to reading biographies and have thrown myself headlong into a crazy round of activity, entertaining the many visitors who have come to stay, anxious to see the truth of our unreal existence for themselves. They, the crazy socializing, and, of course, the children, have kept me more or less occupied, distracting my mind from the dispiriting effect that life on the edge of the Caltech vortex has on anyone who is not a top-notch, international scientific genius.

Caltech is *par excellence* a temple where devotees come to worship at the altar of the gods and goddesses of science, particularly physics, to the exclusion of all else. The Caltech wives' club struggles valiantly to entertain spouses with trips to places like the Paul Getty museum at Malibu (with its genuine underground Roman car park) and the occasional concert or play in the Caltech theatre, but one

cannot get away from the suspicion that there are quite a lot of
disaffected wives who are wretchedly demoralized by their husbands'
obsession with science and their (possibly subconscious) disdain for
any other occupation, walk of life, or interest. These wives
concentrate most of their efforts on their own appearance and the
appearance of their 'homes'.

Gingerly negotiating the rim of this abyss, I have avoided being
swallowed up by it but I cannot remain unaffected by it. A little while
ago, when we went up to Santa Barbara where Stephen spent the
weekend in conference with Jim Hartle, I sat on the beach, wrapped up
against the icy wind, gazing out to sea while the children played. As I
ran the loose sand through my fingers, I asked myself where my life was
going. What did I have to show for my thirty years? I have the children,
'my blessings' as dear Thelma Thatcher would say, and Stephen. His
achievements are extraordinary and I am proud of him yet I don't
really feel that I share in his success.

He is recognized as a leading scientist and is even spoken of in
terms of Einstein's successor. He works hard and provides for us
in material terms as well as any other *père de famille*. Everything that
happens to him is crucial to me, whether it's a gilded honour, sparkling
with fame and glory, or one of those terrifying, life-threatening choking
fits which seize him without warning. I love him for his courage, his
wit, his sense of the ridiculous and the absurd and that wicked charisma
which enables him to twist most people, including me, round his
little finger. Whenever he goes away to a conference, I impatiently
look forward to his return after the first day or two of respite from
the physical strain. The other day I was delighted when he said that
he too feels a great sense of excitement and anticipation when he
returns home after these expeditions.

So, in a sense I am achieving what I set out to do – to devote
myself to Stephen, to give him the chance of fulfilling his genius. But
what have I become in the process? Who am I? What is there left of
me? I ask myself these questions and I'm not sure that I know the
answers. I am beginning to doubt my own identity. Instead of gaining
confidence and a sense of self with age, I am losing my self-esteem.
I am the mother of my darling children but I no longer count myself
a Hispanist or even a linguist. I am Stephen's wife but since I am not a
scientist, I do not command any respect in Caltech – or for that matter
in Cambridge – other than among close friends. Perhaps all this frenzied

socializing and entertaining is my Freudian way of saying 'Please notice me, too!' since for most people – and that, to judge from her attitude, probably includes my sister-in-law who came for Christmas – I am a nobody. I used to have aspirations and a personality. I still have thoughts and feelings. If you prick me, do I not bleed? Am I so dull and so stupid, I ask myself, that I have become nothing more than a robot, a spare set of mechanical parts?

27 January 1975

Mum and Dad are coming back for a second visit because, Mum says apologetically, Robert asked her to come for his birthday! I shall be *so* happy to see them. They were such a marvellous help at Christmas: they entertained the children, shared the driving and helped heave that unwieldy, leaden wheelchair and its batteries in and out of the car hundreds of times. Why is it that at a time when probes are being sent out into space and man can walk on the moon, batteries are still antediluvian – heavy, cumbersome and unreliable? The wheelchair, it has to be said, has become permanently attached to Stephen. For all its excessive mass, it is good to watch him revelling in his independence.

February 1975

Thanks to Trish, I have found a new activity! Choral singing! The glorious music sweeps me away into a new heady dimension, introducing an intoxicating compulsion to my generally banal existence. The music expresses so much that I would like to be able to say and for which I cannot find words – all my anxieties for Stephen, all my yearning to be able to protect him and ease his burdens of frustration and fear, and all my own thoughts about suffering and death. Sometimes as he sits beside me at the piano, thinking out problems in physics, while I tap out the melodies, I hope that through the music, he might realize how deeply I care for him. How strange it is that I should have discovered such spiritual comfort, in such an outwardly materialistic society!

April 1975

Ruth Hughes has just presented me with a Japanese pearl set in a blue velvet case! She said if Stephen is to receive medals like the Papal Medal, I should be given something too! I was very moved that an outsider and comparative stranger should show such awareness and take it upon herself to make such a gesture.

20 June 1975

Our circumstances are luxurious. One might say that we have become true southern Californians, i.e., we are as confident as the rest of them in the firm belief that there is nowhere else to live, not even northern California! We love the sun, the beaches, the deserts and the mountains. I have driven hundreds, if not thousands, of miles, amazed at the extravagant variety of landscape and vegetation and the curiously competitive cohabitation of man and Nature. It's less impressive when you cross the frontier to Mexico as we have just done, and see the poverty of Tijuana, the border town, where cardboard shacks cling to the hillside, the landscape is totally barren for lack of water and the cliffs are a dumping ground for American rubbish. We had come from one of the most luxurious corners of the civilized world foolishly expecting to find picturesque Mediterranean villages. All we found was poverty and squalor, all the way down the coast. I am ashamed to say we scuttled back to the United States as fast as we could.

July 1975

A couple of weeks ago, I was driving along a one-way street, Green Street, when a car on my right suddenly decided to turn left and swerved into us. The damage to our car was not severe and although we were shaken, no one was hurt. The other driver was apologetic and admitted that he was in the wrong, having obviously suffered a momentary mental aberration. Apart from exchanging insurance details, this should have been the end of the story.

We were just getting out our documents when people came running from all directions, wizened little old women and dry, sharp-faced men. They hustled us into a café, made a great fuss of me, my mother and the children and, to my surprise, quite unnecessarily insisted on calling the police. They were rough with the other driver and so were the police when they came. Understandably, he became more and more tense and irascible. I felt very sorry for him. He was black.

3 August 1975

Today has witnessed an historic meeting. For the first time ever, we have met a family in similar circumstances to our own! The Irelands, David, Joyce and John, live over in Arcadia, only a few miles from here. Angelically blue-eyed and blond, John is about Lucy's age. Like Stephen, David is a scientist by training. He studied and taught maths. He is also severely disabled with a neurological illness and is confined to a wheelchair. Like Stephen, there is very little that he can do for himself, though unlike Stephen he is a large man and must weigh quite a lot. Joyce is an athletic, energetic person who seems to be very well organized with a very positive attitude. She married David in the full knowledge of his illness.

Stephen was very nervous about meeting the Irelands. I felt for his anxiety and wanted to protect him, afraid that he might be disheartened on witnessing the full impact of disability, since our lives are built on the brave assertion that his disability is just a minor background inconvenience. He would be brought face to face with another family and would see them as many people see us. In fact, though he was clearly shaken by David's condition, he managed to put on a cheerful smile and together we kept up the bright façade of normality. I wonder what the Irelands must have thought of us. They may have admired our determination but they would not have been fooled by the façade. They know too much themselves about the battles and the struggles involved.

In many respects their battles mirror ours, except that unlike Stephen, David did not suffer a sudden, traumatic diagnosis because his illness crept up on him from the age of sixteen. However he did undergo the same sort of shattering condemnation when his consultant told him to forget all his ambitions, both academic and emotional, that is to say, to forget about living. Joyce and David also experienced doubts and uncertainties during their courtship then, through their marriage, found new resources of determination and optimism. David had to summon a superhuman courage in his fight with the hostile school authorities who, because of his disability, wanted to force his resignation from the job he loved, teaching maths. They then refused to give him the opportunity to take up the alternative job of counsellor for which he was equally gifted and well qualified. Eventually he started his own counselling business and has made a startling success of it.

There the similarities end. There is a fundamental difference between the Irelands and us, as if we are opposite faces of the same coin. That difference lies in the fact that their approach to David's illness is quite open – open with themselves and open with the outside world, not concealing the difficulties and the pain behind a brave smile. David has consigned that spirit of frankness and honesty to a book which he wrote to introduce himself to his son, John, in case he died before John was born or before John was old enough to know him. *Letters to an Unborn Child* is a very honest self-portrait and a moving account of the battles that David and Joyce have undergone together.

In the book David, with Joyce's help, overcomes the physical tribulations of disability, transcending his own experiences and reaching out to a higher knowledge of self. He discovers that each human being is entitled to a birthright, the right to be loved and valued for his or herself, whatever their circumstances, background, or education. As he becomes more aware of his own personality and his own reactions, he confronts his major failing, a tendency to conceal his true self behind a popular, jovial exterior. Having truly penetrated to his inner self, he is then able to deal openly with those able-bodied and physically fit clients who come to him for help, advice and, above all, friendship, in coping with their own emotional and psychological problems. Almost accidentally through his work, David has discovered an enhanced faith in the love of God, a love which is personal, unconditional, outside the realms of time and space, and it is this which enables him to face whatever the future may bring without fear and without bitterness.

In his first letter to his unborn child, David expresses the wish that he might speak on behalf of other people who cannot give voice to their emotions. This gave me grounds for hoping that through David, I might be able to understand Stephen more easily. Certainly David describes many situations where Stephen's reactions have echoed his own: for instance David explains that he, too, was obstinately reluctant to avail himself of medical aids, such as a walking stick or a wheelchair, until they became absolutely essential and it appears that, through necessity, David has developed an iron will equal to Stephen's. I have no doubt that Stephen's concern that his children should have a clearly defined image of him and of his love for them is as passionate as David's wish to convey his personality to John.

On the other hand, David's fluency, his buoyancy, his faith, his appreciation, his depth of understanding, his care for Joyce are aspects of his individual personality. Stephen does allow himself to say to the press these days that everything that has happened to him since that terrible day of the diagnosis has to be seen as a bonus – and this I gladly interpret as a measure of his appreciation – but then in the same breath, he will bravely say that where there is physical illness, there is no room for psychological problems as well: this means that there is always a barrier to the communication of our severest difficulties.

Through reading David's book I have learnt that my tears and frustrations, even the bouts of anger I feel at thoughtlessness and lack of consideration, are all valid emotions since, in David's words, 'they release the poisons which sicken or kill us'. I have always been ashamed when my temper has got the better of me. It usually happens when I am tired and my patience is pushed beyond the limits of endurance. According to David, these shameful emotional outbursts are a healthy assertion of one's birthright, one's individuality, and deserve to be taken seriously. It is imperturbable self-control, the stiff upper lip, bottling up powerful emotions in oneself and suppressing the emotions of others, that is unhealthy and dangerous. I am struck by the irony of discovering these emotional truths through the words of someone who is, if anything, even more disabled than Stephen, someone who, through his own suffering, has learnt to reach out and help other people!

I am sorry that we did not meet the Irelands sooner. Perhaps David could have helped us to improve our lines of communication. As it is, we shall just have to keep up the mask – it has worked well enough to date and it's only occasionally that it does not seem adequate. Anyhow, once we're back in England, marching ever onward, there will be no time for introspection and analysis.

20 August 1975

California has brought us untold material luxury, a social spontaneity unheard of in Cambridge and, with the help of the students, particularly Bernard, a measure of respite from the physical pressures which were beginning to weigh us down at home. These past twelve months have been a year of freedom from the fenland furrow that had become a rut. It has been a time for taking stock of our situation, for bridging the gulf, like a faultline in the surface of the earth, that is inevitably widening between our past and our future lifestyles. Yet, strangely, the brilliance of the Californian sky has defined even more sharply the two extremes between which we oscillate, the bright shining public face – the prizes, the fame, the accolades – on the one hand, and the dark, despairing private image – the creeping paralysis, the anxieties, the tensions – on the other. Sometimes they can be complementary, the one compensating for the other. At other times they conflict and then the joyous applause attending the one is muffled by the anguished cry of the other.

CHAPTER TWENTY-NINE

Establishment

BEFORE WE LEFT Cambridge in the summer of 1974, I knew that we would never again be able to return to live at number 6 Little St Mary's Lane: the house was too small for our growing family and the stairs too perilous. The question of where we might move to was – in physicists' terminology – non-trivial. Cambridge has very few residential properties within easy reach of the town centre, other than a few narrow streets of smallish houses like our own in the Lane. The family houses that do exist are either prohibitively expensive or have been bought up over the years by the colleges and the University. Although our house might be expected to fetch a very reasonable price on the open market, we would never with the proceeds be able to afford to buy a larger, more suitable house anywhere near the Department, certainly not in the Grange Road area, where so many years ago before our marriage Stephen had had lodgings. This time, however, I had no qualms about approaching Gonville and Caius College. The College was eagerly lapping up the reflected glory of Stephen's repeated successes and would be unlikely to treat us with the same harsh indifference that it had shown in the sixties when we were young, unknown and struggling to make ends meet.

Even colleges such as Gonville and Caius eventually respond to changing times, as the Bursar's reply to my enquiry revealed. He explained that his office no longer dealt with the letting of College property in Cambridge as that function had now passed into the hands of the Dean, the Rev. John Sturdy. This was welcome news. Requests for accommodation were much more likely to receive a cooperative response from the Dean than from the Bursar, given the diametrically opposite aims of their respective professions.

John Sturdy had been appointed Dean shortly before Stephen's induction as a Research Fellow in October 1965. The Sturdys had befriended us from that time onwards, always supportive, always concerned for the children, always deeply caring. John, a studious, other-worldly Hebrew scholar of saintly appearance, was well complemented by his lively, bustling, intensely practical wife Jill. I especially respected them for the particular crusade that they had made their own own, although Caius, where pretension always took precedence over humanity, consistently failed to appreciate the extent of their achievement. When first I knew them, the Sturdys already had two children and were expecting their third baby at the same time as I was expecting Robert. Over the next fifteen years they adopted nine more from all backgrounds, colours and creeds. Jill took a degree in English, did a teacher-training course and then founded her own school to support and educate her family. To those children from seriously deprived backgrounds Jill and John gave love, hope, a family and an education that they could never have enjoyed otherwise.

The Sturdys instituted a Christmas party in the College for the children of all members and employees, whether Fellows, kitchen staff or cleaners. John Sturdy or his eldest son, John Christian, would dress up as Father Christmas and the children had a fine time boisterously playing musical chairs round High Table. Exceptionally among the Fellows of Caius, pomposity and privilege knew no place in John Sturdy's outlook, which was determined by the highest Christian principles.

My admiration for the Sturdys knew no bounds and I was sure that I could count on their sympathy. Even so, John's alacrity in responding to my request was surprising. Have you thought about where you would like to live? he asked, as if the range of choice was unlimited, when we met to discuss the prospects on 13 June 1974. 'Somewhere in the Grange Road area, I suppose,' I said, not expecting for one moment that there was even the remotest chance of that pipe-dream becoming a possibility. 'Well,' he replied calmly, 'let's go and look at the properties in that area and see if there is anything suitable for you.'

We looked at half-a-dozen houses belonging to the College on the west side of Cambridge, on the fringes of the Victorian village of Newnham. Like so many other fine houses in the area, all the properties we visited had previously been family homes which had fallen into decline, and had then been taken over by the College for conversion into student accommodation. Some were too distant from the Department for Stephen, some were too close to noisy main roads and others were not spacious enough on the ground floor for a wheelchair.

There was one house, however, in West Road just off the Backs, which immediately caught my attention. Solid and extensive, with the self-assurance generated by Victorian expansionism, it stood in gardens large enough to be designated grounds, next door to Harvey Court, the monstrous sixties development which had replaced a similar Victorian mansion. We were already well acquainted with those gardens since they had been the venue every summer for Robert's birthday parties. My mother would arrive bearing a lavishly decorated birthday cake – sometimes in the shape of a train, sometimes a car, sometimes a fort – and my father and I would organize enough games and entertainments to keep upwards of a dozen small children amused for two hours, the most demanding two hours of the entire social calendar, apart from those dedicated to Lucy's birthday party, which being in the winter was, if anything, even more challenging.

With a few modifications, the ground floor of the West House at number 5 West Road could be made suitable for us in every way, especially because the ground floor consisted of a sufficient number of large, well-lit rooms to accommodate the whole family, plus all the other necessary facilities such as kitchen and bathroom, still leaving room to spare for parties for all ages. It was further from the Department than Little St Mary's Lane but not inconveniently far, and was about the same distance from the primary school that Lucy would be attending. The gardens offered scope for parties and games of all descriptions. It was not until I had a son of my own that I realized how vital those tedious hours spent learning to play cricket correctly on the games field at St Albans High School really were to me. They bore little resemblance to the relaxed games that Chris, Dad and I used to play with a tennis ball in our small garden at home or on the beach. In the gardens of the West House, there would be ample space to put those hard lessons into practice for Robert's benefit.

The house had been vaguely threatened with demolition, I remembered, in the early seventies when the land on which it stood had been earmarked as the possible site for a new college. Mr David Robinson, a business tycoon from Newmarket who had made his fortune in television rentals, had wanted to endow a new college, but not before – so the story went – he had approached the Royal College of Surgeons with an offer of a million pounds. His offer was regarded as a hoax and not taken up. He then turned his attention to Cambridge instead and offered to fund the building of a new college, if the University would provide the land on which to build it. In Cambridge his offer was regarded not so much as a hoax as an embarrassment. Mr Robinson considered that the contribution – of ten million pounds – that he was prepared to make to the enlargement of the venerable institution was of such significance that it should be suitably recognized. Naturally enough, he demanded that the college bearing his name should be built on land on the Backs, as close to the famous view of King's College Chapel as possible. None of the colleges owning land on the Backs were prepared to countenance parting with any of their precious territory and various suggestions for building the college elsewhere were proposed, none of which appealed to Mr Robinson. One of those suggestions was the land owned by Gonville and Caius at Number 5 West Road. However, that site proved to be too small and eventually Mr Robinson was persuaded to spend more money to purchase land from St John's College on the site of the Trinity Hall hostel where Stephen was lodging at the time of the May Ball in 1963.

Number 5 West Road had until recently been a thriving family hotel, the West House Hotel. Its business derived mostly from parents visiting their offspring in the University or at the local boarding schools. Some five years before John Sturdy took me to look at it, the lease had run out and the College had taken it over for use as undergraduate accommodation. The undergraduates had been given free rein to choose their own colour schemes and the once fine Victorian dining-room now had a black ceiling and scarlet walls. This decor did not upset me unduly. As Thelma Thatcher had impressed upon me years earlier, paint was superficial and easily changed. I was much more impressed by the dimensions of the house, so when at the end of our tour John Sturdy asked me for my opinion of the houses we had seen, without hesitation I opted for the West House.

That decision effectively silenced the faction in the College which wanted to demolish any building, including that house, which was more than fifteen years old. Negotiations proceeded without a hitch and it was agreed by 11 July 1974 that on our return from California in 1975, we would occupy the ground floor of those commodious premises. In part-exchange for the rent, the College would have the use of our own house in Little St Mary's Lane for Research Fellows. Times had changed:

over the past ten years, the College had relaxed its rules to allow Research Fellows to rent accommodation.

During our absence, partition walls were erected on the staircase in the West House to screen the ground floor from the undergraduates upstairs; the newly created ground-floor flat was redecorated throughout, eliminating the red and black paint, and ramps were built at the front and at the garden doors. In directing these operations from California, I enlisted the support of a very courageous young man, Toby Churchill, whom we had recently come to know. While still a student, Toby had been struck down by a paralysing illness which had deprived him of the power of speech and the use of his legs. He now lived with his parents in Cambridge not far from us. Toby had used his engineering expertise to adapt his environment to his needs so that he could look after himself – with a little help from nurses – and also to build his own invention, the Lightwriter, a small laptop keyboard with a digital screen into which he could type his conversation.

Quick, intelligent and funny, Toby had been the only disabled person we knew until we met the Ireland family in California. It was a happy encounter since the relationship was devoid of sentiment and built on mutual respect. Toby was someone with whom Stephen could discuss technical, if not scientific matters, and someone whose advice he could seek on communications systems as his own powers of speech were fading alarmingly to a whisper. Unfortunately, Toby's invention was not of much help to Stephen since operating the keyboard required a dexterity which he did not possess, and Toby was not much impressed by Stephen's enthusiasm for electric wheelchairs since he was concerned to keep his arm muscles in good shape by propelling himself around under his own steam. As my intermediary, Toby propelled himself round to West Road many times in the course of the summer of 1975 and reported his findings to me in California, along with all sorts of useful suggestions. I also sought his assistance in advertising free accommodation for any student who, like Bernard, was prepared to give a hand with lifting, but as Toby sensibly pointed out, undergraduate students would go away in the holidays, leaving us in the lurch.

If England seemed small, cramped and dirty on our return from California, the ground-floor flat at Number 5 West Road amply compensated for our disillusionment. For all the sixteen years of our occupancy, we were conscious of our good fortune in being able to live in that house. The rooms were vast and high-ceilinged with decorative plaster cornices and delicately embossed central roses around the light fittings. The tall sash windows gave on to a true English lawn, framed with carefully chosen conifers and deciduous trees: dark, forbidding yew mingled with the light fronds of willow. A giant sequoia – a Californian redwood – evidently a sapling newly introduced to Europe when the house was built, towered above the tumbledown conservatory at one corner of the building, communing with its partner, a *Thuja plicata* or red western cedar of comparable height at the far end of the lawn. The gnarled old apple tree faithfully struggled to produce its blossoms and its crop with such abundance biennially that every two years the ground beneath would be carpeted with an excess of cooking apples from October to December. 'Not stewed apple again!' the children would chorus at the supper table while their father would grin in mischievous collusion. Eventually Stephen decided that he was allergic to stewed fruit but that was not an excuse that the children were allowed to get away with.

In summer we would hang a hammock, swings and climbing ropes from the branches of the apple tree and listen to the twittering of the fledgling blackbirds inside its hollow trunk. To the left of the apple tree, in full view of the living-room window, lay the gracefully curving herbaceous border with its backing of flowering trees and bushes – lilac, almond and hawthorn. Even in the depths of the harshest winter, the beauty of the garden was still magical. Late one night after a persistent snowfall, I peered out through the heavy curtains and held my breath at the sight of the transformation of the dank, brown winter garden outside. The incandescent light of the full moon in a cloudless sky illuminated a glistening blanket of snow, covering lawn and trees with a dazzling purity. The riveting beauty of that scene sent shivers of delight down my spine. I could not drag myself away from the window; I knew that by morning that enchantment would be gone.

In its prime, the garden must have been a splendid sight. Despite the rampant goose-grass and pervasive ground elder, it still conveyed colourful hints of its former glory in its myriad collection of perennials. Like the trees, they must have been planted as part of an overall scheme, perhaps as much as a century ago when the house was built. Legend has it that the gardeners who created the garden received scant reward for their labours: the elderly spinsters who inhabited the house in the early years of the century presented them with packets of marrow seeds culled from the garden as Christmas presents.

I tried to supplement the efforts of the hard-pressed College gardeners with a little weeding and planting in an attempt to subdue the goose-grass. Jeremy Prynne, a colleague of Stephen's in the Fellowship and College Librarian, applauded my efforts and proposed that I should be elected to the College gardening committee since, as he remarked, many of its members could not distinguish a dandelion from a daffodil. His proposal was rejected out-of-hand, however, because it was inconceivable that a non-Fellow, let alone a wife, should be elected to a College committee.

From the time of our arrival in the autumn of 1975, the house, like the garden, was to lend itself enthusiastically over the years to countless parties. There were the family celebrations, the birthday parties and the Christmas dinners. There were also the duty occasions – fund-raising events as I became drawn into supporting charities, coffee mornings and musical *soirées*, Departmental parties, parties for the beginning and the end of the academic year, conference receptions and dinners. In summer there were tea parties (again usually for conferences, mostly of visiting American and Russian scientists) on the lawn with cucumber sandwiches and croquet, and there were the folk-dance evenings, barbecue suppers and firework parties. It was fun and usually appreciated but it was hard work since it was only much later that I had any help with the catering. It was scarcely surprising that sometimes the unofficial companions of the official guests, the hangers-on, mistook me in my working apron for a College servant and condescendingly requested another glass of wine or another sandwich with little of the unctuous charm they would have mustered had they realized that I was their hostess.

We appeared to live in privileged surroundings but there were disadvantages. Despite our occupancy, the house remained under threat of demolition. After the completion of the renovations carried out for our benefit, only minimal maintenance work on it was authorized. In winter, the central heating system, based on the original Victorian radiators, was scarcely adequate when the north wind blew snow through the gaps in the ill-fitting doors and windows. At one stage the gas fires, used to supplement the radiators, were found to be emitting more fumes into the rooms than they were sending up the chimneys. The wiring consisted of an eccentric combination of modern sockets fitted on to old wires of which no one knew the provenance.

Much more alarmingly, ceilings tended to crash to the ground with disturbing regularity, even though my father, with his catastrophic history of provoking the gravitational collapse of many a ceiling, was nowhere in the vicinity. By the grace of God, the damage was never more than material: it was simply the stereo system, not actually any living being, that was crushed when in the middle of one July night in 1978 the living-room ceiling lost its key and descended with an almighty thud amidst a cloud of grime and plaster dust, smashing the furniture to smithereeens in the room beneath and sending the chandelier into orbit. Fortunately we had just gone to bed and the children were sleeping safely in their rooms. Equally luckily, no one was in the bath when later the bathroom ceiling also came down.

Outside, the roof regularly shed its tiles. This latter hazard was rectified thanks to a timely visit by His Royal Highness the Duke of Edinburgh, Chancellor of the University of Cambridge, who came to pay Stephen a private visit. So afraid were we that a tile might crash on to the royal pate as His Highness entered the front door that I asked for a protective screen of wire netting to be put round the guttering to catch any loose tiles in their downward slide. The point was taken and some months later the building was re-roofed. Thanks to the royal visit we also acquired new bathroom fittings.

We were not the sole residents of the house since we occupied only the ground floor. Students, who had a separate entrance, lived on the upper floors, and mice lived in the dark depths of the cellar amongst the equipment belonging to the University Caving Club. The mice kept their distance after Lucy acquired a predatory cat but it was less easy to attain a satisfactory *modus vivendi* with the students. As individuals they were as delightfully friendly a bunch as one could hope to meet, as we discovered on those occasions when we invited them in for a drink or met them on the lawn in the middle of the night when the fire alarm – which had an intermittent fault – roused the whole house for no good reason. But inevitably, the students' lifestyle, their routine and their habits were often at odds with ours. At times their presence made itself felt in a more tangible form than just loud noises and bumps in the night.

About once a year someone would leave the bath water running in the student bathroom upstairs, just above our kitchen. The last time this happened, I arrived home at lunch-time with a quarter of an hour to spare before the expected arrival of some cousins of Stephen's from the Antipodes. I could hear the rush of flowing water the moment I turned my key in the door. With sinking heart, I smelt the familiar musty dankness as I crossed the hall to the kitchen. The floor was already under a layer of water and the best plates and bowls, put out ready on the worktop, were collecting dirty puddles. The cheese, tomatoes, lettuce and bread swam in warm grey pools as more water poured through the ceiling and trickled down the light fitting ... There were times when I regretted that we no longer had a home of our own where we could be in charge of all eventualities.

Such drawbacks had not yet come to our notice, however, when in September 1975 my mother and I cleaned out number 6 Little St Mary's Lane before handing it over to Caius, and I arranged the removal of our possessions to number 5 West Road. Only then did I begin to realize how justified I had been in regarding the year in California as a period of transition. Previously, like so many other young people of our own age, we had lived in modest circumstances: Stephen had no secure employment and had had to struggle hard for recognition, Robert had gone to a state school and, discounting the ravages of motor neurone disease, most of our friends lived in similar situations.

Post-California, our circumstances had changed dramatically. We had come back to England to living quarters which were more akin to a mini-stately home, or a Master's Lodge, and Stephen was assured of his first official post in the University, a Readership. While we were away, rumour had circulated in Cambridge that we were considering staying in California for good. Immediately the old biblical adage about a prophet being without honour in his own country proved itself and the Readership, later to be superseded by a personal Chair, materialized. Far from wanting Stephen to go, as had been predicted by that senior don a year or two earlier, the University had actually been impatient for his return.

The Readership brought with it the much needed services of a secretary in the form of Judy Fella who introduced a fresh vitality and an unaccustomed glamour to the drab realms of the Department of Applied Mathematics and Theoretical Physics. Judy worked for Stephen for many years with tireless loyalty and efficiency. At last there was someone to take over the administration of his official life in England just as his secretary Polly Grandmontagne had in California. She typed his papers, including the hieroglyphs, dealt with his correspondence, organized his conferences, arranged his travels and applied for his visas, all of which amounted to a full-time occupation since he was now something of a celebrity and was much in demand.

America was not unique in its adulation of success. In a more discreet fashion, cloaked in a diffident respectability, the same attitude prevailed in Britain. Afraid of being outdone in the scramble to acknowledge the brilliant scientific star blazing across their horizons, successive scientific institutions took their lead from each other and awarded Stephen their most prestigious medals. On many an occasion over the course of the next few months and years, my parents would come over to Cambridge in time to meet the children from school while I picked Stephen up from the Department, loaded him and the wheelchair into the car, and then set off for some smart London hotel – the Savoy, the Dorchester or the Grosvenor – where the evening's presentation dinner was to take place. Sometimes we were given overnight accommodation to ease the strain on me since I was chauffeur, nurse, valet, cupbearer and interpreter as well as companion-wife, all at once.

When finally all the intervening hurdles between the customary tenor of life in Cambridge and the glitzy London social scene had been surmounted, we would appear, always late, decked out in evening dress, complete with the hand-tied bow-tie on which Stephen insisted, in a sparkling ballroom or dining-room, to be greeted by the assembled ranks of the scientific intelligentsia, peers of the realm and assorted dignitaries. They were all very charming and their wives were often quite considerate, but to me they all seemed so old, older than my parents: they were not the sort of people I was likely to meet in the street or at the school gate where my real friends were.

The same people, along with the most affected members of London's glitterati, also turned up at other notable social occasions in the scientific calendar, particularly the *conversazione*, the evening gatherings in summer, at the Royal Society where the rich and famous mercilessly elbowed each other out of the way in the scrum for drinks and canapés, while the exhibitors, guarding their carefully prepared displays, patiently waited for the frivolous, chattering assembly to show a flicker of interest in their painstaking research.

The artificial glamour of these occasions was simultaneously enter-taining and irritating. As I participated politely in the small-talk, observing the required social graces, I would glance round the room, speculating how many of those people present could possess the insights of Ruth Hughes so far away in Pasadena, how many of them could have even the faintest notion of the reality of our lives, the reality which would return as soon as the party was over. Precious few, I surmised.

At midnight, as soon as the magic had run its course, there would be no coachman to drive us home from the ball and the following morning we would be back in our routine. I would be dressing Stephen, feeding him his breakfast, his pills and his tea, then I would clean the house and put two or three loads of washing into the machine before peeling the onions and potatoes for the next meal. Across the road, the tower of the University Library would loom accusingly, a silent but eloquent reminder of the neglected thesis. There would be no glass slipper either, even though there might be a glistening gold medal, set on a bed of satin and velvet, to remind us that the previous evening had not been just a passing dream. Even the medals disappeared from view after a day or two. Since the house was subject to occasional, opportunistic petty theft – handbags stolen from the hall, bicycles stolen from the porch – the medals had to be consigned to the bank vault, rarely to be seen again.

CHAPTER THIRTY

Buried Treasure

THE REALITY OF everyday life always began the night before, when, after giving Stephen his pills and his laxative and putting him to bed, I would lay out the breakfast things for the children. At long last, Robert's enthusiasm for early rising found its true purpose, since he could be trusted to get his own breakfast and supervise Lucy's as well. Meanwhile I would get Stephen out of bed, dress him and give him a cup of tea and his early morning vitamins before taking Lucy to school on the back of my bike. On my return, usually laden with shopping, I would give Stephen his breakfast and attend to his personal needs before he went to work.

After the freedom he had enjoyed in California, Stephen was in no mind to put up with the frustrations of a push-wheelchair and applied to the Department of Health for an electric model, the fast one, since, according to the propaganda, such appliances were available free of charge. However, the truth, as in so many areas, did not quite conform to the promise of the advertising and all the weight of Stephen's considerable persistence, resolution and doggedness were not enough to shift the grey officials of that particular governmental department into granting his application.

They told him that he could submit another application for the three-wheeler battery-driven car, which he now lacked the strength to control, or, indeed, for an electric wheelchair – but only the slow model, designed for indoor use like the one, purchased by a philanthropic fund he already had at the Institute. We wasted hours trying to argue our case for the faster chair, but repeatedly came up against the same obdurate, wearisome, circular reasoning. The Health Service did indeed supply electric wheelchairs, they said again and again, in the form of the slow indoor model, and we could apply for that. We pointed out that, like

Stephen, most people would want an electric wheelchair for outdoor use and would naturally want the faster model which was scarcely more expensive than the slow one. It was an infuriating moment when the duplicity of the official line dawned on us. Significantly the bureaucrats made no attempt to deny it: the Health Service did not provide the faster outdoor electric wheelchairs because too many people would want them. So much for the Welfare State. It had contributed so very little to our welfare that one might be forgiven for thinking that its purpose was actually to prevent the disabled from working to their full capacity and, consequently, from contributing as taxpayers to the national Exchequer. A handful of vitamin pills on prescription seemed to be the best it could offer with only minimal physical, practical, moral or financial support.

We became even more dependent on family, students and friends in the daily battle to function as a family. Stephen did acquire the wheelchair he wanted. We paid for it ourselves out of our own savings with no help from the National Health Service – and, discreetly accompanied by a student, he travelled to work in it every morning. His route took him along the path through King's College where aconites and snowdrops bloom in winter and daffodils in spring, across the river over the humpbacked bridge and out of the College by a side entrance, to his office in the Department on the opposite side of Silver Street. That Stephen was at last able to enjoy the basic human right to move about freely as and when and where he chose, was not a result of any government provision or benefit, only of his own hard work and his success in physics. The prospects were bleak for those disabled people who had the misfortune not to be geniuses and did not have access to private funding to meet their needs.

Transport for the children was another problem requiring an urgent solution. I took Lucy to school on the back of my bike every morning but Robert's school was some distance away on the Trumpington Road. It was thanks to John Stark, a relative newcomer to Cambridge, that Robert got to school on time. Jean and John Stark and their two children had come to Cambridge from London in the early 1970s when John took up the post of chest consultant at Addenbrooke's Hospital, and had moved into the house that Fred Hoyle had built for himself a decade earlier in Clarkson Road. Luckily for us, John drove past the end of West Road where he picked Robert up on his way to work and dropped him off, together with his own son Dan, at the Perse Preparatory School.

By chance, this arrangement gave rise to one of those memorable moments when our domestic existence coincided fleetingly with the irreality of the public domain, like a crystal raindrop caught on a spider's web briefly illuminating its surroundings with the shimmering colours of the rainbow. This moment occurred at a *conversazione* at the Royal Society. It was one of the more enjoyable of those occasions – a scientist from London Zoo had brought a huge Indian python for the guests to handle. I was enjoying the unexpectedly dry warmth of the snake's smooth body as it slid along my arm, over my shoulder, round the back of my neck and onto the person standing next to me, when one of the onlookers came up to me and said casually, 'You live in Cambridge, don't you?' I nodded. 'And,' she said, 'you live in West Road, don't you?' I nodded again in some surprise. 'How do you know?' I asked. 'I see a little boy who looks just like you standing on the corner of West Road waiting for his lift every morning when I drive past!' she explained. I felt greatly reassured that some of these people were human after all and that some of them realized that there were other facets to my existence than snake-handling at smart occasions.

I reciprocated the Starks' much-valued help in taking Robert to school by collecting the boys from the Perse in the afternoon and delivering Dan to Clarkson Road, where I would occasionally stay and talk to Jean while the children played. After living in London, Jean, a graduate of the London School of Economics, found the male chauvinist attitudes prevalent in Cambridge and the domination of all walks of life by the University cramping and discouraging. She and I had much in common, in education, experience and outlook, and we were both married to dynamic individuals, though they worked in different professions. My marriage to a single-minded scientist found an echo in her marriage to a dedicated doctor, both of whom prided themselves on their high levels of achievement. We shared our frustration at a system which had educated us to compete with men until the age of twenty-one or -two, and then had summarily discarded us, consigning us to second-class status, denying us even the right to claim any spark of intelligence. Not for one moment did we regret our role as wives and mothers but we did resent the low esteem which society, particularly Cambridge society, accorded those essential roles. The women's movement had more or less passed us by: it had improved the lot of women students in that they were now admitted to the men's colleges and, at long last, the Fellows of Gonville and Caius had bowed to pressure from Stephen to amend their statutes to allow wives to dine on High Table; otherwise there was very little support for women who sought intellectual stimulus at the same time as being good mothers. Jean and I tried endlessly to count our blessings and encouraged each other in our respective research projects.

It was Jean who insisted that I take up the thesis again. It seemed to me to be foolish even to contemplate such a hopeless enterprise. The thesis had been a presence in my life, sometimes welcome, sometimes much resented, for nearly ten years. I had completed only one-third of the whole project although I had amassed a vast amount of material, and I could not envisage ever finishing it. The only free time at my disposal was the sparse intervening period between Stephen's departure at midday and a quick round of the shops in the early afternoon before picking Lucy up from school at a quarter past three – two-and-a-half hours at the most. Nevertheless, thanks to Jean's insistence and the extraordinary example of Henry Button, one of my father's old Civil Service colleagues who had begun his research on the *Minnesänger* in 1934 and finished it forty years later, the prospect began to appear less ludicrous. Encouraged by this model of perseverance, I found myself yielding to the strong, silent pull of the University Library, the landmark which, day and night, beckoned and cajoled, accusing me of disloyalty as I stood staring out of the kitchen window, my hands plunged in water at the sink.

As the three areas and periods of my research were so clearly defined, the return to it was less challenging than I had feared. I had already documented my ideas on the earliest lyrics, the Mozarabic *kharjas*, and could now turn my attention to the second area of medieval lyrical flowering – Galicia, the north-western corner of the Iberian Peninsula where the language was more akin to Portuguese than Castilian, and where the city of Santiago de Compostela had attained international renown on account of the shrine of St James whose coffin was said to have been washed up on the Galician coastline in 824. By the twelfth century Santiago had become the end-point of a highly commercial pilgrim route, the *camino francés*, and one of the richest cities in Europe.

The songs of the Galician troubadours ousted the waning Provençal poetry as the favourite amusement at the Castilian court and their composition developed into yet another of the full-scale industries there of that egregious king, Alfonso the Wise. The Galician-Portuguese lyrics fall into four extraordinarily disparate categories, from Alfonso

X's songs to the Virgin, the *cantigas de Santa María*, through the crudely scurrilous diatribes of the *cantigas de escarnho e maldizer*, to the learned love poetry of the *cantigas de amor*, composed under sophisticated courtly influence and aspiring to emulate the abstract ideals of the Provençal school. The fourth group of lyrics, the *cantigas de amigo*, are expressions of love, voiced by women. They betray undisputedly folkloric elements in their style and language and appear to hark back to traditional antecedents. In those few hours at my disposal each day, it was my task to sift out the traditional elements from the 512 *cantigas de amigo*, evaluate any salient stylistic and linguistic features which they shared with the *kharjas*, compare their language with that of learned classical or biblical precedents and situate them against a more general European background.

Like the *kharjas*, the *cantigas de amigo* are women's love songs where the mother figure and the girl's sisters again have prominent roles as her confidantes. As in the *kharjas*, there is in the *cantigas* an established tradition of lovers' meetings, not partings, at dawn, and often the girl has cause to lament her lover's absence. All these parallels are not coincidental: Mozarabic refugees fled north to escape the waves of fanatical Arab oppression, taking their traditions, culture and religious rituals with them. By the thirteenth century close cultural links had been established between the Christian and Moorish kingdoms and the presence of Moorish entertainers and *muwassaha* poets at later Christian courts is documented, while the fine Moorish or *mudéjar* traceries and decorations of northern churches and monasteries provide ample evidence of cross-cultural exchanges.

The *cantigas* differ strikingly from the *kharjas*, however, in that they do not contain any of the clear-cut radiance of *kharja* imagery or any sense of urgent anticipation. Their imagery arises from the natural background of the mountains and streams of the north-western corner of the Peninsula, exposed to the turbulence of the Atlantic winds, and is identified with the emotions of the protagonists. Cultured poets would have read classical and biblical allusions into this imagery of wind and waves, trees, mountains and streams where stags come to trouble the waters. But much more persuasive in the search for its origins is the influence of a distant pagan past, veiled in the mists of a much earlier time than the confident Christian certainties of the *kharjas*.

A girl, closely identified with the beauty and whiteness of the dawn, gets up early and goes to wash tunics in the stream, a stream dedicated perhaps to one of the ancient Celtic fertility gods or goddesses of Galicia whose stones and inscriptions still survive:

> *Levantou-s' a velida,*
> *levantou-s' alva,*
> *e vai lavar camisas*
> *em o alto:*
> *vai-las lavar alva.*

> The lovely girl arose,
> the dawn arose,
> and goes to wash tunics
> in the stream:
> the dawn goes to wash them.

In some of these dawn poems she is interrupted by the playful antics of the wind – in pagan terms, the vehicle of evil spirits – in others by the mountain stag. The stag stirring up the water is symbolic both of the lover's presence and their passionate activity, yet conceals any explicit reference to sexuality:

> *Passa seu amigo*
> *que a muit' ama;*
> *o cervo do monte*
> *volvia a augua*
> *ledo dos amores*
> *dos amores leda.*

> Her lover passes by
> who loves her a lot
> the mountain stag
> stirs the water
> happy in love,
> happy in love

The appearance of the stag at the fountain as a biblical reminiscence recalls the *Song of Songs* and the Psalms, but at the popular level it could well be a vestige of the persistent pagan fertility rites condemned by several scandalized bishops in the fourth and fifth centuries. Similar fertility rituals are also suggested in the pilgrimage songs, the *cantigas de romaria*, where the mothers pray and light candles at a shrine while their daughters dance before their lovers.

Many of the poems conveyed a bleakness and a melancholy which set them apart from the bright immediacy of the *kharjas*. Here the obstacles to true love are fickleness, unfaithfulness and rejection, as well as the practical realities of warfare or social convention, and they find expression through the medium of trees, birds and fountains. Surveying the emotional wasteland that her life has become, the lovelorn girl calls to her negligent lover, reminding him how the birds used to sing of their love. She accuses him of destroying the landscape of their love through his cruelty. The repeated refrain, *leda m' and' eu*, expresses her longing for the happiness she has lost.

> *Vos lhi tolhestes os ramos en que siian*
> *e lhi secastes as fontes en que bevian;*
> *leda m' and' eu.*

> You took away the branches where they [the birds] perched
> and dried up the springs where they drank;
> Let me be happy.

Although the return to the thesis revived my intellectual morale, it was lonely work, sitting at a desk in the Library surrounded by yellowing tomes, trying to evaluate the relative importance of each of the numerous influences which had contributed to the composition of these poems. Stephen's attitude to medieval studies had not mellowed with the years. Indeed when, one morning while feeding him his breakfast, I tentatively interrupted his perusal of the newspaper to show him a letter from my supervisor, Alan Deyermond, in which, ever constructive and encouraging, he enthused over a chapter I had just written, he simply returned to his newspaper without comment. The medieval seminar, formerly such a source of encouragement and enthusiasm, had disbanded; my links with the Cambridge Spanish Department had never been more than tenuous, and although my mother still loyally came to look after the children on Friday afternoons, I felt out of touch with the London seminars.

The plangent voices of the *cantigas* filled my inner world and accompanied me in my solitary activities. They were with me as I went about my household chores, they occupied my mind while I sat feeding

Stephen his interminable meals – diced to small morsels, spoonful by spoonful, mouthful by mouthful – and whenever an opportune moment, however brief, presented itself, I would dash to my table in the bay window of the living-room and jot down a few notes, a few ideas, a few references. Yet studying those songs, annotating them, analysing them was not enough. I passionately wanted to be able to express those emotions myself, through song, the song of any period. After my introduction to vocal music in California, I longed to be able to sing well, especially since I had reached a learning plateau in my pianistic technique. In any case, vocal technique could be practised anywhere at any time, even at the kitchen sink, while piano practice was a much less mobile occupation.

Stephen's contempt for medieval studies was unrelenting and his devotion to grand opera, especially Wagner, continued unabated, but he was keen, nevertheless, to encourage me in my new interest in music. Just once a week he and and the resident student would come home early to babysit so that I could go out for an hour to an evening class in vocal technique. The class was taken by a distinguished baritone, Nigel Wickens, who was both singing teacher and performer. His tall, erect figure was made all the more imposing by his domed cranium and on initial acquaintance he was not a little intimidating, particularly on account of the exaggerated precision of his diction. This, however, was but one of the features of his expansive, eccentric personality. Well versed in the arts of performance, he could hold his class in awed subjection one minute, and the next send them into convulsive laughter. He was both a perfectionist in his insistence on intonation, rhythm, dynamics and enunciation, and a clown in some of the squeaks, squawks and tongue-twisters he demonstrated as practice exercises for his class. Once we had all tried to sing 'fluffy, floppy puppy' or 'cricket critic' to a rising and descending scale, any nervous apprehension gave way to sheer enjoyment.

A veritable musical magician, Nigel would open his box of tricks every week and before our marvelling senses reveal a wealth of glittering gemstones, displaying all the shades and colours of the emotional spectrum. Those gemstones were the rich legacy of a succession of musical geniuses, Schubert, Schumann, Brahms, Fauré, Mozart... geniuses whose songs touched the inner self, reaching in to tap the core of the soul, expressing hopes and fears, an elegiac sadness and the sense of impending tragedy for which words alone were inadequate. Sometimes the sadness of the songs and the ill-defined sense of longing that they evoked were so painful as to be unbearable.

After a couple of classes, I knew that I wanted to learn to sing properly, even though I would have to embark on the arduous process of training my voice from scratch – 'creating the instrument', as Nigel put it. It also meant taking an hour a week from work on the thesis but that seemed an minor sacrifice in return for the satisfaction of finding my own true voice, the ability to express myself effectively that I had so long sought in vain.

Encouragement came from an unexpected quarter, from none other than a Fellow of the College, the composer Robin Holloway. He, however, has always been an exceptional Fellow by the standards of Caius College, both spirited intellectually and sympathetic. He was living in another College house, just across the lawn from the West House, and worked at his compositions in a shed in the garden. Robin had already dedicated a piece of music to Stephen on the theme of the black hole and now he applied his powers of lyrical invention to ten of the *kharjas* in a gratifying synthesis of my musical aspirations and my research into medieval Spanish poetry. He presented me with the manuscript score cautiously inscribed, 'For Jane to sing when she can'. There was nothing disparaging about this dedication. Robin's innovative settings were difficult and I was under no illusions. I well knew that I was a beginner with a great deal to learn and so did he.

CHAPTER THIRTY-ONE

A Board Game

OSTENSIBLY WE HAD resumed our pre-California way of life, with some modifications, and superficially our situation in Cambridge appeared to have changed for the better. We had taken up our old activities – and new ones – and the children were settled in their schools. Robert had entered a school where the educational orientation was much more mathematical and which provided him with opportunities for outdoor pursuits which his father was not able to do with him, such as all the suitably exhausting activities associated with Cubs. As Lucy seemed to regard school as an endless party, she was blissfully happy to be left at the school gate at eight-thirty every morning.

However, when we crossed the river Cam in the move from the Lane, in many senses we really had crossed a Rubicon which forbade any return to our old lifestyle. As far as our living quarters were concerned we had gone from one extreme to the other, from the tiny house only one room wide in Little St Mary's Lane to a palatial residence. The vast rooms on the ground floor of the West House were perfect for manoeuvring the wheelchair and afforded ample space for model railway layouts, dolls' houses and musical instruments. They were so large that at Christmas we were able to have family parties which, in 1975, included the Thatchers, my Great-aunt Effie and my mother's cousin, Jack. It was his heroism that saved us all from incineration after only three months in the house. During Christmas dinner, a paper hat caught light on a candle flame and floated up towards the ceiling – to the children's delight but to the grave consternation of everyone else. Uncle Jack sprang to his feet and, reaching up, extinguished the blaze with his bare hands. As Stephen was quick to point out, it was a useful demonstration for the children of the principle that hot air rises.

Although the house could easily accommodate family gatherings and all those Departmental parties, dinners and lunch parties – of which there were more than forty-five in 1975–6 – as well as conference receptions, it was isolated, surrounded by faculty buildings and undergraduate hostels. I was lonely, sorely missing the daily contact, the mutual support and encouragement of my former neighbours in the Lane. Instead I had to look forward to meeting the band of mothers waiting at the school gate – Caroline Chamberlain, Joy Cadbury and several others – for companionship. As Lucy's sociability, even at the age of five, was already far-reaching, we soon became swept up in a round of after-school tea-parties and, through her, I also made some new friends.

Otherwise we lived in a sort of limbo, somewhere between the undergraduates and the College servants, the only family in the length and breadth of West Road, indeed the only family in the vicinity. For a time a friend from the singing class, Maggie Cawthorne, worked as the librarian of the faculty house next door and would occasionally call for lunch. For Maggie, as for me, Nigel Wickens' singing class represented a kind of therapy from the stresses and strains of existence since she was engaged in her own particular struggle for survival against the severe diabetes which cast a cruel blight over her life. Her brief lunch-hour was never long enough for all that we had to say to each other, comparing our impressions of subjects as contrastingly edifying and depressing as Schubert's ode 'An die Musik' on the one hand and the failings of the National Health Service on the other. The Victorian house where Maggie worked had been designed by a Cambridge architect of considerable renown in the nineteenth century. Along with so many others, it had been acquired and mutilated by the University to serve its new purpose as the Institute of Criminology. As with that house, both Maggie and I felt that circumstances had distorted our identities, forcing us to present an image to the world which was not a truly accurate reflection of the way we saw ourselves.

Secure in his employment in the University, Stephen was changing direction in physics, turning his back on the macrocosmic laws of general relativity and immersing himself more and more in quantum mechanics, the laws which operate at the microcosmic level of the elementary particle, the physics of the *quanta*, the building blocks of matter. This change, which was a consequence both of his black hole research and of his contacts with particle physicists in California, was beckoning him to the heights of a further quest, the search for a theory of quantum gravity which, he hoped, would reconcile Einstein's laws of general relativity with the physics of quantum mechanics.

Einstein had been deeply suspicious of the theory of quantum mechanics, developed by Heisenberg and Niels Bohr in the 1920s, and mistrusted the elements of uncertainty and randomicity implied in that scientific breakthrough because they undermined his belief in the beautifully well-ordered nature of the universe. He voiced this dislike forcibly to Niels Bohr by telling him 'God does not play dice with the universe.'

The origins of the universe had held my imagination for the whole extent of my married life and before. My mother used to point out the constellations sparkling against the bright unpolluted clarity of the Norfolk night sky when Chris and I were children. Still, in the 1970s terrestrial lighting was dim enough for Robert, Lucy and me to be able to look up at the night sky and marvel at the remote, spangled beauty of the glittering stars in the darkness. We could speculate about immeasurable distances and incomprehensible timespans and wonder at the genius, their father and my husband, who could transform that infinite space and time into mathematical equations and then carry those equations in his head – in Werner Israel's words, in the same way as Mozart composed his symphonies. Those equations held the key to many questions about our origins and our position in the universe, not least the all-important question of the nature of our role as the minuscule inhabitants of an insignificant planet revolving round an ordinary star on the outer reaches of an unremarkable galaxy. These questions appealed to my imagination in intelligible poetic and philosophical terms, even if I felt that my knowledge of the physics and the maths was so rudimentary as to be useless.

There was no bridge of poetic wonder and mystery, no long turbulent history of theory, experimentation and intellectual conflict, to link the scientific imperative of quantum mechanics with the realms that I inhabited, the realms where humanity interacted with nature, through cultural, philosophical and historical development on the one hand and the immediate, intense, wondering world of growing children on the other. The collisions of invisible particles, especially when those particles were not only invisible but imaginary as well, neither aroused my curiosity nor fired my interest with the same passion as the extraordinary mental journey through billions of light years to the beginning of space and time. Nor, I have to confess, did the set of scientists with whom Stephen was now associating attract me in the least. On the whole particle physicists were a dry, obsessive bunch of boffins, little concerned with personal contact but very concerned with their own scientific reputations. They were much more aggressively competitive than the relaxed, friendly relativists with whom we had associated in the past. They attended conferences and came to the social functions arranged on their behalf but, apart from a handful of ebulliently jovial Russians, their personalities made very little lasting impression. In among that grey morass it was a pleasure occasionally to see the faces of those cultured, articulate, charming old friends from the relativity days – the Israels, the Hartles, Kip, George, the Carters and the Bardeens. Their dedication to their research seemed to verge on the dilettante by comparison with the driving fanaticism of the quantum physicists, simply because they were able to talk intelligently about other things and show a human interest in people and situations.

Generalizations are unreliable. The most famous quantum physicist of them all left a long-lasting impression, though he was certainly taciturn. Paul Dirac, a Cambridge physicist who in the 1920s had reconciled quantum mechanics to Einstein's theory of special relativity and in 1933 had won the Nobel prize, was regarded as a legendary figure in physics. Stephen and Brandon regarded themselves as Dirac's scientific grandchildren since their supervisor, Dennis Sciama, had himself been supervised by Dirac. I had been introduced to Dirac and his wife Margit Wigner, the sister of a distinguished Hungarian physicist, in Trieste in 1971. It was said of Dirac that when he introduced Margit to a colleague soon after their marriage, he did not say, 'This is my wife' but 'This is Wigner's sister.' After Paul's retirement in 1968 from the Lucasian chair – Newton's chair – the Diracs had moved from Cambridge to Florida, where he became an Emeritus Professor. The story was told that Dirac had once watched his wife knitting a garment. When she reached the end of the 'knit' row, her husband, having worked out the mathematical theory of the craft of knitting, immediately instructed her how to turn the needles and 'purl' the next row.

The Diracs visited us one afternoon in Cambridge. Margit was not dissimilar to Thelma Thatcher in her aristocratic bearing. If anything, though, with her flowing auburn hair, hers was an even more irrepressible personality, unselfconscious and gifted with a natural ease of conversation which contrasted strikingly with her husband's silence. As we sat having tea on the lawn, she talked about their travels, their family and their home in Florida, and she admired the children, chatting with them freely and openly, while her husband listened and watched. Margit more than compensated for his periods of taciturnity, which were attributed to the pressure put upon him by his Swiss schoolteacher father to speak only in impeccable French as a child at home in Bristol. She often spoke for her husband, just as I often found myself acting as Stephen's mouthpiece, especially when the talk did not concern physics. Stephen and Paul Dirac were not unalike in that they were both men of few words and preferred to put those few well-considered words either to the service of physics or to trumping an otherwise meandering discussion. In one particular respect they differed drastically.

In the week of their stay in Cambridge, Margit Dirac rang with an invitation to the ballet at the Arts Theatre. I hesitated, knowing only too well that Stephen would not be best pleased to spend an evening watching *Coppelia*, even in the company of one of the world's most famous scientists. 'No, no, my dear, it's not him we are inviting!' Margit exclaimed emphatically in response to my excuses on Stephen's behalf. 'Paul wants *you* to come with us!' Paul's wishes brooked no further hesitation. A couple of evenings later I joined them at the theatre, slightly surprised to find that Paul really was there too, for I suspected that he would share Stephen's contempt for the dance. I was wrong: he seemed to enjoy the performance as much as anyone else. Despite his silences, he and Margit exuded a comforting reassurance, making me very welcome, as if I were a child protégée who needed to be looked after. For one evening I was not obliged to do anything, to think of anything or to take any decisions. I could trust myself to the generous hands of others and give myself over to the performance without even having to worry whether my companions were enjoying themselves. For a couple of hours my hands let go the taut reins of responsibility.

At home, the routine was eased when a new postgraduate student of Stephen's, Alan Lapedes from Princeton, agreed to come and live in our spare room and, like Bernard in California, help with the more onerous tasks, especially the lifting. Reserved and self-contained, Alan was an uncomplaining helper but I was wary of exploiting his willingness since he also contributed to Stephen's care daily in the Department. There, Stephen's colleagues and his students, particularly Gary Gibbons and Bernard Carr, catered for his needs. Bernard once told me that they had organized an informal rota among themselves so that no one person was obliged to look after Stephen all the time. Nevertheless Stephen was very dependent on their loyal help, even sometimes with the intimate functioning of his body if such problems had not been brought to a satisfactory conclusion at home.

Stephen's bodily discomfort now kept us tied to the house every weekend. During the week it was a perpetual source of anxiety and frustration, despite the efforts of Miss Willis and her assistant, Sue Smith, to make him take more regular exercise, by straightening his body and walking the length of the hall, supported by one on each side. The mother of four and the much-travelled wife of a chemistry don, Sue's background and circumstances were very different from those of Constance Willis but she was equally warm-hearted. She had a frank northern manner and was used to speaking her mind, frequently voicing her candid opinions about Cambridge complacency and pretentiousness. She it was who first brought the concerns of the Chemistry Department about the effect of CFCs on the ozone layer to our notice. Sue also possessed engaging northern humour and generosity. Nonetheless, however much she amused Stephen by telling him all the latest gossip in her own entertaining fashion, she could never persuade him to devote any more than those two hours of her visits to his exercises each week. 'Now, you will do them, won't you, just for me?' she would plead, but he would simply regale her with one of his most beguiling, sphinx-like smiles.

The fact was that since Stephen was sedentary for all his waking hours, his limbs were much wasted through illness and lack of exercise. To outsiders, the mechanical advantages of the electric wheelchair and the independence it conferred hid the true extent of the ravages of motor neurone disease because he was able to get about quite freely, flitting back and forth across the river, to and from the Department. Any obstacle in the way of this revolutionary vehicle, however, required the assistance of not just one able-bodied man but two or three to lift its 120 kilograms over a steep step or up a flight of stairs. If on the way to an evening out together we encountered a single step, we were in trouble.

Unlike me, Stephen, surprisingly, was not usually a prey to the numerous minor ailments which the children brought home from school. He maintained a healthy appetite and a seemingly iron constitution, priding himself on never missing a day's work. Outsiders could have no concept, though, of how painfully emaciated his body had become, like the corpses at Belsen which I once saw in a television documentary. Nor did outsiders generally witness those horrendous choking fits which would come on at supper-time and last well into the night, when I would cradle him in my arms like a frightened child till the wheezings subsided and his breathing slipped into the easy rhythm of sleep.

We tried to avoid these fits by experimenting with different diets, at first eliminating sugar, then dairy products and finally gluten, the sticky protein in flour which binds bread and cakes. They were all suspected of irritating the hypersensitive lining of the throat. Although the children and I continued to eat bread and cakes, and cooking without sugar was not difficult, the challenge of gluten-free cookery required some adjustments in the kitchen since gluten-free flour is one of the most unmanageable substances any cook could possibly have to contend with, although that challenge was infinitely preferable to those terrible life-threatening attacks of choking.

We managed to keep up a pretence of hypernormality throughout the winter of 1975. However, just as we thought that we had escaped the worst of the winter's ills, the spring of 1976 lay in wait with a series of cruel tricks which made of it an obstacle course akin to a snakes and ladders board, though with many more snakes than ladders and with dice which seemed to be weighted to land on the snakes. On 20 March the first small snake on the board snapped us up when Lucy fell ill with chickenpox. This unremarkable though uncomfortable ailment was certainly better disposed of in early childhood than at the age of twenty, as I knew from my own experience as a student in Valencia. By the following Monday, 22 March, poor little Lucy was miserably red with spots, crying for all the attention I could give her by day and by night. As far as the chickenpox was concerned, we were no different from any other family with young children, but there the similarity ended. It was fortunate that Lucy made a speedy recovery during the course of that week, since the next throw of the dice was to send us hurtling down a much more precipitous snake.

On the Saturday morning at the end of that week, we all awoke with sore throats and the next day both Alan and Stephen were distinctly unwell. The inflamed throats were accompanied by a high fever. Inherently mistrustful of the medical profession, still resentful of their shabby treatment of him in 1963 at the time of diagnosis, and as phobic about hospitals as I was about flying, Stephen forbade me to call a doctor even though he was unable to eat or drink and was coughing on every breath. Later the next day, in desperation, I called the duty doctor but Stephen shook his head in furious rejection of all her suggestions for palliative measures, such as cough syrup or any sort of cough suppressant, because he had formulated a theory that such remedies, in suppressing his natural reflexes, could be more dangerous than the cough itself. Effectively he had become his own doctor and was convinced that he knew more about his condition than any member of the medical profession.

Stephen's mother, who had come over for tea on the Sunday afternoon, stayed on and between us, we nursed Stephen through a very disturbed night. The next day – my birthday – though very ill, pale, gaunt and racked by the choking, Stephen, in his fear of losing control of the situation, still refused to allow me to fetch help until late in the day when, as a major concession to me on my birthday, he let me call the doctor. When Dr Swan was finally permitted to set foot in the house at 7.30 p.m., his reaction was pragmatically straightforward: he called an ambulance at once, reassuring Stephen that he would be home again in a couple of days.

It was surely providential that at that blackest of moments when we arrived at the Admissions Unit where Stephen thought that he was about to be confined to a condemned cell and I, in an anguish of uncertainty, stood stroking his arm, the sound of a familiar voice, confident and authoritative, emerged from the doctors' office. In its cheery familiarity, that voice offered the promise of hope and recovery, a veritable ladder bridging the gap between the dire pit into which we had fallen and our normal home-life. It was the voice of John Stark, the chest consultant who drove Robert to school every day. Stephen could not fail to respect John as a friend, whatever his opinion of doctors in general, and I was overjoyed to encounter someone in authority who could take charge of the situation without demanding lengthy explanations, someone with the medical expertise to relieve me of the impossible responsibility of caring for a very sick patient unaided. Nevertheless, because Stephen was so helpless in his inability to communicate with more than a handful of people, and because of his terror of being fed either a medicine or a food which could have harmful effects, I stayed in the hospital at his bedside all night. The next day showed a slight improvement in his condition as he gradually began to climb the first rungs of the ladder towards recovery, and two days later he was so much more cheerful that he seemed well enough to come home.

In the meantime life at home had resumed a semblance of its usual pace. My parents had come to look after the children, Lucy had gone back to school and Robert went on a school day-trip to York. When Alan and I collected Stephen from the hospital on 1 April, we entertained the foolishly optimistic hope that we were going to be able to get back to normal straight away. No sooner had we arrived home, so full of eager anticipation, than Stephen began to choke violently and incessantly and almost immediately slipped back into a desperate state. There was nothing that could be done to help him in his suffering, despite all the advice of the medical experts. He choked whatever position he adopted, whether sitting up or lying down. He could neither eat nor drink and was too weak to endure physiotherapy. My mother, Bernard Carr, Alan and I operated a rota system. One or two of us sat with Stephen all day and all night while the others slept. There was little doubt that the situation was extremely critical. I hardly needed the doctors to tell me that I should prepare myself for the worst.

Where medical science had admitted defeat, a new influence brought an unexpected revival of strength. The concern shown by friends inspired a spontaneous renewal of hope, extending ladders of sympathy and comfort. John Sturdy, the Dean of Gonville and Caius, and his wife Jill came one evening, quietly and unobtrusively, to offer support through their prayers. Stephen's students and colleagues were unwavering in their devotion, visiting regularly and helping with his care, often through the night. Gradually, though still very frail and prone to choking attacks, Stephen began to improve, until on Sunday, 4 April he spent the whole day without choking at all and managed to eat a little puréed food. That night his condition deteriorated again and the following day's dice sent us slithering back down a long, slippery snake. Robert awoke with a high temperature, covered from head to foot in chickenpox blisters and during the day became delirious.

As my father was himself on the point of going into hospital in St Albans for an operation, my parents had returned home when Stephen first began to show signs of recovery. In their absence I had to throw myself on my good friends for help with the children, especially on Joy Cadbury who for several years had hovered in the background, always ready to help with the utmost sensitivity when the need arose. In 1973 Robert had stayed with the Cadburys while we were in Russia and both he and Lucy always felt very much at home with their children, Thomas and Lucy Grace, in the house on the Barton Road. They had already spent a couple of nights there when Stephen was in intensive care and

I was with him staying at the hospital. The magnanimity with which Joy offered to nurse Robert, bespeckled with red blisters as he was, was quite beyond any call of friendship – it was a foregone conclusion that both her own children would most certainly develop chickenpox within the next three weeks. I had no option but to let Robert go since the demands on me were so great and my own resources were so depleted that I could scarcely register what was happening to us. Worry, lack of sleep, responsibilities, decisions and uncertainty had exhausted me to the point where I was incapable of looking after my own children properly.

In Joy's tender care Robert bounced back to health. My father came through his operation successfully and when, a day later, I managed to snatch an afternoon for a flying visit to St Albans, I was glad to find him up and about, walking round the ward. Stephen's recovery was slower and less predictable, mostly because he refused to take the penicillin he had been prescribed. He sat silently in his chair, resting his head on his hand, in the same melancholy posture he had first adopted in the 1960s. He did not speak, he choked frequently, and ate and drank in small, careful sips. He was not strong enough to go out so the Department came to him and held its seminars in our living-room. At last, over the Easter weekend, he began to show signs of gaining strength. Only then could we begin to sleep at nights and I could relax my guard a little. The children came home and the threat of hissing snakes on the board seemed to be fading, yielding to upwardly ascendant ladders, reaching again for the stars. In the one remaining week of the school holidays, we could climb those ladders to regain our previous levels of harmony and activity. In that week, we could learn to function again as a family, enjoying each other's company and relaxing in our lovely garden.

Stephen had other ideas. No sooner had he been released from the clutches of the demon illness than the goddess physics urgently reclaimed him as her own, sweeping him up and away from his family to resume his throne high among her pantheon of demigods. The children and I were no match for such competition. That Easter Monday, still in the early stages of convalescence, Stephen summoned his students, commandeered the car and set off for a five-day conference in Oxford. As I stood in the doorway watching them go, my tearful disbelief at such apparent recklessness condensed into a desperate urge to escape, as far away as possible from the scene of so much anguish.

Dennis and Lydia Sciama, who were as aghast at Stephen's seeming foolhardiness as I was, recommended a hotel in St Ives in Cornwall. In a daze of miserable incomprehension, scarcely knowing where we were going or why, driven by a manic desire to get away from Cambridge, the children and I fled to London and boarded a train at Paddington for the West Country. The train whisked us further and further south. After Exeter it slowed down, crawling along at a snail's pace, snaking along winding branchlines. Oblivious to the slow passing of time, to the children's games, to their laughter and chatter, I gazed blankly out of the window, staring at the primrose-spattered fields of Cornwall without really seeing them, plunged into a stupor of exhausted dejection.

CHAPTER THIRTY-TWO

Celtic Woodland

W<small>E COULD NO</small> longer blind ourselves to the truth: we were living on the edge of a precipice, sometimes staring over the rim into the black void beneath. Yet it is possible to adapt to life even on the edge of a precipice; it is possible to put down roots on the very brink of disaster. The roots grow, penetrating rock and stone, insinuating themselves into whatever soil they can find. Eventually they form a sufficiently secure network to enable the branches above, however stunted, to send forth foliage, flowers and fruit. The precarious, isolated position of the tree on the windswept ledge lends its blossoms a spectacular brilliance, enhancing their magnificence so dramatically that the observer can be deceived into forgetting that the precipice exists at all.

At the end of April, on our return from Cornwall and Stephen's from Oxford, the children went back to school as if the nightmare of the Easter holidays had never happened. Quietly philosophical and undemanding, Robert had always taken his father's illness and disability in his stride. Since Lucy followed her brother's lead in everything, she showed few signs of disturbance at the unconventional nature of her background. Our lives appeared to have taken up their usual rhythms, to be following their usual patterns, though perhaps with an even greater determination to focus on each moment of each day. As Stephen and the children settled back into their routines, I grasped every spare second to jot down a few thoughts on the thesis; redecorated, yet again, the rented house owned jointly by Robert and his grandparents, upon which we depended for paying part of his school fees; attended the singing class whenever possible, and cooked for dinner-parties for the advancing hordes of summer visitors to the Department.

In midsummer, a BBC television crew came to make a film about Stephen as part of a two-hour documentary on the origins of the universe. By chance, the producer, Vivienne King, had been a student at Westfield in the same year as me. Although she had studied maths, she did not adopt a hardline scientific approach to the filming but wanted to present Stephen sympathetically, as a rounded figure set against the background of his family life. This image appealed to me, both because it was how I liked to see Stephen myself – despite the blow this image had received over the past weeks – and because I feared that the hardline scientific approach could well present him as a sinister character, like the malevolent wheelchair-bound Dr Strangelove, played by Peter Sellers in Stanley Kubrick's film of the same name.

The finished product, the first and best documentary of its kind, contained the elements of a poetic idyll, despite its scientific context. Stephen was, of course, seen at work in the Department, interacting with his students, conducting seminars, expounding his latest theories. He was also interviewed at home against the backdrop of the two children playing in the summer sun among the flowers in the garden. When the film was broadcast worldwide the following winter as part of a major BBC documentary – *The Key to the Universe* – a schoolfriend of Lucy's, the daughter of a visiting scholar, watched it back home in Japan. The mother wrote to tell us that her daughter had stood transfixed in front of the television screen when she saw Lucy sitting on her swing under the apple tree. 'Lucy, Lucy . . .' was all that she could say as the tears poured down her cheeks.

This was certainly the image of self-sufficiency to which we continued to aspire, the sweet illusion of success which upheld our self-esteem, without which the darkening reality of our existence would have engulfed us. Sadly the image and the sweet illusion were becoming less and less easy to sustain. Alan was so exhausted on his return from the Oxford conference after Easter that he had to go away for a couple of weeks to recover. After all, he too had been ill but no one had given a moment's thought to his state of health because his help had been urgently required in caring for Stephen. He had unstintingly helped throughout the critical period – and beyond, because when Stephen decided to go to Oxford, he had no choice but to go with him.

Stephen's valiant attempts to appear fit and well may have stood him in good stead in the Department but at home his spirits were alarmingly low and his constitution was dangerously weakened. The cheerful grin had evaporated completely, to be replaced by a mournful sadness expressed in those beautiful, eloquent eyes. He spoke only to voice his demands, which were legion. No sooner had one need been met, one command fulfilled, than another would arise, stretching my powers of endurance to their limits. We needed help more than ever but none was forthcoming from any of the statutory authorities in spite of our doctors' concerted appeals to them. In any case, Stephen still absolutely refused to accept any outside nursing help.

My doctor applied to the local authority for a home help to assist with the domestic chores since all our spare income was spent on augmenting Robert's school fees and did not run to the luxury of a daily help. No help materialized, however, because when the social worker came to assess us, one glance at our favoured surroundings was enough to disqualify us from any benefits. She was only one in a long line of people who in their lack of imagination failed to distinguish between the gilded illusion that we struggled to maintain, and the brutal reality at the core of our situation.

Help when it came assumed a form which in its innocence was so precious that although it eased the physical strain, it increased a hundred times my guilt at being unable to cope on my own. Robert, at nearly nine years old, stepped out of his childhood and began to fetch and carry, lift and heave, feed and wash, and even take his father to the bathroom when I was overwhelmed with the weight of other chores or just too exhausted to respond. In Stephen's pragmatic philosophy of survival, Robert's arms and legs were as good a substitute for his own as anyone else's, as good as a student's in fact, and certainly better, in his opinion, than having a nurse in the house, even temporarily. I could not have disagreed more strongly. It was right that the children should be prepared to lend their father a helping hand voluntarily, providing that was within their capacity, but not that they too should become slaves to motor neurone disease. They had not asked to be born into this situation. It disturbed me greatly that Robert's childhood, that unrepeatable period of freedom, was being brought to such an abrupt conclusion and that he was being used when and where my own power failed. For want of any other regular support, there was no foreseeable solution to this most impossible of predicaments. This was a painfully ironic result of the success of our enterprise: the normal life that I had set myself to create for Stephen had ensnared the children in its tentacles of abnormality.

For the week of half-term at the end of May, I arranged the family holiday that we had not had at Easter – five relaxing days in our favourite hotel, the Anchor at Walberswick, only two-and-a-half hours' drive from Cambridge. There we were well known to the management who generally could be relied upon to cater for our requirements, including a gluten-free diet, with patience and good humour. There, too, the walks over the marshes in the direction of Southwold and the access to the beach were more or less manageable for the wheelchair. The hedgerows were unspoilt, full of the wild flowers which Lucy excitedly searched out and compared with the appealing illustrations in her *Flower Fairy* books.

We enjoyed just one or two very happy such expeditions in an otherwise catastrophic holiday. However hard the hotel chef tried to produce a gluten-free menu, motor neurone disease lay in wait for us each time we entered the dining-room. It pounced on Stephen, attacking his throat with vicious convulsions as we sat down to eat, sending his coughing and wheezing ricocheting off the walls and distracting the other holidaymakers from their meals, whether at breakfast, lunch or dinner. I sat helplessly by, hovering between anxiety for Stephen and embarrassment for the other guests. He was a pitiable sight and they were at some pains to conceal their discomfort.

Stephen was convinced that there was some slight irritant in the atmosphere of that particular room which was causing his throat to go into spasms: perhaps it was a trace of cigarette smoke or cooking fumes from the kitchen, undetectable to anyone else. The manager discreetly suggested that we might like to have our meals brought to our chalet in the garden, an idea which I gratefully seconded. Stephen vetoed it emphatically: he felt that it was a gross insult to his dignity and a denial of his rights, both as a disabled person and a hotel customer. My attempts to suggest – as tactfully as I could – that it would be much more dignified to take our meals together in private and that the other hotel guests had the right to enjoy their meals in peace were angrily rejected as the epitome of disloyalty. Lacking proper nourishment, his strength sapped by the choking, Stephen subsided into a depressed lethargy; he seemed to build a tragically impregnable wall around himself and installed cannons on its battlements to fend off intruders, however hard they tried to reach out to him in his lofty isolation. From the fortress of his suffering he communicated only to express his needs in a morbid game of 'Simon says . . .' Robert's help was called for again and again when I reached breaking-point, as I did often since this situation demanded more stamina and courage than I possessed.

Where could I turn for help, I asked myself frequently and desperately, almost always drawing a blank. Our friends were all keen enough to help in the short term, but they had their own families, their own lives to lead. There was no one who could spare the time or the energy to give us the undertaking, the dedication we needed so badly – I was particularly concerned to relieve Robert of the premature burdens and responsibilities that I felt were being placed on his young shoulders. In my despair I approached Stephen's parents since they were the only people I could turn to. My own parents had given us huge amounts of help throughout our marriage and were wonderful grandparents but there was little that they could do in this extreme situation where medical intervention was required, nor did I feel that it was fair to ask them, especially as my father's mental health was in a rather delicate state at that time.

Stephen's father had promised to help in any way possible in that euphoric period before our wedding in 1965. His intentions were certainly good and in some ways that promise could have been considered fulfilled, had we been a conventional couple in good health, without problems and not under any kind of stress. Frank Hawking had painted the bathroom for us when we first moved into Little St Mary's Lane; he and Isobel had paid for my stay in the nursing home when Robert was born – not that they were in any way responsible for its shortcomings – and they had paid for us to have a cleaner once a week when Robert was a small baby. They had given us a large sum of money to help us buy our house and had generously handed on a couple of family antiques to grace our living room. Isobel had come to look after Stephen when the children were born and she had also been prepared to fly off with him to conferences across the world when small children and flying phobia kept me grounded. On our annual trip to the cottage in Wales, Isobel and Frank could be relied upon to help with Stephen's care, she with controlled good nature often calming her husband's impatience, for clearly it took a considerable emotional effort and self-discpline for him to reconcile himself to the time-consuming restraints of Stephen's severe disability. Although their own property was so dauntingly unsuitable for a disabled person in a wheelchair, they were curiously meticulous about reconnoitring castles and beauty spots for excursions, counting steps and registering any other hurdles in advance of our arrival.

Their visits to Cambridge, however, were always much more formal than my parents'. Mum and Dad were demonstrative and passionate grandparents, involving themselves in every aspect of the children's lives and our own. They would invite the children – singly or together – to stay in St Albans and in later years would take them on extravagant outings to London, to the theatre or to tea at the Ritz. They came over to Cambridge at the drop of a hat to watch Lucy performing as Oliver or Joseph or the Mad Hatter in her Saturday morning Music for Fun Club; they would ferry Robert to Cub camps; they went shopping and helped in the kitchen, and they mixed with gregarious ease with all our friends.

Stephen's parents, on the other hand, behaved like guests rather than close relations and, of late, I had begun to sense a distancing in their attitude, as if the veneer of normality we struggled to maintain was so convincing that no more involvement was required on their part than that of rather correct members of the older generation. Perhaps they assumed that we did not need help because I did not subject them to a blow-by-blow account of every complication. Perhaps, too, the brilliance of their son's success blinded them to the bald, unpalatable facts of his illness. Of Stephen's sisters we saw very little. Mary was established in general practice in Luton, some 35 miles away, and, as she herself said, was far too busy to come to Cambridge often. Philippa, who had come to Cambridge to work with Joseph Needham on the history of science in China, made it quite plain to me from the outset that she wanted as little as possible to do with us.

On our return from Walberswick I wrote a despairing letter to Stephen's parents, begging them to bring their minds and their medical knowledge to bear on the situation and to help resolve – or if that was unrealistic, at least mitigate – the overwhelming difficulties which were threatening us. My promise to Stephen had not altered. I still felt deeply for him and identified with him in all his struggles. However, that promise was becoming much more difficult to sustain, particularly in the face of the unrelenting stress, all day and every day and much of the night as well. The pace of life had accelerated, if anything, since Stephen's illness, with a major conference in Cambridge, more dinners, more sherry parties and more receptions. I was at breaking-point but still Stephen was determined to reject any proposals which might have suggested that he was making concessions to the illness. These were the proposals which might have relieved the children and me of some of the strain. His constant rejection of our need for more help was an alienating force, wearing away the empathy with which I had shared every dispiriting stage in the development of the illness. In his reply to my letter, Frank Hawking promised to confer with Stephen's doctor about the medical aspects of the case and said that there would be ample opportunity to discuss other matters at greater length during our forthcoming summer holiday in Llandogo.

There was actually very little opportunity to do so in Wales because of the characteristic Hawking reluctance to discuss anything of a personal nature. Dutifully Frank helped with Stephen's care every morning and then, usually clad in boots, waterproofs and a souwester, he disappeared into the wilderness to attack the weeds which were making a mockery of his attempts to grow vegetables in the rain-forest conditions of the steep, east-facing hillside. Isobel valiantly did her best to organize interesting excursions for us, dodging the showers in the afternoons – a teddy bears' picnic, a visit to Goodrich Castle, a hunt for four-leaf clover. These were pleasant, sociable family outings, conducted without any reference to the underlying problems and tensions.

One morning Isobel came to me and in a tone of flustered defiance said, 'If you want to talk to Father, you had better see him now.' She pointed outside to where Frank stood in the pouring rain. I donned my raincoat and joined him under the dripping trees. We walked along the road, not speaking, splashing across the rivulets that were rushing straight down the hill to swell the river in the valley below. My thoughts and emotions were churning in such a chaotic whirlpool that they would not be so easily channelled into a coherent flow. I was afraid of appearing disloyal to Stephen yet I had to persuade his family that all was not well, that ways and means had to be sought, and if necessary imposed, to lighten the burdens. If nothing else, it was essential to relieve Robert of the tasks that were oppressing him.

I succeeded in none of my aims. The merest hint of dissatisfaction with our situation was quickly identified as disloyalty to Stephen and summarily dismissed with the implication that it was a symptom of my own inadequacy. Frank did at least offer to discuss the situation with Stephen but doubted that his words would have any effect. In any case, he asserted, there could be no question of forcing Stephen to accept more help. His only other comments were that Stephen was very courageous, that he drew his courage from his determination, and that he, Frank, was sure that Stephen was doing his best for his family. He was providing well for us, we had two lovely children and we were very fortunate in the position we occupied. I did not dispute the truth of all this and no doubt, by comparison with many disabled families, we were well off, but there was little comfort in the repetition of such truisms. These were the blessings that I had conditioned myself to count for so many years. I knew well enough that Stephen's determination was his defence against the illness but I did not understand why he had to use it as a weapon against his family. As for Robert, Frank expressed his concern for him by turning my argument on its head: Robert was too introverted, he said; he should be brought out of his shell so that in the future social ineptitude would not damage his career as Frank believed it had damaged his own, depriving him of recognition for his important work in tropical medicine.

My courage failed me. There was no use in arguing. Though robust and in sterling health, Frank was old, a good ten years older than my father. Perhaps he was too old to understand how I felt and too old to adjust to what was being asked of him. For all his genuine concern for Stephen, he evidently found it difficult to see what was before his very eyes. To try to explain the obvious, to repeat the contents of my letter – that Robert's introversion was mainly a result of the home situation – would have been hopeless, the more so considering that my purely unemotive and practical suggestion that perhaps Frank and Isobel might begin to participate in the running of the rented house in Cambridge, especially when so much redecoration and refurbishing was required between tenancies, had been quashed outright on account of the distance – some 50 miles – between St Albans and Cambridge. The conversation petered out and we returned to the house.

Later the sky cleared. I was sitting on the terrace shelling peas for lunch when Isobel came and sat beside me. 'So I gather you have talked to Father?' she enquired, eyeing me intently. 'Not really,' I replied. She pursed her lips. With the same defiance that she had shown earlier, she announced fiercely, 'You do know, don't you, that Father will never allow Stephen to be put into a residential home?' So saying she stood up, turned on her heel and marched into the house. Her remarks stung me to the quick. I had never so much as thought about a 'residential home' for Stephen, let alone mentioned such a preposterous idea. I had simply asked for help to protect my own young son from the psychological ravages of the physical disease which was afflicting their son.

Humiliated and even more despondent, I stood up. Abandoning the half-filled saucepan of peas, I walked slowly away from the house into Cleddon Wood and there, in utter desolation, sat down on a broad, flat stone, scarcely conscious of the noise of the falls resounding in my ears. Never had I been so alone as there in the forest, on the hillside and by the fast-flowing stream. There was sympathy in nature when human beings could offer none. What timeless truths were buried deep in that damp hillside, what were the hidden secrets of its age-old rocks and mossy stones? Surely this ancient Celtic landscape must have treasures of wisdom to share? The hills offered the comfort of the natural cycle, the colours, the sounds, the dank, earthy smells of nature taking its course, but they offered no defence against hardness of heart.

Nature was powerless to influence intellectual beings who were governed by rational thought, who could not recognize reality when it stood, bared before them, pleading for help. They appeared to jump to conclusions, which distorted the truth to make it fit their preconceptions. Tragedy had struck them and I knew that they had had to struggle to come to terms with the terrible blow of Stephen's illness; it had stretched their intellectual capacity to its limits and left them few resources for coping, helping or indeed understanding. I felt for their grief and, by my efforts, had tried to mitigate its effects. But now it seemed as if, absolved of responsibility by my intervention, they had shut themselves off from the repercussions of motor neurone disease and, in doing so, appeared to have lost whatever inkling of other feelings other concerns, other ideals, whatever sense of other people they might formerly have had. The independence and originality of thought which had initially attracted me to Stephen and the Hawking family as an eighteen-year-old had over the past fourteen years worn away and now appeared to reveal at base little more than the egoism which dictated their largely negative, but always logically plausible, reactions. In contrast my own family, conservative though it was, had proved itself to be dependable, unselfish and generous in its support of us all – of Stephen as much as of me and the children. My parents had never discriminated between the individuals who needed their support, had never refused a call for help, and would never adopt a tone of moral superiority. In my sadness, I recalled, too, how David Ireland, in California, had insisted on having his parents at hand to help so that his treasured wife Joyce would not succumb under the strain of his care. Perhaps I was wrong to expect more of Stephen's family than they were capable of offering.

In the second week of the holiday, when the sun shone brightly and dependably out of a clear sky, the clouds of despair lifted. It appeared that I had been wrong in my opinion of Stephen's parents, particularly of his mother. She took us to a hotel at the seaside on the Cardiganshire coast and was kindness incarnate. She shared in Stephen's care for much of the time, sometimes feeding him his meals, helping to dress him and sitting by him on the path above the beach so that I could play with the children on the sands below and bathe in the sea. My spirits rose as my health and my energies began to revive. It seemed that Isobel was responding to my pleas after all and was genuinely making an effort to help.

I was grateful but I smiled quizzically at some of the remarks she made. 'Looking after Stephen is not really that difficult, you know,' she observed breezily. Was she implying that my tales of woe had been pure fabrication? 'Robert doesn't seem to mind helping his father at all; in fact, I think it's good for them both,' was her next cheerful remark. Had the coolly intellectual workings of her mind failed to grasp my concerns for my elder child? Perhaps such remarks should have been viewed simply as kindly encouragement. That was the interpretation that I was prepared to put on them since the holiday that she had generously provided had been such fun and so beneficial to us all, fortifying us for the hectic term that lay ahead. However, the persistent harping on the ease with which all my responsibilities could be accomplished, the inference that the situation was not as bad as I had made it out to be, in short, the implication that my pleas, my fears, my cries for help were not to be taken seriously, began to dampen my reawakening confidence in her. Although she may genuinely have been trying to encourage me not to dwell on the problems, her bizarre final pronouncement baffled me. 'Really, the wheelchair is not as heavy as you might think,' she announced airily at the end of the week. 'Lucy helped me to put it and the batteries in the car and between us we managed perfectly well.' Lucy was five years old; the weight of the chair and its solid gel batteries had already made many a strapping student blanch.

Sad news greeted us in Cambridge at the end of August. During our absence Thelma Thatcher had been taken into hospital for an operation from which she did not recover. The ten years that we had known her, though a large proportion of our lives, were only a small proportion of hers, yet she treated us as if we were part of her family. Her soul was large, all-embracing, caring and practical, always ready to come to the rescue in times of crisis, always ready to help those worse off than herself, always ready with her quick sense of humour to pinpoint the ridiculous or the absurd. The children adored her and she adored them as their adoptive granny. For me she was a true friend and a staunch ally whose judgement, I knew, was always sound and trustworthy, even though sometimes it might have been hard to digest. I saw her just before we went to Wales. She was philosophical, dismissing her own health problems as insignificant although she already knew that they were serious. Typically she was more concerned to talk about us. 'I wish old Thatcher were stronger and could help her brave girl more,' she said as she hugged me for the last time.

CHAPTER THIRTY-THREE

Retrospective Views

IN THOSE WEEKS after Thelma Thatcher's death we tried to repay a little of her selflessness by taking Mary under our wing as she adjusted to a fundamental change in her life – just as her mother had shown us such enormous practical kindness when we first arrived in Little St Mary's Lane and had watched over us like a guardian angel ever since. Mary often found herself seated at the supper table with one or other of the many scientists who passed through Cambridge that autumn. They would join us for a family meal at the end of long days filled with all the usual bustle associated with children and schools, clubs and after-school activities, as well as Stephen's requirements. Not much had changed in our circumstances, and Robert's help was still often called upon at home, but that week by the sea, the second week of the holiday in Wales had restored both my stamina and my resolve and I was better able to cope. Stephen was also in better health and spirits, although his recovery from the spring bout of pneumonia did not mean that motor neurone disease, which continued to exact its implacable toll of muscle degeneration, eating difficulties, choking fits and respiratory problems, had retreated.

In the Department the latest academic exercise to gain popularity was the symposium, a sort of protracted conference which extended over a whole year. This exercise held great attractions for Stephen since, with increased funding now at his disposal, he could bring scientists to Cambridge from all over the world and work with them at leisure on lengthy projects such as books and papers which would have been an impossible undertaking in the hurried atmosphere of the customary four- or five-day conference. Although he was still wavering in his interests between general relativity and quantum mechanics, most of the visitors to the Relativity Group in the early part of the academic year were the old familiar faces and most of them came from North America. In the course of that term, Jim Hartle came from Santa Barbara, Chandrasekhar from Chicago, Kip Thorne from Pasadena and Abe Taub from Berkeley. Werner Israel, with his wife Inge and son Mark, was still in Cambridge on sabbatical leave from Edmonton.

From my standpoint, the most formidable visitors were the charmingly modest, amiable Chandrasekhars, not because of any clashes of personality but because, just before they arrived for a dinner-party, I learned that they were vegan. I already knew that they were vegetarian, having mistakenly served them a fish sandwich at a conference tea-party, but did not suspect further complications. A last-minute revision of the menu was called for. Out went the recipes from the *1001 Ways with Cheese* that Stephen had brought home from one of his trips to America and the search was on for meat-free, fish-free, cheese- and dairy product-free recipes that were also gluten-free and sugar-free. My old Spanish standby, *gazpacho*, lent a touch of distinction to a meal of mushroom and onion risotto. It was really more appropriate to the Sunday supper table than to a dinner-party for such distinguished guests. Stephen would probably have turned his nose up at it even if it had made an appearance at the Sunday supper table, complaining that it lacked sufficient protein for his requirements.

In the middle of the term, the Cambridge coterie decamped to Oxford, whither Dennis Sciama had moved to take up a Fellowship at All Souls College. Roger Penrose had been appointed Professor of Mathematics at Oxford and he and Dennis regularly organized one-, two-, or three-day conferences. While Stephen and his colleagues gave their seminars, I took the opportunity to get to know the museums and monuments of Oxford better: walking tours were out of the question on account of the driving rain. Indeed, the weather threatened to sabotage the conference dinner in the Cherwell Boat House which was barely accessible because the Boat House itself was on the point of breaking loose and floating down the river.

Oxford, so much vaunted in the Hawking household, was not as forbidding as its reputation suggested. To anyone coming from Cambridge it was superficially remarkably familiar, though less rural in its setting. Over the past few years we had made sixth-monthly visits to meetings in Oxford, even when the children were very small, and I too had begun to appreciate the charm of the place, at once more cosmopolitan and animated than its fenland counterpart. Stephen loved being back in Oxford. He carried the layout of the city in his head and, with a hint of pride, could direct me infallibly to any location, negotiating lanes and back streets with nonchalant confidence.

He would nostalgically point out the wall he had once climbed over, only to fall into the arms of a policeman, and the bridge he and some friends were daubing with a Ban the Bomb slogan in the middle of the night when a policeman sauntered by and arrested the friends, who left Stephen dangling in a cage beneath the bridge. These and other similar yarns had a somewhat apocryphal ring to them, though there were plenty of photos to attest to his disastrous antics on – if not above – the river. There was little doubt, too, that he had been an eager participant in the sconce – a sort of beer-drinking contest, imposed as a fine for a breach of behaviour. Stephen's delight in those memories was touching: they provided a sad reminder, a tantalizing glimpse of the old, active, carefree rebel, the Stephen whom I had just known, the Stephen with whom I had fallen in love, the Stephen I remembered with wry nostalgia. They related, of course, to the days before the diagnosis of motor neurone disease which was, in chronological terms, a Cambridge phenomenon, and to the days before fame and success had cast him in a role of authority. The contrast between the hedonistic youth and the courageous, embattled hero that he had become, invested his image with an intense and undeniable poignancy.

These fleeting images of youth, however, had little relevance to the present. The flippant but determined youth had become hardened both by his fight against illness and by the clamorous competition in the corridors of science. His fortitude in refusing to be overwhelmed by motor neurone disease and his determination to outstrip his competitors in the scientific arena were certainly laudable but I felt that too often he allowed that same obduracy to spill over into our domestic life where it seemed to me to be an unnecessary and destructive force. I only ever wanted the best for Stephen. I never wanted him to be excluded from anything that could give him pleasure, be it a party in rooms at the top of a spiral staircase, a view from a high rock, or a punting trip on the Cam. If these pleasures were available to those of us with two able legs, they had to be available to Stephen as well and I battled to ensure that he could enjoy them too. If the physical restraints were impossible, then I preferred not to partake or participate myself. If I did, the pleasure was muted and the sense of guilt unbearable.

Nevertheless, Stephen's well-being was not the full extent of my responsibilities. I wanted the best for our children as well and I did not want them to suffer from having a severely disabled father. Unbeknown to Stephen, I shared my concerns with their teachers in the hope of protecting them against teasing in the playground and, while encouraging them to love and respect their father, I struggled to compensate for his disability by trying to fulfil the role of two parents: I tried to be both father and mother to each of them and sometimes Stephen's best interests had to be balanced against theirs.

The great black bird of flying phobia still cast its broad shadow over me, feeding pitilessly on my maternal anxieties. I was still terrified both of aeroplanes and of leaving my children, who depended on me for every aspect of their lives. There were other people who could take Stephen to conferences, colleagues and students who were glad of the opportunity to travel and to meet the famous names in physics. This, I felt, was not an area where pressure on me was justified, yet the spectre of conferences here, there and everywhere – often in places like Dallas in the run-up to Christmas – continued to hover over my head. My reluctance to fly only emphasized my own weakness and increased my shame at denying Stephen whose needs were far greater than my own and whose courage in extreme adversity was unparalleled. The corrosive effect of those dilemmas dramatically eroded my self-esteem. How could I, able-bodied, mobile and young, deny anything to the wheelchair-bound victim of an incurable disease, almost totally paralysed and haunted daily by the prospect of his own premature death? If my life was to have any meaning at all, it would result from having done everything I could to make his life tolerable.

Fortunately there were plenty of students and colleagues to accompany Stephen to these functions. On 12 December 1976 he left home at 8 a.m. with some of them to fly off to Boston for one of those pre-Christmas conferences, leaving me free to perform my maternal role unharassed, to attend the nativity plays, ballet shows and school carol services and take the children to the Caius Christmas party. At 9 a.m. on the same day, Alan Lapedes, who had given us so much quietly dedicated help throughout the period of crisis, returned to his home in Princeton. I then spring-cleaned the spare room, our one room in the upstairs part of West House, for the arrival of our new resident physicist, Don Page, whom we had met in California where he was a former graduate student of Kip Thorne's. Don had once invited us to a magnificent performance of Brahms's *German Requiem* at his Baptist church in Pasadena and in September 1976 he and his mother had come to Cambridge on a tour of inspection. Naturally, they wanted to see whether the arrangement we were offering was suitable, and, I suspected, to judge whether I was a sufficiently respectable landlady. Evidently our *ménage* passed the test, for Don bounced energetically into our household like A. A. Milne's Tigger. He arrived with Stephen on his return from Boston on 18 December and eagerly joined in all our Christmas festivities.

I had moved among physicists for long enough to know that they mostly came from somewhat unusual backgrounds. Don Page's background was so unusual that it was exceptional even among physicists. Born of missionary–teacher parents, he was brought up in isolation in a remote part of Alaska, where his parents provided his early schooling. He later attended a Christian college in Missouri, his parents' home state, and from there graduated to Caltech where he joined Kip's group as a postgraduate student. His fundamentalist beliefs were so firmly engrained in his psyche that the apparent clash between them and his field of study, gravitational physics and the origins of the universe, while paradoxical to many onlookers, did not appear to disturb him unduly because he was able to compartmentalize his activities. On the one hand, his Christianity was devout, principled according to absolute values, which as yet unchallenged in their rigidity, could seem to lack sensitivity; on the other, those very evangelical convictions required of him an indiscriminate zeal in all his endeavours.

While I respected his fervour – he attended church twice on Sundays, morning service at the Eden Street Baptist Church, and Anglican Evensong at the Round Church, with additional midweek Bible study classes – and welcomed the supportive religious influence he brought to our lives, I sided with Stephen in refusing to be evangelized, particularly at breakfast-time. Well-meaning in his youthful innocence, Don held out for himself the hope of making a spectacular conversion – comparable to that of the road to Damascus – through his early morning Bible readings and prayers. I could have told him that he was doomed to failure. I was sure that his broad, floodlit highway of biblical certainties was even less likely to meet with success than my own path. My quiet, unpretentious amble along the lanes of simple trust in the power of faith and deeds in the hope that they would convey intimations of a higher influence had led nowhere. That meandering path had had scant attraction for Stephen, whose extreme adherence to the straight and narrow route of scientific rationality forbade any perception of a distracting spirituality.

Belief in the higher influence was my continued source of help and strength. It enabled me to face the rigours of each day and to continue to count my blessings, but I felt myself to be in a spiritual limbo where the signposts, pointing every whichway, were often enigmatic. Was my life destined to end with Stephen's, I wondered. Was I obliged to let physics, the epitome of rational thought, through its contempt and disdain, destroy the essential motivation of my life, the poetry and the spirituality, the persistent, innocent belief that good could triumph over evil? I doubted that Don's earnest readings and literal sermons at eight-thirty in the morning when I came back from taking Lucy to school were going to illuminate the way forward, clarify the signposts or fill my troubled soul with spiritual solace. Only music, particularly song, incompetent beginner though I was, offered a means of satisfying my spiritual needs. The impermanence, even of a Schubert song, was frustrating, however, and left in its place a dark hollow which only a moment earlier a glorious outburst of melody had emblazoned with a golden light.

At breakfast Stephen always hid behind the newspaper, which was propped up on a frame. Many a spare moment in 1977 was to be spent searching for a reliable electronic page-turner. Needless to say, all the models we investigated were expensive although for once, the contribution we could expect from government sources was more generous since a page-turner was an essential aid to his work. Until he finally came by such a machine, Stephen was constrained to rely on a simple wooden frame and human intervention for his early morning encounter with the broadsheets. The upright newspaper was a barrier that the laden spoon had to surmount when feeding him his substantial breakfast of pills, laxative, boiled eggs, pork chops, rice and tea, and it was also a barrier to conversation.

This was not a barrier that Don had anticipated when he came down to breakfast, armed with Bible and edifying tracts in the early days. I said nothing, leaving him to address his invisible congregation, shielded by *The Times*, as best he could. Stephen would not be distracted from his perusal of current affairs, essential for a Fellow who prided himself on having the last word in High Table discussions, whether about Britain's precarious financial position shorn up by loans from the United States, or the test runs of the Space Shuttle. My reading of the newspaper usually amounted to little more than a quick glance at the headlines, whereas Stephen read slowly, mentally photographing and digesting every snippet of information, every fact and figure, for regurgitation on some later occasion, probably at High Table.

As Don was finding his task heavy going, it occurred to me that a distraction was needed. I invited him to help himself to cornflakes, muesli, boiled eggs and toast, and asked if he had ever tried Marmite. He picked up the round, brown jar with its yellow lid. 'No, no, we don't have this in the US; I guess it's some kinda chocolate,' he replied, avidly ladling thick spoonfuls of the dark, treacly substance on to his slice of toast. 'Try it and see,' I said, whereupon he took a large bite. His open, child-like expression creased in wrinkles of repulsion at the pungent, salty assault on his tastebuds when he was expecting the creamy sweetness of chocolate spread. Even Stephen looked up from the newspaper, his broad grin revealing those alluring dimples in his cheeks. Good-humouredly, after a moment's puzzlement, Don was able to take the joke in good part and never again did he bring his proselytizing zeal to the breakfast table.

The great advantage of having an American from Caltech in residence was that whenever Stephen wanted to go to Los Angeles, or anywhere else in the United States for that matter, in the interests of science, the American would want to go too. So although the following summer Stephen pressed me to accompany him to America for three weeks, Don was all too ready to go instead. This unexpectedly easy solution to a previously intractable problem cleared the way for me to fulfil a longing which had lain dormant for many years. It was in fact thirteen years since I had set foot on the Spanish mainland and I longed to renew my contact with that country and its civilization which had played such a significant role in my education before all my modest pretensions and aspirations were swallowed up. Pleasantries exchanged on dining nights with the Spanish butler of Caius had scarcely sufficed to maintain my once fluent command of the spoken language and over the years that skill had dwindled pitifully to a handful of insubstantial polite formulae. The thesis was suffering from a serious lack of inspiration and motivation, partly on account of its length which had become unwieldy, partly because of the copious quantities of scrappy notes which remained to be incorporated into some sort of order, and partly because the topics were so remote that I was losing touch with them.

As always, my parents jumped at any suggestion of a holiday with their grandchildren and together Dad and I planned an extensive tour through northern Spain and Portugal, coinciding here and there with the *camino francés*, the old pilgrim route to Santiago de Compostela. The mere exercise of planning brought back memories of those wonderful European holidays of old, especially because Dad, with his historian's nose, had lost none of his talent for scenting out singular historical treasures which the ordinary tourist would have passed by.

The customary bout of summer entertaining – dinner-parties for a mini-conference, barbecues, lunch-parties and children's tea-parties – competed in the calendar with school sports days, visits to the theatre, College functions, mundane but necessary considerations like servicing the car and cleaning out the rented house for reletting, and, ultimately, a vicious attack of measles which put Lucy to bed just before the end of term. Finally in late July, after Stephen's early departure for California, the children and I prepared ourselves in a more leisurely fashion for our own journey. We collected my parents from St Albans and set sail from Southampton for Bilbao in the early evening. The next day, spent at sea in warm, calm, clear conditions, brought relaxation such as I had not experienced for ages, even on the *QE2* on our return from the year in America in 1975. Then the sea had been rough and the weather not conducive to relaxing on deck. Here in the Bay of Biscay, the family – grandparents, children and I – were setting off on holiday, an unprecedented holiday free of care, free of worry, full of excitement, to the land whose language and culture had once featured so prominently in my youthful experience and which had faded to the vague impression of a half-remembered dream.

Although Bilbao, the grimy, industrial city on Spain's northern coast, gave us a damp, cloudy reception, my heart leaped when I set foot on Spanish soil again. It continued to do so throughout that holiday, not only at the rediscovery of Spain, a liberated country where Fascism was dead and the tender young plant of democracy was tentatively putting forth fresh, green shoots in the arid soil of repression and totalitarianism, but also at perceptible glimpses of my former self, the once hopeful, adventurous teenager, long buried under a heap of taxing burdens and more urgent priorities. By degrees I regained my grasp of the Spanish language, its grammar, syntax and vocabulary, for that too was part of my rediscovery. Spanish, an energetic language, uttered with a forceful staccato assurance, recharged me with its vitality and reawakened my linguistic voice, so long reduced to a timid silence by the oppressive weight of intellectual prejudice in Cambridge where one soon learned to keep quiet rather than make a fool of oneself.

Cities with sonorous names – Burgos, Salamanca, Santiago, León – extravagant cathedrals, medieval monasteries, Mozarabic chapels, sun-baked plains and gnarled olive groves blazed a trail of dazzling light and torrid heat into the chill drabness of our northern lives. There in those scorched landscapes, Africa met Europe and the desert rubbed shoulders with fertile vineyards and mountain pastures. We crossed into Portugal where the children, who had not once complained of the heat, the distance or the endless sightseeing, had their reward in two days by the sea on the Atlantic coast. In northern Portugal and Galicia, too, I found the Celtic resonances of the traditional songs that I had come to seek. There on the windswept coast were the headlands and rocky inlets and inland the blue mountains, the rushing streams and the pine trees of the *cantigas*. This was the landscape in which the troubadour king of Portugal Don Dinis set the song of a lovesick girl:

> *Ai flores, ai flores do verde pino,*
> *se sabedes novas do meu amigo,*
> *Ai, Deus, e u é?*
>
> Oh, flowers of the green pine,
> Do you have news of my lover,
> Oh, God, where is he?

In the mountains we saw modern versions of the colourful local pilgrimages, the *romarías*, which the girl of the *cantigas* longed to attend in the hope of meeting her lover. In the churches, cathedrals, cloisters and shrines stood row upon row of heads, sculpted in wax, of loved ones for whom divine grace was sought. The style of these heads was remarkably similar to that of Roman *ex votos* in pottery on display in the Museo San Marcos in León, suggesting that the custom of bringing the wax image of the lover to the shrine, which still persists in modern Galicia and is well attested in the *cantigas*, might well date back to Roman times.

The exhilaration of the discovery of a living past and unbroken traditions, the sensation that the ponderous weight of scholarship that I was trying to mould into a thesis had some basis in a high-spirited reality, that medieval studies were after all a more relevant, productive field of research than collecting pebbles on the beach, gave a tremendous boost to my motivation. I promised myself that I would finish the thesis, come what may, even though it might not lead anywhere, even though it might simply be an end in itself. I felt eager and impatient to record all that I had seen and relate it to the texts, but not so impatient that I wanted to rush back to Cambridge before we had all squeezed every ounce of benefit from those weeks in Spain and Portugal.

We each stored our own memories of that stay. Lucy, whose imagination was so fertile that she could keep herself and everyone else amused no matter how long the journeys or how searing the heat, was fascinated by the cockle-shell motif of the pilgrim route to the tomb of St James at Santiago. She kept her eyes open for the shell on buildings, statues and signs, letting out a yell of triumph whenever she spied one. Perhaps not surprisingly after so many religious monuments, she and Robert became pretty confused in their grasp of the lives of the saints, with the result that, when we came down to the sea at Ofir in Portugal, they devised a crazy game in which Lucy played the part of John the Baptist, drenching her brother with sea-water while, wrapped in a towel, he played the part of a stoical pilgrim *en route* to the tomb of St James. Any religious connotations of this game were, needless to say, entirely spurious.

While the children were engaged in this heretical and obstreperous pursuit, the one near-disaster of the holiday occurred when Dad found himself unwittingly shut in his room by a faulty doorlock. There was no telephone in the room and the only possible exit was via the balcony: the only way to get off his balcony was to leap over a 70-foot drop on to our balcony and escape through our room. He joined us on the beach, bursting with pride at this dare-devil achievement which, we all had to agree with astonished amusement, was no mean feat for a sixty-three-year-old.

CHAPTER THIRTY-FOUR

Impasse

I N THAT AUTUMN of 1977 I returned to England with my mind once more fired with the glowing impressions of the Iberian Peninsula and determined to attack the thesis with fresh insight and vigour, although the organization of the material remained daunting and time was still a crucial factor. Stephen returned from California to promotion – to a personal Chair in gravitational physics.

Stephen's elevation to a professorship had implications beyond that of a modest salary increase since the title and position assured him of enhanced respect and recognition wherever he went – with a few exceptions, one of them in his own Department. His promotion coincided more or less with the redecoration and refurbishment of the Department and for some time he waited for the carpet, to which as a professor he was entitled, to be laid in his office. After some weeks and months of waiting in vain, he decided to broach the matter to the Head of the Department. The HOD tut-tutted peevishly at his request. 'Only professors are entitled to carpets,' he said. 'But I *am* a professor!' Stephen remonstrated. Eventually, in somewhat belated confirmation of his status, his professorial carpet arrived.

Carpets notwithstanding, Stephen was afraid that the appointment might put a distance between him and his students but took comfort in the fact that the physical help he required of them disarmed any diffidence created by his lofty reputation. Although an undisputed intellectual potentate, he shuddered at the thought of conforming to the image of an Establishment professor, an unapproachable figure, aloof from students and colleagues. He preferred the image of the eternal youth with the boyish grin, poking fun at the very authority of which he himself was now a part.

While Stephen's physical condition may have been an effective equalizer in the sphere of the Department, his promotion, though welcome, created subtle problems for me in our dealings with the world at large, not least because his growing reputation so totally exceeded our circumstances. Only our very closest friends realized that on the home scene the struggle for daily survival continued unabated as before. Despite the pitiless onslaughts of motor neurone disease, Stephen had become a national figure, the youngest Fellow of the Royal Society, the recipient of umpteen awards and medals, Einstein's successor and a professor in the University of Cambridge. The paradox of his situation had made him the darling of the media. Not only in the popular perception but also, I began to suspect, in the eyes of his own family, his success was proof that he had conquered motor neurone disease and therefore the battle was won: we could not possibly be in need of help.

It was the most cruel irony that we had become the innocent victims of our own astounding success. There was not simply a schism between the public face and the private image, they were actually in conflict with each other. Certainly the public functions – like the memorable occasion in the summer of 1978 when Stephen received an honorary doctorate from the University of Oxford – were enjoyable and gratifying but that sort of limelight made not the slightest contribution to the help, both physical and emotional, which we needed more than ever. Motor neurone disease had not been conquered; it was still advancing at a slow but relentless pace, no more perceptibly to outsiders than the natural ageing process. To the immediate family circle, the effects were devastating and the demands punishing. Our earlier blithe assertion that it was just a background inconvenience, a fact of life, rang hollow like a mocking peal of laughter. Motor neurone disease dominated our lives and those of the children in spite of all our efforts to uphold that precious veneer of normality on which our self-respect depended.

From being a bright though reserved little boy, Robert was becoming so withdrawn that I feared he was suffering from depression, a condition which according to my doctor was not unknown in children. For amusement he engrossed himself in computer manuals to the exclusion of other diversions. Stephen tried hard to fulfil his paternal role by buying elaborate electric train sets and complicated lengths of track which Robert was not skilful enough to operate. Even when his old friend, Inigo, brought his more advanced electrical knowledge to bear, the trains never ran smoothly and Robert quickly lost interest. Apart from Inigo, who went to a different school, he had few friends and did not seem keen to cultivate new ones. Rumour reached me that he was not invited to birthday parties because, outside the home, his behaviour was uncontrollable. Evidently the restraints placed on him at home, where his behaviour was exemplary, found their outlet in other people's houses. I began to wonder whether perhaps it was a purely selfish urge that I had accomplished in giving birth to the children. My desire to make Stephen happy seemed to entail the sacrifice of their freedom. Much though he loved and respected his father, it was obvious that Robert needed a male role model, someone who would romp and tussle with him, someone who would ease him out of a childhood already lost into adolescence, someone who would not expect anything of him in return, least of all assistance with their own physical requirements.

Lucy, effervescent and sociable, developed an early sense of independence which enabled her to cultivate a wide circle of friends where she found some compensations for the shortcomings of her home life. From a tender age she threw all her bubbling energies into a giddy social scene which revolved in an unremitting cycle of Brownies, swimming galas, Guide camps, sponsored runs, school plays and concerts, and music and drama at the Saturday club, as well as innumerable parties. Doubtless her huge collection of soft toys and the fantasy world which she and Lucy Grace Cadbury invented for their Snoopy puppets also played a part in helping her evolve subconscious methods for coping with her unusual background, though certainly she remained very sensitive to her circumstances. Both her age and her sex enabled her to avoid the pressures that were falling upon Robert's shoulders.

My parents filled many of the gaps in the children's lives with those trips to London and visits to the theatre. However, there was a deep hole in my own life which I could not even begin to broach to them. Thelma Thatcher was astute and forthright enough to identify it in one of her very last remarks to me before she died in the summer of 1976. 'My dear,' she said, leaning across her highly polished table and looking me straight in the eye, 'I simply can't imagine how you survive without a proper sex life.' I was so astounded by such candour from an octogenarian that I could reply only with a shrug of the shoulders. I myself did not know the answer to her question but my sense of loyalty to Stephen forbade any open discussion of that topic which for him was as taboo a subject as his illness.

I did not allow myself to confide in Thelma Thatcher on that occasion and there was never another opportunity. Nevertheless, I badly needed a confidante in whose age and wisdom I could trust. I needed to be able to talk about my intense anxieties, exacerbated as they were by lack of professional help or advice, for I had reason to fear that the effort involved in sexual activity might kill Stephen in my arms, even though of necessity it was unadventurous and he was and always had been the passive partner because of muscular weakness. My side of the experience was so empty and frightening that it constantly left my nerves raw and jangling and my body unsettled and frustrated.

Quite apart from the physical aspects, the relationship was acquiring profoundly irreconcilable undertones. Intellectually Stephen was a towering giant who always insisted on his own infallibility and to whose genius I would always defer; bodily he was as helpless and as dependent as either of the children had been when newborn. The functions I fulfilled for him were all maternal rather than marital: I fed him, I washed him, I bathed him, I dressed him, I brushed his hair and cleaned his teeth. I had assumed responsibility for every aspect of his well-being, including his appearance. Gradually I had slipped into the role of all-caring mother – only just short of a nurse in that I refused to give injections or intervene in medical matters where I had no training or qualifications. It was becoming very difficult – unnatural, even – to feel desire for someone with the body of a Holocaust victim and the undeniable needs of an infant. Certainly one could admire and venerate the intellect, but the intellect had no arms in which to hold me, no physical strength with which to bring me the comfort for which I yearned. I clutched at the intellectual bond between us for whatever reassurance it could bring, but I foresaw that the marital relationship was inexorably drawing us on to dangerous psychological quicksands which threatened to suck us down, perhaps to sudden death for Stephen and long-term insanity for me. The overall effect of an activity which had united us in the past was becoming bitterly divisive because of the sheer impossibility of talking about it. This was an intrinsic part of the battle against disease which, with better communication, we could have fought together, side by side, supporting each other and developing strategies for coping with the difficulties. Instead it became an alienating force, bringing down a barrier of anguish between us. Like any reference to the illness – even my tentative observation on Robert's tenth birthday that Stephen must have been glad to have lived to see that day – the subject was taboo, trapping each of us in our own vicious circle: Stephen in his refusal to talk about the existence of any problem; me in frustration, despair and ultimately an aching loneliness for which there was no hope of relief.

Not for the first time, I sharpened my eyes and my ears, on the look-out for examples, similar situations, words of advice or crumbs of comfort. My hopes were raised on a rare visit to Lucy Cavendish not long after kind Kate Bertram's retirement from the Presidency. The new President was to introduce herself at a feast, a singular event for that College and one which, despite my reservations about my own academic failings, I was reluctant to miss. After dinner in the dark panelled dining-hall of St John's College, the new President rose to her feet. She recounted the events of her life and of her academic career. Tears came to my eyes as she spoke of her marriage: her husband, too, had suffered from an incurable, disabling disease. Again it seemed for a brief moment that I had met someone with whom I might be able to talk freely and sincerely, someone who would intuitively understand the tiredness and the despair behind the smiling but now hesitant façade, and someone to whom I might turn for advice. To my confusion as the speech progressed, I heard her inviting the audience's sympathy for a choice that had faced her, between her academic career and her husband, when she was offered a prestigious American Fellowship. She had taken up the Fellowship.

Finally, in embarrassed desperation, I spoke to Dr Swan in the clinical atmosphere of his morning surgery. If his tone was one of concerned detachment, his words were as candid as Thelma Thatcher's. 'The problems you are facing, Jane, are much like the problems associated with old age,' he said candidly. 'The irony is that you are a young woman with normal needs and expectations.' He sat back in his swivel chair to consider the situation, as it were, from a greater distance. He then leaned forward and pushed a few papers round his desk. 'All I can suggest,' he said, glancing up at me over his gold-rimmed spectacles, 'is that you should make a life of your own.' This was the prescription which terminated the appointment and I was left to interpret it as best I could.

In an unparalleled moment of chumminess that same autumn, Philippa coolly advised me that the time had come for me to leave Stephen. 'Really no one would blame you,' she added. Whatever her motives, her advice struck me as being singularly inappropriate and ill-judged. Certainly such a solution would have expelled me from the Hawking family circle with alacrity. She seemed not to understand that

I could no more have left Stephen than I could have abandoned a child. I could not break up my family, the family that I myself in my optimism had created. This would be tantamount to destroying the one achievement of my life and with it myself.

To pretend that I had never found other men attractive would be dishonest; however, I had never had an affair and my only relationship had been with Stephen. Those passing attractions had never been more than the briefest of encounters. Far from developing into relationships, they had never consisted of more than a fleeting eye-contact, never surfacing to the light of day, always repressed, never expressed in touch or words. All that remained of them were a few painful and embarrassing scars in the memory. Indeed, I had long since lost my sense of individuality and any sense of myself as an attractive or desirable young woman. I also assumed that I had lost the ability to function in the way that either Dr Swan with his genuine concern for our welfare prescribed or Philippa counselled for whatever reason.

I saw myself as part of a marriage and that marriage had grown from the original bond between two people into an extensive network, like a garden full of diverse plants and flowers, not only comprising parents and children but grandparents, loyal friends, students and colleagues. The central tree in that garden was the home which I had created over the years, whether in Little St Mary's Lane, Pasadena or West Road. The marital relationship from which it had all sprung was now but one aspect of that complex diversity and, although that relationship had changed dramatically from the early passionate embraces, the marriage itself was of much wider import. It brought far-reaching responsibilities which transcended the personal needs of the two people who had initiated it. And for those two people who had founded it, there still existed a web of intimacy which, however difficult open communication could often be, was so binding that words could sometimes be replaced by intuition.

I was prepared to try to suppress my own natural instincts in favour of a calmer, loving relationship based on our intellectual rapport, hoping that we might re-establish harmony and composure; this compromise was not an acceptable solution. A brittle, empty shell, alone and vulnerable, restrained only by the thought of my children from throwing myself into the river, drowning in a slough of despond, I prayed for help with the desperate insistency of a potential suicide. The situation was such that I doubted that even God himself, whoever he was or wherever he was, could find a solution to it, if indeed he could hear my prayer, but some solution had to be found if our family were to survive, if Stephen were to be able to carry on with his work and live at home, if I were to remain sane and a capable mother to the children.

It was an exceptional friend, Caroline Chamberlain – Stephen's former physiotherapist – at once sensitive and practical, who suggested that I might benefit from some diversion, such as singing in the local church choir. 'Come and sing at St Mark's,' she said, 'we need extra sopranos for the carol service.' Late one afternoon in mid-December we left the children with her husband Peter, the Leys schoolmaster, while we went to the final rehearsals. This was the first time that I had sung in a real choir, as opposed to the choral class in Pasadena, and a nerve-racking experience it was. Although the voice was developing nicely, the basic techniques, the sight-reading and the counting were conspicuously absent. The first rehearsal was a sobering reminder of my teenage experiences as a hopelessly incompetent secretary. I was a musical dyslexic, I decided there and then. The other sopranos patiently measured the beat for me while the young conductor, pale and thin, politely internalized his dismay at the musical ugly duckling Caroline had introduced into his carefully trained organization. With practice, my efforts improved so that, come the carol service, my contribution was not as dire as he might have feared, and I was invited to join the choir for carol-singing round the parish later that week.

Lucy came with me and trotted along from street to street, from house to house, calling at many homes where the members of the choir and their choirmaster seemed to be not only well known but well received also. This was the area, Newnham, where Lucy went to school, yet apart from the school and the shops, I scarcely knew it at all. Here was a tightly knit community of friends and neighbours, elderly people and families, for whom the red-brick Edwardian church seemed to represent a nucleus, whether or not they attended it regularly.

In the dark winter night, as the choirmaster, Jonathan Hellyer Jones, walked beside Lucy and me, balancing on the edge of the pavement to protect us from the passing traffic, we struck up conversation and I talked as I had not in years. I had the uncanny sensation that I had met a familiar friend of long acquaintance, a shadowy recollection brought sharply back into focus, given shape and form by this stranger. We talked about singing, music, mutual acquaintances – of whom there were several – and travels, particularly about Poland where he had sung with the University Chamber Choir in the summer of 1976. He told me about St Mark's and its extraordinarily dedicated, warm-hearted vicar, Bill Loveless, who had given him great support and strengthened his faith through a very difficult period. He did not say what that period was but I already knew from Caroline that eighteen months previously Janet, Jonathan's wife of one year, had died of leukaemia.

We did not meet again for several weeks. Our next encounter was quite by chance. In January 1978, while Stephen was away in America with his entourage for three weeks, I went with Nigel Wickens and a group of veterans from the singing class to an evening of Victorian entertainment given by the baritone soloist, Benjamin Luxon, at the Guildhall. In the crowded auditorium, I immediately noticed Jonathan, a strikingly distinctive figure, tall, bearded and curly-haired, on the other side of the hall. I was surprised when in the interval he recognized me and I introduced him to Nigel. 'What a nice man!' Nigel remarked on the way back through King's College to West Road where he had parked his car. I agreed guardedly, preferring to concentrate on the other main topic of conversation, Nigel's forthcoming marriage to a talented American singer, Amy Klohr.

As a result of that chance meeting, Jonathan came to teach Lucy the piano on Saturday or Sunday afternoons, depending on his availability. She quickly warmed to him and his serious-minded hesitancy was soon dispelled by her liveliness. At first he came strictly for the length of the lesson, then he stayed a little longer to accompany me in the Schubert songs I was learning, while Stephen alternately directed the railway operations in Robert's bedroom and provided us with an audience of one for our own private Schubertiades, as we called them. After a few weeks of this routine, Jonathan began to come early for lunch or stay for supper afterwards and to help with Stephen's needs, relieving Robert of all the chores which had oppressed him for so long. Then when we had got to know him a little better, Robert would lie in wait for him by the front door and pounce on him on his arrival, throwing him to the floor and wrestling with him. Jonathan took this unconventional form of greeting in good part and responded in kind to a growing boy's need for a good rough-and-tumble to release his excess energies.

Often during the course of each week we would come across each other quite by accident and wonder at the extraordinary coincidences which seemed to be bringing us together. We would stand by the roadside talking, oblivious to what it was we were supposed to be doing or where we were going. We had so much to discuss – his bereavement, his loneliness, his musical ambitions on the one hand, and my fears for Stephen and the children and my despair at the impossibility of doing everything that was required of me with tolerance and patience on the other. Although younger than me, Jonathan had so much wisdom, so broad a perspective on life with which to enlarge my restricted view, so strong a faith and so luminous a spirituality with which to light my black horizon, that we truly trod the holy ground which, in Oscar Wilde's words, is present where there is sorrow. The holy ground was firmer yet softer underfoot than the rough, rocky pathway over which I had been stumbling and which had been leading us down into a dark pit. The holy ground led away from that pit, climbing a path up into the light. I had met someone who knew the tensions and the intensity of life in the face of death.

Other circumstances conspired to bring us together in the strangest of ways. I still attended dinners once a term or so at Lucy Cavendish simply to maintain the contact rather than because I derived any pleasure from them. On one such occasion, having exhausted my own limited fund of conversation, I was listening to the talk across the table when I heard a distinguished elderly Fellow of the College, Alice Heim, singing the praises of a young man who visited her house regularly to play piano duets with her. The warmth with which she described him and his musical talent startled me. She declared with animation that she had never met anyone like him, in her eyes he was a veritable Apollo. Her ageing companions at dinner were more than a little perplexed by such glowing effusions from their colleague. 'What was his name?' they asked. When she replied, 'Jonathan, Jonathan Hellyer Jones,' my ears burned and I felt myself colouring with pleasure, as though I was the only person present who could really share her appreciation of this champion who had entered our lives. 'Oh, I know him!' I exclaimed with an assurance quite unlike my usual shy diffidence at College dinners. Alice Heim directed a beaming smile across the table and for the rest of the evening fervently treated me to stories of Jonathan's many kindnesses to her, leaving her companions nonplussed, perhaps even a little shocked.

No one could have been more surprised than I, as much at my own blushing reactions as at Alice Heim's enthusiasm. Why was I so keen to talk about my new acquaintance, why did the mention of his name bring the blood rushing to my cheeks? At the same time I was uncomfortably aware that the warm glow resulted as much from embarrassment as from pleasure, as if I stood accused of a guilty secret. Yet there was no apparent reason for this friendship either to be a secret or to be tinged with guilt. The friendship was based on our shared interests, on our concern for each other's situation, on the support we could bring to each other, and above all, on music. Nevertheless, though we had never touched and would not do so for a long time, we were both aware that the guilty secret was an admission of the potentially adulterous nature of the relationship. The attraction between us was strong but adultery is an ugly word and not one which featured in our personal vocabulary for it was contrary to our shared moral code and to the ethical basis on which our lives were built. Was this the price I should have to pay to reignite the flame of my passionate spirit? Was it a price that, in all honesty, I could allow Jonathan to pay? If I were to find myself in the company of the adulterous heroines of the nineteenth century, the price might be even higher. The end-result might be only the jarring sound of a cracked kettle rather than music to move the stars to pity.

CHAPTER THIRTY-FIVE

A Helping Hand

IT WAS DURING the following term that Jonathan suggested I might like to join the church choir. Under his baton, they were rehearsing excerpts from *Messiah* for an orchestral performance at Easter. As Robert and Lucy were old enough to be left for an hour in front of the television in the early evening, I joined the handful of choral parishioners whose musical expertise seemed to be far in advance of my own for the Thursday rehearsals in the church. If they had their doubts about the suitability or the competence of the new member introduced by the choirmaster, they were considerate enough not to voice them. I had no previous acquaintance with *Messiah* – surprisingly, considering the repertoire we performed, it had not appeared on the schedule of the Pasadena City College choral evenings. To me, a comparative beginner, the graphic complexity of Handel's choruses where sheep ran astray with alarming rapidity, 'turning everyone to his own way', represented a challenge which I countered with an obsessive enthusiasm, the more so because, for once, this was not an enterprise which I was tackling on my own, but one in which I had companions.

In joining St Mark's choir, I also joined the church. The services there fell loosely within the bounds of the Church of England formats that I had known since childhood, whether on Sundays, in school or at university, but this was Anglicanism devoid of fossilized ritual, sanctimonious dogma and stifling pedantry, thanks to the visionary dynamism of the vicar, Bill Loveless, whose surname could not have been more ill suited to his personality. Once a journalist on the *Picture Post*, and also an actor, soldier and businessman, Bill had come to ordination in middle age. Happily still blessed with phenomenal vitality, he brought all his experience from other walks of life, and all his contacts too, to assist him in his pastoral work and in his unending search for relevant themes for his sermons or for his monthly forum on topical matters. To the latter he invited a succession of guest speakers – doctors, policemen, social workers, political activists and so on. The forum would give rise to a lively debate which Bill would eventually draw to a close in a sermon on the Christian angle on the subject, whether crime, health, education, homelessness, abortion, violence, old age, wife-battering or politics. The Christian angle was at once pragmatic and generous, disciplined but never judgemental. Thus the congregation of St Mark's – little old ladies and eminent professors alike – was kept in the forefront of the major issues of the final quarter of the twentieth century and was forced to examine those issues from the most profoundly humanitarian perspective.

For Bill, as for David Ireland, true Christianity did not deal in absolutes, bargains with God or divine punishments. Its one guiding principle was a passionate love of humanity, affirming God's unequivocal love for all people, whoever they were, whatever their imperfections. This loving doctrine automatically precluded all selfishness, all intolerance, all cruelty. Its only command was to love one's neighbour. Conversely expressed, its only negative, its only restraint, was the injunction never to harm one's neighbour. In this kingdom there was rest and refreshment for all the weary and heavy-laden. Here I found solace as my eyes began to open to the reality of God's love. At last the crumpled rag of my spiritual being began to revive, gaining shape and substance, vigour and life.

Although I derived comfort from my return to the Church, it also posed imponderable questions in my mind. Some were new and some I had considered before. What was God really asking of me? How great a sacrifice was required of me? The circumstances in which I had met Jonathan when I was at breaking-point were so extraordinary – and yet so ordinary – that I could not avoid the bizarre, perhaps naive, impression that that meeting had been deliberately engineered by a benevolent divine power, acting through our good and caring mutual friends. We were both lonely, deeply unhappy people, in desperate need of help. Could that meeting really have been part of a highly unorthodox divine plan? Or was I just being absurd, even heretical? I dreaded being accused of hypocrisy. I knew my Molière too well to want to find either myself or Jonathan being cast in the role of Tartuffe.

When Stephen and I had first met on that New Year's Day nearly fifteen years ago, we were like two young saplings of roughly equal strength and stature. Although in the early years his sapling had failed to flourish, mine was solid enough to support us both. Despite his failing strength, his tree had put out robust new roots which enabled its spindly trunk to bear a plentiful crop of heavy golden fruit. My own tree braced itself to carry the extra burden but the weight of the fruit had become more than I alone could bear. My tree had become brittle and was in grave danger of snapping from the strain. Just when I needed it most, support miraculously appeared at my side, lifting the burden from my shoulders, sharing the strain in the struggle to keep upright. A happy chance, some would say. Others would marvel at the coincidence. For me, tense and overwrought, it had the hallmark of divine intervention, although at that stage, in the spring of 1978, Jonathan and I had scarcely begun to confront our feelings, let alone give them any expression.

The fundamental question was how to handle this heaven-sent gift. We were presented with a choice, which in the event was no choice at all if one truly subscribed to the Christian ideals of St Mark's. The gift could be used hurtfully, destructively. If Jonathan and I even momentarily contemplated the possibility of going off together, setting up a home together, starting our own family, it would have the potential to break up the family in whose care I had invested so much of myself, so much of my life, so much love and so much energy. I might try to salve any pangs of conscience by claiming that I had fulfilled my promise to Stephen, that I had done my best for him in outrageously difficult circumstances over a very long period and that I simply could not do any more. This was not a viable possibility in the terms of the teachings of St Mark's, teachings which both I and Jonathan believed were the only true basis for human living.

The alternative course was the only one we could follow. Then, that special gift could be used well, for the benefit of the family as a whole – for the children and for Stephen if he were prepared to accept it as such. The family would continue to function as a family, Stephen would be able to live at home and to continue to amaze the world with his scientific discoveries, the children could grow up free of all burdens and I would once again become whole, healthy, happy and capable. The latter course would not be easy since it would require a rigorous amount of self-discipline from Jonathan and me. In caring for Stephen with the love and respect he deserved, we would have to try to maintain a distance from each other. We would continue to live apart and would not allow ourselves to show any outward signs of affection for each other in public.

In principle, our social lives would always focus on at least three, if not five people, rarely an exclusive twosome. The well-being of Stephen and the children would be the justification for our relationship. Never would we allow ourselves to think about or plan for the future. The future was the present and that was full enough to occupy all our energies. In effect there was no future for anyone who became involved with me.

Sometimes I asked myself whether it was not unforgivably selfish of me to monopolize the life of a young man who had already suffered so much tragedy. The answer was always the same: I was too weak and needed him too badly to be able to muster the strength to discourage him. He was the only person who was prepared to save us from the brink of despair. He was young and energetic and had no other commitments, no family of his own dependent on him, no other emotional entanglements to make him impatient to get away. With his help we could survive as a family, without it we were doomed.

As hesitantly we began to admit to the attraction that was drawing us to each other, Jonathan would dispel these doubts by reassuring me that through us – all of us – he had found a purpose which was helping him to alleviate the hollow pain of his own loss. It was during the course of a rare visit to London in May 1978 to see the Blake exhibition at the Tate that he announced that he was prepared to commit himself to me and to my family, come what may. We were sitting in a quiet side chapel of Westminster Abbey away from the hubbub of the tourists when he made that most selfless and most moving of pledges and lifted me out of the dark void that my life had become. The relationship was ennobling and liberating. It was still platonic and would long remain so. The mutual attraction and the unruly emotions it threatened to provoke were sublimated in the music we practised and performed together, usually in Stephen's presence, at the weekends and sometimes on weekday evenings as well. It was enough that someone had come into my life on whom I could depend implicitly.

Stephen at first reacted to Jonathan with a certain understandable male hostility. In true Hawking fashion, he tried to assert his intellectual superiority over him, just as he might when faced with a new research student. He was soon disarmed on discovering that this technique was either unnecessary or unavailing since Jonathan was not competitive by nature. Selfless and highly sensitive to the needs of others, he responded much more readily to Stephen's helplessness, to the charm of his smile

and to the soulful light in his eyes, than he did to the sonority of
his reputation or the legendary agility of his mental processes. Under
Jonathan's influence, Stephen became gentler, calmer, more appreciative,
as if he could allow himself to relax the rigid armour he had assumed
in his battle with fate. He almost seemed glad that there was someone
else who could relieve him of the burden of my emotional insecurities
so that he could get on with the more important business of physics. It
even became possible, in the dead of night, for me to confide in him in
an unprecedented manner. Generously and gently he acknowledged that
we all needed help, no one more than himself, and if there was someone
who was prepared to help me, he would not object as long as I continued
to love him. I could not fail to love him when he was willing to show
such understanding and, most importantly, communicate it to me. On
the occasional days when Jonathan was attacked by the black dog of
depression, it was Stephen who would reassure me that Jonathan would
never let me down. Otherwise, once accepted, the situation was rarely
mentioned. It was however greatly reassuring to me that I could confide
in Stephen.

All pulling together in the same direction, the three of us embarked
upon an exceptional period. There were still those times when the
combination of my tiredness and Stephen's innate cussedness would
bring me to the brink of hysteria but generally we operated on a much
more even keel. For Stephen, it seemed as if the respectability conferred
on him by his Fellowship of the Royal Society and the Papal Medal
constituted an automatic passport to a cornucopia of other honours.
While he continued to advance his understanding of the universe, all
sorts of august bodies continued to trip over each other in their eagerness to cover him with medals, prizes and honorary degrees. These had
already included the honorary doctorate from his Alma Mater, the
University of Oxford, and to his special gratification, an honorary Fellowship at University College, Oxford, his undergraduate college. We
were entertained to six-monthly feasts in the College where, to my
surprise, the Master, Sir John Redcliffe Maud, proved to be the father
of the embassy friends I had made in my student days in Madrid. The
atmosphere in University College was warm and friendly, unsullied by
pomposity. Stephen's undergraduate excesses were a recurring topic of
jovial reminiscence and, as if to lend substance to the recollections, we
were regularly accommodated in undergraduate rooms at some distance
from the nearest bathroom across cold, damp flagstones.

In March 1978 Gonville and Caius College, not to be outdone, commissioned a line drawing portrait of Stephen from David Hockney. While Hockney sketched and drew, Lucy sat curled up, reading and drawing, in an armchair in a corner of the living-room. Unbeknown to her and doubtless to the surprise of the Fellows of Gonville and Caius, Hockney included her in the final version, a gentle acknowledgement of Stephen's family background to offset the official formality of the portrait. On the second day of the sitting, Lucy paid her own tribute to the artist by imitating his mode of dress. We were sitting on the lawn, drinking coffee and taking advantage of a brief spell of spring sunshine, when she burst out of the house, bouncing across the lawn on her hopper, one of her favourite toys, a big balloon made of tough rubber. Her dungarees were pulled up to the knee, deliberately revealing that like Hockney she was wearing odd socks, one white and one brown.

Not only were we beginning to hobnob with famous artists as well as scientists during this period, we also had our first encounter with royalty. One cold wintry evening Stephen and I joined the distinguished gathering of Fellows on the coach going down to the Royal Society for the admission of Prince Charles as an honorary Fellow. (Before coaches were fitted with wheelchair lifts, Stephen had to be hauled aboard bodily by the coach driver and me: this, however, was easier than driving and parking in London.) The occasion gave Stephen cause for some mirth, a welcome reminder of the old irreverent student, scarcely discernible under the present, weighty trappings of Establishment recognition. At the ceremony, the new President of the Royal Society complimented the Prince on the dedicated royal patronage of the Society, founded as he said by Prince Charles's namesake, Charles II, and 'continued by his son James II'. Stephen guffawed incredulously and, in the loudest stage whisper of which he was capable, gleefully announced, 'He's got it wrong! James II was Charles II's brother!' At the reception after the ceremony, Stephen enjoyed himself further by demonstrating the turning circle of the wheelchair to Prince Charles and in so doing, ran close to – or over – the highly polished royal toes, an exercise which he was to inflict at a later date on the Archbishop of Canterbury at a dinner in St John's College, Cambridge.

Jonathan's career was much less meteoric than Stephen's, in fact it had scarcely begun. Quite apart from the devastating tragedy he had suffered, the frustrations of being a struggling musician contributed to the gloom of the bleak, black days he sometimes suffered. A former

chorister and prize-winning scholar of St John's College, he was sufficiently ambitious to find the prospect of a life spent teaching the piano
disheartening, yet his natural reticence and modesty tended to conceal
his very real talent as an organist and harpsichordist. His intense love
and knowledge of baroque music, especially Bach, particularly when
performed on authentic instruments, found scant outlet in the humdrum
routine of piano teaching in schools. A disciple of the tradition established by David Munrow, he was convinced that he had a mission to
educate the ears of the public, accustomed to resonant modern instruments and Romantic interpretations, to the subtleties of baroque performance technique, but he hardly knew where to begin. Authenticity
in performance became one of the subjects under discussion at mealtimes
when the children's chatter allowed the adults to get a word in edgeways.
Stephen would tease Jonathan about the difficulties of managing a harpsichord, insisting that a steel frame would solve all the delicate, time-
consuming problems of tuning and retuning. Jonathan would point out
that the instrument would then not only be unsuitable for authentic
baroque performance, it would no longer be portable either. In fact it
might as well be a piano.

Good-humoured banter notwithstanding, Stephen and I inevitably
became more and more involved in the baroque scene and encouraged
Jonathan to take the plunge, to move away from teaching into performing. This proposition presented him with an intractable dilemma
of which he was already only too well aware. To become a performer
he would have to give up most of his teaching and devote the time to
practising and rehearsing, yet he depended on teaching for his income.
It would be a long time before he could make enough money from
performing alone. He did have one great advantage: he possessed his
own instrument. Not only did he have a fine upright piano in his tiny
house, so reminiscent of number 6 Little St Mary's Lane, on the other
side of Cambridge, but most of the rest of the living space was taken
up with a single manual harpsichord which he himself had built. He
was therefore well equipped to begin performing; he only lacked the
right opportunity.

— The more the three of us discussed the dilemma, the more we
realized that the only way for Jonathan to build up a repertoire and to
become recognized as a performer in a highly competitive environment,
while still earning an income from teaching, was for him to create his
own opportunities. This he could do gradually by self-promotion and

by offering his services to charities. A symbiotic relationship developed between him and the various charities to which he subscribed, particularly the societies concerned with leukaemia and other cancers. He gave recitals free of charge and in so doing trained himself in the techniques of performance, not simply in playing the notes but in overcoming nerves and in planning and presenting the programmes, while the charities benefited from 100 per cent of the takings, minus the costs of publicity.

Meanwhile I was at last catching tantalizing glimpses on the horizon of the end of that long, long road on which I had set foot so many years and two children previously when I embarked upon the doctorate. I was coming to the end of my own intellectual pilgrimage. I scarcely liked to confess how long it had taken me to reach that point, for it was all of twelve years. Alan Deyermond had been right to insist on registering me as a student in London University, as any other university would have thrown me out long ago. The road had been hard and tortuous, and just when I was despondently thinking that there was no end to it, a friend had appeared to cheer me along the final stretch. Jonathan, that new friend on the home front, showed just a sufficient modicum of interest in the subject to spur me on; he it was who would ask me at the end of each day what I had achieved, who would listen to just a few lines of the poetry and lend a hand in sorting out the card index and the masses of notes, scribbled on odd scraps of paper. That interest and a little practical help was all I needed to recover my momentum and bolster my resolve for the final hurdle, the last chapter of the thesis which was to be an analysis of the language of the popular poetry of Castile in the later Middle Ages.

The Castilian lyrics were lively and colourful, full of the medieval iconography of gardens, plants, fruits, birds and animals, symbolizing the multiplicity of the aspects of love. Many of them were also of religious significance and were common to the rest of Europe. The garden epitomizes the attractions of the beloved as well as the virtues of the Virgin Mary. The fountain at the centre is both the spring of life and the symbol of fertility. The apple is the fruit of the Fall and the pear the fruit of divine redemption but, in the secular context, both are potent metaphors for sexuality. The rose is the emblem of the martyrs and of the Virgin yet is the most appealing image of the sensual beauty of the beloved.

Spain introduces its own set of vivid images, drawn from its flamboyant landscape. The fruit which the unhappy nun tastes is the bitter lemon, while happy lovers walk in the shade of the sweet orange grove. The olive grove, similarly, becomes the scene of lovers' meetings. The fact that many of these images have reappeared in the poetry of the Sephardic Jews who were expelled from Spain in 1492, or in the poetry of the New World, is indicative of their early folkloric composition. Thematically these poems present an unbroken tradition with their Galician and Mozarabic forebears, the *cantigas* and the *kharjas*. The songs are usually sung by girls, the motif of the lover's absence recurs, the lovers meet at dawn and the mother is a constant figure.

During sparse weekday minutes and half-hours, the writing began to flow with an unaccustomed ease. At weekends, on Saturday and Sunday afternoons, the songs began to flow as well. Despite my dyslexic handicap in reading music, I voraciously attacked whatever Nigel, my personal Svengali, put before me, whether Schubert, Schumann, Brahms, Mozart, Britten, Bach or Purcell. Thanks to Stephen, I rapidly acquired my own library of music as he showered me with volume upon volume of music for birthday and Christmas presents. Sometimes I would be called upon to sing a solo verse in church. Initially the stage-fright was terrifying. Eventually, with practice, it subsided and then the voice which Nigel had painstakingly crafted into an instrument surprised even me. It was my voice, I was producing it but I could not claim that it belonged to me for it bore little relation to my light, unsure speaking voice. It was strong and confident; it was the voice of someone else, someone with poise and assurance, someone whose identity was at last being affirmed, someone whose grey inmost soul was basking in a warmer, gentler light.

One weekend that spring my brother Chris and his wife Penelope brought their baby daughter to stay. It was quite natural to introduce Jonathan to them as a new friend. They would not demand accounts or explanations of a situation which I myself could not fully explain or understand. They were also a receptive and appreciative audience for a few songs. Afterwards, Penelope remarked on the atmosphere in the living-room that Sunday afternoon. She said that it was magical, as if a great sense of peace and calm had descended on our house. Her remark, warm and comforting as it was, increased my confidence in my new friendship. Chris was much taken with Jonathan. Before he left, he deliberately drew me aside to tell me what a wonderful person he thought he was, especially remarking on his magnificent byzantine eyes.

Later he rang from Devon. We talked for a long time, discussing my situation and the way that it was changing. I took Chris's advice very seriously to heart. 'You have been steering your little boat single-handedly across a very stormy, uncharted sea for many years,' he said, and then continued, 'If there is someone at hand, willing to come on board and guide that boat into a safe harbour, you should accept whatever help he can offer.'

Later that summer we received a visit from my old headmistress, Miss M. Hilary Gent. For some time Miss Gent had regularly included us in her annual progress round the country, which took in former colleagues and pupils from her long career in teaching. She did not restrict her visits to the pupils of St Albans High School but also continued to maintain her contacts with the boys from the prep school where she had started her teaching career. Some of them were now of a relatively advanced age themselves and not a few had achieved high office. Miss Gent's memory for names, faces and circumstances was formidable. She relayed her own news network, linking old girls with old teachers and vice versa, and establishing acquaintanceship between people from different periods of her life who had never even met. Keenly observant, she had shown herself sensitive to my tiredness and low morale over the past few years and had done her quiet best to help by writing formal but encouraging letters and putting me in touch with old girls from St Albans who had come to live in Cambridge.

I rarely followed up her introductions as my life had become too complicated for people who lived normal lives to comprehend. People of my own age had little understanding of the intensity of living in the constant, hovering presence of death. I preferred the company of the elderly, especially since I myself, at the age of thirty-three, was acknowledged to be living the life of an old person and I needed the philosophical reassurance of someone who had come to terms with the dilemmas of old age and mortality which beset me. Once a fortnight or so I would visit the oldest person I knew, a diminutive, white-haired former artist, Dorothy Woollard. As I sat with her in her sheltered accommodation, listening to her tales of the past and commiserating with her malaise at her present restricted circumstances, her room represented a quiet oasis of solitude and reflection in my otherwise frenzied routine. DW, as we called her, had trained in the Bristol School of Art and as a girl she had seen Queen Victoria, a a tiny old woman in a black bonnet, on a royal visit to Bristol. She it was who painted the pictures for Queen Mary's dolls' house in Windsor Castle and during the First World War she worked in the Admiralty, drawing charts. She had never married but had devoted many years of her life to caring for her adored teacher who was wheelchair-bound in old age. His portrait, her greatest treasure, hung in her room amongst her collection of her own masterly paintings and drawings. At an age when most people would have retired from all activity, she kept herself occupied by translating books into Braille. She was still quick and nimble, even in her nineties. She attributed her longevity – she lived to the age of 100 – and her sprightliness in part to her afternoon tea, *hierba mate*, a South American brew which she served to me when I visited her. One Christmas DW demonstrated to my astonished parents her ability to touch her toes. Only Miss Gent, who was probably ten years younger, could compete with her in alertness, clarity of thought and quick-wittedness, yet I never saw *her* touch her toes. Both were blessed with the perceptive wisdom of old age and a sensitivity to the problems of illness which, in my experience, younger people often lacked.

Jonathan was with us when Miss Gent arrived one Saturday afternoon for tea. Immediately she and he began to talk. They talked for the rest of the afternoon while Stephen – the egregious old boy of the preparatory department of St Albans High School for Girls – and I sat listening. It transpired that Jonathan, in his late twenties, and Miss Gent, in her seventies, had many acquaintances in common since music and the musical arena were but one of the many topics with which she was intimately conversant. She interrupted their conversation to follow me into the kitchen when I went to fetch the tea. Unhesitatingly, with an outspoken candour which I found extraordinary for a wizened, elderly spinster, let alone my former headmistress, she declared, 'I am so very glad that you have Jonathan.' She looked at me searchingly, as though wondering whether to be more explicit in conveying her message. 'You have struggled on for so long alone,' she went on, 'I don't know how you have managed; you really need someone to help and support you. He is a splendid young man.' Her message was unmistakable; it was as if Thelma Thatcher, with all her years of experience, was talking to me, telling me that my relationship with Jonathan bore the mark of destiny, that this precious gift was really to be accepted.

My parents met Jonathan that summer. As usual they were reticent about expressing their opinions, traditionally indicated by their reactions rather than words. In this instance they behaved exactly as if Jonathan had been a presence in our lives for as long as they could remember: they did not stand on ceremony nor did they pass any comments on his regular appearances in our household. For his part he tactfully ceded his place at the piano to my father whose passion for Beethoven had fired my own love of music. So while Dad pounded the *Appassionata* out of the keys and my mother plied her needle, replacing the buttons and repairing the cuffs and seams which had fallen off or apart since her last visit, Jonathan would discuss the merits of early instruments with her and tell her about his crusade for authentic performance. It was after we had met Jonathan's parents that I remarked to my mother what wonderful people they were. My mother looked at me in some surprise. 'Well, you ninny, what would you expect?' she said. 'People who have a son like Jonathan are bound to be wonderful. How could they be otherwise?'

At the end of the summer, we parted company already hopefully anticipating our reunion in the autumn. Jonathan left England to attend and teach at a baroque summer school in Austria and we set out, with Don in attendance, for Corsica. Now that the children were growing up and my self-confidence was re-emerging, the fear of flying was beginning to dissipate a little. Air travel no longer held the dreaded threat of separation from tiny dependent beings; instead it held out the enticing promise of a holiday by the Mediterranean on a French-speaking island. The fact that the holiday was also a conference in physics was not a hindrance to enjoyment. In fact it was the perfect compromise because Stephen and his colleagues would be doing what they liked best – genuflecting at the altar of physics – while the families would be enjoying the best sort of beach holiday within a stone's throw of the conference centre. I was particularly looking forward to seeing the Carters again and hearing their news as, since we last met, Brandon and Lucette and their two small daughters had moved to a house at Sèvres on the outskirts of Paris. I promised myself that I would confide in Lucette, telling her about the remarkable change in my life. She with her intuitive understanding of people and relationships would be bound to offer good, sound advice.

CHAPTER THIRTY-SIX

The Unexpected

CARGESE, THE CONFERENCE venue on the west coast of Corsica, was certainly the happiest compromise ever devised for single-minded physicists and their young families. While Stephen revelled in the physics, the children and I revelled in the bright sun, the sand and the sparkling sea. The occasional bomb outrage and the high prices preserved the island from mass tourism, keeping it unspoilt and its beaches and coves clean and uncrowded, as Majorca must once have been before it was exploited. Cargese was established as the home of a colony of Greek refugees from Turkish persecution in the eighteenth century. Their presence was still very much in evidence in street names, family names and the name of our hotel, the Thalassa – the Sea. That name brought back long-buried memories of classical Greek studies as a teenage schoolgirl. In particular, the name recalled Xenophon's *Anabasis* and the whoop of joy the Greek mercenary troops of the Persian Prince Cyrus let out as they came over a mountain pass, tired, hungry, thirsty, lost and footsore after an arduous march across a thousand miles of unknown territory, and saw the sea ahead of them. The relief in that joyful shout of – 'Thalassa! Thalassa!' – had brought the dry ancient text to life with the vivid emotions of real people who had only moments before believed themselves to be at the very limits of their endurance. I echoed their cry every morning at the sight of the calm, glistening waters of the Mediterranean which greeted us as we stepped outside our hotel room.

On promontories overlooking the town, Cargese proudly sported two churches, one Latin and the other Greek. The same priest officiated at both, alternating between the two on consecutive Sundays. Lucette and I attended the Greek rite, fascinated by such an exemplary display of harmony in what might otherwise be a divided community. Both churches contained images of John the Baptist: the Greek icon was compelling for its sharp Byzantine clarity, especially for the haunting depiction of the saint's long, slanting eyes, so reminiscent of Jonathan's. Even that image was not able to inspire me with the courage to tell Lucette about my friendship with him. Whenever I tried to summon the words, whether in English or in French, they stuck in my throat, trapped by my sense of self-reproach at the merest hint of disloyalty to Stephen. The gilded new relationship which promised so much was awakening doubts in my heart of hearts. Was it going to force me to live a lie, to lead a double life? That could turn out to be almost as difficult to bear as the strain and distress of the preceding months and years. I took heart when I recalled Chris's advice and Miss Gent's encouragement but, in the company of physicists and their families among whom Stephen was an awe-inspiring hero, my courage failed me.

In a quiet bay, away from the children's shouts, I wedged myself into a corner in the rock and wrote a long letter to Jonathan. I tried to organize my thoughts and sort out my troubled conscience. I told him how much I missed him and I told him how eternally grateful I was for the light he had brought to my life, like the light of the Corsican sun searching out the green depths of the ocean. I said how appreciative I was of all the unstinting help he had given us, of the transformation he had brought about in our home, easing the tensions and assuming much of the strain. I also confirmed that I could not risk damaging my family, that my first duty was to Stephen and the children, that the bond between my husband and me was indissoluble since we had lived through so much hardship together and that I could not renege on my marriage when Stephen, more helpless than a small child, needed me more than ever.

Resting against a warm rock with the waves splashing at my feet, I was preparing myself for the worst. I knew in my heart of hearts that it would not be at all surprising if, after a period of reflection during his stay in Austria, Jonathan were to decide that association with the Hawking household presented too many physical challenges and too many emotional difficulties for him to continue with us. Such a decision would be understandable. Why should he want to burden himself with all our problems and willingly walk into an emotional trap when he was young and free, with the well-deserved prospect of a full, happy life before him?

Memories of Corsica faded fast on our return home but those weeks had bequeathed us a long-lasting memento. As I took up the reins of the Cambridge routine that autumn, it began to seem even more unlikely that Jonathan would want to involve himself with us again and the prospect of a happy reunion faded into the mists with the waning light of the September sun. As the days grew shorter and a chill crept into the air, I anxiously studied the dates on the calendar, starting to suspect in bewildered amazement that I might be pregnant. For some time I had ceased to bother about contraception in the already fraught marital relationship as it hardly seemed relevant and simply added to the complications. In every waking hour of every day and many a sleepless hour at night, the insistent realization grew that I had been wrong. The combination of the powerfully sensual effects of the Mediterranean climate and my genuine desire to love Stephen, reinforced by the glowing knowledge that I was no longer fighting all the battles single-handedly, had brought us together in fleeting moments of carefree abandon. Passionately though I had adored my babies, the anxious thoughts which now came crowding into my mind – the thought of giving birth to another child, the thought of caring for him or her, the thought of having yet another being totally dependent on me in an intolerably demanding situation without the benefit of the help on which I had come to depend so heavily over the past year – were terrifying. That Jonathan should have considered shoring up the existing family as he had done had been remarkable. To expect him to take on another small Hawking, especially when he had no children of his own and no prospect of ever having any as long as he associated with us, was inconceivable. I was resigned to losing him and with his loss, to losing all hope for the future. I would be alone again.

The pregnancy had only just been confirmed when Stephen left for a conference in Moscow. Since I was already suffering badly from morning sickness, his mother agreed to go with him in my place. Don was also away on a well-earned break from all those duties which he fulfilled most conscientiously. His father had come from Missouri, bearing two inter-rail passes for unlimited travel throughout Europe, and together they had set off to explore the length and breadth of the continent, using the railways both for transport and for overnight accommodation. They had no specific itinerary. Instead they travelled on an improvised basis, choosing their next destination at about nine or ten o'clock each evening, according to the departures available from the city where they happened to be and the length of the prospective journeys. Thus, after spending a day in, say, Madrid, they would look up the trains at the station and decide to take the overnight train to Paris. The next night after a day in Paris, they would board the train for Rome. The longer the journey the better because a long journey could be relied upon to give them a good, uninterrupted night's sleep, especially since their exclusive diet of peanuts and tinned mackerel proved to be extremely effective in deterring other travellers from setting foot in their compartment.

As winter approached in Cambridge, the icy claws of the dark, inner winter from which I had so nearly escaped began to reassert their grip. I wrote Jonathan a note telling him about the baby, wretched in the certainty that this note would amount to a signing off, an abrupt end to those few months of recovery and blissful platonic happiness. I did not know whether he was back from the summer school in Austria and did not expect a reply. For some time I heard nothing but Jonathan had a way of confounding expectations. He did reply eventually, apologizing for having taken time to digest the news and to adjust to its implications. He declared that his commitment to us was unchanged. Although he had no experience of babies, he was sure that I would need his help more than ever and he was ready to offer it unconditionally.

I felt humble and deeply grateful in the face of such unselfishness. I was blessed with the support of someone whose own early tragedy had awakened a sympathy and a consideration for the misfortunes of others which were exceptional almost to the point of eccentricity. It was his hand that reached down and rescued me from death by drowning, not just in deep water, but in deep water under a sheet of ice. It was his encouragement, supernatural in its magnanimity and selflessness, which transformed the long months of pregnancy from a time of desperate anxiety and foreboding to a period of hopeful anticipation and even enjoyment. It was he who gave me the fundamental emotional reassurance that restored me to my old optimistic self and enabled me to prepare to meet yet another challenge, safe in the knowledge that for the first time in many years, this was one I should not have to meet alone. With such reassurance we were all able to fling ourselves back into our positive, forward-looking activities of the months before Cargese.

There was no escaping the fact that a very definite deadline – or rather lifeline – had been sprung on the thesis six months later in April 1979. It had to be finished by the time the baby arrived, otherwise it might as well have been thrown in the bin. I recovered my incentive, setting to work with renewed purpose, even though it was fated always to be done in fits and starts. As usual, the writing had to be fitted in amongst the accustomed round of domestic chores, Stephen's care, children's parties, children's illnesses, speech days, dinners, lunches, visitors and travels. The latter included a physics conference in Dublin. It was our first visit to Ireland and with it we took a step back in time, recalling the London of my childhood, quieter, gentler, unscathed by the monstrosities of modern urban redevelopment. Lucy came with Stephen and me. Her picture, not unlike the Hockney drawing of her, appeared on the front page of the *Dublin Times* when a reporter found her hiding behind a door reading a book at a formal government reception.

Because Jonathan gave so much help with Stephen's needs, with the children and with the chores, even with the shopping, it was actually possible to make good, if fragmentary, progress with the thesis, although it was also competing for time with music and hospital appointments. It was at the first hospital appointment on 7 November that I suddenly became aware of the reality of the fourteen-week-old embryo, a mysterious, ethereal creature, whispering the message of its existence through the clinical medium of a new scientific invention. After putting me through the barrage of usual tests, the doctors wired me up for an ultrasound scan – a test which had been introduced since Lucy's birth – the function of which was to listen to the foetal heart. When they were satisfied with their findings, they asked if I would like to listen too. The rhythmic swish-swish of the tiny heart, beating rapidly against the background of my own – slower, louder, more ponderous – was poignantly moving, awakening in me a deep bond with the new life I had heard but not seen. It was as if the child was appealing to me through the music of its heartbeat: that was a plea I could not ignore. Long before the birth, I began to cherish that unseen presence, already loving the child as much as I loved Robert and Lucy.

Music was to accompany the baby's gestation throughout the winter. Jonathan appointed himself our entertainments officer, frequently bringing home tickets for concerts, many of which were in the newly opened University concert hall five minutes away from West House. We sat on the stage alongside the performers in full view of the audience since there was no other provision for wheelchairs. Often the performers, a host of celebrated musicians from Menuhin to Schwarzkopf, would delay their exits after their curtain calls to come over and greet Stephen. At home I sang whenever I could, practising my repertoire for its first public performance. The baby responded with animated appreciation, kicking hard in time to the music.

We were rehearsing with two musical goals in view. One was my entry in the Cambridge Competitive Festival in March, the other, in February, was a concert we and some musical friends of Jonathan's – Raymond Greenlees, a cellist, and Alan Hardy, a flautist – were giving at home for charity. We invited as many people as we could squeeze into the living-room and, in the tradition of the numerous parties in our establishment, laid on food and drinks in the interval. Afterwards, in an advanced state of pregnancy and an even more advanced state of nerves, I stood up to give my first public performance other than the occasional solo in church. It consisted of two folksongs by Benjamin Britten and a couple of songs by Fauré; these were also to be my entries in the competition. The audience were kindly appreciative and on their departure made generous donations. We divided the proceeds between two charitable causes, leukaemia research and the Motor Neurone Disease Association.

The Association had been founded only recently and Stephen had been invited to become the patients' patron. When, long ago, his condition was diagnosed, we were told that it was very rare, that little was known about it and that since so few people suffered from it, there was no basis for a support group. None of this was true. Through the Association we discovered that the illness, also known in America as Lou Gehrig's disease after a sportsman who suffered from it in the 1930s, was in fact quite widespread and at any one time there could be as many diagnoses of motor neurone disease as there were sufferers from multiple sclerosis, which until then had received much more publicity because there were more survivors. Motor neurone disease ran its course much more quickly, usually within two or three years, distorting the statistics and leaving patients and their families crisis-ridden, with neither the time nor the opportunity to set up support organizations or self-help groups. On the founding of the Association, some information at last became available. It emerged that motor neurone disease could erupt in one of two forms. The acute form paralyses the victim's throat muscles, precipitating an early death. The rarer form, the one which had attacked Stephen, resulted in a creeping paralysis of the voluntary muscles of the whole body, eventually including the throat, over a longer period, perhaps five or, at the outside ten years. Stephen's survival for sixteen years since the time of diagnosis in January 1963 made him a medical phenomenon, as unexplained as the illness itself.

Jonathan had already successfully made his keyboard talents available to raise money for leukaemia research. Over the course of the next few years, he and I gave many joint recitals raising money for the fledgling Motor Neurone Disease Association in churches throughout East Anglia. Increasingly for these recitals I concentrated on a baroque repertoire, since Handel, Bach and Purcell could be more effectively – and authentically – accompanied on the organ or the harpsichord than on the general run of traditionally tuneless, warped and decrepit church pianos. Through these musical undertakings we managed to raise quite respectable amounts of money and also brought the illness to the notice of the public, particularly since Stephen usually featured prominently in the audience. At last the disease had a recognized name. Pinned down, the snarling beast could be identified, targeted and, through communal sympathy and joint endeavour, some of its savagery tamed. It was a small example of the Existentialist philosophy of my youth at work: *angst* or despair was being overcome, or at least dispersed, through shared suffering.

As a local volunteer, I visited some of the afflicted families in the area whose lives were being shattered by the sudden change in their circumstances and expectations. The diagnosis had left all of them shocked and bewildered, as it had left us years before. I felt that I had a duty to try to give these families the benefit of our experience and pass on to them the practical techniques we had devised for managing the condition. I could also give them hope by pointing to the fact that Stephen was a survivor and that he was the living proof that the diagnosis was not necessarily a death sentence if one had the will to fight. Perhaps it was because the people I met were all much older than ourselves that they did not seem prepared to fight with the same vehemence. They were hurt and troubled, certainly, but they revealed a much greater calm and acceptance than I expected. The frenzied lifestyle which had become the mark of our rejection of the disease was not for them. Instead, they lived quietly, appreciating whatever was done for them, thankful for all the love and care they received from their families, often awaiting their fate with resignation. I trod warily, fearing to trespass on their privacy by introducing bright, well-meaning proposals for exercises, diets, injections or vitamins. There was, it seemed, an element in their lives which ours lacked, an element which I found myself envying. It was not defeatism but the element of inner peace.

Stephen's position as Patron of the Association and my attempts to help as a fund-raiser and volunteer brought me face to face yet again with one of those cruel ironies of our situation. Once more, we had been elevated to a pedestal where Stephen was respected and admired. On that pedestal we found ourselves aloof, cut off from the ordinary members of the group. We needed advice as much as anybody but by virtue of our position we were prevented from seeking it because such an admission of our needs would have been a denial of the confident façade on which other people depended for boosting their own morale.

The number of people blessed with the perspicacity to see behind that mask could be counted on the fingers. They included our old friends from the early days in Cambridge, my family, Jonathan and his parents, Sue Smith – Stephen's physiotherapist – and a few exceptional friends like Miss Gent. Among these friends were also Peggy Jacobs and her daughter Angela, who were regular attenders at Nigel Wickens' singing class. Peggy's first husband, Angela's father, had died of motor neurone disease in Canada. She was therefore well versed in the trials and tribulations caused by the illness and was unsparing in the moral support she gave, not only to Stephen and me, but to Jonathan as well, for Peggy was an astute observer of character and situation and she was charitable enough to judge the importance of Jonathan's role in our lives. It was just before the baby was due that we were fortunate to get to know some new friends of comparable sensitivity, Bernard and Mary Whiting from Australia, when they came to one of the West Road musical gatherings.

Bernard had come to work in Stephen's group in the Department; relaxed and easy-going, he, always ready to give Stephen a hand, in much the same way that George Ellis had in the distant past. Mary, a classical archaeologist for whom the chance to live in Europe represented the fulfilment of her dreams, was writing a Ph.D. thesis and working in the Fitzwilliam Museum, compiling a catalogue of the museum's extensive gem collection. Mary was no fossilized museum piece. Her flowing, prematurely grey hair framing her finely-drawn, youthful features lent her a graceful distinction, like a Raphael madonna. Her appearance was well matched by her personality for she was both learned and spirited, her interests extending far beyond archaeology.

Mary and Bernard had come to several Departmental parties at West

Road but as I was mostly too harassed and mind-blown on those occasions to carry on any sort of sensible conversation with the guests individually, it was not until Mary and Bernard met Jonathan that I came to know them better. Mary's fervent interest in archaeology was equalled only by her love of baroque music. She herself played the violin and was immensely proud of her elder sister, an international harpsichordist, who lived with her husband out in the Australian bush surrounded by harpsichords. Mary and Jonathan had plenty to talk about of course. To me Mary sadly confided that she was desperately keen to have children but so far had not succeeded. If ever I needed a salutary reminder of my own good fortune, of my 'blessings', this was it, especially as another little blessing was about to fall into my lap.

Towards the end of March 1979, Robert, who was in the first year of the Upper School at the Perse, went away to Scout camp. I was not at all happy about this camp for eleven-year-olds since it was to be in the corner of a field in north Norfolk, exposed to the biting winds of a reluctant spring. The field, by all accounts, was sodden, under a couple of inches of water, there was a fall of snow during the camp and Robert came back exhausted, soaked to the skin and coughing persistently. Stoical as ever, he declared that the camp had been 'all right' and was not deterred by it from future expeditions with the Scouts. After a couple of days in bed, he recovered sufficiently to be able to go away with Lucy to the cottage in Wales where the two children were to spend Easter with Stephen's parents.

Meanwhile I made my debut on the concert platform at the Cambridge Competitive Festival, singing the Fauré and Britten songs to Jonathan's expert piano accompaniment while Stephen smiled his cheerful encouragement from the audience. The adjudicator politely commended the timbre of the voice and tactfully refrained from commenting on my condition, only allowing himself to remark that he realized that, owing to circumstances, my breath control was somewhat inhibited.

The thesis was very nearly finished; all that remained was the mind-bogglingly boring task of ordering the bibliography alphabetically and attending to all the minutiae therein, upon which Alan Deyermond insisted. Every comma, full stop and bracket had to be in its correct place otherwise he would not pass the thesis for submission.

At St Mark's we were rehearsing for Easter, for the devotional service on Good Friday and for the Easter Festival at which I was to sing a solo,

'Now the Green Blade Riseth', accompanied on the flute by Jonathan's schoolfriend Alan Hardy. After rehearsing in the church in the early part of Holy Week, we were all set for the performance on Easter Sunday. Then, on Maundy Thursday, with an almighty flourish, I put the final full stop to the final entry in the bibliography, thus bringing to a conclusion thirteen arduous years of seminars, research, annotation, card-indexing, organizing, compiling, writing, editing, foot-noting and referencing.

The following day, Good Friday, during the devotional service, I felt dejected to the point of tears. Perhaps this was a reaction to the emotive force of that particular religious commemoration and the music that went with it, perhaps it was the anti-climactic effect of finishing the thesis, perhaps I was missing my children who were to stay with their grandparents until after the baby was born in a week or two's time. The following day the melancholy lifted. Very strong physical symptoms took its place, leaving little doubt that the baby was going to be born quite soon. I spent most of the afternoon in the garden with Stephen beside me, relaxing in the sun and picking bunches of violets. Don drove us to the maternity hospital early in the evening but a routine inspection revealed little movement of any significance so we were sent away again. We called at Jonathan's house on the way home and stayed for a take-away curry, inserting ourselves as best we could in among the musical instruments in the restricted space of the living-room. As Jonathan and Stephen were partial to curries, he often arranged a take-away, especially on Sunday evenings when the West House kitchen, after seven days of churning out three-course meals for all-comers, only ran to scrambled eggs. Exceptionally, this was a Saturday evening curry and it was an exceptionally hot dupiaza.

Back at home I spent a most uncomfortable night and at dawn woke Don to ask him to drive us back to the hospital. Because Stephen wanted to be present at the birth of his third child, special provisions had been made to accommodate him in the delivery room. Sue Smith, his physiotherapist, had offered to attend to him in the hospital for as long as necessary, and Joy Cadbury, who presided over the Friends of the Maternity Hospital, had conferred with the matron to make suitable arrangements for the wheelchair. The upshot of all these deliberations was that when we arrived at the hospital at 6 a.m., we were shown directly into the delivery room because that was the only space large enough for Stephen, Sue Smith and the medical team. I was therefore constrained to spend the rest of the day lying on the hard surface of the delivery table waiting for the birth to happen. Don sat out in the corridor, occasionally peering round the door, while Jonathan wisely took himself off to spend that hot, sunny Easter Sunday with his parents at his father's rectory in the country.

In such inclement conditions, the birthing processes slowed down and then stopped altogether. I sent messages to Don that he could safely abandon his post in the corridor to attend morning service in one or other of his ecclesiastical locations since there was nothing to report. While I lay awkwardly trying to ease my bulk into a comfortable position, I regretted the urgency with which we had come to the hospital, especially when I realized that I could have been singing in church. In St Mark's, Bill Loveless had to announce the cancellation of the musical interlude on account of the absence of the singer who was otherwise engaged.

The various attempts made to accelerate the birth had the sole effect of turning me into a human pin-cushion as the morning slid into afternoon and the afternoon into evening. Don returned and went out again – this time to Evensong. While he was away, a crisis developed: the foetal heart, that infant heartbeat that had introduced itself to me many months ago, showed worrying signs of fatigue. The baby had to be brought into the world without delay. While the medical team had their backs turned, preparing their instruments of torture, I hastily summoned all my remaining energies into an almighty push and my Easter child was born.

When they gave him to me to hold, my heart went out to him. Wrapped in an old green blanket, his face was blue from the battering he had received. Although he was much larger than either Robert or Lucy at birth, he did not display the energy with which they had greeted the world but lay limply, whimpering in my arms. For a moment I was oblivious of the commotion of the cleaning-up operations around us, absorbed by the little creature whom I already knew so well. Then Don burst triumphantly into the delivery room. He was pleased to make the acquaintance of his godson and was even more pleased with himself on account of a little ditty that he had thought up on returning from church. To my embarrassment he would repeat it to everyone he met for several weeks after the event. It went like this:

On Easter Day,
the disciples went to the garden
and found the empty tomb
I went to the hospital
and found the empty womb.

CHAPTER THIRTY-SEVEN

Dissonance

Dur ing the week that Timothy, Stephen and I stayed in hospital, Lucy was brought back to Cambridge to meet her younger brother but Robert was stranded in St Albans for reasons which were not fully explained. Apparently the children had been playing barefoot in the stream in Wales and he had caught a cold. He was coughing again so badly that when the children called on my parents for tea in St Albans, my mother put him to bed and there he stayed for the next week until Stephen's sister Mary, the doctor, decided that he was well enough to come back to Cambridge. His return home coincided with our own homecoming. He nursed his little brother tenderly on his knee, sitting in an armchair in the living-room, but looked suspiciously flushed and unwell. The mother of one of Lucy's friends, Valerie Broadbent-Keeble, a respected paediatrician, came on a social call to see Timothy and me. By coincidence, she arrived at the same time as Dr Wilson. my GP. The two doctors glanced only briefly at Timothy who had adjusted to the business of living and glowed with health; Robert, on the other hand, commanded their full attention. Both were visibly alarmed at his state of health and were fairly sure that he was suffering from viral pneumonia. Valerie went away to organize Robert's immediate admission to the children's ward at Addenbrooke's while Dr Wilson wrote out a prescription for penicillin.

It was a blessing that the new baby was still tired from the ordeal of his birth and consequently slept for long periods both by day and, amazingly, at night as well, otherwise the weeks after his birth would have been an even worse nightmare than they actually were. I was needed by everyone all the time. Stephen's needs were obvious, the baby's needs were indisputable, Lucy needed reassurance now that there was a rival usurping her place as the youngest member of the family.

Above all Robert, who was seriously ill in hospital, needed me most. After one night on the children's ward, he awoke covered in weals from head to foot. Either he had contracted an infectious disease or he was allergic to penicillin. As there was no way of telling which of the two was the cause, he was moved to an isolation ward at the top of the hospital for fear of infecting the other critically ill patients on the children's ward. In isolation, his meals were passed to him through a hatch and the medical staff donned gowns, gloves and masks when they entered his room. He was allowed only restricted visiting and the visitors had to dress up in the same protective clothing as the nurses. Bored, lonely and ill, he lay in bed with the tears streaming down his hot cheeks.

My visits to the hospital had to be timed precisely in between the week-old baby's feeds. Once he was fed, changed and settled, I would dash off to spend the next few hours at Robert's bedside, reading books and playing games, and would then dash home again for the next feed. This became my routine until Robert was discharged from hospital. Stephen's mother did her best to keep the home fires burning, shopping and cooking wholesome meals. There was too much for her to do alone. Never was Jonathan's help more urgently required. He looked after Stephen, he did the heavy shopping, he took Lucy to school and he visited Robert, enabling me sometimes to take a break from a rigorously pressurized routine. He had come aboard and was attempting to stop all the holes in our leaking vessel.

It was unfortunate that he had not been properly introduced to Stephen's mother before this crisis occurred. Since her visits to Cambridge had been much rarer than my parents', the opportunity had not arisen. Although later she accepted our relationship, I realized that at that time I could not expect any of the Hawkings, unlike our close and tactful friends, to divine the significance of Jonathan's presence in our household since none of them were gifted with that much psychological insight or sensitivity. I hoped however that I had earned their respect well enough over the many years in which I had cared for their son for them to trust me at least to try to do my best for him and for the children in the present demanding situation. Though I could not hope for the depth of understanding that Miss Gent, my friends and my own family had shown, I trusted that they might muster some sympathy or discreet toleration. Above all I wanted to reassure them that I was not about to abandon Stephen or break up the home, nor was Jonathan encouraging me to do so.

I waited for a suitable opportunity to broach the matter to Isobel. Such opportunities were scarce and when eventually she and I found ourselves alone in the house with the new baby one afternoon, she took the initiative, catching me unawares. She looked me straight in the eye. 'Jane,' she said, adopting a stentorian tone, 'I have a right to know whose child Timothy is. Is he Stephen's or is he Jonathan's?' I met her steely gaze, dismayed that she had so readily jumped to conclusions and the most uncharitable conclusions at that. All the discipline with which Jonathan and I had forced ourselves to try to sublimate our own desires and maintain a discreet relationship was being trampled under the elephantine tread of Hawking insensitivity. Given the nature of several relationships – affairs, divorces and so on – in her own family, I was surprised that her reaction appeared so blinkered and conventional. The simple truth was that there was no way that Timothy could have had any other father than Stephen and this I told her, trusting that the issue would be swiftly dropped. Then I would be able to reassure her that there would be no change in our way of life and that Jonathan was as committed to the well-being of the family as I was. Alas, she was not content to accept this statement of the truth; instead she continued, carried on the crest of a wave. The force of the wave struck me full in the face, silencing me, stunning my senses and stinging my nerves. 'You see,' she went on, 'we have never really liked you, Jane, you do not fit into our family.' Later, Isobel apologized for her outburst but, from my point of view, it was too late.

The following day Frank Hawking responded to his wife's urgent summons and came over to Cambridge in the early morning. I watched from the house as, together, they went out on to the lawn and disappeared into the shrubbery, engaged in conspiratorial conversation. Soon afterwards they left, huffily defiant, scarcely bothering to acknowledge me at all. The combination of so many apparently traumatic events in such a short space of time after the birth had the predictably disheartening effect of diminishing my ability to feed the two-week-old baby who was emerging from his post-natal stupor, exercising his leonine lungs and his vocal chords with hearty enthusiasm. Stephen brooked no opposition in resolving the situation in his own fashion. He dragooned eight-year-old Lucy to accompany him into town and help him shop at Boots where he bought an array of bottles, teats, sterilizing fluid and dried milk powder. Thus ended my pitiful attempts to nurse my third child and thus commenced a new chore for Jonathan. Every evening before leaving West Road for his own home, he would make up the next day's supply of babymilk and store it in the fridge, ready for use on demand.

Some weeks later, as I was making the preparations for Timothy's christening in early June, Stephen received a letter from his father. The letter announced that he had been in touch with an American team of doctors in Texas, who were treating motor neurone disease with a new drug. These doctors were issuing an invitation to Stephen to become one of the first patients to test the drug. It seemed that it was a *fait accompli*: we would all, Stephen, Robert, Lucy, Timothy and me, by the mere waving of a wand, move lock, stock and barrel to Texas where Stephen would undergo an extended course of treatment lasting months if not years. The letter was passed to me without comment, without explanation, the unspoken implication being that the decision rested with me.

My head swam and my heart sank at the complexity of the responsibility that I was being asked to assume. First and foremost, if there was a chance of a cure for Stephen, I could never deny him that chance. Yet I was only too aware that the demands on the family and on me would be monumental, far in excess of anything we had ever experienced before. The children would be summarily removed from the schools, environment and home where they were happy and secure and would be dumped down in a huge, strange American city. This would not be Pasadena. It was not clear where our income would come from, nor was it clear how our housing or transport would be organized. We were being asked to uproot ourselves, or rather I, the mother of a six week-old baby, was being asked to uproot the whole family, the three children and their paraplegic father, transport them a third of the way round the world and set up home for an indefinite time. There was no indication of how I was to achieve that objective, no promise nor likelihood of any assistance, other than young Robert's, in this mammoth task, nor any certainty that the treatment would be successful. Painful memories of Seattle in 1967 came crowding to the fore, multiplied a thousand times by the experiences of the past several years.

I could not help being suspicious of the timing of this development. If it was a ploy to separate me from Jonathan, the Hawkings could not have found a crueller way of doing so. For a day or two I kept their proposal to myself, restlessly churning over all the connotations of the dilemma it posed, bewildered at the injustice of the burden that had been thrust upon me at such a delicate time. Then finally, one fine June evening when the baby was asleep and the rest of the family were parked in front of the television, Jonathan and I went out for a short cycle ride. It was impossible to conceal from him that something was seriously wrong. We had cycled a couple of miles out into the country when he stopped abruptly to ask what it was that had plunged me into such agitation. He too was disturbed when he heard the news. Since our guiding principle was that Stephen's welfare was our top priority, it appeared that we would have to agree to a parting, the mere anticipation of which, while driving us in deep unhappiness to seek that longed-for comfort in each other's arms, would also tear our hearts out.

As the date of the christening approached, I could not keep this most painful of dilemmas from my parents. The christening party divided squarely into two opposing camps. In a situation which required extreme tact on all sides, the Hawkings stood, indignantly hostile and arrogant, in one camp in a corner of the living-room, turning their backs on the rest of the gathering – my parents, Tim's godparents and their families, and a few friends, including Nigel Wickens and his young wife Amy, who was expecting their first baby. The atmosphere was so unbearable that at one stage I left the room and took refuge in the bedroom.

My father followed me, only too conscious of the intolerable pressure I was under. An intellectual match for the Hawkings but devoid of all affectation or snobbery, he pulled a piece of paper from his pocket. 'Jane,' he said, 'just have a look at this, will you? If you approve, I am going to send it to Frank Hawking.' As I read, gratitude for my father's intervention flooded over me: the letter was a masterly resolution of the dilemma without in any way jeopardizing my loyalty to Stephen. Quite simply it stated that we all wanted Stephen's best interests, but that the Hawkings must be aware that the care of two young children and the new baby – their grandchildren – in addition to the burden of Stephen's care, made it impracticable for me to travel to Texas. He suggested that if they were convinced of the efficacy of the treatment, they should consider accompanying Stephen to Texas themselves. Yet again my father, sometimes exacting, always honourable, always unpretentious, had by quiet, intelligent application behind the scenes, come to the rescue. The letter was sent. He did not receive a reply.

That painful episode finally persuaded me that the Hawking family set little value on me as a human being. I felt that in their eyes, I was just a drudge, the vehicle for producing their three grandchildren and the mechanism for looking after their son. I seemed to have no justifiable claim to the normal needs, hopes and fears of a young woman, let alone any intellectual aspirations. After so many years of thinly veiled tolerance, their dislike of me had emerged when I was at my lowest ebb, soon after the birth of my third child while my eldest child was critically ill. I felt I was the victim of unconcealed hostility. It was stupid of me not to have recognized their animosity and resigned myself to it sooner; it was stupid of me to have lived in innocent hope of better things. As they were Stephen's closest relatives, I had been bound to try to get on with them as best I could. In fact for this very reason, I was still obliged to maintain a veneer of civility. Whether I liked it or not, the close blood tie was the one invariable factor in this predicament.

The following winter news came that the Texan team were offering to send their treatment to Cambridge. However, the consultant neurologist at Addenbrooke's stated quite firmly that the treatment was untested, unproven and inappropriate for motor neurone disease. He suspected that Stephen would be used as a guinea pig and that the researchers were looking for the scientific respectability and publicity associated with his name, possibly to attract funding. The treatment would have to be administered in hospital and the time involved would be considerable, with minimal chance of a positive outcome even in the short term. Motor neurone disease had already done its worst to Stephen; there was little more that it could do and it was a well-known fact of medical science that the body was not able to repair damaged nerve tissue. The greatest risk to his survival these days came from pneumonia, not motor neurone disease *per se*. The proposed treatment would be a waste of Stephen's precious time and scarcely more than one of those chimaera against which Frank Hawking had himself warned so decisively in the 1960s.

Later that summer after the trauma of the period surrounding Timothy's birth, while Stephen set off on one of his international trips and Robert, now well again, went off to another camp, I took Lucy and Timothy to stay with Stephen's schoolfriend Bill Cleghorn, his wife Meg and their small daughter Hester, in Brontë country. It was extremely courageous of the Cleghorns to invite us to stay because only a few months previously Zoe, their newborn baby, had died a cot death.

Bravely suppressing her own pain and with eminently practical good sense, kindness and tact, Meg tried to talk me through some of our seemingly intransigent problems as we sat drinking coffee in her kitchen or steered our little band of children, including baby Tim, on outings over the moors, through the streets of Haworth and round the Parsonage. Despite Meg's valiant efforts at encouragement, the wild landscape of the moors, bleak and cold even in summer, and the turbulent passions of their literary heritage only served to exacerbate my state of emotional and moral chaos. I was stranded, not in literature but in life, on the horns of many an irreconcilable dilemma, many a conflicting hope, many a cause of despair, many a disturbing passion, many a demanding responsibility – too many for one novel or even two – and unlike a novel, life did not promise a linear unfolding of the story from beginning to end and certainly not a simple or tidy conclusion at the dictates of the novelist.

CHAPTER THIRTY-EIGHT

Turbulence

Perhaps I might have been less despondent during that week in Yorkshire had I realized how implicitly I could rely on Jonathan's family. With unassuming goodness, they dedicated themselves tirelessly to the needs of other people, whoever they were, whatever their origins. They made no distinction between family, friends, parishioners or strangers. Anyone in trouble, rich or poor, could arrive on their doorstep by day or by night and be assured of help and sympathy and probably a filling meal into the bargain. Nonetheless, I could not imagine that any parents, however well-meaning, would welcome the sort of family with whom their eldest son had become involved. I was wrong. On our first visit to their rectory, they treated Stephen, me and the children as if we were the most welcome visitors, as if they were really pleased to see us, as if, paradoxically, they were grateful to us for monopolizing their adored son. Never did they pass even the slightest hint of judgement on us or our situation.

Like Bill Loveless, John Jones had been a late ordinand. He had come to Cambridge to train for the ministry, leaving a lucrative dental practice in Warwickshire. In this mid-life change of direction, he was encouraged unequivocally by his wife Irene, so like my own mother in her quietly assured faith. Although Cambridge was familiar territory because both their sons, Jonathan and his younger brother Tim, had been choristers at St John's College from an early age, the strength of John's calling was truly tested by the inevitable decline in the family's standard of living when he came to study at Westcott House. They exchanged a fine family home set in rolling country outside Birmingham for a two-bedroomed Victorian terraced house on a busy, fume-laden main road in Cambridge.

It must have been with delight that they eventually moved out to the country parish of Lolworth, only 5 miles from the centre of Cambridge, one of the smallest villages imaginable and, unusually for Cambridgeshire, situated on a hillside. It was in the little church that in 1974 Jonathan married Janet who was already suffering from leukaemia. For the next year until she died, his parents shared in her nursing, giving her and Jonathan all possible comfort and support.

From their hilltop vantage-point, they tended to their flock in the surrounding fenland and worshipped with a practical tenacity which would have been exemplary in a young incumbent, let alone in one of advancing years. Not only did John, with Irene's assistance, cure the souls in his charge in Lolworth and its associated parishes, he also mended the fabric of the medieval building entrusted to him by an impecunious diocese. In the early 1980s the tower of Lolworth church was badly in need of repairs. As there were no funds available, John and Irene donned hard hats and overalls and set about removing several tons of bird droppings from the inside of the tower before relining and strengthening the structure themselves. At the end of a day's work they would descend from the tower doused in white powder from head to foot, as if they had been working in a flour mill.

Cowed and unsure of myself, I found it unbelievable that these people, not related to us in any way, could find any good reason for wanting to welcome me and my family. I could not understand why they should show such genuine interest in us and so much concern for us that they were prepared to offer stalwart support, practical help and sound advice whenever it was needed. They spread the light of kindness, sympathy and selflessness in darkness. They were the living demonstration of love.

It was not only Jonathan's parents who took us to their hearts but, inexplicably, his entire family as well, his aunts, uncles and cousins, his brother Tim and sister Sara. Formerly a physiotherapist, Sara was blessed with the same sort of intuitive good sense as Caroline Chamberlain in her approach to severe disability; she knew the toll that a paralysing disease could exact on the immediate family as well as on the patient. Sara and I quickly became the closest of friends. We were more or less the same age and we were both producing babies at more or less the same time. Sara's first baby, Miriam, was born in February 1979, two months before Timothy.

Sustained by the generous affection of Jonathan's family as well as my own, I no longer looked to the Hawkings for support. Instead, I began to foster the cool detachment that they had shown for years. Surprisingly, other more distant relatives of Stephen's stepped into the vacuum left by their absence. Many years before, when Robert was a new baby, Michael Mair, a young cousin of Stephen's, had come to call at Little St Mary's Lane, bearing a bouquet of pink and blue flowers. Michael was then an undergraduate in his first year studying medicine at Clare College. He explained that his mother had sent him to call but since he could not remember whether the baby was a boy or a girl, he had brought a bouquet of mixed colours. He proudly demonstrated his medical expertise by testing the curling reflexes on the soles of Robert's minute feet. Mike became a frequent visitor to Little St Mary's Lane and a good friend to both Stephen and me. More than ten years had passed and he had recently returned to Cambridge to work in the eye department of Addenbrooke's Hospital. He and his South African fiancée Salome, a radiographer, were enthusiastic cooks. Every so often they would bring a delicious, ready-prepared, calorie-rich meal for all the family. In anticipation of their arrival, Robert and Lucy would stand in the porch, peering through the glass door and salivating long before they drew into the driveway. Never were those meals-on-wheels more welcome than in the months after Timothy's birth as we struggled to get our little boat and its cargo of passsengers back onto an even keel, desperately weary from the gruelling effort of steering it through turbulent seas.

The truth was that one adult minder was required to attend full-time to each one of the less able members of the family. Disabled to the point of not being able to do anything for himself – except handling the simple joystick controls of his wheelchair and the computer which he had bought when Timothy was born – Stephen had to have a well-known person, whether me, Don or Jonathan, in constant attendance. The baby, previously so docile, had begun to assert himself, responding to all the attention lavished on him with huge captivating smiles, so wide that they could have swallowed us up, but he protested loudly when our attention was deflected elsewhere. On these occasions my mother would laughingly point out his resemblance to his father: he had certainly inherited Stephen's cherubic dimples. Also like Stephen and many a cartoon character, his mouth had a comical habit of drooping downwards at the corners to express extreme, affronted indignation, especially when he was hungry. In other respects, though a larger baby, he was the exact image of his older brother. I called them my twins –

twins nearly twelve years apart. Indeed more than once, passing acquaintances would glance at Tim and cheerily call, 'Hello, Robert!' then in some bafflement wonder if they had fallen into a time warp before they realized their mistake.

Fortunately we were now able to afford the luxury of a nanny/housekeeper on a couple of mornings a week so that I could see to all the administration involved in the production of the four bound copies of the thesis demanded by officialdom. My helper, Christine Ikin, later christened Kikki by infant Tim, was also the mother of three children; she came in from the country as regularly as the unpredictable bus service would allow, and cheerfully hoovered and cleaned and looked after the baby while I contacted typists, proof-read the results of their labours, collated hundreds of pages and sought out bookbinders.

My association with medieval Spanish poetry had well and truly run its course and was coming to a grand finale. Since the thesis did not hold out the promise of any very obvious career, I had already reconciled myself to its being an end in itself rather than the means to greater advancement. In any case, a career was completely out of the question since 99 per cent of my attention had to remain focused on the home and the family. Somehow I had to divide that attention fairly between the children and their father while still finding time to keep my brain alive.

Lucy was apparently finding it hard to adjust to her new position in the middle of the family as neither the eldest nor the youngest child. For weeks while she carried on imperturbably with her school routine and her full social calendar, she expressed nothing more than a passing interest in the baby. It was not until Robert went away to another Scout camp later in the summer that her true, abject misery came to the surface. In Robert's absence, she was suddenly called upon to fetch and carry bottles, nappies, pins and powder for Timothy – chores that Robert had eagerly undertaken until then. At first she resisted defiantly and then she burst into tears. At that moment I realized how badly she, too, had been affected by the trauma we had undergone since Timothy's arrival. Certainly she had felt displaced: that was only natural and to be expected, but it was not the whole story. There had been many other disruptive factors, conspiring as much against her as against the rest of us. Because I had been distracted by Robert's illness and weighed down by all the preoccupations so brutally thrust upon me in the ensuing weeks, Lucy had been left to fend for herself when in fact she needed as much reassurance as anyone else.

I hugged her and tried to persuade her that love does not and should never shut anyone out, and that I had not stopped loving her just because there was another person in the family to care for. In our family there was love for everyone, though it might be expressed in different ways, given the vastly different requirements of each individual member. Implicitly trusting by nature, she believed me without a murmur and warmed to her little brother straight away, as if in all those miserable weeks she had been longing to show her true feelings but had not known how. She fetched and carried just as willingly as Robert had done and thereafter no one could have been more devoted to Tim or more susceptible to his winning ways.

Robert, too, had to be handled with sensitivity and patience. He had been very ill and, although he apparently had made a good recovery and was back at school, he often seemed subdued and forgetful. Dyslexia was still a severe handicap in his schooling. Despite his recognized prowess in science, the compulsory range of arts subjects presented him with horrendous obstacles. The school arranged a few sessions with an educational psychologist who tried to instil into him techniques for coping with dyslexia but failed to identify the true extent of the problem. It was not until many, many years later that I discovered that at the root of it lay an overwhelming sense of inadequacy. From a very early age, he had become aware that his father was a scientific genius and that people, in particular his teachers rather than his parents, had expectations of him that he knew he could not fulfil. His belief in himself swamped by self-doubt, his solution was not to bother with his studies at all since he felt himself doomed to failure in the eyes of the world however hard he tried. The saddest part of it was that from as young as seven years old when he first became aware that his father was a genius, he felt himself to be inferior.

It was foolish of me not to have guessed at the psychological connection between Stephen's celebrity and Robert's underperformance. I could at least have taken him aside – as I had done with Lucy – and assured him that his intrinsic worth had nothing to do with school reports or other people's opinions of his intelligence. Believing inherited dyslexia to be the cause of the trouble, I lacked the deeper insight to be able to free him from the tyrannical misconception that he would never live up to expectations. As it was, that misconception, masked by the deceptive symptoms of dyslexia, was becoming progressively more engrained. His untidiness and his indifference to school subjects were the sad manifestations of some of those much publicized difficulties which beset the children of famous fathers.

Whether I could have reassured him or satisfactorily accounted for another possible cause of disturbance is doubtful, given the difficulty I had in explaining our changed circumstances to myself as well as to other people. It is conceivable that although Jonathan had relieved Robert of the intense strain of helping with Stephen's care and, with discreet respect for Stephen's position, had allowed himself to become the participant in games and the target of all sorts of boyish pranks, Robert – and Lucy too – may have experienced some awkwardness in accounting for his presence. Children, particularly young adolescents, are conformist and like their families to be conventional. Perhaps through fear of peer pressure, they are bound to be sensitive to anything unusual, such as a disabled father, however brilliant he might be. In addition an extra, unrelated adult in the family circle, however caring, might well be unsettling to their perceptions of their families, their parents and, indeed, of themselves. I was thankful that the children were never taunted by their peers on account of their family circumstances and I could only trust that with maturity they would in the future gain some understanding which would enable them to interpret the dilemmas of the past.

Robert had the doubtful advantage of a quick, scientific intelligence. Lucy and Tim, on the other hand, were later to suffer for *not* being of a scientific turn of mind. Lucy acutely remembers her humiliation at being told by her teachers of their disappointment that she was not a scientist, while a good friend of mine smartly rebuffed some of Tim's teachers when they complained at his lack of aptitude for science. Arguably, although their teachers' prejudices cast a passing shadow over their education, Lucy and Tim did not suffer as badly as Robert for whom the expectations of society in general cast the long shadow of his father's reputation, which, because he was instinctively a scientist himself, would follow him everywhere. Really all three children were in a no-win situation.

In the autumn of 1979 Stephen's reputation was enhanced very publicly in Cambridge by his appointment to the coveted Lucasian Chair in Mathematics. The Chair, endowed in 1663 with £100 by Henry Lucas, was one of the most prestigious professorships in one of the most prestigious universities: it was Newton's Chair. Mozart's equal, Galileo's spiritual descendant, Einstein's acknowledged successor, Stephen was now unequivocally ranked with Newton. Later in that academic year, he celebrated his elevation to the dizziest of academic heights by availing himself of the opportunity to give an inaugural lecture, a custom which had fallen into disuse, at least among scientists. A student stood beside him on the stage of the Babbage lecture theatre and interpreted his speech, which had become so faint and so indistinct that only a handful of us, students, colleagues and family, could begin to understand it. With acute embarrassment, even we often had to ask him several times to repeat what he was saying. Hypnotized, as though receiving the words of an oracle, the audience of scientists, many of them young hopefuls, strained to catch his utterances. The words were not designed to offer the comfortable prospect of a secure future for, in his lecture, Stephen gleefully predicted that the end of physicists, if not of physics was in sight. The advent of faster and more sophisticated computers meant that by the end of the century, in a mere twenty years' time, all the major problems in physics would have been wound up, including the unified field theory, and there would be nothing left for physicists to do. He himself would be all right, he declared jovially, as he would be retiring in the year 2009. The audience loved the joke, though I could not see that they really had much to laugh about . . .

Nor in fact did Stephen have much to laugh about. In summarily daring to predict the end of physics he was well and truly making himself a hostage to fortune. His own Nemesis, the demon goddess of physics, aware of his intentions, had tried to pre-empt his lecture and wreak vengeance in advance at the prospect of having her name taken in vain and the demise of her empire over men's minds so irreverently predicted. Just a few months after his appointment, while the inaugural lecture was in preparation, the new decade had opened very inauspiciously for us all, especially for Stephen. After Christmas we all, including the baby, went down with bad colds. By the New Year, the cold had taken up residence on Stephen's chest, racking his body relentlessly with harrowing choking fits at every sip of water or every spoonful of finely chopped food, even at every breath. These fits would come on at the end of the day and would last well into the night. Using the techniques I had learnt in yoga, I would try to encourage him to relax his throat muscles by quietly and monotonously repeating calming phrases. Sometimes I would succeed and would register the change from gasping panic to regular breathing as sleep took over his sad, persecuted frame. Sometimes the sheer boredom of repetition would send me off into an interrupted doze while he continued to cough and wheeze beside me into the early hours. We would both be drained by the morning, though he with true courage would never admit as much and would embark on his normal schedule undeterred by the events of the previous night. While we all feared a repetition of the 1976 bout of pneumonia, Stephen predictably would not let me call the doctor, nor would he take any patent medicines since he was still terrified that the sweetener in cough linctus – even sugar-free ones – would irritate the lining of his throat and the cough suppressant ingredients would either befuddle his brain or plummet him into a comatose state. So he coughed and choked, and choked and coughed, day and night, while the baby snuffled and wailed with a blocked nose and I panted for breath since I was feeling none too well myself.

My mother answered my call for help and promptly came over from St Albans to run the household, while Jonathan, Don and I tried against the odds to care for its ailing occupants. My mother insisted on sending me to bed at least in between the various tasks that I had to attend to. Bill Loveless paid me a visit the following Saturday afternoon. I lay on the bed prostrate from tiredness and breathlessness while Stephen, the real patient, sat reading the newspaper in the kitchen, determined to sit out the crisis. I poured out my troubles to Bill. I still passionately wanted to care for Stephen, to give him a happy home life, to make all things possible for him within reason. Sometimes, as at present, his demands were totally in excess of all that was reasonable and the wall of his obduracy was making life unbearable. In consequence I was becoming more and more dependent on Jonathan to preserve my sanity, to share my burdens, to validate my existence, to make me feel loved. That dependency increased my burden of guilt.

Bill took my hand in his. 'Jane,' he said, thoughtfully but firmly, 'there is something I want you to know.' If I was nervously expecting a stern rebuke, I was much mistaken. Gently he went on, 'In the sight of God all souls are equal. You are just as important to God as Stephen is.' So saying, he left me to ponder this astonishing revelation, and went to talk to Stephen. Later that day Dr Swan called and recommended a short spell in the local nursing home for Stephen who, although ferociously indignant at the affront to his pride, reluctantly accepted his advice.

In a sense Stephen was right and, in my heart of hearts, I agreed. In the nursing home he was not known. The nurses there did not understand his speech nor were they versed in the very precise techniques required for looking after him. He was the first to declare, moreover, that there was nothing wrong with him. In that I emphatically did not agree. As soon as word spread that the Lucasian Professor had been removed to the nursing home, there was no shortage of offers of help. Once more loyal students and colleagues, particularly Gary Gibbons, established an attendance rota so that Stephen should never find himself in the frustrating situation of not being able to communicate his needs to the nurses. Robert's headmaster, Antony Melville, remembering similarly tragic circumstances in his own family, spontaneously offered to take Robert into his own home should the need arise. John Casey, a Fellow of Gonville and Caius who concealed genuine sympathy behind a somewhat mannered façade, decided that the College should pay Stephen's nursing-home expenses and undertook to persuade the governing body and the Bursar. Perhaps that task was less insuperable than it sounds since, it should be noted, the then Bursar, a retired Air Vice-Marshal, Reggie Bullen, was the most humane Bursar ever to hold that office in the College.

The following week while Stephen was in the nursing home, I answered an invitation from Martin Rees, the Plumian Professor of Geometry since 1973, to meet him out at the Institute of Astronomy. Endearingly unconvincing in his efforts to appear a hard-nosed scientist, Martin sat me down in his office and emphatically declared, 'Whatever happens, Jane, you must not let the situation get you down.' The unintentional irony of his words perplexed me but as I was too tired and distraught to comment on them to any effect, I said nothing, neither confirming nor denying his opinion, simply waiting for him to continue. Martin earnestly repeated what he had just said and went on to suggest that the time had come for Stephen to have nursing care at home. If I could find the nurses, he volunteered to find the funds, from various philanthropic sources, to pay for them. I was deeply grateful for his concern and his very practical offer, so carefully and considerately proposed. My gratitude was felt as much for the fact that he had noticed that we needed help as for the help itself.

There were three elements involved in bringing nurses into the home and certainly Martin's benevolent offer would take care of one of them, the financial side. I had no idea how to tackle the remaining two.

Where was I to find suitable nurses and, more significantly, how was I to persuade Stephen to accept them? Whenever the baby and I went to visit him, he ground his teeth in anger at his temporary imprisonment, keeping his eyes firmly fixed on the television screen in front of him and refusing to look at us. Those were the moments when the concentration of his tremendous intellectual and mental energies, tragically constricted and frustrated in a nutshell as they inevitably were, exploded against the rock face of his unyielding physical situation. Woe betide anyone standing close to the explosion. There was little fundamental consolation that I could bring him: rather, my presence seemed to madden him, yet if I did not visit him regularly, I would quickly stand accused of neglect. Panting for breath under the weight of the hefty infant, I would struggle down the long corridor twice a day, rehearsing all the gobbets of information and titbits of gossip that I had been collecting for his entertainment. If the reception we received did not shower us in splinters of sad emotional detritus, it would always have a dampening effect that washed the colour and life out of those little yarns, diluting their impact until they were about as interesting as a firework display in a rainstorm. Stephen's parents paid him a visit one day but they did not call on us at West Road.

By the next weekend the weather, previously gloomy and overcast, had become bright, sunny and very cold, making the roads treacherous with icy patches. We were expecting my father to arrive in Cambridge for lunch when there was a ring at the doorbell. My mother and I were disturbed to find an unfamiliar car in the driveway and a middle-aged woman standing outside the door. Her husband was ushering Dad towards the house. This couple had been travelling behind Dad six or seven miles outside Cambridge when they had seen his car slither across the road on a patch of black ice and crash into the opposite bank and had come to his rescue. Although the car was a write-off, Dad, miraculously, seemed to be unhurt, though badly shaken. Nonetheless, we thought it best to call a doctor to check that all was indeed well. John Owens, the doctor who had delivered Robert twelve years before and who, by a strange coincidence, had also attended Jonathan's wife Janet, came promptly and pronounced Dad to be in remarkably good shape considering the life-threatening ordeal he had undergone.

Only a couple of days later we had reason to call the surgery again. Lucy, who had also had a bad cold, gave us and herself a fright when a capillary in her nose popped and started to bleed. No sooner had one copious nose-bleed dried up than another began. This time the duty doctor was new to us. Rather surprisingly since he was middle-aged, he introduced himself as a trainee doctor. Dr Chester White had taken up medicine as a second career – rather as Bill Loveless and Jonathan's father had gone into the Church – in middle age, and he had only recently qualified. He gave Lucy a check-up, assuring us that there was no cause for alarm since nose-bleeds usually look much worse than they are and in some children, often result from a cold.

As he was about to leave, he turned his attention to me. 'What about you? Are you feeling all right?' he asked to my surprise. 'You look pretty exhausted.' He sat down while I told him about Stephen and the crisis we were in. Little explanation was needed as he knew Stephen by repute and had seen him out and about in the street. He did not know, however, that we had battled on for years with minimal help from the Health Service and was appalled to hear that we had the benefit of home nursing only on two mornings a week when the district nurse came in to get Stephen out of bed and give him a bath and an injection of hydroxocobalamin. Stephen had been obliged to let the district nurses bathe him when, in a cumbersome state of pregnancy with a much larger baby than either Robert or Lucy, I found my room for manoeuvre in the bathroom severely restricted.

Chester White frowned as he registered the details of the unusual case that had dropped on to his plate. As I recounted the same old story of our wearisome struggle to keep going and to find a way through the obstacle course that our lives had become, I was under no illusions: he would listen with the utmost sympathy but would be powerless to effect any improvement. Who could, even with the funds that Martin Rees had promised? Unexpectedly Dr White's expression cleared as I reached the end of my sorry tale, though I myself could hardly believe that a newly qualified doctor, however mature, could even begin to discern a path through the maze of our problems. I anticipated that he would say, as so many others had said, 'Well, I'm terribly sorry but I don't know what to suggest.' I was scarcely inclined to take him seriously, therefore, when with unusual perception, he thoughtfully suggested two courses of action. First, he said, he would prescribe some medication for me, and second, he would get in touch with a male nurse on his list who did some private nursing and might be able to arrange a regular roster of care for Stephen.

The hope that these proposals held out was too beguiling not to be considered briefly, even if with a well-worn scepticism. There was just a chance that another hurdle, that of finding suitable nurses, might be overcome as a result of this chance encounter with a doctor who happened to have the right connections and was prepared to lighten the load of a responsibility which had become far too onerous. Moreover, the last hurdle, and undoubtedly the highest – Stephen's resistance – might also yield in the face of this initiative since it was being imposed by an outside authority. The blame for this most detrimental of steps would not fall entirely on my shoulders.

Within days Martin Rees had found a provisional source of funding to finance some nursing care for Stephen on his return home but, as I feared, Chester White had not managed to get in touch with his nursing contact. That prospect, it seemed, was after all no more than another of those deceptive will-o'-the-wisps, a glimmer of hope extinguished before it had even been ignited. Perhaps it was just as well: in my heart, I disliked conspiring against what I knew to be Stephen's wishes, however intolerable the situation might be. When he came back from the nursing home, there was nothing for it but to return to the routine that we knew so well, a grinding tiredness of body and of mind, long days of worry and sleepless nights of despair, as if a raging storm was forever lashing the hard-pressed vessel of our family life. It was hard to believe that the force of the storm would ever blow itself out or that any gleaming ray of benign calm would ever appear on the horizon.

Then, one morning towards the end of January, Dr White's contact, the nurse Nikki Mantunga, materialized out of the blue. A quietly spoken, hard-working Sri Lankan who had settled with his wife and two children in a village outside Cambridge, he showed no disquiet at my account of the difficulties and the requirements. On the contrary, he was confident of being able to put together a team of nurses from among his colleagues at Fulbourn Hospital, the local psychiatric hospital where he worked. A week later, when he came for his first shift, Stephen adamantly refused to acknowledge his presence, to look at him or to comunicate with him in any way, except by running over his toes with the wheelchair. I apologized to Nikki who persevered with a smile, unperturbed. 'It's all right,' he said, 'we're used to dealing with difficult patients.'

The next week he brought Iolanta Kruschevska, a highly entertaining girl of Polish origins, and introduced her to the system. Then she brought quiet, efficient Sally, followed by Judy, and then Nikki brought his own cousin, Tony. An established nurse came with each new recruit and passed on the details of the routine so that there was always a smooth changeover with minimal intervention demanded of us, the resident carers. Slowly Stephen's irritation subsided as he grew to accept the presence of these dedicated, patient people. Some, like Nikki himself, were unobtrusive and deferential; others, like Iolanta, were an endless source of amusement. Her exuberant personality was such that she could quite unashamedly tell Stephen to his face that only a psychiatric nurse could cope with him – and still evince a broad smile in reply. Sometimes the nurses could be a bit scatty and forget their schedule but that was more or less forgivable because their effect on our lives was generally so beneficial.

Soon Stephen realized that he could allow himself to trust them and regard them as friends. He also realized that he could call upon them for help outside the strict hours of their terms of employment. He could take the nurses with him on trips abroad and be independent of his students and colleagues, even of his family, on whom he would no longer have to rely for help with his personal needs. Through a glass darkly, a different pattern was becoming discernible; it was as if our boat was being steered on to a new course by an invisible hand. There the concatenation of disasters would eventually resolve itself and the force of the storm would die away. A new era was dawning for the master of the universe and, by extension, for the rest of us.

CHAPTER THIRTY-NINE

Rescue

A ROSEATE DAWN SEEMED to shine upon the turning tide of our lives, promising calmer waters ahead. No longer were we in danger of being driven on to the black rocks of despair, or of being torn apart by exhaustion and anxiety. We could contemplate the smoother waters ahead with a glimmer of optimism now that Nikki's team had begun to lift the weight of Stephen's nursing care from our shoulders. In releasing us from the endless toils, he and his colleagues allowed us to start living life rather than just struggling through it. They lifted Stephen out of bed and dressed him in the morning, they administered his medicines and got him ready for bed at night, as well as spending hours attending to his more intimate functions.

Caring for him physically at other times of day was relatively easy by comparison with the previous routine, especially since Jonathan was usually with us most evenings and all day at weekends, helping to feed Stephen, take him to the bathroom and lift him in and out of the car. He too was a helpless witness of the terrifying choking fits which at every meal seemed to be squeezing the last lungfuls of breath out of their victim. We would wait for the fit to pass in a heightened state of nervous anxiety, ready to call the emergency services, knowing that at these critical times the thread by which Stephen clung to life was at its most tenuous. The fit would pass eventually and after a few sips of warm water, Stephen would resume his meal, discarding whatever item he suspected of irritating his throat. Then, just as we were all beginning to relax, he would fall prey to another attack.

Jonathan was by nature susceptible to hardship and struggle, as if those elements attracted his sympathy and attention more than any others. He sensed where and how he was needed and acted correspond-ingly, always with patient good humour, helping with all those necessary domestic chores which formerly I had always done unaided: he brought in sacks of potatoes, emptied rubbish bins, changed light bulbs, checked air pressures in tyres and filled the car with petrol. Now there was someone to help me drag home the mountains of weekly shopping from the market and from Sainsbury's. For years I had struggled across the Backs either pulling the heavy bags in a trolley behind me or carrying them on the pram, slung from the handle and squeezed into the tray underneath. My bike was another useful means of transport, though when laden with bags, compressed in the basket on the back and hanging from the handlebars, it became perilously unbalanced. Jonathan even helped me to redecorate the rented house between tenancies since nobody else was prepared to do so.

Together we looked after the three children but it was usually Jonathan who provided the taxi service to ferry Robert and Lucy to and from their various engagements and it was Jonathan who indulged the baby's favourite activity: Timmie liked nothing so much as being thrown high in the air up to the ceiling, abandoning himself, open-mouthed and wide-eyed, to that split second of suspense before coming back to earth and falling into the safety of Jonathan's arms. Those arms embraced us all with a love and constancy which strengthened our family life and gave me the will to carry on. We could, with even more hands on deck – those of Nikki and his team – confidently resume the all-important façade of functioning as a normal family, each pursuing our own interests to a heightened degree. The fact that our definition of a normal family was widely extended beyond the usual concept of mother, father and children was dictated by circumstances and was quietly accepted as the best possible solution to our problems by those people who knew us well.

Throughout the early 1980s, despite the pall of death which seemed to cling more and more tenaciously to Stephen's enfeebled frame, his ambitions and successes continued to know no bounds. The catalogue of institutions, universities and various scientific bodies vying with each other to shower sonorously named medals – the Einstein Medal, the Franklin Medal, the James Clerk Maxwell medal – and other honours, notably honorary degrees, upon him, read like Leporello's list of Don Giovanni's female conquests in Mozart's opera. There was no shortage of award-giving ceremonies in Britain and when they were near to home, I took Stephen to them myself. On one memorable occasion we drove over to Leicester, only an hour-and-a-half away, for a degree ceremony at the University where the Chancellor was Sir Alan Hodgkin, the Master of Trinity College, Cambridge, and formerly the President of the Royal Society. He had presided when Stephen was made a Fellow in 1974. Genial and unassuming, with a beaming smile even when standing on the platform attired in full black and gold regalia, he warmly welcomed Stephen into the ranks of the honorary doctors of Leicester University by firmly pressing his hand. Unwittingly, he pressed the hand which Stephen was using to control the wheelchair and that unwonted pressure sent Stephen, the wheelchair and Sir Alan, who was still, so to speak, attached to the apparatus, off into an unstoppable *pas de deux*, bringing the whirling ensemble of ceremonial robes, mortar boards, bodies and wheelchair perilously close to the edge of the stage. I leaped to my feet and switched off the joystick control just in time to avert a horrible catastrophe.

Unlike Don Giovanni, however, Stephen's conquests were not all restricted to Europe. Most of the ceremonies were in the United States, and it was fortunate that Nikki and his team were willing travelling companions. In 1982 alone, Stephen crossed the Atlantic five times. Thanks to Nikki's team, he was able to take advantage of every award-giving ceremony on the other side of the Atlantic, for which his fare and theirs would be paid. Then he would go on to the serious purpose of his trip – scientific discussions with his colleagues in other more interesting venues elsewhere. At this time, often as joint editor with Werner Israel, he was particularly involved in the production of several tomes of essays and conference proceedings concerning relativity and attempts to reconcile it with quantum physics.

The conferences – or rather 'workshops', to use their popularizing misnomer – recorded in these tomes were Stephen's new passion. He was delighted to find that his international renown and his distinguished position as Lucasian Professor afforded him an enhanced advantage in attracting funding to the Department, although one of his pet themes for complaint was the lack of money for science. We had been used to receiving and entertaining regular seminar and conference delegates for years on a modest scale. These days Stephen could invite his colleagues – even his adversaries – to Cambridge on a grander scale and preside over all their deliberations as the ultimate authority. The workshops grew into much larger and much more prestigious affairs with money not only to invite the most eminent speakers and delegates, but also to provide dinners and entertainments. Consequently my role as conference hostess was mercifully diminished. The days were over when I found myself putting on buffet dinners for forty or more people; under the new system, the workshop dinners were usually held in the college where the delegates were staying. My involvement was generally limited to hosting receptions and the tea-parties on the lawn for which plates of cucumber sandwiches were ordered from Caius' kitchens. There they had perfected the art – or the machine – for cutting the thinnest cucumber sandwiches ever served in an English garden in summer. Otherwise, dinner-parties at home were more intimate affairs for the intimate band of our closest friends from abroad – the Carters, the Israels, the Hartles, Kip Thorne or Jim Bardeen.

The lion's share of the complex administrative arrangements for these conferences – the delegates' travel, the accommodation, the venues, the methods of payment and all the printed material associated with the conference – as well as typing up the proceedings after the event, fell to Stephen's hard-working secretary Judy Fella, although she was in theory only employed part-time. This was all in addition to her regular workload as the secretary to the Relativity Group. Her children were only about the same age as Robert and Lucy but she often worked long into the night, sometimes having to resort to the more advanced experimental technology which had been installed by the fluid dynamic-ists down in the basement of the Department, to produce camera-ready copy of the hieroglyphic signs and diagrams of the conference proceedings. Although Stephen appreciated her dedication, many of her secretarial colleagues failed to understand the pressures under which she laboured. Since Stephen seldom arrived in the Department before 11 a.m. or even midday, Judy adjusted her work routine accordingly. She would arrive at the same time as him and stay at least until he was ready to leave at seven or eight in the evening. This sensible but unorthodox schedule brought her into conflict with her colleagues who insisted that she should work the same hours as everyone else, arriving at 9 a.m. and leaving at 4.30 p.m. The injustice and stupidity of this petty-minded attitude sometimes brought Judy to tears. She would come across to West Road and collapse on the sofa, overwhelmed by the strain of so much work and oppressed by so much uncomprehending hostility. I would administer the remedy that Thelma Thatcher used to prepare for me long ago – a small glass of brandy diluted with sugar and warm water; it had lost none of its efficacy.

It was in the Department rather than at home that a new wave of pressures, in the shape of the world's media, first made its appearance. For some time Stephen's discoveries had been well documented in the British and the American scientific press: the attitude was always one of deference in the strictly scientific context, with little or no reference to his physical condition. In the early 1980s the popular press began to take a more active interest in the phenomenon of the man himself. The contrast between the restrictions placed on him by his shrunken frame and his croaking speech on the one hand, and the power of his mind which allowed him to roam the outer reaches of the universe on the other, provided a fertile source for many imaginative flights of fanciful prose. Moreover, the subject himself was far from averse to publicity and was a willing interviewee, despite the incursions that interviews made into his already overloaded timetable. Judy took the extra demands imposed on her schedule by the influx of journalists and television crews, not just from national networks but from all over the world, in her stride, although quite a few academics in the Department understandably objected to finding that their tea-room had been turned into a television studio yet again.

In the days before the popular press developed its hysterically prurient obsession with the private lives of the famous, Judy and Stephen conspired mischievously to bewilder the visiting journalists. Blonde and extrovert, Judy would ask Stephen as the *paparazzi* arrived, 'Which bit of thigh shall I reveal today, Stephen?' The visitors' shocked expressions would delight Stephen. Then he, for his part, would exercise his own wicked sense of humour on them. He would apologize for not being able to bring a four-dimensional model of the universe into his office to demonstrate his theories, or, when asked about infinity, would reply that it was rather difficult to talk about it as it was such a long way off. Quite openly he would admit to dismay that black holes had so far evaded detection since proof of the existence of black holes would assure him of a Nobel prize. The journalists made what they could of these witty, often cryptic responses to their questions and then went away to compile reverential articles from their bewildering assortment of notes. Very few of them managed to achieve a balance in their reporting. Often their attempts to describe Stephen's physical presence lacked sensitivity, while their accounts of the science, perhaps understandably, relied on the interpretations of his students and colleagues.

In my opinion the most insensitive journalist of all was a television producer from the BBC's *Horizon* team. When the idea of a programme about Stephen's achievements was broached in 1982, we looked forward with pleasure to another visit from the BBC; an entire programme devoted to Stephen's triumphs was indeed an accolade. The earlier snatch of film made some six years previously by my college friend, Vivienne King, had been a resounding success. With the images that she had produced still clear in my mind, I trusted that the film, to be made in March 1983, would refer back to those earlier images and would follow a similar formula. Vivienne had achieved a balance; she had shown Stephen in context and had avoided the pitfall – or the temptation – of depicting him as the Sellers/Kubrick Dr Strangelove.

It was still one of my worst fears that, in the hands of the wrong producer, Stephen might be portrayed as some sort of grotesque, wheelchair-bound boffin, twisted both in body and mind, destructively intent on the pursuit of science at all costs. In response to my suggestions that some of the filming should take place at home and that Stephen should be set, if only in passing, in the context of the family, the producer observed that the children and I were nothing more than wallpaper in Stephen's life and he was not going to drape his film with such material, because it had far more important matters to digest. Appeals to the BBC had no effect but Stephen exacted from him the grudging promise that Tim, aged three, and I might join the Relativity Group during filming over lunch in the cafeteria of the University Centre.

When the film appeared six months later, the lunch scene was dubbed with a voice-over spoken by one of Stephen's students. He said, 'Neither Mrs Hawking nor their son Timmie is particularly interested in mathematics so when they come to lunch, we try not to talk about work.' Afterwards, I learned that, to his great embarrassment, the student in question had been told to read this, and he apologized to me for it. It was broadcast to the whole nation. My former supervisor, Alan Deyermond, gallantly wrote to the BBC in protest at the injustice and ungraciousness of it. The film, which centred entirely, apart from the lunch sequence, on seminars and discussions in the Department, was saved from the Dr Strangelove fate only by Stephen's sense of humour and his appealing way of guffawing at his own jokes, not by the merits of the production. Irony of ironies, *Professor Hawking's Universe* opened with a shot of one of our wedding photos. The sole people to derive any tongue-in-cheek amusement from it were my parents who featured in the wedding photo: overnight they became television celebrities in St Albans.

The following day, 18 October 1983, the *Times* critic Dennis Hackett paid tribute to Stephen's achievements, although he doubted that the title of the programme was accurate since, he said, 'The universe is ours.' He also complained of the producer's 'mandarin' approach: ' . . .it seemed to be *Horizon*'s presumption that a BBC2 audience contains an extraordinary number of advanced degrees or that it really did not matter as they were giving us a privileged glimpse of something that was above our station.' He also observed that the film might have been more interesting to the general public if some explanation had been given of the CND badge prominently displayed on Stephen's lapel.

Even before the *Horizon* programme, the name of Stephen Hawking had become a household word throughout the nation and indeed the world, penetrating to the most illustrious establishments, including the Royal Household. In 1980 we had been invited to a large gathering at the University Press in celebration of that institution's quincentenary. Although Stephen was not presented to the Queen, she was heard to remark as she walked past, 'Oh, isn't that the black hole man?' The following summer, when Prince Philip, the Chancellor of the University of Cambridge, expressed his wish to meet Stephen in the course of his rounds of the University departments, it seemed most appropriate for him to come for a private visit to the house where he would be able to talk to Stephen without background disturbance. Robert, definitely a budding scientist at the age of fourteen, interpreted his father's replies to the Chancellor's questions about the age of the universe and the nature of black holes and such matters. As the visit on 10 June coincided with our guest's sixtieth birthday, I made and iced a fruit cake, decorating it with half a dozen candles which Timmie and Prince Philip blew out together before the royal visitor was precipitately whisked away to his next appointment, taking the as yet uncut cake with him. Although this domestic informality may not have been quite what the Chancellor of the University was expecting, I received a very appreciative letter afterwards from his Private Secretary, Lord Rupert Nevill, complimenting me on the delicious cake which had been greatly enjoyed in their office. In retrospect it appeared that we had been unnecessarily cautious in our anxiety to keep the visit as secret as possible because when it came to the photo opportunity, we had no photographer present other than Robert. As he had to take the photos he did not appear in them, but a few months later a happy opportunity arose to compensate him for that omission.

When Stephen's name appeared, as a Commander of the British Empire, in the New Year's Honours List of 1982, we decided that, given the potential for calamity involved in controlling the wheelchair, Stephen should not go forward to meet the Queen alone, but that Robert should accompany him at the investiture at Buckingham Palace arranged for 23 February. The occasion demanded new clothes for all of us, except for Timmie who was too young to qualify for an invitation and had to stay with my parents. Robert was kitted out with his first suit, which he never wore again since by the time another formal occasion arose he had outgrown it. Lucy, who was going through a tomboy phase, made it quite plain that she would only allow herself to be forced into a dress and a coat as a never to be repeated exception to her usual mode of dress which consisted of jeans and tee-shirt.

As Robert and I were managing the exercise alone without any extra help from the nurses or Jonathan, we knew that we would be hard pressed to arrive at the Palace from Cambridge at 10 a.m., so we drove down to London the evening before. There we stayed in the flat reserved for the use of Fellows on the top floor of the Royal Society, overlooking the tree-tops of the Mall and the turrets and crenellations around Horse-guards Parade. It was not until I was busily stowing all the new garments and their accessories away in the wardrobes late that night that I realized that Lucy's new patent leather shoes were missing. She was innocently lounging in her scuffed old school clodhoppers and seemed quite content to go to the Palace looking as if she had just come in from climbing trees in the garden. The caretaker's wife thought there might be a shoe shop at the end of Regent Street but doubted whether they sold children's shoes. We resigned ourselves to starting even earlier than planned the next morning.

Leaving Robert to feed Stephen his breakfast, Lucy and I dashed up to Regent Street just as the shops were opening – to buy the only pair of shoes available in Lucy's size. Sensible and unremarkable in brown leather, they were suitably smart but not as pretty as the shiny buckled pair that had been left at home. Ironically, they were to see plenty of wear, whereas the patent leather shoes lay untouched at the bottom of the wardrobe and were eventually given away.

Despite the last-minute crisis, we were still just on schedule when we set out for the Palace. We had not reckoned, though, on joining the mother of all traffic jams in the Mall: the whole population appeared to be converging on Buckingham Palace, giving the Mall the same air of

Above: Conference croquet party on the lawn at 5 West Road, Summer 1980 – with Alan Lapedes and girlfriend (end 2nd row left); next to him Gary Gibbons. Front row: Don Page on Robert's right, Nick Warner on his left and next to him, Bernard Carr; Bernard Whiting behind Lucy and Mary Whiting seated on the grass in front of me.

Right: Visit of the Duke of Edinburgh, June 10th 1981.

Above: Ph.D,
Albert Hall,
March 1981.

Left: Stephen,
Tim and me in
audience with
the Pope,
Rome 1986.
(Fotografia Felici)

Family party 1986 with Jonathan – bottle in hand – and my Uncle Jack
sitting between my parents and Don Page.

Madrid, October 1987. From left to right (seated around the table): Pam
Benson (nurse), Stephen, Pedro Gonzalez Diaz, Elaine Mason (nurse),
Raymond LaFlamme (student), Tim, me, Carmen Sigüenza González.

The Moulin at first sight.

Companion of Honour, Buckingham Palace, July 1989.

In the new house with the children and my parents, November 1994.

At Wimpole Hall, 4th July 1997.

Robert, Lucy, Tim and me, 4th July 1997.

With Jonathan and Bill Loveless, 4th July 1997.

Clockwise:

Lucy and Robert at Lucy's christening.

Tim, aged 2½.

My brother Chris and his wife Penelope with their children, Calendula, Celeste, Peter and William.

A few of my special friends . . .

Rows down from top left:
1. Arthur Bullard, Hanna Scolnicov, Inge & Werner Israel, Nancy Bardeen,
Brandon Carter, Iolanta Kruszewska.
2. Margaret Smithson, Nigel Wickens & Laura, Lucette Carter, Jim Bardeen.
3. Sue & George Ellis & Maggie, Mary Whiting, Don Page, Hiroko Naka,
Bernard Carr, Jim Hartle.
4. Caroline & Peter Chamberlain, Joy Cadbury & Lucy Grace,
Marion Donovan & Jane (my god-daughter).
5. Caroline & George Hill, Tobias & Amelia, Gill & Geoffrey Pinfold,
Mary & John Taylor.

frenzied urgency as the roads leading to Heathrow airport. Just as at the airport, most of the arrivals were being dropped at the gate but it was our privilege to drive through those ornate, oft-televised portals into a world apart, a world which seemed to operate on a different time-scale from our own, a world where everything ran with a clockwork precision yet where no one showed the least signs of fluster or impatience, a bland courtesy and an easy charm being the hallmarks of all encounters.

Leaving the car, which suddenly looked embarrassingly old, battered and dirty, in the middle of the courtyard, we were shown to a different entrance from the other arrivals and were taken up several floors in an ancient lift. Lackeys ushered us with a genteel rapidity through a maze of corridors where we were able to pause only momentarily to glance at the furniture, the paintings, the Chinese vases and the exquisite, glass-cased ivories which lined the walls. When we came out into the main gallery, we were separated: Robert and Stephen were led away to join the waiting queues of national heroes and heroines while Lucy and I were shown to our plush pink seats at the side of the magnificent ballroom.

There was plenty to absorb our attention while we waited for the proceedings to begin. Huge crystal chandeliers sparkled against the white and gold decorations. One end of the immense room consisted of a sort of red velvet temple, bathed in a soft gilded light, where elderly Beefeaters from the Tower mounted guard over the dais where the Queen was to stand. On a balcony at the other end, a military band played a festive repertoire before launching into the National Anthem on the Queen's arrival. The morning's business was briskly introduced and the investiture assumed a remarkably familiar format, combining the time-honoured British traditions of school prizegivings and degree ceremonies with the national penchant for pageantry on a grand scale, as each candidate stepped forward from a seemingly endless line for his or her moment of glory face to face with Her Majesty The Queen. Lucy nudged me in alarm when she saw an elderly Beefeater who was standing behind the Queen keel over, a victim of the heat, the weight of his costume and the hours spent on his feet. He was discreetly removed from the scene, feet first, without any disruption of the cere-monial.

When Robert and Stephen appeared at the side entrance awaiting their turn, about half-way through the proceedings, a tingle of love and pride ran the full length of my spine, making my eyes water. As they crossed the floor to the centre of the room and turned towards the Queen, they made a dramatically impressive pair – the indomitable but frail scientist slouched in his chair grinning broadly, accompanied by our tall, shy, fair-haired son. Stephen had every right to grin in pleasure at his own achievements. Perhaps he was also grinning at the irony. The formerly iconoclastic, angry young Socialist had been nominated by a Tory government to receive one of the highest honours from the Sovereign and was being taken into the bosom of the Establishment which he used to despise so vehemently.

Afterwards, over lunch in a posh hotel in central London, we inspected the insignia, a cross finely worked in red and blue enamel suspended from a red ribbon edged with a grey stripe. The inscription, *'For God and Empire'*, like the Palace itself, belonged to the mysteries and the mythology of another age. When we studied the booklet of information that came with the 'badge', as it was officially called, the only privilege we could discover that might be remotely relevant to us was that, as the daughter of a CBE, Lucy could be married in the Order's chapel in the crypt of St Paul's Cathedral. 'Let's hope she remembers her shoes,' Robert observed drily.

It was not only the British Establishment that was keen to number Stephen among its scions. He had already received the Papal Medal in 1975 and in the autumn of 1981 was invited to attend a conference organized by the Jesuits at the Pontifical Academy in the Vatican. The Pontifical Academy is the close-knit group of eminent scientists of unimpeachable character who advise the Pope on scientific matters. This conference was called by way of a papal updating on the state of the universe. As at that early stage Stephen's nurses had not yet begun to accompany him on trips abroad, Bernard Whiting, the Australian post-doctoral researcher who had been working with Stephen, agreed to accompany him to the conference, interpret his lecture to the audience and help me with his general care.

Since Timothy's birth, all my anxieties about leaving the children had returned and I could only reconcile myself to going to Rome by taking one or at least two of them with me – if not Robert, for whom school was now serious business, at any rate Lucy and Timmie. Happily, Mary Whiting, who knew Rome well as she had studied there, came too. Without the Whitings, the trip would have been an unmitigated disaster. The Hotel Michelangelo, supposedly the closest hotel to the

Vatican though by our standards a good twenty minutes away from the conference venue, served no meals, not even breakfast. It had a lift but to get to the lift on the ground floor, one had first to surmount a flight of steps.

As if that were not enough, Rome was in the throes of cataclysmic rains. The mornings would dawn bright and sunny and we would happily accompany Stephen into the Vatican, bowling along past the Swiss Guards at the gate, through the grounds to the Residence of Pius IV, a beautiful, rustic Renaissance building, constructed for the Pope in the sixteenth century. Later it accommodated female visitors to the Vatican and, since 1936, had housed the headquarters of the Pontifical Academy. There we would leave Stephen gleefully preparing to fight the Galilean corner and instruct the papal cosmologists in his revised view of the universe which had neither beginning nor end, nor any role for a Creator-God.

Until lunch-time at the Academy, the one reliably good meal of the day, I would stroll through the groves of bay trees and the children would play in the ornamental streams which trickled down the hillside. But the fine mornings would deteriorate into sultry, overcast afternoons when majestic clouds, worthy of Michelangelo, would billow over the dome of St Peter's. They would burst spectacularly amidst dazzling lightning and crashing thunder and would go on rending the heavens apart well into the night.

Mary took us on guided tours to the places she loved and knew so well – to the Coliseum, the Forum, the Baths of Caracalla and out to the Catacombs of Callixto – but our excursions were always tempered by the knowledge that we would be drenched to the skin if we were not back in the hotel by four o'clock in the afternoon. Thereafter we would have to hope for a break in the clouds around dinner-time to allow us to dash out, wheelchair and pushchair in tow, for supper.

Needless to say, the permanently gridlocked state of Roman traffic made it impossible to get anywhere near the hotel before the rains descended. Usually four o'clock and the first flash of lightning and roll of thunder found us in the vicinity of the railway station, searching for a bus to take us back across the Tiber. Timmie proved to be the unexpected hero of the hour: he loved the buses, grindingly slow, packed with bodies and suffocatingly steamed up though they were, and the Italian passengers adored him. 'Ché bello bambino!' they would exclaim, making space for me to sit down with him on my knee. 'Carissimo,

carissimo!' they would smile, stroking his fair hair and tickling his chin. He had just begun to discover the art of stringing sentences together in precise, grammatical English and was delighted to have a captive audience on whom to practise his newfound talent. 'Do you have a house?' he would searchingly ask the adoring though uncomprehending secretaries, students, businessmen and corpulent grandmothers. 'Do you have a car?' He would continue with his own answers. 'We have a house. We have a car. We have a garage. We have a garden.' They would laugh, nodding sentimentally, while the rain streamed down the windows and the Roman traffic honked and hooted at a standstill in the darkening evening outside.

Mary took her role as guide so conscientiously that she would not rest until Lucy, Timmie and I had seen every church of note in Rome, including her favourite, San Clemente. The medieval church is noted for its radiantly colourful eleventh-century mosaic of the Triumph of the Cross in the apse. Below ground lies the ancient church, with its early frescoes dating from the sixth century, beside the remains of a Roman house. Having admired the brilliance of the mosaics, we followed Mary warily down into the dimly lit, red-brick lower church which, unaccountably, echoed with the sound of running water. 'Oh,' said Mary blithely, 'that's the Cloaca Maxima, the main drain built by the Romans. It comes through here.' The main drain sounded to me more like a rushing mighty river but I supposed that Mary knew what she was talking about.

The bus ride back to the hotel in the pouring rain took even longer than usual that evening. The whole city had ground to a halt. From the conversation of the other passengers with the driver, Mary found out that the delay was caused by flooding – the Cloaca Maxima had burst the bounds of its Roman conduit and was pouring out into the streets of the city . . . In idle amusement to pass the time, we discussed whether this was a portent, a sign, an indication of divine wrath at Stephen's temerity in professing his heretical theories within the sanctified walls of the Vatican itself.

The Vatican, one of the most powerful, dogmatic and wealthy city states ever known and a massive shrine to art and culture, was presided over by a man whose personal attributes of holiness and courage were not in doubt, yet he sought to impose limitations on freedom of thought – just as rigidly as those atheistic scientists who would dispute our right to ask the question 'why' the universe exists. The very man who should have been addressing that question was busy telling the scientists that they had no right to ask the question 'how' about certain aspects of Creation. At the end of the conference, the Pope told the assembly in his address that although scientists could study the evolution of the universe, they should not ask what happened at the moment of Creation at the Big Bang and certainly not before it because that was God's preserve. Neither Stephen nor I was impressed by such injunctions; they were all too reminiscent of the attitudes behind Galileo's arrest and confinement 300 years earlier.

Prodded by Stephen's campaigning since 1975, the Church was only now beginning to catch up with the history of Galileo's discoveries. There was detectable embarrassment that his theories had lain proscribed for so long. Though they were kept under lock and key, the papers relating to his fate were readily, almost apologetically, produced for Stephen's scrutiny, the implication being that it was simply an oversight that no one had thought of reinstating Galileo sooner. Nevertheless, the papal pronouncement indicated that the Church was still seeking to restrict thought, giving the unmistakable impression that not much had been learnt from the lessons of those 300 years. Instead of embracing the modern scientific quest for truth to its ultimate objective and glorying in the even deeper layers of mystery thus revealed, the Vatican still viewed cosmological science as a contentious issue, a threat to religious stability, which had to be contained.

Furthermore, it seemed to me that the Pope's prohibition was misdirected in that the scientific quest in itself is not reprehensible. The fact that there are exceptional human beings, Stephen among them, who are gifted enough to be able to undertake that quest should be considered as another of the wonders of Creation. What is dangerous is the interpretation and the use to which discoveries are subjected if their exponents have a particular, preconceived axe to grind or if they fall into the wrong hands. Science is wholly amoral. It is we human beings who have been given souls and consciences to invest scientific research with a moral sense so that it can be used for the betterment, not the detriment, of the planet we inhabit and of all living things on our planet. Certainly scientists should be made aware that they have a responsibility to think through the consequences of their research, to point out the potential of their finds and to furnish the public domain with all the available information, since every scientific advance brings its own set of risks and advantages. Even so, there can be no valid argument for imposing religious censorship on research.

For myself, I could not accept a Christianity which was based on dogma or on exclusiveness. Why would a loving God who has given His Creation complete freedom of will seek to restrict that freedom by placing boundaries on the human intellect or by obstructing the quest for knowledge? I could no more sympathize with the Pope's decree that scientists should refrain from asking certain questions about the origins of the universe than I could, as an undergraduate many years before, agree with the Westfield chaplain's insistence that salvation was only for the fully converted, genuflecting, church-going righteous. If the essence of Christianity was couched in the terms of such pronouncements, I could not call myself a Christian since for me, God had to be more broad-minded, more imaginative, more willing to admit the challenge of the human intellect and much more open to the diversity and the limitations of human experience. He also had to be accessible in many more ways than those conceived by religious orthodoxy – through art, through science, through music or through simple faith in the power of goodness. An omniscient God must have anticipated that human beings would discover their own spirituality through a wide range of endeavours in society at large without necessarily subscribing to the preachings of a particular church. Why otherwise would He have created such multiformity? God had demonstrated clearly enough through the life, teachings, death and resurrection of Jesus that the only demand He made of us was that the course of our lives should be dictated by the selfless love of others. I believed that for the fulfilment of that dictum, 'Love thy neighbour as thyself' was the golden rule. Its obverse, selfishness in its many manifestations, had been at the basis of every conflict the planet had ever witnessed.

CHAPTER FORTY

Harmony Restored

MUSIC, THROUGH WHICH I had come back into the Church of England, had become the gateway to my spiritual rebirth and growth. It was thanks to Mary Whiting's insistence that I was able to take up my singing lessons again soon after Timothy's birth. She positively begged to be allowed to take him out for a walk once a week because her doctors had recommended that association with small children and babies might help her conceive a baby of her own. On Wednesday afternoons, therefore, though often tired, I resumed my lessons with Nigel Wickens. Since he too was no stranger to the demands of parenthood after the birth of his daughter Laura, he was sympathetically tolerant of my lapses and my incompetence. Under his guidance and to Jonathan's sensitive accompaniment – as and when his teaching commitments allowed him to play for me – I returned to the rapturous embraces of Schubert, Schumann, Brahms and Mozart. Variously they intensified then assuaged, sharpened then exorcized those competing emotions which jockeyed for space in my deepest self. Meanwhile Mary and Tim went to feed the ducks, walk in the park, sit on the swings and bury their faces in ice-cream.

There were many opportunities to perform the solo repertoire in fund-raising concerts for the causes which Stephen and I had espoused. Sometimes I was brought in to fill the gaps in other programmes; this was how my singing career reached its apogee in the summer of 1982 with a short burst of song in King's College Chapel. Jonathan was giving an organ recital for a medical conference and had arranged for a well-known local singer to perform a vocal interlude between the organ works. At the last minute the singer was detained elsewhere and I was invited to step into the breach. It was an extraordinary experience, as though the sound of my voice was being carried away on angels' wings

to the vaulting where the resonance of the Chapel invested it with
effortless lightness and clarity. Conscious of the inspiration of hundreds
of years of musical tradition, I was much more overwhelmed by the
building than by the audience of 250.

My confidence in both my voice and my ability to learn music
quickly – though not in my sight-reading – had grown sufficiently for
me to feel that it was time to branch out by joining a choral society.
It was just possible to contemplate such a step since I now enjoyed
an unprecedented degree of freedom. While Stephen basked in the
deserved glory of international acclaim, those early years of the 1980s
witnessed my own tranformation. On the one hand, the team of nurses
brought that desperately needed relief from the unrelenting physical
demands which had consumed all my available energy. On the other,
through Jonathan's unwavering support, his spirituality and his devotion
to the family as a whole, aspects of myself which had long been suppressed, lying dormant in a dark corner in the daily struggle, emerged
into the light.

Against all expectation, the knowledge that there really was someone
for whom I mattered, someone who cherished me as a valued human
being, illuminated my outlook. Jonathan appreciated that I had more to
offer than mere drudgery year in, year out, and insisted that partially
living was not enough. With his help and without reneging on my
commitments, I should begin to experience the fullness of life. For the
first time in more than ten years, I grew in the awareness that, after all,
deep within myself, not just on the surface, I was capable of more than
a robotic existence, that the sands which had run through my fingers
on the beach in Santa Barbara years before had not, with the passing of
time, spelt the end of my personal fulfilment.

I did not resent that long period of time: it had been spent supporting Stephen through all the onslaughts of illness and the fluctuations
of success. With the beginning of another decade, the dice seemed to
be falling in a different configuration, one which allowed me a modicum
of individuality. I was entering Karl Marx's kingdom of freedom 'that
begins where drudgery ends'. The white light of that emancipation from
the role of a drudge flooded the vulnerable shell where I had floundered
dumbly. My numbed personality unfolded, expanded, grew stronger,
brighter, more resilient, as though recovering from a long period of
incarceration.

At a concert in the University Church of Great St Mary, I encountered the sort of choir I was looking for – a mixed bunch of people of all ages and all walks of life – performing a wide range of repertoire and aspiring to a high standard. The dynamic young conductor Stephen Armstrong, a recent graduate of the University, took me on and suddenly I found myself thrown in at the deep end. Those early rehearsals revealed that I had the training but not the practice. The voice and the high notes were there but, in the event, not much else, so I had to condition myself to concentrate hard and learn a huge quantity of music at great speed. It was quite as challenging as solo singing and in the once weekly rehearsals demanded intense application for two solid hours at the end of a long day.

The day of the performance, usually a Saturday, was hectic. Concert or no, the family had to be fed and cared for, and the final rehearsal was always gruelling. Then the concert itself would be over in a flash with no opportunity to go back over those missed entries or mislaid notes, no chance of a second take. Eight weeks' work would vanish in a single evening, sometimes creating a wild sense of euphoria at phrases that had gone exceptionally well, sometimes leaving tinges of frustration that others had not come up to expectation. Concert succeeded concert, with quick changes of idiom and musical personality from baroque to modern via the classical and Romantic periods. The first in which I sang – Bach's *Christmas Oratorio* – was followed the next term by the Mozart *Requiem*; this in turn was followed by *Elijah*. Benjamin Britten made frequent appearances, whether in the *Ceremony of Carols*, *St Cecilia* or any other of his choral compositions whose starkly resonant clarity seemed to have been blown, crying in the wind, off the North Sea onto the Aldeburgh coast. *Messiah*, with which I already had a passing acquaintance, recurred quite regularly. I was told it was the best box-office draw for any choir of amateurs struggling to make ends meet, provided that no one else was performing it at the same time in the same area. I did not mind what we sang; each successive work, each successive composer became my passionate favourite for the duration of the rehearsals and the concert. Each oratorio brought about a timeless distillation of the fragile pathos of our lives, transforming painful intensity into consoling spirituality. For days, even weeks afterwards, the music would revolve with manic persistence in my brain until finally it died away with the advent of a new series of rehearsals, another composer and another oratorio.

The most satisfying part of the choral experience lay in the rehearsing and the acquisition of a wide repertoire of glorious and uplifting music. Less enjoyable was the stress which accompanied every concert, an inevitable consequence of the sad fact that choral singing is most definitely the poor relation of the arts in Britain. The onus is on the singers in the choir to bludgeon their families and friends into buying tickets for the concert or to buy the tickets themselves and invite their near and dear to turn out on a dark winter's night and sit on a hard pew in a cold church for the duration of the performance. A full house will send a surge of adrenalin through the choral ranks before the performance even begins: not only does such an occasion create a charged atmosphere of expectation, it also gladdens the choral hearts in the knowledge that the costs will be covered and the society will live to see another season. The reverse is of course also true.

Thanks to Jonathan, I could count on a ready-made audience. He would marshall the family – Stephen, my parents and the children – and lead them in procession to whichever church, college chapel or concert hall happened to be the appointed venue. In Cambridge, where most concerts took place within walking distance of home, this was fairly straightforward, so long as the entrance to the hall was on the level and not up a flight of steps. In the depths of the country it was more difficult. Then Jonathan would willingly drive miles along pitch-black winding lanes to bring Stephen, if not the rest of the family, to every concert. More than once Stephen Armstrong, our conductor, would already have raised his baton, poised to bring it down for the opening chord, when the church doors would be flung wide, letting in a blast of icy air, and the whine of the wheelchair, announcing the arrival of the king of the universe, would usurp the first bar of music. With remarkable composure, for which I am eternally grateful, Stephen Armstrong would relax his hand, lower his arm and smile benignly at the choir, me included, as though such interruptions were of no consequence.

Apart from those occasions in the depths of Cambridgeshire and Suffolk, my parents scarcely missed a concert. Indeed, if Jonathan happened to be playing harpsichord or organ continuo in a baroque oratorio, they would bring Stephen and possibly the children to the concert. Dad even went to the lengths of becoming a 'friend' of the choir. In fact, he was its only 'friend' for many a year.

Although many events stand out in the memory because of their association with the ages of the children at a particular time, certain others stand out because of their association with a particular concert. It was when I was singing in Dvorak's *Mass in D* at a concert in St Ives in February 1982 that it struck me, from my vantage-point in the front row of the sopranos on the platform, that my mother, sitting down in the audience, looked ill. She did not reveal the extent of the illness until the spring when we were already rehearsing for the *Dream of Gerontius* in Ely Cathedral. She and Dad were absent from that concert because she was in hospital recovering from major surgery before embarking on the long haul of weeks of radiotherapy.

Recently she and her only surviving cousin, Jack, had been overburdened with worry on Great-aunt Effie's account. We had celebrated my great-aunt's ninetieth birthday in 1980 with a family party in Cambridge. She had been the life and soul of that party, reciting her favourite snatches of Hilaire Belloc at every opportunity, but her jollity could not mask the fact that she was too old and too physically incapable to continue living alone in her large north London house. She refused even to discuss the possibility of moving to sheltered accommodation, so when my mother or her cousin were not actually visiting her, they were always worrying about her. It was a very unkind twist of fate that decreed that Auntie should miss her way and fall down the stairs in the middle of the night when she was staying with my parents in St Albans. Her fall was not fatal but the shock both to her and to my parents was devastating.

It did not take a genius to identify that particular area of acute stress in my mother's life. Nor, I knew, did one need to look further than my own household to find one very obvious cause of chronic anxiety which could have exacerbated her illness. At least the profound change in our own circumstances, occasioned by the advent of Nikki's nursing team, allowed me to give my parents some moral support at that most critical time and try to repay some of the care that they had shown us for so long.

The revised regime meant that, less harassed and less haggard, I could also give the children more attention. The baby had grown into the most irresistibly funny little child, aware, observant, endlessly enquiring, dancing with an impish vitality. At about eighteen months, long before his encounter with the doting Italian bus passengers, he had started to develop a precocious fascination for astronomy. In the early evening he would watch the moon from his high chair and follow its course as it appeared at the kitchen window distracting him from the important business of his supper. As it moved across the sky – and across the window – he would grow impatient with his food and clamour to be released from his harness. When the moon rounded the corner of the house and disappeared from view, Timmie would dash excitedly into the living-room to await the reappearance of its white shafts through the bay windows. Each evening was for him a triumph of expectation until the moon waned, abandoning him in the darkness of mystified disappointment. Then, at twenty-two months, he demonstrated a poetic though unscientific awareness of other celestial bodies. One cold afternoon in February 1981, when huge snowflakes came drifting down in a leisurely fashion, white and delicately geometrical against a leaden sky, he raced to the living-room window, shouting, 'I see (s)tars! I see (s)tars!' He danced round the room, excitedly chanting his little refrain to the silent music of those softly falling, starry constellations.

Timmie's exuberance was enchanting: it could also be worrying because it could lead him to attempt potentially dangerous feats of independence in imitation of his brother and sister if he was left unguarded for the merest second. A couple of weeks before his second birthday, I was preparing the supper in the kitchen when suddenly I realized that the house was unnaturally quiet. There were no sounds of childish play, of toy cars being pushed across the floor or of the tin drum being thumped, no chattering voices or laughter. The blood froze to icicles in my veins at the terrible silence. I rushed to the front door, only to find it wide open. Timmie had run away.

Robert, charging at full pelt ahead of Stephen and me, had frequently run away as a small boy, but always to some purpose, and he had always put himself in the position of being easily found. Lucy had disappeared only once – on a fine day in the middle of summer when we were still living in Little St Mary's Lane. Thelma Thatcher and I had been anxiously searching the Lane and the churchyard for her without success when some passing Americans told us that there was a tiny girl standing with a doll's pram on the mill bridge. There she was, in her bermuda shorts, one hand resting on the handle of the pram and the other holding up her transparent green umbrella. She was surrounded by an admiring band of undergraduates who were clearly wondering what to do with this very self-possessed infant phenomenon.

Some ten years later in the isolation of number 5 West Road, where there were no friendly adoptive grandparents to call upon for help and where the grounds ran for acres with neither a fence nor a gate, I stood at the open door in a frenzy of blank indecision, not knowing which way to turn. Had Timmie run out on to the road and down to the river, or round the house into the garden? The College staff, who were closing up their workshops for the day, heard me frantically calling his name and came to help. Eventually Pat Parkes, one of the maintenance staff, soberly advised me to call the police. He stood by while, with my heart-beat resounding in my ears and my hands shaking, I dialled the police station. I was upset that the officer who took the call did not react more dramatically. He did not seem to register the urgency of the situation. 'Hold on a minute, ma'am,' he said jovially. He returned to the phone a moment later. 'Can you describe your little boy and tell me what he is wearing?' he asked, still in the same irritatingly cheerful tone of voice. 'Fair hair, blue eyes, blue top and green trousers,' I replied, distraught with worry. 'That's all right then,' the policeman said, 'we've got a little boy in one of our police cars but as he couldn't tell us where he lived, the officer is driving round in the hope of finding his mother.' Timmie was brought home in a police car by a policewoman and the kind person who had picked him up just as he was about to set foot in the road – on his way, apparently, to visit his godmother, Joy Cadbury. That same kind person had held him on her knee until the rather damp, blue and green bundle was delivered back into my trembling arms.

Although they were less dependent on my physical presence, the two older children needed a great deal of understanding. Robert seemed destined to be a lonely child with few companions, while the transfer to secondary school parted Lucy from her band of cherished local friends whom she had known from birth, as she was the sole entrant to the girls' Perse School from the primary school where she had been so happy and secure. Suddenly she found herself thrust into an environment of strangers. Because Robert had received a private education, thanks to his inheritance, we felt that we could do no less for her. I had often urged Stephen to write a popular book to explain his research in cosmology, reasoning that I in particular would benefit from reading it and so would the taxpayers in general, who were financing that research through government funding. In the hope that it might help pay Lucy's school fees, Stephen decided that the time had come to face up to the challenge of describing his science – the study of the origins of the universe – to the public in accessible language, avoiding the barriers of jargon and equations.

Lucy, the smallest girl in a school of 500, meanwhile pined for her friends, struggled with unfamiliar subjects and homework, and resented the draconian discipline imposed on the girls by some of the less sympathetic members of staff. Nearly twenty years after I had left St Albans High School, I was dismayed to find that some of the archaic and negative aspects of girls' schools still existed at the girls' Perse, although such failings had long been discarded by St Albans. Even the smell of the place, a combination of sweaty games boots and disinfectant, was distastefully reminiscent of my own schooldays. We gave Lucy a kitten to comfort and distract her.

Both Robert and Lucy sometimes came with me to St Mark's where, ever inventive, Bill Loveless continued to cater for all ages and tastes. Not only did he keep the congregation of Newnham morally and intellectually awake with his monthly reviews of the state of the nation, he also put a prodigious effort into attracting families to the church by means of the family service at 10 a.m. on Sunday mornings. This service, always entertaining, sometimes unpredictable in the responses it could provoke, influenced a whole generation of children – probably hundreds of them – in an increasingly secular age. It was a favourite with Lucy, who always had a part to play, whether lighting the altar candles or snuffing them out, reading the lesson, participating in the quizzes or performing in various dramatizations.

One Sunday when I had left the children lazily dozing at home, Bill announced the inaugural session of a new youth club to be led by ordinands from the local theological college. It was to consist of a combination of games, fun and serious discussion. Robert showed little interest when I told him about it later that morning, but when I pleaded with him to give it a try – just to please me – he reluctantly agreed to go that evening. At seven o'clock I drove him to the vicarage, promising to wait outside for ten minutes in case the youth club did not appeal to him. He liked it so well, however, that I went home alone after the ten-minute wait and thereafter he never missed a session. He met old acquaintances from primary school and made new friends, both girls and boys. They formed a cohesive and loyal group from that day onwards, encouraging Robert to develop the self-assurance and sociability which previously he had found so difficult. Only two weeks later he met Bill Loveless as he was cycling home from school, and told him that he wanted to be confirmed. Bill became a trusted friend and mentor to both Robert and Lucy. He it was who often reassured them and gently explained the complexities of adult life to them when the anomalies of their background, whether the scourge of Stephen's illness or the unconventional nature of Jonathan's presence in the family, disturbed their preconceived idealized notions of how family life and parents should be.

It was all too obvious that with the best will in the world, our household could not live up to such expectations and needed a sympathetic but neutral apologist to explain its shortcomings to impressionable minds. Inevitably there were those regrettable occasions when Jonathan and I did not quite manage to meet the standards of discretion we had set ourselves and then our relationship became a guilty burden. Sometimes in my more despondent moments, I felt that my life had become one monstrous pretence: I was constrained to keep up a normal façade in totally abnormal circumstances and to keep up that façade, I depended on a relationship which society condemned. It had to be covered with a veneer of respectability to be acceptable: if for a second that veneer fell away, even if for instance Jonathan and I were surprised simply giving each other a much needed hug, our morally divided souls would flinch under the strain.

However, the atmosphere of those years was generally so much more relaxed that I was able to take up with old friends again, particularly my schoolfriends Gillian Pinfold and Caroline Hill, née Berman. They would come with their husbands and families for a Sunday visit once or twice a year. The children, David and Ellie, Tobias and Amelia, were of comparable ages with Robert and Lucy, and their respective fathers, Geoffrey and George, knew us well enough not to be fazed by Stephen's reputation. They, after all, had their own highly successful careers – Geoffrey as a widely travelled engineer and George whose knowledgeable and stimulating leaders in *The Times* won him deserved acclaim. After a leisurely lunch during which many a topic – political, environmental, scientific, literary or musical – would be intensively examined and discussed, the adults would amble round the garden and join the children for the statutory game of hide-and-seek in among the glades and bushes of Harvey Court (the property also belonging to Gonville and Caius next door). This game became a tradition. With Stephen acting as look-out, the rest of us shed our adult reserve and recaptured for just an hour the intense excitement of childhood.

In the comparative harmony of that period, my relationship with Stephen entered a new phase where the tendency for us to slip into the roles of master and slave was arrested. We were companions and equals again, as we had been in our campaigning in the 1960s and early 1970s. The CND badge, which the *Times* critic of the *Horizon* programme had noticed on Stephen's lapel, was but one indication of the several causes which we championed jointly. The inexorable increase in nuclear weapons, of which Rob Donovan had chillingly warned us in the early 1970s, had developed into a fully fledged arms race, a mad, uncontrolled competition between East and West to reach Armageddon as soon as possible and annihilate all living creatures on the planet. The Campaign for Nuclear Disarmament once again became a national force and local groups sprouted all over the country.

Our group, Newnham Against the Bomb, met once a month in the house of Alice Roughton, a retired doctor, a figure of immense and generous energies, trenchant convictions and fabled eccentricity. Over the years she had welcomed foreign students so warmly to her home in Adams Road that in the days when Stephen used to visit her house in the early 1960s, her husband would take refuge in the garden shed. Alice always wore a boiler suit and was reputed to serve her guests roast squirrel with nettles, all culled from her wilderness of a garden.

The dozen or so members of Newnham Against the Bomb would sit round her smoking fire warming our hands on a glass of mulled wine, while we listened to presentations by knowledgeable but despairing speakers. Then we would plan strategies and discuss what we could do to stop the arms race. The prospects were not encouraging. We were after all pitting ourselves against the military industrial complexes of the two Superpowers. There was some slight consolation to be derived from the fact that we were at least making an effort and in any case, Stephen and I were used to playing David against many a monolithic Goliath.

Together he and I composed a letter which I typed and copied and sent off to all our friends around the world, particularly to those in the United States and the Soviet Union. We urged them to protest at the escalation in nuclear weapons which threatened to destroy the population of the northern hemisphere and produce so much radiation that the prospects for remaining life elsewhere would be negligible. We pointed out that there existed four tons of high explosive for every man, woman and child on the planet and that the risk of a nuclear exchange being set off by miscalculation or computer failure was unacceptably high.

Stephen used the same theme in his address to the Franklin Institute in Philadelphia when he was awarded the Franklin Medal in 1981. He remarked that it had taken about four billion years for mammals to evolve, about four million years for man to evolve and about 400 years to develop our scientific and technological civilization. In the previous forty years, progress in understanding the four interactions of physics had advanced to the state where there was a very real chance of discovering a complete unified field theory which would describe everything in the universe. Yet all that could be wiped out in less than forty minutes in the event of a nuclear catastrophe and the probability of such a catastrophe occurring, either by accident or design, was frighteningly high. He concluded that this was the fundamental problem facing our society and was much more important than any political issues of ideology or territory.

We made roughly the same points when we met General Bernard Rogers, the Supreme Commander of Allied Forces in Europe, at a feast in University College, Oxford. General Rogers, a former Rhodes scholar, was the guest at High Table of Lord Goodman, the benevolently rotund Master of the College. On seeing the General's name on the guest list, we felt duty bound to accost him with our concerns on behalf of Newnham Against the Bomb. After the meal, Stephen barred General Rogers' way with the wheelchair as he was about to leave the dinner table. The General listened considerately while in some embarrassment I recited my speech, then he politely acknowledged that he himself was very concerned about the situation and had in fact been engaged in discussions with his Soviet opposite number.

Within a few years, the rapidly changing economic and political situation behind the Iron Curtain overtook our local efforts. We shall never know whether our modest individual and group protests had even the slightest impact on the course of history, whether any of our letters ever reached their targets or whether our messages ever struck home to the heart of the political establishments of the East or the West. In such cirumstances one can only abide by Edmund Burke's famous dictum that 'Evil flourishes when good men do nothing' and hope that by doing something, however insignificant, one can inhibit the spread of evil.

Closer to home, our campaigns concerned less apocalyptic matters though they were equally impassioned, especially when they related to the rights of the disabled. The Cambridge colleges were so remarkably dilatory in implementing the Disabled Persons Act – which in its initial form had first reached the statute book in 1970 – that in the 1980s, new buildings which made no provision for disabled access were still being commissioned. One of them, Clare College, not 100 yards from our house, was sending out an appeal to attract funds for a library and a recital room. According to the advertising material, the recital room was to be a public place, but in direct contravention of the Disabled Persons' Act, the plans made no provision for disabled access. We campaigned vigorously against this attitude and our protests were met with disparaging comments.

We had much greater clout in our campaigning in the 1980s than in the 1970s since we could appeal to various contacts we had made as a result of Stephen's fame. One of those was Lord Snowdon, who had come to photograph Stephen for a glossy magazine. He willingly took up our cause and was heard to berate Clare College for its indifference to the needs of the disabled on a BBC radio programme. He also referred to the situation when he addressed the Further Award Scheme for Disabled Students. 'Not only does the disabled student find it impossible to acquire a wheelchair for outdoor use ... but having reached the stage of further education, he may come up against obstacles like the new library of Clare College, Cambridge, commissioned by the Master and Fellows who adamantly refuse to include a lift to the recital room on the first floor.' By all accounts the governing body of the College was thrown into disarray as a result of this intervention, a vote was called and a decision made to install a disabled lift.

Stephen – and Jonathan – and I had supported the fund-raising activities of the Motor Neurone Disease Association since its inception in 1979. For some time Stephen, as the patients' patron, and I had attended meetings and conferences. In the early 1980s, he was asked to become a Vice-President of the Cheshire Home Foundation as well, and in October 1982, I was invited to join the Appeal Committee to raise funds for converting a Victorian house at Brampton near Huntingdon into a Cheshire Home for the disabled. The target was £600,000. I drove over to Huntingdon for the monthly meetings of the committee and soon discovered that my catchment area for fund-raising was none other than the University of Cambridge – each college within the University and each individual Fellow within each college. Armed with a copy of the University register, my task was to sift through all the hundreds of names of likely donors and personally address pleading, xeroxed letters to each one in preparation for the public launching of the appeal in the summer of 1984. The launch in Hinchingbrooke

House, attended by dignitaries from all walks of life, including the MP for Huntingdon, augured well for the future of the appeal. Stephen and I were not especially keen to meet the Tory MP since we detested the destructive policies of the Thatcher government which were already biting into the life of the nation, encouraging a selfish materialism and an indifference to suffering and poverty. The Tory MP, John Major, and his wife Norma were disarmingly pleasant, however, so it would have been ungracious to blame them for the moral blindness of the then Prime Minister. We could only assume that through some unfortunate oversight, Mr Major had allied himself to the wrong side of the House.

It was unlucky for the Cheshire Home that the launch of the appeal coincided with a six-week postal strike and that the national consciousness was distracted from giving to local charities by the horrendous pictures of starvation in Africa being broadcast daily on television. Not surprisingly, the appeal yielded far less than expected and it took years of fund-raising, bazaars, concerts and coffee mornings before the original target was reached. By that time costs had escalated and £600,000 was only a fraction of what was required. The work for both these charities and our various other campaigns demanded time, conviction and energy. Nevertheless this was a wholly positive activity which gave Stephen and me a united role to play – outside physics.

CHAPTER FORTY-ONE

Unfinished Business

IN THE EARLY 1980s, there were two areas of unfinished business which had to be settled before I could throw myself wholeheartedly into any new activities. First and foremost there was the thesis which was finally completed: I was summoned to Westfield for my oral examination on 17 June 1980 in the presence of Stephen Reckert, the Professor of Portuguese at King's College, London and of my supervisor, Alan Deyermond.

The previous evening in Cambridge, Stephen and I had attended a performance of a Handel opera, *Rinaldo*, as part of the end-of-year celebrations in Caius. Much lauded though the performance was, it failed to make any impression on me because for once music, even the famous aria 'Lascia ch' io pianga' (Let me weep), had temporarily lost its appeal. Like Stephen in those occasions when he had unwillingly found himself at the ballet, I squirmed in my seat in impatience, resenting the misuse of valuable time, despite the commendable performance of the young mezzo-soprano hero. I was fraught with worry that I would never be able to remember every point, every date, every reference in the 336 pages of the thesis the following day at 2 p.m.

My nerves were not eased by losing one of my contact lenses on the way to London the next morning. Tense and partially sighted, I groped my way through the exam until, with a smile, Stephen Reckert asked if I had read a book by David Lodge. Then I was really perplexed. I searched his face for clues to his meaning. Was he teasing me? Could he really be referring to *Changing Places*, the hilariously authentic account by David Lodge of an academic exchange between Philip Swallow of Rummidge University (alias Birmingham) and Maurice Zapp of Euphoric State University (alias Berkeley)? I could not remotely discern any connection between *Changing Places* and medieval Spanish poetry; nonetheless I plucked up courage and tentatively enquired whether Professor Reckert was referring to any of David Lodge's novels, *Changing Places* for instance. He smiled slyly. 'No, no, I mean *Modes of Modern Writing*.' Abashed, I had to admit that I had not yet enjoyed the acquaintance of that work. After that, the exam proceeded in a more relaxed atmosphere. Later Alan Deyermond confessed that he had not read *Changing Places*.

The following spring Jonathan and Stephen, who bought me the flowing red robes of a doctor of philosophy, accompanied me to the Albert Hall and patiently sat through the mammoth degree ceremony. It was the end of a long and arduous journey. The fact that it ended in a blind alley was not significant. I had certainly not entertained any great hopes of a teaching post or even of hourly paid supervisions in the University of Cambridge since my associations with the Spanish Department were slight at best. My tentative enquiries as to whether there might be some teaching were politely ignored and, as my self-confidence was still at an abysmally low ebb, I reconciled myself to more modest ambitions – or to none at all.

The chance to begin an occupation, if not a career, came unexpectedly and centred upon my other language, French, not Spanish, and France, the country whose language I had first encountered with some puzzlement on the side of HP Sauce bottles at the age of four or five. Fortunately the fascination of French engendered by the HP Sauce together with sympathetic teaching in childhood was strong enough to outweigh the powerful disincentive for liking French, imparted by certain features of my secondary school education.

In the upper school of St Albans High School, French was the medium of punishment, meted out with terrifying authority by Miss Leather, the tall, gaunt, imposing figure of the senior French mistress. Wrapped in dark brown furs at all times of the year, she would stalk the corridors of the school with feline resolve, searching out offenders hiding in the cloakroom on wet days or surreptitiously snatching a bite out of a chocolate bar in the classroom. Having upbraided them with biting sarcasm, her green eyes narrowing to slits, she would reduce her stentorian tones to a menacing purr for the dreaded moment of judgement: 'Take fifty French verbs!'

Taking fifty French verbs meant conjugating in all persons, singular and plural, in whatever tenses she chose, practically every verb in the French language, 'in neat' in a special exercise book. Of this petrifying apparition, it was said in her obituary that she was the only known teacher who could maintain absolute silence in a classroom, even in her absence. In fairness, I can truthfully say that she was an inspiring and imaginative sixth-form teacher and also that, thereafter, French verbs never really gave me any serious trouble.

Further down the school, from the age of seven, French had been fun, a living language taught by a young Parisian, never addressed by her name, known just as 'Mamsel'. Occasionally when there were staff absences, we first-formers had to join classes with the top year of the junior department. We of course had to sit on the floor while they lolled at their desks. One particular boy with a mop of unruly brown hair had a desk by the wall and was always leaning against it in an absent-minded attitude of mildly disdainful boredom at the antics of us lesser mortals; I think his name was Stephen. Much of the credit for his understanding of French should go to Mamsel, because I know that thereafter he never devoted himself to the study of the language with overwhelming enthusiasm, despite the 'O'-level pass of which he was moderately proud.

No amount of instruction in the classroom could begin to convey the reality of France herself. In the course of my childhood, my parents began to explore the continent of Europe, twice fought over in their lifetime, still threatened, but always irresistibly attractive. As my father spoke excellent French, rarely a year went by when those glorious summer holidays did not take us to France, either as our destination or later, *en passant*, to Italy or Spain.

It was my first trip abroad, to France at the age of ten, that imprinted the most profound and lasting impressions on my memory, including the consternation my brother Chris and I experienced when we pulled what we thought was the light cord in our bedroom and it summoned the chambermaid. Unquestioningly we accepted our mother's explanation that the *bidet* was for washing our feet. I poignantly remember my childish wonder at the beauty of Brittany, its forests, coastline, beaches and heathlands, vowing secretly that I would return and live there for ever and ever, a resolution soon eclipsed by the intoxicating excitement of an overnight stop in Paris on the way home. Equally vivid is the memory of the sullen frustration into which we children were plunged one swelteringly hot day at Versailles when we were forbidden to have ice-creams. The reason given was that ice-cream in France in those days was made from unpasteurized, untested milk, and Dad, being a senior civil servant in the Ministry of Agriculture, was in full possession of the facts: his reasoning was quite lost on us. During the course of these holidays in Brittany and later in Burgundy, Provence or the Pyrenees, France began to sow the seeds of the spell it was to cast over me.

In the early 1980s, just as I had finished the thesis and Lucy and her contemporaries were looking forward to learning French in primary school, language teaching was summarily removed from the curriculum, a victim of the Tory government's economy measures. One of my much-valued friends from the school gate, Christine Putnis, the endlessly patient Australian mother of a large family of clever children, prevailed upon Rosalind Mays, another of the mothers, and myself to teach French to a group of children after school hours. With some trepidation, we began a project which was to last for ten years. Every Monday afternoon we would greet our pupils with drinks and biscuits, then subject them to an hour's worth of intensive learning, artfully concealed in puzzles, games, songs, drawings and stories. Our aim was to introduce the children to the concept of a foreign language and to French as a natural means of communication before the onset of adolescent inhibitions. They appeared to enjoy it at the time and afterwards many of them went on to study French at higher levels. My own re-emerging fluency and confidence in the language was reinforced by sporadic attendance at the monthly gatherings of the local French Circle, an informal group of Francophiles and native speakers – mostly women, housewives rather than academics. The atmosphere here, at these reunions, was infectiously Gallic, as if for an evening one had stepped across the Channel and left Cambridge inhibitions far behind.

A year or two later I found myself obliged to revise French for GCE O-level with a couple of teenagers, one of whom was Robert. It was his school report immediately before the O-level term that spurred me into action. 'He is unlikely to pass the exam,' it said of his French. The thought of a child of mine failing French was so humiliating that drastic measures were called for. Robert's friend Thomas Cadbury was brought in to provide some competition and to ensure seriousness of purpose, and a minimum of fifty verbs were conjugated in all persons in all tenses. This linguistic onslaught struck its target so successfully that it was actually suggested that the chip off the old scientific block might consider French for A-level, a suggestion given only frivolous consideration as he had been earmarked from birth for physics, chemistry, maths, more maths and, of course, computing.

The move into teaching, initially French at primary level, was intimidating but highly stimulating. Memories of early pictorial attempts at French, inspired by Mamsel's lessons, came flooding back indiscriminately, as if there had been no time lag. The challenge aroused old half-fulfilled interests with increased fervour, and revived that long-dormant love of Europe and fascination with the structure of the Romance languages, now surfacing again with a deeper maturity.

Just as I was beginning to feel confident enough to take on more teaching, either French or Spanish, in a more formal educational situation, another meeting at the school gate provided a golden opportunity. Fleur Houston, one of the cluster of mothers, told me that she worked for a recently established private sixth-form college which was looking for part-time teachers. The advantages were that she could choose her hours and, as the organization had only limited premises, she could teach at home. The arrangement sounded ideal for me too, so Fleur arranged for me to talk to the Principal, Dr Alan Dawson. The interview was extraordinarily informal. We walked round the garden while Alan Dawson told me about the school, the Cambridge Centre for Sixth Form Studies, known more succinctly as CCSS, which he had founded with two colleagues: He suggested that I might like to begin by teaching candidates for Oxbridge entrance. I reeled at this suggestion but Alan Dawson was so persuasive, arguing that university entrance was actually easier to teach than O-level, that he gave me no choice. I supposed that this was some sort of initiation challenge. If I could get his students into Oxbridge, then I myself would probably be given a job.

I spent hours looking up old entrance papers in the University Library, devising teaching programmes for grammar and translations, and ruminating on the moral and philosophical questions set in the general paper. Many of the questions revolved in some way or other around those philosophical and linguistic brain-teasers so beloved of Bertrand Russell such as 'There is a barber in Athens who shaves everyone who does not shave himself. Who shaves the barber?' or 'Generalizations are false.' Epigrammatic quotations were also a favourite of the examiners, who found an ample supply in the works of Oscar Wilde: 'The truth is rarely pure and never simple' rubbed shoulders with essay titles inviting discussion about the ethics of nuclear deterrence or the positive and negative values of science, as for instance, 'The genius of Einstein leads to Hiroshima.' All these topics and many others like them were food to my starving brain.

My appetite whetted by university entrance papers, I next devoured the stuff of the A-level syllabus with voracity. Grammar, translations, reading comprehensions, literary texts – all required hours of thought, preparation and revision but provided a sumptuous feast on which to feed my hungry intellect. Moreover, I actually found that I liked teaching and the age group of sixteen- to eighteen-year-olds who were put into my charge.

As my pupils were always about the same age as one or other of my own children at some stage of their education, I felt a natural affinity with that adolescent group and quickly found that even the most difficult pupils would respond to a friendly, caring approach, whereas they had in all probability rebelled against the repressive authority of their previous schools. More than a few of our pupils had been placed in boarding school at the age of six. By the age of sixteen, they had demonstrated their frustration in some dramatic way or other and had accordingly been expelled. CCSS gave them the independence for which they longed, yet it demanded of them a sense of responsibility which some, in the first term of the sixth form at the age of sixteen, unsurprisingly found rather too challenging.

There was also a clutch of overseas pupils, often multilingual, whose parents wanted their offspring to benefit from an English education within the security of supervised accommodation. These pupils were usually the most highly motivated and the most stimulating, though often, because of their multinational backgrounds, they were uncertain of their true national identity. One might ask what was the point of teaching students who were already bi- or trilingual. In fact, although they might have a fluent command of any number of spoken languages, their written work was seldom as fluent. For them, like all the other pupils, the strength of the A-level course lay in the fact that it encouraged young people to begin to think for themselves, to analyse and to criticize without accepting at face value the import of the texts and articles set before them. It encouraged them, too, to review their own use of language, whether in Spanish, French or English, to expand it and to treat language with care and respect. Above all, the course introduced literature to people who might never have read a book in their lives. It was particular gratifying when, after two years of study, a pupil would come and thank me for opening his or her eyes to the delights of reading.

The pleasure was the more intense when one of those appreciative pupils was dyslexic. Through my own family I had such wide-ranging experience of the multitude of problems associated with the condition that I felt that I could offer special insights and encouragement. Typically in an uncomprehending educational system, whether state or private, the dyslexics in a class, like my own sons, would be told that they were either slow, stupid or lazy, and would be sent to sit at the back of the class. Dyslexics are not stupid. Generally their intelligence quotient is higher than the rest of the population but their overdeveloped brain has squeezed out some other facility, usually associated with language or short-term memory. An intelligent child whose powers of communication are limited and who is sent to sit at the back of the class becomes a frustrated child and may develop behavioural problems. These may eventually lead him into trouble and result in expulsion from the school which has failed to understand him in the first place.

Considerately treated and patiently taught in small classes or on a one-to-one basis, dyslexics can begin to recover their self-esteem and express their latent intelligence. Ideally the problem should be detected at an early age to foster strategies for coping with it. Failing this, the sixteen to eighteen age group is really the last chance for salvaging the mess which conventional education will have wrought in the unhappy pupil. At CCSS we were called upon to salvage many such messes and usually succeeded.

Teaching at home for a few hours a day at my own convenience was the perfect arrangement. Kikki's successor, Lee Pearson, a gentle, reliable girl, took charge of Tim in the mornings while I was teaching. My pupils would arrive as Stephen was leaving for work and when the bell rang, I had only to shed my apron before answering the door. I was happy: the skills that I had to offer were being mobilized and were appreciated. I won the respect of my pupils and gradually discovered a professional identity for myself. I was awakening from an intellectual coma.

CHAPTER FORTY-TWO

Departures

ALTHOUGH THROUGH TEACHING, at first at primary school level and then later for A-level, I was beginning to find some sense of my own worth, there remained the other area of unfinished business, the one major barrier to the recovery of my true self: the fear of flying. Flying phobia, the black consequence of that trip to Seattle so soon after Robert's birth when I nursed my small baby on aeroplanes the length and breadth of the United States, had deprived me of many exciting opportunities to accompany Stephen – to California in midwinter, to Crete in spring or to New York on Concorde. It had forced me to invent patently feeble excuses because every suggestion of travel by air immediately put me on the defensive. It had caused tension in the home and it had made me very unhappy. The anxiety had started to produce physical symptoms so marked that, before the trip to Rome in the autumn of 1981, I was actually sick. I was desperate to find a cure.

It was with great excitement that while idly thumbing through a magazine in the dentist's waiting room later that winter, I came across a reference to a clinic where flying phobia was accepted without embarrassment as a treatable condition. Enquiries and a letter from my GP eventually put me in touch with the York Clinic at Guy's Hospital where Mr Maurice Yaffe, a senior psychologist, treated sufferers, either privately or in groups on the National Health Service. There was nothing clinical about Maurice Yaffe: his personality and manner were absent-mindedly donnish rather than medical; he never mentioned the word 'phobia', only 'difficulty'. He enthused over the delights of the cheap air fares which he could obtain for his patients through a well-placed contact and played down his patients' graphically recounted anxieties with the absolute assurance that they could be overcome.

Gradually we, his patients, became adjusted to a perspective which encouraged us to concentrate on the pleasures of Paris, Rome or New York instead of on the agonies of getting there.

The agonies themselves were dealt with in a practical manner. Meeting and talking to other sufferers – and there were lots of them – helped decrease my sense of isolation. Reading about stress and anxiety encouraged a more objective approach while a basic course in aerodynamics left no doubt in the minds of the sceptical that aeroplanes were meant to fly. Finally Maurice Yaffe delighted his bemused, captivated patients by unveiling his own brainchild, a simulated aircraft cabin, housed in a small room in the basement of Guy's Hospital.

It occurred to me as we wound our way down from Maurice Yaffe's office, perched dizzily on top of the York Clinic, into the underworld – a maze of tunnels under the old hospital with their hissing, steaming water pipes, gloomy lighting and dank, dark walls – that we might well be exchanging one phobia for another. Nevertheless, the simulator room was so well designed that within minutes of taking our seats we found ourselves soaring away to Manchester, because that was where the flight, which appeared on video film in the cabin window, took us. The simulator reproduced all the appropriate sounds and sensations of take-off and flight, the announcements, the revving engines, babies crying, the floor tilting, the undercarriage jolting and a slight bouncing as the plane supposedly passed through cloud.

My first reactions were panicky and uncomfortable, as were everyone else's, but because the experience was so amazingly realistic, after twelve or so flights to Manchester the whole business became so boring that I forgot to be frightened and began to relax. The culmination of the course was a real, not simulated, weekend in Paris, arranged in fine detail by Maurice Yaffe, though not of course paid for by the NHS. Maurice brought his elderly mother, Minnie, along for the ride and Lucy came with me. He took his party through every aspect of the flight to persuade us that nothing was left to chance and that air-travel was not the touch-and-go affair that we had supposed it to be.

Lucy and I spent a delightful weekend staying with Brandon and Lucette Carter and their three daughters at Sèvres just outside Paris. Release from those years of agony brought me in touch with old friends, with France, with the joy of travel and discovery, and it brought me back in touch with the old me who would fly anywhere in clapped-out aircraft on student flights, the true grand-daughter of a magnificent early aircraft engineer who used to test aeroplanes in the First World War by flying out over the North Sea seated on the wing.

If Paris was the first step on my road to liberation, California was but another short step away in psychological terms. There in the summer of 1982, we renewed many old friendships and revisited old haunts. Jonathan had arranged to attend a conference on early music in Vancouver that August and combined the conference with a visit to us in Santa Barbara where he was often taken for one of Stephen's students. Indeed, he lived with the students in their accommodation and to all intents and purposes shared their rota of duties although, unlike them, he was paying his own way. In the neighbouring apartment, Stephen, the children and I set up home for six weeks. Although we were living apart just as we did in Cambridge, Jonathan's help and support, even though from the house next door, enabled me to enjoy California as never before, even to the extent of revelling in Disneyland with the children.

Little Tim was amazed at the size of the country. 'They did build a big country!' he would mutter to himself as he gazed out of the car window over deserts and mountains. As we watched the sun setting over the Santa Inés mountains from our apartment every evening, he would declare solemnly, 'It's the end of the world, it's the end of the world.' Some time later, I asked him what he liked best about California – the Getty Museum, the deserts, the mountains, the sea, or the Huntingdon Museum and gardens? It was a stupid question to ask a three-year-old. He answered me in what he considered to be my own terms for, as quick as a flash he replied, 'The Mickey Mouse Museum . . .'

I was now ready to fly East again as well as West. With a cautious eye on future employment, Lucy had begun to study Russian for O-level. In retrospect, this was not a good choice since, despite changing times, it did not lead to a brilliant career and produced only anxiety and frustration. A frivolously sunny language like Italian would have been much better suited to her wide-ranging cultural interests and her temperament. However, the rigours of studying seventeenth-century Church Russian at Oxford and a winter spent in Moscow amid the privations of 1992 were still on the distant horizon when Lucy flew with her father, a bevy of nurses and me to a conference in that city in October 1984. Lucy's attempts to speak Russian were met with ecstatic delight, especially when she stood up to propose a brief toast to '*mir i drujba*' – peace and friendship – at the closing banquet of the conference.

It was one of those Russian banquets where the hors d'oeuvre are lavish – caviar, smoked fish and meats, nuts, pickles and, of course, the ubiquitous cucumber – and last for hours, interrupted by toasts and speeches. The main course, the usual lump of unidentifiable meat and mashed potato, arrived at the tables just as everyone was leaving.

Hospitality at the personal as well as the official level relieved the drear sadness which pervaded the country. Eleven years earlier, our acquaintances had demonstrated the utmost caution in their dealings with us. Now they seemed not to care a fig for officialdom. The young guide who was sent to 'mind' Lucy and me was much more concerned to accompany us to buy clothes in the hard currency shops to which we had access than she was to direct our movements. Two of Stephen's closest colleagues, Renata Galosh and her husband Andrei Linde, openly invited us to dinner in their small flat on the outskirts of Moscow. They provided a delectable meal, in part the result it appeared of an amicable relationship with the manager of some restaurant or other. For the other part, Renata produced preserves from her *dacha* in the country, among them home-made strawberry juice strained from precious home-bottled fruit.

That meal was memorable in more ways than just for the delicious food. Renata's elderly mother, who lived with the family, had taught French at Moscow University before the war. She had not been to France since 1936 but had kept her fluency alive by reading and listening to broadcasts. Her French, fossilized for almost fifty years, was unnervingly competent: it was also elegant and precise, devoid of anglicisms, reminiscent of an earlier more gracious age. I sat with her conversing in French at one end of the table while the rest of the company spoke a mixture of English, Russian and Polish. Iolanta, Stephen's Polish nurse, was with us on this trip and found to her surprise that her native Polish, learnt at home in Cambridgeshire, stood her in good stead in understanding Russian. She was less conversant with other aspects of Russian life, however.

On arrival at Sheremetyevo airport, Stephen, Lucy, the students and I had flinched as we passed under the scrutiny of the Customs officers in their forbidding military uniforms, even though we knew our papers, visas and passports to be in good order. Once through the control barriers and past the reflecting mirrors and the inquisitorial gaze, we waited for Iolanta to join us. Had a problem arisen on account of her Polish background, we wondered. When at last she came through,

beaming as ever, she announced with cheerful indignation that she had
been detained by the Customs because they had had the nerve to query
the photograph in her passport. She went on to explain that she had
not liked the official photo in her passport and had decided to change
it herself before leaving home, by sticking another one in its place. The
new one, of course, had not been sealed nor did it bear the official
stamp of the British passport authorities. In the circumstances we were
amazed that she had been allowed into Russia at all.

Although flying phobia was more or less under control, it was
simply not practicable for me to accompany Stephen on each of his
international expeditions: travel had become an obsession with him and
he regularly seemed to spend more time in the air than he did on the
ground. He found it hard to accept that, quite apart from Lucy and
Tim, I was not prepared to abandon either Robert at home or my
students at CCSS, as their A-levels approached in the spring of 1985, a
period which he had designated for an extensive tour of China. Bernard
Carr and Iolanta manfully took charge, heaving Stephen on and off
aeroplanes and trains, and valiantly manoeuvring the wheelchair up onto
the Great Wall. They came back exhausted – nor was Stephen in the best
of health, though he was triumphant at his achievement. He coughed
frequently and appeared to be even more sensitive to irritants in foodstuffs. Many nights would be spent nursing him in my arms, trying to
calm the panic which itself precipitated even worse choking fits.

However, the summer holidays promised a respite. We were to
spend the whole of August in Geneva where Stephen was planning
to have discussions with the particle physicists at Cern while the rest of
us enjoyed the environs of Lake Geneva. Stephen would be working on
the implications for the direction of the arrow of time of quantum
theory and of the observations from the particle accelerator. This was a
topic upon which he had expatiated at some length, with Robert's help,
to the Astronomical Society at the Perse School. It was at this lecture
that I resigned myself to the realization that physics had become so
abtruse and so abstract that even when explained in pictorial form, it
was beyond my comprehension. No amount of film played in reverse
of broken cups and saucers jumping back on to tables and reassembling
themselves could persuade me that the direction of time could be
reversed. Such a supposition could potentially alter the course of human
history if visitors from the future could interfere with the past. It seemed
however that it was essential to prove mathematically that this was not

a possibility since the proof would ensure that nothing could travel faster than light.

Stephen's travels in time and space notwithstanding, it had been a good summer. Lucy completed her first French exchange with a Breton girl whose boatman father had won the lottery. As far as we knew at the time, the exchange was a reasonable success, given the reluctance of teenagers when subjected to such an experience designed solely for their benefit. Only some ten years later did we discover the real truth of the two girls' nocturnal escapades which, had we known about them earlier, would have sent every hair on our combined heads into a state of permanent electric shock.

There were parties, too. Robert set the style by celebrating his eighteenth birthday, just before the onset of his exams, with a ceilidh on the lawn on a warm, clear night under a full moon. There were concerts of every description, choral and instrumental, recitals and even a pop concert. This latter was for Tim's entertainment since he had become an addicted fan of the group Sky. For his sixth birthday, Bernard Carr had given him tickets for a Sky concert in the Albert Hall and thereafter he devoted himself single-mindedly in his every waking moment to emulating the tremendous sustained drum rolls he had heard and seen performed in the concert. An unscheduled concert of a different nature took place on our back lawn when, one Sunday at the beginning of July, just as Stephen and I were returning home from an expedition into medieval Suffolk with the delegates to that summer's physics conference, the lights failed in the University Concert Hall up the road. Jonathan was to play the harpsichord in the concert that evening and brought news of the disaster. The weather was fine and dry so the obvious solution was for the players to set up their instruments on the lawn while the audience grouped round, sitting *al fresco* on whatever rugs, cushions and mats we could muster.

Although Jonathan was regularly asked to play with modern and amateur orchestras such as the one which performed on our lawn, he had long lamented the lack of authentic baroque performance in Cambridge where many young keyboard players vied for the few opportunities available. On the other hand, he was too remote from the London scene for involvement there to be a feasible prospect. Sadly I realized that, had it not been for his commitment to us, particularly to me, he might well have moved to London where he could have advanced his career much more easily. The only course was for him to start his own orchestra but that was a daunting prospect in terms of the time, commitment and money required.

He was becoming so frustrated by the musical isolation in which he found himself and hankered so desperately to be able to perform as part of an ensemble that when, in the spring of 1984, he went into hospital for an operation, I decided to take charge of the situation. First I picked up the telephone and booked the University Concert Hall and then I rang various contacts and booked a small but complete orchestra of baroque players. Jonathan came round from the anaesthetic to the news that he had been appointed the director of the newly formed Cambridge Baroque Camerata which was due to give its inaugural concert on 24 June. Frenzied planning, programming and publicity filled the intervening weeks which were also the weeks of his convalescence.

On the night, Robert ran the box office, Lucy sold programmes and various friends acted as ushers while I ran to and fro, liaising between the front of house and backstage and attending to Stephen who sat at the side of the platform. To our amazement, the queue for tickets stretched out into the forecourt. We counted each member of the audience as they filed into the concert hall that June evening since a full house was crucial to the financial success of the enterprise. 'Financial success' did not mean making a profit; it merely signified breaking even. All seats were taken and the performance, entitled *The Trumpet Shall Sound*, received rapturous applause. Emboldened by the success of the 1984 concert, the Cambridge Baroque Camerata ventured on to the concert platform again in 1985 with another own-promotion, a programme to mark the tercentenary of the births of Bach, Handel and Scarlatti. Fortunately the gamble paid off a second time, although on some later occasions, unexpected rival attractions such as an international football final on television would decrease the size of the audience discouragingly. The elation generated by a concert which was successful both musically and financially was intoxicating because these promotions were always high-risk activities fraught with uncertainty. As his savings oscillated according to box office receipts, Jonathan resigned himself to a philosophical point of view, regarding the concerts and the publicity they engendered as investments for the future. This was the only realistic attitude to take to the London debut of the ensemble, planned for October 1985 in the Queen Elizabeth Hall.

Thus, despite its innate tensions, our household seemed to have recovered some degree of equilibrium. It would always be subject to anxiety and insecurity because it still stood on the edge of a precipice but its foundations had been reinforced, lending it an unaccustomed stability. This stability was not to be enjoyed for its own sake, indulging us in a more restful life and the assumption of comfortable habits; it was to be put to good use as a firmer basis from which to reach out eagerly for self-fulfilment, modestly or more flamboyantly, depending on circumstances. For no one were the results more spectacular than for Stephen himself, who had finished writing the first draft of his popular book about cosmology and the origins of the universe. The book ranged wide – from a discussion of early cosmologies to modern theories of particle physics and the arrow of time, with particular reference, of course, to the significance of black holes. In conclusion the author looked forward to the time when mankind would able to 'know the mind of God' through the formulation, at some not too distant date in the future, of a complete unified theory of the universe, the theory of everything. Stephen had been given the name of an agent in New York where the book was being offered to publishers and meanwhile in England we discussed tax-efficient methods of receiving royalties which we expected to bring in a modest, supplementary income regularly over the years, like textbooks which were said to be far more reliable in the long run than bestsellers. It was unlikely to fulfil the original aim of paying Lucy's school fees as she was already well into her secondary education.

The harmony which prevailed at home was never more evident than on Sunday afternoons when Stephen would take Tim down to the ice-cream van at the end of the road – or perhaps it was Tim who took Stephen. They both enjoyed these excursions, indulging each other's desire for greater independence. They were close enough to home for Tim to be able to run back for help if the wheelchair broke down, but generally there were few hazards in their path, especially since the traffic always respectfully slowed down for Stephen to pass. Tim would return home, beaming with chocolatey delight, his tee-shirt spattered with the creamy drips which had not quite reached his mouth.

At the end of July, a few days in advance of the rest of us, Stephen, his new secretary Laura Ward and some students and nurses, flew out to Geneva. I was anxious to stay to see Robert off on a Scout expedition to Iceland before leaving Cambridge myself. The plan was that within the week we would meet Stephen and his entourage in Germany at Bayreuth, the Wagnerian mecca, for a performance of the

Ring cycle and then all travel back to Geneva to a house rented for the duration of the holidays. At last I had begun to achieve a balance in my life: the sinuous chromatic dissonances of Purcell mitigated the effects of Wagner's sinister modulations, the ebullience of Handel countered depressive pessimism, the soaring spirituality of Bach fortified the soul against disconcerting ambiguities. In addition, I had become converted to Stephen's worship of the composer to such an extent that I could contemplate a complete performance of the *Ring* at that shrine to megalomania with a certain measure of good-humoured tolerance.

I waved goodbye quite casually to Stephen as he left home on 29 July. Geneva after all was no distance away by comparison with China and it was renowned for its Swiss standards of hygiene. We were all concerned for Stephen's father who was in the throes of a chronic illness and feared that he might die during our absence. Frank Hawking bore his illness with the same gruff stoicism that he had brought to all situations and which he used to conceal pain or embarrassment. Despite the vicissitudes of my relationship with the Hawking family, and although in the past I might have hoped for a more sympathetic approach from him, I had not ceased to respect him, the more so because of late he had begun to write me truly appreciative letters, praising my care of Stephen and the children and my management of the letting house. But my greatest anxiety was for Robert, my eldest son, whom I saw off in the company of the Venture Scouts three days after Stephen's departure. Their plans to trek across a glacier and to canoe round the north coast of Iceland filled me with foreboding.

Part Four

CHAPTER FORTY-THREE

Darkest Night

IT WAS SELDOM that Jonathan and I were alone together for any length of time. We tried to maintain our code of conduct in front of Stephen and the children whereby we behaved simply as good friends, suppressing, sometimes with difficulty, any display of closer affection or intimacy in our attempts to avoid hurting anyone. Every evening I would stand behind Stephen at the front door as he saw Jonathan off, despatching him to his own house on the other side of Cambridge. In our efforts to keep the home going by this unconventional method we had the support of many people, among them my elderly home help Eve Suckling, Lee Pearson's successor; these were people who had witnessed the situation from the inside and who were wise and experienced enough not to draw hasty conclusions.

Only slightly younger than my parents, Eve had worked as a caterer in St John's Choir School while bringing up her five children. Her attitude to life was down to earth and pragmatic. In her view there was no doubt about it: Jonathan, whom she remembered as a chorister, was essential to the well-being of our household. Even Don, whose absolute values had been shaken to their core one evening in the spring of 1978, just before Tim's birth, when he found us sitting on the sofa lounging comfortably against each other, had conceded that the situation often demanded of him much more than he had expected and sometimes more than he could give, certainly more than he could give indefinitely. He admitted that he had lived with us long enough to find that the ceaseless rigours of our way of life often brought him into uncomfortable conflict with his own conscience. Always, too, we knew that we could count on the guidance of Bill Loveless to strengthen our resolve and help keep our perspective within the disciplined framework that we had tried to establish for it while viewing our weaknesses with compassion.

More than once he was heard to say that our situation was unique and that he could not prescribe how we should deal with it.

For once, the closed nature of Cambridge society worked to our advantage. People did not ask impertinent questions but rather took situations at face value. There may have been some people, among them one or two members of the clergy, who lived by absolute standards, usually people whose prejudices and preconceptions had never been put to the test, who looked askance at the apparent irregularities of our lifestyle. The challenge to conventional morality presented by our arrangements was more than they could accommodate and they were unable to believe that Jonathan and I had indeed struggled with our own consciences, well aware that our lifestyle was extremely and uncomfortably irregular, and that we had decided that the greater good – the survival of the family unit, Stephen's right to live at home within that family unit and the welfare of the children – outweighed the means required for achieving that goal, namely our illicit relationship.

Occasionally when Stephen went abroad or when we were to take the car to join him somewhere on the Continent, we tentatively allowed the poor, sickly plant of our relationship to come out into the open for an airing and to blossom. Even then it was often watered with tears of tension and guilt since an incomprehending reaction or an unthinking word from one of the children or an unexpected encounter on a beach or campsite could quickly destroy the brief, heady illusion of freedom and send our consciences plummeting into despair.

Discretion and deceit were divided by only the finest line of conscience and it was never easy to judge on which side of the line we stood. There were a couple of other celebrities in the public eye who were seriously disabled and it was public knowledge that their spouses had found solace with other partners while still caring responsibly and lovingly for them. Perhaps it was because those spouses were husbands rather than wives that it was easier for them to bring their new relationships into the open than it was for me. As a wife, my back-room role was so inextricably identified with support and caring that society at large, as represented by an increasingly prurient press, would not willingly credit me with needs or a personality of my own.

Nevertheless those short periods of respite, even if spent under canvas in a raging wind or sometimes sharing a small foreign hotel room with the children, allowed us a freedom from nagging anxiety and constant care; it restored our flagging morale and, paradoxically, reinforced our loyalty to Stephen. Those fleeting holiday periods often took us to or through France where I was at last able to introduce Jonathan to Brandon and Lucette. Lucette was immediately impressed with, though perplexed by, him: he was sharing a tent with Robert in the garden of the Carters' rented cottage in Brittany while the rest of us camped indoors, and she could not quite decide what part he played in our lives. She had supposed that the 'Jonathan' mentioned in my earlier letter was a friend of Robert's. As one of my dearest and closest friends, Lucette deserved the explanation of his presence which I had not been able to give her in Cargese in 1979, so one day after lunch, she and I cycled along the coast to the next village where we sat in a café till sundown discussing my situation. She was fervent in her support of Jonathan and me, declaring that it was not until she and Brandon had children themselves that she realized how heavy my burden of a family and a totally paralysed husband really was.

Sometimes when travelling across Europe to meet Stephen, Jonathan and I and one or more of the children would stay in Paris overnight, either with the Carters or with Mary and Bernard Whiting, our Australian friends, who had left Cambridge and taken up residence in a very small flat just off the rue Mozart. In the early 1980s, Mary had begun to resign herself to her childless state; she had taken up her career in archaeology again and then she found herself expecting their daughter, Ruth. While the Whitings were in Paris their son Mark was born, so the flat which would have been small for two people was distinctly crowded. That, however, was no bar to the Whitings' enthusiastic hospitality. Sometimes we would call on them on our way to take the overnight sleeper from Paris and would pack a year's news into an animated hour or two. In 1985, however, our route took us through Belgium and Germany rather than France. It had become an accepted part of the family routine that Stephen would attend a summer school in some desirable part of Europe and would fly out with his students and nurses, and that Jonathan and the children and I would arrive by car in a more leisurely manner, taking a few days' holiday on the way. Thus it was that on Friday, 1 August 1985 after Robert's departure to Iceland, Jonathan, Lucy, Tim and I set out for Felixstowe to board the ferry for the overnight crossing to Zeebrugge.

We had planned to spend the weekend by the sea on the Belgian coast before driving through Belgium and Germany to Bayreuth where we were to meet Stephen on 8 August. One night on the coast, where stinging sandstorms were blowing along the beach under leaden skies, was enough to turn us inland to look for campsites in the Ardennes, the hilly forested area near the German border. Not only did torrential rain begin to lash our windscreen before we had even reached Brussels, but a strange itchy feeling also began to creep around the nape of our necks, like prickly burrs caught in our pullovers and anoraks. I suspected that we had brought more than just four human travellers with us on our journey.

The stowaways were not hard to identify. Just before the end of term, Tim's primary school had been subject to yet another plague of head-lice, the recurrent scourge of all English primary schools at the time. We had all carefully washed our hair with the prescribed shampoo while Stephen, for good measure, had insisted on also having his ample locks doused with a foul-smelling lotion which he wore throughout a whole day in the Department. He remarked in the evening that apart from his faithful attendant-student, no one had come near him all day.

On that summer holiday in Belgium, we were little better than tramps, soaked to the skin and lice-ridden. In the French-speaking Ardennes, I called to mind one of those improbable nouns which had been impressed upon us in school and which I in turn jokingly impressed upon my pupils for its irregular plural form, never expecting to have to put it to the test – *poux*, lice, *poux de tête* – for which I went in search of the appropriate *shampooing*. Stephen would not be best pleased if we arrived in Bayreuth accompanied by an army of *poux*. It was all too easy to imagine the face he would pull at that news and the discomfort of sitting in their company throughout interminable Wagnerian operas. The scourge was brought under control as we sheltered from the rain in a charming small hotel in what appeared, through the deluge, to be a pretty little riverbank town, and listened with pleasure to the hotelier's impeccable French while sampling the delights of his cuisine.

We ambled on, still in the pouring rain, from Belgium into Luxembourg. If the skies seemed to be clearing, we would put up our tents for the night, otherwise we would come to roost in a warm, dry, inexpensive guest house. In a break in the clouds, we paused for a picnic lunch in Echternach, a leafy town on the German border. After being cooped up in the car all morning, Tim raced gleefully up and down a long alleyway of trees in a park, supervised by Lucy. Inevitably he stumbled and fell flat on his face in a muddy puddle. The apparition which rose from the dirt was of an unrecognizable small boy, previously blond, caked in mud from head to foot, from the very tips of his eyelashes to his shoelaces; every item of clothing, including his anorak, oozed brown mud. Jonathan steered me onto the front seat of the car and then hastily opened the back. He brought out the washing-up bowl and set up the camping stove on the pavement. He warmed some water and then washed the offending creature and his clothes as best he could in full view of all the passersby – to Lucy's intense mortification. We spent the rest of the day dodging the showers and climbing up the stairways and round the passages of the Porta Nigra, the massive Roman gateway to Triers, and that night our German landlady took Tim's wet clothes and dried them for us. The rains, the mud and the *poux* were at last behind us.

The next day in Mannheim we visited musical friends of Jonathan's, whom he had met on an earlier visit to Bayreuth, and then set off on the final leg of the journey to Rothenburg, a medieval showplace within easy reach of the Wagnerian holy of holies. We pitched our tents in the early evening and lingered drowsily over food and wine in a pleasantly atmospheric restaurant. On the way back to the campsite, I stopped at a phone box to ring through to Geneva to check the arrangements for meeting Stephen in Bayreuth the next day. The phone was answered by Stephen's new secretary, Laura Ward. She had replaced Judy Fella when the latter had left to go on an extended trip to South Africa with her husband.

Laura's voice was tense with unexpected urgency. 'Oh, Jane, thank goodness you've called!' she almost shouted down the phone. 'You must come quickly, Stephen is in a coma in hospital in Geneva and we don't know how long he'll live!'

The news was shattering. It plummeted me into a black pit of anxiety, misery and, above all, guilt. Quite irrationally forgetting all those travels to distant places that he had survived perfectly well without me, I asked myself how I could ever have let Stephen go off alone with his entourage, deprived of the protection of my intimate knowledge of his condition, his needs, his medicines, his likes, his dislikes, his allergies, his fears. How could I, his mouthpiece, have left him at the mercy of a medical profession which would undoubtedly put him into hospital at the first opportunity? How could I have seen him off without a qualm of anxiety and then have set out on holiday myself – with Jonathan of all people?

Stephen had rung, as he usually did on arrival, to say that all was well. He was living in a nice house in Ferney-Voltaire, well situated, if some distance from the laboratory. He had wished us well for our journey and looked forward to seeing us in a week's time at Bayreuth. After that, in the mishmash of all my other concerns, especially my anxiety for Robert, I had scarcely given him another's moment's thought, knowing him to be safe and in good hands. Apart from the troublesome cough, he had been fine when he left home. It was incredible that he could have fallen into a coma.

We sat in the car numbly discussing the news. We decided to strike camp and set off for Geneva forthwith, but on our return to the campsite we found everything closed for the night: the main gate was shut and the only entry or exit was by means of a wicket gate for pedestrians. The office was dark and empty. There was no way we could leave until the early morning. I lay awake in my sleeping bag, listening to wolves howling and farm animals cackling somewhere in the distant black night. 'Please God, let Stephen be alive!' I whispered, impatient for dawn.

As soon as the campsite opened, we loaded the car and set out on the mad dash across Europe to Geneva. Hundreds of miles of German pasture land sped by without our noticing as we drove like fiends to the Swiss border. The one advantage of being in Germany was that there were no speed restrictions. We paused at the border for some refreshments for the children, though I had no stomach for food, and then resumed our frenzied progress along the heartlessly tranquil shores of the blue Swiss lakes, Lake Neuchâtel and then Lake Geneva. We spoke little, each absorbed in an unhappy turmoil of confusing reflections. Even the children were quiet in the back of the car. Geneva glistened in the late afternoon sun as we approached it, impervious to its charms. For us it was the scene of disaster and we had only one goal, the Hôpital Cantonal, where the fearsome truth of life or death awaited us.

A combination of Jonathan's map-reading expertise and my ability to ask for directions in French brought us to our destination, a clean, clinical complex of buildings, white and glowing on the outside, highly polished and chromium-plated on the inside. We were taken straight up to the intensive care unit and there Stephen lay, quiet and still, his eyes closed in a comatose sleep. A mask covered his mouth and nose, and tubes and wires attached to various parts of his body trailed in all directions while across monitor screens an endless dance of luminous green and white wavy lines traced the rhythmic patterns of the life forces battling to maintain their superiority over the old enemy, death. He was alive.

The medical staff on the ward gave me a curt reception. 'How many years is it since you last saw your husband?' they asked coolly. It was obvious that they thought that Stephen and I lived separate lives and that his illness had developed since we last met. They were surprised when I replied that I had seen him only last week. 'Well then, why is he travelling in his state of health?' they asked with the shocked incomprehension of inbred medical caution. I could no more answer that question than they could themselves, though I tried to recount the usual story of Stephen's indomitable courage combined with his scientific genius, etcetera – an oft-repeated tale that was too long and too complicated in the telling for my drained emotional state. So far removed were these facts from the reality of their own experience that they proved indigestible to my audience, who decided to overlook what sounded like a totally implausible story. Instead they gave me a garbled version of what had happened.

Apparently Stephen's cough had worsened after his arrival in Geneva. Perhaps, because they did not live with him every day and every night, his companions had not realized that this was fairly normal. Much to his annoyance, they had insisted on calling a doctor. After hours of argument, the doctor in turn had insisted on consigning him to hospital in Geneva. There pneumonia was diagnosed and, after more argument, Stephen was put on a life support machine. He was not in fact in a coma, as his secretary had said, but had been drugged to permit a potent mixture of antibiotics and nourishment to be fed into his system through various drips, while the ventilator did his breathing for him. He was not at present in danger since all his functions were governed by machines.

I could sadly and all too easily imagine that this had been the realization of his worst, most terrifying nightmare. His fate, which lay in his own control of his medical care, had been taken out of his hands by strangers who knew next to nothing about him. They did not even know who he was, let alone how to manage his case. They were doing their best in the circumstances but I well knew that Stephen would think that medical intervention had over-reached itself dramatically and disastrously. Like his hero, Siegfried in the *Ring* cycle, my sad warrior had been felled by the enemy's attack on his weak spot, in Stephen's present case his throat and his difficulty in communication. It was not Wagner but Bach, however, who inspired the thoughts and sounds which revolved with an obsessive urgency in my head as I kept vigil by his bedside. The sublime words and melody of the final great chorus of the St Matthew Passion – *Ruhe sanfte, sanfte ruh! Ruht, ihr aus gesognen Glieder, ruhet sanfte, ruhet wohl!* – Rest thou softly, softly rest. Rest thy worn and bruised body, Rest softly, rest well – brought me far more consolation and inner peace and spoke more poignantly to my heart than any of those Wagnerian declamations.

At the rented house in Ferney-Voltaire, our arrival was greeted with relief by the students, nurses and the secretary – all at a loss since, with the removal of the key player, their presence was superfluous. They were all in a muted state of shock, as we were, each silently questioning what else or what more they could have done. While Stephen lay drugged in hospital there was nothing for them to do. However, when in the succeeding days I found myself sucked into a vortex of administrative, emotional and ethical problems, they invented new roles for themselves which they fulfilled with quiet efficiency. The students did the shopping and the cooking, the nurses looked after the children and took them on outings – this, after all, was supposed to be their summer holiday – and Laura, the secretary, was in perpetual contact with Cambridge and Cern, trying to sort out our financial, insurance and other problems.

The news was a bitter blow for Stephen's family, especially for his mother. Her husband was an invalid with a poor life expectancy and now her son's life was critically threatened too. We were in touch by phone daily and she was consistently supportive and philosophical. In her unemotional way, she already seemed to have resigned herself to Stephen's death. It was cruel that three generations of Hawking menfolk were at risk at the same time, yet so far apart: Frank was old and ill in the small, more manageable house in Bedfordshire to which he and Isobel had recently moved; Stephen was critically ill in Geneva, and goodness knows what had become of Robert. It was just as well that I did not know that his canoe had overturned in the North Sea.

There was no anxiety about the well-being of the fourth and youngest Hawking male, Tim. His immediate future was a problem, however, since he had to be returned to England by some means or other and entrusted to my parents; I was far too preoccupied in Geneva to be able to look after him, and the nurses would shortly be leaving. Although Lucy had her own passport, Tim was registered on mine, so I approached the British Consulate for help in getting him home. One could have been forgiven for thinking that the consular officials were being deliberately obstructive. The hard-faced, dark-haired woman at the consular desk summarily waved me away after I had spent ages waiting for an interview, even though I explained the extraordinary circumstances fully. There was no chance of Tim's returning to England without a passport, she said harshly: for that, I would need to produce his birth certificate. I grimaced. Tim's birth certificate was in the living-room at home, in the William and Mary desk which had belonged to Stephen's grandmother.

On an off-chance I telephoned our home number, not expecting it to be answered. To my surprise Eve's voice came on the line at the other end: providentially, she was in the house doing a spot of spring-cleaning. She went to the desk, found the birth certificate and sent it out to Geneva by express delivery. Triumphantly I waved the document at the same consular official a couple of days later, but she was not impressed. 'That will not do,' she said, as acerbic as ever, 'that's only a short birth certificate and we need the full one – from Somerset House.' I stared at her in disbelief. 'And in any case,' she went on, 'there are papers to fill in that your husband will have to sign.' 'I have already told you,' I replied through clenched teeth, 'that my husband is unconscious and paralysed on a ventilator in intensive care in the Hôpital Cantonal. He cannot possibly sign anything.' 'Well,' she continued obtusely, 'if your husband does not know that you are taking the child out of the country, you certainly cannot have a passport for him.'

In one final attempt, near to tears in exasperation, I pleaded with her, 'I am only trying to send the child home.' She paused for a second in which her mood mollified slightly, as if only at that moment had my words registered on her brain. 'If you can get someone else, a British person with some qualifications, a teacher perhaps, to sign the papers, and bring a photo, then we might consider it,' she replied.

To our private amusement, Jonathan filled in and signed the forms since he fulfilled all the official requirements. We took Tim to a photo booth and made him practise his signature. At last on 13 August, a full British passport was issued in the name of Mr T. S. Hawking; it bore the appealingly innocent photograph and the untried spidery signature of a six-year-old. Thus equipped, Mr T. S. Hawking travelled home – business class for want of a seat in economy – to England with Lucy and the nurses, and went to stay with my parents.

In absentia, Robert was the source of the only piece of good news that summer. Bernard Carr, always a loyal and dependable ally in extremity, flew out to Geneva to take over from the students as the situation began to change. He brought Robert's A-level results which were excellent, the only glimmer of light through the blackest of clouds. Those results assured Robert a place at Cambridge, at Corpus Christi, my father's college, to read Natural Sciences.

CHAPTER FORTY-FOUR

A Slender Thread

IF THE COMPARATIVE triviality of Tim's passport took an inordinate amount of time to resolve, it was in the topsy-turvy nature of things during that period that a far more serious matter was resolved in seconds. Two days after our arrival in Geneva, the doctor in charge of Stephen's case asked to see me as a matter of some urgency. He took me into a bare grey side room. At first, as I responded to his questions, I thought that he was simply wanting to verify the facts of Stephen's extraordinary existence. The nursing staff had begun to accept by now that Stephen was no ordinary patient, nor was he the victim, as they had originally supposed, of neglect by his family. Having ascertained various details about his phenomenal longevity and his self-management, the doctor came abruptly to the point of the interview. The question that he wanted me to answer was whether his staff should disconnect the ventilator while Stephen was in a drugged state or should they try to bring him round from the anaesthetic.

I was shocked. The possibility of switching off the life support was unthinkable. What a travesty, what an ignominious ending to such a heroic fight for life, what a denial of everything that I, too, had fought for! My reply was quick and ready. I did not need either to think about the question or to discuss it with other people. There was only one possible answer. I held only the power of life, not death, in my hands; a single moment's contemplation of any other course would have been a denial of everything that mattered to me. 'Stephen must live. You must bring him round from the anaesthetic,' I replied.

The doctor went on to explain the complications of the procedures that would ensue. Stephen would not be able to breathe unaided and would eventually, when he was stronger, have to undergo a tracheotomy operation. This would be the only way of weaning him off the ventilator as it would bypass the hypersensitive area in his throat which had been giving him so much trouble. The technicalities of the tracheotomy, a hole in the windpipe below the vocal chords, would require permanent professional attention. I did not pay much attention to this gloomy, if realistic, prognosis. I had made the decision that was required of me and what would be, would be. The important truth was that Stephen was alive and would remain alive as long as I had any power to influence events.

I emerged from the interview room to a remarkable sight. There, standing in the corridor, was a Fellow of Gonville and Caius College, though not someone whom either of us knew at all well. James Fitzsimons and his Swiss wife, Aude, had been on holiday with Aude's family in Geneva when word had reached them from the College that Stephen was ill in hospital there, and they had come to investigate and offer help. They could not have arrived at a more propitious moment. I was profoundly shaken by the events of the past week and was disturbed, though defiant, at the interview. I had ingested sufficient information to realize that the crises were by no means over and indeed a worse crisis could be looming, for it was not at all certain that Stephen would even survive resuscitation from his drug-induced sleep.

James and Aude Fitzsimons brought fresh energy and buoyant, though sensitive, resolve to bolster our resources. As Stephen was slowly restored to us, James joined our long vigils, taking a share in the rota which consisted of Bernard, Jonathan, the remaining students and myself. We were not there to act as nurses – there were plenty of those in the hospital – but to strengthen Stephen's fragile hold on life and reawaken his interest and his curiosity from their unprecedented state of inertia. Fortunately James was a fluent French speaker and was able to relieve me of some of the pressures of communicating Stephen's every indistinct request to the nursing staff. His attempts to mouth those requests were impeded by the tubes and masks covering his face. Those of us close to him had to try to anticipate his needs and ask the right questions; he would respond in the negative or the affirmative by means of his painfully expressive eyes, now open again, and by raising his eyebrows or frowning.

To alleviate the tedium, we read aloud from whatever holiday material we happened to have with us. My teaching that year had drawn me into Latin American literature – not only on account of the syllabus. One of my most talented and likeable students, Gonzalo Vargas Llosa, was the son of the Peruvian novelist Mario Vargas Llosa, and with him I had begun to explore the works of the Colombian writer Gabriel García Márquez, and the blind Argentinian multi-lingual polymath, Jorge Luis Borges. Borges had come to Cambridge to address an informal gathering in Trinity Hall to which one of my few linguistic contacts in the University, Dr Joe Cremona, had kindly invited me. Borges' ideas excited me: I was particularly fascinated by his preoccupation with paradox and ambiguity, time and timelessness and the cyclical nature of historical events. His writing appeared to mirror in literary, even poetic, form much of the substance of scientific discovery in the twentieth century and might be likened to literary versions of Martin Escher's spatially irreconcilable drawings, themselves artistic representations of a mathematical concept, the Möbius ring. I had intended to read Borges' *Libro de Arena*, The Book of Sand, over the summer holidays, so, hoping that its conundrums and enigmas might appeal to Stephen, I commissioned Bernard to bring an English translation to Geneva with him.

Whether Stephen appreciated the rather complex, cerebral games of Borges' writing, I did not discover. Rather selfishly I relished the stories for the intellectual escape they offered from the nerve-racking tension and the clinical monotony of the intensive care unit. But my fascination was stronger than that of an objective reader when I found that I was being absorbed into the puzzle of the literature myself, especially through the first story, 'The Other'.

'The Other' is apparently autobiographical. Borges is seated on a bench in Cambridge, Massachusetts in 1969, looking out over the Charles river. A young man comes to sit beside him and the two converse. The young man, however, asserts that they are sitting on a bench overlooking the Rhône in Geneva in 1914. He is, of course, Borges' youthful self and recounts details of his home life at number 17 Malagnou Street in Geneva. The ideas in the story – of identity, time travel, dreams, prediction, history repeating itself, of knowing the future – were stimulating in themselves. The coincidence that I had, unknowingly, chosen to read this story to Stephen in Geneva gave me the startling impression that I had entered it myself and become a part of it, adding yet another dimension. Bernard, still engaged on parapsychological research as an antidote to physics, enjoyed the coincidence.

One afternoon as Jonathan and I were leaving the hospital, I suggested driving out of the city to catch a glimpse of the Alps. To my astonishment, I saw from the map that our route took us along the rue Malagnou. Both on the way out of the city and on the way back, we scoured the street for number 17, the house in Borges' story. We could see numbers 15 and 19, 14 and 16, but of number 17 there was no trace. I wanted to write to Jorge Luis Borges to tell him of the coincidence and to ask him about the missing house. Was it, I wanted to know, another of his games? The next days, weeks and months were so fully occupied that there was neither the time nor the opportunity to write – and then Borges died.

Once Stephen had regained consciousness, the pace quickened. As soon as possible an air ambulance, paid for by Caius, was commissioned to bring us back to Cambridge. Carrying an enormous amount of luggage, Jonathan set out for home by car on the same day that Stephen and I, accompanied by a doctor, paramedics, portable ventilators and other equipment, were loaded carefully into an ambulance, whisked to the airport, decanted into a small, red jet and sent hurtling into the sky the moment the hatch was closed. Had it not been for the circum-stances of our flight, I might rather have enjoyed it; even Stephen roused himself sufficiently to peer out of the window as we soared above the clouds. This was the way to fly: our private plane was given priority over all the other airliners queuing up for space on the runway; there was no time for anxiety, none of the usual hassle and no delays. At Cambridge airport, John Farman, the head of the intensive care unit at Addenbrooke's, was waiting to meet us with an ambulance on the tarmac.

Although Stephen had undeniably received excellent treatment in Geneva, there was an irrepressible sense of relief at being back home where we and our situation were well known. Many a familiar figure appeared in the intensive care unit that day, including Judy Fella, Stephen's former secretary. She had already been active on his behalf and was ready to give whatever help was needed. There were no gasps of surprise from the staff at Addenbroke's at Stephen's ambitious travelling schedule, or incredulity at his domination of motor neurone disease. The minimum of general explanation was needed. Nevertheless, detailed explanation was required of the management of his case, of the routines that he himself had developed, of the precise quantities and frequencies of the medications he took, of the positions he liked to adopt when lying in bed, of his insistence on a gluten-free diet, even when being fed by tube. Each and every one of these matters and many more like them became the subject of lengthy discussions and investigations.

Three days after the flight, by which time Stephen's condition had stabilized in intensive care, John Farman thought it might be possible to ease him off his dependence on the ventilator; he was keen to encourage him to breathe unaided in the hope of avoiding the threatened tracheotomy operation. By Tuesday, 20 August, Stephen seemed to be making good enough progress for the experiment to be tried. He was comfortable and gaining strength and we, that is, as many friends and relations as could be mustered, had devised a rota, mounting guard over him by day and by night. Usually the long-suffering students, or our team of nurses or physiotherapists, including Sue Smith and Caroline Chamberlain, would sit with Stephen by night, while the family and other friends took turns by day. The nurses promised to ring if Stephen needed me that night as they embarked on the delicate process of detaching him from the ventilator.

The telephone rang in my bedroom in the early hours of the morning. The ward sister said little, except that she thought I should go to the hospital straight away. She offered no explanation. As my parents were looking after Tim, I had only to dress and leave a note before slipping out at first light. Stephen was very ill; a blotchy grey pallor had taken the place of his whitish complexion and his bulging eyes were drained of all colour. His limbs were rigidly frozen in spasm while a brutal cough, the old demon, had returned to torment his throat, like a cat toying with a mouse, letting it go, then pouncing with sharpened claws. In between each attack, he desperately tried to draw breath. Fear was written large all over his face.

The expression on the nurses' faces gave me to understand that they thought that very little could be done for him and that the end was near. I thought differently. That the old demon was back and currently had the upper hand was obvious, but I detected a familiar element in the choking. That element was Stephen's own understandable tendency to panic. But it had been controlled before and there was just a chance that it could be brought to heel, using the simple relaxation techniques I had learnt in yoga classes and which I had practised successfully on him at home in past crises.

I sat at the head of the bed and put one arm round the back of his neck. While I stroked his face, his shoulder and his arm with the other hand, I slowly whispered soothing words into his ear, as one might when trying to calm a fretful baby. I chose my words carefully for their soft, sibilant or liquid, palatal sounds, and tried to create a gentle, rocking rhythm to ease away the panic. I conjured up scenes of calm, blue lakes and balmy, clear skies, rolling green hills and warm golden sands. Gradually, over the next few hours, as the tension subsided and his body relaxed, the paroxysms yielded to a quieter, more regular breathing pattern. Finally he dozed off. I was exhausted but jubilant: my home-spun attempt at hypnosis had worked! There was no escaping the fact, however, that Stephen was still critically ill.

I went away for a rest, leaving the telephone number of some good friends, John and Mary Taylor, who lived close to the hospital. The Taylors had come to Cambridge from Oxford with their schoolboy sons in 1980 when John had been appointed to the Chair in Particle Physics in the Department. Modest and retiring but endowed with a wry sense of humour, he was strikingly untypical of the unsmiling breed of particle physicists whom I had met. Mary, his wife, was not only immediately sympathetic for her spontaneity and her concern for others, she was also a professional pianist. She and Jonathan had quickly become friends and musical companions, often playing duets together. Mary also took singing lessons with Nigel Wickens and under his tuition had developed a lovely floating, high soprano voice. As well as being regular visitors to Stephen's bedside, the Taylors had offered me the use of their house. That morning I took up their offer at 7 a.m.

Mary offered me a bed but I preferred to sit for a while in the garden to breathe in the fresh morning air, so welcome after the sterile, dry atmosphere of the hospital, and to let the early sun caress my weary frame. Mary brought me some breakfast and we sat talking. I was incoherent with tiredness but I had one overwhelming desire and that was to speak to Robert.

It was so long since I had last seen him and so much had happened in the interim. I had to assume that he was well and that no news was good news. According to the schedule he was due to be back at base camp before setting off on the final expedition, and was therefore no longer incommunicado. I felt that the time had come to warn him that his father was critically ill, though I did not intend to ask him to come home. 'Phone him from here,' Mary suggested with her customary generosity. I had not the will to protest: I did as she said, dialling through to Iceland with trepidation. When I heard Robert's voice, my resolve crumbled and I broke down. Whatever my intentions, they were overriden by a cry which leapt up from the heart and escaped before I could suppress it. 'Please come home!' I heard myself pleading into the phone. 'Right!' he said without the slightest hesitation. He came home the next day and was met by the Taylors at Heathrow. I did not realize that, had he completed the expedition, he would have qualified for a Queen's Scout Award. When later I heard about the canoe-capsizing episode, he laughed it off as a triviality.

My return to the hospital revealed the sort of variations on the theme of illness that had become familiar over the past two interminable weeks. Stephen's life still hung by a thread, new strains of bacteria had been found in his lungs and the medication had been changed. He was breathing through the ventilator again but cheered up considerably at the news of Robert's return. I discussed with John Farman the possibility of bringing in a professional hypnotist to encourage him to alleviate the panic attacks and relax those muscles which went into spasm when he tried to breathe. John readily agreed and brought in a GP of his acquaintance who was also a trained hypnotist. She had moderate success, using the same techniques that I had been using, but not enough to warrant parting Stephen from the ventilator for any extended period. There was, it appeared, no alternative to the tracheotomy, the operation which would allow him to breathe through a hole in the windpipe bypassing the troublesome membranes and muscles in his throat.

As August slid into September, the doctors started to talk seriously about performing the operation; the lung infection was at last responding to treatment and Stephen was getting stronger. Whatever they may have felt about the risks of such a step, I was beginning to feel confident that Stephen would survive. How could he not, with so many people contributing in every imaginable way to his recovery? Some offered invaluable practical help at his bedside, nursing and communicating; some helped with the day-to-day administrative problems or with running our home; others, more distant, offered moral support; others prayed. Many, like Jonathan who had arrived back from Geneva, his parents and mine, did all of these.

The operation was a success and Stephen made such a rapid recovery that, after four weeks in intensive care, it became possible to lift him out of bed into his wheelchair, though he was still too weak to operate it himself. The prognosis improved daily until it was considered safe to move him out of intensive care on to one of the neurological wards. There was a price to be paid for recovery, however: the operation had deprived Stephen entirely of the power of speech.

CHAPTER FORTY-FIVE

The Burden of Responsibility

IN GENEVA WE had been protected from the bustle of the wider world. There we had been able to focus on Stephen and his illness, our movements restricted to the route between the hospital and Ferney-Voltaire. Of that small border town, I saw only the statue of Voltaire, its most famous resident, who had settled there in 1759, putting a comfortable distance between himself and the French government, ready to flee into exile in Switzerland at a moment's notice. Apart from the several arrivals and departures, the outside world which existed at the end of the telephone line was unreal, remote from the intensity of the tragedy of which we were part. In Geneva, too, we took each day as our measure of time. We neither looked forward to, nor planned for, anything weeks or months ahead.

Back in Cambridge that protection fell away, leaving us exposed – as it always does on return from even the best of holidays. On the one hand, there were all the usual matters associated with our normal way of life at home that had to be dealt with. Children had to be fed and cared for, bills paid, Tim taken to school every morning and collected in the afternoon, school functions attended and my teaching commitments fulfilled. On the other, the preoccupation with the fluctuations in Stephen's condition continued to be just as harrowing as in Geneva and the hospital visiting consumed just as much time. My teaching hours had to be squeezed into the middle of the day, after leaving the hospital in the morning and before returning in the afternoon. It was only because my parents and Jonathan operated a comprehensive back-up system and many friends, particularly Tim's godmothers, Joy and Caroline, generously offered help in some productive or reinforcing way or other that as a family we survived this most exacting and exhausting period.

Keeping the home going while ministering to Stephen in hospital was by no means the full extent of my responsibilities. There were many pieces of unfinished business to be sorted out, not least the future of Stephen's book. It existed in a first manuscript draft which had been accepted by the publishing house of Bantam. As soon as the contract was signed in the summer of 1985, Peter Guzzardi, a New York editor, started working on the manuscript and his letter outlining preliminary criticisms was waiting for Stephen, though he was in no fit state to read it, on our return to England. It was no surprise that the manuscript was not publishable in its draft form as many of the concepts it contained were far too abstruse for popular consumption. I myself had read it and marked in red the passages where the science was incomprehensible. Understandably, the publishers pointed out that every equation would halve the sales. In his present circumstances, it was unlikely that Stephen would be able to effect the fundamental change of tone and the expansion required himself. Unless the manuscript could be amended by a ghost writer, we might have to return the advance paid by Bantam just before the beginning of the summer holiday. I approached one of Stephen's former students, Brian Whitt, to enlist his help with the rewriting but I put all other unpalatable considerations on that score temporarily to the back of my mind since there were others, much more pressing, in the forefront.

As Stephen began to make progress and was transferred to the neurological ward, his eventual return home was mooted as a distinct possibility by all the participants in the drama, from the senior consultant downwards. It was not at all clear how this was to be achieved since, plainly, Stephen would need specialist nursing twenty-four hours a day. Our previous relaxed system of support by psychiatric nurses at specific times and for limited periods would no longer suffice, nor was their psychiatric training adequate to deal with what was essentially a critical medical situation. The tracheotomy operation which had saved Stephen's life also brought its own concomitant risks because the tracheotomy tube, inserted in his throat, had to be cleaned regularly by a sort of mini-vacuum cleaner to bring up the secretions which perpetually accumulated in his lungs, and the device itself was potentially a source of damage and dangerous infection. He was frighteningly frail and vulnerable. It was impossible to imagine a more extreme disability of the body.

Twenty-four-hour nursing for 365 days a year would cost an

enormous sum; predictably, only a tiny fraction of this expense would be borne by the National Health Service. Funding would have to be found privately and nurses engaged privately. The philanthropic foundations that had funded nursing for a couple of hours a day would be unlikely to pay for twenty-four-hour nursing at a minimum of between thirty and forty thousand pounds a year on an indefinite basis.

Then, at that most critical time, a message arrived from Kip Thorne in California. The news of Stephen's illness had travelled far and fast, thanks to Judy Fella's concerned intervention and, in response, Kip advised me, as a matter of urgency, to make a representation to the John and Catherine MacArthur Foundation, an American philanthropic organization based in Chicago. In Kip's opinion, there was a chance that the MacArthur Foundation might be prevailed upon to make a large grant on the scale needed for permanent nursing for Stephen if the case were well presented. Murray Gell-Man, the particle physicist, was on the board of the Foundation and Kip was sure that he would encourage the other directors to give our case a fair hearing, although there was some uncertainty as to whether the Foundation would sanction a grant outside the United States. Speed was of the essence since their next meeting was but a few weeks away.

I had no practice in writing begging letters but whatever reluctance I might otherwise have felt about such an exercise evaporated in the face of the overwhelming need. I put down all the information which I considered appropriate and which might influence the committee, not omitting to mention that Stephen had been a frequent visitor to the United States and had received many honorary degrees there. I also included photographs, taken in happier times, of smiling family groups. It was essential to assure the Foundation that any grant donated would be handled by a team of professional accountants, so my next task was to negotiate with the University authorities to persuade them to administer the fund on our behalf. The negotiations were both complex and time-consuming, although the good-will demonstrated was encouraging.

The need to set up a private nursing scheme was the more pressing since certain aspects of the treatment Stephen was receiving in hospital were less than satisfactory. On the intensive care ward, he had received the full attention of the specialist nurses. The situation changed when he went on to one of the neurological wards. If the ward sister was generally cheerful and competent, some members of her staff appeared to be much less so. There were far fewer of them in proportion to the number of patients than in intensive care, but sometimes their lack of continuity alarmed me, particularly since many of the patients were in a vegetative state, unable to protest, think or even speak for themselves.

One nurse in particular appeared to take advantage of that state to mete out treatment that Stephen and I considered was less than human. She was on duty when I arrived for an afternoon visit. Stephen, now sitting up in his wheelchair, was grimacing and squirming in discomfort while the young nurse, totally impassive in expression, busied herself about the room, deliberately – or so it seemed – ignoring his urgent need to pee. I helped Stephen myself and sent the nurse out of the room. That was her usual attitude, Stephen explained, quivering with anger. She always ignored his needs when she was on duty. He did not trust her and was afraid of what she might do or omit to do. I could see what he meant. In her impervious expression and blank, pale blue eyes I sensed a chill hint of sadism. There was little redress except to get Stephen home, and that meant sorting out all the problems associated with twenty-four-hour nursing as quickly as possible.

That Stephen was able to protest about the nurse's behaviour was thanks to a miraculous piece of equipment which had arrived out of the blue for his use. We, the family, students and friends had done as much as we could to make him comfortable: we had tried to keep the rota of attendance constant with no more than a gap of a few minutes here and there, and I had bought a television for his room. Nothing could compensate for the terrible loss of the power of speech, however, and just when that loss appeared depressingly irremediable, the new means of communication arrived unforeseen and unannounced.

In fact it was the result of Judy Fella's tireless efforts behind the scenes. She recalled having seen a feature about communication for the severely disabled on the BBC science programme, *Tomorrow's World*, and, after a global search for information, she managed to locate the British inventor of the equipment that had been featured. She brought him and his invention – a set of electrodes which when attached to the head could measure rapid eye movement – to the hospital, and persuaded the Cambridge-based computer firm Acorn to contribute the necessary computer free of charge. Stephen balked at the intrusive discomfort of the electrodes attached to his temples, but when one of his students adapted the mechanism to a hand-held control box, he was more willing to experiment with the device.

The computer was loaded with a programme which combined dictionary and phrase-book. Using the control, the operator could scan the screen for the words he wanted to use: as he clicked on each one, it would take its place in the sentence which was forming in the lower part of the screen where the observer could read what Stephen was wanting to communicate. Frequently used phrases could be incorporated complete and verbal endings could be added to infinitives as required. Initially it was a slow, laborious and silent way to communicate, requiring patience and concentration both of the operator and the observer. I found that, given one or two words to point me in the right direction, I could often interpret Stephen's thoughts telepathically and save him the bother of tapping them all out, though often he insisted on writing out the whole sentence to give himself practice. Once his hand and finger muscles had recovered some movement, the new device absorbed much of the tedium of that final period in hospital. Painstakingly, he began to master the novel technique which allowed him once more to reach beyond the drab surroundings of his hospital room and make contact with the outside world. He could begin to talk to his students about physics again and to experiment with writing, as well as directing his own medical care.

Having set the wheels for raising money in motion, Laura Ward and I embarked on the search for nurses. Neither of us had any experience in interviewing or employing staff, least of all nurses. I trusted that the various social service departments, in the hospital and the community, would give us support and advice in this process. Many social workers and nursing officers called and sat chatting and drinking coffee while they talked about their pet animals. The amount of useful information I gleaned from them could have been consigned to the back of the proverbial postage stamp. Laura and I were left to advertise and engage nurses and then set up a working rota of three eight-hour shifts, as best we could.

Laura repeatedly placed advertisements in the local newspaper. She dealt with the responses initially, asking for references which she followed up. As time was short, we decided to interview all the candidates who showed any suitability before receiving the responses to our requests for references. They all seemed plausible, likeable even, and I was in a hurry to set up the nursing system with as many nurses as possible so that Stephen could come home. I assumed that nurses were by nature dedicated and idealistic and that I could trust them. I explained the situation as best I could and made it clear that, although we wanted Stephen to be able to live at home, it was important that the home, also the home of three children, should not be turned into a hospital. I expected to treat nurses as guests in my house and in return I assumed that they would respect our right to privacy.

It transpired that even among the people we had interviewed and liked, my preconceptions of idealism and service were not always well based. When the references started trickling in, we had to erase many of the names we had thought to employ. Some were said to be slovenly, others unreliable, a few even criminal. How was it, we wondered, that there was no central control over the movements of the latter when the jobs in home nursing for which they would be applying would almost all, by definition, take place in vulnerable and delicate circumstances? We were still left with a handful of good candidates even after eliminating the undesirables but, alas, when Laura wrote to the promising applicants offering them work, a depressing number either declined to reply at all, or replied saying that they had found other jobs or that they did not think the situation suitable. To our own deep dismay, there were some eminently suitable people whom we had to turn away, on the advice of Stephen's doctors, because of their lack of training in tracheotomy technique.

The alternative was to employ agency nurses. The severe disadvantage of these was that the essential element of continuity would be lost: a different nurse at every shift could only add to the considerable frustrations which Stephen, and the rest of us, were bound to experience. Equally prohibitive was the financial aspect: agency fees, over and above the nurses' pay, would fritter away the MacArthur grant in no time at all. The money had been approved, despite some understandable suspicion on the part of the Trustees about the role of Britain's much vaunted National Health Service. Why, they had wanted to know in their ignorance, was Stephen's care not covered by the NHS? I had to choose my words carefully in explaining how the American-inspired monetarist policies of the Thatcher government – which had been in power for the whole of Tim's lifetime – were destroying our already overloaded free Health Service. The truth was that in encouraging a new self-seeking materialism, those policies were destroying not just the Health Service and our educational system but the very fabric of society itself. Indeed, Mrs Thatcher had denied the existence of society: for her it consisted of nothing more than a set of individuals with no sense of common purpose. It was an inopportune time to be ill, unemployed, very young, elderly or otherwise socially disadvantaged. Disproportionate amounts of money were pouring into the pockets of the so-called yuppies, the stockbroker class in their early twenties who flocked on to the floor of the Stock Exchange and whizzed about London in Ferraris and Lotuses while in other parts of the country, the destruction of the manufacturing base was leading to wholesale unemployment. The money at the disposal of the yuppies made a mockery of academic salaries and of those of many other dedicated professional people.

A couple of months later, Laura Ward fell seriously ill and had to leave. She had stretched her capacities to the utmost in helping to cope with our situation and had shared much of the intense stress and pressure, always positively and efficiently. By great good fortune, Judy Fella, who had already given so much unstinting help, was willing to resume her old post as Stephen's secretary until a full-time replacement could be found. Judy was more circumspect than I in selecting nurses, urging caution in the face of my impatience to bring Stephen home. She was wary even of some of the nurses whose written credentials appeared to be impeccable but such was my desperation to be able to bring Stephen home, I had to take nurses as I found them during the recruitment process, trusting still to the honourable calling of the profession. In the circumstances, I refused to listen to gossip which, in any case, might be maliciously inspired, and if a prospective employee struck me as reliable and efficient and otherwise appeared to come from a dependable background – the mother of a family, say, or a church-goer, I would gladly be inclined to trust her.

During the month of October, I brought Stephen – with a hospital nurse in attendance – home from the hospital each Sunday afternoon. It was a delicate, worrying undertaking. Sometimes the change of atmosphere would frighten him and precipitate choking attacks. He was still very weak and coughed a great deal. The mini-vacuum cleaner was often in use, clearing the sputum from his chest. I had a horror of that mechanism; its brutal functioning and its revolting noise evoked a torture chamber. Sometimes we would have to return to the hospital before the afternoon was out because the strain was too great; occasionally he would relax and enjoy being at home, although I sensed that he found the outside world intimidating after three months' incarceration. In those three months of crisis, his indomitable instinct for survival had stubbornly maintained its hold on life. Now everything looked strange and unfamiliar to him, as if he could not trust what he saw. Part of him wanted to re-enter the flurry of unpredictable normality, part of him wanted the predictable security of the hospital. Nevertheless a date, Monday, 4 November, was set for his discharge.

In those three months since early August, I had escaped for just one evening's respite from the harrowing routine in order to attend the London debut of the Cambridge Baroque Camerata on 1 October. The evening was warm after a hot, sunny day, giving London a carnival atmosphere in the midst of which I felt alien and uncomfortable. The concert, played to an appreciative audience, went well, though the atmosphere lacked the buzz of excitement which attended the orchestra's full houses in Cambridge. It was a mystery how Jonathan had succeeded in putting it on at all, since his every spare moment had been spent either in the hospital looking after Stephen or at West Road looking after the family. Unruffled, he had calmly pursued his own activities – organization, administration, practising and rehearsing – late into the night ensconced in his own little house. As he performed and directed, always with an unassuming simplicity and understated elegance of style, there, beneath the lights on the stage of the Queen Elizabeth Hall, no one could have guessed at the pressures of the preceding weeks. I was glad to be in London to witness his success, yet I was smitten with guilt at having left Stephen forlornly behind in hospital, sitting out of doors in the sun on a bare patch of ground which apologetically called itself a garden.

By the end of October, the situation was different: Stephen was much stronger but I was completely exhausted. I had developed chronic asthma and I slept badly, increasingly dependent on sleeping tablets which kept me in a fog of drowsiness for the best part of the next day. I was also subject to welts which came and went, producing sore tingling spots on the palms of my hands and in my mouth. All these were, of course, nothing more than the symptoms of severe stress. The doctors recommended a break, even if only a weekend, before Stephen's return home. It was as if they knew something that I was not aware of.

In September, Robert had left Cambridge to spend his gap year in Scotland. He went to live with the Donovans outside Edinburgh and started working on the shopfloor at Ferranti, where he learnt basic engineering techniques under the eye of an exacting foreman. Eventually he moved into digs in Edinburgh. It was not an easy life for an eighteen-year-old and I was afraid that he was not looking after himself properly.

The last weekend before Stephen's return home – which also happened to be the first weekend of half-term – was an opportune moment to get away, to benefit from a change of air and routine, an opportunity to calm my stinging nerves and to see Robert's circumstances for myself. I was comforted to find him in good form; the Donovans were kindness itself and Edinburgh was at its glorious, autumnal best. Three days, however sunny and bright, however clear and crisp, however stimulating with new sights and sounds, however reassuring in the warm presence of old friends, was scarcely long enough to erase the incessant, intense, traumatic strain of the past three months. Not three days or months or even three years could have prepared me, or I suspect anyone else, physically and mentally for what was yet to come.

CHAPTER FORTY-SIX

Mutiny

STEPHEN DID INDEED return home – in the early afternoon of 4 November. It was like bringing a new baby home from hospital. There reigned a sense of excitement tinged with nervousness, a protective fear lest the helpless, fragile being might suddenly cease to draw breath within moments of entering the house. Stephen, too, was tense and nervous, suspicious of the competence of the nurses engaged to care for him and anxious about every speck of dust in the atmosphere which might upset his breathing. He had little respect for the intelligence of other people at the best of times. Now, at the worst of times, he was inclined to regard them all as morons. His fears were often warranted, but not altogether for the reasons one might have supposed.

The nurse who came that first afternoon was herself unwell; she was little more than an elderly waif and although she fulfilled her duties admirably, she rang afterwards to say that she would not be able to come again as the strain of looking after the patient was too great for her. This was a bitter blow because that particular nurse had been booked for many of the twenty-one weekly shifts. There were others like her, pleasant, well-meaning people who could not cope with the stress. Agencies were the only recourse, whatever the cost. For the next few weeks, as Judy and I tried to shore up the collapsing rota with a frenzied round of advertising, interviewing and instructing of prospective candidates, the agency nurses were of varying degrees of competence. In fairness, these nurses probably had little advance notice of what would be expected of them.

Never were Stephen's worst anxieties – and mine – more fully justified: a different nurse came on every occasion. Although generally they were well intentioned and well qualified, none of them easily understood what was required. Either Jonathan, if he were with us, or

I, spent as much time repeating the same instructions over and over again as we would have spent looking after Stephen ourselves. Some never mastered the angle of the cup to prevent tea from dribbling down his front into the tracheotomy tube or onto his clothes, some did not chop his food into small enough morsels, others mashed it to an unacceptable purée. Some tried to give him his pills in the wrong order, some jogged his hand on the joystick of the wheelchair, sending him off into a spin, others made a complete shambles of the bathroom routine. Despite their medical experience, many were terrified of the tracheotomy tube in his throat and were nervous of using the suction unit.

Very rarely did the same nurse come back twice. When occasionally one of them was brave enough to cross the threshold for an encore, I greeted him or her as a long-lost friend in my relief at not having to repeat the whole procedure until I was sick of the sound of my own voice. I tried hard to be patient, reassuring and welcoming but my nerves were on edge, bristling with suppressed frustration, worry and dejection. Stephen's frustration was understandable, of course, and he made no attempt to conceal it.

If the daytime routine verged on the impossible, at night the problems were of a different order. Once in bed, Stephen no longer had the use of his computerized means of communication and was again deprived of speech. There were just two devices to help him. One, an alphabet frame, must have been the stock in trade of occupational therapists in the Dark Ages. The alphabet, in groups of large letters, was displayed around a transparent frame: Stephen was supposed to fix his eyes first on a group of letters, then on an individual letter within that group to spell out his needs letter by letter. The attendant was supposed to follow his eye movements and construct his meaning from them. The device demanded extraordinary patience and remarkable powers of deduction from all concerned. I tried to simplify the procedure by developing a short-hand code so that Stephen only had to focus on one letter for his meaning to become apparent. Either my code got lost in the muddle in his room, or the nurses thought they could do better, in any event, my invention did not last long.

The other device, which eventually superseded the alphabet frame and marked a considerable technological advance over it, was a buzzer. All night Stephen would hold the control in his hand, in much the same way as he held his computer control by day, and would exert pressure on it to illuminate a small box where any one of a limited number of commands would appear in sequence on a panel to indicate his needs – whether he needed suction, whether he wanted to be turned over, whether some part of his body was uncomfortable, and so on.

For a long time, even when he was in good health, it had been difficult to settle his rigid limbs comfortably in bed, and now that he was seriously ill, the process took most of the night. In those early months I would stay with him until I was confident that he was well settled since I knew that he was afraid of being left with an unfamiliar nurse. Then at two or three in the morning I myself would fall into bed, often to be woken soon after by the night nurse who found that she could not cope alone.

Quite apart from the day-to-day and night-to-night problems, the months after Stephen's return were marked by many other life-threatening dramas. These usually occurred late at night when the tracheotomy tube either blocked off or came unstuck. While the nurse tried to clear or adjust it, I would dial through to the intensive care unit in search of the doctors who were versed in the technique of changing it. A dash to hospital and endless hours waiting in the casualty department would follow, until a new tube was inserted and Stephen could breathe again. Since our last student helper, Nick Warner, a cheerful Australian, had left in the summer and had not been replaced, Jonathan slept in the upstairs room so that he could look after Tim and take him to school first thing in the morning when I was still recovering from the disturbances of the night.

It was fortuitous that Robert had left home just before Stephen came out of hospital. Robert's room, large and airy at the front of the house, was quickly converted into a room for Stephen. It was particularly suitable because it had a washbasin and adequate cupboards for nursing and medical equipment, of which we received regular, massive deliveries. There was also plenty of space for an orthopaedic bed, bins, computers, desks, armchairs, all sorts of other paraphernalia and, of course, the wheelchair.

This last item was becoming ever bulkier and heavier. The computer equipment which Judy had acquired for Stephen when he was in hospital had been superseded by a more sophisticated version, sent from California. The new computer had the added advantage of a voice synthesizer so that Stephen could be heard to speak the sentences that he typed up on the screen. No matter that the synthesized voice sounded unnervingly like a Dalek: Stephen was once again endowed with the power of speech. David Mason, the husband of one of the nurses, was a skilled computer engineer. He set to work to adapt the computer and add the several parts to the wheelchair so that Stephen would no longer be desk-bound but could carry his voice with him wherever he went. The weighty computer and voice-box were strapped on to the back of the chair and the screen was attached to the frame where Stephen could see it. Once, some time later, when we happened to come across an industrial weighing machine, we levered Stephen and all his contraptions on to it. The weight of the chair, batteries, computer, screen, various cushions and occupant amounted to 130 kilograms.

There were recurring crises when the newly invented mechanism developed teething troubles, just as there were recurring crises with Stephen's own state of health. If David Mason were not called round as a matter of urgency at all hours of the day, then it was our faithful friend John Stark, the chest consultant, or long-suffering Dr Swan or another duty doctor from the surgery who would be summoned at all hours of the night. Physiotherapists were called out at weekends and our local chemist was roused after closing hours. In short, we floundered in an endless state of crisis throughout November into December, with its usual round of school carol services and other preparations for Christmas. We were again piloting our boat across troubled waters. These uncharted waters were shrouded in darkness and we had on board a potentially mutinous crew.

The lion's share of my energies and my time were devoted to Stephen. I drank every sip of water with him, ate every spoonful of food and breathed every gasp of air. When my strength failed, Jonathan shared the burden, quietly and always reliably available in the background. What little time and energy I had left I gave to my children and to my pupils. Teaching was my one opportunity to concentrate for a few hours a day on other matters – the time when language and literature could fill and enliven the vacuum created by despondency and crushing weariness. The pupils of that year became very special to me. One in particular, Ana Malison, the daughter of Russian–American parents who had settled in Madrid, showed exceptionally mature understanding and perception for a teenager. From her I received the fulsome appreciation which strengthened my resolve to continue teaching, come what may, so long as I was capable of doing the job properly. It was essential to my own ragged mental health.

Stephen did not view my modest attempts to keep up my intellectual interests in the same light. He had suffered – and was still suffering – a horrendous ordeal and was still very frightened; like Lear, he was child-changed – into a child possessed of a massive and fractious ego. On the one hand, his pathetic physical state bespoke all too clearly his need for constant loving reassurance; on the other, he made himself inaccessible, barricading himself behind defiance and resentment. From being authoritative in the past, he became authoritarian, even – or perhaps especially – with those of us who had been through so much with him. He was indignant at some of the decisions I had been forced to take in family matters during his period in hospital and would insist on his rights as a matter of principle. It was natural that he would want to reassert himself but no one disputed his right to be king of the universe, master of the house and father of the children. It was difficult therefore to understand why he seemed to want to make the daily routine even more fraught than usual by means of various disobliging ploys, often in the evening stationing his wheelchair obstructively between the cooker and the table or in the morning, between the front entrance and my teaching room when my students arrived. He insisted on his right to go anywhere he chose in the house – for example into Lucy's bedroom, her only haven, pursued by a bevy of inquisitive nurses. This intrusion was resented by fifteen-year-old Lucy whose teenage years were being turned upside down by her father's illness.

Lucy and I were very close companions. Her open character, brimming with enthusiasm, and her independent spirit were endless sources of strength and encouragement even in the depths of despair. She and I talked at length, discussing all manner of subjects from perfume, clothes and make-up, to literature, art, the theatre and personal relationships without any constraint. It was obvious over the following months that in our extraordinary situation Lucy needed space to herself. Her room had to be respected as her sanctuary, away from the constant commotion caused by nurses and wheelchairs. It was not that she did not want to see and talk to her father: she was as intensely loyal to him as she was to me but she longed for privacy, away from the prying eyes, listening ears and gossiping tongues of the nursing staff.

I recounted my dismay at Stephen's apparently unreasonable attitudes to a doctor friend, Rachel Lewinsohn, another of those remarkable ladies who in mid-life had taken up medicine. Rachel, with the typical outspokenness of a Jewish matron, replied, 'Just think, Jane, what he has been through! He nearly died, he was kept alive by machines and drugs. Can you tell me that all that would have no effect on his brain? There must have been times when his brain was starved of oxygen and it's more than likely that that shortage caused minute, undetectable lesions which are now affecting his behaviour and his emotional reactions, although, thankfully for him, his intellect is intact.'

Meg Cleghorn, the superbly comforting and perceptive wife of Stephen's schoolfriend Bill, was herself a senior nurse in a hospice for the victims of incurable degenerative diseases in Hitchin where she and Bill and their family had set up home after their move from Yorkshire. Her long experience in treating neurological patients had convinced her that the families of those motor neurone patients struck down in the prime of life rather than in old age were the ones who were subjected to most anguish. In one sense these opinions and advice were comforting. They implied that Stephen was not completely responsible for his actions and that it was not just his excess of innate egoistic energy that was determining his lack of consideration, but the combined effects of motor neurone disease, pneumonia and the recent trauma. Rachel's opinion, however, bore little weight elsewhere, even in medical circles, since it was apparent to all that intellectually, Stephen had come through hell unscathed.

That, nevertheless, was not the full story. Judy, Lucy and I thought that Stephen's tendency to self-assertion was being fed by his nurses. I might as well have voiced my concerns about keeping the home a happy place for all the family and not allowing it to become a hospital to a concrete wall, for all the impact they had on some of the nursing staff. They appeared to be indifferent to the fact that the house was also home to a shy, sensitive six-year-old and a spirited, intelligent teenager immersed in O-level studies. One of the very first nurses on the rota started turning the whole house inside out as soon as she stepped through the front door. Fretting at the lack of sterility, she scrubbed everything in sight, trying to bring our home up to intensive care standards, while Eve, who continued to give valiant service, washing, cleaning and hoovering daily, watched incredulously, then declared, 'She's daft!' Finally the new broom must have decided that it was too stressful to work in such an unhygienic atmosphere and left.

There were, it has to be said, nurses who were dedicated and perceptive. Generally these were older women – or men – trained in a more disciplined age, people who had achieved a higher level of education, or people who were no strangers to problems themselves. Their names shine like lights in that darkness: in particular I think of Pam Benson, the disciplined Irish girl whose regular job was with one of the transplant teams at Addenbrooke's and who had read modern languages in Dublin before becoming a nurse; quiet, shy Theresa; Jenny, hard-working and down-to-earth; Elizabeth Hughes, analytical, intelligent and practical; Jean Benfield, wise and far-sighted; Gilbert Dodd, much-travelled, elderly, devoted, uncomplaining, and later Joan Godwin, utterly reliable and, like Jean Benfield, a stalwart of the old school. There were others of similar ilk who promised to be as dependable but who, in the event, found the physical strain too much for them.

There was also the gentle, softly spoken Mr Johaheer, known to all and sundry as Mr Jo. He was extremely popular and not only for his calm professional skills: he was also an excellent cook. Sometimes on a Sunday evening he would treat us to a homemade curry. Our taste buds would tingle in impatient anticipation as his chicken tikka masala marinated for hours in its colourful aromatic sauce and then simmered slowly in the oven. By contrast, the third stage, when the dish came to the table, was over with frustrating speed. Unable to restrain their eagerness any longer, the family demolished that most fragrant of recipes in double-quick time as if to make up for the methodical slowness of its preparation.

Obviously few nurses could compare with Mr Jo. Undoubtedly there were those who genuinely tried to do their limited best and for whom one had to be grateful, but my cruelly lasting impression was of those for whom the words 'professional discipline' and 'understanding' meant little and for whom self-interest was paramount. Our tales of the harrowing months before their arrival meant nothing to them, nor did they give a moment's thought to the stress we lived under all the time. A seven- or eight-hour shift might be stressful, but the nurse who performed that shift could go away to recover in her own home. That was not an option open to members of the family.

One common problem was that nurses, like social workers before them, tended to be easily deceived by our surroundings. Because we lived in a large house, they supposed we must be super-rich. Discreet attempts to explain that we rented our flat from the College fell on deaf ears. None were deafer than those of a nurse who misread the combined impressions given by our outward circumstances and Stephen's professorship as evidence of wealth and power. Late one evening she came to me in the kitchen as I was putting out the breakfast things, and brazenly demanded that I obtain a mortgage for her from the University. I was not sure that I had heard correctly so asked her to repeat her request in front of Stephen who was already in bed. We went into Stephen's room where, standing beside the bed, she repeated what she had said. I apologized and explained that there must have been some misunderstanding; I had no influence with the University and was not in any position to obtain a mortgage on her behalf. Whereupon, at midnight, she started screaming and writhing, stamping and beating her chest, before whirling into a frenzied war-dance round Stephen's bed. I ran to the phone and rang Judy who came straight away. She smartly but tactfully removed the wailing banshee who stood screeching her protests and threats of litigation out in the drive while I tried to find a replacement.

Another nurse, a sad, lonely woman whom I befriended, soon turned out to be a dipsomaniac. She would arrive for her shift with her speech blurred, her gait unsteady and her breath smelling strongly of alcohol. I suspected that in the dead of night she was imbibing judiciously measured thimblefuls of liqueur from our modest assortment of spirits stored at the bottom of the kitchen cupboard. Stephen liked her, and in her lucid moments she was an excellent nurse, but Judy and I were scared that she might either sleep through her shift or catastrophically mishandle the equipment or medications. I also suspected that she was helping herself to more than just the alcohol. We were searching for ways to deal with the problem diplomatically when suddenly, to our great relief, she left of her own accord. The taxi driver who drove her to Heathrow happened by chance to be an acquaintance of Judy's. He reported back that the nurse had not only paid his fare – some £45 – in small change, pennies, 2- and 5-pence pieces – but had spent the whole journey regaling him with the intimate details of life in our household. I did not doubt that she had laced the story with many a fabrication of her own invention.

That nurse might well have been party to everything that went on under our roof because privacy was non-existent. It was virtually impossible to have a private, let alone intimate, conversation with Stephen – or anyone else for that matter – without first making an appointment and asking the nurse on duty to be so good as to leave the room for five minutes. She would then, of course, find good reason for fussing about, tinkering with the tracheotomy tube, adminstering more pills or cleaning a piece of equipment until finally, with ill-feigned curiosity and reluctance, she would step outside. Because of the scarcity of time and the slowness of communication, I got into the habit of preparing what I wanted to say to Stephen in advance. I hoped that by presenting him with a succinct and logical argument, I could simplify the matter, be it financial or family, under discussion. Stephen objected to this technique, implying that yet again I was denying him his rights. He would insist on returning to first principles and would dispute my reasoning at every stage, sure of the superiority of his own arguments. Thus minor matters became major issues and the optimistic frame of mind in which I had entered his room would quickly disintegrate into defeat and disillusionment at the negligible esteem in which my judgement and opinions were held.

As Stephen recovered his power of speech, I became nervously withdrawn again, unsure of myself and so uncertain of my opinions that I ceased to voice them. I was becoming as much the victim of psychological pressure, battered by circumstances and by people, as Stephen was the victim of illness. I observed this process in the full knowledge that it was happening, yet there was nothing I could do to bring it to a halt because it was part and parcel of the situation. I was caught in a trap and began to have nightmares two or three times a week. The nightmare was always the same: I was buried alive, trapped underground with no means of escape.

In a last-ditch attempt to stem the tide of insurrection, Judy and I decided to provide the the nurses with uniforms in response to a request from some of them who complained that their clothes were getting spoilt by splashes and spills of fluid. One of the more senior of them had access to a supply of second-hand white overalls and brought us a dozen or so. A white overall worn with a belt and buckle would look smart and official; the agency nurses always wore uniform so it seemed appropriate for ours to do so too. A uniform would also clearly draw a distinctive line between the nurses and the family and, we hoped, instil some sense of professional discipline. Stephen, however, protested. He did not want his nurses to wear uniform: he wanted to maintain the illusion that his attendants were just friends. Thereafter nurses had free rein to wear whatever they liked. Often the mode of dress and make-up adopted by some would have been more appropriate to a street-corner in Soho than the home of a severely handicapped Cambridge professor and his family.

Lucy soon became used to having the newspaper whisked from

under her nose by the duty nurse as she sat eating her breakfast before school in her O-level year. It would then be ceremoniously set up in Stephen's place to await his arrival some ten minutes later. Quickly, the rest of us became second-class citizens as if we, the family, were the lowest of the low, crouching on the bottom rung of a ladder, at the top of which the angels – the Florence Nightingales – administered to the deity – the master of the universe. In between there were the several echelons of students, scientists, computer engineers, all of whom were obviously more important than we were.

When one of the nurses, Elaine Mason, asked why I did not give up teaching and take up nursing, learning to use the suction machine so that I could look after Stephen myself, it seemed to be the final confirmation of the prevailing perspective: nursing was the highest calling and the patient's wishes were the only valid commands. What was the point of trying to answer a question like that? It had no connection with the philosophy of our former way of life and little in common with the vision of the way forward for the whole family that I was desperately trying to foster. We felt that such questions simply consigned the rest of us, who had no medical qualification or any desire to acquire them, to a despised obscurity where our role was to serve the great and the good of medicine and science.

The facility with which Elaine used her religion certainty to gloss over profound issues I found disconcerting. When she airily announced in Stephen's hearing that looking after him was easy, so much easier than bringing up her own two sons, I hardly liked to point out that she was nursing Stephen for only a couple of sessions a week. Such remarks were all too reminiscent of the Hawking attitude that I had encountered in the past. I was similarly disturbed by her reactions to other people's misfortunes – accidents, birth defects and deaths. It seemed that these were willed by God and should be accepted as such – even joyfully. As she was an efficient nurse and otherwise appeared to be warm and friendly, I tried to overlook the fundamental differences of outlook between us. I was inwardly frustrated, nonetheless, that yet again we were confronted with the assertion of absolutes which bore little relation to my experience of the deeper truths of Christianity.

In these circumstances, I found even greater solace in my attachment to St Mark's and the compassion of Bill Loveless. I listened to his sermons intently and also to those of his fellow preacher, a scientist and former missionary, Cecil Gibbons, who at an advanced age made it his duty to keep abreast of scientific developments and interpret them in a religious context. They both always had something pertinent and measured to say to me personally, whether about suffering, Man's place in Creation, or good and evil.

Under their guidance, I began to formulate my own simple philosophy about some of the stumbling blocks to faith, principally by understanding that free will is a prerequisite of the human condition. If belief in God were automatically decreed by the Creator, the human race would simply be a breed of automatons. There would be no evolution of thought, no motivation for discovery, no spirit of enquiry or sense of wonder, no freedom of choice. However in giving His whole Creation complete freedom, God forfeited the right to interfere in it. Consequently He had no power to prevent suffering, so much of which was provoked, directly or indirectly, by the human race itself. Evil, I reasoned, was often reducible, even if distantly and hazily, to human greed and selfishness – predatory animal instincts, dictated by nature for survival in a distant evolutionary past, long before the development of finer intelligence and the dawn of conscience. Conscience became our means of asserting our superiority over nature and instinct. Selfish, instinctive reaction, the root of evil, is outside the reach of God precisely because free will prevents His intervention. However loving His nature, God could not prevent suffering, but He could alleviate its effects by restoring hope, peace and harmony.

There was still the stumbling block of illness, degenerative, incurable, paralysing and devastating, which did not fit into this system – unless, that is, illness also sometimes happened to be the result, however remotely, of human fallibility, an error in research or treatment, in a chosen way of life or in the environment. If the cause of Stephen's illness was really a non-sterile smallpox vaccination given in the early 1960s, it might be accounted for thus and Stephen's courage in overcoming it could be seen to be divinely inspired. As for the present chaos, one could only hope that by keeping faith, by still trying to give of one's best, a brighter, calmer light would one day appear on the horizon.

On the administrative front, Judy was beleaguered. She would prepare an agreed rota of nursing shifts a month in advance, only to find, in the event, that her careful organization had been mysteriously overturned by persons unknown, and that the working rota bore little resemblance to the one she had prepared and distributed. Neither she nor I would have any idea whom to expect at any given time; the system would inexplicably break down and agency nurses had to be called in. Shattered and demoralized by all the unforeseen – and often unnecessary – complications which had accompanied our best efforts to enable Stephen to return to the family and the community, Judy and I called a series of meetings to try to settle various differences once and for all. Word had reached her indirectly that, quite apart from the interference in the organization of the rota, trouble was being whipped up among the staff on issues which had no relevance to our private nursing scheme.

The grants from the MacArthur Foundation came in six-monthly instalments. Every six months the University accountants would prepare a balance sheet to show the Trustees of the Foundation how their money had been spent, and I would submit a report on Stephen's health and care, together with another begging request for a further grant for the next half-year. In my second letter to the Foundation in March 1986, I explained how we had tried to engage our own team of nurses by placing regular advertisements in the local paper. I referred to the 'indescribable problems' that this method had occasioned, with the result that we had often had to resort to agencies – hence the considerable bills for agency nursing.

The grants, though generous, were only just enough to cover the bills. They certainly were not adequate to meet the demands which some mischiefmakers among the nurses were now devising and which Judy thought to answer by calling a first meeting. At that meeting I thanked those present for all their help and said how much it was appreciated. I went on to explain how the finances were obtained and organized in the hope that they might have a better idea of the difficulties we had experienced. I pointed out that the nursing bill came to at least £36,000 a year and was financed from the United States. I also emphasized that there was never any certainty that it would be renewed. It was therefore impossible to provide the nurses with anything more than casual employment on a part-time basis, which was strictly how the work was advertised. Consequently there was no scope for sickness pay, holiday pay, pensions or any of the other perks for which they had begun to agitate.

Thereafter a subdued audience concentrated their attention on requests for laundry baskets, towel rails, adequate lighting, shelving and suchlike, and repairs to the potholes in the driveway. Judy and I took the opportunity to distribute the UK Council of Nursing's code of conduct which Pam Benson had obtained for us and asked the assembly to give its fourteen clauses their attention. Those recommendations had as much impact as the concerns I had already voiced about keeping the home a happy and well-balanced environment for Stephen and the children alike, yet as far as we, the inmates, were concerned, there was no scope for movement or for doing things differently. This was our home, Stephen was living at home and needed nurses, however wilful, exploitative and manipulative they might be. We had to live with the situation and make the best we could out of it. Even with hindsight no other genuinely feasible solution has ever presented itself.

CHAPTER FORTY-SEVEN

Out of the Ashes

DESPITE THE MAYHEM wrought in the home by outside intervention, Stephen rose like a phoenix out of the ashes of 1985 and
by early December he was well enough to attempt short sorties to the
Department. At first I drove him there by car but, unless the weather
was bad, he was soon wheeling himself in his chair over his usual route
across the Backs, the only difference being that he was accompanied by
a nurse instead of a faithful student. All expeditions took longer than
before, involving much careful preparation of the patient before setting
out. Many essential accoutrements had to be strung on to the back of
the wheelchair, giving the whole contrivance an extraordinarily quixotic
air. Lumbering, cumbersome and festooned with eccentric appliances,
rather like a tinker's cart, the chair dwarfed its occupant who, small and
wasted, drove it fearlessly into battle to reassert his sovereignty over his
intellectual domain.

It was unwise to dwell for too long on the vulnerability of the
occupant, though it was difficult not to fall into the snare of sentimental
overprotection: many had fallen into that trap. Some of us had striven to
achieve a balance between a deep concern for the minimal, evanescent,
physical presence and a somewhat mischievous irreverence of the
immense psychological and intellectual power. This delicate balance, so
essential to a healthy family life where no one person should claim to
be more important than anyone else, had become impossible to maintain. At best, it entailed nerve-racking attention to every detail of
Stephen's care, yet a healthy scepticism at some of his more outlandish
and outrageous pronouncements. On a Sunday evening, for instance,
Jonathan would bring in the usual take-away curry. Mistrustful of the
ingredients of my carefully prepared, guaranteed gluten-free home-
cooking, Stephen would on Sundays resolutely consume a huge plateful

of curry, with never a thought as to the ingredients. The children and I considered this glaring inconsistency fair game for a little gentle teasing.

These were also occasions for wide-ranging discussions. Private conversation had become impossible but in the relaxed atmosphere of those Sunday evenings, sometimes too at Sunday lunch when Robert, who came back to study in Cambridge in 1987, would bring his under-graduate friends home for a square meal, questions of science and faith would form the basis of sustained, good-natured argument. Cecil Gibbons had pointed out in one of his sermons that scientific research required just as broad a leap of faith in choosing a working hypothesis as did religious belief. Stephen usually grinned at the mention of religious faith and belief, though on one historic occasion he actually made the startling concession that, like religion, his own science of the universe required such a leap. In his branch of science the leap of faith – or inspired guesswork – centred on which model of the universe, which theory, which equation, one chose as the most appropriate object of research. Then this, at the experimental stage, had to be tested against observation. With luck, the guess – or leap of faith – might, in Richard Feyman's words, prove 'to be temporarily not wrong'. The scientist had to rely on an intuitive sense that his choice was right or he might be wasting years in pointless research with an end result that was defini-tively wrong. Any further attempts to discuss the profound matters of science and religion with Stephen were met with an enigmatic smile.

Insensitive to the subtleties of our relationship and unable to distin-guish the mind from the body, some of the nurses, on the other hand, tended to smother Stephen in a blanket of sentimentality. This belied his strength of mind and undermined my attempts to keep the correct balance. For them he had become an idol, immune from criticism or even from the healthy scepticism which Iolanta and the other psychiatric nurses had generated. They seemed to concentrate on the calamity of the illness rather than the victory over it, kowtowed to the patient's every whim and interpreted any innocent bantering as a blasphemous insult to their idol.

I considered that the same sentimental mistake had been made earlier in 1985 by an artist commissioned jointly by the College and the National Portrait Gallery to paint Stephen's portrait. The paintings, unveiled that summer, all too clearly showed the pathos of the body, slumped disjointedly in the chair, but I thought they failed to show the willpower and the genius, conveyed with such persuasion in the set of the face and the light of the eyes. I regarded the portraits as a travesty and said so – to the exasperation of the bodies who had commissioned them.

In the early months of 1986, the light of determination returned to those eyes as Stephen recovered his mobility and with it his unassailable position in the Department. The effect of his period of illness was not unlike the effect that Newton's exile from Cambridge had had on his creativity when the University was closed because of the Great Plague in 1665. In the isolation of the manor house at Woolsthorpe near Grantham, Newton had found time for the contemplation and calculation needed to develop his theory of gravity. In those months when he was too weak to leave home, Stephen had learnt to use the new computer with the same single-minded motivation he had shown in memorizing lengthy equations when, in the late 1960s, he lost the ability to write.

Through the loss of his voice, he discovered that he had gained a much improved method of communication. He could converse with anyone, not just the small band of family and students as in the past, and he was no longer dependent on having a student at hand to interpret his lectures for him. By turning up the volume on the speaker, he could address an audience as effectively as, if not more so than, anyone else. His synthesized speech was slow because it took time to select the vocabulary, but there was nothing unusual in that since his speech had always been measured. Stephen had always taken time to think before speaking to avoid cliché or inanity and to ensure that the last word on any subject was his and his alone.

Not only was he empowered to express his own thoughts directly, deliver his own lectures and write his own letters, he was also able to work again on his book. His former student, Brian Whitt, had over the past months begun to help him with the methodical organization of the material and continued to help, particularly with diagrams and seeking out research material, but the project was now firmly back in Stephen's grasp. The book gave him the motivation to exploit the full potential of the computer and the computer gave him the means of writing a revised version of the manuscript, incorporating the suggestions of the American editor. It began to look as if the book might become a reality: not only should we not have to repay the advance, but we had, at long last, the prospect of financial security. The book might not make a fortune but it might bring in a regular supplementary income, heralding the end of nearly a quarter of a century of economizing.

At home I endeavoured to juggle my own interests, teaching, music and the children, with the tiresome demands of wayward nurses. With Judy's stalwart help, I fended off impending chaos by conducting weekly interviews with new candidates and by attending to the requests for improvements from those already on the rota. We sensed that we had become the scapegoats for the frustrations which the nurses could not vent on Stephen himself. I discussed our predicament with an old school-friend, Mary Douglas. Mary, the daughter of the orthopaedic surgeon in St Albans who long ago had attended to my broken wrists, had trained as a nurse herself. She had gone on to become a lecturer in nursing. She recognized the syndrome and could account for it, though she had no easy solution. 'Nurses, like soldiers, are trained to act, not to think,' she said. 'If there is a patient needing treatment, their first duty is to that patient to the exclusion of all else. They act at an intensely physical level which does not involve the intellect. Imagination is not a quality that is prized in nursing.' This information certainly clarified the problem but offered scant comfort since it implied that nurses operated at the opposite end of the philosophical spectrum from the rest of us, and however much we might try to compromise, they, by definition, were unable to do so.

Meanwhile Stephen celebrated his return to normality. In the immediate short term, this took the form of a visit to the pantomime for his birthday and the College ladies' night two days later. In the long term, he was already planning his travels for the forthcoming year, rashly undaunted by the Geneva experience. Paris and Rome were on his itinerary for the autumn, to be preceded by an experimental trip abroad in June, to an island off the Swedish coast for a conference in particle physics. How all this was to be achieved was another matter, especially since the dates for the Swedish conference coincided with Lucy's first O-level papers and I was reluctant to leave her at such a critical time.

In fact attention shifted dramatically from Stephen to Lucy in the spring of 1986. In March, she set off with a school party to Moscow but not, as we parents had all expected, under the exuberant auspices of her Russian teacher, Vera Petrovna. It was Vera Petrovna's custom each year to dress up her charges from the Perse School, like Michelin men, in layer upon layer of clothing acquired from secondhand shops and jumble sales. In Moscow the girls would tour the city, visiting all Vera Petrovna's friends and relations, peeling off a layer of charitable clothing at each stop. In 1986, Vera Petrovna was inexplicably refused a visa for the first time, so other non-Russian speaking teachers had to accompany the party to Moscow and Leningrad. It was a potential catastrophe when Lucy fell ill in Moscow with only her own knowledge of Russian to help her. Terrified of being abandoned in a Russian hospital, she told no one how ill she was feeling; she ate nothing and clutched her stomach for ten days. When she arrived home, she was too ill with a high fever and excruciating abdominal pain to go anywhere except straight to bed. The doctor came and diagnosed acute appendicitis which required emergency surgery. So there we were again, walking the all-too-familiar corridors of Addenbrooke's Hospital, sitting on the same plastic chairs, drinking out of plastic cups and waiting for news, though of a dangerously inflamed appendix rather than a dangerously obstructed respiratory tract. We were told the next day, when Lucy was already recovering, that she was very lucky not to have had a burst appendix in Moscow. Even then, the hospital was reluctant to release us from its clutches: later that summer, Tim was also rushed there as an emergency. While picking blackberries in a friend's garden he had fallen while carrying a bowl and had slashed his right wrist on the broken china.

Nevertheless, the arrival of warmer weather alleviated some of the tensions associated with winter susceptibilities, allowing us to spread our wings again like frail butterflies emerging from the chrysalis. Life began to assume at least a thin veneer of its former hard-won normality, even if we were always conscious of the fifth column in our midst, never free to relax at home without suspecting, as in the Soviet Union, that the walls were listening to whatever we said. All future plans, all political preferences, all financial discussions, all reference to personal interests were best suppressed because whatever might be laughingly bandied around our dinner table I suspected would predictably be circulating within hours among the nursing team, their friends and relations, stamped with the certain authority of gospel truth and the subject of prurient speculation and gossip.

Defiantly determined that the home should still be worthy of that name, I tried to consign the complexities of full-time nursing attendance to the background, pretending, as we had so often in the past, that it was just another minor inconvenience. Once more we gave dinners and drinks parties for scientific visitors and participated in local activities at the schools and the church. Tim invited seventeen of his classmates to his birthday party where a good old-fashioned Punch and Judy show kept the guests enthralled for part of the time, while for the rest of the afternoon my father, in time-honoured tradition at the piano, kept them amused with musical games. There were also those matters which respected neither persons nor illnesses: the interminable bills had to be paid, again and again cars had to be serviced, and the letting house which I continued to administer had to be redecorated and prepared for incoming tenants.

As Stephen's health gradually improved, I ventured to take up some of my old activities, notably singing in the church choir and with Fairhaven Singers, the choral society which I had joined in the early 1980s. Since the latter's weekly rehearsals took place in Caius College Chapel by kind permission of the Dean, John Sturdy, this activity was quite compatible with Stephen's movements. Accompanied by a nurse, he would dine in the College while I sang – or tried to sing my way through an endless succession of colds – in the Chapel. Often he would call in there after dinner to listen to the final stages of the rehearsal and we would then proceed home together.

Lucy was adopting an increasingly independent lifestyle, which revolved more and more round the theatre and kept her out of the house. Even Tim was becoming more adventurous. Like Robert at the same age, he too had a close friend of a similar nature and similar interests in a thoughtful little boy, Arthur Bullard, who lived half a mile away. Like Inigo ten years earlier, Arthur was cared for by a nanny while his mother, a biological scientist, worked in a research laboratory. The two boys were as close as brothers: they went to school together in the mornings and in their free time after school they played together, building Lego houses and model railways. Wendy, Arthur's nanny, had often looked after Tim in the critical period of Stephen's illness so he was used to staying in Arthur's house. In the summer half-term of 1986, he went with Arthur, his mother and Wendy to stay in Germany with Arthur's father who worked in Heidelberg, leaving me free to oversee the final arrangements for Stephen's trip to Sweden.

Three nurses and a doctor were engaged for that expedition, stretching the MacArthur budget to its limit. It was however a profitable investment since Murray Gell-Man, one of the trustees of the

MacArthur Foundation, was also a participant at the conference and could see at first hand just how dire Stephen's circumstances were and just how much costly professional care was needed to sustain his life and *ergo* all-importantly his contribution to physics. In my next application to the Foundation in September of 1986, I was able to refer to our meeting with Murray Gell-Man and to report that Stephen's health, though much more stable, continued to require the same degree of professional nursing: I confidently predicted that it would be required indefinitely. Thereafter, the MacArthur Foundation agreed to support Stephen's nursing expenses on an indefinite basis. The trustees accepted my explanation that the National Health Service provided only an occasional morning visit from the district nurse to check the supplies, a weekly visit from the GP, one eight-hour shift out of the twenty-one, and additional help with bathing on a couple of mornings a week.

The small, traffic-free island of Marstrand off the west coast of Sweden proved to be the most delightful and suitable place for a convalescent physicist to flex his intellectual muscles and stretch his wings, ready to take flight for ever more ambitious projects. While Stephen and his comrades explored the universe by means of the trajectories of elementary particles, I relaxed, cherishing peace and solitude in the rocky coves and walking along the woodland tracks where daffodils still bloomed in June and the sun shone late into the night.

The freedom of those few days in Sweden was a rare luxury but one which just occasionally came my way thanks to the unexpectedly helpful intervention of Stephen's mother after the death of his father in March 1986. Stephen's father was not an easy patient in his final illness; the frustration of immobility was too burdensome for one who in earlier years had thought little of driving single-handed across Africa to enlist for service at the beginning of the Second World War, and who habitually in his late seventies would spend whole weeks camping and walking in the Welsh mountains. His funeral marked a sad end to a distinguished but inadequately recognized career in tropical medicine. I suspected that I was not the only person present whose feelings towards him were decidedly ambivalent. I admired him and respected him yet I found him disturbingly unpredictable. He could be sensitive and considerate, even appreciative; he could also be cold, harsh and distant.

After his death, Isobel's formerly stringent inflexibility appeared to mellow as she showed signs of greater liberality and compassion. She seemed anxious to share the stresses of our family life in a new way and became popular with the children for her coolly sardonic sense of humour and for her apparently easy-going nature which made few demands of them. She also showed a surprising and benevolent tolerance of my relationship with Jonathan, as if she had finally come to realize that he was not intent on destroying the family but was genuinely supportive of us all, including Stephen. Indeed she accepted the relationship to the extent that she offered to keep house in Cambridge from time to time so that we could escape, either, say, for a quick trip to the sea, or for a longer spell of summer holiday with Tim, sometimes with Lucy as well, under canvas somewhere on the Continent, usually in France.

I was grateful for her help and understanding. If I could reliably look forward to the occasional weekend or a couple of weeks' summer holiday away from the strains of a half-life in a house where I was on duty in every capacity for seven days a week for a minimum of forty-nine weeks a year, juggling all my roles, trying to be all things to all the inhabitants, I felt that I could summon the strength to continue, however onerous those duties might be. Then, like Persephone emerging from the Underworld, I could come out into the light and bask in the sun. Often we chose to camp, both to save money and to capture a gypsy sense of liberty which enabled me to rejoice in a precious freedom of movement and freedom from encumbrance, responsibility and care. Living in basic simplicity on a campsite, I could forget the restrictions and pressures of Cambridge. We could pretend that we were just any ordinary family from any ordinary background with a young son whose skin turned golden and whose hair was bleached in the sun as we built castles in the sand, played French cricket and taught him to catch a ball. Those were blissful weeks for all three of us, camping among the pines on the Atlantic coast of France, cooking on a *Gaz* stove, and listening to the wind rustling in the trees at night and blending with the roar of the sea. At the end of the allotted time, I returned without question to Stephen.

There were times when re-entry was difficult. Once, on arrival, the first thing I noticed was that Lucy's new bicycle had gone from the porch – in my absence, no one had bothered to lock the front door. Nonetheless, however much I might sometimes have longed for just a little more freedom, a little less duress, my place was in Cambridge with Stephen. Force of circumstance might have driven me into the morally un-comfortable position of being unfaithful but I would never be disloyal.

The situation that I dreaded most was finding myself forced to make a choice. Jonathan never asked me to do that.

In all fairness to Stephen and his mother and their methods of housekeeping, it should be said that even when I was at home, the front door was often left unlocked or even wide open. The nurses would come and go as they might in a hospital, heedless of the fact – frequently impressed upon them – that it was usual to keep the front door of a private house locked against the outside world, especially at night. We had learnt that lesson as a result of minor burglaries in the past. Fortunately, apart from the missing bicycle, the nurses' carelessness led to only minor disruptions: for example, late one evening when I was reading in bed, I heard a scuffling in the hall. Just as I came out of my ground-floor bedroom to investigate, two terrified-looking girls came hurtling down the stairs. They stared momentarily at me wide-eyed with fear and then ran out through the open front door into the night.

My parents were staying in our only upstairs room at that time. They had already gone to bed and had put out the light when their door opened and a female voice called, 'Neil, are you there?' Dad, dozing in a half-sleep, sat bolt upright in bed and, using one of his favourite exclamations, shouted out, 'What the policeman?' The two girls fled in fear of their lives only to meet me at the bottom of the stairs. Presumably, poor things, they had found themselves in the wrong house or the wrong entrance to the right house if in fact they were looking for one of the students who lived upstairs on the other side of the partition.

Having spread his phoenix wings in Sweden without mishap, Stephen was eager to use them again and again. In September, the travelling circus, which now included a young physics graduate as Stephen's personal assistant, set off for Paris for a conference at the Observatoire de Paris at Meudon where Brandon Carter worked. I was delighted to be able to spend time with Lucette, bringing her up-to-date on the events of the past year, and there I also discovered a new role for myself as chauffeur and interpreter for the party. As a result of overnight stops in Paris in previous years, I knew the layout of the city reasonably well and could take even the Place de la Concorde in my stride. I was pleased, too, to have an outlet for my linguistic skills instead of finding myself cast in the role of a mere hanger-on. I could even make a passable attempt at translating Stephen's scientific terminology for the press since his computer was no better at modern languages than its operator. At least the nurses could hear, if not see, that I was good for something.

Only a month later we found ourselves again in Rome where Stephen was to be admitted by the Pope as a member of the Pontifical Academy of Sciences, despite the heresies he was still preaching about the universe having neither a beginning nor an end. Tim came with us, as did the retinue of nurses and the young personal assistant whose responsibility it was to attend to the workings of the computer and the mechanics of Stephen's lectures. We tried to choose nurses whom we knew to be Catholic and who would appreciate the significance of the occasion. We were lucky in that two of the most reliable and pleasant nurses on the rota, Pam and Theresa, were both Catholic and were overjoyed to be invited. We needed three nurses, however, and not all were as keen as Pam and Theresa. It was only at the last minute that Elaine Mason agreed to come with us: she did so only on the understanding that she would not have to shake hands with the Pope as such a gesture would be against her principles.

The second visit to Rome was more formal than the first in 1981. The weather was better and so were the provisions made for us: we stayed in a much more comfortable hotel, closer to the Vatican. Special tours of the art treasures of the Vatican were put on for wives and children while the scientists conferred in the Renaissance headquarters of the Academy. The climax of the visit was an audience with the Pope to which all members of Stephen's party were admitted. With his hand gently resting on Tim's head, the Pope talked quietly to Stephen and me pressing our hands and giving us his blessing. He then shook hands with the others; carried away by the power of the occasion none of them, of course, resisted. I was moved by the genuine warmth of his personality, the softness of his big hands and the holiness of the light in his bright blue eyes. I had no religious prejudices and had come to Rome with an open heart and mind. The Pope touched my heart and my mind, for, politics and dogma apart, I sensed that he sincerely cared about the people he met and kept them in his prayers.

Before leaving Rome we had a free day. As we had a car and a driver at our disposal, it seemed an ideal opportunity to drive out of Rome to visit the famous Tivoli Gardens at the Villa d'Este. The drive took longer than expected, and lunch, out in the autumn sun under a pergola of trailing vines, was a leisurely affair. After lunch, Tim and I went ahead to the Villa d'Este while the nurses administered to Stephen's needs. We strolled round the gardens playing hide-and-seek in the alleyways and running our hands under the fountains. At about a quarter past four, we climbed back up to the entrance to find out why Stephen had not joined us. He was sitting outside the entrance, fuming. When I found out why, I fumed as well. The gardens were to close at five. At half past four he was denied entry by an all-too-officious guard who would not even let him drive through to the terrace – which was all he would have been able to do in any case – for a panoramic view of the scenery. In some respects, it appeared that the Vatican was well in advance of this part of Italy which was fossilized in the sort of attitude towards the disabled that we had encountered in the National Trust in the 1960s. It was with great satisfaction that by contrast, the following year in Spain I noticed that attitudes to the disabled were civilized and helpful, although the hotel in Madrid where the booking had been made for us had a flight of steps inside the main door worthy of a Stalinist memorial.

Encouraged by the success of these tentative trips abroad within Europe, Stephen's aspirations knew no bounds. That December he soared away to the usual pre-Christmas scientific conference in Chicago to reclaim his place on the international circuit. These days he travelled with all the ceremonial due to an Arab sheikh, surrounded by hordes of minions, nurses, students, the personal assistant and the occasional colleague. He was attended by so much luggage that the chassis of the limousines that came to whisk him away to the airport often had difficulty in clearing the ground as they left the driveway.

The airlines were learning to treat Stephen with respect as a valued customer rather than an inconvenience, and had begun to accord him the sort of deference and assistance which, had it come twenty years earlier when I was struggling to look after Stephen and a tiny baby, might have spared me much unhappiness. Nowadays, my presence was almost superfluous on the international travels. Alone among so many people, I often took Tim along for companionship, just as Robert had been my small companion in days gone by. Tim fulfilled this role admirably. He loved air travel and, as the plane was gathering speed for take-off – my worst moment – he would gasp, 'Faster! faster!' dispelling my lingering fears with his contagious excitement. There was much that

I could teach him and interest him in on these travels, not least a grounding in the Romance languages. In Spain, with patience and a total lack of competitiveness, he taught me to play chess, something his father had never succeeded in doing.

CHAPTER FORTY-EIGHT

Maths and Music

ALTHOUGH EIGHTEEN MONTHS previously Stephen's chances of survival had been dismissed as negligible and the likelihood of his ever returning to work was discounted as unthinkable, he had confounded the pessimists yet again: he had survived and was back in the forefront of scientific research, theorizing on abstruse suppositions about imaginary particles travelling in imaginary time in a looking-glass universe which did not exist except in the minds of the theorists. His phenomenal resurrection and the consequent transformation of his prospects had galvanized him into even more intense industry. He was travelling again, terrestrially and universally, whenever and wherever he chose. He was at the centre of a court where his every word was law and where his courtiers bowed and scraped, adoring the ground beneath the wheels of his chair. Above all, just over a year since his first painstaking attempts to come to grips with the workings of the computer and his cautious return to the Department, he had completed the second draft of his book and was searching for a title.

His state of health continued to be extremely precarious, the subject of perpetual anxiety, but with all the aids of modern medicine and twenty-four-hour nursing care at his disposal, he virtually carried his own mini-hospital with him wherever he went. The nurses had learnt emergency techniques for changing the tracheotomy tube themselves and Stephen himself had taken charge of his medication as he reckoned, rightly, that he knew more about his case than any doctor. With the reassurance which his new improved circumstances and his own native intelligence afforded him, he pursued a hedonistic way of life, compensating ever more tenaciously for his disability, ever more assured of his own invincibility, mocking the untimely death whose grasp he had evaded.

Another nurse, Amarjit Chohan, had joined the rota. Tall, elegantly swathed in veils and saris, she came from an aristocratic family in the Punjab. By night she worked in the operating theatres at Addenbrooke's and by day and in her free time, she came to look after Stephen. She was used to commanding and, convinced of the superiority of her own approach to medicine, could behave with a patrician intolerance of lesser mortals. If she was also capricious at times, that was the price we had to pay for her dedication and her devotion, not only to Stephen but to us all as a family. In lonely exile from her own home, the victim of thinly veiled racism in a hostile foreign environment, she adopted us with a passionate intensity which soon began to upset the other nurses. Stephen was flattered to find himself the contested prize in the battles which the more volatile, less stable of his attendants fought for his favours and regarded their squabbles with bemused complicity. In Spain, Tim and I were astounded to watch while one of the nurses flirted unashamedly with a student and then actually resorted to fisticuffs with another nurse over some petty rivalry associated with nursing practice. Like distant thunder, rivalry between assertive personalities and alternative methods of care rumbled menacingly. It was an additional wearisome problem at home and a source of embarrassment in public. The ultimate catalyst which would consume us all by sparking off a blazing conflagration was as yet in its formative phase.

The big event of 1987 which, in among the imaginary trajectories and illusory universes, was exercising Stephen and all those caught up in his orbit, was the celebration of the tercentenary of the publication of Newton's *Principia Mathematica* with an international conference to be held in Cambridge. Stephen was firmly established at the centre of this event since the Newtonian tradition of leading cosmological research in Cambridge was consigned to his care as Lucasian Professor, and his work was the logical extension of Newtonian physics modified by the twentieth-century influence of Einstein's theory of relativity.

Isaac Newton was born in 1642, the year in which Galileo died and 300 years before Stephen was born. Although Newton's education as a schoolboy in Grantham and as a 'sizar' or servant-student in Trinity College was conservative, his major work, *Principia Mathematica*, was directly influenced by the mechanical and mathematical principles formulated by René Descartes, the great French philosopher of the seventeenth century. In Cambridge in the 1660s Descartes' theories provoked 'such a stir, some railing at him and forbidding the reading of him as if he had impugned the very Gospel. And yet there was a general inclination, especially of the brisk part of the University to use him' (from *Never at Rest: A Biography of Isaac Newton* by Richard Westfall). Newton took Descartes' principles home with him to Woolsthorpe Manor just after his graduation when the Great Plague closed the doors of the University of Cambridge. It was during that extraordinary period of creativity at Woolsthorpe that, at the age of twenty-three, Newton developed his three major discoveries, the calculus, the universal theory of gravitation and the theory of the nature of light.

Newton may have been 'brisk' in adopting Descartes' theories but was not at all brisk about publishing the results to which those theories had led him. *Principia Mathematica* was finally published in 1687 at the insistence of Samuel Pepys, the President of the Royal Society, and Edmond Halley, the young astronomer. In this *magnum opus*, Newton not only proposed the Law of Universal Gravitation, predicting the elliptical movement of the planets around the sun, but also developed the complicated mathematics of such motions. It is in *Principia Mathematica* that mathematics is harnessed to the service of physics and is rigorously applied to the visible universe.

Opticks, Newton's other great work, also developed in the Plague years but not published until 1704, described light as a spectrum of colours which in combination formed white light, but which could be split into seven component bands. Newton set up a prism in the path of a sunbeam and watched in amazement as the white light entering the prism split into the colours of the rainbow, producing not the rounded image of the sun on the opposite wall, but an oblong image where the seven colours from blue to red separated and fanned out 'according to their degrees of refrangibility'. If *Principia Mathematica* was inspired by the fall of an apple in the garden of Woolsthorpe Manor, the inspiration for *Opticks* was commercial, the improvement of the glass in the telescope, the instrument which Galileo had first turned on the heavens in the winter of 1609. Although Newton would have described himself as a natural philosopher, one might anachronistically designate him the first great modern mathematician and physicist.

The product of an unhappy childhood, Newton could be arrogant, dictatorial and not a little devious. He earned a reputation for vindictiveness in his treatment of the German philosopher, Gottfried Leibniz, who claimed to have discovered the calculus first. Newton's discovery of the calculus, or 'fluxions' as he called them, was prompted by his need in the mid-1660s for a general method of mathematical calculation, essential for dealing with the dynamics of planetary motion; it was put to immediate use in his theory of gravitation. Typically, however, he failed to publish his results and was then incensed when Leibniz published his independent findings in 1676.

There was nevertheless a humbler aspect of this embittered genius which appealed to me. When writing of his role in science, he speculated about his own importance, unsure of the significance of his discoveries: 'I do not know what I may appear to the world; but to myself I seem to have been only like a boy playing on the sea-shore, and diverting myself in now and then finding a smoother pebble or a prettier shell than ordinary, while the great ocean of truth lay all undiscovered before me' (from *Never at Rest*). 'Collecting pebbles on the beach' was the very image Stephen had used in 1965 to pour scorn on medieval studies.

Newton left no stone unturned on his particular beach. Although in the opinion of contemporaries he was said to be tone-deaf, he had in 1665 produced a theory of music. *Of Musick* was a fairly unremarkable treatise containing nothing new; in it he considered questions of tuning the scale and compared in logarithmic terms the just and equal temperaments. In *Opticks* he also used music to draw synaesthetic analogies between the seven notes of the diatonic scale and the seven bands of colour in the spectrum, basing those analogies on the breadth of the colour bands and the seven string lengths required to produce a scale.

The link between Newton's personal tastes and music was rather tenuous but, taken with all the other considerations, his theoretical interest was strong enough to justify putting on a concert of the music of his era to celebrate his tercentenary. Another of the considerations centred on the fact that Newton's genius was initially fired by the new approach to science coming from France, while with the Restoration of the monarchy in 1660, a wave of enthusiasm for the innovative French style in music came to England with Charles II and inspired the other great English genius of the period, Henry Purcell.

Since, together with the music of Bach and Handel, the music of Henry Purcell formed the basis of the Cambridge Baroque Camerata's repertoire, there could have been no more appropriate way of entertaining the delegates to the Newton tercentenary conference than with a concert of the music of that period. However much Stephen might have preferred it, a performance of the *Ring* cycle was hardly feasible.

The great advantage of such a prestigious occasion, to be held in Trinity College, was that it attracted commercial sponsorship for the orchestra and enabled Jonathan not only to put his musical enterprise on a secure footing at last, but also to make a recording of the programme, entitled *Principia Musica*.

Again, Stephen, Jonathan and I seemed to have struggled back to some sort of synthesis of our various talents and interests. Although the modern physics of quantum theory was completely beyond my ken, I could research Newtonian physics with some understanding of the concepts if not of the mathematics, and I could make myself useful liaising between the mathematical and the musical aspects of that summer's major endeavour. I enjoyed concert organization: it was hard work but, like teaching, it gave me a sense of self-worth. Jonathan's appreciation and gratitude were profuse and compelling to a psyche which had become used to regarding itself as inferior and whose endeavours were usually either met with disdain or ignored.

As well as the practical business of concert promotion, arranging the venue, the advertising, the ticketing and so forth, there was the intellectual stimulus of researching the background to the music for the programme notes. In pursuit of information about the late-seventeenth-century musical scene, I found myself inveigled back into the venerable precincts of the University Library where the frenetic tempo of daily existence slowed to a reverent, unhurried pace along lofty, tranquil corridors. My researches yielded surprising results: an eminent seventeenth-century musicologist and undergraduate contemporary of Newton's, Roger North, provided a welcome connection between Newton and Purcell. In his *Notes of Me*, written at the end of the seventeenth century, Roger North concluded that the great 'practical diversions' of his life have been 'reducible to two heads: one is Mathematicks and the other Musick'. His delight in mathematics culminated in 'Mr Newton's new and most exquisitely thought' hypothesis of light 'as a blended mixture of all colours'. As for music, there can be little doubt that 'the devine Purcell' afforded him the greatest pleasure as he came 'full saile into the superiority of the musicall faculty'.

As in days past, the hours I could spend in the University Library were lamentably scarce; there was time only for dashing in to check a few references before rushing out with a pile of books under my arm; no time for browsing through the treasury of literature and information which lined those shelves, no time to satisfy curiosity – not that I wanted to do so – by penetrating the forbidden sanctum of the tower which, rumour had it, housed the world's greatest collection of pornography. Before the Newton celebrations in July, there was a flurry of other activities to be fitted into the calendar so that nobody could complain that their interests were being overlooked.

The trap that I was falling into was not unlike the one that had ensnared me in California in 1974: each time Stephen gained a new independence or received a new honour, I felt bound to fling myself into a feverish round of activity as if further to justify my own right to existence. Now in the late 1980s, much, though by no means all, of the day-to-day physical burden of his care had ceased to be my responsibility, so I had to find other ways of proving my worth. Being a mother and a part-time teacher was not enough; I had to prove that I was still a worthy companion to a genius who set a pace which was impossible to sustain. Like Newton and his heavenly bodies, I was never at rest, propelled by an inner tension which pervaded every aspect of my being, physical, mental, intellectual, creative and spiritual. Above all, I had to prove to the world at large that we were still operating as a normal family. Apart from our academic activities, there were more parties and dinners, more work for charities, more concerts and conferences, more travel and more honorary degrees. Though other families led busy lives, I failed to notice that by comparison with theirs, ours was not normal; it was insane.

The more daring and the more death-defying Stephen's exploits became, the more I was brought face to face with my own inadequacies. My needs were insignificant by comparison with his, yet I depended for my survival on all the support and reinforcement that my myriad activities and my family, friends and Jonathan could give me. Stephen's nursing companions, gifted in neither insight nor imagination, viewed these pit-props, whose function was to shore up my fumbling efforts to keep the home a bright, wholesome place rather than a dark tunnel of despair, as counter to Stephen's interests rather than supportive of them. Soon I, and the rest of the family, felt that we should be apologizing for our presence, for our existence, for breathing the same air as the man of genius. Sometimes, when compatible nurses like Pam Benson were in attendance, it was possible to achieve a happier balance, but more often than not, it was Lucy who helped me keep a sense of perspective and Jonathan who encouraged me to retain some self-respect.

As Lucy was continuing with her Russian studies and was in her first year of A-levels, she came to Moscow again in May 1987 with Stephen and me for yet another conference at the Academy of Sciences. The Academy, like so many other Russian institutions, was quietly dropping its former 'Soviet' nomenclature in recognition of the dramatic change which was taking place in Russian society. In the days before the harsh reality of a clumsy, ill-managed, precipitate conversion to a free market economy had begun to hurt, *perestroika* and *glasnost* were the words dancing on everybody's lips with an excitement bordering upon euphoria. 'What do you think of the changing state of affairs in this country?' journalists asked Lucy and me after Stephen's public lecture. 'The very fact that you can ask such a question is proof enough of the extraordinary change,' we replied. Freedom of speech, freedom from oppression, freedom to travel – these were astoundingly precious liberties to people who had been restricted to the chill, grey confines of a shadowy one-party state.

We, too, were much freer than on previous visits to Moscow. We could go where we liked without being accompanied or trailed, and the entertainment provided for us was not just the obligatory visit to the Bolshoi but a concert in a church outside Moscow as well. Religious fervour had gripped Moscow. In the church of the monastery of Novodievichy, for example, the air was thick with the smoke of hundreds of lighted candles, around which the faithful were chanting and genuflecting as if to make up for lost time. By coincidence, the Fairhaven Singers had spent the winter months rehearsing Rachmaninov's *Vespers* – in Russian – for performance in Jesus College Chapel in March. To my delighted surprise, the concert to which we were taken was performed by a similar group of amateur singers and consisted of unaccompanied Russian liturgical settings, sounding very much like the *Vespers*, in an atmosphere that was tense with the novelty and promise of suppressed history and reawakening tradition. Against a richly gilded backdrop of icons, the majestic basso-profundo voices summoned up dark Russian vowels, rolled them on the tongue and emitted them into the resonant spaces of the ancient church where their deep-toned sonorities held the audience enraptured.

Not all Russians had taken to the new freedoms with equal enthusiasm, as Lucy and I found out before the concert began. Feeling distinctly uncomfortable after too much tea, the bumpy bus ride to the church and a long wait for the rest of the audience to assemble, she and I were searching around the churchyard for non-existent facilities. We were just about to take advantage of the shelter of a gravestone, when a grey statue, half-hidden under the dripping trees at the end of an alley, caught our eye. The statue blinked and we hastily abandoned our comfort station. On closer inspection the 'statue' proved to be one of the lingering vestiges of a moribund communism, a young soldier, presumably on guard lest the coachloads of highly distinguished Western scientists and their spouses were to start an insurrection – or perhaps take cover behind a gravestone for want of any other convenience. On the other hand he may simply have been posted there and forgotten. He may still be there now.

In the shops, too, it was clear that the prospect of a change in policy was not going to be welcomed. Shopworkers used to full employment and an assured pay packet, however small, were not likely to take kindly to productivity agreements and redundancies. When we tried to buy a Russian–English dictionary, they gave us to understand, just as in the old days of rampant communism, that customers were a bore and a nuisance, interfering with their private conversations or their nail-painting sessions on the other side of the counter. In this attitude, they had much in common with certain Cambridge dons for whom undergraduates were a nuisance and a hindrance to research.

Through being in Moscow, I missed an occasion in Cambridge which was of profound significance not only to the children, Jonathan and me, but to the whole of the parish of St Mark's. Our vicar, Bill Loveless, was retiring. So devastated was the congregation at losing its dearly loved incumbent that the parish went into a state resembling collective mourning for a long period after his departure to the customary exile which is cruelly expected of parish priests and their wives on retirement. In the spring Lucy had taken the opportunity to attend Bill's final series of confirmation classes. At about that time, in honour of his forthcoming retirement, the choir had put on a concert at which I sang a couple of his favourite Schubert lieder, including 'Die Forelle', and afterwards we held a large farewell supper party at West Road. Even so, I was sad not to be present at his last Sunday service. He had a fund of wisdom of which I had only scratched the surface and I was not sure that I would be able to confide in a newcomer who had no intimate knowledge of our situation.

One of Bill's last sermons as Vicar of St Mark's had made a deep impression on me. His theme, based on the Collect for the day, was the search for a quiet mind. In it he uncovered every aspect of my own lack of peace: my anxieties, my concerns, my fears for Stephen, for my children and for myself; my inability to rest, the tensions and the cares, the frustrations and the uncertainties which beset me every day and every night. He also broached that other group of manifold emotional disturbances associated with an unquiet mind, those evoked by guilt, to which I was no stranger. Self-reproach trailed me like a menacing shadow. Bill considered the repercussions of guilty thoughts and deeds, and also the profound complexities of guilt affecting bereavement and illness. I listened for whatever scraps of comfort he, with his inspired perception, could throw in my direction.

His prescription for dealing with anxiety contained elements which were not new to me. Live in the present, he said, and disregard the wordly cares of mammon. This I had long tried to do but my obligations to three children and a paralysed husband had forced anxiety into a prominent position in the foreground of my personal stage. I had to recognize, though, that even in the most extreme circumstances, our needs had always been met through a combination of sheer hard work, willpower and the coincidence of the right thing happening or the right person appearing when most desperately needed. Bill went on to advise us to trust in God through darkness, pain and fear. Here his words struck me with the force of a revelation as he quoted the biblical passage from Corinthians: 'God will not suffer you to be tested more than you are able.'

Bill turned to the redemption of guilt. Guilt, he said, is the risk that comes from striving always for the highest and the best; love is the only answer to guilt. Only in love can we sustain each other. His words offered a new resolution to the gnawing dilemma. Love was most certainly the force that sustained our household. According to that reckoning, I was being true to my promise: I had love for everyone, abundant maternal love for each of the children, love for Stephen as well as love for Jonathan. Love had many facets, Agape as well as Eros, and I wanted to continue to prove my love for Stephen by doing my best for him. Since his physical presence was now as insubstantial as a wraith, love for him had developed into a fathomless compassion, stronger and more lasting than any eroticism, born of a quarter of a century of shared hardship and perseverance. Sometimes that love became so entangled with the legion of worries that responsibility for his care generated, that it was hard to know where anxiety ended and love began. Stephen himself was insulted by any mention of compassion; he equated it with pity and religious sentimentality.

CHAPTER FORTY-NINE

Extremes

With a little help from Shakespeare, Stephen had devised a title for his book, the manuscript had been moulded into a form acceptable to the publisher and a date in the summer of 1988 was set for publication. The American edition was to be published in the spring before the British edition in June. The first edition had to be pulped at the last minute because of the fear of legal action on account of certain aspersions cast in the text on the integrity of a couple of American scientists. This misfortune allowed a minor omission to be rectified. Stephen had dedicated *A Brief History of Time* to me, a gesture which came as a much appreciated public acknowledgement, but the dedication had been left out of the American edition. The presses were put into overdrive to produce 10,000 copies of the amended edition within days, the potential libel was erased, my name featured in the dedication and the book was launched in the United States.

While Stephen was in America for the launch, Tim and I went to stay with his friend Arthur and his parents, Kevin and Belinda, all of whom were now living together in Germany. The two little boys saw each other rarely these days, yet neither of them had made other close friends; when they met, they happily settled into their familiar routine, like long-lost brothers. As there had been a late fall of snow in the Black Forest, Kevin surprised us by asking if we would like to go skiing. I had never skied in my life and never expected to do so, although rumour had it that Stephen used to be a competent skier and Lucy regularly went skiing with her friends. Indeed at that very moment, she was in the Alps recovering from an arduous run of rehearsals for the play which she and her companions in the Cambridge Youth Theatre were to perform in Cambridge in April before appearing at the Edinburgh Festival in the summer. Since his gap year in Scotland, Robert had taken to the mountains but in a more strenuous fashion – with crampons and ice-axe. Tim and I jumped at the chance to learn to ski.

Tim learned quickly, hurling himself down the slopes at breakneck speed, threatening to overshoot the car park at the bottom. I watched helplessly while Belinda desperately shouted instructions at him to snow-plough – that is, to slow down by turning the skis inwards. The memory of broken arms when learning to ice-skate made me much more wary and more nervous until I realized that snow was a soft bed, if cold and wet, to fall into or onto. In that weekend in the Black Forest, I recovered some of my lost bravado. High up on the hillside, with the wind in my face and the sun shining on the glistening white snow, I rejoiced at an unprecedented release from the treadmill of care, responsibility and the divisive, tedious squabbles of petulant nurses which had made our home life such an unendingly depressing struggle. Skiing demanded 100 per cent concentration, both physical and mental: the immediate objective was the bottom of the slope and the only question the brain could accommodate was how to get there in one piece. Once safely at the bottom, the next question was how to negotiate the T-bar lift to get up to the top again. Going up, braced against the lift, proved a far worse challenge than skiing down. With my customary physical incompetence, I fell off the lift into the piled-up snow at the edge of the track at every attempt. Not only that, but I usually managed to push anyone else who happened to be on the T-bar off into the snow as well.

Stephen was in America for over three weeks. After our return from Germany, we often invited the sons of Elaine Mason, his accompanying nurse – always his eager and willing companion – to play and sometimes gave them and their father supper, thus attempting to repay some of the kindness David Mason had shown in building and maintaining Stephen's voice-box. It was a mystery to me that Elaine, the boys' mother, could bear to be away from them so often and for so long. The elder boy was only the same age as Tim, and his brother two years younger. Her dedication to duty made me feel small, apologetic and inadequate, particularly as she often continued to assure me that looking after Stephen was so easy by comparison with looking after her family. Elaine volunteered to travel with Stephen at every opportunity and had gone off with him to America, whereas I still felt a tremendous wrench whenever I had to leave home and the children. However, despite certain misgivings on that and other scores, soon after his return from America I had promised to accompany him to Jerusalem where he was to collect the prestigious Wolf Prize, awarded jointly to him and Roger Penrose for distinction in physics. The Wolf Prize differed from many of the other honours which had been showered upon him in that it brought with it a handsome cheque.

My misgivings about the Israeli trip were not solely caused by my reluctance to leave the family or to take time from teaching. Although I was looking forward to meeting Hannah Scolnicov, my friend from Lucy Cavendish days, I was not looking forward to visiting the holiest, most ancient city in the world in the company of a party of physicists; I should have preferred a pilgrimage with more like-minded people, but I had no choice. There was a discernible tension in the air when Stephen said that if I did not want to go, he was sure that Elaine would be happy to go in my place.

He had resented my refusal to go to America with him in March; since his return the communication lines between us had become brittle and taut. My suggestion that he should sack some of the troublemakers among the nurses met with the blank, incontestable reply, 'I need good nurses.' When I offered to collaborate with him on a proposed autobiography, a project which I hoped would bring us closer together, his reaction was impassive and dismissive: 'I should, of course, be glad of your opinion,' he replied tartly. Only then did I start to perceive the truth of what other nurses had been trying to persuade me for some time, namely, that one of their number had developed a strong influence over Stephen, which tended to provoke and exploit disagreements between us. Naturally, they implied, my relationship with Jonathan featured in the web of wile and deceit that was being woven around me and as far as that was concerned, there was little I could say in my own defence since clearly in the eyes of the world our relationship was a guilty one.

Before the Israeli venture began, there was just time to see Lucy performing in the lively spectacle of *The Heart of a Dog*, a staged adaptation of the political satire written in the 1920s by the Russian writer Mikhail Bulgakov. The novella in which Bulgakov voiced his concerns at the take-over of Russian society by the proletariat was considered too abrasive for publication at the time and was not published in the Soviet Union until 1987, the year of our most recent visit. On 5 May 1988, as a precursor to the trip to Israel, we were invited to a reception at the Israeli embassy with Roger Penrose and his second wife, Vanessa, and on the following Sunday, leaving my parents in charge of the home, we set out for Israel.

All the benefits of Maurice Yaffe's treatment for pterophobia (which, I have discovered, is the official medical term for fear of flying) were quickly dispelled by the hassle we encountered at Heathrow. There was, of course, the customary hassle of travelling with an entourage, a wheelchair, stacks of luggage and a disabled person. There was also the strain of flying with the Israeli airline, El Al, which required an inordinately long check-in period and a detailed search of every passenger and his or her luggage. This I did not mind too much, since safety first on the ground was undisputedly an entirely laudable policy. I did however feel a considerable surge of unease that our plane appeared to be undergoing a major overhaul, but four hours later we took off.

Fortunately the main stretch of the flight passed without incident. Jonathan, who was away on tour with the Cambridge Baroque Camerata, had given me a Walkman and tapes of the B Minor Mass for my birthday, and with that I whiled away the time, occasionally peering out of the window down to the distant blue depths of the Mediterranean. As night fell and the sky and the sea darkened, a strip of neon lights appeared far below, clearly marking the coastline, and we were told to fasten our seat-belts for landing in Tel Aviv in just a few minutes. The plane began its descent, flying lower and lower. I watched as we skimmed lighted buildings and roadways. I heard the rumble of the undercarriage being lowered and waited for the jolt of the landing on the runway. The bump never came. Instead the plane lumbered its way back up into the night sky. To my own surprise, I was fascinated, not frightened. There were no announcements. A hush descended on the cabin and I sensed that the same questions were passing through the minds of all the passengers: had we been hijacked and were we heading for Lebanon? The prospect was quite exciting. What on earth would the hijackers do with us?

Ten minutes later the captain's voice came over the address system. We had not been able to land in Tel Aviv because of fog, he explained, and had been diverted to the only other available runway, a landing strip at a military airbase in the Negev desert, the neck of Israeli territory narrowing down to the Red Sea between Eygpt and Jordan. The explanation was perplexing and not satisfactory; there had certainly been wisps of cloud as we descended to Tel Aviv but nothing like a London fog. The plane droned through the night to the desert where it made an abrupt and bumpy landing on a short runway, not built to accommodate 747s. There we stayed the night. By the time the fog had cleared in Tel Aviv, the period of duty for our crew had expired, so we – and they – had to wait for another crew to come out from Tel Aviv to collect us. We were offered stewed coffee but I preferred to draw down the blind, curl up and go to sleep. Stephen's assistant, Nick Phillips, nudged me the next morning just as the engines were beginning to turn. I drew up the blind and looked out on a perfect introduction to the Holy Land. Outside was a scene of timeless peace and beauty, golden sands, silken dunes and barren, purple hills, all tinged with the soft pinkish hue of dawn. I watched the unfolding landscape, entranced by its primeval stillness all the way back to Tel Aviv.

The focal point of the official visit was the presentation of the Wolf Prize in the Knesset against the backdrop of Chagall's immense tapestry of the history of the Israeli people. The ceremony took place in the presence of both the highly respected, liberal-minded President of Israel, Chaim Herzog, and the notoriously hardline right-wing Prime Minister, Yitzak Shamir. They epitomized the two ends of the political spectrum in a country where good sense and fanaticism co-existed in equal measures. After the completion of the ceremonials, Stephen and Roger Penrose were so much occupied in scientific meetings, lectures and seminars with their Israeli colleagues that I was often left to wander and explore at will through Jerusalem. 'You can go into the Jewish quarter of the Old City,' I was advised, 'but don't go into the Arab quarter; it's too dangerous because of the *Intifada*.' In my impatience to be independent of the official party, I shrugged off such caution with indifference, happy to find that the hotel, a modern block in new Jerusalem, was within easy walking distance of the Jaffa Gate of the Old City. Here I should not have to conform to any schedule or wait for an official driver to take me out.

Like a magnet, the grey walls on the opposite hill, as austere and forbidding as the walls of the Alhambra on the Albaicín in Granada, drew me to them, giving not a hint outwardly of their inner richness. Unprepared for the bustling, noisy mass of colourful humanity which ebbed and flowed in and out of the gate beneath David's Tower, I paused in the gateway, looking about me and wondering which way to go, to the right or to the left. I was tempted to let myself be pulled along with the crowds and be sucked down the narrow street on my left but remembering the advice to keep out of the Arab quarter, I resisted the temptation and set off to my right, past the grey stone Anglican cathedral into a street which ran along the inside of the city walls. It was disappointingly dull and quiet. Hammering came from the occasional workshop, a few people going about their daily business hurried down the street, the sounds of a piano wafted from an upper window, otherwise there was little to claim my interest. It was pleasant but unremarkable. I carried on walking and came to a new housing development which was even more disappointing. However, an alleyway between the new houses on the left gave on to a steep flight of steps. These descended to a leafy little square where I stopped for a drink, before continuing on down the next long flight. At the bottom was a broad open expanse, enclosed on the far side by a high wall of mellow sunburnt stone. Black-coated men were praying and kissing the wall, and bridal parties were being photographed against it. I had reached the Wailing Wall. I ambled across the open space watching the crowds, some earnest and devout, others laughing and talking.

On one side of the space was a short tunnel, guarded by soldiers, under a mass of buildings. People were coming and going through it quite freely so I joined them. In passing through that tunnel, I discovered – without the aid of complex mathematical equations – that time travel is a real possibility. In practical and political terms, that tunnel divided the Jewish and the Arab quarters of the Old City. In historical terms it divided uninspiring, secular modernity from an ancient past which vibrated with the sounds, the colours and the traditions of biblical times. Pilgrims and tourists mingled like visitors from another planet with the local inhabitants who, with their children and donkeys, got on with their daily lives as if the twentieth century had not happened. I walked on alone, pausing now and then on the edge of a group of pilgrims. I listened to the guide's explanation of each site and I joined in their prayers and hymns at a couple of the stations of the Cross on the Via Dolorosa.

It was a strange experience suddenly to be alone, neither responsible for nor answerable to anyone else, as if I had cut loose from my moorings and was as light as air, without all the habitual trappings which pursued our usual progress. I was free to make my own discoveries and form my own judgements. I shuddered at the gloomy, repellent sense of intrigue which pervaded the Church of the Holy Sepulchre with its squabbling, rival sects and its queues of tourists waiting to pass through the inner sanctum. I could not wait to get out of its morbid atmosphere into the bright daylight. The view from the tower was its one redeeming feature. The panorama of flat white rooftops was as striking as the view of the red roofs of Venice from the top of the Campanile. Far below, chickens cackled, cocks crowed and a donkey brayed.

It was with reluctance that I dragged myself away from the grey stone Church of St Anne, close by the excavations of the pool of Bethesda, only 100 yards from the Lion Gate with its views across to the Mount of Olives. The Church of St Anne, immense and domed, light and airy, was deserted when I went in. I clicked my fingers – a trick Jonathan had taught me to test the acoustics of a building – and was surprised to find that the church was even more resonant than King's Chapel. Emboldened by the silence of the empty church, I hummed a few bars of Purcell's 'Evening Hymn', 'Now, now that the sun has veiled his light and bid the world good night . . .' This was a favourite though difficult piece which I had performed a couple of times with the Camerata. I listened in astonishment as the sound of my voice was caught by the pillars and flung up into the dome. There the hymn took on a life of its own and escaped its earthly provenance, rotating and dancing with ecstatic delight before sliding back to earth in a whisper. The friendly Arab guardian of the church appeared from a side door. He said that he liked to listen to the pilgrims who came to sing in his church. Apparently I was lucky to have had it to myself; usually choirs queued up for their turns. He invited me to return whenever I liked.

The Arab quarter of the city held no terrors for me, so another day I made for the Dome of the Rock, the spectacular holy place of Islam and the site of the stone where Abraham prepared to sacrifice Isaac. The entrance was closed and guarded by Israeli soldiers. It would be closed, except to worshippers, for the foreseeable future. In disappointment I made my way back up the street through the Arab bazaar with its motley assortment of tourist goods – Bethlehem blue glass, pottery and leather. I browsed among its antique stalls which displayed bits of Roman glass, copper and coins, and its food stalls, spilling over with all the delicacies of the eastern Mediterranean, nuts and olives, Turkish delight and halva as well as a cornucopia of fruits and vegetables. Like the stall-holders I had met in Tangier twenty-five years earlier, the Arabs here were polite and friendly. Having haggled over a pretty Roman glass bead at one of the antique stalls, a malachite and silver necklace at a ridiculously low price then caught my eye. The proprietor came out to talk to me without attempting to pressurize me into a purchase. He spoke good English and was just telling me about his cousin in Middlesex when he glanced down the street and hastily pushed me into his shop. He then took up a position, arms akimbo, in the doorway. His alarm was understandable. A troup of armed Israeli soldiers was forcing its way noisily up the alley. They did not seem concerned about respecting any property, barrows or stalls, in their path, and from the stance adopted by my shopkeeper and others nearby, it appeared that they had a reputation for being light-fingered. When the noise of their passage, their boots on the cobbles and their shouts, had died away, the shop-keeper came back inside. He apologized for pushing me through the door and simply said, 'You see, we have to be very careful.' I bought the necklace and a richly decorated, hand-painted plate and said goodbye, promising to return. I did return on the last day only to find everywhere closed; the shops were boarded up and, apart from stray cats, the streets were deserted. The ancient pageant of light, life, noise and colour had vanished. Everywhere, every street, every corner, every square, was supernaturally dark, eerie and intimidating – a ghost city which had closed its doors to time travellers.

As well as my sympathy for the Arabs, I felt a natural affinity with the Jewish people: many of our friends were Jews, highly intelligent, articulate and sensitive, whose families had been ravaged by the Holo-caust. When I compared the tragedies of that inferno with our own situation, I continued to count my blessings and tell myself that we had plenty to be thankful for. We had never lived under the threat of separation and extermination, of gas chambers, brutality and starvation. I sympathized, too, with the fears of my Israeli friends, the Scolnicovs, who had brought up their three children in Jerusalem throughout the years of conflict and who faced the imminent prospect of their eldest child, their daughter, being called up for military service, followed in succession by their two sons.

I could not, however, sympathize with the inhuman tactics of the Israeli army that I had witnessed in the Arab quarter of Jerusalem; even less could I sympathize with the loathsome man who had been allotted to us as our driver. An American Jew of Central European origins, he voiced his opinions loudly and coarsely wherever we went. As he drove down the winding road to the Dead Sea, he gestured to a row of white houses up on the hills. 'See there,' he said proudly, 'That's one of our settlements, we're building all those homes. The Arabs had this land for two thousand years and didn't do anything with it. They've had their chance but now it's our turn and they want to push us into the sea.' I had heard these wearying arguments before, delivered in the same Americanized monotone by other immigrant speakers. Further down the road, we came across a simple Bedouin encampment. 'What can you do with people like that? Just look at them!' the driver expostulated. 'They haven't advanced in two thousand years!' I could hardly contain my indignation. 'Perhaps they like their traditional lifestyle,' I retorted.

Such ill-informed, entrenched opinions, reflecting those of the country's Prime Minister, constituted an insurmountable obstacle to peace. The best Jews and the best Arabs had a lot in common. They could both be intelligent, generous, friendly and amusing. Perhaps the Jews had the edge over the Arabs in rational argument, in science, technology and mathematics, but the Arabs had superior intuitive and artistic skills. Between them, they held the key to the most successful and gifted culture the world has ever seen. They had only to look to medieval Spain to see how the harmony of their cultures could produce a highly positive and creative society. A thousand years later in Israel, instead of uniting to exploit that wealth, each side had been commandeered by mindless fanatics who were bent on exploiting their historical and religious differences.

There were, inevitably, many official expeditions. Television cameras and reporters followed Stephen to all his meetings, eager for his reactions to a wide range of questions. Unfailingly one question recurred at every interview. I watched and listened from the sidelines and my heart sank as I heard it repeated again and again in some form or other. 'Professor Hawking, what does your research tell you about the existence of God?' or 'Is there room for God in the universe you describe?' or, more directly, 'Do you believe in God?' Always the answer was the same. No, Stephen did not believe in God and there was no room for God in his universe. Roger Penrose was more tactful. When asked the same questions, he conceded that there were different ways to approach God; some people might find God in religious belief, others in music, others conceivably in the beauty of a mathematical equation. Roger's answers could not, however, dispel my sadness. My life with Stephen had been built on faith – faith in his courage and genius, faith in our joint efforts and ultimately religious faith – and yet here we were in the very cradle of the world's three great religions, preaching some sort of ill-defined atheism founded on impersonal scientific values with little reference to human experience. The blank denial of all that I believed in was bitter indeed.

I sat in miserable silence in the back of the van as the driver conducted us round all the holy places of the Old and New Testaments – the dark little cave in Bethlehem, the bleached stones of Jericho, the parched mountains of the Wilderness, the rippling green flow of the river Jordan and the Sea of Galilee. Dumbly in my corner of the careering van, I mused on the conflicts and dichotomies which the Holy Land seemed only to exacerbate: Jew and Arab, war and peace, progress and tradition, secularism and religion, atheism and religion, science and art, reason and emotion. One could be forgiven for thinking that this tragic land bred conflict. Against the impenetrable landscape, the sense of conflict was all-pervasive and insidious. Even Stephen and I were in danger of succumbing to it since we rarely seemed to be of one mind.

While Stephen finished his lunch in a lakeside restaurant at Tiberias, I swam alone in the turquoise waters of the Sea of Galilee and for a few precious minutes I felt myself to be at peace and in harmony with the landscape and its history. The threat of war over the Golan Heights had preserved Galilee from the ravages of the tourist industry with the result that little could have changed in 2,000 years. Tiberias was possibly even less of a resort in 1988 than it had been in Roman times and the Lake was as calm and as unspoilt as a Scottish loch. Had it not been for the heat, Galilee seen from the Chapel of the Sermon on the Mount could well have been Loch Lomond.

On the final day, we all bathed in the Dead Sea. Encouraged by me and supported by Pam, Amarjit, Nick and the natural buoyancy of the salt, Stephen lay back, floating in the warm water, briefly re-establishing contact with the reality of nature, long denied him, rather than its theory with which he was in ceaseless communion. There was silence all around us. The only witnesses of Stephen's peaceful bathe were the hazy purple mountains of Jordan in the distance, the blue sky and a solitary bird of prey. It was impossible to drown or even to swim. My attempt to strike out in a breast-stroke collapsed in splashing and floundering and filled my nose with stinging salt. My swimming sessions would have to be reserved for the hotel pool up on the roof where I swam a few lengths every evening after each day's hot, dusty excursion. The novelty of swimming with the whole of Jerusalem spread out below would have been an entirely agreeable experience had it not been for the presence of a suspiciously spotty child in the water. I recognized the spots of chickenpox but trusted that I was well enough protected with anti-bodies against that particular virus as a result of my experience in Spain as an undergraduate.

CHAPTER FIFTY

The Red Queen

THE TRIP TO Israel was a prelude to the demands of that summer which proved to be even more intense than usual. Although there was no escape anywhere from the endless bickerings of the nurses, the epicentre of the rumbling discontent had moved to the Department as that was where Stephen spent most of his day. The young assistant, Nick Phillips, wrote me a sad note apologizing because he intended to hand in his resignation before the end of his year: he explained that it was impossible for him to carry out his work for Stephen properly because he was tired of being the target of the ill-humour and criticism of one of the nurses. 'Bad-mouthing' was the term he used in his note. I sympathized with him but there was little that I could do to help. The nurses were a law unto themselves and neither Judy Fella nor I had any influence. Whatever went on in the Department was completely beyond my reach; my concern was focused on maintaining a civilized atmosphere in the home.

With the start of the A-level exams and the end of those particular teaching commitments for the year, I turned my attention to the plans for Robert's twenty-first birthday party. We celebrated the actual day with a large family dinner at home, in advance of the party which was to take place a week later. We planned another evening party on the lawn with a band, a repeat of his eighteenth birthday party, though this time it was to be a jazz band, and Robert sent out invitations to a 'Mad Hatter's Fancy Dress Party'. Just as preparations for the party were in full swing, three weeks after returning from Israel, I awoke one morning with a splitting headache and itchy spots around my waist. The only comparable headache that I could remember was the one that had preceded the chickenpox in Spain when I was an undergraduate. Lucy took her younger brother to school and I fell back into bed.

I saw no one until Eve came in as usual at ten o'clock. Her comforting Brummie accents were clearly audible outside my bedroom door. 'Where's Jane?' she asked. Elaine's unmistakably languid tones rang out in prompt reply, 'Oh, she's lying in bed... shamming.' Eve took no notice but came directly into my room. One look at me sufficed. 'You need a doctor!' she pronounced firmly and loudly enough for all to hear.

The doctor diagnosed shingles, explaining that it was the reactivation of the chickenpox virus as a result of renewed contact with that illness, exacerbated by stress. He prescribed bedrest and a new drug to relieve the itching. Ruefully I remembered the spotty child in the rooftop swimming pool in Jerusalem and wondered how I was to fit bedrest into the long list of all those things to be done.

Thanks only to Eve – who was herself suffering, having broken her arm – Lucy and Jonathan, I managed to rest a little. Jonathan shopped and ferried Tim to and from school and Cub camp, in between organizing and rehearsing his next run of concerts, while Lucy interrupted her usual whirl of social activity to bring me cups of tea, cook and ward off unwelcome intrusions.

Luckily Jonathan was no longer dependent on my administrative skills in the running of his baroque orchestra, since that enterprise was now established on a firm enough financial basis for him to be able to employ an administrator, a superbly efficient local lady who, with her willing husband, attended to every minute detail of every concert. She handled all the secretarial chores, the publicity and the printing, and together, she and her husband toured the country, measuring up doorways to see if the harpsichord would pass through, putting up posters and manning box offices. Since the Camerata was now a going concern and was giving concerts regularly even in the remotest parts of the land, Jonathan was frequently away from Cambridge. He worked hard, rehearsing and performing long hours and often driving back from distant concerts in the small hours of the morning. His irregular schedule, typical of the life of an itinerant musician, was incomprehensible to the nurses. Not having witnessed or appreciated his talent in practice, the less imaginative of them appeared to suppose that his presence in the house during the day suggested that he was a ne'er-do-well, a lounger, sponging off Stephen's munificence. His comforting presence gave rise to much whispering and tight-lipped drawing-in of breath.

Lucy, meanwhile, was juggling her social life and rehearsals for the

Edinburgh Festival with her summer exams. As the shingles improved only slowly, she found herself obliged to squeeze yet another unforeseen commitment into her already hectic routine. I had been intending to accompany Stephen to Leningrad for a conference in the third week in June, but it was obvious to everyone, except to Stephen and perhaps his minions, that I would not be well enough to travel. It was understandable that he should be dismissive of illnesses other than his own. As he made such a superhuman effort to overcome all obstacles, it was difficult for him to see why others, above all his wife, should not be capable of similar exertion and will-power, especially since all other illnesses were insignificant by comparison with motor neurone disease.

It was clear that I could no longer live up to his expectations. I found myself having to open every sentence with awkward apologies, and each attempt to apologize for my dysfunction – to apologize for myself, for being me – made me even more aware of my inadequacy. In every area, I was letting him down. The more my sense of deficiency grew, the more intense the shingles became. The neuralgia and dizziness intensified to blinding proportions while my nerves tingled like a thousand bee-stings to the very tips of my fingers whenever I tried to communicate my feelings or my ideas over any family matter, however trivial.

There was one function which I could not miss, ill though I felt: that was the launching of *A Brief History of Time*, scheduled to take place at a lunch party for family and friends at the Royal Society on 16 June, just a week after the shingles struck. *A Brief History of Time* was the tangible expression of Stephen's triumph over the forces of nature, the forces of illness, paralysis and death itself. It was a triumph and an achievement which involved us both in a way that was reminiscent of those passionate struggles and heady victories in the early years of our marriage. This triumph, however, was not a private affair but a very public event, attended by intense publicity. The figure I cut at that feast was little more than spectral: I lacked the stamina even to maintain a coherent conversation, let alone confront the onslaught of ensuing media interest with any display of confidence.

The day after the launch I rose from my sick-bed again, donned my red dressing-gown and a red paper crown, applied patches of violent rouge to my cheeks and appeared at Robert's party as the Red Queen: I made a rueful joke of the fact that, like the Red Queen, I was always running to stay in the same place. That night Stephen insisted on staying up very late, well after the end of the party, until all the clearing away and washing up was finished. Unaccountably and uncharacteristically, he had dismissed Gilbert, his faithful male nurse – to Gilbert's bewilderment – earlier in the evening and was evidently expecting me to put him to bed single-handed well after midnight. Jonathan was away on tour and by that stage of the night I was beside myself with exhaustion, dizzy, aching in every limb and blinded with the persistent headache. My brother Chris, who had driven with his family from Devon for the party that day, came to my rescue and offered to help with Stephen.

This capriciousness on Stephen's part was incomprehensible and disturbing. Maddeningly obstinate he could be; he could also be unashamedly self-centred, a forgivable failing considering the severity of his disability. Ruthlessly determined he certainly was and, from time to time, his lack of consideration could be deeply hurtful, but he had never been deliberately cruel, vindictive or malicious. Despite a certain justifiable intellectual arrogance, his nature always tended to generosity, particularly when his droll sense of humour was engaged. But the sense of humour seemed to be evaporating; towards me, the limpid eyes were becoming hard and unrelenting and the candour which long ago had drawn me to him was fading. The laudable spirit of determination appeared to have degenerated to deliberate stubbornness as immoderate forces outside his control – forces against which I had no defence – gained influence over his nature, affected his personality and changed his behaviour.

Perpetually tired and listless, I battled on to the end of term through a long string of engagements and the last lessons of the academic year. I had neither the energy nor the inclination to intervene again in the feverishly explosive rivalry among a few of the nurses which was exacerbated with the meteoric rise of *A Brief History of Time* to the top of the bestseller list. So long as the nurses' squabbles did not further threaten the balance of life in the home, I tried to treat them with the contempt I thought they deserved. The minimum amount of time I was – in theory – prepared to grant them stretched to eternity as they aired their mounting grievances at length over the telephone, oblivious to the fact that I might have better things to do, but all too ready to be mortally offended if I replaced the receiver without hearing them out.

The situation continued to deteriorate until finally I asked Elaine Mason, whose behaviour was seriously implicated in the troubles, to come one evening with her husband for a discussion. I intended to point out that she was a professional employee in our house and that she should take care to behave as such and treat the other nurses with respect. I intended to impress upon her that I could not stand by and see my home and my family torn apart and the nursing rota destroyed by her machinations. I might as well have saved my breath. With a smug complacency and a grin more suitable to the Cheshire Cat than a professional nurse, she condescendingly denied all such malicious intent, calling upon her husband to vouch for her immaculate character. Then she sailed out of the house, her head held high, while I sank into a hollow of all-enveloping despair.

As if the daytime disturbances were not bad enough, we had also begun to find ourselves at the mercy of crank intruders who would ring – usually from America – in the middle of the night with no consideration for the time difference. At all hours, they would imperiously demand to speak instantly to 'the Professor'. Like a certain Mr Justin Case, they had all, to a man, solved the riddle of the universe and were impatient to tell the Professor where his calculations had gone wrong. Mr Justin Case had to vie for the phone line at 3 a.m. with a Mr Isaac Newton who was a regular caller from Japan. Lucy answered one call from a man who asked her to marry him. 'Fair Lucy,' he pleaded, 'will you marry me? But read my thesis to your father first!' Another desperate caller from Florida insisted on speaking to Stephen because he was sure that the world was going to blow up in half an hour. 'Sorry,' we said, 'he's away.' 'Well, then,' came the forlorn reply, 'its the end of the world and there's nothing I can do to save it!' Some actually turned up at the front door and lay in wait for Stephen there, not always to their own best advantage however. One, his upper half clad only in a string vest, was unprepared for the front door opening outwards. As the door was flung wide for Stephen to emerge at full pelt in his chariot, the poor man was thrown into a rose bush. His string vest caught on the thorns and Stephen was well away by the time he extricated himself.

There was also the Hollywood film star, Shirley MacLaine, who wanted to test out her own questionable theory of the universe. She descended on a group of us, Stephen, me, a nurse and some students, one lunch-time in the University Centre. She spoke only to Stephen and largely ignored the rest of us. Although to me she looked like an ordinary middle-aged lady, her presence dazzled the staff who by their awed deference actually exaggerated her glamour. I did not suppose that she had a clue about Stephen's theories any more than he understood her trendy beliefs, but each appeared to be well satisfied with the meeting; the science was immaterial, all that mattered was the historic encounter which flattered both of them. Less entertaining were the fraudulent journalists who came promising to make donations to charity in payment for the interviews we granted them but never paid up, and the would-be unauthorized biographers who were obviously out to make a quick buck at our expense. It was with impatience that I looked forward to the summer holiday when we were to lay the ghost of the Geneva episode with a return to that city. Anywhere had to be better than Cambridge.

Hollywood stars and domestic tensions notwithstanding, when we managed to communicate, Stephen and I gave some thought to the mundane matter of how to spend the accumulating funds in our bank account. The Wolf Prize and the anticipated proceeds from *A Brief History*, together with the modest savings that I had made over the years, amounted to enough to allow us to think of buying a second home. Stephen was interested in buying a flat in Cambridge as an investment, but I cherished the dream of a country cottage, somewhere away from all the razzmatazz, the tensions and the persistent invasions of our privacy. A cottage on the north Norfolk coast would have been my ideal but that was beyond our means. A place in the country could give us longed-for peace and anonymity, I reasoned. It would allow Stephen the time and the quietude to think and consign his thoughts to computer away from the constant interruptions of which he complained in the Department. The children could relax and revise for exams in peace and I would be mistress of my own establishment, house and garden, responsible for the upkeep of the premises but free of the irksome discomforts of living in an institution, free of overhead student disturbances in the middle of the night and of crank intruders on the telephone, free of squabbling nurses since the entourage would be handpicked, and free to create my own herbaceous border without fear of its being grassed over for 'economic' reasons, as the College was threatening to do to the garden.

It was not until Jonathan, Tim and I came across an eccentric Englishman as we ambled through northern France on the way south to meet Stephen in Geneva that August, that the thought of buying a property in France began to cross my mind as a viable proposition. This gentleman, who had a minimal command of Franglais, was cheerfully setting himself up in business, buying and renovating French country properties and selling them to the British at prices which were extraordinarily cheap by comparison with those at home. As he unfolded his plans to a rapt audience of mystified French and fascinated English bystanders in a wayside restaurant, the exciting truth began to dawn that this was a possible outlet for our resources – not enough to buy a cottage by the sea in Norfolk, but enough to buy and renovate an old house in France. We would enjoy all the advantages of a cottage in England and in addition we and our children would be true Europeans, with a foothold in Europe, part of a broader cultural heritage, and, hopefully, bilingual into the bargain. All interests would be catered for. Fired with enthusiasm, I left a message for the Englishman at his lodgings the next day but I never heard from him again.

With all the hurly-burly of the start of the new academic year just after returning to England, I let the idea drop and it passed into the category of a pipe-dream, one of those things we might have done, with all the attendant ifs and buts. Our holiday with Stephen in Geneva had been a heartening success from the moment we met him at the airport, and after that harmoniously restorative spell, Jonathan, Tim and I had spent ten days camping in the south of France. We came back to Cambridge, refreshed and ready to take up the reins, altogether unaware of the new chaos that awaited us.

First of all, Lucy's application to the University of Oxford – to her father's and paternal grandfather's old college, University College – had to be withdrawn and hastily resubmitted because of the unexpected success of the Cambridge Youth Theatre's visit to the Edinburgh Festival. Moreover, her headmistress had to be prevailed upon to support the revised application for entrance in the autumn of 1989. She did so with extreme reluctance, pointing out that since Lucy would not be available to sit the entrance exams, because of her new theatrical commitment, she would have to apply only on the basis of an interview and her A-level results the following summer, instead of one straightforward exam in November. We were warned that no one at Lucy's school had ever got into Oxford simply on the results of the interview. Second, the tenant in the letting house belonging to Robert and his grandmother was threatening legal action because in my absence Stephen had thought to resolve a problem that had arisen by writing to her and ordering her to leave. Third, the administrator of the Cambridge Baroque Camerata was finding the workload too great and wanted to resign. Fourth and above all, most untypically for the discreetly private world of a scientific institution, the Department had turned into such a cauldron of intrigue that Judy, unable to enforce any discipline among the nurses and consequently incapable of doing her job properly, was brought to the point of tendering her resignation in the same week that Nick Phillips finally left his job as Stephen's assistant. This was a sad turn of events for those of us who had witnessed and appreciated Judy's devotion to Stephen over a span of almost fifteen years.

I was afraid that the volcanic eruptions in the Department might overflow and engulf the house at the worst possible time when Lucy was under greatest pressure. She was now studying for her A-levels and for Oxford entrance at the same time as rehearsing for yet another run of *The Heart of a Dog*. The Cambridge Youth Theatre's performance at the Edinburgh Fringe had met with such acclaim that they had been awarded one of the top prizes in the Festival, the *Independent* award for the best Fringe performance, which entitled them to a two-week run on a London stage. Unfortunately the London performances were scheduled to take place just before the crucial Oxford entrance interviews. Lucy would have to go down to London to perform every day after school and then return to school as usual the next morning. As her resilience would be tested to the limits, it was essential for her to be able to count on a quiet, stable background at home from which to sally forth to meet all her disparate challenges. This simple piece of common sense did not impinge at all on the consciousness of the majority of the people who regularly came in and out of the house.

A rearguard action to keep the nurses' battles at bay was simply not enough to maintain calm at home. From being a well-known scientific figure in Britain and America, Stephen had suddenly achieved worldwide fame: he had become a cult figure with the success of the book. We had the first taste of this in October 1988 when Tim and I accompanied him to Barcelona for the publication of the Spanish edition of *A Brief History of Time*. Everywhere he was recognized, attracting crowds who stopped to applaud him in the street. So much sudden attention was gratifying and disturbing at one and the same time. I felt ill-at-ease in the public eye, conscious of the way I walked or I held my head or even at the way I smiled. However, the crowds and the cameramen were not very interested in Tim or me, often pushing us out of the way in their eagerness to film Stephen, so it was not difficult for us to blend unnoticed into the throng.

The Spanish edition was subcontracted to Latin America and a poorly translated Portuguese edition soon followed. Although I could be sure that the Spanish was accurate because I had proof-read it myself and had marked errors in the text, my Portuguese had not advanced much beyond the language of medieval lyric poetry and was not sufficiently reliable to check a scientific treatise, so I was not responsible for that proof-reading. In Spain I was again called upon to translate for journalists in press conferences and television interviews and, in my own right, was asked to give interviews for women's magazines. There was a satisfaction in working in tandem with Stephen again as his intellectual partner.

The demand for interviews was reaching fever-pitch, not only in Spain but everywhere, at home and abroad. It was easier to cope with the publicity abroad because we were there expressly to sell the book and that Mephistophelian pact required us to make ourselves available to the media. At home where we had our daily routine to accomplish in quiet anonymity, the intrusions of the press became an irksome dislocation of family life. That television equipment should become a regular feature of Stephen's office where nurses vied with each other to pose for the cameras, was not a problem. The problem arose when the journalists asked for an interview or pictures at home as well; this I was extremely loath to grant and the children objected vociferously. It was bad enough having nurses in the house all the time: with television cameras and reporters as well there would be no privacy for anyone anywhere. My arguments cut no ice. Quite the contrary, they were represented as yet further evidence of my disloyalty to the man of genius. It was obvious that with my dependence on Jonathan and my refusal to train to be a nurse, I was already condemned. My reluctance to regale the press with stories of life with that genius within the walls of my home was just one more admission of my perfidy.

On 7 November, Lucy's two-week run in London began at the Half-Moon Theatre on the Mile End road. She came out of school at 4 p.m. with just half an hour to spare before catching the coach. The play demanded huge reserves of energy and concentration of its young cast who changed roles with every scene, sometimes appearing in individual parts, sometimes in the chorus. She would arrive home after midnight and the next morning, by nine o'clock, would have to be back in school for a full day's work. Her schedule was punishing but the general stress was eased somewhat by Stephen's decision to go off to California with his retinue for a whole month the day after the first night. Thereafter the quality of life improved dramatically at home and we all heaved a long sigh of relief as we withdrew into comparative peace and seclusion.

With unaccustomed self-indulgence, I was sitting idly thumbing through the Sunday paper the next weekend when an article on the availability of property in France caught my eye. Beneath it there was a modest advertisement for an English agency, based in Sussex, offering to search for suitable houses in the French countryside for its customers. I made a note of the number and, determined to follow it up, found a few minutes in which to dial the Brighton number – rather nervously, for I had visions of financial sharks expecting me to part with vast sums of money. It was a reassuring surprise to hear a pleasant female voice at the other end. She listened attentively and took my request for information seriously. Her firm had various contacts in northern France and she promised to put me in touch with them.

Only a few days later, xeroxed flysheets started arriving in the post from northern France. The quality of reproduction was not good. The photographs looked as if they had all been taken in thick fog or a snowstorm and the terminology used often sent me searching for the dictionary, but there could be little doubt about the prices. They were remarkably low, none of them more than about half the price of a two-bedroomed Victorian terraced house in southern England, and, although it was impossible to tell what state the houses were in from the hazy photos, all the properties were patently much more substantial in terms of ground area. Clearly further investigation was warranted, which was how Tim, Jonathan and I came to be sailing to France one Saturday in mid-November, itself a daring and liberating exploit, as none of us had ever dreamt of crossing the Channel in winter before.

CHAPTER FIFTY-ONE

Prospecting for Paradise

FRANCE IN NOVEMBER was bleak and dreary indeed, and bitingly cold and dark. But at seven o'clock in the evening, Arras, our destination, was still brimming with life and activity as the shops disgorged their last customers out into the brightly lit streets. They were full of enticing displays of Christmas delicacies and toys which promptly made a hole in our pockets. Moreover, much to our surprise, signs everywhere announced that *Beaujolais Nouveau* had arrived! The weekend began to assume a different perspective, especially after an excellent meal in the bar of our *pension* where the ruby-red new arrival met with general critical acclaim. If all else failed, the weekend held the promise of dealing with most of the Christmas shopping and a certain amount of pleasure in liquid form as well.

The next day was the sort of day which at first sight sends one back under the sheets, vowing never to emerge. The heavy sleet was hard and relentless. I could summon no interest whatsoever in quaint little houses dotted about the landscape and virtually had to drag myself along to the office where the pleasant, helpful agent and his assistant were waiting, prepared to give up the best part of their Sunday to escorting us round what they considered to be the most suitable properties on their books. What a Sunday that was and what sights we saw as we huddled in the back of the agent's car! The rain beat down mercilessly, now and then giving way to driving snow. When finally the sleet and snow had exhausted themselves, a dark, penetrating mist set in.

We were looking for an old house with character but basically in good condition, possibly with some opportunities for renovation and with plenty of ground-floor accommodation for the elderly and infirm members of the family, especially Stephen. Nice views were desirable and the distance from the main road was a prime consideration. We saw many hopeless houses, most of them very close to a busy *route nationale*, before returning to Arras, cold and depressed, and taking our leave of our helpful guide and his companion. As darkness fell, we sat in a café in one of the beautiful medieval squares, mulling over the day's experiences, none of them at all encouraging. I was thoroughly disgruntled, prepared to abandon the project altogether with no wish to visit any more French houses, large or small, old or new. I had seen enough to convince me that the whole idea had been a mistake and that the sooner we abandoned it the better. Sympathizing with my disappointment and suspecting that the scheme might be dead, my travelling companions could afford to be encouraging. 'Isn't there just one more agent lined up for tomorrow?' they asked. Tim was afraid that school would loom earlier than promised if we went straight home. 'Yes, but let's give him a miss,' I replied irritably. Inspection of the map undermined my resolve for it revealed that the little town where the agent lived was directly on the way to Boulogne, so, with the greatest reluctance, and with all sorts of provisos about the weather, I was persuaded to consider the possibility of just one more consultation.

As it happened, the day dawned bright and clear and the countryside sparkled under a fine layer of crisp, fresh snow. It was market day in St-Pol-sur-Ternoise, the small town on the way to the port, and some of the main thoroughfares were blocked off. Directions to the agency were hard to interpret as the people I asked either were strangers themselves or had no teeth. With any luck, I thought, we shall not manage to find the street and can go on our way, forgetting all about this nonsense. Suddenly we stumbled upon the narrow old street quite by accident and I was sent off to negotiate with the agent, a Monsieur Maillet. Uncertainly I rang the door-bell. The agency was not a shop with a glass front but a private house with only a name-plate advertising its business function.

It was not Monsieur but Madame Maillet who attended to me. If we would follow her, she said, she would lead the way to various suitable properties in her blue Renault. She headed out of the town on the *route nationale* in the direction of the coast. The road climbed out of the hollow in which the town nestled, up on to the windswept reaches of an extensive plateau, in fact, a broad ridge between two river valleys. We passed a small race-track on the right and sped through a tiny village. There was little sign of habitation, only the occasional church spire, water tower or ruined windmill. Then, suddenly, Madame Maillet turned right; we followed and there it was, a kilometre or so away from the main road, long and low, whitewashed and red-tiled. 'That's our house, Mum,' said Tim, then aged nine. And so it was, unmistakably beckoning us across the fields, an old friend from a past existence, instantly recognizable, immediately appealing.

'*Un vrai coup de foudre*,' the French would say – love at first sight. Nor were we disappointed when we turned into the driveway of the Moulin – for that was what it was, an old mill house, its windmill long since destroyed. The low, smiling façade we had seen from the road proved to be but one of the three sides of the house which embraced a courtyard, rather in the style of a Roman villa, the sort of house that Stephen and I had dreamed of in the golden days of our engagement. The aspect inside the courtyard was as delightful and welcoming as the exterior had been from the road.

With a nervous, slightly subdued sense of excitement in case this might all prove to be a dream, or there might be some unsuspected fatal flaw in the property, we made our way from room to room, making swift mental notes of dimensions, drawbacks and potential. It was difficult to gain an accurate impression of the size of the rooms as their proportions were in some measure obscured by the heavy furniture of the present occupants. The living-rooms, including the kitchen, all looked on to the yard or out to the garden and pasture at the back; they were wild and unkempt, at the mercy of a flock of hostile geese, except for a corner of traditional vegetable garden.

The sleeping quarters, consisting of two ground-floor bedrooms, ideally suited to Stephen's requirements, were all in the long side of the building which had first caught our eye, and our imagination, from the road. The accommodation could be considerably expanded by completing the conversion of the vast, light, airy attic which ran the whole length of that wing of the house. To Tim's delight but my dismay, it was accessible only by means of a rickety ladder, notwithstanding the agent's description of access by a staircase, but the perilous climb was rewarded by the sight of majestic old beams, holding up the roof structure like the ribbing of an upturned boat and dwarfing the clutter beneath. A quick leap of the imagination did away with the old bicycle frames, the heaps of onions, the broken bedstead, legless chairs, a fridge on its side and the discarded paraphernalia of several generations, and envisaged instead whitewashed walls, a polished wooden floor and brightly coloured covers and curtains.

It was almost too good to be true. As far as we could tell, the house fulfilled every requirement; it was within an hour's drive of the coast, no farther away from Cambridge than parts of the West Country and certainly closer than Wales. It enjoyed lovely views sweeping across fields to woods and châteaux; it was well away from the main road yet the access was easy. There was plenty of ground-floor accommodation and facilities, including a large ground-floor bathroom; all the main rooms and the main entrance were on the level and it was old and bursting with character but apparently in reasonably good condition. There was obvious potential for further improvements, and, most significantly, the price left a sufficient margin for any renovations.

Muted and overawed by this unforeseen development, we took our leave of the owners and followed Madame Maillet to yet another property, which, although infinitely pleasanter than anything we had seen the day before, was not a patch on the Moulin and held little charm for us. Tentatively, before setting out across the glistening landscape for the ferry, I asked a few hesitant questions about the procedures governing house purchase in France. Madame Maillet said that she could handle all the formalities for us and agreed, if required to do so, to arrange a survey with a local architect who was a colleague of her husband's, though surveys were not usually conducted in France; he could also advise on further conversions. She reckoned that we had about a fortnight to make up our minds but promised to let us know if any competitors for the Moulin appeared on the scene.

All the way home my mind was fixed on the Moulin, programming in the impressions, the excitement, the ideas. The contrast with the previous day's reactions was astounding. Once back in England, I hastened to write it all down and, with pen, paper and ruler, to make rough sketches of the property and plans for its adaptation to our needs and fax them all to Stephen in southern California. Many ideas reached the drawing-board but were then scrapped as being impractical or in all likelihood too expensive. Stephen replied positively. It was much less complicated to communicate with him by fax across the Atlantic than face to face, and I interpreted his terse comment 'sounds good' as approval.

Given my degree of timidity about embarking on such a major

endeavour, the wheels for the purchase of the Moulin were set in motion at remarkable speed. Equally quickly I had to learn the language and the procedures for house purchase in France which, from the outset, proved to be very different at every stage from the English equivalents. I had to get to grips with French law and legal terminology, the French banking system, French building terms, insurance French-style, local taxation and the eccentricities of the public utilities. The pound sterling was buoyant against the franc at the time so I had the consolation of benefiting from a favourable exchange rate. The comforting thought was that the same amount of money could not have bought us anything worth having in England.

Nevertheless, having committed the family to the purchase, I lay awake at night wondering what I had done and how Stephen would react. We were committed to spending a large sum of money, most of our savings in fact, on a property I had seen for three-quarters of an hour at most. I had taken everything at face value; I had inspected the house, outbuildings, garden and pasture only cursorily. I knew nothing of the area or of the people. Suppose I had misjudged the size of the rooms? Suppose when all the heavy furniture were removed there was less space than envisaged, not sufficient for the wheelchair with all its computerized trappings to turn easily? Suppose a child were to fall down the well in the yard? Suppose the main road were nearer and noisier than I remembered it? Suppose the sound of cars roaring round the race track were unbearable?

I lay awake going hot and cold at the thought of all the ghastly mistakes I might have made. Yet deep down inside me I felt an assurance and a certainty that I had not known in years. This project, based on my input, my knowledge of French, would be my contribution to family life, although, of course, it would be jointly financed. So many of our excursions in the past had had a single objective, the pursuit of science. This project would combine all our interests and talents – languages, love of France and the French way of life, relaxation, gardening and music as well – with that scientific pursuit. The more I looked at my plans and drawings, the more I realized that the Moulin had an even greater potential than I had at first deemed possible. There was an old barn attached to the house. It was ripe for conversion into accommodation upstairs, and a conference room downstairs, permitting Stephen to have his own summer school to which he could invite his scientific colleagues and their families. I had visions of establishing our own version of the Les Houches summer school in the undulating countryside of northern France and it was my hope that there we would once again find the unity and the harmony, the *modus vivendi*, which we had achieved before the events of 1985 and which since then had eluded us in England.

CHAPTER FIFTY-TWO

A Homecoming

NINETEEN EIGHTY-NINE BEGAN innocently enough, much as any other year except that I spent the first week proof-reading the French edition of *A Brief History of Time* in Belinda Bullard's isolated cottage in Norfolk. The English edition opened with an introduction by the American scientist Carl Sagan and I was perplexed to find that this had not been translated into French and that unknown to Stephen, Flammarion, the French publisher, had commissioned an introduction from a French physicist to replace it. I considered the disparaging tone of certain remarks in the French introduction to be distasteful and I took it upon myself to delete them. The launch of *Une Brève Histoire du Temps* was scheduled for the beginning of March in Paris and would coincide neatly with the completion of the house purchase. The weeks before the launch brought a procession of French journalists and television cameras to Cambridge, while the completion of the conveyancing process focused my attention more and more on the other side of the Channel. My horizons were expanding, no longer constricted by the four walls of the home in England.

The intricacies of the French legal system, the mechanisms for setting up a bank account, the plans for improving the facilities at the house for Stephen's use and converting the attic into bedrooms – all these I attacked with vigorous enthusiasm helped by the delightfully idiosyncratic characters with whom I was coming into contact in the quietly rural Ternois region of northern France. The first of these was Monsieur Pierre Vasseur, the portly, bespectacled patriarch of the local building trade whose custom it was to appear in a cloud of smoke, speak a language that was totally unintelligible to the uninitiated, and leave his audience gasping for breath. Amiable and benevolent, he was treated by all the locals with respect and affection, and he and I quickly built up a good working relationship. He slowed down his speech to what must have been, for him, a moronic pace and, by means of diagrams and written instructions, we reached a consensus which allowed us to plan alterations yet keep within our budget. These plans were already in the pipeline when, *en route* for Paris, I signed the house purchase agreement in St-Pol-sur-Ternoise on 1 March.

Tim and I had slept at the Moulin once, at the February half-term, before the purchase was completed. In keeping with the gathering pace of that year, half-term had been ridiculously busy: a frenzied dynamism drove me onwards and then brought me cruelly up against my limitations. Tim, Lucy and I had spent the first weekend of half-term skiing with Arthur and his parents in Switzerland. Rather, they skied while I floundered, all my hopes of fulfilling the previous year's exhilarating promise utterly dashed by the high pistes and the thin, icy snow. While the children went off to the top of the mountain, I stayed behind, marooned at the middle station or at the bottom, frequently falling off the T-bar, incapable of moving gracefully either up or down. I sensed that my clumsiness was making me an embarrassing burden to my companions, not least to my own children.

No sooner had we returned to England than Tim and I effected a quick turn-around, and set off for France in gales and sleet in eager response to an invitation from the current owners to visit the Moulin. Whatever the weather, I felt more confident about my French than I did about my skiing, but even that confidence was to be quickly shaken. We crossed the Channel amid mountainous seas and relentless hail and it was already dark when we arrived in Boulogne. As this was only our second visit to the Moulin, I was not at all certain of the route and my map-reading – of questionable accuracy at the best of times in broad daylight – was absolutely useless in the dark. Increasingly nervous in the lashing rain and the pitch-black night, we drove up and down the main road several times before we spotted the concealed turning to the village. Our hosts had closed the shutters and barred the gates, having given us up for lost. Inside they welcomed us with roaring fires and a hot meal.

The demands of those three days were every bit as challenging as the ski trip but, thanks to the kindly guidance of our hosts, I swiftly gained a life-time's experience of France and the practicalities of the living language. I opened a bank account, applied for the telephone and the electricity supply, arranged insurance, had long planning consultations with Monsieur Vasseur and bought furniture and appliances. I hoped against hope that all would be ready for the family at Easter. Only then would Stephen see his new/old house for the first time as he had decided that he could not spare the time from the book launch in Paris to attend the completion ceremony. That decision caused a last-minute crisis as it meant that I had to be given power of attorney, in a form acceptable under French law, for the purpose of buying the house in our joint names in Stephen's absence. The document had to be prepared in France and sent to England. Then Stephen had to put his thumbprint to it, not simply in the presence of a solicitor, but before a Notary Public whose own signature had to be authenticated as well. Finally all the documents had to be sent to the Foreign Office for the official seal of approval before being despatched to France. I thought it highly unlikely that the papers would arrive in St Pol in time for the completion a mere six days later.

In the meantime, Stephen went gallivanting off to New York on Concorde, taking Tim with him. When news of the house in France began to percolate through to friends and relations in England, I was upset by some of the reactions. 'Stephen doesn't like the country,' his mother announced adamantly in his hearing, as if intent on predisposing him against the Moulin before he had even seen it. Had she forgotten Llandogo? Certainly Stephen's mistrust of the country might be justified after that experience. But to condemn the Moulin, which had been chosen so carefully and was being prepared so meticulously for his enjoyment, seemed very unfair. The image of Stephen that was being cultivated by his relations and some of his nurses was that of a playboy roué who lived for the bright lights of the city and who found the rural life boring. This image of him conflicted with my own perceptions of his character, and the aspersions cast on my venture were already undermining his interest in it.

On 1 March, I attended the formal proceedings for the completion of the house purchase in the lawyer's office in St Pol. To my astonishment, the completion took the form of a legal ceremony at which all parties to the transaction were present. Everyone except me was dressed in their best for the occasion. If afterwards they were expecting the customary celebratory drink – at ten o'clock in the morning – they must have been disappointed because I was in a hurry to leave for Paris where Stephen was to arrive by air in the middle of the afternoon. Before leaving, however, I called on Monsieur Vasseur in his office. As I entered the room, he hastily shovelled the contents of his brimming ashtray into the top drawer of his desk. The reason for all the fag-ends was quite understandable: his computer had crashed and all the carefully prepared plans and estimates for work on our house had sunk without trace. It would take him days to rewrite them.

The next few days in Paris certainly intensified Stephen's love of the bright lights. He was fêted and pursued wherever he went, the darling of the media and the prized possession of the publisher. As I loved Paris too, it was no hardship for me to enjoy the bright lights as well. We dined at La Coupole, the restaurant where famous artists left their marks on the walls in lieu of payment; we ate in the restaurant in the Eiffel Tower where Stephen was invited to add his name to the signatures of the rich and famous in the visitors' book; we visited the newly opened Musée d'Orsay and we entertained friends and Stephen's French relations, including his cousin Mimi, to a dinner in celebration of the launch. Photographers followed us everywhere and journalists clamoured for interviews, for which either I or a French colleague of Stephen's did the interpreting. I was flattered to be asked for an interview by a leading radio journalist, J. P. Ekkerbach, at the radio station Europe 1. When I arrived my interviewer was involved in a long and heated discussion with Jean Le Pen, the nationalist leader. J. P. Ekkerbach quickly recovered his composure and treated me with Gallic charm and deference. The interview was broadcast all over France and as a result we and our circumstances were introduced to our new neighbours in our village in the north before we had even taken up residence.

Within three weeks I was setting out for France again, this time with Tim and Lucy, in a car laden to the roof with packaged cupboard and bookshelf kits, linen, crockery, cutlery, utensils and food. As if in our honour, we found that a new motorway had just been opened, cutting twenty minutes or so from the journey from Calais, so when we arrived, earlier than expected, at the Moulin, we found the house full of workmen, putting the finishing touches to the herculean effort which they had completed in seventeen days. Their beaming pleasure in our delight was obvious as we toured the house that they had so swiftly transformed. They had installed a proper septic tank in place of the previous owner's rather inadequate arrangements, gravelled over the muddy yard, enlarged the entrance to the bathroom for the wheelchair, covered the well, divided the attic into bedrooms and installed the electrical appliances that I had bought earlier.

The next morning as I lay in bed in one of the attic rooms, gazing up at the rafters, I thought how lucky we were to have our own house, so old and full of character. Then I wandered through the rooms feeling free, ethereal, unburdened, beholden to no one, far removed from the unwelcome attentions of the media and the venomous wranglings of the nurses. I walked round the patch of garden at the back and into the meadow beyond, debating where to establish a lawn, where to plant a beautiful flower garden and where to grow vegetables. I peered into the old barn festooned with cobwebs and wondered whether it might really be feasible to carry out my more ambitious plan of converting it into a conference centre for Stephen and his colleagues – for our old friends, the Carters, the Bardeens, the Hartles, and our new scientific friends from Madrid, Pedro and Carmen González-Díaz, to whom I had become particularly close. When we were in Spain, they had raced hither and thither across the country to see us and to run errands for Stephen. I looked forward to repaying the kindnesses of so many of those loyal friends and fondly imagined that we might re-create the happy, carefree atmosphere of the old days when we were young, before cosmology had acquired cult status and Stephen had become its guru.

That day, after doing a huge amount of shopping, Lucy, Tim and I set to work to redecorate the ground-floor rooms, especially Stephen's bedroom, in readiness for his arrival. We were interrupted by a call from our nearest neighbours across the fields who invited us to lunch. Having heard my broadcast on Europe 1, they were anxious to meet us and offered to help us settle in, in any way possible. This was the first of many gestures of extraordinary warmth and generosity, not only from that family, the old-established aristocratic family at the château, but from many other people from all walks of life and all political persuasions. Over the latter, they may have differed vociferously among themselves, but that was of no consequence to me. With them all, I was at ease, open and confident, a startling change from my unhappily repressed English self. It was as if by changing language, whether to French or Spanish, I could change my character and assume a different personality, expansive and uninhibited, so unlike my harassed, diffident Cambridge image.

Stephen had recently bought a Volkswagen van which had been

fitted with a ramp and fixtures to hold the wheelchair steadily in place. It also proved invaluable in transporting large items of furniture. Late that evening, Jonathan arrived at the wheel of the van which was packed with yet more furniture and luggage and the following day he drove to the airport at Le Touquet, so fashionable with the British in its heyday, to meet Stephen, Robert and the entourage of two reliable and trusted nurses, Pam and Jenny, and Jenny's little daughter, Kerrie. The advances and royalties coming in from the several editions of *A Brief History of Time* permitted Stephen the luxury of chartering a small aeroplane from Cambridge airport to bring him to France by the simplest and most comfortable means possible. The genial Australian pilot had opened up spaces in the wing to store suitcases and bits of the wheelchair and invited one of the passengers, on this occasion Robert, to sit beside him in the cockpit of his tiny six-seater aircraft.

The weather was so kind during the Easter holiday that northern France acquired a deceptively Mediterranean aspect. The long white walls and low red roofs of the house and outbuildings glowed in the bright sun against a clear sky, while clouds of white blossom fluttered to earth like silken snowflakes in the meadow and the shrubbery. Even Stephen was impressed, although he complained that the countryside was as flat as Cambridgeshire. This was not actually true, as Robert was to discover when he set off on a bicycle ride. The house stood on top of a plateau which was divided by many a meandering river valley with villages, water mills, ruined châteaux and *abbayes*, poplar trees and trout streams. Stephen appeared to like the house – though of course he would never allow himself to admit it – and made his own welcome contribution in the form of a mini-stereo system which I took as a token of his approval. Nevertheless, my burgeoning plans for expansion, when I eventually broached them, were firmly rejected. As ever, a compromise was called for and reached: I could go ahead with further renovations so long as I paid the greater share of the cost myself.

Whatever his opinions about country life and quaint old houses, Stephen certainly enjoyed the social scene. He and the children went out to buy pink champagne for the house-warming party which we gave for all our neighbours and all the people who had helped me with the purchase or worked on the house. The carpenter, Jean-Paul Régnier, came with his wife, Andrée-Marie, and their shy little daughters. The insurance agent, Jean-Pierre Degand, brought his boisterous family of three sons, all in Tim's age range. Sybille and Philippe de la Borde came from the château with their three sons, the two eldest of whom were more or less contemporary with Lucy. Sybille's parents, Huguette and Alain de Courson, regaled us with stories of life in the village in the war and, of course, Monsieur Vasseur descended in a cloud of smoke. Madame Maillet, the house agent, probably the most imaginative person ever to grace that profession, presented us with a visitors' book, *un livre d'or*, the pages of which we began to fill there and then. Stephen was the willing centre of attraction: to everyone's amusement, he demonstrated his computer and its ability to speak a garbled, Americanized version of the French language and graciously acknowledged the abundant congratulations showered on him on the success of his book.

I was very pleased that my faith in the project which I had taken on more or less single-handedly had been justified. All tastes were catered for: Stephen could work in peace, the children had quickly made new friends and even Tim was communicating effectively in French with a few well-chosen words and gestures, like '*football?*' or '*jouer?*' He was delighted with his ready-made band of friends, Benjamin, Maxime and Gautier, the sons of our insurance agent, but he objected strongly to being kissed on both cheeks at every encounter and I often had to apologize for his apparent bad manners by explaining that he was not used to it – 'Il n'a pas l'habitude.' Robert remarked to Tim's mystification that in a few years' time he would be only too pleased to be kissed on both cheeks by the girls. Jonathan was having some difficulty in finding an organ to play that had all its keys and pedals intact, but so far the gastronomic attractions of France were keeping him happy. Pam, Jenny and Kerrie were discreetly helpful, never intrusive, always considerate, and as for myself, regular meals for nine were not a burden since there was an abundance of excellent local ingredients and no shortage of willing hands.

There was one potential crisis when a sudden power cut indicated that the supply to the Moulin was not sufficient to cope with the large household and Stephen's requirements. To my great relief the extensive measures to increase the power did not involve us in further cost and many other people benefited as well, either from the statutory payment they received for accommodating new pylons on their land, or from having their hedges trimmed, or from an enhanced supply. This successful outcome was superficially a subject of amusement. For me, however, there was a much deeper dimension to the whole exercise of the Moulin, the renovations, the problems and their solution. In France, unlike England, I found that I commanded an unaccustomed respect. The fact that I was a woman and the fact that I was married to a recognized genius of superior intelligence were irrelevant. My opinions were courted and taken seriously. Sometimes they were contradicted with a frankness of manner which could have been disconcerting, were it not for the unfailing courtesy which accompanied it. However, I appreciated that forthrightness. It represented a straightforward approach and an assurance in a society which for 200 years had set great store by the equality of the individual. The sudden realization of myself as a worthwhile individual was startling; not surprisingly, it enhanced my growing love of France and the French way of life where the assumed priorities seemed so much better balanced than their English counterparts.

From the French perspective, the frenzied rat-race across the Channel appeared quite ludicrous. Respect for others and a self-confident directness of approach meant that the French had few qualms about defining their priorities and no shame in admitting to enjoyment and a judicious amount of self-indulgence as essential components of a well-balanced existence. Those essential components – sometimes envied, sometimes ridiculed by less refined nations – were manifest in sophisticated tastes in food, wine, personal appearance, clothes and all the small artistic details of presentation. They were also apparent in a respect for privacy.

These attitudes contributed to an unapologetic enjoyment of the fullness of life without any of the guilt-laden, self-conscious, puritanical hang-ups which beset the British as a nation in general, and which appeared to have taken over our home in Cambridge in particular. In England I was cowed. Each barely concealed insinuation was a stab at the raw wound of my guilty inferiority complex. The pain was intense; to ease it I could only retreat into myself, sliding further into my pit of despair. In France I could be French, spontaneous and natural and true to myself, neither having to justify my actions nor apologize for my existence.

CHAPTER FIFTY-THREE

The Price of Fame

THE SHOOTS OF my budding self-esteem, cultivated in the soil of French society, were to be quickly crushed back in England. Gullible and optimistic as ever, I did not anticipate that the arrival in late April of a Hollywood film producer would signal the first tentative shots in the next onslaught on our home life. He seemed friendly enough, inspiring my confidence with stories of his young family, and conveying a genuine sense of purpose in his plan to make a film of *A Brief History of Time*. His would be a serious, informative film of the book in the form of a journey through time and the universe, as witnessed through the eyes of a child. The idea was appealing. So long as the film remained strictly scientific and could be imaginatively done, using the innovative technology of graphics, his plans augured well and there was no reason to object to them.

Hot on his heels came an American film crew, directed by a lively woman who also won my confidence with her sympathetic approach. It had become the accepted routine that film crews would first wreak havoc in the Department before turning their attention to our home for a reassuring touch of cosiness in the otherwise enigmatic portrait of the disabled genius. Their routine always followed the same pattern. On initial acquaintance the directors would all appear to be pleasant, considerate, ordinary people, effusively assuring me that any disturbance would be kept to an absolute minimum. Their fly-on-the-wall approach would take no time at all and would require only a few shots, causing no disruption to our normal activities. Cameras, cables, arclights, microphones would all remain at a discreet distance; the furniture would not be moved; we could dress informally and go about our daily business as usual.

Such were the assurances which preceded every filming: the reality bore little relation to them. Without exception, in the short interim between pleasantries and filming, the procedures would – before our shocked eyes – become devastatingly intrusive. With little regard for the assurances they had given, the teams would plead shortage of time or scarcity of funds in mitigation of their sudden change of approach as soon as the cameras started to whirr. Items of furniture would be shoved around, never to be returned to original positions; blinding arc-lamps and glaring reflective screens on cold metal supports would supplant well-worn, familiar clutter, obscuring antique chairs, walnut tables, comfortable sofas, books and newspapers; lengths of cable would snake hazardously across the floors in and out of every room; microphones would be hung from any available hook or shelf and we, strangers in the harshly transformed landscape of our unrecognizable tubular steel home, would be typecast in our parts as the principal – though untrained – actors in the drama, expected to react with natural grace and aplomb for the eye of the camera.

That all-seeing eye was the sacred object of worship in this alternative religion, the twentieth-century cult of media power. By comparison the religion of science appeared old-fashioned, dignified and almost spiritual. When the great high priests set up the camera, all other competing sounds had to be silenced: normal, healthy background noises – music playing or children chattering – were stifled. For the length of each take, an unnatural stillness reigned with despotic authority, creating a false impression of calm compliance, fossilizing us for all time in artificial attitudes and poses which were a manicured travesty of our real lives. As I watched helplessly and participated reluctantly, a despairing voice inside me protested. Surely, it complained, there had to be a middle way between this insatiable nosiness and the starkly impersonal approach of the BBC *Horizon* film some years before. But an imaginative middle way would demand both time and money, more time and money than any of the directors had at their disposal as they rushed frenziedly from one project to the next.

For want of any outlet, my silent rebellion at this extra burden rumbled beneath the surface. Despite the complaints of the children, especially of Lucy, for whom the glare of publicity and the intrusion of the cameras were most distressing as her exams approached, I was in no position to bar the cameras from the house for fear of further antagonizing Stephen who had positively developed a taste for the publicity. Yet again, I had refused to accompany him to America that spring, at the beginning of the summer term, pleading my own teaching commitments, Lucy's A-levels and Robert's Finals. Although Robert did not, of course, live at home and these days sensibly kept well out of the way, I felt that it was important for him to know that he had my support at a critical time and could come home even if all he needed was a square meal or clean washing. As for my job – for that was all it was, just a job with no career prospects, no status, no advancement and only meagre pay – to me it was indispensable. It represented my only hope of maintaining any self-respect in the chaotic world which I now inhabited. This period confronted me with choices at every turn; I was forever having to weigh up the needs of one member of the family against those of another and constantly encountering terse disapproval when I made the wrong choice. Not that my opinion was ever sought when it came to deciding on travel dates: I was simply expected to abandon everything and conform to whatever arrangements had been made.

It has to be said that there was a further dimension to travelling with Stephen, quite apart from the actual flying, which only increased my reluctance. Even with the help of the nurses, assistants and students, every such expedition was now indescribably nerve-racking, attended by some twenty to thirty pieces of luggage and so many unforeseen factors that an expedition to the Himalayas would have seemed like a children's picnic in comparison. The first nail-biting question was whether the taxi or limousine summoned at dawn for the drive to Heathrow would be large enough to take the luggage as well as the travellers. Check-in at the airport would be a confrontational experience. While we held up a long queue, the check-in clerk would find it difficult to suppress his or her disbelief and irritated frustration at the amount of luggage and the apparently impossible demands of the frail but commanding body in the wheelchair. Whatever seating had already been allocated, Stephen's requirements admitted no opposition and accordingly hasty rearrangements would have to be made to seat him and his entourage wherever he chose. He would pay scant regard for the airline's normal policy for dealing with disabled people because he had devised his own. Come what may, he would insist on driving his wheelchair to the door of the plane, suspecting that to do otherwise might mean the loss *en route* of a vital part. Only there would he allow it to be dismantled with strict instructions as to the disposition of the various parts: the main frame could be taken to the hold but all the bits and pieces, the armrests, footrests, headrests and cushions, had to be stowed away in the cabin, in the overhead lockers or such spaces as the cabin crew could conjure up. He himself would then have to be carried on board. As often as not, the seat he had chosen would not be suitable after all and he would want to change yet again. The laptop computer would then have to be set up so that he could argue out the details of his gluten-free meal – if indeed one had been provided – with the steward. The flight itself would usually pass with little disruption, apart from umpteen requests for warm water to wash down his medications – until, that is, Stephen bought himself an altimeter to check the cabin pressure. Woe betide the airline that tried to economize on fuel by minimizing its cabin pressure. Often the duration of the flight would pass in a flurry of messages from Stephen to the captain, conveyed by one or other of us to the cabin crew, insisting that the cabin pressure should be brought to the equivalent of atmospheric pressure at 6,000 feet. Each of these demands, taken singly, was reasonable enough, even justifiable; all together they would fray the nerves of even the most rugged travelling companion. To preserve my sanity, I was forced to invent more and more excuses and contrive to stay at home.

Even so, the respite afforded by Stephen's most recent trip to America did not arm me with sufficient strength to combat the depredations of the film crew at what was always for me the worst season of the year when tree pollens settled like pepper dust in my sinuses. The American director, who at first sight had appeared so friendly and likeable, rapidly became assertive, indeed embarrassingly so, when her cameras trailed us into town to film my usual routine of Saturday morning shopping. It was unusual for me to be accompanied in this weekly chore by Stephen and his retinue, even more so that we should all have a fully-fledged film crew trailing our steps. There was no possibility of taking evasive action. It might not have been so bad if they had actually lent a hand with the shopping instead of following us like shadows, poking their cameras and microphones into my face as I loaded the shopping trolley to the rim, and then impassively registering my efforts to drag its heavy weight home behind me. Had I been a war or famine victim, the intrusion would have been intolerable. In the event at least the market stallholders derived some amusement from such a ludicrous charade.

The primary function of this film was supposed to be a portrait of Stephen for an American television news channel; subsequently it was to serve the dual purpose of providing a snippet of biographical background for the scientific documentary based on *A Brief History of Time*. Only the thought that this spate of filming would be serving both purposes made that horrible weekend bearable. By the time the urbane interviewer-journalist and his wife arrived for drinks that Saturday evening, I was in no mood to welcome any more film or television personalities or technicians into the house.

Scarcely had I introduced myself to them than the journalist's wife casually asked, just as I was handing her a drink, 'Do you have a religion?' Her enquiry was delivered with the same unabashed coolness as that shown by an American visitor who many years before had asked whether we had a bathroom in the house at Little St Mary's Lane. Perhaps in the eyes of some Americans, thankfully not my best friends, a bathroom and a religion come into the same category of desirable acquisitions, something everyone should possess but which is kept well hidden from view. Either can still form the fascinating subject of patronizing enquiry in a backward foreign land.

That clumsy question revealed to me in a flash of startling clarity that my life and everything in it, however private, had become such public property that I was at the mercy of the idle curiosity of all strangers, whether film directors, journalists, television interviewers or camera-men, and all their hangers-on. All that I had toiled for, slaved for, agonized over, all the love, the vision, the commitment, the heart-break and the faith, was reduced to a few trivial clichés for prurient mass consumption. This was in addition to the disruptive, meddlesome, often spiteful scrutiny of our very own resident KGB, some of the nurses within our walls. I, together with everything about me, was little more than a spectacle for mindless curiosity, an object of amused fascination or hostile criticism. That time my frayed nerves snapped and, like a cornered animal, I turned angrily on my vapid interrogator more or less telling her to mind her own business, but then, instantly overcome with remorse, I heard myself foolishly inviting the entire team to dinner in compensation for my rudeness.

Alone, late at night, I lay in bed writhing in the trap that was closing over my head. The situation was entirely artificial and unnecessary. The stress it produced was forcing me to behave in ways that were uncharacteristic and untrue to myself yet there was no clear way out. It was obvious that, in the eyes of the media, I had become an appendage, a peep-show, relevant to Stephen's survival and his success only inasmuch as in the distant past I had married him, made a home for him and produced his three children. Nowadays I was there to appease the media's desire for comforting personal detail by performing like a well-behaved circus animal, obeying the commands to accomplish certain familiar tricks, jumping through hoops, balancing balls on my snout and bowing to the audience, while inwardly my spirit rebelled both at the indignity and at my own helplessness.

Ten days after that bout of filming had come to an end, Stephen gave the Schrödinger lecture in a hot, stuffy lecture theatre, packed to capacity, at Imperial College, London. Schrödinger's equation, the fundamental equation for the science of quantum mechanics which he developed in 1926, bears the same relation to the mechanics of the atom as Newton's laws of motion to the movement of the planets. Stephen's lecture about imaginary time was as lucid as it could be, and afterwards he was fêted and pursued by representatives from IBM, the firm that had sponsored the lecture, who hankered for a photograph with him, presumably as one of the perks of their job. I stood diffidently to one side, thinking in some embarrassment that I was the only non-scientist present, until I was introduced to Schrödinger's daughter whom I had encountered once before at a similar occasion in Dublin in 1983. She was quiet and apologetically unassuming, informing me for the second time that she was Schrödinger's daughter by someone other than his wife but that she had later been adopted by Mrs Schrödinger. I was sorry for her; she was uncomfortably pursued by her father's legacy – as much embarrassed perhaps by his reputation as a womanizer as she was haunted by his scientific fame – and walked in his shadow. I feared for my children – hers was not a fate that I wanted for them, although recent indicators suggested that unless a satisfactory balance between public exposure and personal privacy could be achieved, their futures were not going to be easy. Like Schrödinger's wave functions, they and I lived in a state of oscillation, fluctuating between desperate attempts to pursue normal, healthy lives and the adoption – as and when required – of a suitable show of family unity for the delectation of the cameras.

The following Saturday, before setting off into town to sell flags outside Sainsbury's for the National Schizophrenia Foundation, I opened Stephen's mail for him as usual. It contained a letter from the Prime Minister in which she proposed recommending his name to the Queen as a Companion of Honour in the forthcoming birthday honours' list. The proposal sent us running for the encyclopedia. It revealed that this singular honour was one of the highest in the land, ranking above a knighthood and discreetly conveyed, without title, simply by the letters C.H. placed after the name. As Stephen was on the point of leaving for America, it fell to me to reply to the Prime Minister for him; I thanked her and accepted her offer.

As Stephen had already been nominated for an Honorary Doctorate of Science in the University of Cambridge, the summer promised to mark the apogee of his career, although how that, with its inevitable flood of media interest, was to be reconciled with Lucy's A-levels and Robert's Finals, let alone stability and harmony, was not at all obvious. Our priorities were diverging drastically. Mine was the preservation of the sanctity of the home and the privacy of our family life – or such tatters of it as remained after the nurses and the media had plundered every corner of it. While I applauded Stephen's success, I could not genuflect and worship reverentially at his feet whenever he entered the house. He was, for all his fame, but one member of a family where no one person had the right to be more important than any other. Although his medical condition demanded more attention for him than for anyone else, the home had still to cater fairly for the needs of all its occupants, adults and children alike. The children must never have cause to resent the circumstances into which they had been born through no fault of their own.

Stephen, for his part, appeared to delight in the publicity and revel in the symbiotic relationship which had made his name a household word all over the world. His delight was understandable. His fame in the face of a sceptical and sometimes hostile society represented the triumph not only of his mind over the secrets of the universe but also of his body over death and disability. For him any publicity was good publicity and could often be justified by claiming that it would increase the sales of the book. A case of champagne arrived from Bantam Press later that summer in celebration of *A Brief History of Time*'s fifty-second week on the bestseller list. In the fifty-third week, it returned to its commanding position at number one. It seemed that Stephen had succeeded in reconciling two extremes in the task he had set himself: in his description of his branch of science, the most fundamental and the most enigmatic of all the sciences, he had managed to placate the scientific intelligentsia and attract the popular reader.

Although there was no denying that the book was a phenomenal success, I did not consider it necessary for the world at large, or even for our close circle, to know the details of just how successful it was in financial terms, so I tried to keep the correspondence relating to the handsome royalties confidential. If our sudden flush of wealth were to become generally advertised, I knew that I risked losing many of my real friends with whom in the past I had scraped and saved to make ends meet and who even now, many years later, lived on a modest scale. I was also well aware that any publicity given to our enhanced financial status would attract exactly the sort of people with whom I did not want to associate. In the past, while Stephen's mind was focused on weightier matters, I had handled our financial affairs, always with an anxious eye on that uncertain future when Stephen might be too ill to work and the money might run out. I had run the family budget prudently and had accumulated sufficient savings to pay Lucy's school fees and to provide a buffer against the rainy day which for us could run to months and years. The financial situation was now much eased but old habits died hard. Since the signing of the contract for *A Brief History* in 1985, I had also dealt with the correspondence on that subject with the agent in New York. Maybe I was too cautious; maybe I controlled the family finances too strictly when Stephen would have liked a more profligate lifestyle. If I had gained a reputation for penny-pinching, this was only because he, given free rein, was spendthrift in his habits. Invariably in the past in restaurants he would choose the most expensive item on the menu, leaving me to select the cheapest in order to be able to settle the bill with equanimity. Unaccountably the arrangement whereby I handled the royalties of *A Brief History* was suddenly overturned behind my back. It was from the agent in New York that I learned of this change: he told me that he had been instructed to send all correspondence relating to the book to Stephen in the Department and no longer to me at home. I had no idea what had provoked this change and Stephen gave no explanation. It was as if after many years of mutual trust, my ability to handle financial affairs efficiently and with discretion was being called into question. In the resulting confusion, even the most casual helpers were allowed to open and read private correspondence; it was spread out on desks and tables, left strewn around for all to see, as if in black and white confirmation of the undisputed supremacy of genius.

Stephen's second trip to America that spring allowed us all a breathing space from impossible tensions in which to return to those other elements of a more regular lifestyle, the teaching, the studying, the literature and the music, and to settle into simpler, more relaxed habits without the vain and wearisome distractions of fame, publicity and contentious nurses. Tim and I fulfilled one of his passions by taking off for a promised weekend to Legoland in Denmark where we met Arthur and his parents, and later in May we returned to France for half-term.

The Moulin, welcoming us in its summer garb for the first time, opened its box of delights in a new guise. Under Monsieur Vasseur's auspices, further renovations had been completed, a bathroom had been added for Stephen's sole use, work on the barn had been started and the garden was beginning to take shape. Like the down on a baby's head, a faint haze of green was starting to show where grass seed was sprouting and vegetables and herbaceous plants were putting out vigorous growth. My dream of an English country garden was being realized in France so satisfactorily that even Claude, my valiant workman, confessed that he had begun to plant flowers in his own garden where previously he had grown only vegetables. I drew courage from the dependability of the natural cycle, the succession of the seasons, the time to plant, the time to harvest, all predictable and reliable. In that garden my creative efforts were not all in vain but were repaid with interest, with gratitude even, by Mother Earth.

Even more significantly, the Moulin opened the door to another world, the world of a past era, where the impossible whirlwind of our Cambridge lives slowed to a leisurely pace under the influence of the land and the sky, and where the only sound was the song of the lark, soaring high into the blue above the green cornfield in the morning sun. The place had already engraved itself on my heart. Its crisp, clean air and broad patchwork of fields fading to a distant grey horizon, its sleepy shutters and its aroma of newly chopped logs and old wood, its backdrop of tall conifers and shrubs shimmering in the sun, all sang of unaccustomed peace, solitude and salvation. There I could be alone, undisturbed by nurses, by the press, by cameras, by the clamour of incessant demands. I could dig my garden, intent on creating a beautiful display of shape and colour; I could immerse myself in books without fear of interruption, and I could learn and listen to music without fear of criticism at such wasteful self-indulgence. There I could find my true centre, in close touch with nature, old-fashioned, perhaps, contemplative certainly, a daydreamer whose favourite occupation was gazing out at the wide expanse of the western sky each evening. I would stand spellbound at the everchanging magnificence of the setting sun as it dropped

behind the silhouetted line of trees across the fields. The brilliant interplay of light and colour, luminosity and radiance, creating a sense of
primeval majesty, touched me with a poignancy that the bald scientific
statistics, however startling, about the speed of light or the distance of
the nearest star, even the age of the universe, could never match.

In those periods of reflection while I dug the garden, sowed seeds
and planted rose bushes, I identified with the hero of one of the set
texts that I had been teaching for the French syllabus in the past year.
The story of Candide, Voltaire's young hero whose optimism in the
'best of all worlds' – as taught by the philosopher Dr Pangloss – is sadly
betrayed by experience, had captured my imagination as much as it had
my students'. In despair at his inability to correct any of the horrendous
wrongs that he sees perpetrated around him, Candide finally turns his
back on the world and takes refuge in his garden. 'Il faut cultiver notre
jardin' is his ultimate, pessimistic, personal solution to the malfunction
of society.

Voltaire held a particular attraction for me, though I had only a
sketchy student acquaintance with his writing when in the ill-fated
summer of 1985 we stayed at Ferney, the village on the French border
near Geneva where he had settled. It was there that the present unstoppable train of events had been set in motion with the critical illness which
had deprived Stephen of the power of speech and made constant nursing
care a baleful necessity. Voltaire now began to emerge as yet another of
those writers and thinkers who held a special significance in my relationship with Stephen. Through *Candide*, his philosophy was accessible to
the teenagers in my class, yet in 1738, in *Eléments de la Philosophie de
Newton*, he had explained Newton's discoveries to the rest of Europe.
In its way, this endeavour to bring Newton's new science and its implications for philosophy to a wider public in intelligible language was an
eighteenth-century forerunner of *A Brief History of Time*.

Indeed, Stephen had much in common with Voltaire who made no
secret of his contempt for superstition and the stranglehold of the vested
interests of organized religion or of any other institution. Stephen would
have applauded Voltaire's insistence on reason as the only acceptable
basis for the government of society and the actions of civilized men,
and he might well have sympathized with his deist approach to Creation.
God for Voltaire was the supreme clockmaker: He wound up the spring
of his invention and set it in motion. Then He stood aside, not inter-

fering in either human or physical events but leaving His Creation to develop independently of His intervention.

I had less sympathy for Voltaire's insistence on rationality as the sole criterion for behaviour. In my experience reason – with its ally, the purely theoretical approach – could be as damaging to human relationships as dogma and superstition had been in the past. If the discipline imposed on my life by theory and reason was not as abstractly rigorous as that of Thomas Gradgrind in Dickens' novel *Hard Times*, I was nevertheless all too aware that scientific reason denied the validity of sensitivity, poetry, emotion and faith. Theory was often so far distant from practicality as to render the two incompatible. It was to a twentieth-century Spanish author and philosopher, Miguel de Unamuno, whose writings I had also been teaching in that year, that I turned for solace in confronting that dilemma and found myself taken back to the theories and philosophy of Existentialism which had inspired my youth.

Unamuno's elaboration of Kierkegaard's Existentialism found expression not only in his philosophical works but also in his novels, where he conveyed the basic Existential creed of the discovery of self through constant choice and decision-making. It was one of Kierkegaard's tenets that reason destroyed faith and denied all hope of an afterlife. Unamuno expanded this notion of the destructive power of reason, making it a central theme in all his novels. For Unamuno, *carne y hueso*, flesh and bone – or as we would say, flesh and blood – symbolizing emotion and willpower, are as important as reason and should be involved and respected in any decision-making process. While emotion has to be kept under control in a civilized society, the suppression of one's true emotional self, under the pressure of excessive rationality, leads to an inability to share suffering and then an inability to share love. Suicidal despair is the inevitable result. Unamuno confirmed my fervent belief that reason, cold and imperious, could not provide all the answers to the human condition. Reason ridiculed faith, it disregarded poetry, it derided emotion, it decreed that novels were a waste of time; it rang with the resonance of a cracked bell.

The clash of inexorable, but often zany, logic and searing, unresolved emotional problems lay like a corrosive material at the root of our existence in Cambridge, and that root was succumbing to the insidious effect of an invasive poison. In France the soil was fresh and fertile, and there the garden was full of the promise of a future, a cyclical, foreseeable future, decreed by the immutable laws of nature. There it might still be possible to re-create some of the harmony of the past, but only in peaceful seclusion, away from the seductive distractions of fame and fortune.

CHAPTER FIFTY-FOUR

Honoris Causa

SUMMER IN CAMBRIDGE did not permit any private philosophical discussion with Stephen about either Voltaire or Existentialism. All attention was concentrated on his multiple triumphs and the avalanche of media interest in them. The date for the conferral of the honorary doctorate by the Chancellor, the Duke of Edinburgh, was set for Thursday, 15 June while, known only to ourselves, the royal honour from Buckingham Palace was to be confirmed the following day and published in the media on Saturday the 17th. By a fortunate coincidence this was also the date of a concert to be performed in Stephen's honour by Jonathan and the Camerata, two days after the honorary degree ceremony, also in the Senate House.

Although the Newton celebrations and concert in 1987 had provided an attractive lure for commercial sponsors to support the Camerata, the sponsors themselves had become extremely vulnerable to the harsh vicissitudes of life in Thatcherite, monetarist Britain. The ink was barely dry on the signatures to a generous sponsorship deal when the sponsoring business, a very gentlemanly British firm, was gobbled up by Prime, an American computer corporation, which had no compunction in declaring that they were in business to make money, not to support the arts, music or any other charitable organization. Prime promptly pulled out of the sponsorship deal, leaving Jonathan, whose schedule of contracted concerts for two years hence was based on the calculations of the sponsorship deal, potentially with a huge debt, when he himself at the best of times earned little more than a subsistence income from music. At that most inauspicious moment for Jonathan and the Camerata, Stephen's fame and success offered the hope of salvation. A concert in Stephen's honour could be counted on to attract a large audience of people who would come to applaud Stephen as well as to listen to the music. It might also appeal to new sponsors for whom the high scientific profile would be attractive. Stephen would be fêted with his favourite pieces of baroque music and a retiring collection could be divided among the charities we all supported. This piece of planning, of my own devising, augured well for everybody, and Stephen gave it his approval, along with his approval of the Prime Minister's letter, before he left for America in May.

The challenge of concert planning, forever flying in the face of sound economic sense, had previously added a certain spice and bravura to my other various dilettante occupations. That concert would have been no exception, had it not been for the perpetual incursions of the media. Now the additional obligation to meet the press had to be accommodated in each weekly schedule to the exclusion of other more worthwhile occupations, so my part in organizing that concert was reduced to minimal intervention and other helpers were co-opted in to deal with the nitty-gritty of the arrangements.

The journalists who came to interview me were a mixed bunch: some were reasonably pleasant, some were clinical, others were demanding. It was impossible to tell in advance what sort of gloss they would put on an interview, as I discovered to my cost when one of the long succession of French journalists began her article 'Elle est furieuse . . .' This was a very unfair, sensationalized exaggeration of a little scene she had witnessed during the interview. One of Stephen's students had arrived at the house unexpectedly to collect the car keys so that he could drive Stephen to visit a sick friend in hospital. Perhaps Stephen enjoyed the prospect of being a hospital visitor rather than a patient for once, but I was worried that he might be exposing himself to the risk of infection – in an unnecessarily foolhardy manner – because the friend's condition had not been fully diagnosed. Only I knew the potentially devastating effects for us all of Stephen's falling ill. Upset I may have been but not furious, not nearly as furious as the journalist herself when her taxi failed to arrive to take her to the airport at the end of the day. There was nothing for it: I had to offer to drive her there myself. Naturally that 50-mile round trip in the rush hour did not merit any mention whatsoever in her article.

French journalists, Spanish journalists, representatives of all nations, came in an endless stream, all wanting a different slant on the science and on the background. They brought their superficial interviewing techniques to the situation; in turn, I developed my own techniques for dealing with them by deciding in advance how much information I was prepared to part with. I saw no reason why I should confide all the intimate complexities of my life to a journalist, a stranger whose interest in me was purely objective, governed by the imperative to sell more newspapers. If I wanted to confess, I would turn to a priest; if I needed psychiatric treatment, I would turn to a doctor, and if I had a story to tell, I might one day write it myself, although regard for privacy – my own and other people's – might well outweigh the desire to tell that story. If, therefore, the questions posed by journalists overstepped my boundaries, I would try to turn the interview into a conversation, asking for their opinions and reactions rather than telling them my own. Inevitably I became the target of disparaging remarks. For example, one journalist reported that I had 'cared for Stephen for just a couple of years after our marriage'. My old headmistress and stalwart supporter, Miss Gent, angrily wrote to the editor of that newspaper, *The Times*, to rectify the mistake. She was shocked at his arrogant reply: far from offering any redress or apology it confidently suggested that the facts in the article were correct. Our loyal friend George Hill, ever anxious to protect us from the prying eyes of the gutter press, said that he knew about the misrepresentations in *The Times* because he had peered over the journalist's shoulder when he was writing the piece. However he, George, had been so relieved to find no mention of Jonathan and his part in our household that he had thought it better to let the article stand as it was rather than reveal his close association with us.

It was refreshing in the midst of all the media hysteria to be interviewed for an article for the *Sunday Telegraph* by an old acquaintance, John Casey, the right-wing Fellow of Caius who had so often supported our cause in the past. Ostensibly he came merely to check the details of his article, the ages of the children and so on, but in fact we settled into a stimulating discussion about Voltaire, deism, optimism and various other-isms in relation to Stephen's theories. As ever, John was witty and amusing and, unlike many other journalists, so unsentimental about Stephen that he could liken him in force of character to that imperious matriarch of the Tory party, Margaret Thatcher herself. She at this time clearly suffered delusions of grandeur since she frequently used the royal 'we' and had taken to dressing in a style akin to that of Elizabeth I. Egoism, the disease of the successful in any walk of life, had stamped its mark on her. Where in the past she had sonorously promised to bring commitment, there was now arrogance at her own success, hand-in-hand with the insincerity born of complacency. She was lamentably blind to the fact that the adulation which surrounded her was little more than thinly veiled sycophancy.

There were just two professional journalists whose writings about our situation I respected: Bryan Appleyard, writing for the *Sunday Times* in the summer of 1988, had difficulty in suppressing his irritation and scepticism at Stephen's adamant, all-embracing, atheistical pronouncements and seemed to share my unease that such pronouncements uttered by a respected public figure, who also had the charisma of a rock star, could have a cynically damaging effect on susceptible minds. His angle on the story was a philosophical one and he it was who reported my heartfelt cry that my role no longer consisted in promoting Stephen's survival and success: instead I found myself telling him that he was not God. The truth was that the supercilious enigma of that smile which Stephen wore whenever the subjects of religious faith and scientific reasearch came up was driving me to my wits' end. It seemed that Stephen had little respect for me as a person and no respect at all for my beliefs and opinions. Had our discussion ranged wider, I suspected that Bryan Appleyard would have shared my sympathy for the conviction that reason and science alone could not furnish all the answers to the imponderable mysteries of human existence.

There was also Pauline Hunt, sent by the local paper, the *Cambridge Evening News*, whose interview was later to be syndicated and published by the *Guardian*. I felt more at ease in discussing our home life with Pauline than with other journalists. We had met socially and she well knew how our lives were ordered. By this stage, however, I was severely dissatisfied with the trite old clichés about the rewards of living with a genius, those oft-repeated truisms which dwelt on fame and fortune as if illness and disability were not fundamental factors in our lives. If I continued to perpetuate the myth of cheerful self-sufficiency without even mentioning the hardships, I would be cheating the many disabled people and their families who were probably suffering all the heartache, anxieties, privations, stresses and strains that we ourselves had undergone in earlier years. It would be all too easy for an uncaring society to point accusingly at other disabled people and declare, 'If Professor Hawking can do it, why can't you?' There was also the fear that the hard-pressed carers might be pressurized into performing even more impossible tasks because of the unrealistic image of our way of life presented through the media. I could no longer truthfully present the carefree, smiling façade, giving the erroneous impression that our lives were contented and easy, marred only by a little inconvenience.

This time my assessment was candid and truthful: I noted the triumphs but did not gloss over the difficulties. I used the interview to voice our criticisms of the Health Service and emphasized the fact that Stephen's success, even in procuring funds to pay for his nursing, had been due entirely to our own efforts. I described how we fluctuated between the glittering peaks of brilliant success and the black sloughs of critical illness and despair, with very little level ground in between. In a tribute to my old school and Miss Meiklejohn's dictatorial domination of the games field, I admitted that greatly to my surprise, I had found my experiences on the cricket pitch, inept though they were, extremely useful in bringing up my two sons since I often had to be both mother and father to them.

Such simple and fairly obvious truths appeared to be most unpalatable to those people who had come to believe in Stephen's immortality and infallibility, and had conveniently detached themselves from the reality of his condition, namely, his family and certain of his nurses. My comments were interpreted as a measure of extreme disloyalty where no hint of criticism could ever be countenanced. Such reactions only served to increase my sense of isolation. Were the people around me blind or mad, or was I losing my mind? Were those people living in a parallel universe where the roles were reversed and, where, as they seemed to suggest, it was I who was infirm?

Further accusations of disloyalty were flung thick and fast on the showing of a BBC film made that summer. In it I repeated the misgivings voiced in the two newspaper interviews in a vain attempt to restore a sensible balance both to the depiction of our way of life and to the representation of Stephen's scientific theories as the basis for a new religion. My performance before the cameras, which rolled throughout the period of the honours and celebrations and afterwards, was not enhanced by a streaming cold and a raging sore throat – just a couple of the recurring infections and ailments to which I was constantly subject. The heavy cold lent my interview and voice-overs a jaundiced tinge, deadening any humorous nuances and betraying an unintentional touch of bitterness.

That bitterness was the unfortunate outward manifestation of a profound inner sense of desolation and foreboding. Cassandra herself could not have forecast more accurately or with greater dread the catastrophe that I knew was looming over us all. Even Nikki Stockley, the young television producer, remarked how Elaine Mason had disrupted the filming process when she had tried to film in the Department. In public and at home, she seemed to be busily usurping my place at every opportunity, sometimes apeing me, sometimes undermining me, often flaunting her influence over Stephen. She had an unassailable stranglehold over the nursing rota and had so successfully ingratiated herself that all remonstrance was useless: any comments would be reported back to Stephen and I would be castigated for my interference. My appeals to the secretary of the Royal College of Nursing for help met with a flat refusal to become involved. Such was the background of physical chaos and emotional torment against which the tapestry of the traditional honorary degree ceremony unfolded, briefly transporting us into a fantasy realm of theatrical grandeur and champagne celebrations where all the froth of new clothes, archaic ritual, fixed smiles, polite chatter and endless handshakes spread like an insubstantial layer of white foam over the smouldering reality beneath.

In a modest bid to ensure some privacy, Lucy had optimistically marked the calendar from 8 June as follows: 'Lucy starts A-levels and becomes a complete recluse(!)' The day of Stephen's honorary doctorate, 15 June, she noted as, 'L does 2 A-levels.' Although she missed the accompanying festivities on account of the exams, there was little hope of fulfilling her reclusive intentions, so it was hardly surprising that on 22 June an impassioned appeal appeared in brackets: '(Give me the sympathy I deserve!)'. In the circumstances, it was a credit to her that she managed to do her exams at all, let alone succeed in them. Unintentionally, I too added to her trauma in a way that I subsequently regretted.

In a flush of genuine enthusiasm for Stephen's moment of glory, I had commissioned a family portrait from a young artist who had painted a Rembrandt-style canvas of the Fellows of Gonville and Caius. I trusted that he would respect Stephen where the National Portrait Gallery commission, in my opinion, had failed so dismally. In the event, it was a bad mistake on my part to add that extra engagement to our already overloaded schedule. It was neither fair to the family nor to the artist who had to work quickly, uncomfortably harassed by the ever-present television cameras that were filming around his easel while he painted. The resulting group portrait of Stephen, Robert and Tim poring over a chessboard in the living-room was an excellent likeness, capturing the three personalities engrossed in thought. To that extent the portrait was much more successful than the National Portrait Gallery commission. However, Lucy and I, seated on the *chaise longue* to one side, appeared as mere sketched afterthoughts, appendages set apart from the main group. This apparent slight was hurtful at the time, particularly in view of all the other tensions about which the artist could not have known. Perhaps it was not surprising that Lucy and I appeared as little more than broad brushstrokes since, in my state of perpetual motion, it was hard for me to sit still for more than a couple of minutes consecutively, and Lucy objected so strongly to the project and the inconvenience that the artist had only a passing glimpse of her on which to base his picture.

15 June, the day of the two most intensive A-level papers, was bright, hot and sunny, which was not of much help to Lucy. For Stephen's honorary degree ceremony, however, the weather was ideal. Never had the discrepancy between the best interests of different members of the family been more marked. Lucy left early for school in an advanced state of nerves while the rest of us looked forward, with a tinge of guilt on her account, to a day of pomp and rejoicing, a true holiday from stress and dissenting voices. The nurses attended to Stephen's *levée*, while Tim and I had a leisurely breakfast before dressing up, like bemused actors, in our fancy clothes – a short-sleeved white shirt and navy cotton trousers for him, and a grey silk suit and a broad-brimmed grey hat for me. We all left the house at 10 a.m. and strolled down the road to the Backs. Never had the lawns and meadows by the river looked more pastoral and peaceful: every blade of emerald grass and every leaf, green, gold or bronze, rippled in the bright morning sun, while the river gleamed like a silvery mirror, reflecting the infinite brilliance of the sky in mid-stream and the shady overhanging fronds of willow at the water's edge.

We arrived in Gonville and Caius to find it abuzz with unaccustomed excitement: the whole College had assembled to applaud Stephen in Caius Court, the Renaissance court near the Senate House. It took a few minutes to robe the honorary graduand in the ante-Chapel and a little while to get him comfortable in the chair in the heavy red gown, which would have been fine for midwinter but was unbearably hot in midsummer. He refused to wear the gold-rimmed black velvet bonnet, so Tim wore it instead. As we emerged from the Chapel, the Fellows, all begowned, preceded us, taking up positions along the path to the Gate of Honour. From another gate, the Gate of Virtue, came a brass fanfare and then the choir struck up the anthem 'Laudate Domino'.

Another fanfare resounded round the court, chasing Stephen as he raced at full speed through the Gate of Honour, up Senate House Passage and into the Yard of the Senate House.

Robert had enlisted the help of muscular undergraduate friends to lift the wheelchair and its occupant up the long winding staircase to the Combination Room in the Old Schools building where the other honorary graduands, including Perez de Cuellar, the Secretary General of the United Nations, were assembling. Stephen just had time for a sip of apple juice before Prince Philip, the Chancellor, arrived. Good-humouredly he came over to talk to us and recalled coming to West Road in 1981. He teased Tim about his hat and stayed to watch Stephen's demonstration of the computer before being whisked away to meet the other dignitaries. We passed the royal personage as we made our way out to prepare ourselves for the procession in advance of the rest of the party. 'Self-propelled, is it?' he asked. 'Yes,' I replied, 'watch out for your toes!'

The procession, which had already formed by the time we joined it, began to move forthwith. The four of us, Stephen, Robert, Tim and I, walked slowly round the Senate House lawn at the tail end of the line-up, watched by the crowds outside the railings and the cameras within. The clouds of tension, friction and confusion evaporated in the fierce sunlight and for a fleeting moment, it was hard to believe that they had ever existed. In the Senate House, all was cool, dark and solemn. The assembly of red-robed Masters of Colleges and Professors and the Chancellor in his gold-braided black robes took up their positions, and the audience of families and friends, dressed with the formality befitting an occasion of such pageantry, sat waiting in silent expectation.

As the great oak doors closed on the midday brilliance and the thronging informal crowds of tee-shirted tourists outside, the combined choirs of St John's and King's opened the proceedings with an anthem by Byrd, followed by a twentieth-century piece, and then the presentations began. A German theologian, the Lord Chancellor Lord Mackay, Perez de Cuellar and then Stephen were all introduced by the Public Orator, in witty Latin, delivered with such panache and such flourish that when he concluded his oration in honour of Stephen, Tim, not renowned for his Latin scholarship, burst into spontaneous applause. Perez de Cuellar was described as 'having brought peace to the Persians and Mesopotamians' while the substance of Stephen's encomium was adapted from the first atomic theory as described by Lucretius in *De Rerum Naturae*.

Amid much bowing, handshaking and doffing of hats, the Duke of Edinburgh conferred the degrees one by one, each presentation ending with a round of applause which, when Stephen's turn came, attained rapturous proportions. Some of the graduands, like the diminutive and frail figure of Sue Ryder, looked as nervous as young undergraduates; others, like the opera singer Jessye Norman and Stephen himself, were old hands at the game and received their ovations with confidence and style. The only disappointment was that Jessye Norman did not break into song there and then. The ceremony came to an end with more anthems and two verses of the National Anthem. Leaving Tim with his grandparents, Robert and I processed out with Stephen, sedately walking round the green again before heading down King's Parade in the blazing sun. Crowds cheered, smiling and waving, and cameras clicked.

When we reached Corpus Christi College – which by coincidence was Robert's college – for the luncheon, we found ourselves surrounded by the nation's great and good, all wilting visibly in the heat inside the marquee where champagne was being served. Sue Ryder seemed most ill at ease and Michael Bevan, the Lord Lieutenant of the county, weighed down by the trappings of his office, like Stephen in his robes, mopped his brow. Numerous people came to greet us. Some were well known, others were less familiar. I was particularly pleased to be introduced to Sir Crispin Tickell, the British Ambassador to the United Nations, a committed ecologist about whose efforts to preserve the South American rain-forests I had recently been reading in the *Independent*. However, no sooner had Sir Crispin and I started to discuss the depletion of the rain-forests than a loud-mouthed, ill-mannered don – of whom there are plenty in the University – interrupted our conversation. In time-honoured Cambridge fashion he monopolized the distinguished Ambassador, pushing me to one side and confirming my long-held belief that I must be invisible to some people. I left them to it and went over to compliment James Diggle, the Public Orator, on his splendid orations, and to share cherished memories of the medieval seminar of long ago with an old friend, Derek Brewer, the current Master of Emmanuel College.

Lunch was served in a stiflingly hot marquee in the main court and to add to Stephen's discomfort, the food, apart from the salmon, was not suitable for him. Lady Huxley, sitting on his left, readily kept up an animated flow of conversation with him but I had a fairly hard time with my neighbour, a well-known authority on French history who seemed to have nothing to say for himself until I mentioned our house in France. Then he came to life. His wife had just bought a property in Normandy, he said, but he was a city man and did not much care for the country. Whereupon there was much mirth as he shared his views with Stephen and the latter grinned in agreement.

In the rising temperatures, the speeches were mercifully short. Starting with Stephen, 'because everything begins with him', the Duke of Edinburgh expressed his admiration of the graduands who 'reflected the best of our civilization'. Lord Mackay replied briefly and then it was all over. The Duke of Edinburgh paused on the way out to enquire if all was well with us; I did not like to speculate what he could have done had it not been.

The rest of the day was a disturbing mixture of frivolity and encroaching normality, as if the harsh reality of the gathering storm could not extend its reprieve for much longer. At home, where a select group of relatives and friends had gathered and the College had laid out a tea of smoked salmon sandwiches and strawberries and cream on the lawn, one of those minor though typically exasperating crises lay in store. The champagne had not been delivered. The defaulting wine store was prevailed upon to send it round in a taxi.

Robert was not at that party as he had another engagement: early that evening he was to row in the Corpus second boat, racing in the Bumps, the May races which, Cambridge being Cambridge, always take place in June. Subconsciously, though for no apparent reason, I had a feeling that he needed some support at that particular moment and I managed to dash away from the lingering guests just in time to see him row. The day, however long and eventful, was not yet over. Lucy came home in dire distress as neither of her A-level papers had gone at all well, and then, late in the evening when all the guests had left and I was clearing up, the telephone rang. It was Robert. We chatted for a bit and then he blurted out that his Finals results were out and they were not as good as he had hoped. He was understandably very upset but at that time of night I could find few words to comfort him, though I too felt his humiliation and the irony of the situation keenly.

Robert, loyal and uncomplaining as ever, had dutifully assisted his father at the Senate House, had accompanied him in the formal procession and had provided the team of helpers from among his friends, to lift him up steps and over obstacles in Corpus Christi College. With thoughtful reticence, he had witnessed his father's good fortune without presuming on it, though always overshadowed by it. All through the ceremony in his father's honour, the excesses of media exposure, the compliments, the ovations and the accolade, Robert had kept to himself the galling news that his Finals results, published that very day, were a severe disappointment. The underlying truth of the situation was that his profound sense of individuality had rebelled against the overpowering shadow of his father's genius by mutely refusing to compete with it. I could not help feeling a much deeper pain for my son in his dismay than joy for my husband in the full glory of his many-faceted success: I identified with Robert in his humiliation. I could only stand on the sidelines of Stephen's success.

I groped for a comforting message hidden somewhere in the day's events. Pomp and ceremony, the company of the high and mighty, honours and fame are fine in their place and all very well, but to be successful as a person in the deepest sense, the sense of compassion, selflessness and integrity, is a much greater challenge, and with the possible exceptions of Lord Mackay and Sue Ryder – and Stephen of course in terms of courage – there had been very few people present on that day who would have merited that sort of praise. Robert, I knew, would aspire to that challenge and would fulfil it. The contrast between the children's experiences and ours that day was striking proof that pleasure would never be unalloyed.

If Robert had not achieved the academic success he had been hoping for, he made up for his disappointment on the river. Pursued by the BBC film crew, I took Stephen down to the river the following afternoon. Despite taking a wrong turning off the motorway – the races take place on a stretch of the river at Fen Ditton, 5 miles or so out of town – we arrived just in time to see the Corpus boat flailing past, hot on the stern of the Lady Margaret boat. News filtered back up the river in their wake that the Corpus boat had bumped its prey.

My father, who in his day had also rowed for Corpus, was much happier with Robert's prowess on the river than with any success in exams. He always regretted that under constant pressure to aim high, he had not been able to relax and enjoy his years at Cambridge in the 1930s. In his grandparentally indulgent opinion it was much more important that Robert had made the most of his time as an undergraduate.

CHAPTER FIFTY-FIVE

Honourable Companionship

Late on the evening of 16 June, we sat up to watch the announcement at midnight of the Birthday Honours. Inexplicably, Elaine Mason, the nurse in attendance, appeared disparaging and disapproving but my father hopped up and down with excitement at his son-in-law's elevation to the higher echelons of the Establishment as a Companion of Honour. Like Stephen's own father before his death, he derived a vicarious enjoyment from his close proximity to the sort of public success that circumstance had denied him.

The next morning I awoke to the more practical consideration of how to open the day in a suitably festive manner. I had not given any thought to the start of the day and Stephen's most important meal, his breakfast. Then I remembered that there was probably some caviar left over from a trip to Moscow and champagne from Thursday's celebrations in the fridge. The consequence of that extravagant breakfast was that none of us achieved very much that morning, only managing to stumble across the fen to the University Centre where I had booked a table for lunch. In the early afternoon, however, I cycled into town to check on the organization of the evening's concert in the Senate House and found Jonathan's family busy arranging the seating and the general layout while he rehearsed the orchestra. I left them to it and raced back home to collect Dad for a lightning trip down to the river. We arrived just in time to see the Corpus second boat rowing down bearing a willow branch, the sign that it had made yet another triumphant bump.

That warm, cloudless June evening saw us back at the Senate House, astonished at the sight of the long line of friends and admirers who were patiently queueing to get in for the concert, aptly entitled 'Honoris Causa'. I steered Stephen away from making a tactless beeline for the exam results, the Class lists, which were posted up outside the Senate

House, and left him sitting on the same lawn around which we had processed only two days before. There he had his photo taken in company with various distinguished guests from the firm sponsoring the concert, from his College and from the University, while I went to investigate why the queue was moving so slowly. Its length was partly explained by the fact that ten-year-old Tim was the only programme-seller inside the building, although Lucy and Dad were hard at work ushering the crowds to their seats. Having enlisted more help for Tim, I rejoined Stephen outside. The manager of the Senate House, Michael Hughes, who had given us much valuable advice and assistance over the previous weeks, insisted to my embarrassment that Stephen and I should make a formal entry and detained us outside until the rest of the audience was seated. We were greeted by a standing ovation. While Stephen beamed at the audience and pirouetted in his chair, I felt painfully shy and gauche and was glad to be able to sit down and conceal my flushed face from all those well-wishers seated behind me.

A couple of minutes later, the sounds of the baroque trumpet in Purcell's sonata for that gloriously commanding instrument opened the concert, soaring above the heads of the audience to mingle with the ornate plasterwork of the eighteenth-century ceiling. The trumpet reappeared with a companion at the end of the first half in a marvellously fluid rendering of Vivaldi's concerto for two trumpets. The oboes, horns, recorder and strings provided the filling in the trumpet sandwich with the First Brandenburg Concerto. In the interval, the audience spilled out on to the lawn where Stephen was soon surrounded by admiring crowds. Several people took the trouble to wish me well and a good few remarked that they hoped I felt I shared in the honour. The warmth of feeling generated by so many people was moving, almost overwhelming. Back in the Senate House, the audience in their elation took no notice of the orchestra's attempts to tune their capricious baroque instruments – a process which always takes place on the stage when the orchestra has assembled – so I had to ask Stephen's dear old nurse, Gilbert Dodd, one of the few reliable stalwarts of the nursing team, to call them to order. This he did admirably in what he called his 'public speaking voice', allowing the concert to proceed with Brandenburg Six and then to conclude with a thrilling performance of the Water Music.

Just as I had hoped, the audience were so well satisfied with their evening's entertainment that they contributed generously to the retiring collection. The result was that we were able to send handsome cheques to the three charities – the Motor Neurone Disease Association, Leukaemia Research and the Leonard Cheshire Foundation – as well as covering the costs of the concert from ticket sales. Ostensibly the evening had been a spectacular success: the charities had benefited, the Cambridge Baroque Camerata had secured a new sponsorship deal and had given a spectacular performance to a full Senate House, and, most importantly, Stephen had been fêted and applauded in lavish style by hundreds of well-wishers. There had also been a reception and meal provided by the sponsors after the concert.

Stephen, however, was edgy and disgruntled. His perceptions of the event seemed to be coloured by the grudging view that Jonathan and the orchestra had obscured his share of the limelight. This was as unjust as it was unlike Stephen's formerly generous nature. He had entered into the project with excitement and, when he had not been in America, had involved himself in its development with enthusiasm. Jonathan with his natural reserve had carefully stepped aside to allow Stephen to revel in the audience's adulation at the end of the performance and indeed there could have been no doubt that it was Stephen's show. It was even less like Stephen that he should remind me that since the honour bore no title, I had no part in it.

The conclusion was as inescapable as it was unpalatable: like Mrs Thatcher, he had fallen prey to flattery. The sources of this flattery were not disinterested and seemed to be feeding him ideas which were contrary to his formerly liberal nature. These ideas, when sweetened with the saccharin of sycophancy, became addictive and flourished by opening up an old wound – the impossibility of a marital relationship. It was only too easy for the same malevolent source then to rub salt into that wound by persistently criticizing and drawing attention to Jonathan's presence.

All that was left of me withered under this insidious infiltration; I was a hostage to guilt, vulnerable to the least hint of accusation and powerless to defend myself. The communication lines between Stephen and me were trampled and twisted like the wires in a telephone line brought down in a gale. He seemed to have lost that essential sparkle, his sense of ironic humour which in the past had made all things bearable and to which I had always been able to appeal. In its place I saw an implacable, unsmiling gravity of purpose which spurned any light-heartedness or attempt at wit as beneath his attention.

The limelight was blindingly focused on Stephen for the rest of that summer, never more so than when we made our second visit to Buckingham Palace a few weeks later, though by comparison with the first visit seven years earlier, this one was surprisingly intimate. We followed a similar routine – again staying at the Royal Society the night before – but with the difference that this time Tim and Amarjit Chohan, Stephen's Indian nurse, came with us and Lucy had remembered to pack her smart shoes to go with the dark brown dress which set off her blonde hair beautifully. Again, just as before, the traffic in the Mall was at a standstill, although this time it was on account of the Changing of the Guard. To avoid the congestion around the main entrance, we were directed to the Queen's private entrance and were suddenly transported into a quiet, colourful country garden away from the hot stuffy turmoil of London and its traffic. An equerry, footmen and a lady-in-waiting greeted us with graciously imperturbable smiles and ushered us into the Palace, past Prince Charles's toy car and a couple of bikes, and up into the vast marble-pillared hall, lit along its entire length and furnished in red and pink damask. Huge displays of lilies stood like decorative sentinels, guarding the treasures.

In its immaculate condition, the marble hall recalled many a National Trust stately home, with the fundamental difference that this hall was inhabited, not at present by its resident occupants, but by apparently prospective purchasers from the Middle East who were strolling up and down, as if measuring up its length, and lolling in their flowing white robes on its velvet sofas, testing them perhaps for comfort and size. Our companions, the Palace officials, regarded the visitors with suspicion as one might the prying eyes of prospective purchasers of one's own home. In a cordoned-off area in the gallery at the top of the very grand white and gold staircase, the débris of the previous evening's state banquet for the Arab guests and their hordes of friends and relations was being cleared away. We turned a corner and doubled back along the picture gallery, quickly retracing our steps over the marble hall with scarcely a moment to glance at the portraits of Charles I and his family, gazing in mute detachment at each other across the floor. A couple of Canalettos, a Dutch genre painting and lots of portraits of a Princess Augusta caught my eye. We turned into a passage, so narrow that it might have led to servants' quarters, and were shown into the Empire Room, a small side room full of paintings and furniture. After a brisk briefing from the equerry, Stephen and I were hurried away from the family to meet the Queen who was waiting in a room at the end of the passage. 'Good luck!' Amarjit called after us. 'It's not an exam, is it?' I replied as I followed the wheelchair out of the room.

True to form, Stephen charged ahead towards the open door across the passage. There by the mantelpiece stood the Queen, wearing a royal blue dress streaked with white. She glanced in our direction with a friendly but apprehensive smile. This soon changed to a look of absolute horror when Stephen, bursting in haste into her reception room, rolled the carpet up in his wheels with the effect of a cross between a cow-pusher on an American locomotive and a vacuum-cleaner. The chair hoovered up the edge of the thick coffee-coloured carpet, tying it up in knots, bringing Stephen to an abrupt halt and blocking the way into the room. From behind the chair I could not easily see what was happening and there was nothing I could do to release the royal pile. The Queen was the only person inside the room. She hesitated and then for one moment made a gesture which suggested that she herself was about to step forward and lift the heavy mechanism and its occupant out of the snare. Fortunately the equerry who had announced us squeezed past the chair, lifted the front wheels and sorted out the mess.

Naturally, Her Majesty was a little flustered – as was I – so we failed to shake hands or I to curtsey as she uttered a short formal speech of welcome. After an awkward silence she must have decided that the best course of action was to go ahead with the presentation without delay, and so proceeded to announce that she was pleased to invest Stephen with the insignia of the Companion of Honour. I received the medal on Stephen's behalf and showed it to him, reading the inscription aloud as I held it out for him to see. 'In Action Faithful, in Honour Clear' it read, like the first line of one of those resounding hymns we used to sing at school. The Queen remarked that she thought it was a particularly lovely wording and Stephen typed up, 'Thank you, ma'am.'

We in turn presented her with a thumbprinted copy of *A Brief History of Time* which rather nonplussed her: 'Was it a popular account of his work such that a lawyer might give?' she enquired. It was my turn to be nonplussed since I could not imagine anything remotely approaching a popular account of the law. I recovered my composure sufficiently to say that I thought *A Brief History* was more readable than that, especially the first chapters which provided a fascinating account of the development of the study of the universe before the physics became too complicated with elementary particles, string theory, imaginary time and that sort of thing. Thereafter the conversation continued haltingly for another ten minutes or so, ranging from a basic explanation of Stephen's science and interests to a demonstration of the workings of the computer and its American voice. Stephen apologized for his transatlantic accent, to which she replied that it was unfortunate: 'Was there not an English voice available?' Her questions were all directed to me with a piercing blue gaze, as bright as the large sapphire and diamond brooch on her shoulder. Although there was warmth and consideration as well as keenness in that gaze, it transfixed me. I was too terrified even to move my eyes, much as I would have liked to glance round the pretty turquoise reception room with its paintings and mementoes, but stood awkwardly rooted to the spot, hardly daring to turn my head to left or right.

As for the nationality of the vocal system, I explained that it had been pioneered in the United States and that it was now so closely identified with Stephen's personality that I found it quite upsetting if one of the children played around with it. As the conversation turned to the children, I fleetingly entertained the vain hope that they, and Amarjit too, might be invited to join the audience, just as in Rome, despite the remoteness of audiences at the Vatican from the common experience, our entire entourage of family and nurses had been invited to meet the Pope: this was not to be; Court protocol allowed no place for spontaneous gesture. The Queen simply expressed the hope that they were enjoying their visit to the Palace.

Meanwhile, lest Her Majesty receive any false notions about his mobility, Stephen the jetsetter was busily typing up that he travelled a lot and had already spent ten weeks in America that year, that he had been in France and Spain and would be returning to Spain in the autumn to collect the Príncipe de Asturias prize. It transpired that the Queen was already aware of the latter. 'And hadn't Philip given Stephen some award lately?' she asked. I was taken aback. Philip? Who was he? 'Ah, yes,' I answered quickly, 'Stephen received an honorary doctorate from the Chancellor of the University in Cambridge on 15th June, such a hot day, it must have been unbearable for the Chancellor in those heavy robes.'

On this relaxed note the audience came to an end. After the Queen had repeated her congratulations to Stephen, we formally said our good-byes, with plenty of handshaking and curtseying to make up for the unconventional manner of our entry, and cautiously made our way to the door without mishap. Out in the passage, the children were waiting for us. They had been evicted from the Empire Room to make way for a Middle Eastern Ambassador and his grim-faced wife who passed us in the corridor on their way to be presented. 'Poor Queen!' I thought.

During our audience the personnel had changed – even they worked shifts, it seemed – so it was a different team that escorted us back to the car. They regaled us with stories of some of the problems caused by guests to the Palace. Certain State visitors apparently had no compunction about demanding politically sensitive invitations to banquets for all and sundry at the last moment while other potentates had filled the Palace with such dense clouds of pungent incense that it had taken six months to clear the smell. Our mild request, which was willingly granted, was to be allowed to stroll in the gardens and take some photos before returning to the roar of the London traffic. Those idyllic moments brought us back to earth and braced us for re-entry into the roaring real world outside the Palace walls.

Over lunch on the top floor of the Hilton we recounted the details of the audience to the family, not omitting the carpet episode which appealed to their irreverent sense of humour. We described the subsequent conversation as somewhere between an oral exam and an interview with an intense but well-meaning headmistress, both equally terrifying. I had little doubt that the Queen had found it pretty difficult as well. Did we give the right answers, we wondered, as we looked out over the London skyline. There, directly beneath us, was the Palace, a bastion of privilege, like a model in a glass bubble, surrounded by the Elysian Fields where, unbelievably, we had just walked. Stephen complained that he had not been able to converse as much as he would have liked because of a problem with the setting of the hand control of the computer, disturbed by the contretemps with the carpet. Be that as it may, the overall impression was that the occasion had gone well and, moreover, unlike an oral exam or an interview with the headmistress, Stephen had another impressive medallion to add to his already extensive collection. Just as we were leaving the restaurant, I was surprised to be presented with an enormous bouquet of orange and yellow lilies by the management. Although it came from a commercial institution, one of the chain of Hilton Hotels, the gesture was quite affecting. It reminded me of the pearl that Ruth Hughes had given me in California when Stephen was awarded the Papal medal in 1975 and it told me that somebody had noticed me.

When we reached my parents' house in St Albans after a slow, tiring drive out of London, I lay on their lawn musing on the extraordinarily anachronistic institution of the monarchy. It was a weird Faustian pact that elevated one family to the rank of a dynasty, vested it with divine significance, endowed it with unlimited wealth and privilege, and then took away its freedom, condemning it to life in a giant goldfish bowl. The Queen would never have to negotiate a Volkswagen van with its cargo of offspring, husband, wheelchair, nurse and equipment through London traffic jams in the heat of the day, nor would she run the risk of dirtying her best dress when stopping for petrol, but neither was she at liberty to kick off her shoes and stretch out on the grass in that vast garden under a clear blue sky as and when she chose. The outmoded formalities that protected the royal family from the dreaded horrors of familiarity, even in their own domain, contributed, as we had just seen, to the barrier of unreality which divorced them from the ordinary lives of the public.

After the rest in St Albans, we resumed the journey home. There we feasted yet again on what had become that summer's staple diet – cold salmon and champagne.

CHAPTER FIFTY-SIX

Dies Irae

A WEEK LATER TIM and I were in France again. The Moulin yawned and blinked sleepily in the evening sun as we drove towards it up the track. 'Oh, there you are!' it seemed to say in its international language. 'So you've come back. Exhausted and stressed as usual, I suppose. Just as I said, you should have stayed here.' Although that had been my opinion too, it was easier said than done. I nodded in silent communion with the wise old house as I got out of the car to open the wrought-iron gates. The air was crisp and fresh, penetrating deep into my asthmatic lungs, reviving my spirits, physically tired after the long journey and emotionally taut after the recent peaks and troughs. The inner courtyard was quiet and still, so quiet that the silence was audible, tangible almost. Like a soft blanket it enveloped us, burying us in its folds. In it I could hide myself away from the tyranny of the outside world.

The silence was broken only by the chirruping of sparrows echoing off the white walls: Tim added his piping voice to theirs, impatiently urging me to open the door so that he could get in and clamber up to his attic to check the state of his model aeroplanes, swooping vertiginiously over the stairwell, suspended from the banisters by an intricate web of thread and sellotape. I turned the key in the door and let him in, and then I hesitated. Should I inspect the house first or the garden? He called me after him so I followed him into the house.

We ran from room to room, inspecting every nook and cranny, renewing our acquaintance with every old beam. To our astonishment, the dusty black barn had undergone a Cinderella-like transformation. Its rubble, cobwebs and rotting rafters had disappeared and in their place downstairs was a large room with a tiled floor and a kitchenette, and upstairs two bedrooms with a bathroom. A blend of solid new beams and usable old ones held up the structure, so confident in their age-old tradition that were it not for the sheen of newness on all the fittings, they could have been there from time immemorial.

Then we ran out into the garden, anticipating more discoveries. Some strange enchantment had been exercised over the Moulin in our absence. Tim gasped, 'It's just like Buckingham Palace!' and indeed he was right. The plants and seeds in the herbaceous border had leapt to maturity and, where in May there had been small isolated clumps and diminutive seedlings, now a riot of densely nodding flower-heads and dancing colour shouted ecstatic greetings to us.

There were still things to be done, walls to be painted and floors to be covered, but the essential work was completed. The Moulin was ready to receive us and the whole crowd of our summer visitors. My brother was to bring his rumbustious family at about the same time as Arthur and his parents would be arriving for a weekend visit, Jonathan would be bringing my parents and Stephen would be coming out by air to Le Touquet, faithfully attended by Pam Benson and accompanied by Elaine and David Mason and their family. Still incorrigibly optimistic, despite my forebodings, I had invited the whole family in the hope that the experience of living with us for a while in the same house but in more relaxed circumstances than in Cambridge would encourage a more reasoned approach and a greater respect for the bedrock of self-discipline which was basic to our routine. While I had no intention of interfering in any fond attachment that might have developed between Elaine and Stephen, I thought that she might just be persuaded to see that the success of our task depended on finely balanced teamwork which admitted of no disruption through whim or personal preference. There was no room for troublemakers in this situation. Naively I trusted too that if she realized that Jonathan and I did not, as a matter of course, sleep together in the same room or indulge in riotous orgies, she would learn to respect the *modus vivendi* which enabled us to go on caring for Stephen and the children indefinitely, come what may. Surely she could not be blind to what we were trying to achieve and the effort and restraint that we put into that endeavour? It was ironic that in days gone by, Stephen would have been scathing in his intolerance of conventional views and would have laughed to scorn anyone who tried to preach them. 'You're very brave,' some of the nurses remarked on hearing that I had invited that particular nurse and her family to France.

'I don't think that is a very wise thing to do,' said my mother. Of course she was right.

We – that is, my handyman Claude, Cécile, a very helpful girl from the village, Tim and I – were still energetically applying white emulsion to the walls of the new part of the house downstairs when my absent-minded brother and his family, which now included twin boys as well as two daughters, arrived a week earlier than expected. With Tim's help, I had struggled back late the night before from the do-it-yourself store in St Pol with a long roll of carpeting which somehow, between us, we managed to heave up the stairs and lay in the two large bedrooms, giving them a semblance of habitability, even if the effect was rather makeshift. Chris more than compensated for his early arrival by taking over the cooking. In his opinion, the best tourist attractions of France were the supermarkets where he would happily spend his days browsing along the shelves in search of ever more extravagant ingredients to add to his cooking pot, the aroma of which, wafting from the new kitchen, would make our mouths water every evening with the promise of gas-tronomic delights in store.

By the time Stephen and his entourage flew in to Le Touquet in the middle of August, the new wing of the house had been well and truly tested by successive waves of visitors, including my parents, who had pronounced it entirely satisfactory both for its charm and its con-venience. A perceptible tension reigned amongst Stephen's party, however, and my delight at his arrival met with a cool response, arousing my suspicions that the underhand mutterings about his dislike of the French countryside had struck home, persuading him that he really did not want to spend any time on holiday in France, let alone in the country. All efforts to interest him in the glorious views from the house across sun-drenched fields to the distant blue line of hills and forests met with the same bored, disdainful expression.

Day after day, the truth forced itself remorselessly on me that his smiles and his interest were reserved for someone else. Although perhaps he was still fond of me, as one might be of an old garment, I suspected that he was being encouraged to despise me and disregard me as a person of any worth because I was flawed and did not conform to the image of perfection with which he was constantly being tantalized. Was he being persuaded that I was no longer of any use to him; that I was good for nothing? The other person was in a position of strength; her responsiblities were minimal and she could indulge Stephen by doing anything he asked, and her specialized training enabled her to attend to his every whim. Since his work and his physical condition were his two principal preoccupations, my role was logically much diminished and hers was ostensibly greatly enhanced. The familial and intellectual bonds which I had valued and through which we maintained a semblance of normality had apparently become insignificant. Probably with her he had found someone tougher than me with whom he could again somehow have a sexual relationship, whatever the other dimensions of their affair. In all fairness I could not deny him this and was prepared to acknowledge that it was important to him. I was also prepared to accept their relationship in our scheme of things – in the same way that Stephen had generously accepted my relationship with Jonathan – provided that it was discreet, posing no threat to our family, to our children, to our home or to the running of the nursing rota achieved at such wearisome cost – provided, too, that it did not negate my relationship with Stephen.

Whatever the seductive charms and attractions of his nurse, I remained convinced that he needed me, that without me he would be like a lost child. Indeed he had become my child – an unruly, demanding, assertive child who needed my protection both on account of his physical helplessness and of that peculiar naivety, born of his hyper-intelligence, which can blind the famous to the Machiavellian subtleties of personalities and motivations. I may not have been able to respond to all his individual physical needs but overall I held the keys to the management of his condition and to our family life. My fate had been bound up with his so closely and for so long that I could never be indifferent to him however difficult, however ruthless and however selfish his peculiar set of circumstances – those of a disabled genius – had made him. Everything that affected him mattered to me. Care for his well-being had become second nature to me and I could no more have cut that instinctive element out of my mentality than amputate one of my arms. Whether it was the slightest sign of distress, discomfort or disapproval that his mobile features betrayed, I could not ignore him. Deprived as he was of the use of his limbs, he was nevertheless a masterly puppeteer and I was his puppet.

It was hard to say how I felt about him, except that, unlike Eros, the more volatile form of love, Agape, or compassion, never dies. In that emaciated body, despite the power of the mind, his suffering was all too painfully apparent and it was through that suffering that my feelings for him were constantly being aroused and channelled in an inexhaustible flow of protective compassion. However maddening or exasperating the recipient might be, compassion always makes allow-ances for that person's special conditions or misfortunes, and compels the giver to imagine how that other person might have been in happier circumstances. This attitude was never intended to be patronizing; indeed it often could lead one on to an emotional tightrope because compassion implicitly also demanded deference for the other person's dignity. Sometimes the balance between the required allowances and respect for dignity was a delicate one to achieve and and a weighty one to sustain, especially when in other circumstances the demands would have seemed to be quite unreasonable.

Our marriage, and the large and complex structure that it had become, lay at the foundation and was the definition of my adult life, summing up my most important achievements: Stephen's continued survival, the children, the family and the home. It was the long history of our joint battles against his illness and the story of his success against all the odds. To it I had dedicated most of myself, even if I had sought help in a morally unconventional manner to allow me to persevere without becoming suicidal. True, I sometimes longed for more freedom of movement and resented the strict limitations it imposed, but I had never thought of running away from it except, when driven to utter despair, by drowning myself. The structure may have become danger-ously top-heavy and unstable but it was unbelievable that all that the marriage implied might now be swept away in a flush of irresponsible, unbridled passion.

The fact that Elaine had a family of her own was beyond the scope of my comprehension. I was sorry for David, her husband, who, though previously so supportive of her, was now evidently baffled by his wife's obsession with the patient for whom he had constructed a voice-box. To judge by some of his remarks, he was unhappy about the holiday, but the communication lines between us were somewhat tangled and indistinct since he too subscribed to fundamentalist doctrines and he seemed to have been persuaded that I was the root cause of all the trouble.

The situation might have resolved itself peaceably had the combi-nation of personalities involved been different. Had some been more considerate, less determined, less self-centred, less bent on the fulfilment of their own desires to the exclusion of all else and others stronger and less confused, then perhaps I could have handled the situation differently and with more assurance. As it was, the prophets of doom were right about the holiday: it was a disaster. Stephen's distaste for the country, even for the Moulin – so unlike his reactions in the spring – became more pronounced, though sometimes for good reason. On one excursion the wheelchair broke down, on another he was grossly insulted by the proprietress of a café in Doullens, a small town on the way to Amiens, who hurled insults at the English, the disabled and Stephen – and refused to serve us lunch. Museums we wanted to visit were closed and the weather changed for the worse.

The inauspicious combination of mishaps did not dispose Stephen to be obliging, either to the family or to Pam Benson who was understandably upset at the capricious treatment she was receiving from him and from her supposedly professional colleague. They seemed to expect her to remain at their beck and call, by day and by night. This was not a civilized way to treat anybody, least of all Pam, and it was the sort of behaviour which would make a mockery of all efforts to maintain a regular and reliable nursing system. After one particularly disrupted night which had followed a long day out, I took it upon myself to point this out to Stephen and his companion.

This was the match, struck by my own hand, that set fire to the conflagration which would consume us all. The firestorm that engulfed the old house that day and the following night, shattering the cherished silence and shaking the aged beams, raged around me. Flames of vituperation, hatred, desire for revenge leapt up at me from all sides, scorching me to the quick with accusations – the unfaithful wife, the uncaring partner, the selfish career woman, work-shy and frivolous, more intent on singing than on looking after her frail, defenceless husband. I had had things my own way for too long, they said. I should 'put Stephen first'.

I faced the attacks alone. I would not demean Jonathan by bringing him into this uncivilized fray, but neither were there any weapons in my armoury with which to douse the flames. It was hopeless to try to point out that throughout all the alienating distractions of physics and the grinding demands of illness, I had honestly tried to be a good wife to Stephen, that through the paraphernalia of medicines, medical equipment and nursing rotas, and the plethora of scientific papers, equations and meetings, I had honestly tried to do my best, however distorted my own life had become. That Jonathan's love and help had preserved us and saved me from ultimate despair would never be countenanced as a valid defence. My best was not good enough and now I was being cast aside in favour of someone who seemed to offer more constant and devoted nursing care and travel companionship than I ever could. It was the beginning of the end. It signalled the death of the marriage.

Alone in my room when the first wave of attack had finally subsided, helplessness reduced me to hot, angry tears. My spirit rebelled at the apparent shallowness of so many of the people who had recently come into our lives. Had they ever come face to face with multiple crises? Had they ever had to confront the overwhelming trauma of living in the face of death, day in, day out, for more than a quarter of a century? Had they ever plumbed the depths of emotion or been torn apart by moral dilemma? Had they ever been stretched to and beyond the utter limits of their physical and mental capacities? Perhaps because of their ignorance of our past history, I felt myself criticized by them and treated as an automaton with neither feelings nor aspirations, devoid of all human needs and instincts. Indeed in their eyes I had no justifiable claim to any human reactions at all. My need to be loved for myself alone was dismissed as preposterous and quite untenable.

After this fiasco Stephen and the Masons returned to England and Tim and I stayed on at the Moulin. The lovely old house and garden gathered up my spent body and charred mind into the comfort of their embrace as the calm of rural France descended once more. If Stephen really did not want me, I reasoned, I could make a good life for myself in France. I could support myself by teaching English and Spanish and Tim could become completely bilingual. At the beginning of September he started going to the village school where he quickly made friends, unperturbed by the demands of the language. He would cycle off down the road to the village every morning while I stood waving and watching as he climbed the hill opposite and disappeared under the trees. At home we often spoke French. English and England had become alien to me, a country and a language which harboured and expressed both extreme personal torment and widespread political injustice, while France offered a new lifestyle, new friends and a sense of equality which England in general and Cambridge in particular had denied me.

Moreover, France, a predominantly Catholic country, worshipped and prayed to the Mother of Jesus, the feminine intermediary to the masculine figures of the Trinity. There a woman had a recognized place in the divine order of things. Mary had a human presence which was tragic, loving and comforting. She epitomized the joys and the suffering of motherhood with which women could identify and which men were bound to acknowledge. A society which respected her and prayed to her would respect and protect its women, especially the mothers of its children, however secular the constitution of that country. Often in French country churches and cathedrals, I would be drawn to the figure of the Virgin Mary – a crudely painted plaster saint perhaps but she emanated sympathy for my heartache and offered solace, the solace of shared suffering. By contrast it was a sad comment on English society that in England, women – even the Prime Minister – had to behave like men, adopting masculine mannerisms, to win any respect or achieve any prominence.

Tim and I quickly settled into a routine which I was confident of being able to sustain. We could live in France permanently if need be, or eventually we could return to England when Stephen had resolved his problems. Jonathan, who had returned to Cambridge to play a series of organ recitals, kept in touch regularly, urging us to stay in France if that was where we felt at ease. Stephen also telephoned almost daily but he urged us to return to England. He missed us, he said, and he needed us. He was so persuasive that I trusted that he really intended to restore some harmony to our lives and keep his nurses under control. Later that September, believing that my lost child really needed me, we set out for England across stormy seas, determined to avoid confrontation. The family, that is my parents and Robert, were delighted to see us when we arrived home late at night after long delays on the motorways. The reception I, but not Tim, received from Stephen was distinctly frosty. It was not the lost child who came to greet us but the despot. At once I knew that I had made a grave mistake in coming back to England.

CHAPTER FIFTY-SEVEN

Too Much Reality

THE FOLLOWING MONDAY, Tim returned to his primary school and I took up my teaching again, committing myself at least for the term if not for the whole academic year. Then, exactly a week after our return, Stephen gave me a letter announcing his intention of going to live with Elaine Mason. That evening, by a sorry coincidence, Robert was dealt a broken jaw by muggers who attacked him on his way home.

The execution of Stephen's decision was considerably delayed for the extraordinary and eminently practical reason that he and Elaine Mason had nowhere to live. In the meantime we lived in a maelstrom of chaos and confusion where open discussion was impossible because an insurmountable barrier had arisen between us. I clung like a limpet to the belief that the storm would eventually blow itself out and that, despite his present sad confusion, Stephen would choose to stay with his family. Quite suddenly and for no apparent reason, calm would descend for a couple of days but then the storm would rage over us again, acquiring a frightening predictability. Yet it was not really predictable because unforeseen elements would be introduced at each new turn. Reports reached me that the nurse was already announcing her forthcoming marriage to Stephen and I lived with the constant fear that there might be a battle to gain custody of Tim. Jonathan was banned from West Road under threat of a court injunction and had no choice but to keep to his own home. The more Stephen appeared to lose control of his own situation, the more I felt he sought to control me, as if I was simply a piece of property. Letters were posted through my car window by the duty nurse just as I left for work each day, and impossible demands were made of me each evening. Unpleasant remarks and motives, which were not true, were attributed to me. I was told to give Jonathan up and 'to put Stephen first in everything'. I found myself reluctantly drawn into clashes about money, not just with Stephen but with Elaine Mason as well.

I was well aware that I could be classed as a wicked woman – one of the insults hurled against me – in terms of conventional morality, indeed I was so in terms of the moral creed to which I myself subscribed; as such I had no defence to offer. I had not become immoral out of selfishness or lasciviousness but on account of a basic instinct for survival – my family's and Stephen's – as well as my own desperate need to feel loved and respected. The days of heroic gestures were long gone. In fact I saw myself as a hopeless misfit in terms of any moral creed, social doctrine or cultural movement: I had transgressed the moral code of the Church to which I belonged; I was a dismal failure both in terms of the fictional heroines, the Jane Eyres and the Maggie Tullivers, who had inspired my youth, and in terms of the liberating independence of spirit demanded by the women's movement, the overwhelming social force conceived by my own generation but irrelevant to my way of life, except in that feminism had legitimized women's aspirations and validated their need for physical love and sexual expression. Pragmatism, expediency and care had dictated my movements and my relationship with Jonathan. He had been the real hero, sincere, gentle, patient, long-suffering, and undemanding. In effect the simple charge that was being directed against us both was that we were human. As for the money, although I found the prospect of wealth unsettling, I had no wish to be left destitute, nor did I see any good reason for relinquishing the rewards of a quarter of a century's joint struggles to an outsider.

The course I had taken, with all its obstacles, dilemmas and tribulations, had been called into question and rejected, leaving me in mental and emotional disarray. Through the concentration required by teaching, especially by teaching the wholly absorbing, intellectually teasing novels and short stories of García Márquez, I managed to preserve some sanity, while among my colleagues in the staff room I found a quiet sympathy and supportiveness which brought a sense of stability to the few hours each day that I spent away from home. At other times music soothed and solaced my battered emotions, though often its intensity caused my voice to falter and fade. Otherwise bedlam reigned and our home became the scene of unprecedented violence as other people's madness forced itself into our household.

Madcap schemes were devised for whisking Stephen away to live in the other party's small terraced house with her, her husband and family.

My various ruses for calling his bluff – by putting his suitcase outside the locked front door, for example – not only did not work, they backfired, as I knew they would in advance because such behaviour was not really in my character. They resulted only in bricks being hurled through windows, shattering the glass and whatever fragile sense of security Tim and I, quaking with fear inside the house, still retained. Again I appealed to the Royal College of Nursing and the UK Nursing Council for help. They would not intervene unless I could furnish them with concrete evidence, a photograph, say, of the nurse's actions, and also medical evidence that the patient was not in full possession of his senses. These conditions were both impossible to fulfil. How could one claim that one of the great geniuses of the twentieth century was not in full possession of his senses or of his emotional reactions or that he was being manipulated in ways that he could not control?

Later that month, as I waved the two eldest children goodbye on consecutive days – Robert to Glasgow for a postgraduate degree course in information technology and Lucy to Oxford – it seemed that my entire existence and the structure on which it rested were crumbling away to dust. The personal identity which I had desperately tried to construct over the years from all the disparate fragments – the jigsaw pieces of everyday life – had been assassinated. I was alone and without shelter in the midst of a private war. Distant impressions of earliest childhood – visions of bombed sites, hollow blackened buildings and broken glass – came marching with urgency and frightening clarity out of the deep recesses of memory to the chaotic foreground of the present. Wherever I looked, I saw the rubble and ruins of the brave, bold but fragile edifice that Stephen and I had built. A dark chasm had opened up in the ground, swallowing up that edifice and with it more than twenty-five years of my life – all the years of my youth and young adulthood, all the hopes and all the optimism. In their place there was left little more than an insubstantial, vacant shroud, ghostly and withdrawn. The only certainty for the future was that my youngest and most vulnerable child, Tim, had to be protected and, however crushed and broken I might be, I had to muster the strength and the courage to fight for him.

The future had no clarity or distinction; it was scarcely discernible, a vague jumble of shattered aspirations and emotions, lacking all shape or form. The past was known, identifiable and familiar, full of people and events, and I wanted to hold on to it. It could be read like an old map where the roads were never straight and fast; they meandered, twisting and turning through a landscape that was often forbidding, frightening even. Although the going had been rough, taking us over steep mountain passes and across parched deserts, those roads had always led somewhere, following signposts which pointed, however uncertainly, to the next destination – a birth or a birthday, a celebration or an award, a conference or a concert. These dates and events, which included the crises and the death-defying illnesses, were like populous cities on the map, while the changing countryside of calm valleys and craggy peaks reflected the whole gamut of emotions associated with those events. In recent years the way forward had led us down many wrong turnings and along many a detour, often in pitch darkness with many fractious passengers on board. Nonetheless there was still security in that knowledge of the past from where we had come. Unbroken, it should have continued to run into the future as far as the eye could see. The map had been torn up, however, and there were no longer any signposts pointing the way ahead. The road had come to an abrupt end at the edge of a precipice. The future had fallen into the abyss and lay somewhere at the bottom in a confused welter of broken rubble and illegible, smashed signposts.

Jonathan and I had never contemplated the possibility of a future together without Stephen. We had no fantasies, no dreams. The thought of change was alien to our thinking; I had closed my mind to it and did not seek it. In the past I thought that we had achieved a balance whereby everyone could flourish, even if that demanded considerable contortion, restraint and self-discipline at a personal level. This had evidently proved to be nothing more than complacent wishful thinking for I was now forcibly given to understand that Stephen had been dissatisfied with our way of life for some time. I found this revelation quite surprising. If Stephen had been seething with resentment for so long, why had he not told me about it? How had he managed to be so successful, creative and dynamic if he was really unhappy? It now became apparent to me that he had not liked being treated as but one member of the family when he considered his rightful place to be on a pedestal at the centre. Someone had come along who was prepared to worship at his feet and make him the focal point of her life. That someone was promising him that he would never have to employ nurses again since she alone would care for him twenty-four hours a day, seven days a week and would travel everywhere that he wanted to go. Patently I could not match such single-minded devotion, and as a result, change of the cruellest kind was being forced upon me. I was threatened with being thrown out of the family home and my role in Stephen's life was being systematically denied, as if all reference to me, all memory of me had to be erased from all the records.

I deeply regretted coming back from France. I had returned to a daily diet of mental torture as if I were merely some inanimate chattel that could be kicked around at will. I could not understand why Stephen had begged me to come back unless he himself was so unhappily confused that he did not know what he really thought or wanted. But the latter was not a line of approach that was easily pursued because to persevere in it would, with absolute certainty, close down all communications indefinitely. It represented an insult to a towering intellect and an indomitable will, both of which had far outgrown the luminous courage which had first ignited them. The all-powerful emperor spurned the image of the lost child.

Once the term had started and Tim and I were entrenched in the Cambridge routine, there was no going back to France, yet I badly needed a bolt-hole. Jonathan's house was out of the question since a move there would signify that I was ending the marriage, which was not and never had been my intention. Any bolt-hole had to be neutral territory where Tim and I could escape the tensions, the battles, the venom and the recriminations which were creating bitter chaos at number 5 West Road. There was just one option open. Although the College had been in possession of our house in Little St Mary's Lane for years – in exchange for the College flat – the property still technically belonged to us. As I knew that the house was unoccupied, I wrote to the Master pleading with him to allow Tim and me to use it temporarily until the battles had died away and the crisis had resolved itself for better or for worse. The Master was new to the College; I scarcely knew him nor he me. In fact I had scarcely ever known any of the Masters well in person, though in the past their wives had always been well disposed towards us. Lady Wade, the wife of the previous Master, would, I was certain, have espoused my cause. The reply of the current Master was unequivocal: much as he regretted it, there existed a formal agreeement between Stephen and the College for the exchange of the two properties, and until Stephen revoked that agreement, I could have no access to the house. The College had appointed yet another Bursar following the retirement of the sympathetic Air-Vice-Marshal Bullen.

The new Bursar, as if embarrassed by his official role, considerately offered me the use of his house which was empty during the day, but that fell far short of our needs and, in any case, I did not want to find myself beholden to anyone.

With that one escape route closed off, I resorted in desperation to the doctor's surgery. By day asthma stifled my breathing and befuddled my mind while my hands tingled to the tips of my fingers with fright each time that Stephen announced that he wanted to speak to me. Every night the terrible nightmares returned, waking me in a terrified panic: my heart pounded as buildings collapsed on top of me, burying me in a dark underground tomb. Tim too had nightmares. He dreamt that he was being chased by baddies along corridors and down streets. By day he became excessively introverted and anxious. Dr Wilson prescribed beta-blockers to calm my heartbeat and recommended me to see a counsellor. The only remedy for Tim was to distance him from the troubles but since Little St Mary's Lane was denied us, that was not easily done. I went to see his head teacher and told him of the tensions in the home, asking him to warn his staff that Tim was under great strain and should not be put under pressure at school. Too late I discovered that for reasons best known to himself, the head did not pass my expressed anxieties on to his staff and poor Tim often came home from his primary school in tears.

Anthea, the counsellor recommended by my doctor, encouraged me to clarify the miserable confusion that possessed my mind almost to the exclusion of all else. 'How much do you really love Stephen?' she asked. As I could not answer that question because I myself did not know, she suggested a technique for finding out. The test would indicate my true feelings amidst the present turmoil and would clearly show whom I really cared for. She told me to close my eyes and imagine a row of boxes, laid out on a familiar piece of furniture. She asked how many boxes I could see in my mind's eye. There were five, spread out along the chiffonier in the hall. She then asked me to look in each box in turn and tell her what I saw. I peeped into the first box. There was Tim, sad and anxious. In the second I saw Robert's face, pensive, enquiring, philosophical. Lucy's vivacious personality bubbled out of the third as soon as I removed the lid. Jonathan was in the fourth box, calm, gleaming, golden. Finally I lifted the lid of the fifth box. There from the bottom of the box a pair of huge, grey eyes, Stephen's eyes, stared up at me. His face was nothing more than a blurred, featureless setting for those enormous sorrowful eyes. Those were the irresistible eyes whose anguish I had longed to share and to comfort. At that moment I knew that I still loved them, though it was seldom these days that they showed that intensely heart-rending, imploring expression. Rather they flashed with the frightening, cold light of hard resolution and self-absorption. I told Stephen of this experience, hoping that he too would be impressed by it and would be persuaded that I really did still love him, but he took no notice.

The battles continued to rage furiously for the rest of the term with only a short truce during the visit to Spain for the presentation of a prestigious award by the heir to the Spanish throne, the Príncipe de Asturias, in Oviedo. Spain lifted my spirits and made that visit bearable. Although the truce brought its own minor superficial tensions in the form of repeated public appearances, press conferences and interviews, at least these gave me the opportunity to prove myself professionally again and reassert my own qualifications as a linguist and my role as Stephen's companion. The underlying tension which resulted from his lately announced resolve of buying a flat for his favourite nurse was much more severe. As for Stephen's coterie, all that mattered to them was the soap-opera question of whether I had slept with him in the course of that visit. On our return from Spain one of the nurses – a flighty, self-regarding woman – was actually heard to pose that question to his face. I sensed that she and her companions chose to be deliberately oblivious to the bald facts of the situation: the obvious fact that one of them was always, had always, to be present all night, the fact that Stephen was draped with tubes and pipes which gurgled and spluttered frighteningly at the slightest provocation, that he scarcely went to bed, except in the early hours, and had to be turned at regular intervals; the fact that the light was kept on in his room all night; the fact that he was all mind and no body, an all-too-powerful rational mind and an enormous fund of restless energy trapped in a pathetic paralytic shell of a body, as emaciated and enfeebled as any victim of Belsen.

The mind which had mastered the mathematical secrets of the universe was no match for the emotional upheaval which now over-whelmed it. Like his Wagnerian hero, Siegfried, Stephen had wrapped himself in a protective cloak, the stiff cloak of determination, inspired by unrelenting reason, steeling him against sentimental frailty in the belief that he was invincible. But like Siegfried he, too, was vulnerable, and was helpless when his vulnerability was exposed to attack. Stephen's physical weak spot had been his throat which had succumbed to infection in Geneva but he also had a second, psychological, weak spot: it was an utter lack of resistance to emotional pressure. He had never been subjected to it before and had no armour against it. He had never liked to admit to emotions, regarding them as the fatal, irrational flaw in my character, and I had never succeeded in exerting such pressure in any circumstances, although I had watched from time to time in amazement as more powerful women bent otherwise strong men to their will. The techniques they employed remained a mystery but I knew that these women were to be avoided. This was the sort of pressure being exerted on Stephen: it built up a head of steam, hissing with relentless energy until it erupted in a series of emotional explosions, surges of volcanic force, which engulfed all obstacles with a red-hot flow of anger and passion. Then, quite miraculously, each new eruption would subside as quickly as it had exploded, and peace, like a cloud of silent, white ash, would descend once again on our homelife as we turned our backs on the devastation, ready to believe that it was nothing more than a bad dream or a temporary aberration. In those precious times of respite, Stephen and I would reach out to each other. He would become gentler, more docile and regretful, genuinely concerned to put the turmoil behind him and resume the family life on which he had thrived in the past. Then he would admit that he was being tossed by conflicting emotions and needed support and understanding and the possibility of a reconciliation. This I was all too willing to give for I shared the tragedy of his situation and wanted to help him live through it.

The lull would last only until the awful moment when another missive, another ultimatum, another summons, would seek out its target. I learned to dread the outcome as Stephen dashed off, abandoning meals and social engagements to become even further enthralled. My pleas and attempts to reassure him in his confusion were feeble by comparison with the magnetic force which exerted its pull over him. I, after all, was just the scapegoat for all the disasters, major and minor, of his life – for everything that had gone wrong, from his illness to every small irritation. Predictably the volcano would erupt again, plunging us into the black slough of chaos, sweeping him helplessly away beyond my reach, revoking all the resolutions so recently agreed. And so it went on until Christmas. My parents' plans for celebrating their Golden Wedding were a catastrophe of the ebb and flux of that tidal force.

With a randomness which had become perversely predictable,

Stephen spent Christmas Day in the bosom of his family observing the time-honoured and cherished routines, presents round the tree, Christmas dinner, the Queen's speech, an afternoon walk, films on the television and a salad supper. Late at night his van drew up outside and he vanished into the darkness, leaving home to go and stay in a hotel before setting off for a conference in Israel the following day.

We did not see him or hear from him again until early January when the children, Jonathan and I arrived home from a blissfully untroubled break in France to find him waiting for us at number 5, for all the world as if he were expecting to resume business as usual. No explanations were proffered and I knew better than to ask for any. In this I followed the good counsel of Bill Loveless's successor at St Mark's, Philip Spence, a priest who combined sensitivity and spirituality with a sense of humour which was sometimes outrageous. Philip was also pragmatic: he advised me to wait and let Stephen resolve the situation one way or the other. He also suggested that I should take legal advice. I knew that the latter was vital. Twenty-five years of living with Stephen had persuaded me that I could never win an argument, whether trivial or important. It was a foregone conclusion that in my present weakened state, I – and perhaps Tim too – would inevitably be the losers if I tried to handle the case myself. Legal fees were a comparatively small price to pay to avoid the far greater psychological toll of a confrontation on legal and financial matters.

However, the day after our return, as the family gathered to celebrate Stephen's birthday with due ceremony, I felt tremendous relief at the apparent and unexpected resumption of our own brand of normality. That evening thoughts of legal wrangles faded as we gathered round the candle-lit table, feasting on roast duck and orange sauce. Our normality was always eccentric, frequently witty and amusing, often difficult, but it was the only normality we knew and it seemed to be re-establishing itself, particularly when Stephen tossed me a verbal invitation for later that week to Bishop Shaxton's Solace, the Caius Ladies' Night. Dinner amongst the largely pompous Fellowship and their long-suffering wives promised the reassuring familiarity of an age-old tradition of which we had become part.

The relief prompted me to write a cheerful letter to Stephen's mother the next morning, genuinely expressing my joy that the disruptions appeared to be over, and that we could resume our attempts to lead a creative family life: this after all, at last seemed to be the reconciliation which Stephen in calmer moments over the past turbulent months, had proposed and which I had been only too willing to accept. I should have realized that this was a foolish move since Isobel had already quite pointedly, angrily even, taken it upon herself to inform me how much she liked and approved of the nurse in question. She wrote back on 12 January. From that letter it became clear to me that she discounted, even doubted, the effort and the love that I had so long put into caring for Stephen and, on the contrary, viewed me as the hedonistic beneficiary of his fame and success, intent now on denying him his chance of happiness.

In true Hawking style, I felt she had again misjudged the situation – and me. I had never had any intention of denying Stephen happiness – I knew more than most that our unique circumstances required unique remedies. All I asked was that our family should not be smashed to pieces; after all, Tim was only ten. From this and subsequent letters she sent, I realized that she did not seem disposed to believe my side of the story. I replied in kind to her letter, venting my fury in unequivocal terms for the first time. Nevertheless, the College feast had reinforced the notion of a return to stability. Its time-honoured format was unchanged, though now jiving took turns with ballroom dancing and Stephen could take to the floor swirling and whirling in his wheelchair to the admiration of the other dancers.

The stability was short-lived; all too soon the situation began to deteriorate again. I heard rumours that Stephen's sole reason for returning home was that there had been some hitch in the construction of the flat that he had bought for himself and Elaine Mason, and that as soon as the drainage malfunction was corrected, he would be moving out. I found this hard to believe since he himself had given not the slightest indication to that effect. After several more weeks in which the threats, the recriminations and the abuse once again gathered force, the children and I left to join Arthur and his parents for a few days' skiing in Austria over half-term. On our return to Cambridge, there was no sign of Stephen. He had gone. He had finally moved out, aided apparently by Elaine's husband, on the day we left for Austria, 17 February 1990. The end had come. I felt neither sadness nor relief. I was numb.

It was not the end, however. The very next day, Stephen telephoned from Elstree Studios where the film version of *A Brief History of Time* was being shot and asked me to join him there to participate in a family portrait, a biographical background for the film. It was an astonishing request. First and foremost, it was incredible that having just left his family, he could expect us to go on performing like Pavlov's dogs for the cameras, still conveying the outdated happy and united façade. Secondly, I was highly suspicious of the whole project. What, I asked, had become of all those fine promises that this film was to be entirely scientific, not biographical, and the assurances that the family sequences from the earlier American television film would be quite sufficient for introductory shots? There was no longer any timid hesitancy in my voice. In taking his decision to leave us, Stephen had unwittingly relinquished his power over me, leaving me free to make up my own mind, no more in dread of his imperious reactions. I refused to go to Elstree. I had gained control of my life.

Thereafter the high tragedy descended into farce. The phone rang incessantly as one after another the American producers and directors tried to cajole, flatter and persuade me into playing in their film. When they moved to Cambridge to set up an exact replica of Stephen's office in a disused church, they beat a path to the door, bringing with them their pathetic arguments. Millions of dollars were at stake, they lamented, wringing their hands; my absence would upset all their plans; without the biographical element, the film would be unbalanced. I shrugged my shoulders and quoted back their original assurances, enshrined in the contract, about the nature of the film – a purely scientific documentary with only the briefest of biographical references. The more they revealed their unreliability by denying their assurances, the easier I found it to hold my ground; and the easier I found it to hold my ground, the stronger I became.

CHAPTER FIFTY-EIGHT

Null and Void

WHATEVER SMALL COMFORT I may have derived from my new-found independence of spirit, the cataclysm had in truth left me a shattered wreck. In the darkness of defeat, I felt myself discredited and disowned, fumbling to find an identity, as if the preceding twenty-five years had been discarded without trace. Indeed that impression was not simply subjective; it was given substance by the two charities, the Motor Neurone Association and the Cheshire Foundation, for whom I had worked so hard, even when my strength was at its most depleted and I was at my most depressed. They gave me to understand that they could not risk their public credibility by continuing to have the two partners to a separation or divorce associated with their efforts so they no longer required my services. Naturally Stephen's name was more useful to them on their letter-heads than mine. Charity was big business, its ethos determined by market forces and bald economic considerations. This was a bitter blow. I thought that I had a great deal to offer in terms of first-hand experience of disability, its demands and consequences; I also had practical knowledge, insight and enthusiasm, and above all, care and sympathy for people living in the desperate circumstances I myself had known for so long. The door was slammed in my face, barring me from any viable public role with people I wanted to help. As I had suspected, outside the marriage and apart from Stephen, I was nothing.

It was nevertheless from despair and the blind maze of disorientation that I began to sense the stirrings of an unprecedented, almost palpable strength vibrating in the air around me and welling up inside me, a spiritual force, unrelated to my sapped physical state. Gradually I became aware that this force was the spontaneous expression of concern and love reaching out telepathically to me from our many friends worldwide. These were the true friends, people who had known us for many years; friends who had witnessed the struggles and had often helped in times of crisis; friends who had generously delighted in the successes without being blinded to the harsh underlying reality. These were friends, too, from whom my attempts to come to terms with the situation had been no secret, friends who had known and admired Jonathan for his dedication to the family as much as for his musical talent. Many said that they wept when they heard what had happened. Their support was comforting and enveloping, like a warm house on a cold winter's night.

It was then that I became convinced that God does exist as the ultimate power of goodness. Powerless to intervene when human selfishness prevails because humanity enjoys free will, he is ready and waiting to heal the wounds and repair the damage inflicted by that selfishness. Like a parent, unable to pass on the wisdom of experience to the next generation, and forced to watch from the sidelines in silent frustration as a much-loved child makes a terrible mistake in choosing the wrong career, the wrong friends, the wrong partner, he has to wait, unable to intervene knowing that blows will inevitably rain down and that lives will be torn apart. Only afterwards will he be able to bring his healing power to those who will accept it and keep faith with him.

The healing power did not make me any more or less religious. Still under Stephen's rational influence, I preserved a healthy scepticism about formal religion and dogma, and I detested religiosity. I still disliked any cliquishness associated with religious groups and still reacted badly to any pretension or pomposity in the name of Christianity. Religion for me had to be a personal relationship with God and through it, in my heart of hearts, I found the germinating seeds of an incipient peace and a wholeness which I had not known for a very long time.

The sense of peace enabled me to look to my own resources. Rather than dwell on Stephen's behaviour and wallow in resentment, I would put the energy which I had previously devoted to his well-being to a new project, a project of my own, through which I could prove to myself, if to nobody else, that I had a brain which was both capable and inventive. I would write a book but not the book of my memoirs for which various publishers were already clamouring, since that was far too painful a subject and it was much too soon for me to have gained any clear perspective on all those years of marriage. This would be a book of my own devising which would combine narrative skills with the largely unused research techniques that I had acquired when working on my doctorate. I would write a book about my experiences in setting up home in France; it would consist of amusing anecdotes and practical information, aimed at the considerable market of British buyers of homes in France. Moreover, as not many of those Francophiles seemed to have any great command of the French language, I would compile a phonetic lexicon of useful terms relating to all areas of house purchase and residence in France, legalities, insurance, renovation, the utilities, the telephone system, local government and healthcare.

Most of the time which used to be spent running the home, attending to Stephen's needs, accommodating his nurses, organizing rotas, answering the phone to disaffected nurses and putting on parties, I gave to the book, since in Stephen's absence there was an extensive hiatus in my timetable and the home virtually looked after itself. In writing the book and compiling the lexicon, I learned – like Stephen in the period after his critical illness – to use a computer. I wished that one had been available in those years when I was working on my thesis. The computer and printer were a magnanimous parting gift from Stephen. Quite why he bought them I never discovered but suspected that that gesture was typical of the state of confusion in which he found himself, though which as ever he was too proud and self-contained to admit. I was, however, duly appreciative since I could not have compiled the dictionary of useful terms without it.

I was much encouraged, too, when a literary agent, who had initially been keen for my memoirs, offered to find a publisher for the French book. He said the manuscript read well and in his view the idea was saleable. All that was required was my signature on his contract which I signed willingly, not liking to query the four-year term. I scarcely read the conditions, because in my demoralized condition I was so grateful for his interest. Indeed he appeared to be as good as his word and set about contacting publishers straight away. No sooner had I finished the first draft than I received a letter announcing that the Virgin publishing house was interested in the book. Together Peter Tauber, the agent, and I went to meet the Virgin editor in a chaotic, dingy back room some-where in north London. He predicted that his staff would be able to read and use my computer disks without any difficulty at all and once they had reviewed the disks, he would most certainly offer me a contract. I despatched a disk to him forthwith and then heard no more. After some months' silence, I prevailed upon Peter Tauber to get in touch with the Virgin editor who told him that the disk they had received was blank. In my innocence of computers, I supposed that the disk had been damaged in the post, so I sent off another by special courier straight away. After several more months' delay, the same reply came back from Virgin via the agent: the disk was found to be blank again. By now I was highly suspicious of the Virgin publishing outfit: I rang their offices myself and learned my first unpalatable lesson about the world of publishing: it was not the disk that was at fault but it transpired that the publishing house did not have the hardware to read my disks.

The news of the separation remained concealed from the press for several months. Because it had not hit the tabloid headlines, we were allowed a period of respite which was beneficial to us all. This limbo enabled Stephen and me to try to put our relationship on a new footing without the rub of media attention. We could meet as old friends without the stress of the day-to-day friction which had soured our relationship: he could come to West Road to see Tim at mealtimes and we could discuss matters of family concern calmly and sensibly. The only difference was that he lived elsewhere with someone else.

There was one half-hearted attempt at a reconciliation when Stephen announced one evening that he was intending to live at home with us for part of the week and the rest of the week in his flat with his lady love. The proposal was absurd and dictatorially conveyed, conjuring up visions of a headlong plunge back into the spinning, rapacious vortex from which we were just beginning to emerge and from which I was just starting to collect up the tattered fragments of my life. There would be more wrangling, more in-fighting, more tearing apart of our bodies and souls. There could be no turning back.

It was shortly after this that the press learned of our separation, literally as the result of an accident. One night as Stephen was on his way back to his flat, he and the nurse in attendance (not Elaine Mason) were knocked down by a speeding taxi. The wheelchair was overturned and he was left lying in the road in the dark. It was a miracle that he suffered nothing worse than a broken shoulder and spent only a couple of days in hospital. Inevitably the press got to hear of the accident and naturally wanted to know why his home was no longer at West Road. Reporters and cameramen, especially from the tabloids, came clustering round the gate, like a pack of baying hounds, scenting scandal and terrifying Tim and me with their persistent prowling. We were being hunted. It was thanks to the good sense of the head porter at Harvey

Court, Ken Britt, that they were put off the scent and Jonathan, of whose existence they were unaware, managed to escape out of the back door.

Once the separation had entered the public domain, the College lost no time in sending the Bursar across to enquire when we were going to move. He reasoned that as the College had provided the accommodation for Stephen's benefit and he was no longer living there, it was logical that the rest of the family should move out. He was quite explicit: the College felt itself under no obligation to house the family. He was in effect giving me notice to quit. While he rattled on, telling Lucy the details of his daughter's twenty-first birthday party, I sat by in stunned silence. I should have pleaded my rights as a sitting tenant, I should have consulted my solicitor, I should have refused to move. In my reduced state, I had neither the presence of mind to protest nor the will to fight. The previous day would have been – technically was – our twenty-fifth wedding anniversary. On that Monday morning in July, my intimations were being confirmed by the College authorities: everything that had occurred in those twenty-five years was of no relevance or importance to anyone other than me. Those twenty-five years had all been obliterated from the records. They might as well never have happened for all that they mattered. Stephen was the only person who mattered. I was of no consequence, nor were the children. I had been given my marching orders and we were effectively being thrown out into the street. It was time to wake up to a new reality.

Perhaps it was because I meekly agreed to move without protest that the Bursar relaxed his aggressive stance and agreed to my request for a period of grace, a year say, in which to readjust. Tim had been entered for King's College School, directly across the road, and it would have been the height of irony if we had been forced to move just as he was changing to a school less than five minutes from our front door. A further advantage of King's for Tim was that his friend Arthur was coming from Germany to school there as a boarder, so whatever the upheavals at home, he could count on seeing his best friend every day in school. In fact Tim saw Arthur not only in school but at home as well because Arthur came to live with us for the next two years. It was a very happy arrangement for all concerned. Arthur became part of our family and gave Tim invaluable moral support in his changing circumstances: potentially as much of a computer wizard as Robert, my mentor, he also filled the gap created by Robert's absence. Whenever I encountered a problem with my new computer, Arthur came to my rescue.

It was my infinite good fortune that I was not, in fact, alone. Jonathan had stood discreetly and steadfastly by my side despite being the target of considerable hostility. Equally discreetly and steadfastly and with endless patience, he began to reassemble the broken shards of what used to be my personality, the while trying to come to terms himself with what had happened. From the outset he had been under no illusions: he knew that our relationship depended on a fine balance and on Stephen's acceptance of the assurance that it was dedicated to the perpetuation, not the destruction, of the family. Jonathan had feared the possibility of Freudian repercussions but had underestimated the havoc that the intervention of an outside party could wreak by gossip and misrepresentation. There had not been any viable alternative since he cared so deeply for me and for the family, including Stephen. For my part, not only could I not cope, I could not survive without him: he shouldered the physical burdens and in his arms I found the longed-for emotional security which marriage had always denied me.

The new reality flung us together, though not with any joy or elation, only with sadness at the betrayal of our best intentions, coupled with muted relief that the long ordeal was over. Our mood was akin to that of a couple of survivors of a shipwreck stranded on a desert island. It was not a question of the simple equation that some less sensitive people seemed to imagine; they supposed that Stephen's departure would leave me free to rush into marriage with Jonathan forthwith. That simplistic appraisal ignored the unfathomable complexity of long-suppressed feelings; it underestimated my attachment to Stephen on the one hand, and on the other, glibly ignored my rejection of all thoughts of remarriage. Although Jonathan and I started to live together and began to look for a suitable house to buy, I was not intending to compromise my new-found independence and liberty. That precious independence meant the simple freedoms to keep my own counsel, manage my own affairs, to travel and spend my money as I chose without having to defer to any other dogmatic opinion – not that Jonathan's opinions were ever dogmatic, nor did he force them upon me. These were the only freedoms that I valued. In every other way I was ready to commit myself to Jonathan as a life-long friend, partner and companion, but without the public ceremony and the legal document. In addition I was in no fit state physically or emotionally, to marry anyone, let alone someone who deserved so much more than I could offer. In any case, since there had been no mention of divorce, I was technically still married to Stephen.

It was some consolation that, for all the chaos that *A Brief History of Time* had plunged us into, at least it had not left me destitute. We were able to buy and enlarge a detached house on a modern estate on the same side of Cambridge. At first sight I found the house and its garden depressing to the point of heartbreak. The house was cramped, featureless and uninspiring, a modern brick and concrete box, its inner walls covered in torn and faded hessian and its garden pitifully bare and sombre, shaded from the neighbours only by a row of overgrown Leylandii. Yet again I would have to start from scratch and try to re-create a home in that characterless house and a flower garden from the unyielding grey clay which passed for soil. The attraction of the house was its position; it was still within cycling distance of the centre of town and of Tim's school. It also happened to be quite close to Stephen's luxury flat, which had to be regarded as an advantage since Stephen insisted on seeing Tim twice a week. With uncomplaining loyalty, Arthur accompanied Tim on these regular visits, the outcome of which was never predictable and always disturbing, a tragic sit-com of grotesque proportions. I was relieved that Stephen showed no urgency in pressing for divorce because I dreaded that Tim might become a pawn in yet another acrimonious battle between his parents. Occasionally a demanding letter would arrive but as this clearly was Stephen's response to domestic pressure, these letters could be taken lightly; whatever their contents, generally our discussions were civilized and even affectionate whenever we met. As long as no divorce proceedings were filed, Tim was safe from legal wranglings over custody. Eventually that aspect, because of his age, ceased to be an issue.

For my part, I was leading a normal life, a tremendous indulgence after more than twenty-five years of a life which had never really been normal. Jonathan and I cherished our normality and our privacy, though still living in fear of detection by the gutter press who, we knew, would not hesitate to exploit our situation to please the salacious tastes of their readership. On one occasion, when Jonathan was away on tour, the boys and I received an unannounced visit from a young woman journalist. I invited her in, uttered a few carefully chosen clichés, introduced her to Tim and Arthur, and then to my relief, she left. I did not bother to read what she wrote in the now-defunct *Today* newspaper. It was sufficient that the local greengrocer told me that the coarse representation of me bore little resemblance to his customer of long standing. Some time later a neighbour enquired whether the young woman who had called at her door claiming to be an old friend of mine had actually found our house.

It was no secret that both the University and the College had designs on the land on which the house at number 5 West Road stood. The two institutions were engaged in negotiations for the redevelopment of the end of the garden as a library for the Law Faculty, while for many years the College had been intending to demolish the house and build a hall of residence on the rest of the site. In that last year of our occupation, we watched from the house in a silent state of siege as surveyors stalked the garden, armed with measuring rods, marking out distances with stakes and poles, while down by the holly hedge a pile-driver forced its way deep into the light alluvial soil. With our removal the fate of the whole property, the old house, its lovely tranquil garden and its majestic backdrop of trees would be sealed. In the name of progress, the University and the College seemed to be intending to perpetrate the worst sort of vandalism, official vandalism, by which Cambridge would lose yet another of its shady green spaces to glass and concrete. The perpetrators would shelter behind the anonymous façade of collective decision-making – large-scale vandalism conducted by committee being so much more socially acceptable than the vandalism conducted by disaffected youth. In the mayhem of moving, there was little that I could do to save the house and garden except to ensure that the trees, especially the two magnificent sentinels, the wellingtonia by the house and the red western cedar, the *Thuya plicata*, at the end of the lawn, were protected by tree preservation orders. I called the appropriate department of the city council and asked the self-styled arboreal officers to conduct a survey. They came, counted and inspected the trees and assured me that they would conduct a survey but that I had no need to worry since the trees were protected in any case because they were in a conservation area. I moved house satisfied that I had done my civic and environmental duty.

During the course of the next year, I visited the garden frequently on my way home from town to check that nothing untoward had happened. The threat appeared to have receded. All was quiet apart from the constant grinding action of the pile-driver. The garden, the lawn, the trees were untouched, just as we had left them. I wandered in that sanctuary of nostalgia, sadly remembering the parties, the dancing, the games of croquet and cricket, and gazing at the blank, unseeing windows of the house, those windows that had contained so much joy and so much anguish. The house guarded its secrets closely, revealing its past in only a few scattered remnants, like the forgotten spoils of a battle – the rain-washed remains of Tim's sandpit, a battered toy bucket, a deflated football, a cracked flowerpot and the rusting umbrella washing-line which had given such good service. They told of lives and events of which the current student occupants of the house were scarcely aware.

Lulled by the unchanging tranquillity of the scene, my concerns for the garden were replaced by other more pressing matters. Peter Tauber, my agent, was having scant success in finding a publisher for *At Home in France*, my handbook about buying houses in France. After the Virgin fiasco, he had managed to arouse the passing interest of an editor at Random Century who said that if I would expand the text with more autobiographical material, she would be pleased to issue a contract. I did as requested, adding a few light anecdotes, and submitted a revised manuscript, only to receive a reply some months later to the effect that Random would be prepared to publish the book on France on one of two conditions. Either I could sign a joint contract for my memoirs or contribute £15,000 towards the costs of publication of the French book. I flung the letter in the bin in disgust. The offer was preposterous. Even if I published the book myself, it would cost less than £15,000, and as for writing my memoirs, the time was not right, as I had repeatedly told Peter Tauber. He was becoming suspiciously restive in that respect, despite my assertion that the pain was far too severe, the wounds still too open: I explained time and again that I had not come to terms with the change, I had not gained a reasoned perspective, I had not found the voice for the narrative, I had no starting point.

Naively I suggested to him that I might consider publishing *At Home in France* myself since he had met with such a singular lack of success. His response was immediate and cutting: he sent me a copy of his contract, pointing out that I was bound by its terms until the summer of 1994, unless, that is, I would sign a new one giving him rights in perpetuity over any biography I might write about Stephen. He warned me that 'the market might lose interest in the story' and went on to paint a lurid picture of 'the possibility, God forbid, of you [sic] becoming incapacitated before you have written up the book, which would not only be a financial tragedy for yourself but also your children and their children'. I was furious, as much with myself for being so naive, as with the slippery customer of an agent who had taken such blatant advantage of my inexperience and my dejection. His deviousness fired my determination to publish my French book myself, whatever the cost, and to deprive him in perpetuity of any commission on any other book that I might write. He seemed quite unable to comprehend that if I were ever to write such a work, it would have to be in my own good time, when I was ready. In any case, in those years in the early 1990s, I was far too preoccupied with more mundane and tiresome matters than literary aspirations.

At about the same time as the literary agent revealed himself in his true colours, the special compliance branch of the Inland Revenue turned their attention to the profits made from *A Brief History of Time*. As a result of the high rate of unemployment caused by deliberate Tory government policy, the Treasury was short of funds and was instructing the Inland Revenue to increase its income from compliance investigations. They were particularly advised to direct their snooping to situations where a marriage break-up might have caused fiscal confusion. Although I was no longer involved in the handling of Stephen's book, I still kept the accounts and, as far as I was concerned, there were no irregularities in the recording of advances, royalties, expenses and outgoings relating to *A Brief History*. The fault lay with the inefficiency of a newly engaged tax consultant who had taken over from our trusted accountant on his retirement. Despite my best efforts to placate the tax inspector, he brought the full force of his bullying professional belligerence – usually employed in pursuit of jobbing builders and moonlighting agricultural labourers – down on my head. He pursued me with letters and phone calls, even ringing up at Christmas when my hands were deep in flour and my mind on carols, puddings and presents. He made no concessions to Stephen's exceptional circumstances. We were at liberty to appeal against his decisions, he told us, but if we lost the appeal, he would increase the already monumental fine. Or possibly we might go to prison. Although his attitude raised my hackles and I was almost curious to see how the authorities planned to handle Stephen if a prison sentence were handed down to us jointly, Stephen capitulated, having first protested that he had already paid enough tax to build a small hospital. Nor did he want to pursue the accountant for restitution of the lost funds. His fighting spirit seemed to be in abeyance.

These and other preoccupations distracted me from the issue of the trees and the garden at number 5 West Road at a critical time. It was not until one Monday in July 1993 that I found myself thinking about them again; strangely, these thoughts grew in strength until they became a compulsion, an irresistible urge to go to the garden. The feeling was unfamiliar and puzzling. I did not know how or why it had come and my rational self suppressed it since I was far too busy that Monday with preparations for the summer holidays as well as other activities. It was not until later in the week that I found the time to call in at West Road on my way home from a final, pre-holiday shopping spree in town.

As I rounded the corner of the house, I encountered a vista of horrendous proportions. Where I expected to find the well-known, much-loved haven of flowers and greenery, all I saw was wanton mass destruction. The far end of the garden had been ransacked, obliterated. Where previously there had been trees and shrubs, roses and poppies, birds, hedgehogs and squirrels, now there was nothing more than a huge black hole in the ground, a muddy crater where Mother Earth was laid bare, ravaged and exposed. A quick mental count suggested that as many as forty trees had been felled, the most spectacular being the red western cedar, the *Thuya plicata*, under whose shady branches Cottontail, Tim's little rabbit, had had her hutch. As I stood paralysed with shock, anger and disbelief at the scale of the devastation, I remembered the strange call I had felt earlier in the week. Could those trees really have been calling me to their rescue? What had become of my attempts to protect them with preservation orders?

Pat Parkes, the College maintenance man, came out to talk to me. Together we stared blankly into the hole in the ground while he recounted the ghastly tale. Bulldozers had arrived on the site early on the Monday morning and before any of the College gardeners or workmen had an opportunity to protest, the land had been cleared, the trees swept away. 'We would have chained ourselves to the trees if we had known what was going to happen,' he said sadly. 'They'll have the rest down too before we know anything about it,' he added, waving his hand in the direction of the house and the remaining trees. I vowed there and then that 'they' would not, not if I could stop them.

In response to my enquiries, the City Council could find no record of my earlier requests for a tree survey of the site and for preservation orders to be placed on the trees. The plans for the new building when presented to the planning committee had made only passing reference to a few insignificant shrubs and saplings, so the planning committee had given the go-ahead without further enquiry. The protection to the trees afforded by the conservation area was worthless. The site had been cleared to allow a glass and concrete dinosaur, the product of megalomaniac architects, to assert the imperious sway of modern technology unthreatened by any competition from nature, not even a blade of grass. There was a sense of poetic justice in the tragedy. The fate of the trees and the garden mirrored the fate that had befallen the children and me. There could not have been a more potent or poignant metaphor for the end of our family life than that hole in the ground.

Only a year later my vow that I would not allow the same fate to befall the remaining fifty or so trees, including the towering giant sequoia, the wellingtonia, at the side of the house, was put to the test when Gonville and Caius submitted plans for the demolition of the house, the wholesale destruction of the rest of the garden and the erection over the site, from front to back, of a ninety-room hall of residence, supposedly for second-year undergraduates, but more probably for lucrative conferences, complete with ensuite bathrooms and underground car park. My protests, supported by local councillors, over the previous slaughter of trees had at least awakened the local authority to its environmental responsibilities but only by means of a major time and energy-consuming campaign. I had been forced to capitalize on all the publicity and media coverage that the name 'Hawking' could generate, to prevail upon the City Council to acknowledge those responsibilities and place tree preservation orders on the threatened trees. Letters of protest in response to my plea for help to the multitudes of scientists and friends who had at some time or other attended parties in that garden rained down on the Planning Department from all corners of the globe.

The press chose to concentrate on the issue of the house as the birthplace of *A Brief History of Time*. That slight misrepresentation did not trouble me, although the Bursar, on behalf of the College, sought to pour scorn on my misplaced sentimentality, announcing that the reputation of their illustrious Fellow would survive through his work rather than through the place where he had lived. As far as I was concerned, the house and the garden were so closely linked that it would be very difficult to destroy the one without harming the other. Ultimately the ecological value of the trees proved a more cogent weapon than the historic value of the house. The City Council rejected the development plans because of the trees and placed tree preservation orders on them, but English Heritage, despite having just declared a council housing estate from the 1950s a listed monument, refused to place a protection order on the house, one of the few fine mansions in Cambridge from the Victorian era. Ironically English Heritage later approved a grant for the completely spurious renovation in mock Graeco-Roman style of rooms in the College for the use of the Fellows.

Perhaps, in the light of this battle, I was naive to expect that the College would grant the children and me a key to the Fellows' tennis court which I politely requested some months after these events. Nobody ever used that court and it was inconvenient to have to ask Stephen for the key whenever we wanted to play. Given that I had learnt over the years that arguments in Cambridge colleges are always said to be purely objective, totally devoid of personal involvement, I assumed that the battle for the trees would logically have been viewed in the same way. This was a grave misapprehension. My request was curtly dismissed on the entirely logical grounds that I was not a Fellow of the College, which was the same argument that had been used years before to bar me from membership of the College Garden Committee . . .

Postlude

1997

IN A SENSE that was the end of the story in as much it was the end of an era, the era of my marriage to a phenomenal and courageous genius, the era which historically may be of interest to succeeding generations. Readers who are interested only in the Hawking aspect may wish to close the book here. However, as far as I myself am concerned it was not the end because I am still alive, as is Stephen, and my life continues. Indeed, some say that Stephen has outlived motor neurone disease and is getting stronger. Certainly he is a major player on the world stage and goes from success to success in the company of the rich and famous. I, too, have grown in strength, thanks to regular acupuncture sessions, and in self-assurance, thanks to the support given me by Jonathan, my family, and my friends. I have only to think of my several young namesakes worldwide and my seven godchildren, one of them a little French boy, Bryan Régnier, and another, the youngest, Helena Wilson, the daughter of Sue, one of my closest colleagues at CCSS, to realize what a rich fund of loyalty I enjoy in my caring friends.

After our trip to Seattle in 1995, there were two thought-provoking letters amongst the huge pile of mail commanding my attention. One was a letter from a generous admirer who had taken the trouble to write and tell me how useful and enjoyable she had found *At Home in France*. The book had finally seen the light of day in the summer of 1994, when, after the expiry of Peter Tauber's contract, I published it myself under my own imprint, Allegretto Publications. There were expensive mishaps in production caused by the inefficiency of one or two of the professionals whom I had the misfortune to employ. One error in production threatened to make me a laughing-stock: my acknowledgement to my excellent proof-reader, inserted after she had finished her work, maddeningly thanked her for her '*rigirous* attention to detail'. I was however satisfied to have proved to myself that my brain was actually still capable of functioning creatively and to some worthwhile purpose. The same kind correspondent also urged me to write more.

The second letter came from Susan Hill, a respected editor at Macmillan, enquiring whether I would like to write about my life, in my own terms, in whatever way I chose. The arrival of these two letters preceded Stephen's remarriage that September by a few days, four months after the divorce was finalized in May 1995. Stephen did not instigate divorce proceedings for a long time, and when he finally did, I handed the matter over to my solicitor, as was always my intention. The weekend of Stephen's remarriage, my parents took me to Norfolk and both they and the proprietor of our hotel deliberately shielded me from the media coverage of the event. They say that recovery from a broken marriage takes one year for every five years of the marriage. That is no exaggeration, especially when the marriage has been as demanding, unpredictable, heart-breaking and eventful as ours had been. With his marriage, Stephen effectively slammed the door on our remaining lines of communication. By an unjust and whimsical quirk of English law, he was free to marry as soon as he liked after the divorce but, because the financial settlement was not yet agreed – and indeed would prove to be the subject of hard bargaining over the next eighteen months – I could not avail myself of the same freedom without severely jeopardizing my financial status.

With Stephen's remarriage, I had no choice but to reconcile myself to the end of an era, even to the extent of realizing that the end was probably inevitable. Many, many factors – fame, fortune, diverging aspirations, priorities and outlook, as well as many people – had come between Stephen and me and they proved stronger than the pull of home and family. Perhaps the end could have been foreseen. Certainly the Hawkings were busy telling people that they had not expected 'the' marriage to last as long as it had. An exception to the general Hawking attitude, which was one of indifference, was to be found in Stephen's Uncle Bill, his father's youngest brother. Uncle Bill had had an uneasy relationship with the rest of the family, perhaps not unlike my own. He had moved south from Yorkshire on remarriage and he and his friendly, outgoing wife Margaret frequently called on Jonathan and me when they came into Cambridge on shopping expeditions. They were disturbed by what had happened to us and showed us kindness and understanding, enlivened by Uncle Bill's sense of humour, often directed against his own eccentric relations. Uncle Bill employed a Yorkshire bluntness in his speech which was refreshing after all the innuendo and gossip that I had endured. His remarks could be searching, they could also be complimentary. Once he paid me a handsome compliment which recalled William Thatcher's expressed opinion in those early days in Little St Mary's Lane when he had remarked that, though small, I must be tough. Uncle Bill, doubtless referring to his relatives, observed: 'You know, Jane, *they* used to say that you were an insignificant slip of a girl but now that I know you better, I really think you have great presence and strength of character.' Such an encomium from one of Stephen's relatives was music to my ears.

The realization in Seattle that my life, or a major part of it, had come full circle, had prepared me for a reassessment of the past and had eased me into a change of perspective. The two letters on our return encouraged me to think seriously about using that new perspective as a starting point from which to consign the experiences of those years to paper. My initial reluctance, arising from diffidence about the loss of privacy that the exercise might entail, gave way before the gradual awareness that I had no choice in the matter. My privacy was compromised anyhow because my life was already public property as a result of Stephen's fame, and it would be only a matter of time before biographers started to investigate the personal story behind his genius and his survival, and that would inevitably include me. I had no reason to suppose that they would treat me with any more consideration than the press had in the past. It would therefore be far better for me to tell my own story in my own way. I would be revealing truths which were so deeply and painfully personal that I could not bear to think that their music might resound only with the ring of the *chaudron fêlé*, Flaubert's cracked kettle. Writing the story in my own way, I would be able to relieve myself of the burden of so many contrasting and conflicting experiences and exorcize the strain, the tensions and ultimately the overpowering toll of unhappiness. The exercise would certainly be cathartic. It might also be healing.

Although Stephen and his family might wish to deny my role in his life, I could not close my mind to a quarter of a century of living on the edge of a black hole, especially when the undeniable, paradoxical, living proof of the extraordinary successes and early happiness of those twenty-five years was to be seen in our three handsome, well-adjusted, very loving children, as well as in the acclaim which Stephen enjoyed.

For the sake of the children as well as for myself, I had to retain a window on the past which would allow it to be integrated with the present. As I began to write, I discovered that the voice and the register were there within me, ready and waiting to surface and express that mass of memories accumulated over the years, memories which might simply be seen to relate the saga of an English family in the latter part of the twentieth century. Much of it would be quite ordinary, quite common to most people's lives, were it not for two factors: motor neurone disease and genius. I set to work in the autumn of 1995; thereafter writing and teaching, interspersed with frequent choral concerts and intensive bouts of gardening in France, became my absorbing occupations for two winters and more.

In the summer of 1996 we stayed in Seattle again after touring the length and breadth of California where I met many old friends and plumbed their memories and their scientific expertise. In Seattle Robert was heavily committed to producing Microsoft's new programme, Office '97, and had little free time to spend with us. With only ten days' leave a year, he could not afford to take much time off. The time that we did have together was well spent, not only in sightseeing and walking in the mountains but also in attending services at St Mark's Cathedral, above all the mystical service of Compline sung by a male choir late at night to a hushed congregation of young and old, seated wherever they could find space in the packed cathedral. After the stillness of the service, like many a service in Ely Cathedral in its medieval resonances, Jonathan made the organ ring out with a magnificent rendering of Bach's Prelude in C Major. St Mark's, Seattle, though of course much larger, bears a strangely reassuring resemblance to St Mark's, Cambridge, both in style and in atmosphere; this somehow reinforces my transformed relationship with Seattle.

We did not go to Seattle in the summer of 1997 but some of our closest American friends came to England. They came to join our wedding celebrations. Between the courses of the Christmas dinner of 1996, Jonathan grasped the fleeting opportunity of a private moment out in the utility room to ask me to marry him. At long last, having consigned much of the past to the computer, if not yet to paper, I felt sure enough of myself to be able to accept. It was the happiest of parties, that Christmas around the table with the faces of all three children, Jonathan's parents and mine, and Robert's girlfriend, Katrina – a talented young sculptress from Seattle – glowing in the candle-light.

We celebrated the promise of a new future, carefree, hopeful, contented, with the exciting prospect of six months to prepare for the wedding, marred only by the inconvenience of Tim's A-level exams. As we began to draw up plans, our original idea of a small, discreet wedding developed into a huge party to express our thanks to those legions of friends who had stood by us through so many tribulations.

The reality of those six months developed into an unbelievably cruel sequence of crises and tragedies, some of which affected us directly, some of which concerned our dearest friends. In early January news came that two-year-old Bridget Whiting, the youngest of the three children of Mary and Bernard, the Australian couple who had given us all such sterling help and support, both practical and moral, in the early 1980s, was seriously ill with leukamia in Florida where the family had been living since their move from Paris some years before. Then soon afterwards there was the sudden and premature death while out jogging on Hampstead Heath of our loyal journalist friend George Hill, a man of luminous intelligence and integrity. Not long after spending Christmas with us, my mother quite suddenly became immobilized with arthritis, not in itself a terminal condition, except that the painkilling drugs that she was prescribed destroyed her digestive system with devastating results. That vital, busy person, with an exceptional memory for, and interest in, people and their families, rapidly shrank to an ailing but indomitable shadow of her former self. The contrast between her expansive personality, still fighting courageously to assert itself, and her wasted frame was pitiful. As my father, at eighty-two, struggled to look after my mother and keep their home going, it soon became apparent that 'community care' was as meaningless a term for my parents, who had assiduously paid their taxes since the 1930s and done their patriotic duty during the war, as it had been for Stephen and me in all the years of our struggle against motor neurone disease.

In March Jonathan loaded his harpsichord into the car and went off on a tour of northern England with a Swedish orchestra. Touring is a routine part of any musician's life and since Jonathan is a careful driver, I was used to such absences as a matter of course. On this occasion, however, I was distinctly unhappy about his leaving, although there was no specific cause for my anxiety that I could pinpoint. As always, we kept in touch as and when he could get to a phone. I was beginning to dismiss my fears as nonsense when he rang from Liverpool to tell me that he had been rushed to hospital as an emergency with severe but

undiagnosed pains in his back. He eventually underwent a kidney operation and was in hospital for the next ten days. Meanwhile his car, which
he had had no choice but to leave in a hotel car park, was burgled, the
windows smashed and all his music and personal possessions, including
the house keys, taken. There was little that I could do to help as I was
hobbling around at home on crutches after a skiing injury. I had the
locks on the house changed immediately and then promptly locked
myself out. Jonathan's convalescence was a long one and interfered not
only with the planning of the wedding but also with his careful preparations for a recording with the Cambridge Baroque Camerata of all
Bach's six Brandenburg Concertos, plus a seventh arranged from a
harpsichord and viol sonata, scheduled for August, a month after the
wedding.

Only a week before the blow came from Liverpool, Lucy had arrived
home from New York, where she was working as a journalist, to
announce that she was expecting a baby, and she and the baby's father,
Alex Mackenzie Smith, a member of the UN Peace Corps in Bosnia,
were intending to set up home together in London. This was not bad
news but it was somewhat unexpected. It demanded time, energy and
finance in support of the young couple as they hastily attempted to find
accommodation and work in London in anticipation of the baby's arrival.
Thus, with the wedding only a few weeks away, we were overwhelmed
by a host of anxieties including a near fatal car crash in Devon involving
my niece, her husband and three-year-old son. None of these crises
could be shelved or ignored or even taken lightly, since they all involved
the health and well-being of my closest friends and my family.

It was ironic that at about the same time Microsoft confirmed a deal
struck with Cambridge University according Bill Gates the right to
build a Microsoft Seattle-style campus in Cambridge. The University
congratulated its collective self on having extracted a deal worth £50
million from Bill Gates. The fact that it had granted one of the world's
richest men, at current estimates worth around US$40 billion (so many
noughts that they are meaningless to me), the rights to all its invaluable
computer research in the future appeared to have been underestimated
in the equation. According to press reports and television coverage, the
deal was brokered by Stephen. When I asked Robert what he knew
about it, he said that he was the last person to find out: it had all been
done over his head and he had not been consulted in any way. One of
the rumours in circulation had it that the so-called campus might be

built on the meadow – according to the press 'a piece of wasteground' – at the end of our road.

Against this tumultuous background, Jonathan and I were married on 4 July. An elderly Newnham resident who happened to be passing St Mark's reported back to his family that there had been a French wedding at the church. His confusion was entirely understandable because he had indeed seen us, the newly-weds, being driven away from the church in an open-top, left-hand-drive car with French number plates. The driver, Jean Pierre Degand, one of our remarkable friends from St-Pol-sur-Ternoise, had generously insisted on putting his splendid vehicle at our disposal. Jean-Pierre and his wife and sons were part of the international congregation from far and wide – from France, Spain, Germany, Nigeria, the United States and Japan – as well as all those friends and relations, in varying degrees of health, who had driven across the country or had just walked down the road to the church to be with us on that day.

The catalogue of illnesses and accidents that had befallen us and ours had left little time for the practicalities of planning, let alone for any mental, emotional or spiritual preparation. In truth, nothing could have prepared us for the emotional and spiritual power of that day. Just a minute or two before leaving home, I suddenly became aware to my embarrassed amazement that a mile down the road there was a church full of people awaiting me. Then, on arrival at St Mark's in the company of my three adult children, even our new vicar Christine Farrington's calm, friendly greeting could not allay that mounting sense of awe and wonder. Perhaps indeed her resplendent white and gold ceremonial vestments only added to the potent, dream-like quality of the occasion, a quality which became overwhelming as Robert, Lucy, Tim and I took up our positions in the porch from where we glimpsed my future husband, rising to his feet at the chancel steps. A wave of emotion engulfed us as the organist, at the organist's wedding, launched into the majestic opening chords of 'The Arrival of the Queen of Sheba' and my children bore me, trembling and incapable of looking to right or left, up the aisle and deposited me at Jonathan's side. In a space to my left, looking wan and frail, sat my mother in the wheelchair to which she had recently become confined.

There followed the hymns, the prayers, the readings and the anthems, their words carefully chosen, pored over, analysed, translated into French and Spanish, typed into and extracted many a time from the computer. All those words came alive in speech and song, lent breadth and depth, truth, urgency and clarity in the voices of the choir, the clergy, the readers and the congregation. Our own voices quavered, caught in our throats, captive to the intensity of strong feelings as Christine Farrington guided us with gentle authority through the vows. The choir, composed of old friends, many of them professional musicians, moved many eyes to tears with their sublime rendering of 'How lovely are thy dwellings fair' from Brahms's German Requiem.

As for the preacher, there was only one possible choice. Only Bill Loveless, who had known us both for so long and had sustained us through such times of trial, could have given the address. Despite ill-health and old age, he climbed into the pulpit and launched into a passionate address which bore all the hallmarks of his customary vigour and commitment. He spoke with heartfelt candour and honesty of the dilemmas and anguish of the past without glossing over the reality of our relationship. He spoke, too, of his and the vicar's support for our application to the Bishop of Ely for a marriage service as opposed to a service of blessing which has been the norm for the remarriage of a divorced person in church. As he recalled times past, it occurred to me that so many of the friends who had given us so much valuable support in days gone by and for whom I regularly said a silent prayer from my pew on a Sunday morning were in the church, with us and around us – all, that is, except Stephen, my companion over such a long period and the father of my children.

There were the odd moments which were enough to distract anyone's concentration from the proceedings. The image of darling Lucy standing at the lectern to recite Shakespeare's sonnet about the marriage of true minds was quite unforgettable. She stood, radiant in cream silk, with her hands clasped under her six-month bulge as if to gain confidence from her tiny, foetal son while Alex beamed with pride from the congregation. Then there was the horrible scratchy pen which turned my signature on the registers into an untidy scrawl, bringing back humiliating memories of a failed art exam in calligraphy at St Albans High School. Finally there was that silly moment when I knelt at the altar and realized that I had forgotten to remove the price labels from the soles of my new shoes . . .

All too soon the service was over and Jonathan and I were gliding down the aisle, borne aloft by the strains of Bach's 'St Anne Prelude' and by the joy on the faces of the congregation. We stepped out into the sun – it was the first fine day in weeks – there to kiss and hug all our guests and well-wishers before setting off at the head of the long, slow-moving, French-led motorcade to Wimpole Hall for photographs, the reception, dinner and festivities which lasted into the night.

'A true marriage' – '*un vrai mariage*', Danièle, one of our French friends remarked, adding that she would not have missed it for anything. She was right – a true marriage, made at St Mark's which, as Bill Loveless said in his address, is our spiritual home. A spiritual home as well as a dependable family home is essential for every person born into this world. It is at our peril that we neglect those deep-seated needs in favour of materialism, egoism, science or the extremes of rationality.

October 1997

Lucy's baby is even now embarking on the long, arduous journey into independent life. In a few hours, within months of becoming a step-father, Jonathan will become a step-grandfather and Stephen, against all expectation, will have lived to see his first grandchild. The prospect of becoming grandparents and of having to help the young family establish themselves has united us again with a strength of purpose reminiscent of the distant past, and it helps us to communicate harmoniously. Some-times I catch a glimpse of the old Stephen, untouched by fame and fortune, the Stephen who is prepared to confide in me that he hates going anywhere near number 5 West Road, because it brings back so many memories, and I share his feelings. As West Road is on my route into town, I cycle past the house often but only rarely do I stop to look at its gaunt, blank, roadside façade. If my footsteps stray into the remains of the desecrated garden and I find myself contemplating the smiling, sunlit back of the house, then I am overcome with melancholy and I hear voices, shrill children's voices calling and laughing in the sepulchral silence of the place. My solitary contemplation leads me to consider unanswerable questions: perhaps I had become overprotective in my well-intentioned attempt to provide a secure home for Stephen and the children; perhaps I would not have been capable indefinitely of the super-human effort which that endeavour demanded without collapsing under the strain. However, life continues. I myself am a much happier, more confident person now and I am glad for Stephen that he continues to enjoy resounding success with, I hope, a due measure of happiness.

On his *Desert Island Discs* programme, he paid me a tribute which was all the more touching for being completely unexpected.

He has admitted recently on television that his prediction in his inaugural lecture in 1979 that the laws of physics would be wound up by the end of the century erred on the side of optimism. However, he predicts that the current technological developments, which will enable scientists to probe the universe back in time to the Big Bang, will mean that the outstanding questions will be resolved twenty years from now. He is working, with some success it seems, on the theory of everything.

It is a depressing comment on the priorities of modern scientific research that, despite those extraordinary advances in space technology which will soon capture the beginning of the universe 15 billion years ago on film, the short, very basic, earthly journey into life is still every bit as painful for the mother and as stressful for the child as it was thirty years ago when Robert was born. Childbirth is certainly safer in terms of mortality, but a comparison of experiences over three generations in our family suggests that there has been little improvement in alleviating the pain or expediting the process since the days when Stephen and I were born. Staff shortages and inadequate training in the new technologies have actually brought about a deterioration in the maternity services. To judge by the way that Lucy is at present being treated, or rather ignored, in her bed in the flagship London hospital of the NHS, the Chelsea and Westminster, there is even less concern and care today within the system for a young mother experiencing the frightening force of the pain of childbirth for the first time. The same degree of incompetence and callous disregard still prevails, as if among the staff there is a conspiracy to ignore the pain because the period of suffering is finite and in most cases, at the end of it, the mother will be rewarded with an adorable baby. Although the incompetence may be occasioned these days by lack of proper funding, the callousness exemplifies the same old primeval undercurrent of hardened indifference.

This child, when he is born, will inherit a remarkable scientific legacy from his grandfather. He will not grow up to be a successful human being, however, unless he is also aware of his spiritual birthright. Only through the knowledge of his own soul, that innermost contact with the voice of God working deep within each of us, will he discover the power of love and compassion, the essence of goodness and concern for others, and the ability to distinguish right from wrong. As he and his generation grow up in the new millennium, they will have the chance of using this knowledge to try to redress some of the horrendous wrongs perpetrated in the twentieth century. We must hope that in the place of cruelty, violence, political and religious dogma, poverty and despair, they will substitute a spirit of unselfish generosity and tolerance, respect for life in all its forms and concern for the planet. They can only achieve this end by building on a renewal of faith in goodness.

Faith, the outward expression of spirituality which can make sense of all the wonders of Creation and of all the suffering in the world, gives substance to all our hopes. However far-reaching our intellectual achievements and however advanced our knowledge of Creation, without faith and a sense of our own spirituality there is only isolation and despair, and the human race really is a lost cause.

Index